MALE VIOLENCE

Most human violence is carried out by men, yet a book which highlights this by being called 'Male Violence' is very different from one simply entitled 'Human Violence'. The contributors to *Male Violence* take as their starting point not the generality of aggression in the human species, but the predominantly male nature of most acts of violence.

Male violence is clearly a problem in the modern world, and may even be *the* major source of human suffering. It is, however, intractable, as it is deep-rooted in biology and culture, and is supported by male vested interests of many kinds.

This book contains accessible contributions from a wide range of psychologists who have studied the many faces of male violence: in childhood and adulthood; on the street and in the home; towards men, women and children; and in its sexual and non-sexual forms. These varied topics, together with an emphasis on naturalistic rather than laboratory-based investigations, distinguish these researchers from those aiming to make generalizations about human aggression without considering issues of sex and gender.

In later chapters a variety of theoretical frameworks are brought to bear on this subject. Emphasis on *male* violence leads one to consider, on the one hand, the consequences of natural selection for the two sexes, and on the other, the gendered nature of the cultures in which we live. In line with current evolutionary thinking, the contributors emphasize the complementary nature of these two approaches.

John Archer is Professor of Psychology at the University of Central Lancashire. He is the author of *Ethology and Human Development* and *The Behavioural Biology of Aggression*, and co-author (with Barbara Lloyd) of *Sex and Gender*. He also co-edited (with Kevin Browne) *Human Aggression: Naturalistic Approaches* (Routledge 1989).

ALSO AVAILABLE FROM ROUTLEDGE

HUMAN AGGRESSION
Naturalistic Approaches
Edited by Kevin Browne and John Archer

PSYCHOLOGICAL PERSPECTIVES ON SEXUAL PROBLEMS
New Directions in Theory and Practice
Edited by Jane Ussher and Christine Baker

PSYCHOLOGICAL AND PSYCHIATRIC PROBLEMS IN MEN
Joan Gomez

GENDER ISSUES IN CLINICAL PSYCHOLOGY
Edited by Jane Ussher and Paula Nicolson

MALE VIOLENCE

Edited by John Archer

ROUTLEDGE

London and New York

First published 1994
by Routledge
11 New Fetter Lane, London EC4P 4EE

Simultaneously published in the USA and Canada
by Routledge
29 West 35th Street, New York, NY 10001

Typeset in Baskerville by
Pat and Anne Murphy, Highcliffe-on-Sea, Dorset
Printed and bound in Great Britain by
Mackays of Chatham PLC, Chatham, Kent.

British Library Cataloguing in Publication Data
A catalogue record for this book is available from
the British Library.

Library of Congress Cataloging in Publication Data
Male violence/edited by John Archer.
p.   cm.
Includes bibliographical references and index.
1. Aggressiveness (Psychology) – Sex differences.
2. Violence – Sex Differences.   3. Men – Psychology.
I. Archer, John, 1944–   .
BF575.A3M   1944   155.3'32–dc20
93-10055 CIP

ISBN 0–415–08961–1
0–415–08962–X (pbk)

CONTENTS

Part III Violence towards women and children

Part IV Explanations and theoretical perspectives

ILLUSTRATIONS

CONTRIBUTORS

Yvette Ahmad is Lecturer at Sheffield Hallam University. She is in the process of completing her PhD on bullying in schools. She is also involved in the Department for Education project concerned with effective intervention strategies on combating bullying in schools.

Bernice Andrews has been Lecturer in Psychology at Royal Holloway, University of London, since 1992. Previously Research Officer at the Department of Social Policy and Social Sciences at Royal Holloway, her past and current research activities have included a particular focus on antecedents and consequences of family violence.

John Archer is Professor of Psychology at the University of Central Lancashire. He is co-author, with Barbara Lloyd, of *Sex and Gender*, and author of *The Behavioural Biology of Aggression* and *Ethology and Human Development*. His research interests are aggression, gender roles and grief and loss.

Michael J. Boulton was formerly Senior Lecturer in Psychology, Sheffield Hallam University. He is now Lecturer in Psychology at Keele University. He has carried out extensive research on children's and adolescents' participation in playful and aggressive fighting and is currently involved in a major DFE-funded project that is examining unprovoked aggression in junior, middle and secondary schools.

Kevin Browne, a Chartered Psychologist and Chartered Biologist, is Senior Lecturer in Clinical Criminology at the University of Birmingham. He is Chair of both the Research Committee of the International Society for the Prevention of Child Abuse and Neglect (IPSCAN) and the Editorial Board of the British Association for the Study and Prevention of Child Abuse and Neglect (BASPCAN), as well as Co-editor of *Child Abuse Review*.

Anne Campbell gained her PhD in Experimental Psychology from Oxford University. Formerly Associate Professor of Criminal Justice at Rutgers University, she spent eleven years working on female gang membership and violent interactions in the United States. She was until recently Principal

Lecturer in Criminology at Teesside University, and is now Senior Lecturer in Psychology at the University of Durham.

Martin Daly is Professor of Psychology and Biology at McMaster University and President of the Human Behavior and Evolution Society. His research interests include the evolutionary psychology of human conflict and the behavioural ecology of desert-dwelling mammals. He is co-author, with Margo Wilson, of *Sex, Evolution and Behaviour* and *Homicide*.

Neil Frude is Senior Lecturer at the University of Wales, teaching courses on family relationships, abnormal psychology, human aggression and counselling. He has written and edited a number of books, including *Psychological Approaches to Child Abuse* and *Understanding Family Problems: A Psychological Analysis*. He is a Fellow of the British Psychological Society.

Paul Gilbert is a Top Grade Clinical Psychologist in the National Health Service and Honorary Professor of Clinical Psychology at the University of Derby. Having worked in the National Health Service for fifteen years, he has published several books, including *Human Nature and Suffering*. His current research is in interpersonal behaviour and shame.

Arnold P. Goldstein is Director of the Syracuse University Center for Research on Aggression. He is Professor of Special Education, Syracuse University, Co-Director of the New York State Task Force on Juvenile Gangs, and a member of the American Psychological Association Commission on Youth Violence.

Robin Goodwin received his PhD from the University of Kent, Canterbury. Formerly Lecturer in Psychology at Keele University, he is now Lecturer in Social Psychology at the University of Bristol. He is particularly interested in cultural and historical variations in personal relationships, and currently conducts research on this theme in Eastern Europe.

John P. Hoffmann received his PhD in Criminal Justice at the State University of New York at Albany. He is currently Post-Doctoral Fellow at Emory University School of Public Health, Atlanta. He is also an Assistant Professor in the Department of Criminal Justice, University of North Carolina, Charlotte.

Timothy O. Ireland is a doctoral student at the University at Albany, School of Criminal Justice, and an Assistant Editor of the *Sourcebook of Criminal Justice Statistics*. His research interests include long-term consequences of childhood maltreatment, theoretical criminology and modelling deviant behaviour.

Barry McCarthy obtained his PhD in 1976 and is currently with the Department of Psychology at the University of Central Lancashire. His main research pursuits are in personal relationships and sex biases, but he also has a long-standing interest in social and military history and in psychological concomitants of participation in warfare. He is Reviews Editor for the *Journal of Social and Personal Relationships*.

Steven Muncer gained his PhD from the Institute of Psychiatry, University of London. He worked as a research Associate in Psycholinguistics at Columbia University and has been involved in research on language, cognition and aggression. He is currently Senior Lecturer in Psychology at Teesside University.

Paul Pollard obtained his PhD in Cognitive Reasoning in 1979. He is presently lecturing at the University of Central Lancashire on aggression and social inference. His research interests have moved from cognitive to social psychology, with particular focus over the last five years on sexual aggression.

Peter K. Smith is a Professor of Psychology at the University of Sheffield. He is co-author, with David Thompson, of *Practical Approaches to Bullying*. In addition he is Director of the Sheffield Bullying Project funded by the Department for Education.

Angela K. Turner is a science editor and writer, currently based at Sussex University. She obtained her PhD in animal behaviour from Stirling University. Since 1986 she has been Editor of the journal *Animal Behaviour*. She is co-author, with Felicity Huntingford, of *Animal Conflict*.

Glenn Weisfeld received his PhD from the University of Chicago. He has conducted research on street gang youths; stability, predictors and nonverbal behaviour of dominance in Hopi Indian children, Chinese adolescents and other populations; and dominance relations and marital satisfaction in Britain. He is Editor of *Human Ethology Newsletter*.

Cathy Spatz Widom is Professor of Criminal Justice and Psychology and Director of the Criminal Justice Research Center at the State University of New York, Albany. Her recent research focuses on the intergenerational transmission of violence. She was Winner of the 1989 American Association for the Advancement of Science Behavioral Science Research Prize.

Margo Wilson is Associate Professor of Psychology at McMaster University. Her research interests include homicide, violence against women, the evolutionary psychology of male sexual proprietariness, risk-taking and discriminative parental solicitude in both humans and nonhuman species. She is co-author, with Martin Daly, of *Sex, Evolution and Behavior* and *Homicide*.

PREFACE

Most human violence is carried out by men, yet a book which highlights this by being called *Male Violence* is very different from one simply entitled *Human Violence*. Psychologists have constructed general theories to explain human aggression, which is at the root of violent acts. We take as our starting point not the generality of aggression in the human species, but the predominantly male nature of most acts of violence. It is clearly a vast problem in the modern world, and may even be the major source of human suffering. It is, however, intractable, as it is deep-rooted in both biology and culture, and is supported by male vested interests of many kinds.

This book contains contributions from psychologists and others who have studied the many faces of male violence: in childhood and adulthood; on the street and in the home; towards men, women and children; and in its sexual and non-sexual forms. These varied topics, together with an emphasis on naturalistic rather than laboratory-based investigations, distinguish these researchers from those aiming to make generalizations about human aggression without considering issues of sex and gender.

A variety of theoretical frameworks are brought to bear on this subject. Emphasis on *male* violence leads us to consider, on the one hand, the consequences of natural selection for the two sexes, and on the other, the gendered nature of the cultures in which we live. I have sought to emphasize the complementary nature of these two approaches, rather than seeing them as part of a nature-versus-culture dichotomy.

The initial idea for the book arose from a workshop on 'Gender and Aggression' held in 1990, financed by the Nuffield Foundation of London. I would like to thank them, and also the University of Manchester, for granting me a Simon Fellowship during 1991–92, during which my two chapters were written, and much of the editing undertaken. Special thanks are due to Tony Butterworth, Pat Bateson and Tony Gale for encouraging and supporting my application. The completion of the book and the writing of the Introduction took place while I received further study leave financed by the University of Central Lancashire. I would like to thank Peter Young and Alan Roff for supporting my application, and Val Service, Sheila Glenn, Christine Anderson, Paul Pollard and Ros Bramwell for undertaking extra work caused by my absence.

John Archer
January 1993

1

INTRODUCTION
Male violence in perspective
John Archer

Deliver me, O Lord, from the evil man: preserve me from the violent man.

(Psalm 140, i)

This book concerns violence by human males. As Paul Gilbert remarks in the concluding chapter, 'Male violence may even outrank disease and famine as the major source of human suffering.' He goes on to say that in terms of mental health intervention, targeting male violence would probably be the single most significant form of community prevention programme that could be mounted. It would also be amongst the most difficult, as it would strike at the root of so many entrenched cultural beliefs which justify a wide range of vested interests. Materialism, consumerism, capitalism, militarism, racism and sexism provide shorthand and value-laden descriptions of some of the ideologies supporting these interests.

In this book we explore the many forms of male violence: in childhood and adulthood; on the street and in the home; towards men, women and children; in its sexual and non-sexual forms. Later chapters explore particular theoretical frameworks which may be relevant for explaining such violence, notably the legacy of natural selection, genes and hormones, socialization, the social representations of violence, and power relations. In the final chapter, Paul Gilbert provides a more discursive and speculative overview of the subject, in particular identifying obstacles to change, and to the more pro-social and co-operative alternatives to the ideologies underlying much male violence.

In this chapter I shall introduce several contentious issues connected with the study of male violence, and then provide an overview of the contents of the remainder of the book. Terminology is always a minefield in areas where there is a rich – but often imprecise – everyday vocabulary, and this applies to terms such as 'aggression' and 'violence'. I shall therefore begin by trying to distinguish between these two terms. Choosing to examine *male* violence will be a controversial choice in the eyes of some readers. I shall therefore seek to justify this emphasis. I shall also consider who are the victims of male violence, and finally discuss the connection between sexual and aggressive motives for sexual aggression.

VIOLENCE AND AGGRESSION

Throughout this book, the reader will encounter both the terms 'violence' and 'aggression'. We are particularly concerned with violence, although in order to consider the background to violent acts we also have to consider the broader category of behaviour which psychologists and behavioural biologists refer to as 'aggression'. In many instances, these terms have been conflated. For example, Gerbner (1974), in a study of television violence, defined violence as 'the overt expression of physical force', a phrase which could equally well have applied to 'physical aggression'. In a later study of the same subject, Williams, Zabrack and Joy (1982) qualified this definition, referring to violence as 'physically aggressive behaviors that do, or potentially could, cause injury or death' (p. 366). This added emphasis on the damage caused is, in my opinion, the crucial distinction between physical aggression and violence. The first concentrates on the act and the second on the consequences.

This distinction has not been clearly drawn in a number of areas of aggression research. One area where it is particularly important to do so is the study of aggression and violence in sexual relationships, notably between marriage partners. As indicated in the next section, this lack of clarity has contributed to very different interpretations based on studies emphasizing either behavioural acts or their consequences.

Studies which have sought to estimate the frequency of so-called 'violence' in community samples of married or 'dating' couples have generally used a series of rating scales devised by Straus (1979), referred to as the Conflict Tactics Scales, or CTS. Respondents are asked to indicate on a questionnaire which of various methods they have used to solve conflicts within the relationship. These vary from having talked the problem over calmly through to verbal argument and abuse, to threats of, and actual, physical aggression. The latter consists of a series of items which gradually increase in severity, culminating in use of a knife or a gun.

The problem with using this scale to investigate *violence* in a relationship is that it consists of items which are behaviourally defined, such as kicked, slapped or hit the other. In adopting this approach, researchers have excluded consideration of the possible damaging consequences of these acts, which is the principal concern when studying violence (Dobash *et al.* 1992). In addition to its potential for causing physical damage, a physically aggressive act may have a psychological impact. The behaviourally based approach is likewise unsuited for addressing this issue, since it removes the action from its context: thus the mood of the respondents, the attributions for their actions, and the meaning these have for the relationship are not considered.

Reliance on the behaviourally based CTS is likely to give the impression of a more equal level of 'relationship violence' in the two sexes than would be warranted had the impact of such acts been considered (see the next section). This is largely because men are in most cases bigger, stronger and more familiar with the use of physical aggression than their female partners. For example, when a woman punches her husband this counts on the CTS as the same as when he punches her. But, in most cases, the man has the potential to do more damage with his punch than the woman has with hers.

Many researchers have perpetuated the confusion between physical aggression and violence by labelling studies involving the behaviourally based CTS as 'marital violence' or 'dating violence'. The second of these refers to studies of aggression between sexual partners who are not married, mostly carried out on North American student samples. The CTS have been widely used in these studies, which have been consistently labelled as 'dating *violence*', when they really concern acts of physical aggression. I have to admit to contributing to this confusion in a British study of physical aggression among premarital heterosexual partners (Archer and Ray 1989).

WHY MALE VIOLENCE?

In the book *Sex and Gender* (Archer and Lloyd 1985), we endorsed the view of those feminist writers who claimed that violence was a *male* rather than a human problem. The male had for so long been the model for human beings in general that the two had often been conflated (see Miedzian 1992; Hoffman, Ireland and Widom, this volume). It is still the case that there are vast sex differences in overt acts of violence when we look at homicide statistics (for example, Daly and Wilson 1988, 1990), violent crime statistics (for instance, Dobash and Dobash 1977–8; Wilson and Herrnstein 1985), accounts of violent acts in public (for example, Felson, Baccaglini and Gmelch 1986), major acts of violence in a domestic context (Dobash and Dobash 1977–8; Dobash *et al.* 1992), and the use of violence by organized groups, whether the police, army or politically motivated groups outside the law.

Nevertheless, it is true to say that some women do commit acts of violence. For example, they accounted for 14 per cent of aggravated assaults in Wilson and Herrnstein's (1985) US crime survey, and 8.6 per cent of violent assaults which resulted in police charges, in two Scottish cities in 1974 (Dobash and Dobash 1977–8). A slightly lower proportion was reported for same-sex homicides in a larger scale study carried out in Canada by Daly and Wilson (1988). When self-reports of aggressive crimes are examined, the sex ratio narrows, but it is still just under three to one (Campbell 1986). Campbell examined reports of fighting in samples of 16-year-old schoolgirls, young female offenders and older convicted women prisoners. Overall, the occurrence of physical fights at some time in these women's past was widespread, although it is difficult to assess how their frequencies would compare with equivalent male populations.

Campbell's study considered physical aggression, which may or may not have damaged the opponent or victim. If we move into the realm of what psychologists cover by the term 'aggression' – for example reactions to minor provocations, self-assessments of hostile feelings, and verbal abuse – the scales become more evenly balanced between the sexes: however, men are still on average found to be more aggressive than women (Frodi, Macaulay and Thome 1977; Eagly and Steffen 1986). If we consider self-reported episodes of anger, the sexes are very similar (Averill 1983), and indirect aggression has been found to be more frequent in girls than boys (Lagerspetz, Bjorkqvist and Peltonen 1988). However, none of these categories is likely to apply to the sorts of problematic acts of violence that are involved in cases of violent crime. Instead, they represent the day-to-day annoyances which we all experience and which are typically negotiated without recourse to any act of physical violence, however minor. One possible exception to this is the systematic use of indirect aggression by girls as a form of bullying (see Chapter 4, by Ahmad and Smith). However unpleasant such actions are, it still remains that most acts of aggression which result in injury or death (and fear of these) are carried out by males, and in particular young males.

Because of this, the approach we adopt in this book is to acknowledge that females are quite capable of aggression, and may even be violent in some cases. But we do not let this side-track us from the much greater social problem of male violence by mistaking aggression for violence or by over-emphasizing the relatively unusual, but highly newsworthy, cases of the seriously violent wife, the female sexual abuser of children or the woman serial killer.

As indicated in the previous section, there is controversy over the level of female violence in relationships. Some commentators have suggested that assaults on men by their wives constitute an extensive social problem which goes largely unrecognized. When Walker (1989) characterized domestic violence as violence by men towards women, this provoked a sharp exchange in the correspondence columns of *American Psychologist*. Two critics disputed this claim: one (Mills 1990), by attacking Walker's feminist stance, and the other (Mould 1990) by citing studies using the CTS showing that equal numbers of men and women commit acts of physical aggression to their partners in community samples (for example, Straus and Gelles 1988; O'Leary *et al.* 1989). In fact, this sort of evidence has been widely used both in academic articles and in the media (for instance, Smyth 1992) to support what Dobash *et al.* (1992) referred to as 'the myth of sexual symmetry in marital violence'. Support for this position has also been derived from spousal homicide statistics in the United States, which – unusually – show equivalent numbers of male and female victims.

We have already considered the objection to equating violence with the counting of acts of aggression, irrespective of their seriousness. The CTS has other problems which may obscure difficulties between male and female aggression and violence. It does not distinguish offensive and defensive acts

(Walker 1990); it does not consider the meaning and intentions behind the acts (Dobash *et al.* 1992). It also relies on victim and offender measures from one member of a family, without attempting to validate such measures by asking the other person involved. Where such checks have been carried out, agreement has been found to be little different from chance (Dobash *et al.* 1992).

We can only speculate about the reasons for such discrepant reporting. It has been suggested by those who seek to publicize the plight of male victims of marital violence (such as Smyth 1992) that male under-reporting of victimization is responsible for the greater proportion of female victims in published statistics. It is said that such men do not disclose their plight because of the ridicule, social stigma and outright victimization they would receive (Smyth 1992). However, as Dobash *et al.* (1992) pointed out, there is considerable evidence that women under-report marital violence, whereas the claim that men do so is purely speculative. Married women have many reasons for not reporting their partners' violence, including fear of retaliation, homelessness, economic dependence, and concern for their children's welfare. Altogether it would seem that the situation of the woman victim usually presents fewer viable escape routes.

US homicide statistics are another source of data sometimes used to support the case for the level of marital violence being similar in men and women. In the United States – but not in other countries – almost as many husbands are killed by wives as vice versa (see Wilson and Daly 1992a). Some commentators have interpreted these figures as implying that the reasons for the killings are equivalent. But, as Dobash *et al.* (1992) demonstrated, practically all the killings by wives were motivated by self-defence, often following years of physical violence from the husband. Men's reasons for killing their wives rarely, if ever, follow this pattern. Instead, they are often related directly or indirectly to a proprietary attitude, and to jealousy based on real, possible or imaginary infidelity (Wilson and Daly 1992b).

To base the case for sexual symmetry in marital violence on evidence from the CTS and US homicide statistics is to neglect contradictory evidence from other sources, such as women's refuges and national crime surveys. The latter consistently indicate that a large majority of victims of spousal violence are women, and that they are much more likely than men to suffer injury. The view that these measure problematic violence whereas the CTS does not is further supported by a single large-scale study which found no sex difference when isolated acts of physical aggression were counted, yet women were much more likely than men to be the victims when consequences (injuries) were considered (Dobash *et al.* 1992).

I have dealt with these claims in some detail in relation to marital violence. There have been similar efforts to emphasize cases of female sexual abuse towards children (for example, Barwick 1991), and a more general assumption that mothers are the main offenders when considering physical abuse

(Andrews, Chapter 11). These all have in common an attempt to offer a 'gender-free' interpretation of these events, in opposition to feminist accounts which challenge the behaviour of men and the power relations between the sexes which underpins it (Dobash *et al.* 1992; Felson, 1993). Incidentally, the evolutionary framework coincides with the feminist perspective in emphasizing that the sex of the interactors is of primary importance in understanding the outcome of their interactions, for different, but potentially reconcilable reasons (Gowaty 1992).

Recognition that there are *some* cases of abused husbands and that women may sometimes contribute to the sexual abuse of children is not incompatible with the present emphasis on *male* violence. The position adopted by most authors is that a critical assessment of the present evidence indicates that men commit the bulk of the serious cases of physical violence towards women and children, and of course are largely responsible for sexual aggression. If we add to this the much higher rate of within-sex violence by males than females, it more than justifies singling out *male* violence. As Dobash *et al.* (1992) and others have realized, denying the connection between the male sex and violent acts severely distorts the development of adequate theory. In this book, acknowledgement of the connection has led us to explore a wide range of theoretical approaches to explaining male violence, from the feminist power explanations referred to above, to an exploration of social representations of violence, a critical assessment of socialization explanations, genes and hormones and the theory of natural selection.

THE VICTIMS OF MALE VIOLENCE

The victims of male violence can be men, women or children, but the context in which each becomes a victim tends to differ. Inter-male violence has been less studied than the other two, partly because it tends to be more dispersed and to occur between strangers in more public places. It is also the case that violence within the family has been of concern in relation to prevention of child cruelty and in family studies, and that violence towards women has been spotlighted by feminist researchers. There have been fewer ideological, practical or theoretical reasons for studying violence between men, although it still presents a vast social problem, with repercussions not only for the men involved but also their wives, children and other relatives. We consider inter-male violence in Chapters 6, 7 and 8, and discuss possible explanations in the later chapters of the book.

Violence against women and children involves more repeated and systematic attacks on the same people in the same place. They therefore show much more of an immediately coherent pattern and hence there is greater scope for intervention. As indicated above, violence against women was initially studied because it aroused concern and interest from a feminist perspective, and it was viewed in terms of political power exerted by men over women (Walker 1990).

This type of explanation is considered in Chapter 14. Violence by men towards their wives can also be understood in terms of male proprietary attitudes towards women, which have originated from the different evolutionary selection pressures on the two sexes (Wilson and Daly 1992b; see also Chapter 14). As I argue in Chapter 16, these two types of explanation are not incompatible: it is important to understand that the two sexes do not share the same interests in terms of the activities which will maximize their contributions to future generations. I argue that this difference has provided the basis for social organizations which give priority to male interests at the expense of those of females.

Physical violence by men towards children may be overlooked. Indeed, research has tended to concentrate on the mother in cases of physical abuse. Research described by Bernice Andrews (Chapter 11) challenges this emphasis, finding that men were implicated much more frequently than women. Of course, in the case of sexual abuse it is men who are nearly always the perpetrator (see Chapter 12). Even this research area has strong political implications, and it has been suggested that women play a much larger part than is generally suspected (Barwick 1991).

One British male journalist, noted for his anti-feminist views, wrote the following in his weekly column in the London *Observer*:

> The consensus, widely adopted by the media, is one that has been promoted by feminists. It states that the threat to children comes from the male sex and especially from fathers. A climate has been successfully created in which a father is seen as a regrettable necessity in the business of procreation and thereafter someone to be regarded with acute suspicion.
>
> (Ingrams 1992: 22)

The rest of the piece packs as much prejudice as is possible in five paragraphs, attacking those who run children's homes and what is sneeringly referred to as the 'sex-abuse industry' (that is, those seeking to minimize child sex abuse). For the present, we should note that the research evidence indicates that the main threat to children – even in the case of physical abuse – does arise largely from men.

SEX AND VIOLENCE

So far, I have mainly considered violence associated with aggressive motives; namely, angry or instrumental aggression. Here the physical damage inflicted on the victim is the primary defining feature of the violence, although the accompanying psychological trauma also needs to be taken into account. In the case of sexual violence, which includes rape and other forms of non-consensual acts with adults, and all forms of sexual acts by an adult with a child, the defining feature is the psychological trauma of the experience, rather than any accompanying physical damage – which may or may not have occurred.

Sexual violence – used in this broad sense – is linked to physical violence in the following ways. If a sexual act does not involve consent, physical force will often be necessary to carry it out: for example, studies of marital rape indicate that it rarely occurs without physical assault (Fagan and Browne 1990). A second link arises because the same sorts of men commit both types of violence at different times (Fagan and Wexler 1985, cited in Fagan and Browne 1990). Thirdly, men who endorse extreme masculine role attributes and values show, on the one hand, physical aggression in relationships (Thompson 1991), and on the other a proclivity towards sexual aggression (Smeaton and Byrne 1987). These last two connections are further explored in Chapter 10.

There has been much debate about the immediate motive for rape and other forms of coercive sexual acts. Do they primarily arise out of frustrated sexual motivation? If so, the accompanying physical violence can be viewed as a form of instrumental violence whose aim is sexual access or gratification. However, another suggestion is that in at least some cases the motive is to dominate women. Advocates of this view point to evidence that at least a large proportion of rapes are carried out by men who have sexual partners, and that rape proclivity and actual incidence of rape are linked to attitudes towards women which emphasize the legitimacy of male power and control.

Felson (1993) counters such evidence by arguing that it is subjective sexual deprivation that is important, rather than whether the man has access to a sexual partner at all: for example, married rapists show high rates of both marital and extramarital intercourse. In arguing that the motive for rape is sexual in most cases, he points out the high degree of preoccupation with finding sexually willing females amongst young men, and the degree to which access to attractive females is unavailable to most men. Coercion, he argues, is one strategy that some men adopt, and he also notes evidence that non-coercive strategies are preferred if they are effective.

I would add that the use of a coercive strategy to obtain sex is underpinned by an adversarial attitude to women (and in the case of prison, to subordinate men: Felson 1993), which views them largely in terms of sexual gratification. Power – the exercise of which is inevitably involved in all acts of coercion – enables the man to obtain sex in this way, rather than being the goal of the coercive act. This interpretation is also consistent with the finding noted above, of a link between using violence to obtain sex and for other reasons. A similar view is provided by Paul Pollard (Chapter 10), where he argues that it is important to distinguish between the immediate motive for a typical rape – namely, sexual access – and the use of sexual conquests, whether with or without consent, to bolster male self-esteem and reputation within a peer group. In this respect, terms such as 'scoring' and 'conquests' point to the competitive nature of the enterprise when viewed in terms of its social presentation to the male group. It may not be too far-fetched to point out a parallel between keeping a tally of such conquests and a similar record of killings among the males of some non-state societies (see Daly and Wilson 1988).

Although this dual interpretation, of an immediate sexual motive with longer-term implications for male status, is consistent with the majority of the evidence, there are still cases in which coercive sex may be used for the main or sole purpose of humiliating the victim. This is likely to be the case in some serial stranger rapes, when a man deliberately sets out to humiliate his victims – for example, by taking their clothes (Davies 1991). It is also seen in an extreme form in the use of sexual torture – the purpose of which seems to be to destroy the victim's sense of identity through sexual violation (Agger 1989).

OUTLINE OF REMAINING CHAPTERS

The book is divided into a number of sections. The first one contains three chapters on various aspects of aggression in children, to indicate some of the developmental origins of adult male violence. Chapter 2 is concerned with the differences and similarities between aggression and play-fighting, since in both cases there are pronounced sex differences amongst children. Michael Boulton first outlines the difficulties in distinguishing between 'rough-and-tumble play', as it is usually called, and real aggression. He describes the ways in which researchers make the distinction, and to what extent children can tell the two apart. The widespread sex differences in rough-and-tumble play, which are also found in other mammals, have been attributed to biological differences, notably those in prenatal hormones. An evolutionary functional explanation has been offered in terms of rough-and-tumble play being necessary preparation and training for later male aggression. This argument leads to the second half of the chapter, which concerns the relationship between the two in childhood and adolescence. Boulton concludes that although they are not closely related for most children, there may be a minority of children who use play-fighting as an opportunity to hurt another. During adolescence, the two may be used for similar ends, such that some boys may be using rough-and-tumble to assert their capacity to dominate another physically. Boulton goes on to describe some of his own recent research on between-sex rough-and-tumble incidents in the playground, suggesting that some boys use them as a cover for brief physical assaults. Finally, one recent study raised the intriguing possibility that during young adulthood, rough-and-tumble (termed 'horseplay' at these ages) may be more closely linked with physical aggression, but, as Boulton acknowledges, this remains a possibility to be investigated further rather than a definite conclusion at this time.

Boulton's chapter tells us that rough-and-tumble episodes may form part of the various ways in which older boys work out physical dominance relations. The third chapter concentrates on the importance of dominance in boys' groups. Adopting a perspective derived from studies of dominance in other social animals, particularly primates, Glenn Weisfeld argues that children – and in particular boys – compete so as to form dominance orders. In arguing that there is a motive to strive for rank or status, Weisfeld raises one important issue which crops up in various places throughout the book when dealing with aggression and violence towards other males: it concerns why these acts are so much more common than comparable acts between females. In Chapter 16, I consider the notion of striving for status as an example of a power explanation, and come to a rather different conclusion about the motive to gain status from that of Weisfeld. In editing this book, it was apparent that there were several instances where individual contributors had different ways of viewing their subject matter. Rather than smoothing over what some would regard as discrepancies, I have chosen to highlight them so as to clarify where the different theoretical perspectives produce not only different interpretations but also different predictions for future research, and different practical suggestions for alleviating and controlling violence.

Weisfeld discusses the way in which boys' dominance relations are similar to those of other primates, and their importance for providing access to resources (and hence for biological fitness: see Chapter 14, by Daly and Wilson) in social animals generally. This becomes accentuated at puberty, an observation which is again understandable from an evolutionary perspective, since this signals the onset of reproductive competition, which is particularly marked among males (again see Chapter 14). Weisfeld also discusses the stability of dominance relations during development, and the correlates of high dominance rank with other attributes such as attractiveness, athletic ability and popularity. He also outlines the association of aggressiveness and dominance position with social problems such as delinquency.

In Chapter 4, Yvette Ahmad and Peter K. Smith describe their research on bullying, which was built on earlier research by Olweus in Norway. It also incorporates findings from Finnish researchers (Lagerspetz *et al.* 1988 – see earlier section) showing the widespread use of indirect aggression by girls. Following from this, Ahmad and Smith found that British boys and girls on the receiving end of bullying also reported a sex-linked pattern in the aggression: boys were more likely to be hit, whereas girls were more likely to experience indirect forms such as having rumours spread or no one talking to them. Nevertheless, even with indirect aggression included, boys were still involved in more bullying than girls. For male victims, it was usually other boys who were the bullies. For girls, it depended on age: at 8 and 11 years, they were more likely to be bullied by boys, whereas at 13 and 15 years it was other girls who were the most frequent bullies.

Part II is concerned with male violence towards other men. Arnold Goldstein discusses the male gang, concentrating on studies carried out in North America. He traces the different views of gangs held by researchers since early this century, and elaborates theories about gang behaviour, most of which are sociological in nature. National surveys in the United States show gang members to be mainly males from 12 to 21 years of age, from poorer areas, with Afro-Americans and Hispanics highly represented. The gang provides an alternative way of obtaining resources and social standing for young males from poor and educationally disadvantaged groups. This view is echoed in other chapters more specifically concerned with individual inter-male aggression (for example, Chapters 3, 7 and 14). However, Goldstein emphasizes that delinquent behaviour forms only a small part of the gang's total activities. Mostly they just hang out, and mark their allegiance to their territory and to the gang in diverse ways. Over recent years, however, gangs have increased their level of violent crime, which is typically three times that of delinquents who are not gang members.

Goldstein goes on to describe the various intervention programmes that have been attempted to tackle gangs as a social problem. He concludes that neither the earlier attempts to provide agency workers in the field, nor pro-viding opportunities for gang members, have been adequately evaluated. Since the late 1970s, the rise in street gangs and accompanying violence has produced a more punitive response to gangs. At present there are signs of more comprehensive programmes incorporating aspects of all these earlier approaches, which seek to combine the needs of gang members with protec-tion of the wider society.

Barry McCarthy adopts a historical and cross-cultural viewpoint in considering the values behind men who adopt the warrior role. He shows that warrior values are closely linked with concepts of masculinity, and that such values – although they may differ in terms of specific attributes – are wide-spread amongst young adult males in non-state subsistence cultures. In politically and economically more elaborate societies, a distinct warrior caste of high status has developed. McCarthy provides historical examples of the warrior caste from the officer elite of the Roman Republic, the knights of medieval Europe, and the samurai of medieval Japan, before considering its twentieth-century manifestations, culminating in the Waffen-SS. Warrior values in their various forms are shown to accentuate and glorify certain recurrent themes in more broadly based conceptions of masculinities.

In Chapter 7, I consider violent disputes between pairs or small groups of men. Various sources of evidence indicate that the most severe forms of within-sex violence occur between men. So do most other forms of physical aggression (with the exception of the usually less damaging forms such as pinching and scratching). Such inter-male violence is concentrated among teenagers and young adults, and is more likely among those outside the main-stream of society. It tends to occur on the streets of poor urban areas, and the bar may serve as a focus by bringing a violence-prone section of the population together.

The typical precipitating act involves violation of perceived social rules reflecting on status and self-esteem. However, this is only the beginning, and the subsequent moves which escalate the contest are crucial for understanding its outcome. Similar escalated sequences occur prior to fights between animals, and game theory modelling has been used to elucidate the evolutionary rules on which these are based. Perhaps the most important feature is that the escalated sequence involves assessment of the opponent's fighting potential. Although this is still true of human exchanges, the influence of alcohol and weapons has considerably changed the circumstances of fighting. Nevertheless, such changes can still be understood within the evolutionary game theory perspective. The chapter finishes with a consideration of how masculine beliefs and values provide the background for understanding the cultural significance of male violence.

Part III is concerned with male violence towards women and children. Violence in a domestic context has been the subject of much research and public concern over the last twenty-five years in the United States and other modern western societies. This has now extended to extramarital relationships in the form of studies of 'dating violence' (see above). Some of the concerns expressed earlier in this introduction are elaborated by Robin Goodwin in a chapter which takes a critical look at research on relationship aggression and violence. He is concerned not only with the limitations of the counting approach outlined earlier, but also with the way in which such research has been approached without concern for its historical and cultural context. In this respect, the commonly used term 'dating violence' says it all. Dating is a (middle-class) North American cultural institution (see Mead 1950, chap. 14), which does not extend too well to Basingstoke, let alone to Baghdad. The 'violence' that is supposedly investigated is the physical aggression of the CTS (see above). Goodwin therefore refers instead to 'relationship aggression', and includes both physical and sexual aggression in his discussion of the importance of the cultural background for understanding the significance of these acts.

In Chapter 9, Neil Frude specifically concentrates on marital violence, viewing it from an interactional perspective – that is, as the outcome of social interactions placed in a cultural and societal context. He is concerned with the precise ways in which more global concepts such as social class affect the likelihood of violent interactions, and also how this is affected by characteristics of the relationship and by the personal attributes of the individuals. These influences all form a background to the violent incident itself, which is commonly sparked off by quarrels about sex or money. (These themes are readily understandable from the perspective of evolutionary biology outlined in Daly and Wilson's chapter.)

Frude is careful to point out that viewing marital violence in an interactional context does not imply that both protagonists are equally responsible. He, like other authors, emphasizes that it is usually husbands who are the violent partner. Nevertheless, it is worth highlighting some aspects of this way of looking at marital violence which differ in their implications from those of alternatives. The interactional perspective is potentially gender-free: it essentially looks at the ongoing interaction between a couple, albeit in the context of variables which link this interaction with the wider societal context. In contrast, both the evolutionary view (derived from the principle of sexual selection) and the feminist view (emphasizing power inequalities in society) stress first and foremost the imbalance in any relationship between a man and a woman. This is seen as fundamental for understanding the nature of the relationship, which entails a conflict of interests (the evolutionary view), or unequal power (see Gowaty 1992 for a more detailed discussion of the convergence between these two apparently different viewpoints).

Paul Pollard (Chapter 10) is concerned with male sexual violence towards women, in particular to identify the characteristics of men who carry out such aggression. He first reviews studies which indicate that rape and other forms of sexual assault are far more common than is generally supposed and that the typical rapist is not the convicted criminal who rapes a stranger, but an acquaintance of the victim who does not have a criminal record and who is not reported to the police. This leads on to consideration of studies assessing variations in the tendency to rape in the general male population, and to the identification of variables associated with 'rape proclivity'. Thus the values which enhance the likelihood and acceptance of rape are also those that foster inter-male violence and relationship violence.

Pollard discusses two common beliefs about rapists: first, that they have poor social skills or are for some other reason limited in their access to women; and secondly, that they are mentally unstable. Neither is supported by the available evidence. Instead, a cluster of beliefs, consisting of greater acceptance of rape myths (essentially greater tolerance of rape and blaming the victim), traditional gender-role attitudes, and attitudes supportive of violence towards women, were all associated with self-reported sexual aggression. So were higher arousal to rape depictions, greater sexual experience and belonging to a sexually exploitive peer group. Further research indicated that when several of these variables are present together, they have greater predictive power than would be expected from their summation. In general, although rape proclivity seems to be a continuous attribute within the male population, 'the "macho male" whose sense of self worth is bolstered by the pursuit of dominance and exploitation of the opposite sex, is particularly likely to translate his basic misogyny into sexual violence' (Pollard, this volume).

In Chapter 11, Bernice Andrews describes her research on both physical and sexual violence by men towards children in a domestic context. She concludes that in the case of physical abuse, although previous research has tended to focus on the mother, men were implicated much more frequently than women in her studies. Of course, in the case of sexual abuse it is men who are nearly always the perpetrator. Examination of the contexts in which such violence is likely to occur suggested that a maternal psychiatric condition, particularly depression, or poor mothering, increased the chances of both forms of abuse.

The next chapter, by Kevin Browne, provides an overview of current research on the sexual abuse of children. He reviews evidence of a high rate of sexual victimization, for example, from retrospective community samples. Most offenders are male, the most common age being 35 to 40. They are usually known to the victim, but are not from his or her immediate family. As also found by Andrews, certain family factors, indicative of poor care, are associated with increased risk. Although various personality and behaviour problems can be identified in offender populations, they are not restricted to child sex abuse, and there is no agreed profile of the typical abuser.

The consequences of this form of abuse are likely to be widespread, and include the traumatic results of the sexual act, a sense of betrayal of trust, a feeling of powerlessness, and stigmatization. Later psychological problems include drug abuse, sexual dysfunction, personality and eating disorders. In males, they also include aggressive and antisocial behaviour and child sexual abuse, so that one generation's victim becomes the next's offender. Such individuals typically show cognitive distortions about the acceptability of their actions.

The final part of the book is concerned with explanations of male violence. Explanations may vary in several different ways. For example, in explaining sex differences, emphasis may be placed on biological or environmental influences on the person's psychological disposition, or on the impact of the overall social structure on people's behaviour at an individual level (Archer 1992b). In the case of male violence, the first would be represented by an explanation in terms of the effect of the male hormone on the brain and on fighting capability; the second involves the way in which boys learn to suppres their more empathic side, and to associate masculinity and self-esteem with toughness and violence; the third involves the direct effect of being in a powerful position in society: it includes the way in which the social position of husband has throughout history permitted wife beating (Chapter 16) and the social position of soldier or warrior (Chapter 6) has permitted – or rather made obligatory – violence towards the enemy.

The explanations distinguished in the previous paragraph vary in terms of an emphasis on nature or nurture as the controlling influence, and whether they focus on the individual or the whole society. As is indicated below, the nature–nurture distinction is in practice a false one in terms of whether both sorts of influence occur, but perhaps not in terms of which has most control on the development of a specific attribute (Archer 1992a). Another type of distinction concerns proximal or immediate causes versus the distal or ultimate ones. Hormonal action or a particular type of environment would be immediate influences, whereas the evolutionary background of the hormone, or the cultural origin of the immediate environment, would be ultimate explanations.

In the final part of the book, a number of different perspectives are explored in individual chapters. These include: the immediate biological influences of hormones and heredity; the ultimate biological explanation of evolutionary adaptation; power explanations – which are structural explanations involving people's positions in society; socialization; and the social representations of violence by men and women – which provide the cultural background to socialization. In the final chapter, Paul Gilbert provides an overview which seeks to integrate at least some of these and to link male violence to mental health concerns and wider societal values.

Angela Turner considers the evidence for male violence being influenced by biological variables within the individual. Males and females are different genetically, hormonally and in average size and strength. After providing an overview of the extensive research in this area, Angela Turner concludes that there is at most a small genetic component underlying delinquency, aggression and violence, but a greater one for the personality traits underlying these, such as sensation-seeking and impulsivity. Even so, the route from genes to adult behaviour is long and complex, leaving much scope for variability in different environmental conditions. As regards the possibility, often voiced, that male aggression may be enhanced or even caused by high testosterone levels, the evidence does support a moderate association between testosterone and aggression. However, interpretation of this association as indicating such a causal link is complicated by the consequences of competition and aggression affecting hormone levels, including testosterone. Turner concludes that neither a simple genetic and hormonal explanation nor a simple environmental one can by itself explain male violence. Her conclusions coincide with those in the book *Boys Will be Boys*, in which the philosopher Myriam Miedzian set out to examine the link between violence and masculinity from a broad feminist perspective. She concluded that, 'while there appears to be some biological base to greater male violence, this potential can be reinforced or diminished depending on socialization' (Miedzian 1992). She argued that because men have such a potential it is all the more important to do everything possible to discourage its development and expression, and to emphasize alternative patterns of behaviour. This conclusion echoes that of Gilbert in our final chapter (see below).

Martin Daly and Margo Wilson present a Darwinian perspective on male violence. They first introduce the background to this way of thinking about psychological attributes, since it involves a viewpoint that has been little represented in mainstream psychology (and the social sciences generally), where it is often misunderstood (or purposely ignored). They argue that an understanding of the principle of natural selection is crucial for any endeavour which seeks to explain general psychological dispositions – general, that is, in terms of the species, the sex and the age group. Male violence is one such general disposition.

The overall pattern of male violence, whatever its specific cultural or historical context, can be understood in terms of past selection pressures, particularly those outlined by Darwin as 'sexual selection'. As was realized a century later by Trivers (1972), these derive ultimately from the specialization

15

of males and females in gamete production. This, combined with anatomical and ecological conditions which make it more or less feasible for one sex (usually the male) to leave the other to take care of the offspring, provides an understanding of why males and females have come to have different reproductive strategies. These different strategies involve greater competition and risk-taking between males than females, and a conflict of interests between males and females. Most male violence – to men, to women and to children – can be understood in terms of these two principles.

As Daly and Wilson argue, although violence is abhorrent and a severe social problem, from an evolutionary viewpoint it cannot be viewed as a pathological form of human behaviour. They go on to consider the evidence for male violence having its origins in evolved adaptations. They highlight its association with reproductive competition, its concentration in the years following puberty, and its enhancement by certain developmental and current environmental conditions: these are principally ones which indicate that an individual has much to gain and little to lose (in terms of fitness) by adopting a violent strategy. Thus an evolutionary explanation is not incompatible with one which emphasizes developmental history or the current cultural milieu. Instead, it makes the impact of these environments understandable from a wider perspective, rather than appearing to be arbitrary.

John Hoffmann, Timothy Ireland and Cathy Spatz Widom critically examine traditional socialization explanations, which have concentrated on aggression rather than violence. In psychology, these have their roots in psychoanalytic and social learning theory. Perhaps the most influential version in relation to aggression has been that of Bandura, which concentrated on the impact on the person of aggressive models, from family, peer group and the mass media. Bandura later emphasized cognitive mediators of these influences in the form of self-regulation and self-efficacy; that is, observing violent actions will only lead to the person enacting violence in a future interaction, if it is viewed as a positive way of enhancing self-esteem, and is within the person's perceived capabilities. This theoretical framework has led to studies which more directly examine the family backgrounds of aggressive individuals.

Hoffmann and his colleagues point out that, although the social learning view is supposed to apply to learning aggressive behaviour in general, it has been developed and applied almost exclusively to males. Although it provides a basis for understanding the transmission of aggressive actions to individuals from their family, peer-group and media backgrounds, there remain a number of outstanding issues, which the authors consider in their chapter. They include: the extent to which these theories of *aggression* can be applied to *violence*; the lack of a developmental perspective (since they are concerned with processes which can potentially occur at any time in the life cycle); the need to take into account the entire family and peer-group relationships; the role of macro-level situational and social variables, such as social class and unemployment (see

Chapter 9 by Frude for a consideration of how such variables influence marital violence); the need to consider the sex of both the perpetrator and the victim in this theoretical perspective (which was originally 'gender-free' – see above).

In the chapter on power explanations, I consider first the feminist argument that male violence towards women forms part of a wider societal and historical system often called the 'patriarchy': the evidence is consistent with this as an explanation of why it is women who are the major recipient of marital violence. Why particular men are violent is explained in terms of variations in male expectations and female actions. This structural power explanation of marital violence can be contrasted with an interpersonal status explanation for inter-male violence: this concerns the exercise of personal power through violence under conditions of minimal structural power. The two explanations can be linked in terms of a common set of masculine values which endorse the use of violence to attain status in the eyes of other men, and as a way of keeping women in a subservient position to men generally. I also seek to place the origin of these two forms of male power in an evolutionary context (see also Chapter 14), arguing that the first has its origins in the conflict of interests between the optimum reproductive strategies of males and females, and the second is a consequence of inter-male competition, arising from sexual selection.

Anne Campbell and Stephen Muncer consider the ways in which men and women think about aggression and violence, and advance their hypothesis, supported by a growing body of empirical evidence, that this is fundamentally different. Men consider violence in instrumental terms, connected with obtaining tangible or abstract benefits, whereas for women it represents a discharge of emotion, a sign of not coping. The evidence indicates that these different 'social representations' of aggression are generally divided along sex-linked lines, but are also closely related to masculine and feminine occupations requiring the attributes of aggressiveness or nurturance. They are not, however, closely associated with individual gender-linked personality traits. Overall, these different meanings attached to aggressive acts by men and women will be very important in relation to violence between the sexes, since these would involve mutual misunderstanding which will compound the original source of conflict.

In the final chapter, Paul Gilbert first provides his own integration of explanations for male violence, ranging from sources as diverse as psychoanalysis to evolutionary biology. He views physical aggression as a strategy for a variety of ends in a variety of situations. Principally, human conflict concerns issues such as coercion of others and with self-presentation and achieving status in the eyes of others. It is either directed to the intimidation of others or to gaining their admiration. The two tactics often go together in a single act of violence. In the second half of the chapter, Gilbert argues that the problem of male violence lies not so much in 'there being too much of something' – namely, anger and aggression – but of there being 'too little of something' – namely, empathy and affiliation. This takes us back to a recurrent theme in this book, that male violence needs to be looked at in the context of a set of values associated with a particular view of masculinity. This provides the link across various forms of male violence, physical and sexual, to other men, to women and to children. This view of masculinity can ultimately be understood as a particular reproductive strategy rooted in our evolutionary history.

As Gilbert indicates, we first have to identify the conditions which foster and encourage such a view of masculinity. He looks at these in the widest possible cultural context, concentrating on the impact of economics and religion. The first, via capitalism, rewards competitive and individualistic values which promote a certain form of ruthless and competitive masculinity, and which devalue attributes traditionally associated with femininity such as empathy and compassion. The second involves hierarchical and male-dominated structures, and encompass values which are antithetical to female sexuality in particular and to women in general. The specific values associated with most of the main religions help to perpetuate male domination, and a view of women as contaminated and dangerous to men, hence easily blamed when they are the victims of sexual and physical violence. With both capitalist economic values and the major religions providing firm supporting structures for traditional notions of masculinities that legitimize and condone both inter-male conflict and violence towards women in the 'appropriate' circumstances, it is clear that the problem of male violence raises fundamental questions about values which are accepted and unquestioned by the majority of people – men and women alike – living in the modern world.

REFERENCES

Agger, I. (1989) 'Sexual torture of political prisoners: an overview', *Journal of Traumatic Stress*, 2: 305–18.

Archer, J. (1992a) *Ethology and Human Development*, Hemel Hempstead, UK: Harvester Wheatsheaf.

—— (1992b) 'Childhood gender roles: social context and organisation', in H. McGurk (ed.) *Childhood Social Development: Contemporary Perspectives*, Hove, UK, and Hillsdale, NJ: Erlbaum, pp. 31–61.

Archer, J. and Lloyd, B. B. (1985) *Sex and Gender*, New York: Cambridge University Press.

Archer, J. and Ray, N. (1989) 'Dating violence in the United Kingdom: a preliminary study', *Aggressive Behavior*, 15: 337–43.

Averill, J. R. (1983) 'Studies on anger and aggression', *American Psychologist*, 38: 1145–60.

Barwick, S. (1991) 'Not only men', *The Spectator*, London, 266 (no. 8499): 8–10.

Campbell, A. (1986) 'Self-report of fighting by females', *British Journal of Criminology*, 26: 28–46.

Daly, M. and Wilson, M. (1988) *Homicide*, Chicago: Aldine de Gruyter.

—— (1990) 'Killing the competition: female/female and male/male competition', *Human Nature*, 1: 81–107.

Davies, A. (1991) 'The language of rape', Paper presented at the British Psychological Society Social Psychology Section Conference, University of Surrey, Guildford, UK, 20–22 Sept.

Dobash, R. E. and Dobash, R. P. (1977–78) 'Wives: the "appropriate" victims of marital violence', *Victimology: An International Journal*, 2: 426–42.

Dobash, R. P., Dobash, R. E., Daly, M. and Wilson, M. (1992) 'The myth of sexual symmetry in marital violence', *Social Problems*, 39: 71–91.

Eagly, A. and Steffen, V. J. (1986) 'Gender and aggressive behavior: a meta-analytic review of the social psychological literature', *Psychological Bulletin*, 100: 309–30.

Fagan, J. and Browne, A. (1990) *Marital Violence: Physical Aggression Between Women and Men in Intimate Relationships*, Washington, DC: National Academy of Sciences.

Felson, R. B. (1993) 'Sexual coercion: a social interactionist approach', in R. B. Felson and J. T. Tedeschi (eds) *Aggression and Violence: Social Interactionist Perspectives*, Washington, DC: APA.

Felson, R. B., Baccaglini, W. and Gmelch, G. (1986) 'Bar-room brawls: aggression and violence in Irish and American bars', in A. Campbell and J. J. Gibbs (eds) *Violent Transactions: The Limits of Personality*, Oxford: Blackwell, pp. 153–66.

Frodi, A., Macaulay, J. and Thome, P. R. (1977) 'Are women always less aggressive than men? a review of the experimental literature' *Psychological Bulletin*, 84: 634–60.

Gerbner, G. (1974) *Cultural Indicators Project: TV Message Analysis Recording Instrument* (rev. edn), Philadelphia: University of Pennsylvania.

Gowaty, P. A. (1992) 'Evolutionary biology and feminism', *Human Nature*, 3: 217–49.

Ingrams, R. (1992) column headed 'Richard Ingrams', *The Observer*, London, 11 Oct., p. 22.

Lagerspetz, K. M. J., Bjorkqvist, K. and Peltonen, T. (1988) 'Is indirect aggression typical of females? gender differences in aggressiveness in 11- to 12-year-old children', *Aggressive Behavior*, 14: 403–14.

Mead, M. (1950) *Male and Female*, New York: William Morrow.

Miedzian, M. (1992) *Boys Will be Boys: Breaking the Link Between Masculinity and Violence*, London: Virago.

Mills, M. E. (1990) 'The new heretics: men', *American Psychologist*, 45: 675–6.

Mould, D. E. (1990) 'Data base or data bias?', *American Psychologist*, 45: 676.

Nelson, S. (1992) 'Deadlier than the male?', *The Guardian*, London, 25 March, p. 37.

O'Leary, K. D., Barling, J., Arias, I., Rosenbaum, A., Malone, J. and Tyree, A. (1989) 'Prevalence and stability of physical aggression between spouses: a longitudinal analysis', *Journal of Consulting and Clinical Psychology*, 57: 263–8.

Smeaton, G. and Byrne, D. (1987) 'The effects of R-rated violence and erotica, individual differences and victim characteristics on acquisition of rape proclivity', *Journal of Research in Personality*, 21: 171–84.

Smyth, A. (1992) 'Do only women bleed?', *The Guardian*, London, 15 July.

Straus, M. (1979) 'Measuring intrafamily conflict and violence: the Conflict Tactics (CT) scales', *Journal of Marriage and the Family*, 41: 75–88.

Straus, M. A. and Gelles, R. J. (1988) 'Violence in American families: how much is there and why does it occur?', in E. W. Nunnally, C. S. Chilman and F. M. Cox (eds) *Troubled Relationships*, Newbury Park, CA: Sage, pp. 141–62.

Thompson, E. H. (1991) 'The maleness of violence in dating relationships: an appraisal of stereotypes', *Sex Roles*, 24: 261–78.

Trivers, R. L. (1972) 'Parental investment and sexual selection', in B. Campbell (ed.) *Sexual Selection and the Descent of Man*, Chicago: Aldine, pp. 136–79.

Walker, L. E. A. (1989) 'Psychology and violence against women', *American Psychologist*, 44: 659–702.

—— (1990) 'Response to Mills and Mould', *American Psychologist*, 45: 676–7.

Williams, T. M., Zabrack, M. L. and Joy, L. A. (1982) 'The portrayal of aggression on North American television', *Journal of Applied Social Psychology*, 12: 360–80.

Wilson, J. Q. and Herrnstein, R. J. (1985) *Crime and Human Nature*, New York: Simon & Schuster.

Wilson, M. I. and Daly, M. (1992a) 'Who kills whom in spouse killings? on the exceptional sex ratio of spousal homicides in the United States', *Criminology*, 30: 189–215.

—— (1992b) 'The man who mistook his wife for a chattel', in J. H. Barkow, L. Cosmides and J. Tooby (eds) *The Adapted Mind*, New York and Oxford: Oxford University Press, pp. 289–321.

Part I

AGGRESSION IN CHILDHOOD

2

THE RELATIONSHIP BETWEEN PLAYFUL AND AGGRESSIVE FIGHTING IN CHILDREN, ADOLESCENTS AND ADULTS

Michael J. Boulton

Complex behaviour that has implications for society at large, such as aggression and violence, pose an almost irresistible challenge to researchers from a variety of disciplines, including the biological and social sciences. Attempts to understand such behaviour have had varied levels of success. Developmental psychologists have been at the forefront of these endeavours, most notably in their attempts to identify precursors of adult aggression/violence in the lives of children and adolescents. A full review of their achievements in this respect, however, is not the aim of this chapter. Rather, I shall attempt to consider what developmental psychologists have found out about the relationship, both concurrent and developmental, between aggression and a category of behaviour that in many ways appears to closely resemble it. This category of behaviour is widely known as 'rough-and-tumble play', and basically includes fighting and chasing action patterns that are playfully motivated and delivered. The surface similarity between such playful actions and their aggressive counterparts has meant that it has been tempting for some adults to make certain assumptions about the role of rough-and-tumble play in the aetiology of aggressive tendencies. Such assumptions have included the notion that participation in rough-and-tumble play somehow causes children to be more aggressive or that highly aggressive individuals also engage in elevated levels of rough-and-tumble play. It is only in the past decade or so that developmental psychologists have begun to address systematically these specific issues. As I shall argue in this chapter, many of the assumptions about rough-and-tumble play and its relationship to aggression have received only partial support, and many have not been supported at all. However, I first address the issue of what rough-and-tumble play is, what action patterns it involves, and how often children of either sex participate in it.

IDENTIFYING ROUGH-AND-TUMBLE PLAY

Harlow and Harlow (1965) were among the first researchers to identify rough-and-tumble play as a separate category in the behavioural repertoire of rhesus monkeys. Blurton-Jones (1967) then applied this category to his observational research with human children. Another important landmark was the publication of Aldis's (1975) book *Play Fighting*, which contained descriptive accounts of the behaviour in a range of locations, including playgrounds, parks and beaches. Following on from this innovative early work, rough-and-tumble play has been defined in a variety of different ways. In a recent paper, Fry (1988) classified episodes

> as either serious aggression or play aggression on the basis of the facial expressions and gestures of the actors. . . . Smiles, laughs and play faces were common play signals, while low frowns, bared teeth, fixated gazes, and crying/weeping were interpreted as indicating serious intent.
>
> (1975: 1013)

The definitions that have been adopted in the past, although diverse in some respects, generally share the common notion that rough-and-tumble play contains behaviour that looks aggressive but that is essentially playful and so lacks the intent to hurt or intimidate another person. In arriving at a satisfactory definition, two problems in particular have to be overcome. First, the definition must be able to distinguish between playful and serious/aggressive intent on the part of the participants, and secondly, it must be able to handle the diverse range of physical action patterns that could, potentially, be involved.

One recent approach (Boulton 1988; Boulton and Smith 1992) has been to break down rough-and-tumble play into a taxonomy with several categories, and then to apply three main identifying criteria to ensure that these categories can be considered playful. These criteria involve the characteristics of physical action *per se*, particularly the strength of a blow, kick and so on, the presence/absence of signs of injury/distress/annoyance by the recipient, and the presence/absence of signs of regret by the perpetrators of injury/distress/annoyance. Thus, apparent fighting behaviour is judged as playful if it does not involve powerful blows, or cause injury and/or distress and/or annoyance to one or other party or, if it does involve these things, the offender shows signs of regret and suggests that they were accidental. Behaviour would be seen as aggressive if powerful actions which caused injury and/or distress and/or annoyance were neither accompanied by signs of regret nor were accompanied by insults and other negative statements.

This taxonomy was not presented as the 'finished product' but rather as one which was applicable to a specific sample of children. It may have less relevance or usefulness for samples drawn from other ages or geographical locations. For example, the 'other' category accommodates patterns of behaviour that occurred so infrequently in the sample of children studied that to have included them as individual categories in the taxonomy would have rendered the taxonomy too unwieldy. In other samples these same patterns of behaviour might occur with greater frequency and hence it would be sensible to include them as distinct categories in the taxonomy. Alternatively, some action patterns that occurred with relatively high fequency in the sample of children studied may occur only rarely in other samples, and hence it would be prudent to subsume these under the general category of 'other'. For example, the categories, 'boxing' and 'kung fu' may only be applicable to children who are exposed to media images of adults engaging in these activities.

ROUGH-AND-TUMBLE PLAY AND AGGRESSION: EVIDENCE FOR A DISTINCTION IN CHILDHOOD

There is a growing body of evidence that rough-and-tumble play and aggression should be seen as distinct categories of behaviour for most children. Some of the earliest studies were carried out with preschool children, and sought to identify criteria upon which a distinction could be made. Many investigators focused on facial expressions. Using factor analysis, Blurton-Jones (1967, 1972) found that rough-and-tumble play was characterized by 'laugh' and the 'play face', whereas aggression was loaded highly for 'frown' and 'fixate'. Several subsequent studies provided evidence for a distinction along similar lines (Konner 1972; McGrew 1972; Eibl-Eibesfeldt 1974; Aldis 1975; DiPietro 1981; Humphreys and Smith 1987; Fry 1988). However, Boulton (1991a) recently sounded a note of caution about relying too heavily on facial expressions. He observed many episodes which were playful (that is, the participants themselves said so when asked) but which involved negative facial expressions, such as frowns. In most of these cases, the negative facial expressions appeared to reflect fantasy themes that are often part of the rough-and-tumble encounters of young children.

Several researchers have also used the outcome of encounters to make a distinction between rough-and-tumble play and aggression (McGrew 1972; Aldis 1975; Humphreys and Smith 1987). Play encounters are seen as being characterized by partners remaining together after the bout is over, whereas aggression usually involves participants moving away from one another when it ends. As we shall see later, more detailed research suggests that outcome is heavily influenced by the sex composition of the participants.

Smith and Lewis (1985) extended these investigations by combining the use of these two important criteria. They observed preschool children in free-play situations and recorded both facial expressions and the outcome of episodes. Almost half of the episodes were positive on both criteria, about a quarter were positive on one criterion and neutral on the other, and about a tenth were negative by both criteria or negative on one and neutral on the other. Based on this evidence it appeared that the two criteria of facial expression and outcome were especially useful in helping to distinguish between rough-and-tumble play and aggression.

In a recent study, Boulton (1991a) compared structural and contextual features of rough-and-tumble play and aggression. The former was found to contain a greater variety of actions than the latter, and both wrestling and chasing were more often observed as constituents of rough-and-tumble play than of aggression. In a similar study, Fry (1987) observed differences between play fighting and serious fighting among 3- to 8-year-old Zapotec children in Mexico. Play-fighting episodes occurred significantly more often than aggressive episodes (5.3 per hour versus 0.6 per hour), lasted significantly longer (16 seconds versus 4 seconds), were more variable in content, were more likely to involve restraint and were more likely to include multiple participants. Thus, there is a large body of observational data to support the distinction between rough-and-tumble play and aggression during childhood.

There is also convergent evidence from questioning children who have watched both forms of behaviour on videotape. Smith and Lewis (1985) carried out individual interviews with eight nursery-school children and two adults as they were being shown discrete episodes of behaviour recorded on videotape. After viewing each episode, which either showed children engaging in rough-and-tumble play or aggressive fighting, the participants were asked to indicate whether they thought the episode involved playful or aggressive behaviour, and also why they had arrived at their decision. The latter responses were collated into a number of categories. Both of the adults and six of the children showed significant agreement about whether the episodes were playful or aggressive. Almost half of the reasons given by the children as the basis for their discriminations were founded on the physical actions of the participants. In over a third of cases they were unable to give a reason, perhaps because of poor powers of expression, or even boredom with the 'game' they were being asked to play.

Boulton (1993a) used a similar technique with 8- and 11-year-old pupils, and obtained results similar in many respects. Thirty-four out of forty-four of the younger children, and forty-two out of forty-five of the older children, agreed with a standard view of some nineteen episodes. Again, the most common reason underlying these decisions related to the physical actions of the participants (43 per cent), followed by reference to the (presumed) reasons underlying the participants' actions and/or their intentions (9 per cent), whether the participants remained together or separated after the episode (8 per cent), and to facial expressions of the participants (5 per cent).

While the video technique has yielded some useful data, they are limited in a number of important ways. The judgements of the children will be influenced by the nature of the episodes shown. In some episodes, for example, facial expressions may not be very clear so that the children would be forced to pay attention to, and report using, alternative features of the episode when deciding upon the playful or aggressive nature of such episodes. A complementary technique is to interview children. In one such study (Smith and Boulton 1990), about 90 per cent of children aged 8 to 10 indicated that they could tell the difference between rough-and-tumble play and aggression, and the most frequent reasons for making this decision were the presence of laughter or crying (20 per cent), presence or absence of a specific action (18 per cent), facial expressions (17 per cent), the force of a blow or kick (15 per cent), verbal expressions accompanying the actions (11 per cent), causing a partner pain or injury (8 per cent), outcome (4 per cent), and actions of onlookers (3 per cent). Data obtained in this way suggest that facial and vocal expressions are more widely used as a basis for judging real-life situations than it would appear from the videotape studies.

SEX DIFFERENCES IN PARTICIPATION IN ROUGH-AND-TUMBLE PLAY AND AGGRESSION

In reviewing the evidence, Humphreys and Smith (1984) stated that 'one of the most consistent findings of the studies on rough-and-tumble play is that there is a sex difference: boys do more of this kind of play than girls' (p. 255). Data on this issue have been collected mainly in the United Kingdom, but also in a range of other cultures: Blurton-Jones (1967, UK), Smith and Connolly (1972, UK), Brindley et al. (1973, UK), Blurton-Jones and Konner (1973, UK and Kalahari San), Whiting and Edwards (1973, India, Japan, Mexico and the Philippines), Smith and Connolly (1980, UK), DiPietro (1981, USA), Smith and Lewis (1985, UK), Humphreys and Smith (1987, UK). In a recent study of ninety-three middle-school pupils in the United Kingdom, Boulton (1991a) found that boys engaged in more rough-and-tumble play than girls at 8 years of age (forty-one versus thirty episodes per hour) and at 11 years of age (thirty-five versus fifteen episodes per hour).

The sex difference in participation in rough-and-tumble play has been explained in a variety of different ways, ones which incidentally mirror some common explanations of the relative frequencies of aggression in boys and girls. Some of these accounts draw heavily on biological, especially hormonal, mechanisms, some on environmental, especially social learning, mechanisms. More recently, others have tried to integrate the contribution of both sets of influences. With respect to biological influences, evidence comes largely from an examination of the effects of anomalous amounts of prenatal sex hormones, which are usually associated with exogenous reasons such as mothers being given treatment that includes gonadal hormones during pregnancy, or endogenous causes such as the adrenogenital syndrome. Money and Ehrhardt (1972) found that girls who had been exposed prenatally to higher than usual levels of androgens were more likely to be tomboyish and to enjoy rigorous physical activities including rough-and-tumble play. Ehrhardt and Meyer-Bahlburg (1981) suggested that intense physical energy expenditure and participation in rough-and-tumble play 'seems to be an essential aspect of psychosocial development and it appears to be influenced by sex steroid variation before birth' (p. 1313). Quadagno *et al.* (1977) disagreed with some of Money and Erhardt's conclusions. They argued that since the androgenized girls were born with masculinized genitalia that required surgical correction, parents may have encouraged more tomboyish behaviour in these girls. This view in turn was seen as unlikely by Erhardt and Meyer-Bahlburg (1981) who argued that parents would be more likely to encourage femininity in these circumstances.

Even if the evidence for hormonal effects was widely available, the effects of environmental factors cannot be ruled out. Previous studies have examined differential parental reinforcement and the effects of gender perceptions and values on rearing practices. Lamb (1981) found that fathers treated sons and daughters similarly soon after birth, but by the second year they began to direct more social behaviour towards sons than daughters. Thus, it is possible that fathers encourage more rough-and-tumble play in sons, both by modelling the behaviour and directing more of it towards sons. However, a study involving 20- to 24-month-old infants provides little support for such a view. Fagot (1978) found that parents responded positively to rough-and-tumble play almost to the same extent in sons and daughters – 91 per cent versus 84 per cent, a non-significant difference. To be in a better position to test the differential reinforcement hypothesis we must await a longitudinal study involving older children as it is quite possible that parental responses to rough-and-tumble play may become more gender-stereotyped as children age.

As noted above, more recent explanations of the sex difference in rough-and-tumble play (and other behaviour such as aggression) have emphasized the interaction between biological and social factors (Archer and Lloyd 1985). Thus, differential reinforcement by parents and other adults of the rough-and-tumble play shown by sons and daughters could act to magnify a gender-differentiated predisposition to engage in the behaviour that may have been caused by differential exposure to gonadal hormones prior to birth.

Humphreys and Smith (1984) recently stated that 'an interactionist model . . . is . . . the most promising for understanding *how* the sex difference develops, although it does not ultimately explain *why* this difference exists' (p. 258, italics in original). Progress in this area, and also progress in understanding the wider issue of male violence, may come from taking an evolutionary approach (see Chapter 14, by Daly and Wilson). Such a view considers the likely environmental pressures on our ancestors, pressures that shaped the evolution of specific behaviour such as rough-and-tumble play and aggression. Obtaining data with which to derive and test evolutionary hypotheses is difficult, but two fruitful areas have been to consider present-day non-human primates and contemporary hunter-gatherer societies (since they inhabit environments which are likely to have many features in common with those of the earlier hominids).

With respect to the evolution of rough-and-tumble play, what might the selection pressures have consisted of? Several candidates have been proposed, including the need to hunt effectively, to avoid predation, and to develop intra-specific fighting skills (Boulton 1991b; Boulton and Smith 1992). As an illustration of what is involved in taking an evolutionary approach, and what benefits might be on offer for explaining sex differences and the ontogeny of aggression, I would like to consider the view that rough-and-tumble play evolved because it helped to practise the skills that would be used in aggressive fighting. This hypothesis is based on the finding that amongst a variety of primate species, competition for reproductive success is higher for males than for females, and that skill in fighting is an important factor influencing success (Wilson 1985; Symons 1978). For example, Symons (1978) observed rhesus macaques in their natural habitat and found that males engaged in significantly higher levels of rough-and-tumble play than females. Symons suggested that such forms of play provide physical training for fighting skills, and that males play more than females because these skills are of greater importance to them in terms of their reproductive success. Wilson (1975) similarly proposed that human males were exposed to the same sorts of pressures over the course of their evolution. This view has led to the practice fighting hypothesis of rough-and-tumble play in humans. Smith (1982) argued that 'the adaptive value of play-fighting as practice for adult fighting skills would have been maintained through hominid evolution' (p. 15). The validity of this hypothesis has been examined in a number of ways. To provide practice for skills that will be employed in aggressive fighting, rough-and-tumble play would necessarily have to resemble it in some way. As we have seen, this does appear to be the case, although there are some important differences, such as the greater levels of restraint that are characteristic of rough-and-tumble play. Similarly, data on sex differences in rates of participation are also compatible with the practice fighting hypothesis: males need to fight more than females, therefore males need more practice, therefore males engage in more rough-and-tumble play.

An alternative approach to examining the practice fighting hypothesis was adopted in the innovative research carried out by Humphreys and Smith (1987). They combined the collection of observational data on who children selected as partners in rough-and-tumble play, with sociometric data about the children's views of how much they liked these partners and how strong they were perceived to be. They argued that, 'a tendency for partners to be particularly closely matched for perceived strength would suggest an element of competition and possible practice of fighting skills' (p. 202). This turned out to be the case among 11-year-old children (but not 7- or 9-year-olds). Boulton (1991b) replicated Humphreys and Smith's study, with some improvements to the methodology, and obtained data that provided 'some, though not absolute, support for the view that rough-and-tumble play is functionally related to . . . the development of real fighting skills' (p. 177).

A central notion underpinning the practice fighting hypothesis is that *at some time in our evolutionary past*, those individual males who were most adept at

29

intra-specific fighting would have had a distinct advantage in terms of their inclusive fitness. Given that our present circumstances, or at least those in industrialized societies, are much changed from then, and that fighting ability is unlikely to be an important factor in a human male's ability to find a suitable partner and raise a family, why then, it might be asked, should boys of today still engage in rough-and-tumble play when the main advantage this conveys (namely, the practice of fighting skills) is no longer adaptive? Such a question might be asked by proponents of the so-called correspondence programme who believe that since organisms evolved to be inclusive-fitness maximizers, organisms should therefore behave adaptively in their *present* circumstances. According to this point of view, rough-and-tumble play is redundant at least in so far as practice for real fighting is concerned, and so modern boys should no longer engage in it. However, such a view as this is strongly countered by proponents of the so-called adaptationist programme, such as Tooby and Cosmides (1990). They argue, convincingly to my mind, that, 'our inherited design is the same regardless of our (present) circumstances, and it can only be understood with reference to our evolutionary history' (p. 420). Thus, we do have a theory, rooted in evolutionary thinking, for why modern children continue to engage in rough-and-tumble play and for why there is a sex difference. A temptation might be to go one step beyond the practice fighting hypothesis and argue that by engaging in rough-and-tumble play, modern boys are somehow 'made' more aggressive. After all, boys generally do engage in more rough-and-tumble play *and* aggression than girls. It is to this issue that the next section turns.

THE RELATIONSHIP BETWEEN ROUGH-AND-TUMBLE PLAY AND AGGRESSION IN CHILDHOOD

A number of hypotheses have been presented which suggest that there is a close relationship between playful and aggressive fighting during the childhood years. Three of these hypotheses will be considered here.

Accidental injury

In some schools in the United Kingdom, and amongst some parents, rough-and-tumble play is discouraged or even banned because it is thought that it leads to an increased risk of accidental injury which would precipitate an aggressive retaliation and hence fighting. Certainly, rough-and-tumble play can be a vigorous activity on some occasions, but data from a number of sources seem to indicate that banning it may be an over-reaction on the part of schools and parents. In a recent study, Boulton (1993b) observed seventy-nine fights on middle-school playgrounds and categorized the causes of each one. A small but noteworthy proportion of these aggressive interactions (14 per cent) were caused when a playful 'assault' received an aggressive retaliation.

However, it is not clear what proportion of the aggressive retaliations occurred because of an accidental injury *per se*. They may have been made for another reason, such as cheating or honest mistakes about the intentions of the original actor (see below). In another study, Boulton (1992a) reported the causes of a further forty-eight playground fights. Seven of these were caused by accidental injury, but, on further examination, in only one case did the injury occur in the context of rough-and-tumble play. Thus, the weight of evidence goes against the view that participation in rough-and-tumble play elevates levels of aggression as a consequence of accidental injury, although on a few occasions this link may exist.

Cheating

Participation in rough-and-tumble play may require an adherence to a number of implicit rules, guiding such matters as how hard one may strike an 'opponent', and the need for participants to exchange roles (Smith and Boulton 1990). As with all rule-governed behaviour, individuals might abuse the system and 'cheat' in order to benefit in some way. This notion stems from the work of Breuggeman (1978) and Fagen (1981) with non-human primates. According to Fagen's cheating hypothesis, 'animals may exploit opportunities to change play into agonistic fighting. An animal would begin play, then make an escalated attack on its playmate. By doing so it would damage or intimidate its opponent, thus gaining access to a current or future resource' (p. 337). Smith and Boulton (1990) applied this hypothesis to children's rough-and-tumble play encounters. They suggested that, 'even though most [rough-and-tumble play] bouts . . . are . . . motivationally straightforward . . . some bouts or invitations to bouts, involving some children some of the time, might be deliberately used to inflict hurt or maintain, improve, or display dominant status' (p. 280). Such a view, it must be said, has yet to be systematically tested, but my own impression, based on many hours of observation of rough-and-tumble play in naturalistic settings, is that such a tactic is not common amongst children. Indeed, evolutionary theory would not lead to such a prediction. During the course of hominid evolution, play partners of individuals who did cheat in this way would quickly learn to avoid playing with them, and would instead choose to play with individuals who, like themselves, were willing to compromise with the needs of others, overtly by following the 'play conventions'. Individuals who persisted in cheating would probably have ended up with few if any play partners and so would have received few if any benefits from this type of social play. While it is true to say that we need more data to allow formal tests of the cheating hypothesis as describing a link between rough-and-tumble play and aggression in childhood, there are good theoretical reasons why at best it may only apply to a minority of individuals.

31

Honest mistakes

Another scenario underlying a possible link between rough-and-tumble play and aggression involves the social skills that regulate children's interactions. As we saw earlier, most children are adept at distinguishing between the two types of behaviour. However, a growing body of evidence also suggests that a minority will have problems. At the infant-school level, Sluckin (1981) argued that 'undoubtedly a certain number of children . . . fail to distinguish and react appropriately to rough-and-tumble (pretend) and real aggression' (p. 40). The study by Boulton (1993a) described earlier found that a small but noteworthy proportion of 8- and 11-year-old middle-school pupils were relatively poor at making this distinction. In the United States, Pellegrini (1988) found evidence to support the view that poor decoding skills in this domain are associated with elevated levels of aggression and low popularity with peers. Pellegrini examined the transitional probabilities of rough-and-tumble play leading into other activities. Playground encounters that involved children who were poor at making the distinction between play and aggression, and who tended to be rejected by their peers, were more likely to turn into aggression, whereas those of children who were skilled in this area, and who tended to be popular with their peers, were more likely to turn directly into games with rules.

This sort of evidence suggests that in some individuals, the social skills that normally ensure that rough-and-tumble play bouts *remain* playful are in some way 'faulty', and this may contribute to their becoming aggressive members of their peer group. Other research suggests that once a child has acquired a reputation for being aggressive this is highly resistant to change even if the individual learns to regulate his (or her) behaviour in the future. Peers continue to interact with the child as if he (or she) was still aggressive, and this in turn may lead to a re-emergence of aggressive tendencies in the individual.

One implication of this work is that an inability to decode playful intent correctly may, in the long run, contribute to the development of aggressive behavioural tendencies. Where do these social skills come from? Boulton (1993a) considered this issue, which is directly relevant to the question of the development of aggressive behavioural tendencies, at least in a minority of individuals. Abilities in this domain could be largely independent of actual experience, suggesting that they have been heavily canalized during phylogeny. In some non-human primates, the ability to make a distinction between a play-face and a threat-face may not require social experience (see Fagen 1981). In humans, smiling, which as we have seen is an important play signal, is shown by very young infants in such a wide variety of different cultures that an innate basis seems very likely (Hinde 1987). Alternatively, these skills may be dependent to some extent on children's experiences of rough-and-tumble play and/or aggression. Neill (1991) suggested that, 'even when nonverbal signals have strong innate basis, but their expression, and even their meaning may be altered by experience and cultural influences' (p. 14).

Boulton (1993a) correlated the rates at which 8- and 11-year-old children participated in rough-and-tumble play (and aggression) and the number of mistakes they made on the videotape test. In three out of the four classes that participated in the study, these correlations were non-significant. Thus, the hypothesis that by engaging in rough-and-tumble play children might benefit in terms of their ability to distinguish between playful and aggressive intent was not generally supported. Moreover, in the other class that participated, the correlation was significant but in the other direction to that predicted by the hypothesis: those children who were observed to engage in high levels of rough-and-tumble play were found to make most errors on the videotape test. Boulton sounded a note of caution about rejecting the hypothesis on the basis of the evidence he provided. He stated that

> it is possible that most children in the present study had reached an age where they had already engaged in enough rough-and-tumble play (with parents and or with peers) for them to have developed their skills in decoding peer's affects and/or intentions to some adequate level. In contrast, some other children may have lacked these early experiences and even their relatively high present rate of engagement in the activity may not have yet compensated for this deficit.
>
> (Boulton 1993a: 260)

A study that examines these issues in younger pupils is clearly warranted.

The weight of evidence discussed above suggests that rough-and-tumble play and aggression are not closely related during childhood for most individuals, although they may be in a minority of cases in which faulty social skills or the tendency to cheat is present. However, Gergen (1990) recently sounded a note of caution and outlined a number of reasons why these two categories of behaviour may be conjugated at this age range. As an example, she applies some of the predictions from Huesmann's (1988) information-processing model to this issue. The model proposes that experiences during childhood lead to the development of cognitive scripts. These scripts are then evoked later in life under relevant social conditions and they influence which response out of a set of alternatives will be shown. Gergen states that,

> applied to the present question of horseplay [her term for rough-and-tumble play], we might anticipate that the use of physical means of expressing one's feelings and of gaining instrumental and affiliative goals becomes a well-established 'script' for many children; later this script lends itself to actions in other circumstances, either friendly or provocative. Thus, for example, a boy who often wrestles and punches his brothers in fun may more easily use the same response in less friendly circumstances than a boy who does not do so.
>
> (Gergen 1988: 383)

This point of view, although not systematically tested, assumes that if there was going to be a link between rough-and-tumble play in childhood and the occurrence of aggressive tendencies at some later time, it would be because participation in the former during childhood somehow *led* to a greater propensity to engage in aggression in later life. As we have seen, there is no direct evidence to support such a view. Moreover, the fascinating work of Doug Fry (1988) among Zapotec communities of Mexico suggests that it is the levels of aggression among *adults* that is more likely to influence the behaviour of children, including their participation in rough-and-tumble play, rather than the other way round. Fry found that both rates of aggressive fighting and rates of playful fighting among Zapotec children were significantly higher in a community with relatively high rates of adult aggression than in a community with relatively low rates of adult aggression. He suggested that participation in rough-and-tumble play might provide a practice of the fighting skills that are sometimes used in hand-to-hand fighting among adults. Fry concluded that

> patterns of aggressive and prosocial behaviors are being passed on from one generation to the next, as the children learn to engage in different behavioral patterns that are modelled and accepted by adults in their respective community. . . . It would seem that the learning of aggressive and prosocial behaviors begins at an early age among the Zapotecs.
>
> (Fry 1988: 1017)

ROUGH-AND-TUMBLE INTERACTIONS BETWEEN GIRLS AND BOYS IN THE PLAYGROUND

One of the most obvious and well-documented aspects of the social structuring of children's peer groups is a propensity for same-sex partners. In a comprehensive review of sixteen studies that examined sex segregation within the school environment among 3- to 11-year-old pupils, Lockheed and Klein (1985) noted that a preference for same-sex peers emerges during the third year and lasted throughout the middle-school period. Scott (1984) also documented a similar pattern of preferences in children's playgroups throughout the preschool and infant-school years. This is not to say that there is no mixing of the two sexes on the playground. Despite the findings, discussed above, that boys generally engage in more rough-and-tumble play than girls, my own observations, although not yet quantified, confirm that a noteworthy proportion of such encounters involve both boys and girls. An examination of these interactions may provide further useful information relevant to the issues of the concurrent and future relationships and interaction patterns between members of the two sexes, including interactions that involve aggression. One possibility, proposed independently for children by Boulton (1988) and for adolescents by Gergen (1990), is that rough-and-tumble play 'allows' physical contact of a fairly (sometimes highly) intimate nature between males and females, without at the same time violating the social norms that operate in the peer group. During the middle-school years, many boys (though by no means all) strive to appear 'tough', 'macho' or 'hard', and at the same time regard girls as 'sissy' or 'weak'. Attitudes and values such as these are very unpalatable to many adults, and often appear quite resistant to change. They may also present boys with a dilemma given that they may be experiencing the beginnings of 'romantic' interests in girls. While I could find no references in the literature to young boys' romantic inclinations or interest in the opposite sex, my observations in playgrounds suggest that they do exist for some individuals at this stage. Based on these observations, I suggested that rough-and-tumble play might provide an interactional context in which physical contact with opposite-sex peers may take place, but in which boys can still be 'macho', and so on by displaying their (often only perceived) greater strength than girls, and without having to spend too much time with them to risk being ridiculed by other boys. As a preliminary test of this hypothesis, I have examined the extent to which same-sex and mixed-sex dyads who participated in rough-and-tumble play were (1) together or apart prior to the interaction, (2) showed a rough-and-tumble play response to the initial 'invitation' to participate, and (3) remained physically together or separated after the interaction. The results are summarized in Table 2.1. For same-sex interactions, most participants were together beforehand and most participants remained together afterwards. Conversely, in mixed-sex interactions, most participants were apart beforehand and a large proportion of participants separated afterwards. A rough-and-tumble play response was about equally likely in both types of interaction. Although not yet analyzed in detail, my impression is that many of the mixed-sex interactions involved boys approaching girls, restraining them or playfully assaulting them in some way, before being driven off by friends of the female 'victim'. In one case, an 8-year-old boy cried out to his friends, 'I want to have a baby', as he was restraining a girl of the same age by pulling her close to his body. These early data do provide some support for the physical contact hypothesis, and suggest it is worthy of further study. In terms of the aetiology of male violence towards women, such a hypothesis has some negative undertones that have yet to be explored. Specifically, boys could be learning to view girls as legitimate targets for physical assaults, possibly with sexual elements, albeit playfully at first during childhood. We might speculate that in a minority of individuals, this tendency could become more pronounced, and be an important variable in their tendencies to assault women. Of course it would be unreasonable to posit this as the single most important variable, but it would appear to merit more attention from researchers. Huesmann's (1988) information-processing model, outlined above, may apply here as well. Specifically, cognitive scripts that influence actual behaviour could be formed during male–female rough-and-tumble interactions, scripts that may be evoked in later life to influence how a man might behave towards a woman.

Table 2.1 Proximity prior to interaction, percentage of rough-and-tumble responses, and outcome of interactions in same-sex and mixed-sex rough-and-tumble play encounters

	Proximity prior to interaction		Proportion of rough-and-tumble responses	Outcome of bout	
	Together	Apart		Stay	Separate
Same-sex bouts (%)	74	26	41	80	20
Mixed-sex bouts (%)	37	63	46	52	48

Source: Data come from an analysis of 1,754 bouts of rough-and-tumble play observed in a sample of 93 8- and 11-year-old children

THE RELATIONSHIP BETWEEN ROUGH-AND-TUMBLE PLAY AND AGGRESSION IN ADOLESCENCE AND ADULTHOOD

Whether the separation between playful and serious aggression that applies to the majority of children also applies to adolescents and adults is only beginning to be investigated. Firm conclusions would be premature at this stage as only three published studies to date have focused on this issue. Nevertheless, the available evidence seems to suggest that the boundary between the two types of behaviour becomes more blurred for an increasing number of individuals. A number of researchers working in this area have evoked the concept of social dominance (see Chapter 3) to help account for their findings. In the first study to be reported, Neill (1976) factor analysed observational data on 'fighting' behaviours in 12- to 13-year-old boys. One of the two main factors that were identified was labelled 'vigorous fighting' that was 'usually playful but often causing distress to the victim' (p. 220). Typically, these interactions began and ended with playful signals but were more hostile in the middle. Neill suggested that interactions of this type might serve a dominance function in that the boy who introduced the hostile elements might be attempting to challenge his partner's position in the dominance hierarchy or to maintain his superior position by intimidating his partner. The stronger boy would gradually escalate the encounter by introducing more aggressive elements until the weaker boy showed submission in some way. The stronger boy could then ease off, as it were, and the episode would revert to a playful mode.

Boulton (1992) investigated this hypothesis further. As a first step, it was established whether or not the general distinction between rough-and-tumble play and aggression which is so apparent during childhood also applied during adolescence. This view was supported by the finding that over three-quarters of the respondents out of a sample of 505 13- to 16-year-olds indicated that it was possible to tell if two people are engaged in a play-fight or are having a real fight. Moreover, 47 per cent of the sample indicated that they personally try to win play-fights, and the most common reason offered for this concerned a desire to show their supremacy/dominance over another person and/or to deter others from teasing them or picking fights with them. Some pupils indicated that as they had grown older their rough-and-tumble play had become rougher, and almost one-fifth of these pupils said this was because they tried harder to win play-fights with increasing age. Again, this supports a link between rough-and-tumble play and dominance relations. The results from this study also indicated that for this age range more males than females were concerned with issues surrounding participation in both playful and aggressive fighting. In particular, more males than females reported that (1) they engage in playful fighting, (2) they can tell who is the strongest person in a playful fight, (3) they think it is important to win a playful fight, (4) they themselves do try to win playful fights, (5) they try to win playful fights in order to show that they are tough/to prevent unwanted teasing/to avoid the need for a real fight, and (6) as they have grown older, their playful fighting has become rougher. With respect to real fighting, more males than females reported that it was important to be good at real fighting, and that they would like to be the best fighter in their class. This study also clearly indicated that not *all* males value playful or aggressive fighting or use playful fighting in relation to dominance relations, and similarly that these things do apply to *some* females.

Some recent research by Gergen (1990) has suggested another reason why the links between rough-and-tumble play and aggression become closer after puberty. Her research was based partly on a relational theoretical perspective. She stated,

> from this theoretical position the definitions of actions emerge within social interaction and are dependent on the negotiation of the participants. Thus whether an action is defined and responded to as horseplay or aggressive depends on the mutual defining procedures of the actors. The line between what is playful and what is hostile thus becomes fuzzy and unstable depending on the actor's responses within the larger relational context. The relational approach relies heavily on the notion that interpretations are somewhat flexible within certain cultural constraints.
>
> (1990: 383)

Gergen considered the influence of a number of mediating factors in determining the amount of horseplay and aggression, and their relationship, in a sample of 18- to 20-year-old college students. One of these factors was the level of involvement with a heterosexual partner. She noted that previous studies had found that the more involved the couple, the greater the likelihood of violence between them. Consequently, she contrasted couples who were 'going steady' and those who were not. The second mediating factor was level of alcohol consumption. For both sexes separately, Gergen found significant correlations between self-reported levels of horseplay and aggression with same-sex friends, and separately, with other-sex friends. Gergen also found that this relationship was more robust for women than for men. With respect to the mediation variables, going steady was found to increase the likelihood of both horseplay and aggression for men and women, and drinking alcohol was shown to be associated with increased horseplay for both sexes. Heavy drinking was associated with increased aggression for men with men but decreased aggression for women with women. Consuming alcohol did not appear to influence the level of aggression with the opposite sex.

Gergen interpreted her data in the following way: 'the extent to which each gender is physically playful within the gender *predicts levels of aggressiveness*' (1990: 393, emphasis added). Again, the implication is that participation in horseplay was the precursor of participation in aggression. This view was 'based on the social conventions of viewing a horseplay-aggression scenario temporally, beginning at a neutral or low-conflict level and ending at a high-conflict one' (p. 393). However, such a conclusion would be premature for a number of reasons. Gergen is correct to state that this pattern of findings does not rule out the possibility that aggressive behaviour is the antecedent of horseplay, and that aggressive episodes could become de-escalated and change directly into horseplay. I have observed such a change several times in middle-school children. One case involved two 11-year-old boys, and the incident began when one boy kicked another boy's football across the playground even though he wasn't involved in the game. The second boy was so incensed that he shoved the other boy very hard in the chest with both hands. The first boy responded with the same actions. This continued in a tit-for-tat manner, and was accompanied by low frowns and verbal insults, for some 20 seconds. Over the course of the next few minutes the heavy shoves changed to light ones, then to light taps and eventually to light flicks of the ear lobes, accompanied by broad smiles. This episode is a clear reminder of the possibility that aggression can precede horseplay directly in children and hence may do so in adults. More data are clearly needed on this issue.

Another reason why Gergen's conclusion may be premature relates to the methodology she adopted. An anonymous questionnaire was given to subjects who were asked, 'Which of the following [behaviours] have you engaged in either with a boy or a girlfriend, or with a close same-sex friend?' The problem is that these instructions are ambiguous so that some respondents may have considered one friend/sub-group of friends for the horseplay items but a *different* friend/sub-group of friends for the aggression items. If so, then Gergen's conclusion that aggression and horseplay are related would be invalid. Other methodological limitations must also cast doubt on Gergen's conclusion that alcohol is (partly) responsible for elevated levels of horseplay. Gergen asked respondents about how often and in what ways they had participated in horseplay *during the past three years*, but asked about their *weekend* alcohol consumption. Thus it cannot be assumed that those respondents who indicated a heavy level of alcohol consumption and an associated high level of horseplay actually engaged in any of this horseplay immediately after drinking alcohol. The possibility that her finding represents a spurious correlation looms too large for comfort.

Despite the methodological problems, Gergen's work is innovative and important because it has raised the issue of a potential close temporal link between horseplay and aggression beyond the childhood years. Her findings do seem to warrant further studies, using direct observations and experimental manipulations.

CONCLUSION

In this chapter, I have endeavoured to review much of the evidence concerning the relationship between playful and serious aggression both in childhood and beyond. As noted above, many of the important issues have yet to be fully resolved, and some are only just finding their way on to the agenda. Consequently, we must at present resist the temptation to cast too critical an eye over play-fighting activities or to view them as developmental precursors of serious aggression. Thus, to my mind, the old cliché of the jury being out on this particular issue would not be a case of hedging one's bets, but rather a sensible stance based on current knowledge. I would also argue that our understanding of the developmental changes in aggression will benefit from a closer study of it's (apparently) physically similar, and (apparently) motivationally distinct cousin, rough-and-tumble play.

REFERENCES

Aldis, O. (1975) *Play Fighting*, New York: Academic Press.

Archer, J. and Lloyd, B. (1985) *Sex and Gender*, New York: Cambridge University Press.

Blurton-Jones, N. (1967) 'An ethological study of some aspects of social behavior of children in nursery school', in D. Morris (ed.) *Primate Ethology*, London: Weidenfeld & Nicolson, pp. 347–68.

—— (1972) 'Categories of child–child interaction', in N. Blurton-Jones (ed.) *Ethological Studies of Child Behavior*, Cambridge: Cambridge University Press, pp. 97–127.

Blurton-Jones, N. G. and Konner, M. J. (1973) 'Sex differences in behavior of London and Bushman children', in R. P. Michael and J. H. Crook (eds) *Comparative Ecology and Behavior of Primates*, London: Academic Press.

Boulton, M. J. (1988) 'A multi-methodological investigation of rough-and-tumble play, aggression, and social relationships in middle school children', Ph.D. thesis, University of Sheffield.

—— (1991a) 'A comparison of structural and contextual features of middle school children's playful and aggressive fighting', *Ethology and Sociobiology*, 12: 119–45.

—— (1991b) 'Partner preferences in middle school children's playful fighting and chasing: a test of some competing functional hypotheses', *Ethology and Sociobiology*, 12: 177–93.

—— (1992) 'Rough physical play in adolescents: does it serve a dominance function?', *Early Education and Development*, 3: 312–33.

—— (1993a) 'Children's abilities to distinguish between playful and aggressive fighting: a developmental perspective', *British Journal of Developmental Psychology*, 11: 249–63.

—— (1993b) 'Proximate causes of aggressive fighting in middle school children', *British Journal of Educational Psychology*, 63: 231–44.

—— (1993c) 'Aggressive fighting in British middle school children', *Educational Studies*, 19: 19–39.

Boulton, M. J. and Smith, P. K. (1992) 'The social nature of playfighting and play chasing: mechanisms and strategies underlying co-operation and compromise', in J. H. Barkow, L. Cosmides and J. Tooby (eds) *The Adapted Mind*, New York: Oxford University Press.

Breuggeman, J. A. (1978) 'The function of adult play in free-ranging Macaca mulatta', in E. O. Smith (ed.), *Social Play in Primates*, New York: Academic Press, pp. 169–91.

Brindley, C., Clarke, P., Hutt, C., Robinson, I. and Wethli, E. (1973) 'Sex differences in the activities and social interactions of nursery school children', in R. P. Michael and J. H. Crook (eds) *Comparative Ecology and Behavior of Primates*, London: Academic Press.

DiPietro, J. A. (1981) 'Rough and tumble play: a function of gender', *Developmental Psychology*, 17: 50–8.

Eibl-Eibesfeldt, I. (1974) 'The myth of the aggression-free hunter and gatherer society', in R. Holloway (ed.) *Primate Aggression, Territoriality, and Xenophobia*, New York: Academic Press, pp. 435–57.

Erhardt, A. A. and Meyer-Bahlburg, H. F. L. (1981) 'Effects of prenatal sex hormones on gender-related behavior', *Science*, 211: 1312–18.

Fagen, R. M. (1981) *Animal Play Behavior*, New York: Oxford University Press.

Fagot, B. I. (1978) 'The influence of sex of child on parental reactions to toddler children', *Child Development*, 49: 459–65.

Fry, D. P. (1987) 'Differences between playfighting and serious fights among Zapotec children', *Ethology and Sociobiology*, 8: 285–306.

—— (1988) 'Intercommunity differences in aggression among Zapotec children', *Child Development*, 59: 1008–19.

Gergen, M. (1990) 'Beyond the evil empire: horseplay and aggression', *Aggressive Behavior*, 16: 381–98.

Harlow, H. F. and Harlow, M. K. (1965) 'The affectional systems', *Behavior of Non-human Primates*, 2: 287–334.

Hinde, R. A. (1987) *Individuals, Relationships, and Culture*, Cambridge: Cambridge University Press.

Huessmann, L. R. (1988) 'An information-processing model for the development of aggression', *Aggressive Behavior*, 14: 13–24.

Humphreys, A. D. and Smith, P. K. (1984) 'Rough-and tumble in preschool and playground', in P. K. Smith (ed.) *Play in Animals and Humans*, Oxford: Basil Blackwell, pp. 241–66.

—— (1987) 'Rough-and-tumble, friendship and dominance in schoolchildren: evidence for continuity and change with age', *Child Development*, 58: 201–12.

Konner, M. J. (1972) 'Aspects of the development ethology of a foraging people', in N. Blurton-Jones (ed.) *Ethological Studies of Child Behavior*, Cambridge: Cambridge University Press, pp. 285–304.

Lamb, M. E. (1981) 'The development of father–infant relationships', in M. E. Lamb (ed.) *The Role of Father in Child Development*, New York: John Wiley & Sons.

Lockheed, M. and Klein, S. (1985) 'Sex equality in classroom organization and climate', in S. Klein (ed.) *Handbook for Achieving Sex Equality through Education*, Baltimore, MD: Johns Hopkins University Press, pp. 262–84.

McGrew, W. C. (1972) *An Ethological Study of Children's Behaviour*, London: Academic Press.

Money, J. and Erhardt, A. A. (1972) *Man and Woman, Boy and Girl*, Baltimore, MD: Johns Hopkins University Press.

Neill, S. R. (1976) 'Aggressive and non-aggressive fighting in 12–13 year old pre-adolescent boys', *Journal of Child Psychology and Psychiatry*, 17: 213–20.

—— (1991) *Classroom Nonverbal Communication*, London: Routledge.

Pellegrini, A. D. (1988) 'Elementary school children's rough-and-tumble play and social competence', *Developmental Psychology*, 24: 802–6.

Quadagno, D. M., Briscoe, R. and Quadagno, J. S. (1977) 'Effects of perinatal gonadal hormones on selected nonsexual behavior patterns: a critical assessment of the nonhuman and human literature', *Psychological Bulletin*, 84: 62–80.

Scott, K. P. (1984) 'Teaching social interaction skills: perspectives on cross-sex communication', *ERIC Document No. AN ED 252445*.

Sluckin, A. M. (1981) *Growing Up in the Playground: The Social Development of Children*, London: Routledge & Kegan Paul.

Smith, P. K. (1982) 'Does play matter? functional and evolutionary aspects of animal and human play', *Behavioral and Brain Sciences*, 5: 139–84.

Smith, P. K. and Boulton, M. J. (1990) 'Rough-and-tumble play, aggression and dominance: perception and behaviour in children's encounters', *Human Development*, 33: 271–82.

Smith, P. K. and Connolly, K. J. (1972) 'Patterns of play and social interaction in preschool children', in N. Blurton-Jones (ed.) *Ethological Studies of Child Behavior*, Cambridge: Cambridge University Press.

—— (1980) *The Ecology of Preschool Behaviour*, Cambridge: Cambridge University Press.

Smith, P. K. and Lewis, K. (1985) 'Rough-and-tumble play, fighting and chasing in nursery school children', *Ethology and Sociobiology*, 6: 175–81.

Symons, D. (1978) *Play and Aggression: A Study of Rhesus Monkeys*, New York: Columbia University Press.

Tooby, J. and Cosmides, L. (1990) 'The past explains the present: emotional adaptations and the structure of ancestral environments', *Ethology and Sociobiology*, 11: 375–424.

Whiting, B. and Edwards, C. P. (1973) 'A cross-cultural analysis of sex differences in the behavior of children aged three through eleven', *Journal of Social Psychology*, 91: 171–88.

Wilson, E. O. (1975) *Sociobiology: The New Synthesis*, Cambridge, MA: Belknap Press.

3

AGGRESSION AND DOMINANCE IN THE SOCIAL WORLD OF BOYS

Glenn Weisfeld

This chapter concerns dominance and other types of aggression in boys. The main theoretical orientation is ethological. Ethology essentially adopts an evolutionary, comparative and naturalistic approach to behaviour including that of humans. Rather than provide a detailed description of the ethological approach, the reader is referred to sources such as Weisfeld (1982), Eibl-Eibesfeldt (1989) and Archer (1992a) for accounts of how this approach is applied to the study of human behaviour. The use of ethological research in this chapter is principally concerned with aggression in the context of dominance relations. However, before proceeding with this, it is necessary to consider where dominance aggression fits into the overall typology of aggression.

Moyer (1976) identified several functional types of aggression, including predatory, maternal and defensive. Each of these types is species-wide and has a fairly obvious adaptive advantage. Aspects of Moyer's typology are supported by neural research indicating that different types of aggression are mediated by more or less distinct neural pathways (Buck 1988). The existence of somewhat characteristic forms of attack and display for each type also supports this typology.

On the other hand, Moyer's typology has been criticized on various grounds (Archer 1988). These include failure to distinguish the neural bases of the following supposedly distinct types of aggression: inter-male, territorial, maternal and irritable (angry). Secondly, the criteria for inclusion are inconsistent. Sometimes Moyer relies mainly on the behavioural form of the aggression, and at other times on its function. Different types of aggression sometimes take the same behavioural form, such as defensive aggression occurring in response to predatory attack and to attack by a territorial resident. This may reflect the confused way in which the various types of aggressive behaviour evolved, and the fact that different types of aggression can occur in rapid succession.

Given these and other criticisms, I shall present a modified version of Moyer's scheme. Types of aggression will be identified mainly by their under-lying motive, or emotion, which in turn usually has a clear function for the individual. That is, each type generally enhances the biological fitness – survival and reproductive success – of the individual (see Chapter 16). The following are Moyer's (1976) types of aggression, interpreted in functional terms.

The function of *fear-induced* aggression is defence. Fear-induced aggression is observed when the animal defends itself against a predator or a stronger rival (Blanchard and Blanchard 1989). Fear-induced, or defensive, aggression occurs when flight is not possible and freezing or other defensive behaviour does not deter the opponent from approaching. These observations confirm that fear is involved in this type of aggression.

Fear-induced aggression has a typical communicative display, or emotional expression. The animal usually threatens its opponent initially, as by hissing, vocalizing, teeth-baring and pilo-erection. Attack comes as a last resort, and is often aimed at the vulnerable structures of the face.

The function of *maternal* (or, more broadly, parental) aggression is also defence – not self-defence but defence of offspring. Because of this functional similarity to fear-induced aggression and the likelihood that fear is involved in both types, they should perhaps be lumped together. However, maternal hormones may influence maternal aggression in distinctive ways in some mammals (Buck 1988; Svare 1983). Further complicating the matter, maternal aggression in rodents resembles territorial aggression in some ways (Archer 1988).

The function of *predatory* aggression is feeding. It is probably best to view this form of behaviour as part of feeding behaviour, as a manifestation of the hunger motive (Archer 1988).

Moyer (1976) recognized *territorial* aggression, which is certainly important in many species but which is debatable in ours (see Eibl-Eibesfeldt 1989, for discussion). Deciding whether or not humans are territorial may be a definitional issue.

Moyer's (1976) *sex-related* aggression is doubtful. It refers to male aggression in subduing a female during courtship. This does not fit the common definition of aggression as harming another. Although injuries to females do sometimes occur during mating, this is not typical and would seem to be contrary to the male's fitness interests. Forced copulation (see Chapter 16), which was not discussed by Moyer in this context, has evolved in some species, but may belong under the next category.

Instrumental aggression is a miscellaneous category that does not correspond with any single motive. Aggression may be used to subdue a rival for some tangible object, or to gain some intangible goal. As one example, in some Old World monkeys the new male leader of a group may kill off the previous leader's young offspring (van der Dennen 1992). In humans, aggression in warfare may involve some elements of instrumental aggression, such as fighting for pay or to avoid shame. See Eibl-Eibesfeldt (1989) for a discussion of this important and neglected topic.

Most of the examples of human aggression that are of interest to us here constitute either *dominance* aggression or *angry* aggression. Therefore, separate sections will be devoted to each of these two types. By understanding how these two types of aggression operate, we may be better able to analyse specific cases of aggression in boys.

DOMINANCE AGGRESSION

Dominance aggression functions to allow the individual to gain the prerogatives that accompany attaining high rank in certain species. Dominance hierarchies tend to be observed in group-living species in which resources are strongly contested; for example, in polygynous species. Dominance aggression is labelled 'inter-male aggression' by Moyer (1976) because it is more prominent in the male of most species. However, this term excludes dominance behaviour amongst females (for instance, hens), and between females and males. Inter-male aggression also might be construed to include territorial aggression. For these reasons the term 'dominance aggression' is used here.

Some investigators, such as Archer (Chapter 16), see no reason to recognize a dominance motive. I would argue for doing so. If an animal possessed such a motive, it would seek to defeat opponents and thereby gain prior access to certain resources. 'Pacifists' in a hierarchically organized species that lacked this motive and always declined to compete would fall to the bottom of hierarchy and might well be selected out (unless they adopted an alternative means of gaining resources).

Animals might conceivably be motivated to fight only by the prospect of gaining a resource. If so, they would probably not fight as vigorously as an opponent that, in addition, liked winning for its own sake. Also, a dominance motive might dispose an animal to seek opportune occasions on which to challenge an opponent, even when no resource was present. On these occasions, the animal would probably defeat its opponent, and hence would gain a cheap victory that might favourably affect its future encounters with that opponent. 'Animals may initiate dominance interactions outside the immediate context of competitive encounters . . . if this enhances their ability to compete successfully in future' (Clutton-Brock and Harvey 1976: 217).

Thus, a dominance motive would seem to be adaptive in many group-living, competitive species. But does a distinct dominance motive actually exist? Archer claims that the dominance concept should be restricted to describing the relationship between two individuals – namely, which has won the competitive encounter(s). '[T]he reasons that they fight in the first place is another matter' (p. 318).

One problem with claiming that these fights are only attempts to gain a resource (that is, instrumental aggression) is that sometimes they occur in the absence of any contestable resources. In some species inter-male fighting occurs in the absence of females, such as domestic cats (Huntingford and

Turner 1987). In many species the males abruptly begin fighting with each other during their first breeding season, before they can foresee the tangible advantages that accrue to dominant individuals.

It is difficult to imagine that these fights in the absence of resources occur because the animal foresees that it will eventually gain resources by establishing dominance over an opponent. Most other motives do not seem to work this way. Animals probably do not figure out that they will get more mates by holding a territory, more descendants by defending their offspring, fewer injuries by fleeing a predator, more food by migrating where it is warm, and so on. Simpler proximate mechanisms seem to be the rule in motivation (Pugh 1977). Foresight is a fairly rare neuropsychological ability, being most notable in primates with a well-developed prefrontal cortex, and is probably weak in many species that exhibit dominance.

Moreover, there are indications that dominance contests are controlled by direct mechanisms rather than entailing foresight. Prenatal and pubertal testosterone enhances this type of aggression (Buck 1988). Also, in numerous animals fighting is triggered by exposure to a mature male of the same species.

Washburn and Hamburg (1968) are amongst those who have argued for recognizing a distinct dominance motive. They maintained that animals fight for dominance not simply out of desire for the tangible resources that accrue to high-ranking individuals, but because of a desire to be dominant. 'Being dominant appears to be its own reward – to be highly satisfying and to be sought, regardless of whether it is accompanied by advantage in food, sex, or grooming' (Washburn and Hamburg 1968: 473).

Animals certainly act as though they like to win and hate to lose. Mice that have won fights tend to seek out fights subsequently; those that have lost tend to avoid fights (Ginsburg and Allee 1942). By homology to humans, we might say that they have a capacity for the emotions of pride and shame (see Gilbert, this volume). It may seem anthropomorphic to impute to animals affects analogous (or homologous) to human pride and shame. Yet we do the same thing when we refer to a hunger motive in animals.

Numerous other parallels exist between various aspects of dominance behaviour in humans and other species, such as dominance and submission displays (Weisfeld and Linkey 1985). These parallels (discussed below) argue for a distinct dominance motive in humans that evolved from simian dominance behaviour. For discussion of this viewpoint, see Mazur (1985), Barkow (1975), Rajecki and Flannery (1981), and Omark, Strayer and Freedman (1980).

Having made a case for recognizing a dominance motive, I wish now to enter into a less controversial area and describe dominance behaviour further. Dominance goes beyond the simple tendency to fight for resources. Animals in dominance hierarchies recognize one another's rank – relative fighting ability – and behave accordingly. They can predict the outcome of fights. They can issue and respond to dominance challenges appropriately. Why challenge a much stronger opponent? Why back down from a weaker one?

Armed with this knowledge, animals in a stable group tend to fight only infrequently; there is no need to run the risks of a fight when the outcome is a foregone conclusion. If the outcome is uncertain, on the other hand, fighting is more likely, as when a group is forming, when a new animal appears, and between closely ranked opponents.

Thus, an essential element of dominance hierarchization is the animal's recognition of the fighting abilities of its opponents in the group. This process of recognition is aided by the use of dominance and submission displays, which are essentially memory aids that reflect the animal's past fighting success. Animals 'size one another up' on the basis of these displays (or emotional expressions), their memory of past encounters, and other cues such as size, vigour and weaponry.

Each animal benefits from this knowledge. Resources are distributed in an orderly fashion and with a minimum of fighting, albeit not equally.

Rank orders are orderly and peaceful in other ways as well. First, once a dominance relationship is established, the subordinate usually defers to the dominant animal in subsequent encounters. Secondly, submission displays are respected, meaning that the dominant animal will desist from attack once its opponent submits. Thirdly, dominance aggression is often highly ritualized; that is, fighting remains within the bounds of fairly innocuous 'rules of combat'. For example, giraffes fight for dominance by swinging their necks together. Ranks are usually settled with a minimum of injuries. Fear-induced attack, on the other hand, consists of kicking, a much more dangerous form of attack. A giraffe can subdue even a lion by means of kicking.

As mentioned below, all of these social regularities are enforced by the threat of a vehement (angry) attack by the victim if they are violated. They are not agreed upon by the participants or upheld as matters of principle, of course. Thus, they are not conventions but they may constitute rules, in the sense that they connote regularity of action and a minimum of contention.

Thus, I would conclude that it is in the interests of the individual animal (1) to strive for dominance, (2) to utilize information and cues about an opponent's competitive ability and intentions, and respond appropriately, and (3) to stay within the 'rules' governing dominance hierarchies. If the functional utility of these tendencies is recognized, the otherwise mysterious competitive behaviour of humans (especially males) makes some sense and need not be denied as being fundamental to our nature.

In summary, I am maintaining that dominance is a motivated behaviour. Like other motives, it is a distinct, whole-body, voluntary behaviour. Like other emotions, it is characterized by a specific affective capacity (pride and shame), a characteristic overt behaviour (attack or other forms of competition), a phylogenetic distribution and an evolutionary function (gaining resources by judicious competition), emotional expressions (or displays), specific subcortical and biochemical mechanisms, and a typical developmental pattern.

In this chapter, dominance will not be treated as just one thing. It is not merely an operationally defined relationship between animals that reflects their competitive abilities (cf. Chapter 16). Like other motives, it has various facets, no one of which alone captures the whole concept. Adding to this complexity, dominance interacts in complex ways with other social motives, such as affiliation and play (for example, Strayer 1992), grooming, leadership and attention. These connections are only beginning to be understood (Archer 1992a).

The concept of dominance was never intended to explain all of social behaviour and organization, but it is certainly one of the most fruitful ideas for analysing individual differences that we have yet developed. If we recognize it as one motive amongst many, we may be able to avoid exalting it as a concept capable of explaining all aspects of social organization or dismissing it as a mere behavioural measurement concept.

ANGRY AGGRESSION

Angry aggression is also referred to as rage, affective aggression and irritable aggression. As some of these terms imply, angry aggression usually includes prominent threat displays, as does fear-induced aggression.

It has been proposed that angry aggression arises when the animal is unable to attain a goal. This is the famous frustration-aggression hypothesis (Dollard *et al.* 1939). Indeed, when a variety of animals are given continuous reinforcement which then stops, they attack any nearby target (Archer 1988). Many critics have doubted the generality of this explanation, saying that although frustration can lead to aggression, often it does not; sometimes it simply prompts trying another tack or withdrawing (Huntingford and Turner 1987).

Anger in humans may arise from a specific type of frustration. Pastore (1952) noted that in the examples provided by Dollard *et al.* anger was greatest in response to scenarios in which the subject was 'arbitrarily' frustrated. In one of these examples, subjects reported they would be more angry if a bus driver failed to stop for them when he was scheduled to stop than when the bus was a 'special' on its way to an athletic event. Pastore's own results supported this distinction, as did those of Allison and Hunt (1959).

Interest in this topic led me to propose a 'transgression-aggression' hypothesis (Weisfeld 1972). The crucial releaser of anger may not be frustration but, more specifically, the perception of the violation of a social norm. Similarly, Blanchard and Blanchard (1989) referred to violations of rights. In my test of this notion, aggression was elicited when subjects merely observed, but were not themselves victimized or frustrated by, an act that violated social norms.

Archer (1976) referred to aggression as resulting from a discrepancy between

47

what is expected and what is actually received. To phrase the matter in terms of norms or rights is somewhat more complicated; it involves social expectations, or proprieties, not just the anticipation of certain outcomes. Archer's discrepancy model has the advantage of applying to animals as well as humans. However, it has the disadvantage of not easily accounting for the observation that transgression aggression in humans and simians (for example, Simonds 1965) can be exhibited by a third party.

This transgression-aggression explanation is similar to Trivers' (1971) widely accepted notion of moralistic anger, which he said arises in response to failures to return favours. However, it seems to me that any behaviour that violates existing social norms, not just norms regulating the exchange of favours, can evoke anger. Social norms govern virtually every behaviour in human society, and violation of any of these norms, such as a traffic law, social convention, food taboo or religious observance, can evoke anger.

Angry aggression is observed in other species too. These 'rage reactions' characteristically occur when some dominance or territorial norm is violated. For example, a vehement attack often occurs in response to a subordinate trying to take something from a dominant animal, or when one animal exceeds the ritualistic rules of combat for dominance contests, or when the victor continues to attack even after the loser has submitted (Bernstein and Gordon 1974). Likewise, territorial claims are respected; intruders are vigorously attacked. Incidentally, note that in these examples there is a social agent of frustration; agents of frustration such as the weather or an obstacle do not usually evoke aggression.

Other norms are unrelated to dominance or territoriality. Baboons respect the possession of females by males (Kummer 1971). Chimpanzees respect the possession of food by another, as indicated by a stronger animal begging from a weaker one (Teleki 1973) – although they may become angry if their persistent begging is denied (Goodall 1986). In some primate species, dominant males aggress against an animal that strays from the troop (Kummer 1967), against subordinate males that harass females (Simonds 1965), against females that attempt to mate with subordinates (Kummer 1967), and against juveniles that play too roughly (Eimerl and DeVore 1965). An adult female sometimes attacks animals that threaten not only her own young but also any other infant (Mitchell 1969). Note that some of these examples involve third-party aggression.

Furthermore, there seems to be a certain capacity for flexibility in social norms. My dog barks indignantly when denied an expected reward (Leila, canine communication). The same tendency was demonstrated by the wild child Victor of Aveyron, studied by Itard (Malson 1972). These might be cases of simple frustration, but they seem to be specific reactions to being unexpectedly thwarted by another – that is, thwarted by socially abnormal behaviour.

Violations of social norms are often punished vigorously by the victim

(Bernstein and Gordon 1974; Maynard Smith and Ridpath 1972). The intensity of these attacks makes sense given the stakes: an animal cannot afford to be half-hearted if its basic rights in competition are threatened. Without the protection of these social norms, the animal would be open to repeated exploitation. It must demonstrate a willingness vigorously to oppose violations of its customary prerogatives.

In our species, third parties and groups often intervene to punish wrongdoers, so the individual does not have to act alone in defending him- (or her-) self. In settings in which this element of policing is somewhat ineffective, such as prisons and playgrounds, individuals are thrown back upon their individual resources (see Chapter 7).

Real-life examples of aggression often involve more than one type (Archer 1989–90). When an animal is attacked without provocation, it may experience anger as well as fear, in that it alternately attacks and retreats. In Chapter 2, Boulton discussed the complex relationships between 'play-fighting', or rough-and-tumble play, and angry aggression and dominance.

Despite such interactions amongst types of aggression and with other types of behaviour, it is useful to try to specify the type of aggression involved. We need to identify the type in order to analyse a given aggressive situation functionally, and to recognize which factors predict which types of aggression. In practice, the type of aggression can usually be specified by simply asking oneself what emotion the aggressor is probably feeling. Is the aggressor experiencing fear, anger, a desire for pride (dominance), interest (play-fighting), or the desire for a tangible object (instrumental aggression)? Emotional expressions and the form of attack provide important information for making this assessment.

DOMINANCE IN COMPARATIVE PERSPECTIVE

Because the dominance hierarchy model has been useful for analysing aggressive behaviour in children and adolescents (Omark et al. 1980; Smith 1989), I wish to describe this comparative model more fully at this point.

Is human dominance in fact species-wide and evolved, and hence amenable to comparative analysis? What is the evidence for the universality of human dominance? Do children indeed fight for dominance, as do the young of many other primate species?

Cross-cultural research suggests that dominance aggression occurs in children everywhere, and especially in boys. By about 6 years of age, a consensual dominance hierarchy based on fighting ability ('toughness') has been found to emerge in playgroups in Ethiopia, Switzerland, England, Canada and the United States, and among the Hopi Indians (Omark et al. 1980). Rank orders based on who pays attention to whom have been described in Germany, in Japan, and among the G/wi Bushmen (Hold 1976, 1977). Similarly, a rank order based on social influence was described in a group of US children (Barner-Barry 1980).

To be sure, not all of these studies demonstrated all of the aspects of dominance behaviour that have been described. But enough convergent evidence exists to conclude that dominance behaviour in children is homologous to that in other primates. Some of the evidence for this homology is listed below:

1 ranks based on fighting ability ('toughness') in childhood (Dawe 1934; Omark *et al.* 1975; Smith 1988);

2 high-ranking ('tough') children exercising prerogatives such as leading the group at play (Omark *et al.* 1975; Savin-Williams 1987);

3 high-ranking children attracting more attention (Hold-Cavell 1985; Vaughn and Waters 1980);

4 ranks being generally rigid (few instances of a subordinate defeating a dominant child) (Strayer and Strayer 1976; LaFrenière and Charlesworth 1983);

5 ranks being generally linear (few cases of A dominating B, B dominating C and C dominating A) (Hanfmann 1935; McGrew 1972; Strayer and Strayer 1976); but see Archer (1992a) for a compelling critique of conclusions concerning the rigidity and linearity of ranks;

6 fighting falling in frequency over time (Savin-Williams 1976; LaFrenière and Charlesworth 1983; Strayer 1992);

7 ranks remaining stable (LaFrenière and Charlesworth 1983; Savin-Williams 1976; Strayer 1992), even over years (Weisfeld 1980);

8 threat, fear, dominance and submission displayed in typical primate forms (Blurton Jones 1967; Camras 1980; Weisfeld and Berger 1983; Zivin 1977);

9 sex differences, with most males outranking most females and being more aggressive or competitive (Jersild and Markey 1935; McGrew 1972; Omark *et al.* 1975; Strayer and Trudel 1984), and non-verbally dominant (Dovidio *et al.* 1988);

10 species-typical age of onset, i.e., shortly after infancy (Weisfeld and Linkey 1985);

11 most dominance contests occurring between closely ranked individuals, i.e., between individuals uncertain about their relative rank (Savin-Williams 1976);

12 homologous structures of the brain involved in dominance in humans and in simians – for example, stimulation of the amygdala enhances aggression in dominant animals and submissiveness in subordinates (Huntingford and Turner 1987), and the orbitofrontal cortex seems necessary for normal dominance behaviour in simians and for social status striving in humans (Weisfeld and Linkey 1985);

13 biochemical parallels, e.g., testosterone and serotonin levels rising with competitive success in men and male primates (Mazur and Lamb 1980; McGuire *et al.* 1984).

The homology between human and animal dominance is obscured by the fact that adult humans do not compete for status merely by fighting. The criteria for dominance expand beyond physical traits as we get older, and the criteria differ across cultures. Nevertheless, the same dominance motive is operating even after we outgrow fighting for rank; status-striving is universal, even if the criteria for status are multiple and do vary across cultures (Barkow 1975, 1989). Analogously, we gain nourishment from a wide variety of foods (after weaning), but we all possess the hunger motive.

DEVELOPMENT OF AGGRESSION IN CHILDREN

Now I wish to describe the development of some of these types of aggression, making liberal use of ethological concepts and particularly the dominance model. Analysis of the different types of aggression shows that each takes a characteristic developmental course.

Starting in the second year of life, children often use force to secure a toy (Cairns 1979; Smith and Boulton 1990). This may be *instrumental aggression*, since the objective seems not to be hurting the other child but simply securing the toy (Hartup 1974). In animals, instrumental aggression over resources is more likely if the resources are scarce, valuable and easily defended (Wilson 1975). Analogously, reducing the number of toys per preschooler has been shown to increase the rate of fighting (Smith and Connolly 1980). The frequency of instrumental aggression declines during the preschool years (Dawe 1934; Jersild and Markey 1935), presumably because of socialization effects.

Dominance aggression seems to emerge at around 3 years. A great many researchers, using a variety of terms and theoretical concepts, have reported increases in competitiveness at this age. This takes such forms as running races, play-fighting, seeking approval and comparing heights; tangible resources do not seem necessary to motivate these comparisons (Weisfeld and Linkey 1985). Actual fights sometimes result from verbal challenges which, if refused, result in loss of face (Smith and Boulton 1990). For example, Italian children sometimes employ singsong mocking, called *cantilena* (Corsaro and Riozzo 1990). In these challenges self-esteem is at stake, not just tangible resources. This behaviour is distinguishable from angry aggression because the challenge to self-esteem precedes any anger of the target and hence itself needs to be explained. Play-fighting also increases during this period (Hartup 1983), and sometimes includes a competitive element.

Although some observers have reported dominance relationships to occur as early as 6 or 8 months (Missakian 1980; Strayer and Trudel 1984), these results may simply reflect consistency in the outcome of object struggles. The fact that one child consistently aggresses against or intimidates another may just be due to strength differences, rather than the existence of a dominance motive.

In their detailed cross-cultural, cross-sectional research, Omark et al. (1975)

found that 4-year-olds expressed great interest in being tough (especially the boys, who greatly overrated themselves on toughness). Dominance motivation may be manifested by this competitiveness and overrating of self (which may function to enhance self-confidence and hence rivalry). Agreement on ranks emerged first for the highest and lowest positions; those in the middle were confused. Omark *et al.* explained this by referring to the emerging Piagetian concepts of transitivity and seriation. A true dominance hierarchy featuring prerogatives of rank and a stable, consensual hierarchy did not emerge until about 6 years. Similarly, Blurton Jones (1967) observed that consistent leadership in a children's group did not appear until after a hierarchy had crystallized.

As the hierarchy stabilizes, the rate of dominance aggression seems to decline (LaFrenière and Charlesworth 1983; Strayer and Trudel 1984). However, this conclusion is complicated by the fact that verbal assertiveness increases over the same period (Hartup 1974; LaFrenière and Charlesworth 1983). Children gradually come to use verbal aggression instead of physical aggression in their disputes. During middle childhood, the rate of 'unprovoked physical attacks' continues to fall (Kagan and Moss 1962).

The total amount of aggression has been found to peak at 4 years (Hartup 1983). However, the rate of positive social behaviour (for example, attention, approval, submission and generosity) also increases from 3 to 4 years of age (Charlesworth and Hartup 1967). It is important to remember that children greatly increase their activities with peers starting at about 3 years of age, the approximate time of weaning for our species cross-culturally.

Cross-cultural evidence indicates that the presence of adults and their threats of punishment reduce physical aggression between children (Huntingford and Turner 1987). In the United States, middle-class (but not always lower-class) socialization tends to increase the proportion of friendly versus aggressive interactions with age (Hartup 1983). In violent neighbourhoods, pacifism may be a particularly unsuccessful individual strategy (Chapter 7). A parent withdrew her son from Peace Lutheran School in Detroit on the grounds that he was not learning how to fight!

Angry aggression in the context of peer interactions was reported to begin at age 4 by Goodenough (1931). Hartup (1974) also reported 'hostile' aggression among peers as early as 4 years. It makes functional sense that the capacity for enforcing dominance rules should emerge by the time that dominance hierarchies do. Anger in other contexts, as when an infant is denied the breast, occurs much earlier (Bridges 1932).

In Hartup's research, physically aggressive retaliation for an insult or violation of the possession norm was more typical of younger children. Older children (6–7) were more likely to retaliate verbally.

Sex differences in aggression are present in our species throughout development. Starting early in childhood, the sexes show a pronounced tendency to play separately (Archer 1992b). Amongst older children each sex usually forms its own hierarchy (Sluckin and Smith 1977) – although children of both sexes generally agree on the ranks of all the children (Omark *et al.* 1975). Starting in preschool and continuing throughout childhood, boys initiate and receive more attacks of all kinds than do girls (Cairns 1979), and exhibit more play-fighting (Blurton Jones 1967; Boulton and Smith 1992). In some cross-cultural studies no sex difference is reported, sometimes because of few instances of aggression recorded. Another problem is that the type of aggression is often not specified. However, whenever there has been a statistically significant sex difference, males have proved to be the more aggressive sex (Rohner 1976; Whiting and Whiting 1975).

The cross-cultural sex difference in aggression is consistent with the pattern for other primates (Boulton and Smith 1992; van der Dennen 1992). It also makes functional sense: in most mammalian species, more aggressive competition for mates occurs amongst males than females. Consequently, selection pressure for aggressiveness was doubtless stronger upon males than females, accounting also for their generally greater size and strength (Daly and Wilson, this volume). Consistent with this explanation, the sex difference in size and agressiveness is associated with mating systems with pronounced sexual competition amongst the males.

DEVELOPMENT OF AGGRESSION IN ADOLESCENTS

At reproductive maturity, an essential new resource must be sought: mates. Before then, some dominance aggression is to be expected because non-sexual resources are contested and because the outcome of early fights may affect later ones ('conditioning to success'). This carryover would also occur if dominant juvenile males fed better and grew to be stronger and, at maturity, proved more successful in fighting for mates.

But at maturity the advantages of being dominant, especially for males, greatly increase in many species. An animal will be unsuccessful in passing on its genes if it does not secure mating opportunities.

Dominant males do tend to produce the most offspring. In most hierarchically organized primate species, most studies show that dominant males gain the most reproductive opportunities (Barkow 1989; Chalmers 1980). Cross-cultural research has demonstrated that high-ranking men are sought as husbands (Buss 1989) and have the most offspring (Barkow 1989). Although rank is often defined as having wealth in this research, dominant behaviour may be more directly attractive to women (Weisfeld and Feldman 1982; Weisfeld *et al.* 1992). Dominant adolescent boys also tend to be attractive to and popular with girls in the United States (Weisfeld *et al.* 1980, 1983, 1987) and China (Dong *et al.* in preparation).

Increased dominance competition amongst males at reproductive maturity occurs in many vertebrate species, due to the rise in testosterone levels (Archer 1988). Androgens do not seem to influence fear-induced or parental aggression in mammals (Ellis 1986). Likewise, in humans the sex difference in aggression mainly concerns dominance aggression (namely, initiating aggression), rather than angry aggression (retaliation) (van der Dennen 1992).

One might therefore expect increased dominance competition at puberty in boys, linked to rising androgen levels (Neill 1985; Weisfeld 1979). Neill (1985) concluded from various observational studies that 'roughness peaks in adolescence' (p. 1381). Verbal repartee contests become more common in adolescent boys cross-culturally (Apte 1985). These competitions may remain friendly but sometimes escalate.

There is some evidence that androgen levels are correlated with various measures of individual aggressiveness in adolescent boys and young men, but it is weak and variable (Archer 1991). These studies, and the complications in their interpretation, are discussed in Chapter 13 (by Turner), and by Archer (1991). Prenatal testosterone may also play a permissive role in the development of male aggression (Ellis 1986).

It may be the case that as long as pubertal androgens are within the normal adult range in men, individual differences in aggressiveness seem not to be consistently observed. However, as adolescents enter puberty, aggression may be correlated with androgen level because pubertal androgens are not yet within this range. At least two studies have reported such correlations in adolescents or young men but not in adults (Kreuz and Rose 1972; Persky et al. 1971).

Leaving aside the question of hormonal factors in adolescent dominance, we turn now to observational studies of this behaviour. The most important ethological research on dominance amongst adolescent peers was conducted at a US summer camp. Savin-Williams (1987) found that a rank order stabilized within a few days, and remained stable until the end of camp several weeks later. Boys' dominance contests were observed to involve more aggression and physical threats than did those in the girls' cabins. However, for both sexes most of the dominance contests were characterized by verbal ridicule. Dominant boys were recognized as such by the subjects, prevailed in most dominance contests, and exercised various prerogatives.

Similarly, the social psychologists Sherif and Sherif (1964) observed that adolescent boys spontaneously formed recognizable, increasingly stable hierarchies. High-ranking boys exercised more control over group decisions.

Dominance competition may be especially intense between adolescent sons and mothers. Conflict between them, as observed during family discussions, peaked at mid-puberty, controlling for chronological age (Steinberg 1985, 1989). Subsequently, sons generally emerged as dominant over mothers in decision-making. A process whereby adolescent sons compete with and come to dominate mothers may occur universally: in all cultures, males have higher ascribed status than females, and elders higher status than juniors. This means that sons eventually overtake mothers. Likewise, in chimpanzees young males overtake adult females in dominance (Goodall 1986). Similarly, Beynon

(1989) observed that the most humiliating event for his Welsh schoolboys was to be hurt or embarrassed by a woman teacher. In a Japanese study, filial violence by adolescents was most often directed at dominant mothers (Kumagai 1983).

Steinberg's research showed that fathers remained dominant over sons, and both parents over daughters, again consistent with the cross-cultural pattern. Along the same lines, Patterson and Cobb (1971) showed that supervision by the father, including merely paying attention, was effective in inhibiting aggression in aggressive boys. Sons with fathers (even stepfathers) in the home have lower rates of criminal arrests than sons of single mothers (Daly and Wilson 1988). Similarly, in several primate species, the adult males exercise a 'control' role over juvenile males.

CRITERIA FOR DOMINANCE

Which children are likely to become dominant? In childhood, dominant children tend to be good fighters, or 'tough'. This occurs cross-culturally (Omark and Edelman 1976), even amongst the peaceful Hopi (Weisfeld et al. 1984). Dominance relations may be sorted out mainly in the context of play-fighting, during struggles over toys or during angry altercations. Actual fighting may not be necessary, however; size comparisons, the use of dominance and submissive displays, and staring contests may suffice in a given confrontation.

Abundant research in the United States demonstrates that dominant, popular, influential boys at all ages are those who are attractive and athletic (Dodge 1983; Hartup 1983; Savin-Williams 1987; Weisfeld et al. 1987). In other words, socially successful boys tend to possess desirable physical traits from childhood through adolescence. All of these physical traits – toughness, attractiveness, athletic ability, strength and early maturity – seem to form a stable constellation throughout development (Tanner 1978; Weisfeld and Billings 1988). Boys with one of these traits tend to possess them all. The reasons for some of these correlations are obvious. For example, strength probably underlies toughness and athletic ability (Klissouras 1984).

As for the correlation of attractiveness with these other physical traits, it would make evolutionary sense for females to be drawn to males who were strong and athletic. These males would make good hunters and protectors, and would sire sons who were successful in dominance competition and hence high in reproductive success (Weisfeld and Billings 1988). Indeed, the attractiveness of adolescent boys to the opposite sex is correlated with their athletic ability (Weisfeld et al. 1980). I am suggesting that natural selection favoured females who were attracted to males with an appearance that connoted strength and athletic ability. In many other animals too, females prefer males that are strong and physically dominant.

Boys who are dominant and popular with girls are also dominant and

55

popular with other boys, and are seen as leaders by both sexes (Weisfeld *et al.* 1980). The common factor explaining this may be these boys' physical attractiveness; attractiveness is important for social success in both sexes throughout development (Adams 1977; Jackson 1992). It would make sense for males to defer to these strong, athletic rivals, and follow their leadership. These dominant males will tend to make useful allies and commanding leaders.

Does this mean that the social world of boys is simply a struggle for social success based on physical traits? Not at all; other traits also influence dominance and popularity. For example, popular boys tend to be relatively pro-social even independent of their attractiveness (Dodge 1983). Parents and other adults evaluate children by other criteria besides physical ones, and these judgements affect self-esteem even in adolescence (Walker and Greene 1986).

Furthermore, the criteria for dominance multiply as development proceeds. Various skills, personality attributes and, especially for men, wealth are respected by others. In research conducted at an academically excellent US high school, by the senior year (age 17) boys' dominance status was based on intelligence as well as physical traits (Weisfeld *et al.* 1987). However, in most US high schools, intelligence bears no significant relation to peer status (see, for example, Coleman 1961).

Recently we collected data on Chinese adolescents. For both sexes, popularity and dominance were associated mainly with intelligence and academic success (Dong *et al.* in preparation). Athletic ability counted for very little. However, attractiveness played a significant role. At present we are working with Sean Neill on a study of English adolescents.

Our tentative conclusion is that the appeal of physical attractiveness is evolved and is an important criterion for social success throughout development in both sexes. However, culturally imposed values can greatly affect the importance of other criteria, such as intelligence. Perhaps in a society with a strong 'youth subculture' such as the United States, adolescents judge one another mainly on the basis of physical criteria. Where adults exercise stricter control, as in Japan and China, culturally imposed criteria may be more influential.

Carrying this further, I would suggest that the respect that street-gang youth and prisoners exhibit for fighting ability (see, for example, Sherif and Sherif 1964; Weisfeld and Feldman 1982) likewise represents a default to the evolved respect for physical prowess in dominance relations. Consistent with this, boys in street gangs (Goldstein, this volume) exhibit clear-cut dominance displays, including swaggering, threatening, swearing (to indicate anger), and spitting (to indicate fearlessness). Gang leaders are consistently the best fighters, and exercise various prerogatives such as receiving monetary tributes from their followers. Gang leaders also tend to be the most popular with girls.

Respect for fighting is utilitarian in these rough settings, as well as consistent with the evolutionary scenario I am proposing. Many disputes are settled by physical force or intimidation, and violence is sometimes employed in committing property crimes. A youth who is not willing and able to defend himself, his girl and his property will be left with nothing but disgrace. Homicides frequently occur over what appear to be petty altercations (Daly and Wilson 1988). However, the value of not backing down – of maintaining one's dominance status, or saving face – is apparent given the realities of a violent environment. Humiliating affronts or threats to reputation are the most reliable predictors of violence in assault-prone subjects (Worchel 1978).

This is not to say that affection and co-operation do not occur in such environments; these virtues are indeed to be observed. Rather, violence is very important in these settings – important in competition and in co-operation. In rough neighbourhoods, a person fairly frequently defends himself physically and also backs his allies by force; words alone may be unavailing.

STABILITY OF DOMINANCE STATUS

Dominance ranks are strikingly stable, at least among boys. Dominance hierarchies formed at 6 or 7 years show significant stability as long as ten years later (Weisfeld et al. 1987). Boys who were tough children tended to become dominant, popular leaders in adolescence who exhibited the erect posture of dominant primates (Weisfeld and Beresford 1982). Similarly, Bronson (1966) reported that the trait of dominance versus passivity was stable from ages 5–7 to 14–16 in boys. Kagan and Moss (1962) found that dominance of peers was stable from ages 3–6 to ages 10–14 for both sexes. They also reported that boys' (but not girls') competitiveness at ages 6–10 predicted competitiveness in adulthood.

Thus, dominance is an unusually stable trait. The stability of dominance seems to be due largely to its high heritability (.49 as reported by Gottesman [1966]). This is consistent with the notion that strength and other traits that seem to underlie athletic ability are also highly heritable (Klissouras 1984). As stated above, a stable constellation of physical traits characterizes dominant boys. Since these traits seem largely to determine dominance status and are themselves highly stable, one would expect dominance status to exhibit stability, which indeed it does.

Much has been made of the fact that early maturity in adolescent boys is associated with dominance, popularity and other desirable social traits, even well into adulthood (Jones and Bayley 1950; Mussen and Jones 1957). However, dominance seems to be more closely tied to athletic ability than to early maturity in adolescent boys (Savin-Williams 1987). The correlation of early maturity with dominance is probably derivative; early maturity is associated with strength and athletic ability (Tanner 1978). Early maturity probably does not directly cause high social status (Weisfeld and Billings 1988), since it existed previously.

CONSEQUENCES OF BEING DOMINANT OR SUBORDINATE

Being a dominant boy leads to a number of desirable social results. Dominant children take the lead in play (Jones 1984); they mediate conflicts (Ginsburg and Miller 1981; Hold 1976, 1977), and therefore gain experience exercising leadership. Dominant boys tend to be verbally assertive (LaFrenière and Charlesworth 1983). Tough boys become recognized as leaders when they reach adolescence (Weisfeld *et al.* 1987). Dominant children tend to be popular with peers (Coie and Dodge 1983; Deluty 1981; Weisfeld *et al.* 1987). A developmental history of approval by peers doubtless enhances self-esteem or, in our terminology, pride. These cumulative positive social experiences doubtless enhance happiness and social skills.

Boys who are submissive suffer from the opposite kinds of experience. These less popular boys have suffered repeated social rejection and shame. They tend to be socially withdrawn (Dodge 1983), anxious, low in self-confidence, poor in social skills, depressed and lonely (Perry *et al.* in press; Weisfeld 1980).

Perhaps the criterion of dominance and overall social success easiest to identify is attractiveness. Attractiveness is highly stable (Adams 1977) and is perceived even by 3-year-olds in terms of adult standards (Dion 1973). The crucial role of attractiveness in social development is indicated by a number of studies (Jackson 1992). Judgements of attractiveness are made instantaneously, and show consistency across cultures. The attractiveness of a face affects behaviour even in 3-month-old subjects. A person's attractiveness leads to many advantages. Attractive children tend to exhibit desirable social traits (Dodge 1980; Styczynski and Langlois 1980). In a crucial study, Langlois and Stephan (1981) found that some time between 3 and 5 years of age, unattractive children as a group began to manifest the aggressiveness that others have reported to characterize unpopular boys later on. Attractive children tend to be privileged; unattractive ones tend to struggle socially.

Why should we have evolved to be so sensitive to others' attractiveness? If attractiveness connotes fighting prowess in males and high mate value in both sexes (good genetic quality, health, full sexual differentiation and so on), we can identify individuals possessing these qualities at a mere glance. Having identified them, we can be emotionally disposed to them in ways that will enhance our individual fitness. Specifically, we can be deferential to formidable rivals of the same sex, and sexually attracted to opposite-sex individuals of high mate value.

DEVELOPMENT OF EXCESSIVE AGGRESSIVENESS

The dominance model may eventually prove useful for understanding cases of excessive aggressiveness. In this section a preliminary attempt will be made to interpret some of the existing data on excessive agressiveness in light of this model.

Differences in dominance status are inevitable. In most cases, a child accepts his or her status with good grace. However, sometimes the child continues to be aggressive. Four patterns of response to the outcome of dominance interactions will now be described.

Excessive aggressiveness seems to result in some cases when a subordinate does not submit. Pierce (1990) called these children 'high-conflict victims' – *aggressive subordinates*, in ethological terminology. They provoke other children but wind up losing, resulting in great distress. They insist on having their own way, blame others, persist in attempting to socialize when rejected, and exhibit excessive anger.

Similarly, Lesser (1959) observed that unpopular boys sometimes exhibit excessive angry aggression. This seems to occur because they habitually receive hostile treatment (Dodge 1980), tend to expect harsh treatment from peers (Waas 1988), and react accordingly (Dodge and Frame 1982). They also act less pro-socially than do popular boys. The evidence suggests that these unpopular boys are correct in expecting ungenerous treatment from their peers. Rather than lacking social skills, they accurately perceive this bias against them. They simply resent their low status; they refuse to submit. Moreover, they bring their aggressiveness to new groups, thereby incurring rejection anew (Coie and Kupersmidt 1983; Dodge 1983).

This persistent aggressiveness may result from either anger at perceived past injustices and/or high dominance motivation. In line with the latter interpretation, Patterson (1982) observed that problem children are often poor at fighting, yet behave as though a dominance hierarchy does not exist and persist in challenging their superiors. Thus, a failure to accept low status and its humiliations may lead these children into further difficulties.

In contrast with these aggressive subordinates, 'low-conflict victims' (*non-aggressive subordinates*) yield quickly and accept exclusion from the group. They are less disliked than high-conflict ones (Pierce 1990). Moreover, they seem to dislike their chronic attacker less than do violent subordinates theirs (Dodge *et al*. 1990).

Analogously, there are high-conflict victors (*aggressive dominants*), whom Dodge and Coie (1989) called bullies. In this case, excessive aggressiveness results from a different cause. These children typically settle on a non-resistant victim and torment him. They frequently do this by initiating ambiguous rough play towards their partners (Dodge *et al*. 1990). Then, having provoked a fight, they ignore their victim's submissive displays. Perry *et al*. (in press) reported that aggressive children are less likely to desist in attacking when the victim shows signs of pain. Bullies' relations with other children are usually normal. However, both the bully and the angry, resisting victim tended to be low in popularity, and to dislike each other intensely (Dodge *et al*. 1990).

Bullies may have high dominance motivation, or be angry at their low popularity or have some other motive (see Chapter 4). They may differ from aggressive subordinates only in being less compassionate or more capable of dominating at least one other child.

The last category is what might be called low-conflict victors (*non-aggressive dominants*). These boys are willing to defend themselves against victimization (Lesser 1959); that is, to aggress in anger. On the other hand, they resort to relatively little aggression, simply because they are seldom challenged or offended. These children have the best developmental outcome, as explained above.

APPLIED IMPLICATIONS

The greatest problems seem to result from refusals to accept the resolution of a dominance conflict (aggressive subordinates and aggressive dominants). Why do certain children persist in being violent even when they are either defeated or submitted to?

Some evidence suggests that aggressive children highly value the various rewards that aggression offers, such as control over others, tangible rewards and being submitted to (Perry *et al.* in press). Perhaps their dominance motivation is relatively high; they have a great need for pride. Thus, just as males tend to be more aggressive than females because of a greater dominance motive, certain individuals are more aggressive than others.

Interestingly, children who exhibit impulsive aggression tend to have low levels of serotonin (Pines 1985), a neurotransmitter released in vervet monkeys when they are submitted to (McGuire *et al.* 1984). Serotonin also tends to be low in adults who commit violent crimes or suicide (Goodwin and Post 1983; Kalat 1992). Perhaps aggressive children do not receive enough respect, either from peers or at home. If they perceive this rejection as unfair, an element of anger may also underlie their combativeness.

Some more specific recommendations may now be tentatively advanced. Concerning the aggressive subordinate, it may be possible to introduce such a child to other activities at which he may succeed. Not everyone can be the toughest – dominance hierarchization is a zero-sum game – but each child can try to develop his or her talents to the fullest. Also, the parents can be urged to be as warm and encouraging as possible. Of course, the latter is good advice for every parent.

In the case of the aggressive dominant, or bully, two additional remedies suggest themselves: parental intervention and angry retaliation by the victim. Savin-Williams (1987) reports an example of the latter: the victim of chronic bullying suddenly retaliated, which put an end to the bullying (see Chapter 4). According to Appel (1942), self-help is likely to be more effective and less humiliating than parental intervention. Lauer (1992) has suggested that adult interference can prevent the emergence of a stabilizing dominance hierarchy. However, adult intervention is probably better than no solution at all. If adults tolerate or ignore bullying, it may persist. If they think that punishing aggression is actually rewarding because the aggressor receives attention, then they probably need to use unequivocal punishments.

In trying to understand the origin of excessive aggression, one must recognize that aggressiveness shows considerable long-term stability in boys (Parke and Slaby 1983; Olweus 1984). In Kagan and Moss's research, aggression towards the mother (presumably, angry aggression) predicted adult anger arousal starting at ages 3–6, for males but not females. In two English longitudinal studies, juvenile delinquency at age 18 was predicted from teacher- or peer-rated aggressiveness at age 8 (Parke and Slaby 1983).

This long-term stability of aggressiveness from an early age may be attributed to several factors. For example, early experience may be crucial, especially within the family. Hartup (1983) concluded that delinquency stems from disturbed family relations, which lead to aggressiveness towards peers, followed by exposure to delinquent norms.

Rutter and Giller (1983) also document the importance of family factors in delinquency, including weak parental supervision and divorce. In traditional cultures, supervision of children by family members is much closer than in modern societies with higher rates of violence, notably the United States. Economic and social policies that support the intact family may be the most efficient means of elevating the quality of parental behaviour and decreasing the prevalence of violence and other social problems. The presence of a 'control male' may be especially effective (Patterson 1982), particularly the biological father (Daly and Wilson 1988).

A child may persist in seeking to dominate peers because of insufficient emotional support at home. The ideal parental style seems to be characterized by warmth, frequent explanations of norms, and relatively high expectations (Olweus 1984; Patterson 1982). Affection, consistency in punishing, and general respect by the parent – towards the child and towards the spouse – seem to reduce aggressiveness and promote co-operation (Perry et al. in press). Also, role-playing (Chandler 1973), empathy training (Feshbach 1989), and other remedial programmes that teach juveniles to anticipate the consequences of their actions have proved useful. Generally speaking, educational and custodial programmes that feature warmth, respect, explanations and high expectations show the greatest success (Rutter and Giller 1983).

In neighbourhoods where violence is endemic and hence all but necessary for the individual's self-defence and self-esteem, an interpretation in terms of individual pathology is inappropriate. Instead, community-wide remedies are called for, such as opportunities to gain status through employment, and improved police and legal services.

Some further ideas for reducing aggression in children can be derived from considering our prehistory. In hominid evolution, instrumental aggression before the age of 3 would have been uncommon because infants were constantly carried about by their mothers or other caregivers and (except for twins) would not have had much opportunity to interact with peers. Even

61

after the age of 3, fighting amongst children was probably rare, because few children were similar in age and hence in fighting ability. In a US study it was indeed found that conflicts were few when children differed in age (Blume 1989). Thus, age segregation as occurs in classrooms may intensify competition.

Crowding of children may also be a factor. Fighting amongst preschoolers increased once a critical social density of 25 sq. ft./child was reached (Smith and Connolly 1980). Our hominid ancestors probably seldom crowded their children together to this extent, since most play occurred out of doors. Also, toys were simple and easily made, and hence probably seldom in short supply.

Lauer (1992) noted that the presence of a new member tends to increase fighting in a primate group. Thus, it would seem desirable to reduce geographical mobility, a factor that has also been associated with juvenile delinquency (Rutter and Giller 1983). One main reason why people move house is to find employment. Therefore, bringing jobs to areas of high unemployment, on the Swedish model, would seem desirable. This would also tend to preserve the extended family.

Adults, perhaps, should encourage and model amicable means of settling disputes. The constructive role of appropriate retaliation in enforcing social norms should be recognized too. Without it, children would need to rely completely on adult supervision of their activities, and would not develop the social skills needed to interact independently. When they are older, children can go beyond insults and develop subtler, face-saving negotiation skills, such as compromise, supportive criticism, apology, restitution and forgiveness.

CONCLUSION

The ethological approach seems to hold promise for identifying the basic types of aggressive behaviour, recognizing their functions, and showing how they can be deranged. By analogy to the medical model, we need to understand normal processes before we can understand pathology. An ethological approach to human behaviour seeks to identify universal forms of behaviour whose functions can be discerned. If we wish to intervene, we can do so by working with human nature, rather than against it. Ethology is by no means the only useful approach to the study of aggression, but it may be especially important because of the comparative overview that it affords, and its functional perspective (see Chapter 16).

No one would claim that all social behaviour reduces to dominance behaviour. But I would maintain that dominance does constitute a basic behavioural system that influences practically every social interaction. Yet seldom is any mention even made of this behaviour, which entails so much of what we humans do, from age 3 onward. Whether we call it dominance behaviour, competitiveness, approval seeking, pride and shame, or social evaluation, this behavioural system is conspicuously absent from most textbooks dealing with developmental psychology and social psychology.

Other motives, such as play, aesthetics and parental behaviour, are also neglected by many textbook authors. If more attention were paid to our basic human motives, we might develop a more balanced view of human behaviour, and one that gave functional considerations the importance they deserve.

ACKNOWLEDGEMENTS

I wish to thank John Archer and Peter K. Smith for their unfailingly constructive and insightful criticism of earlier drafts of the manuscript. Those errors that remain are my own.

REFERENCES

Adams, G. R. (1977) 'Physical attractiveness research: toward a developmental social psychology of beauty', *Human Development*, 20: 217–39.

Allison, J. and Hunt, D. E. (1959) 'Social desirability and the expression of aggression under varying conditions of frustration', *Journal of Consulting Psychology*, 23: 528–32.

Appel, M. H. (1942) 'Aggressive behavior of nursery school children and adult procedures for dealing with such behavior', *Journal of Experimental Education*, 11: 185–99.

Apte, M. L. (1985) *Humor and Laughter: An Anthropological Approach*, Ithaca, NY: Cornell University Press.

Archer, J. (1976) 'The organization of aggression and fear in vertebrates', in P. P. G. Bateson and P. Klopfer (eds) *Perspectives in Ethology*, New York: Plenum Press.

—— (1988) *The Behavioural Biology of Aggression*, Cambridge: Cambridge University Press.

—— (1989–90) 'Pain-induced aggression: an ethological perspective', *Current Psychology: Research and Reviews* (Winter), 8: 298–306.

—— (1991) 'The influence of testosterone on human aggression', *British Journal of Psychology*, 82: 1–28.

—— (1992a) *Ethology and Human Development*, Hemel Hempstead, UK: Harvester Wheatsheaf.

—— (1992b) 'Childhood gender roles: social context and organization', in H. McGurk (ed.) *Childhood Social Development: Contemporary Perspectives*, Hove, UK and Hillsdale, NJ: Erlbaum.

Barkow, J. H. (1975) 'Social prestige and culture: a bisocial interpretation', *Current Anthropology*, 16: 553–72.

—— (1989) *Darwin, Sex and Status: Biological Approaches to Mind and Culture*, Toronto: University of Toronto Press.

Barner-Barry, C. (1980) 'The structure of young children's authority relationships', in D. R. Omark, F. F. Strayer and D. G. Freedman (eds) *Dominance Relationships: An Ethological View of Human Conflict and Social Interaction*, New York: Garland.

Bernstein, I. S. and Gordon, T. P. (1974) 'The function of aggression in primate societies', *American Scientist*, 62: 304–11.

Beynon, J. (1989) 'A school for men: an ethnographic case study of routine violence in schooling', in J. Archer and K. Browne (eds), *Human Aggression: Naturalistic Approaches*, London: Routledge.

Blanchard, D. C. and Blanchard, R. J. (1989) 'Experimental animal models of aggression: what do they say about human behaviour?' in J. Archer and K. Browne (eds) *Human Aggression: Naturalistic Approaches*, London: Routledge.

Blume, L. B. (1989) 'Social-role perception and social behavior of preschool children in a mixed-age setting', Paper presented at the Society for Research in Child Development meeting, Kansas City, MO, 28 April.

Blurton Jones, N. G. (1967) 'An ethological study of some aspects of social behaviour of children in nursery school', in D. Morris (ed.) *Primate Ethology*, London: Weidenfeld & Nicolson.

Boulton, M. J. and Smith, P. K. (1992) 'The social nature of play fighting and play chasing: mechanisms and strategies underlying cooperation and compromise', in J. Barkow, L. Cosmides and J. Tooby (eds) *The Adapted Mind: Evolutionary Psychology and the Generation of Culture*, Oxford: Oxford University Press.

Bridges, K. M. B. (1932) 'Emotional development in early infancy', *Child Development*, 3: 324–41.

Bronson, W. C. (1966) 'Central orientations: a study of behavior organization from childhood to adolescence', *Child Development*, 37: 125–55.

Buck, R. (1988) *Human Motivation and Emotion*, New York: Wiley.

Buss, D. M. (1989) 'Sex differences in human mate preferences: evolutionary hypotheses tested in 37 cultures', *Behavioral and Brain Sciences*, 12: 1–49.

Cairns, R. B. (1979) *Social Development: The Origins and Plasticity of Interchanges*, San Francisco: Freeman.

Camras, L. (1980) 'Animal threat displays and children's facial expressions: a comparison', in D. R. Omark, F. F. Strayer and D. G. Freedman (eds) *Dominance Relations: An Ethological View of Human and Social Interaction*, New York: Garland.

—— (1984) 'Children's verbal and nonverbal communication in a conflict situation', *Ethology and Sociobiology*, 5: 257–68.

Chalmers, N. (1980) *Social Behaviour in Primates*, Baltimore, MD: University Park Press.

Chandler, M. J. (1973) 'Egocentrism and antisocial behavior', *Developmental Psychology*, 9: 326–32.

Charlesworth, W. R. and Hartup, W. W. (1967) 'Positive social reinforcement in the nursery school peer group', *Child Development*, 38: 993–1002.

Clutton-Brock, T. H. and Harvey, P. H. (1976) 'Evolutionary rules and primate societies', in P. P. G. Bateson and R. A. Hinde (eds) *Growing Points in Ethology*, Cambridge: Cambridge University Press.

Coie, J. D. and Dodge, K. A. (1983) 'Continuities and changes in children's social status: a five-year longitudinal study', *Merrill-Palmer Quarterly*, 29: 261–81.

Coie, J. D. and Kupersmidt, J. B. (1983) 'A behavioral analysis of emerging social status in boys' groups', *Child Development*, 54: 1400–16.

Coleman, J. S. (1961) *The Adolescent Society*, New York: Free Press.

Corsaro, W. and Riozzo, T. (1990) 'Disputes and conflict resolution among nursery school children in the US and Italy', in A. Grimshaw (ed.) *Conflict Talk*, Cambridge: Cambridge University Press.

Daly, M. and Wilson, M. (1983) *Sex, Evolution and Behavior*, Boston: Willard Grant.

—— (1988) *Homicide*, New York: Aldine de Gruyter.

Dawe, H. C. 'An analysis of two hundred quarrels of preschool children', *Child Development*, 5: 139–57.

Deluty, R. H. (1981) 'Adaptiveness of aggression, assertive and submissive behaviour for children', *Journal of Clinical Child Psychology*, 10: 155–8.

Dennen, J. M. G. van der (1992) *The Nature of the Sexes: The Sociobiology of Sex Differences and the 'Battle of the Sexes'*, Groningen: Origin Press.

Dion, K. K. (1973) 'Young children's stereotyping of facial attractiveness', *Developmental Psychology*, 9: 183–98.

Dodge, K. A. (1980) 'Social cognition and children's aggressive behavior', *Child Development*, 51: 162–70.

—— (1983) 'Behavioral antecedents of peer social status', *Child Development*, 54: 1386–99.

—— (1989) 'Bully–victim relationships in boys' play groups', Paper presented at the meeting of the Society for Research in Child Development, Kansas City, MO (April).

Dodge, K. A. and Frame, C. L. (1982) 'Social cognitive biases and deficits in aggressive boys', *Child Development*, 53: 620–35.

Dodge, K. A. and Coie, J. D. (1990) 'Bully–victim relationships in boys' groups', Paper presented at the meeting of the Society for Research in Child Development, Kansas City, MO (April).

Dodge, K. A., Price, J. M., Coie, J. D. and Christopoulos, C. (1990) 'On the development of aggressive dyadic relationships in boys' peer groups', *Human Development*, 33: 260–70.

Dollard, J., Doob, L. W., Miller, N. E., Mowrer, O. H. and Sears, R. R. (1939) *Frustration and Aggression*, New Haven, CT: Yale University Press.

Dong, Q., Weisfeld, G., Boardway, R. and Shen, J. (in preparation) 'Social success among Chinese adolescent boys'.

Dovidio, J. F., Ellyson, S. L., Keating, C. F. and Heitman, K. (1988) 'The relationship of social power to visual displays of dominance between men and women, *Journal of Personality and Social Psychology*, 54: 233–42.

Eibl-Eibesfeldt, I. (1989) *Human Ethology*, Hawthorne, NY: Aldine de Gruyter.

Eimerl, S. and DeVore, I. (1965) *The Primates*, New York: Time-Life Books.

Ellis, L. (1986) 'Evidence of neuroandrogenic etiology of sex roles from a combined analysis of human, nonhuman primate and nonprimate mammalian studies', *Personality and Individual Differences*, 7: 519–52.

Feshbach, N. D. (1989) 'Empathy training and prosocial behavior', in J. Groebel and R. A. Hinde (eds) *Aggression and War: Their Biological and Social Bases*, Cambridge: Cambridge University Press, pp. 101–11.

Ginsburg, B. and Allee, W. C. (1942) 'Some effects of conditioning on social dominance and subordination in inbred strains of mice', *Physiological Zoology*, 15: 485–506.

Ginsburg, H. J. and Miller, S. M. (1981) 'Altruism in children: a naturalistic study of reciprocation and an examination of the relationship between social dominance and aid-giving behavior', *Ethology and Sociobiology*, 2: 75–83.

Goodall, J. (1986) *The Chimpanzees of Gombe*, Cambridge, MA: Harvard University Press.

Goodenough, F. L. (1931) *Anger in Young Children*, Minneapolis: University of Minnesota Press.

Goodwin, F. K. and Post, R. M. (1983) '5-hydroxytryptamine and depression: a model for the interaction of normal variance with pathology', *British Journal of Clinical Pharmacology*, 15: 3938–4058.

Gottesman, I. I. (1966) 'Genetic variance in an adaptive personality trait', *Journal of Child Psychology and Psychiatry*, 7: 199–208.

Hanfmann, E. (1935) 'Social structure of a group of kindergarten children', *American Journal of Orthopsychiatry*, 5: 407–10.

Hartup, W. W. (1974) 'Aggression in childhood: developmental perspectives', *American Psychologist*, 29: 336–41.

—— (1983) 'Peer relations', in P. Mussen (ed.) *Handbook of Child Psychology*, 4th edn, New York: Wiley.

Hold, B. (1976) 'Attention structure and rank specific behaviour in pre-school children', in M. R. A. Chance and R. R. Larsen (eds) *Social Structure of Attention*, London: Wiley.

—— (1977) 'Rank and behaviour: an ethological study of pre-school children', *Homo*, 28: 158–88.

Hold-Cavell, B. C. L. (1985) 'Showing-off and aggression in young children', *Aggressive Behavior*, 11: 333–5.

Huntingford, F. and Turner, A. (1987) *Animal Conflict*, London: Chapman & Hall.

Jackson, L. A. (1992) *Physical Appearance and Gender: Sociobiological and Sociocultural Perspectives*, Albany, NY: State University of New York Press.

Jersild, A. T. and Markey, F. V. (1935) 'Conflicts between preschool children', *Child Development Monographs*, Teachers College, Columbia University, 21.

Jones, D. C. (1984) 'Dominance and affiliation as factors in the social organization of same-sex groups of elementary school children', *Ethology and Sociobiology*, 5: 193–202.

Jones, M. C. and Bayley, N. (1950) 'Physical maturing among boys as related to behavior', *Journal of Educational Psychology*, 41: 129–48.

Kagan, J. and Moss, H. A. (1962) *Birth to Maturity: A Study in Psychological Development*, New York: Wiley.

Kalat, J. W. (1992) *Biological Psychology*, 4th edn, Belmont, CA: Wadsworth.

Klissouras, V. (1984) 'Factors affecting physical performance with reference to heredity', in J. Borms, R. Hauspie, A. Sand, C. Susanne and M. Hebbelinck (eds) *Human Growth and Development*, New York: Plenum.

Kreuz, L. E. and Rose, R. M. (1972) 'Assessment of aggressive behavior and plasma testosterone in a young criminal population', *Psychosomatic Medicine*, 34: 331–2.

Kumagai, F. (1983) 'Filial violence in Japan', *Victimology*, 8: 173–94.

Kummer, H. (1967) 'Tripartite relations in hamadryas baboons', in S. A. Altmann (ed) *Social Communication among Primates*, Chicago: University of Chicago Press.

—— (1971) *Primate Societies: Group Techniques of Ecological Adaptation*, Chicago: Aldine.

LaFrenière, P. and Charlesworth, W. R. (1983) 'Dominance, attention, and affiliation in a preschool group: a nine-month longitudinal study', *Ethology and Sociobiology*, 4: 55–67.

Langlois, J. H. and Stephan, C. (1981) 'Beauty and the beast: the role of physical attractiveness in the development of peer relations and social behavior', in S. S. Brehm, S. M. Kassin and F. X. Gibbons (eds) *Developmental Social Psychology*, New York: Oxford University Press.

Lauer, C. (1992) 'Variability in the patterns of agonistic behavior of preschool children', in J. Silverberg and J. P. Gray (eds) *Aggression and Peacefulness in Humans and Other Primates*, Oxford: Oxford University Press.

Lesser, G. S. (1959) 'The relationship between various forms of aggression and popularity among lower-class children', *Journal of Educational Psychology*, 50: 20–5.

McGraw, K. O. (1987) *Developmental Psychology*, New York: Harcourt Brace Jovanovich.

McGrew, W. C. (1972) *An Ethological Study of Children's Behavior*, New York: Academic Press.

McGuire, M. T., Raleigh, M. J. and Brammer, G. L. (1984) 'Adaptation, selection, and benefit-cost balances: implications of behavioral-physiological studies of social dominance in male vervet monkeys', *Ethology and Sociobiology*, 5: 269–77.

Malson, L. (1972) *Wolf Children and the Problem of Human Nature*, New York: Monthly Review Press.

Maynard Smith, J. and Ridpath, M. G. (1972) 'Wife sharing in the Tasmanian native hen, *Tribonyx mortierii*: a case of kin selection?', *American Naturalist*, 106: 447–52.

Mazur, A. (1985) 'A bisocial model of status in face-to-face primate groups', *Social Forces*, 64: 377–402.

Mazur, A. and Lamb, T. A. (1980) 'Testosterone, status and mood in human males', *Hormones and Behavior*, 1: 236–46.

Missakian, E. A. (1980) 'Gender differences in agonistic behavior and dominance relations of Synanon communally raised children', in D. R. Omark, F. F. Strayer and D. G. Freedman (eds) *Dominance Relations: An Ethological View of Human Conflict and Social Interaction*, New York: Wiley.

Mitchell, G. D. (1969) 'Paternalistic behavior in primates', *Psychological Bulletin*, 71: 399–417.

Moyer, K. E. (1976) *The Psychobiology of Aggression*, New York: Harper & Row.

Mussen, P. H. and Jones, M. C. (1957) 'Self-conceptions, motivations, and interpersonal attitudes of late- and early-maturing boys', *Child Development*, 28: 243–56.

Neill, S. R. St. J. (1985) 'Rough-and-tumble and aggression in schoolchildren: serious play?', *Animal Behaviour*, 33: 1380–2.

Olweus, D. (1984) 'Development of stable aggressive reaction patterns in males', in R. J. Blanchard and D. C. Blanchard (eds) *Advances in the Study of Aggression*, vol. 1, New York: Academic Press.

Omark, D. R. and Edelman, M. S. (1975) 'A comparison of status hierarchies in young children: an ethological approach', *Social Science Information*, 14: 87–107.

—— (1976) 'The development of attention structures in young children', in M. R. A. Chance and R. R. Larsen (eds) *The Structure of Social Attention*, London: Wiley.

Omark, D. R., Omark, M. and Edelman, M. (1975) 'Formation of dominance hierarchies in young children', in T. Williams (ed.) *Psychological Anthropology*, The Hague: Mouton.

Omark, D. R., Strayer, F. F. and Freedman, D. G. (1980) *Dominance Relations: An Ethological View of Human Conflict and Social Interaction*, New York: Garland Press.

Parke, R. D. and Slaby, R. G. (1983) 'The development of aggression', in P. Mussen (ed.) *Handbook of Child Psychology*, 4th edn, New York: Wiley.

Pastore, N. (1952) 'The role of arbitrariness in the frustration-aggression hypothesis', *Journal of Abnormal and Social Psychology*, 47: 727–31.

Patterson, G. R. (1982) *Coercive Family Processes*, Eugene, OR: Castilia Press.

Patterson, G. R. and Cobb, J. A. (1971) 'A dyadic analysis of "aggressive" behaviors', in J. P. Hill (ed.) *Minnesota Symposium on Child Psychology*, vol. 5, Minneapolis: University of Minnesota Press.

Perry, D. G., Perry, L. C. and Kennedy, E. (in press) 'Conflict and the development of antisocial behavior', in C. U. Shantz and W. W. Hartup (eds) *Conflict in Child and Adolescent Development*, New York: Cambridge University Press.

Persky, H., Smith, K. D. and Basu, G. K. (1971) 'Relation of psychologic measures of aggression and hostility to testosterone production in men', *Psychosomatic Medicine*, 33: 265–77.

Pierce, S. (1990) 'The behavioral attributes of victimized children', Unpublished master's thesis, Florida Atlantic University; cited in Perry, D. G., Perry, L. C. and Kennedy, E. (in press) 'Conflict and the development of antisocial behaviour', in C. U. Shantz and W. W. Hartup (eds) *Conflict in Child and Adolescent Development*, New York: Cambridge University Press.

Pines, M. (1985) 'Aggression: the violence within', *Science Digest*, 93: 37–68.

Pugh, G. E. (1977) *The Biological Basis of Human Values*, New York: Basic Books.

Rajecki, D. W. and Flannery, R. C. (1981) 'Social conflicts and dominance in children: a case for a primate homology', in M. E. Lamb and A. Brown (eds) *Advances in Developmental Psychology*, vol. 1, Hillsdale, NJ: Lawrence Erlbaum, pp. 87–129.

Rohner, R. P. (1976) 'Sex differences in aggression', *Ethos*, 4: 57–72.

Rutter, M. and Giller, H. (1983) *Juvenile Delinquency: Trends and Perspectives*, New York: Penguin Books.

Savin-Williams, R. C. (1976) 'An ethological study of dominance formation and maintenance in a group of human adolescents', *Child Development*, 47: 972–9.

—— (1977) 'Dominance in a human adolescent group', *Animal Behaviour*, 25: 400–6.

—— (1987) *Adolescence: An Ethological Perspective*, New York: Springer-Verlag.

Sherif, M. and Sherif, C. W. (1964) *Reference Groups*, Chicago: Regnery.

Simonds, P. E. (1965) 'The bonnet macaque in South India', in I. DeVore (ed.) *Field Studies of Monkeys and Apes*, New York: Holt, Rinehart & Winston.

Sluckin, A. and Smith, P. (1977) 'Two approaches to the concept of dominance in preschool children', *Child Development*, 48: 917–23.

Smith, P. (1988) 'The cognitive demands of children's social interactions with peers', in R. W. Byrne and A. Whiten (eds) *Machiavellian Intelligence*, Oxford: Oxford University Press.

—— (1989) 'Ethological approaches to the study of aggression in children', in J. Archer and K. Browne (eds) *Human Aggression: Naturalistic Approaches*, London: Routledge.

Smith, P. and Boulton, M. (1990) 'Rough-and-tumble play, aggression and dominance: perception and behaviour in children's encounters', *Human Development*, 33: 271–82.

Smith, P. K. and Connolly, K. (1980) *The Ecology of Preschool Behaviour*, Cambridge: Cambridge University Press.

Steinberg, L. (1985) *Adolescence*, New York: Knopf.

—— (1989) 'Pubertal maturation and parent–adolescent distance: an evolutionary perspective', in G. R. Adams, R. Montemayor and T. P. Gollotta (eds) *Biology of Adolescent Behavior and Development*, New York: Sage, pp. 71–97.

Stephens, W. N. (1963) *The Family in Cross-Cultural Perspective*, New York: Holt, Rinehart & Winston.

Strayer, F. F. (1992) 'The development of agonistic and affiliative structures in preschool play groups', in J. Silverberg and J. P. Gray (eds) *Aggression and Peacefulness in Humans and Other Primates*, New York: Oxford University Press.

Strayer, F. F. and Strayer, J. (1976) 'An ecological analysis of social agonism and dominance relations among preschool children', *Child Development*, 47: 980–9.

Strayer, F. F. and Trudel, M. (1984) 'Developmental changes in the nature and function of social dominance among young children', *Ethology and Sociobiology*, 5: 279–95.

Styczynski, L. E. and Langlois, J. H. (1980) 'Judging the book by its cover: children's attractiveness and achievement', Unpublished manuscript, University of Texas at Austin, cited in W. W. Hartup, 'Peer relations', in P. Mussen (ed.) *Handbook of Child Psychology*, 4th edn, New York: Wiley.

Svare, B. (1983) 'Psychobiological determinants of maternal aggressive behavior', in E. C. Siommel, M. E. Hahn and J. K. Walters (eds) *Aggressive Behavior: Genetic and Neural Approaches*, Hillsdale, NJ: Lawrence Erlbaum, pp. 129–46.

Tanner, J. M. (1978) *Fetus into Man: Physical Growth from Conception to Maturity*, Cambridge, MA: Harvard University Press.

Teleki, G. (1973) 'The omnivorous chimpanzee', *Scientific American*, 228: 33–42.

Trivers, R. L. (1971) 'The evolution of reciprocal altruism', *Quarterly Review of Biology*, 46: 35–57.

Vaughn, B. E. and Waters, E. (1980) 'Social organization among preschool peers: dominance, attention and sociometric correlates', in D. R. Omark, F. F. Strayer and D. G. Freedman (eds) *Dominance Relations: An Ethological View of Human Conflict and Social Interaction*, New York: Garland.

de Waal, F. B. (1982) *Chimpanzee Politics*, London: Jonathan Cape.

Waas, G. A. (1988) 'Social attributional biases of peer-rejected and aggressive children', *Child Development*, 59: 969–75.

Walker, L. S. and Greene, J. W. (1986) 'The social context of adolescent self-esteem', *Journal of Youth and Adolescence*, 15: 315–22.

Washburn, S. L. and Hamburg, D. A. (1968) 'Aggressive behavior in Old World monkeys and apes', in P. C. Jay (ed) *Primates: Studies in Adaptation and Variability*, New York: Holt, Rinehart & Winston.

Weisfeld, G. E. (1972) 'Violations of social norms as inducers of aggression', *International Journal of Group Tensions*, 2: 53–70.

—— (1979) 'An ethological view of human adolescence', *Journal of Nervous and Mental Disease*, 169: 38–55.

—— (1980) 'Social dominance and human motivation', in D. R. Omark, F. F. Strayer and D. F. Freedman (eds) *Dominance Relations: An Ethological Perspective on Human Conflict and Social Interaction*, New York: Garland Press, 1980.

—— (1982) 'The nature–nurture issue and the integrating concept of function', in B. B. Wolman and G. Stricker (eds) *Handbook of Developmental Psychology*, Englewood Cliffs, NJ: Prentice-Hall.

Weisfeld, G. E. and Beresford, J. M. (1982) 'Erectness of posture as an indicator of dominance or success in humans', *Motivation and Emotion*, 6: 113–31.

Weisfeld, G. E. and Berger, J. M. (1983) 'Some features of human adolescence viewed in evolutionary perspective', *Human Development*, 6: 121–33.

Weisfeld, G. E. and Billings, R. L. (1988) 'Observations on adolescence', in K. MacDonald (ed) *Sociobiological Perspectives on Human Development*, New York: Springer-Verlag.

Weisfeld, G. E., Bloch, S. A. and Ivers, J. W. (1983) 'A factor analytic study of peer-perceived dominance in adolescent boys', *Adolescence*, 18: 229–43.

Weisfeld, G. E. and Feldman, R. (1982) 'A former street gang leader re-interviewed eight years later', *Crime and Delinquency*, 28: 567–81.

Weisfeld, G. E. and Linkey, H. E. (1985) 'Dominance displays as indicators of a social success motive', in J. Dovidio and S. Ellyson (eds) *Power, Dominance and Nonverbal Behavior*, New York: Springer Verlag.

Weisfeld, G. E., Muczenski, D. M., Weisfeld, C. C. and Omark, D. R. (1987) 'Stability of boys' social success among peers over an eleven-year period', in J. A. Meacham (ed) *Interpersonal Relations: Family, Peers, Friends*, New York: Karger.

Weisfeld, G. E., Omark, D. R. and Cronin, C. (1980) 'A longitudinal and cross-sectional study of dominance in boys', in D. R. Omark, F. F. Strayer and D. G. Freedman (eds) *Dominance Relations: An Ethological View of Human Conflict and Social Interaction*, New York: Garland Press.

Weisfeld, G. E., Russell, R. J. H., Weisfeld, C. C. and Wells, P. A. (1992) 'Correlates of satisfaction in British marriages', *Ethology and Sociobiology*, 13: 125–45.

Weisfeld, G. E., Weisfeld, C. C. and Callaghan, J. W. (1984) 'Peer and self perceptions in Hopi and Afro-American third and sixth graders', *Ethos*, 12: 64–84.

Whiting, B. B. and Whiting, J. W. M. (1975) *Children in Six Cultures: A Psycho-Cultural Analysis*, Cambridge, MA: Harvard University Press.

Wilson, E. O. (1975) *Sociobiology: The New Synthesis*, Cambridge, MA: Harvard University Press.

Worchel, S. (1978) 'Aggression and power restoration: the effects of identifiability and timing of aggressive behaviour', *Journal of Experimental Psychology*, 14: 43–52.

Zivin, G. (1977) 'Facial gestures predict preschoolers' encounter outcomes', *Biology and Social Life*, 16: 715–30.

4

BULLYING IN SCHOOLS AND THE ISSUE OF SEX DIFFERENCES

Yvette Ahmad and Peter K. Smith

Bullying can be regarded as a subset of aggressive behaviour and shares the main elements of most forms of aggressive behaviour in that it involves the intention to cause harm, either physical or psychological, to one or more individuals by one individual or a group. However, bullying has certain characteristics which are not necessarily shared by other forms of aggressive behaviour. It involves an imbalance of power, with the more powerful individuals oppressing the less powerful ones. The aggressive act is either unprovoked by the victim(s), or at least the action of the person doing the bullying would not be considered justified by onlookers. Finally, the action is a repeated one between the same individuals; an incidence that happens just once or twice would not usually be called bullying. Bullying can occur in different contexts – for example, prisons, children's homes, army camps, office environments. This study specifically looks at bullying in schools.

Sex differences in all forms of aggression have been repeatedly found, and bullying is no exception. Most research findings agree that, in general, males are consistently physically more aggressive than females. Olweus (1987), carrying out research in Norway, reported that boys are more violent and destructive in their bullying than girls. Boys were found to use more overt forms of bullying, such as physical aggression and direct threats. Girls, on the other hand, were more likely to use malicious gossip and ostracism. Girls were more likely to bully other girls, whereas boys bullied both boys and girls. Roland (see Munthe 1989) has also reported differences in the ways in which boys and girls are bullied. He found that both boys and girls tease, whereas boys use more physical violence and girls often use exclusion as a method of causing distress to others.

Physical aggression has usually been contrasted with verbal aggression. Definitions of bullying often comprise both. For example, Hoover *et al.* (1992) define it as 'any activity from teasing to physical attacks where one or a group of youngsters pesters a victim . . . over a period of time'. Rigby and Slee (1991) cite 'systematic verbal or physical harassment of one child by another or others'. In these and similar studies, the overall incidence of being bullied tends to be higher in boys than in girls. However, sex differences may be

70

greatly affected by the inclusiveness of the definition of bullying. The concepts of direct and indirect aggression and bullying have emerged recently as important, especially for the clarification of sex differences.

Indirect aggression itself needs to be clearly defined. In some earlier studies, verbal and indirect aggression have been lumped together. Frodi *et al.* (1977) defined indirect aggression as aggression with a substitute target, either a substitute target person or no concrete target at all (but without giving clear examples). However, a more comprehensive scale and refined use of the terms 'direct' (physical and verbal) and 'indirect' aggression has recently been devised by Björkqvist and colleagues (Björkqvist, Österman and Kaukiainen 1992; Björkqvist, Lagerspetz and Kaukiainen 1992; Lagerspetz, Björkqvist and Peltonen 1988). They view indirect aggression as still being directed at the main target, but without using direct means. Their items are as follows:

Physical aggression: hits, kicks, trips, shoves, takes things, pushes, pulls.
Direct verbal aggression: yells, insults, says (s)he is going to hurt the other, calls the other names, teases.
Indirect aggression: gossips, tells bad or false stories, becomes friend with another as revenge, plans secretly to bother the other, says bad things behind the other's back, says to others: let's not be with him/her, tells the other one's secrets to a third person, writes nasty notes about the other, tries to get others to dislike the person.

Lagerspetz, Björkqvist and Peltonen (1988) measured direct and indirect aggression by means of peer estimation techniques using 11–12-year-old schoolchildren. They found indirect aggression to be more common with females than males. Björkqvist, Lagerspetz and Kaukiainen (1992) measured all three types of aggression from peer estimation, in 8-year-olds and 15-year-olds. Direct physical aggression was more common in boys; there was little difference between the sexes in direct verbal aggression, but indirect aggression was more common in females. Together with the earlier data on 11–12-year-olds, age profiles showed a movement away from direct physical forms of aggression to other forms, as children got older.

The purpose of our study was to examine sex differences in the nature and extent of bullying between males and females; for example, the kinds of bullying, and the location of the bullying. In the past, definitions of bullying which failed to include explicitly indirect means may have underestimated its frequency among females. For example, the definition used by Olweus (1987, 1991) in his extensive studies of bullying in Norway clearly included physical and verbal (that is, direct) bullying, but did not include indirect bullying; although Olweus has a separate scale for 'indirect bullying' based on lacking friends at playtime, this is not quite the same as the indirect aggression described by Björkqvist, Lagerspetz and Kaukiainen (1992). We planned to see whether the sex differences found by Björkqvist and colleagues for aggression in Finnish schoolchildren would apply to bullying in English schoolchildren, with a combination of qualitative (interview) data and quantitative (questionnaire) data.

INTERVIEWS WITH PUPILS WHO HAVE BEEN BULLIED

As an initial inquiry, ninety-three interviews were carried out with pupils from one middle school and one secondary school in the South Yorkshire region of England. The samples were from a selected number of classes in middle school (8 and 11 years) and secondary school (13 and 15 years). Interviews were carried out individually and privately, in a separate room; the interviewer guaranteed anonymity for anything that was said. Each interview took approximately half an hour (the actual time depending on whether pupils were bullied or engaged in bullying).

Below are given some summaries of the kinds of bullying experienced by pupils, from these interview data. The first six case studies are from the middle school.

Case study 1 was with a white female. She reported that her older brother and friend tease her a lot, swear at her and call her names such as 'stupid idiot' and 'baby'. He sometimes hits her. She gets very angry with him but says it doesn't upset her.

Case study 2 was with a white female. She reported that she is consistently bullied. She is teased, hit and kicked by both boys and girls, but mainly by boys (same age and older). They mainly tease her because (according to them) her boyfriend is 'smelly', 'scruffy and can't afford decent clothes'. She gets extremely upset when they tease her.

Case study 3 was with an Asian female. She reported that she has been bullied repeatedly. It started with name-calling, 'blackjack', 'blackie' by another Asian girl. She has also been punched repeatedly by this girl and a group of boys who go round with her.

Case study 4 was with a Chinese male. He reported that he is teased a lot with name-calling, but he did not want to say what he is called. He gets upset more by rumours that girls spread about him in his class.

Case study 5 was with a white male. He reported that he is teased by boys and mainly called 'skinny'. He doesn't like playing football, as they start to hit and kick him.

Case study 6 was with a white male. He reported that he is repeatedly beaten up while going to and from school, by a few different groups of boys. One of the groups involves his best friend. They all laugh and joke at him and say they are just messing with him and he shouldn't take it seriously. This boy is upset and distressed by the repeated hitting and kicking.

The second six case studies are from the secondary school:

Case study 7 was with a white female. She reported that a group of third-year girls are teasing her. The leader of this group harasses her and calls her 'bitch' and 'slag'. She has not been physically abused by these girls.

Case study 8 was with a white female. She reported that the bullying started when she took up defence position in the netball team but was changed to centre position when the games teacher realized she was a good player. The girl who was originally in centre position became jealous and set up a gang against her, called her 'bitch' and 'hussy' and threatened to hit her on several occasions.

Case study 9 was with a white female. She reported that she mainly experiences name-calling. Both boys and girls tease her, call her 'snob' and say she is stuck up; they also write on her chemistry book.

Case study 10 was with a white male. He reported that he was bullied when he went out with a girl because another boy was jealous and told him to 'lay off her'. He was punched, hit and kicked. When he finally stopped seeing her the bullying stopped.

Case study 11 was with a white male. He had joined the school in the second year. He reported that he is bullied by boys in the same class. He is called 'four eyes', and he is hit and kicked during break time.

Case study 12 was with a white male. He reported that he has had a long history of being teased about his ears. Girls tease him more than boys; they call him 'Dumbo' and pull his ears and say he can fly with them. He is also hit, punched and kicked by boys.

What appeared to emerge from these and other interviews was that name-calling was as common amongst the boys as the girls, the difference being that boys engage in verbal *and* physical abuse whereas girls are mainly involved in verbal abuse. Girls do seem to be more involved in perpetrating indirect bullying (for example, case studies 4 and 8). Different types of bullying between the sexes become more apparent when the pupils move into secondary school.

A QUANTITATIVE SURVEY OF BULLYING IN SCHOOL

To ascertain whether these apparent differences could be replicated with a larger sample, we carried out a survey using a modified version of the Olweus questionnaire (Ahmad *et al.* 1991). This questionnaire incorporated Olweus' definition of bullying, but this was modified following pilot interviews with the children. During the interviews, many females reported being called nasty names (sometimes behind their backs), being deliberately excluded from groups, and having tricks played on them; others were bullies and carried out these kinds of behaviour but they didn't always see it as 'really bullying'. Some saw only physical behaviour as bullying. Some possibly 'female forms' of bullying were often not included spontaneously as bullying when pupils were asked to define what bullying was, even though these kinds of action were clearly intended, and hurtful to the victims. As forms of indirect bullying were not explicit in Olweus' original definition, we included two examples in our own definition, as follows:

> We say a child is *being bullied*, or picked on, when another child, or a group of children, say nasty or unpleasant things to him or her. It is also bullying when a child is hit, kicked, threatened, locked inside a room, **sent nasty notes, when no one ever talks to them**, and things like that. These things can happen frequently and it is difficult for the child being bullied to defend himself or herself. It is also bullying when a child is teased repeatedly **in a nasty way**. But it is *not bullying* when two children of about the same strength have the odd fight or quarrel.

The phrases in bold-face type are additions to Olweus' original definition. 'Sent nasty notes' and 'when no one ever talks to them' were seen as indirect forms of bullying which most often were mentioned in pupil interviews. ('In a nasty way' was included as a qualifier to teasing, since from interviews we found that many pupils felt that some teasing could be friendly, and not bully-ing. Olweus has in fact included the similar qualifier 'in a negative way' in his latest version of the questionnaire definition.)

The questions in the questionnaire were similar in format and content to those designed and used by Olweus (1991), with slight modifications to suit the British school system. Questions asked about whether pupils had been bullied or taken part in bullying others, this term; and (if so) details of the type of bullying, where it took place, which sex and class the victim(s) was from, if anyone had been told, and how the pupil felt about bullying. There were nine-teen questions for middle-school children (aged 8 to 11) and twenty questions for secondary-school level (aged 11 to 16). All questions required a single response, except for one question about the way pupils were bullied, where pupils could circle as many responses as had happened to them.

The total sample consisted of 1,433 pupils. Five schools (two middle, three secondary) participated; three from the South Yorkshire region, one from the West Yorkshire region and one from a London borough. All five schools were different in racial mix, location and size, so as to provide a variety of experi-ence with the questionnaire: four of the schools were located in inner cities, and one in a rural setting. Schools varied in size from 100 to 1,000 pupils. Racial mix varied; two schools had almost 100 per cent white pupils, whereas the other three schools varied from 10 per cent to 54 per cent pupils of non-white ethnic origin (their families mainly originating from the Indian sub-continent).

Altogether 226 pupils provided questionnaires from the middle schools (8–11 years); 108 boys (48 per cent), 118 girls (52 per cent). A total of 1,207 pupils provided questionnaires from the secondary schools (11–16 years): 615 boys (51 per cent) and 592 girls (49 per cent).

Schools were provided with the questionnaires and given a package with detailed instructions on how to administer the questionnaire. Questionnaires were administered by the teachers to the pupils (usually by a teacher from a different year). A standardized procedure was given to all the schools to follow. Before the questionnaire was filled in, teachers read out the definition of bullying so that pupils were clear about what was meant by the term 'bullying'. The questionnaire was anonymous, so confidentiality of pupils' responses was guaranteed, except to identify whether they were male or female and which class they were in. The questionnaires were given in December 1989 (three schools), late February 1990 (one school) and May 1990 (one school), and returned to the university for analysis. Selected items from the questionnaire were analysed concerning general aspects of bullying and sex differences.

Tables 4.1 (a and b) show the frequency of bullying and being bullied at both middle- and secondary-school level. The questions were as follows:

(Middle) How often are you bullied at school this term?

(Secondary) How often have you been bullied at school this term?

(Middle) How often have you joined in bullying other children at school this term?

(Secondary) How often have you taken part in bullying other young people at school this term?

Pupils could respond, 'I haven't been bullied this term' and 'I haven't bullied others this term'; any other responses are totalled in the right-hand columns of Tables 4.1 (a and b). Many of these responses were, 'It has only happened once or twice'; since this would not normally be thought of as (repeated) bullying, most workers with the Olweus questionnaire only consider the responses 'sometimes' or more frequently, which are shown separately in Tables 4.1 (a and b) (two categories in middle school, three categories in secondary school).

There is clearly a significant difference in reported bullying between middle and secondary school. For being bullied, boys tend to score higher at middle school, but the difference is slight; at secondary school boys clearly report more bullying overall, but this sex difference disappears at the most frequent category of 'several times a week'. So far as admitting to bullying others is concerned, boys generally score higher at both middle and secondary school. However, there is again little sex difference at the high frequency categories in secondary school (with what difference there is being higher for girls).

Overall, these results confirm that boys are more involved than girls in bullying others. This is true even when indirect bullying is explicitly included. The reversed sex difference for very frequent bullying may relate to types of bullying to be reported shortly. In secondary school more girls' bullying involves social exclusion (Table 4.3), and this could be perceived as continuous ('several times a week'), whereas boys' physical bullying may be more discontinuous and spasmodic.

Table 4.1a Pupils (boys and girls) who reported being bullied during the school term (percentages)

Middle schools			
	Sometimes	Several/week	Total ever bullied
Boys (N = 180)	22.2	8.3	52.7
Girls (N = 118)	18.1	6.9	50.9

Secondary schools				
	Sometimes	Once/week	Several/week	Total ever bullied
Boys (N = 615)	13.2	3.3	3.0	47.6
Girls (N = 592)	7.3	2.3	3.4	38.9

Table 4.1b Pupils (boys and girls) who reported bullying others during the school term (percentages)

Middle schools			
	Sometimes	Several/week	Total ever bullied
Boys (N = 180)	12.3	4.7	53.8
Girls (N = 118)	12.1	0.0	33.7

Secondary schools				
	Sometimes	Once/week	Several/week	Total ever bullied
Boys (N = 615)	9.1	2.3	0.1	42.8
Girls (N = 592)	5.0	2.6	1.9	29.6

Table 4.2 shows (for those children who were bullied) whether boys or girls were reported to do the bullying. The questions were as follows:

(Middle)   Is it boys or girls that bully you?
(Secondary)   What sex is the young person or young people who bully you?

Table 4.2 Who does the bullying? (percentages for boys and girls)

	Middle schools		Secondary schools	
	Boys	Girls	Boys	Girls
A boy/boys	88.0	58.0	89.0	28.0
Boys and girls	10.2	23.0	9.0	22.0
A girl/girls	1.8	19.0	2.0	50.0

The results show that boys are usually bullied by other boys, and rather rarely by girls; the picture changes very little from middle school to secondary school. However, there is an interesting change for girls. At middle school, they too are most likely to report being bullied by boys (though more likely to be bullied by both boys and girls, or by girls, than boys are). But at secondary school, they are most likely to be bullied by girls.

An explanation for the increasing trend of bullying between girls at secondary school could be rivalry of other girls or jealousies which develop for the competition of certain male partners. Puberty is a time when sexual awareness of oneself and others develops and the testing out of one's attractiveness becomes a focal point – earlier for females than for males. This explanation would tie in with the qualitative research which was carried out. It was interesting to note that at middle school terms such as 'bitch', 'slag' or 'hussy' were rarely mentioned, if at all. However, at secondary school these terms were the most frequently mentioned for girl 'victims' when talking of girls who bullied them. However, these names were not only used in incidents of rivalry for male partners but were also used in general; for example, see case study 8 (secondary school). These terms are probably some of the most hurtful to an adolescent girl as strong stereotypes remain for a young female to be 'respectful', 'nice' and a 'good girl'. It is interesting to note that 'poof' was a term mentioned a fair amount amongst male victims: again, adolescent males are pressured to conform to stereotypes of what is 'masculine'. All this coincides with the rapid change in physical growth and development in adolescence.

Table 4.3 shows (for those children who were bullied) the type of bullying that occurred; direct physical forms are shown at the top of Table 4.4, followed by direct verbal, indirect and other. The question was as follows:

'In what way have you been bullied at school this term?'

It is clear that boys who are bullied are more likely to experience direct physical bullying than girls who are bullied; this is most obviously true at secondary school, where boys seem to be just as likely to be hit or kicked as at middle school (girls much less so). Having belongings taken is more common in boys, though it decreases for both sexes at secondary school. Being threatened (sometimes more physical, sometimes just verbal), also more common in boys, does not vary greatly from middle to secondary school.

Verbal bullying is the most common form of bullying, both at middle and secondary school; over half of bullied pupils report experiencing it. The sex difference favours girls, but the difference is not large, especially if racist name-calling (more common in boys) is included.

Indirect bullying is also quite common, especially having rumours spread about one. This is slightly more common in boys at middle school, but in girls at secondary school. There is a relatively small proportion of pupils reporting that no one would talk to them, or that bullying happened in other ways.

A small proportion of pupils checked the item 'I was bullied in another way'; the pupil was then asked to give details. These were content analysed. Very little can be discerned from the middle-school results because of the small number of such responses (four boys and three girls) and because of repetition (for example, 'called nasty names' or 'threatened' were already listed). However, the secondary-school results showed that girls reported the most common 'other' form of being bullied as 'sexual harassment', being pestered by boys to go out with them; refusal led to either physical or verbal abuse. The second most common category was 'hair-pulling', often coupled with being called a 'slag' (although this latter could come under being 'called nasty names'). Other miscellaneous responses were: 'sarcastic remarks', 'sending nasty notes', 'getting others to fall out with them' and 'being tripped up'.

Table 4.3 Types of bullying behaviour for boys and girls (percentages)

Types of bullying behaviour	Middle schools		Secondary schools	
	Boys	Girls	Boys	Girls
I was physically hurt e.g. hit and kicked	30.1	33.3	36.1	9.2
I have had my belongings taken away from me	20.6	15.1	9.7	6.3
I was threatened	26.9	15.1	24.6	19.8
I was called nasty names	55.5	59.0	57.2	74.2
I was called nasty names about my colour	17.4	18.1	12.1	6.3
No one would talk to me	6.3	6.0	3.1	8.0
I have had rumours spread about me	22.2	16.6	17.3	30.3
I was bullied in another way	6.3	4.5	7.9	9.7

For boys 'being tripped up', 'having belongings destroyed', 'being spat at' and 'hair pulled' were responses which were listed, with 'being tripped up' being the most common response.

Since secondary-school girls reported sexual harassment as the most common 'other', it would be useful to include this in future research as a category to check, just as racial harassment is already included.

Table 4.4 shows (for those children who were bullied) where it was reported to take place. The question was the same for both middle- and secondary-school children:

Where did you get bullied in school this term?

At middle school the playground was the most common place to be bullied for both boys and girls. Nevertheless, bullying in corridors, classroom and other places were all more frequent for girls. At secondary school boys still report the playground as the most common place to be bullied, but the corridors and classrooms follow closely behind. Girls reported the classroom as the most likely place they were being bullied, followed by the corridors and the playground, with other places still reported more frequently than boys.

Table 4.4 Where in school boys and girls were bullied (percentages)

| | Middle schools | | Secondary schools | |
	Boys	Girls	Boys	Girls
In the playground	65.0	54.0	31.0	21.4
In the corridors	24.0	14.0	28.0	25.6
In the classroom	8.0	18.0	26.0	33.0
Other places in school	3.0	14.0	15.0	20.0

A content analysis was carried out of responses to the 'other places in the school' (pupils were asked to state where, if they circled this option). The most common responses given by boys and girls were noted. At middle school, 'at home' was the most common response for both boys and girls; a few mentioned elder brothers; parents or other siblings were not mentioned. (This does not mean that the latter would not have been involved in bullying, as many of the respondents did not mention who was bullying them at home.) The second most common response, again the same for both boys and girls, was 'to and from school'. The third most common place for boys was 'when they were playing football'. For girls there was no clear third most common place. A few boys and girls also mentioned 'in town', 'in the dinner queue', 'in the toilets','at the shops'. (Some of these locations are of course outside school. It was not the intention of this question to elicit out-of-school locations, but obviously pupils of this age slightly misunderstood the question to include being bullied regardless of where it took place or from whom.)

At secondary school the pupils generally included answers closely related to the school experience. The most common response for boys and girls was 'to and from school'. This included answers such as: 'on the school bus', 'on the way to/from school' and 'at the bus stop outside school'. Girls reported this more than boys. The second most common response for boys was 'the playing field' and the remainder were miscellaneous: 'library', 'lockers', 'shops' and 'dinner hall'. There was no clear second common category for girls – again a series of miscellaneous answers such as 'toilets', 'sports hall' and 'dinner hall'.

The playground is probably the most common place to be bullied at middle school (for both boys and girls) since pupils have to go out at breaktimes; this is not so at secondary school, where the level of bullying in the playground for both boys and girls drops considerably. At secondary-school level, pupils have more access to the school grounds inside and outside at breaktime. At both middle and secondary school, girls more often report being bullied in corridors, classrooms and elsewhere (other than the playground). In part this may be due to the well-known preference of boys for more outdoor play; in the 'other' responses, boys at middle school mentioned playing football, and secondary-school boys mentioned the playing field, more than girls. In addition, it may be explained by the fact that the types of bullying each sex engages in can be quite different; as seen, girls tend to use more 'covert' forms of bullying and boys more 'overt' forms. It would be an obvious reaction of a teacher to reprimand any physical forms of bullying in the classroom. However, if girls are engaging in spreading rumours, sending nasty notes or 'sending a girl victim to Coventry', it's quite possible that this would go unnoticed in the classroom.

Table 4.5 shows, for all pupils, the response to witnessing another pupil being bullied. The questions were as follows:

(Middle) What do you do when you see a child of your age being bullied at school?

(Secondary) What do you usually do when you see a young person of your age being bullied at school?

Table 4.5 Pupils (boys and girls) who reported their response when witnessing another pupil being bullied (percentages)

Response	Middle schools		Secondary schools	
	Boys	Girls	Boys	Girls
Nothing, it's none of my business	18.0	22.0	22.0	32.0
Nothing, but I think I ought to try and help	26.0	23.0	44.0	41.0
I try to help him or her in some way	56.0	55.0	34.0	27.0

Three response categories were provided as shown in Table 4.5. Interestingly, fewer pupils give 'helping' responses at secondary school than at middle school. Sex differences are small, but suggest that girls had slightly less sympathetic attitudes to victims than boys, especially at secondary school. This is surprising in the light of the usual 'caring' image of girls compared to boys. Possibly, at secondary school, girls may be more admiring of 'tough', successful boys, and more despising of the (by now relatively smaller number of) victims who have still not been able to cope with bullying behaviour.

IMPLICATIONS OF THE FINDINGS

These results are based on a fairly large sample of children, especially at secondary-school level. Many of the results are very similar to those found by Whitney and Smith (1993), who also used the modified Olweus questionnaire, on a sample of more than 6,000 pupils in the Sheffield LEA. Their study was carried out in different schools from those reported here, about one year later. They report summary results only, and no qualitative data. However, as in our study, bullying decreased from middle to secondary school. There was little or no sex difference for being bullied, but boys more often bullied others. Boys were more likely than girls to report being bullied by one or several boys; girls, however, were more likely than boys to report being bullied by one or several girls, or by both boys and girls. It was unusual for boys to report being bullied by one or several girls. Boys were more likely to be physically hit, and threatened, than were girls. Girls were slightly more likely to experience verbal forms of bullying such as being called nasty names (in other racist ways, which boys experienced more); and much more likely to experience indirect bullying such as having no one to talk to them (being 'sent to Coventry') or having rumours spread about them. These sex differences were found in both junior/middle and secondary schools.

The one different result is that the greater incidence in middle-school boys of 'I have had rumours spread about me' (Table 4.3) was not replicated by Whitney and Smith, who found it more frequent in girls throughout the age range. This strengthens the supposition that indirect bullying tends to be more characteristic of girls, in the United Kingdom, as in Finland (Björkqvist, Lagerspetz and Kaukiainen 1992) and probably in Norway (Munthe 1989).

Bullying was less at older ages for both sexes, as also reported from Norway by Olweus (1991). This difference between the age groups has received surprisingly little discussion. One possibility (Olweus, personal communication) is that pupils are usually bullied by other pupils the same age or older than them (Olweus 1991; Whitney and Smith 1993); and that as they get older, there are fewer older pupils to bully them. As this theory would predict, there is a rise in bullying rates at year of entry to secondary school (Olweus 1991; Whitney and Smith 1993); but the rise is relatively small if the above explanation was the primary cause of decline in school bullying. Another possibility is that pupils become more 'socialised' as they get older, more aware of what is acceptable behaviour and perhaps more aware of others' feelings when bullied. Certainly, there is a relative decrease in serious bullying such as having belongings taken (Table 4.3), and, for girls, of direct physical bullying. However, there does not seem to be a change to more positive attitudes (Table 4.5), as this explanation might predict.

Two other studies have examined age and sex differences in attitudes to bullying. Oliver et al. (in press) surveyed 207 children aged 7 to 12 years in small schools in the US Midwest. They found no significant age changes, but they did find that girls, significantly more than boys, agreed with the statement that bullies had higher status (that is, were more popular) than those children they picked on. This might support the supposition mentioned above that (at secondary school) some girls may admire the bully as being of high status. Rigby and Slee (1991) gave a Provictim scale to 685 Australian children

81

aged 6 to 16 years. They too found that Provictim (helpful to victim) scores were higher in younger children (in this case, the under-12s). However, they found that girls generally scored higher on the Provictim scale than boys, perhaps through being more emphatic. They conclude that 'the postulated growth in the capacity for empathy as a child becomes older did *not* result in a growing tendency for them to sympathise with the victims of bullies in the school context. Indeed, there is evidence of a contrary effect, especially among girls of high school age' (1991: 625–6). Although the evidence for their final clause is not entirely clear, it certainly corresponds closely to our findings.

In summary, a clear picture of sex differences in bullying is now emerging from studies in England, Norway and Finland. Bullying is quite frequent in schoolchildren, but declines from middle to secondary school. The most common form is direct, verbal (name-calling), with little sex difference. Sex differences in other types of bullying are particularly marked at secondary school; by then, girls have greatly decreased direct physical bullying, but it is still common in boys. On the other hand, girls have (relatively) increased their involvement in indirect forms of bullying, especially spreading rumours about someone behind their back.

Boys bully both boys and girls, but focus more on other boys at secondary school. Much of this boy–boy bullying takes place in playgrounds, which are often poorly supervised. Girls usually only bully other girls (though they are quite often bullied by boys, especially at middle school). Girl–girl bullying, often indirect, is relatively more common outside the playground, in class-rooms and corridors. At times, it can be seen as more or less continuous.

The 'female forms' of bullying, which tend to increase with age relative to other forms (Table 4.3) may not always be recognized as bullying, or described as such if scale items or definitions are not sufficiently inclusive. The recently developed scale by Björkqvist, Österman and Lagerspetz (1992) deserves serious consideration for research purposes. There are several items listed which might be included in questionnaires such as those of Olweus, particularly items included in the indirect aggression category. Although we included two similar items in our own modified version of Olweus' definition, we did not include others such as 'becomes friends with another as revenge', 'plans secretly to bother the other', 'tells the other one's secrets to a third person', 'tries to get others to dislike the person'. These might be included in the definition of bullying, but this might risk making the definition too long to remember; they could alternatively be added to the list of possible responses for types of bullying.

Both the qualitative and quantitative research confirm that there do appear to be 'male' and 'female' forms of bullying, but this does not mean they are exclusive to each sex. Our qualitative research, as well as the figures in Table 4.3, still show females involved in physical forms of bullying and males involved in verbal bullying, although the occurrence is less frequent when compared to more sex-specific forms of bullying. Finally, even though 'female bullying' occurs, and perhaps has been underestimated in some past studies, its frequency still does not equal that of male bullying. Nevertheless, studies on sex differences in bullying are important not only for the detection of bullying by teachers and parents, but for awareness-raising in pupils, and for focusing efforts to reduce school bullying and improve the lives and happiness of many children during their school careers (Smith and Thompson 1991).

REFERENCES

Ahmad, Y., Whitney, I. and Smith, P. K. (1991) 'A survey service for schools on bully/victim problems', in P. K. Smith and D. A. Thompson (eds) *Practical Approaches to Bullying*, London: David Fulton, pp. 103–11.

Björkqvist, K., Lagerspetz, K. M. J. and Kaukiainen, A. (1992) 'Do girls manipulate and boys fight? developmental trends in regard to direct and indirect aggression', *Aggressive Behavior*, 18: 117–27.

Björkqvist, K., Österman, K. and Kaukiainen, A. (1992) 'The development of direct and indirect aggressive strategies in males and females', in K. Björkqvist and P. Niemala (eds) *Of Mice and Women: Aspects of Female Aggression*, Orlando, FL: Academic Press, pp. 51–64.

Farrington, D. P. and West, D. J. (1990) 'The Cambridge study in delinquent development: a long-term follow-up of 411 London males', in H. J. Kemer and G. Kaiser (eds) *Criminality: Personality, Behaviour and Life History*, Berlin: Springer-Verlag, pp. 115–38.

Frodi, A., Macaulay, J. and Thome, P. R. (1977) 'Are women always less aggressive than men?', *Psychological Bulletin*, 84: 634–60.

Hoover, J. H., Oliver, R. and Hazler, R. J. (1992) 'Bullying: perceptions of adolescent victims in the Midwestern USA', *School Psychology International*, 13.

Lagerspetz, K. M. J., Björkqvist, K. and Peltonen, T. (1988) 'Is indirect aggression typical of females? Sex differences in aggressiveness in 11–12-year-old children', *Aggressive Behavior*, 14: 403–14.

Munthe, E. (1989) 'Bullying in Scandinavia', in E. Roland and E. Munthe (eds) *Bullying: An International Perspective*, London: David Fulton.

Oliver, R., Hoover, J. H. and Hazler, R. (in press) 'The perceived roles of bullying in small-town Midwestern schools', *Journal of Counselling and Development*.

Olweus, D. (1987) 'Bully/victim problems among schoolchildren in Scandinavia', in J. P. Myklebust and R. Ommundsen (eds) *Psykologprofesjonen mot or 2000*, Oslo: Universitetsforlaget.

—— (1991) 'Bully/victim problems among schoolchildren: basic facts and effects of a school-based intervention program', in D. J. Pepler and K. H. Rubin (eds) *The Development and Treatment of Childhood Aggression*, Hillsdale, NJ: Lawrence Erlbaum Associates, pp. 411–48.

Rigby, K. and Slee, P. T. (1991) 'Bullying among Australian school children: reported behavior and attitudes toward victims', *Journal of Social Psychology*, 131: 615–27.

Smith, P. K. and Thompson, D. A. (eds) (1991) *Practical Approaches to Bullying*, London: David Fulton.

Whitney, I. and Smith, P. K. (1993) 'A survey of the nature and extent of bullying in junior/middle and secondary schools', *Educational Research*, 35(1): 3–25.

Part II

INTER-MALE VIOLENCE

5

DELINQUENT GANGS

Arnold P. Goldstein

Delinquent youth gangs in the United States, as a social (or, better, anti-social) phenomenon, ebb and flow in terms of both their numbers and societal impact. As America enters the 1990s, there seem to be, and are, more of them, more gang youth drug involvement, and greater levels of violence being perpetrated by such youth. The present chapter describes the sources and substance of this phenomenon and, with particular focus on gang violence, examines an array of preventive and rehabilitative interventions which have been employed towards the reduction of delinquency and aggression.

Let us begin by defining the domain of this chapter. Many definitions have been put forward. What constitutes a gang has varied with time and place – with political and economic conditions, with community tolerance and community conservatism, with level and nature of police and citizen concern, with cultural and subcultural traditions and mores, and with media-generated sensationalism or indifference to law-violating youth groups. The answer to the question 'What is a gang?' has varied chronologically from a playgroup formed out of unconscious pressures and instinctual need (Puffer 1912), to an interstitial group derived from conflict with others (Thrasher 1927/1963), to an aggregation demarcated as 'a gang' by community and then self-labelling processes (Klein 1971), to singular definitional emphasis on territoriality and delinquent behaviour (Gardner 1983), and, most recently, to particular definitional focus on violence and drug involvement (Spergel *et al.* 1989). Spergel *et al.* (1989) comment with regard to this definitional progression:

> Definitions in the 1950s and 1960s were related to issues of etiology as well as based on liberal, social reform assumptions. Definitions in the 1970s and 1980s are more descriptive, emphasize violent and criminal characteristics, and possibly a more conservative philosophy of social control and deterrence (Klein and Maxson 1989). The most recent trend may be to view gangs as more pathological than functional and to restrict usage of the term to a narrow set of violent and criminal groups.
>
> (1989: 13)

The contemporary American juvenile gang may have structured organization, identifiable leadership, territorial identification, continuous association, specific purpose, and may engage in illegal behaviour – as largely characterizes many of the gangs in California, Illinois and elsewhere as America enters the nineties (California Youth Gang Task Force 1981). Or, rather less characteristic of the typical, contemporary gang, they may – as is largely the case in New York City – be loosely organized, of changeable leadership, be criminally active and not territorially oriented, associate irregularly, pursue amorphous purposes, and engage in not only illegal, but also legal activities (New York State Task Force on Juvenile Gangs 1990). Nevertheless, they are more violent and more drug-involved, and these two characteristics must also be included in establishing an accurate, contemporary definition of 'gang' in America.

How else may the nature of delinquent youth gangs in the United States best be clarified? Thinking about causation – that is, *why* gangs form – aids such attempts at clarification. Early theorizing, reflecting the heavy reliance on both Darwinian thinking and *instinct* as the core explanatory construct in the behavioural science of the day, asserted that one ought to

> look upon the boy's gang as the result of a group of instincts inherited from a distant past. . . . we must suppose that these gang instincts arose in the first because they were useful once, and that they have been preserved to the present day because they are, on the whole, useful still.
>
> (Puffer 1912: 83)

Thrasher (1927/1963) looked for causative explanation both within the youths themselves and the community of which the youth was a part. The typical gang member, in his view, was 'a rather healthy, well-adjusted, red-blooded American boy seeking an outlet for normal adolescent drives for adventure and expression' (Hardman 1967: 7). Yet the youth's environment was equally important to Thrasher. Inadequacies in family functioning, schools, housing, sanitation, employment and other community characteristics combined to help motivate youths to turn elsewhere – to a gang – for life satisfactions and rewards. This focus on social causation blossomed fully during the next era of gang research, the 1930s into the early 1940s, which Hardman (1967) appropriately labelled 'the depression studies'. It was an era in which social scientists sought explanation for many of America's ills – including delinquent ganging – in 'social causation, social failure, social breakdown' (Hardman 1967). Landesco (1932) emphasized the effects of conflicting immigrant and American cultures. Shaw and McKay (1942) with more complexity stressed a combination of slum area deterioration, poverty, family dissolution and organized crime. Tannenbaum (1939) analogously proposed that the gang forms not because of its attractiveness *per se*, but because 'positive sociocultural forces' – family, school, church – that might train a youth into more socially acceptable behaviours are weak or unavailable. Wattenberg and Balistrieri

(1950) similarly stressed socio-economically sub-standard neighbourhoods and lax parental supervision. In the same contextual explanatory spirit, Bogardus (1943) – in one of the first West Coast gang studies – emphasized the war and war-like climate in America as underpinning the aggressive gangs forming at that time. Dumpson (1949), more multi-causal, but still contextual in his causative thinking, identified the war, racism, and diverse political and economic sources. Although the social problems of the day have over the decades largely formed the basis for explaining why youths form gangs, Miller (1982) has offered a more fully inclusive perspective, which appears to us to capture more adequately the likely complex determinants of gang formation. He observed that

> Youth gangs persist because they are a product of conditions basic to our social order. Among these are a division of labor between the family and the peer group in the socialization of adolescents, and emphasis on masculinity and collective action in the male subculture; a stress on excitement, congregation, and mating in the adolescent subculture; the importance of toughness and smartness in the subcultures of lower-status populations; and the density conditions and territoriality patterns affecting the subcultures of urban and urbanized locales.
>
> (1982: 320)

DELINQUENT GANG THEORY

The early periods in the history of the interest of social science in delinquent gangs were thus largely descriptive. What gangs were and the societal or familial conditions that were their antecedents and concomitants were the focus of concern. Little emerged during this time in the way of formal gang theory – that is, conceptualizations of the structural and dynamic variables underlying gang formation, organization and, especially, the delinquent behaviour which characterized a substantial amount of gang functioning. This theoretical lacuna was later filled, beginning in the 1950s. By far the largest part of this effort to develop theory was sociological in nature. It focused primarily on seeking to explain the delinquent behaviour of individual and groups or gangs of youths, and included the following.

1 *Strain theory*, which emphasized the discrepancy between economic aspiration and opportunity, as well as such discrepancy-induced reactions as frustration, deprivation and discontent. Cohen's (1955) reactance theory, and Cloward and Ohlin's (1960) differential opportunity theory are both elaborations of strain theory.
2 *Subcultural theory*, or *cultural deviance theory*, which holds that delinquent behaviour grows from conformity to the prevailing social norms experienced by the youth in his or her particular subcultural group. These norms are largely at variance with those held by society at large and include,

89

according to Cohen (1966), gratuitous hostility, group autonomy, intolerance of restraint, short-run hedonism, the seeking of recognition via anti-social behaviour, little interest in planning for long-term goals, and related behavioural preferences. Differential association theory (Sutherland 1937; Sutherland and Cressey 1974), Miller's (1958) notion of lower-class culture as a 'generating milieu' for gang delinquency, differential identification theory (Glaser 1956), culture conflict theory (Shaw and McKay 1942), illicit means theory (Shaw and McKay 1942), and what might be termed 'structural determinism theory' (Clarke 1977) are the major varieties of subcultural theory.

3 *Control theory*. Whereas both strain and subcultural theories seek to explain why some youngsters commit delinquent acts, control theory operationalizes its concern with the aetiology of delinquency by positing reasons why some youngsters do not. Everyone, it is assumed, has a predisposition to commit delinquent acts, and the theory concerns itself with how individuals learn not to offend, primarily by a process of social bonding (Hirschi 1969).

4 *Labelling theory*. In 1938, Tannenbaum described an escalating process of stigmatization or labelling which he asserted can occur between the delinquent individual or group and the community of which it is a part. The process of making the criminal, accordingly, is a sequence of tagging, defining, identifying, segregating, describing, emphasizing, making conscious and self-conscious. In labelling theory, a person becomes the thing he is described as being.

5 *Radical theory*. Radical theory is a socio-political perspective on crime and delinquency (Abadinsky 1979; Meier 1976). Its focus is the political meanings and motivations underlying society's definitions of crime and its control. In this view, crime is a phenomenon largely created by those who possess wealth and power in the United States. America's laws, it is held, are the laws of the ruling elite, used to subjugate the poor, minorities and the powerless. Thus, the theory holds as its target for intervention the social and economic structure of American society.

CURRENT GANG DEMOGRAPHICS

Data on the number, nature, structure and functioning of delinquent gangs, especially accurate data, are hard to come by. No national-level agency in the United States has assumed responsibility for the systematic collection and reporting of information relevant to gangs. Each city or region is free to (and does) formulate its own definition of 'gang', and decides what data to collect. Police (who are the major source of information on gangs in most American cities), public service agencies, schools, mass media representatives, and others regularly exposed to gang youth not infrequently exaggerate or minimize their numbers and their illegal activities as a function of political, financial or other impression management needs. Compounding the difficulty in obtaining adequate, accurate, objective and relevant information are gang youths themselves, who have their own reasons, real and imagined, for exaggerating or diminishing the purported size, activities and/or impact of their gang. Thus, caution in accepting the available data, and conservatism in its interpretation, are requisite. Given these provisos, what is currently known about the structure and demographics of the contemporary delinquent gang?

In 1974, Miller conducted a major national survey seeking information related to gangs from a spectrum of public and private service agencies, police departments, probation offices, courts, juvenile bureaux and similar sources. Particular attention was paid in this effort to the six American cities reporting the highest levels of gang activity. Philadelphia and Los Angeles reported the highest proportion of gang members to their respective male adolescent populations (6 per 100). Gang members in the surveyed cities were predominantly male; aged 12 to 21; residing in the poorer, usually central, city areas; and came from families at the lower occupational and educational levels. Gang youths were Afro-American (1/2), Hispanic (1/6), Asian (1/10) and non-Hispanic white (1/10), and strongly tended to form themselves into ethnically homogeneous gangs.

Needle and Stapleton (1982) surveyed police departments in sixty American cities of various sizes. Delinquent youth gangs were no longer to be seen as only a big-city problem. Though the popular mythology is that most of these other gangs are branches intentionally exported to such locations by particular big-city gangs or mega-gangs (especially Los Angeles' Crips and Bloods), the reality appears more complex. While a modest amount of such 'franchising', 'branching', or 'hiving off' may occur, many mid-sized and smaller city gangs either originate in such locations or are started by non-resident gang members via kinship, alliance, the expansion of turf boundaries, or the movement of gang members' families into new areas (Moore et al. 1983).

By 1989, according to yet another, and particularly extensive, survey conducted by Spergel et al. (1989), delinquent gangs were located in almost all fifty states. As a group, thirty-five surveyed cities reported 1,439 gangs. California, Illinois and Florida have substantial gang concentrations. Spergel et al. reported that three jurisdictions in particular have especially high numbers of youth gangs: Los Angeles County (600), Los Angeles City (280), and Chicago (128). Of the total of 120,636 gang members reported to exist in all the surveyed cities combined, 70,000 were estimated to be in Los Angeles County, including 26,000 in Los Angeles and 12,000 in Chicago.[1] But it is clearly not only these three jurisdictions which are expressing concern. Spergel et al. (1989) report that whereas 14 per cent of their survey's law-enforcement respondents and 8 per cent of other respondents believed that the gang situation in their respective jurisdictions had improved since 1980, 56 per cent of the police and 68 per cent of the non-law-enforcement respondents claim their situation had worsened.

Males continue to outnumber female gang members at a ratio of approximately twenty to one. Gang size is a variable function of a number of determinants, including density of the youth population in a given geographical or psychological area (that is, the pool they draw upon), the nature of the gang's activities, police pressures, season of the year, gang recruitment efforts and relevant agency activity (Spergel 1965). Only 5 per cent or less of gang crime is committed by females. Females join gangs later than do males, and leave earlier. The age range of gang membership appears to have expanded, to from ages 9 to 30, as gang involvement in drug-dealing has increased. Younger members are often used as look-outs, runners and so on, with the knowledge that if they are caught, judges and juvenile law tend to be more lenient when the perpetrator is younger. Older members tend to remain in the gang as a result of both the profitability of drug-dealing and the paucity of employment opportunities for disadvantaged populations in the legitimate economy. Blacks, Hispanics, Asians, and whites are America's gang members.[2]

Why do they join? Largely to obtain what all adolescents appropriately seek: peer friendship, pride, identity development, enhancement of self-esteem, excitement, the acquisition of resources, and in response to family and community tradition – goals which often are not available through legitimate means in the disorganized and low-income environments from which most gang youths originate.

How do they leave? They may marry out, age out and find employment in the legitimate economy. They may shift to individual or organized crime. Many go to prison. Some die.

What do gangs do? Mostly they just 'hang out', engaging in the diverse interpersonal behaviours characteristic of almost all adolescents. They may claim and topographically define their territory; make (sometimes extensive) use of graffiti – to define their turf, challenge rivals, or proclaim their gang; incorporate distinctive colours or colour combinations within their dress; tattoo their bodies; and make use of special hand signs as a means of communicating.

Not infrequently they commit delinquent acts and engage in various forms and levels of aggressive behaviour. Although the absolute amount of such behaviour is small, its effect on the chain of media response, public perception of gang youth behaviour, and police and public agency counter-measures is quite substantial.

Through the 1970s and 1980s, the levels and forms of gang violence in the United States have substantially increased, in line with the levels and forms of violence elsewhere on the American scene.[3] Whereas the Roxbury Project (Miller 1980), Group Guidance Project (Klein 1971), and Ladino Hills Project (Klein 1971) gang intervention programmes of the 1950s and 1960s collectively revealed almost no homicides and only modest amounts of other types of gang violence, there were 81 gang-related homicides in Chicago in 1981, 351 such deaths in Los Angeles in 1980, and over 1,500 in Los Angeles during the 1985–89 period (Gott 1989). Spergel *et al.* (1989) report that only about 1 per cent of all the violent crime committed in Chicago was perpetrated by gang members. The seriousness of such figures, however, resides not only in their relative increase from past years, but also, and especially, in their nature: primarily homicide and aggravated assault. Such violent offences, Spergel *et al.* (1989) observe, are three times more likely to be committed by gang members than by non-gang delinquents, a finding also reported by Friedman *et al.* (1975) and Tracy (1979).

What do they fight over? Drugs, territory, honour, girls, perceived insults, 'bad looks', reputation, ethnic tensions (see also Chapters 7 and 16).

INTERVENTION

Detached workers

Gang intervention programming may be conveniently described chronologically as shown in Table 5.1. As can be seen, until approximately 1950, gangs themselves were not a major American phenomenon, and hence nor were gang intervention efforts. As the post-war gang problem grew in the United States, so too did intervention programming – at that time largely in the form of social work procedures to be utilized by agency staff detached from their offices and working where the young people themselves were, on the streets.

Table 5.1 Gang intervention programming

Past	
–1950	Indifferent or unsystematic
1950–65	Detached worker, youth outreach, street-gang work
1965–80	Social and economic opportunities provision
1980–90	Suppression/incarceration, gang-busting, just deserts
Present	
1991–93	Suppression/incarceration, gang-busting, just deserts
1991–93	Comprehensive programming
Future	
1993–	Comprehensive programming

According to Spergel (1965):

> The practice variously labeled detached work, street club, gang work, area work, extension youth work, corner work, etc., is the systematic effort of an agency worker, through social work or treatment techniques within the neighborhood context, to help a group of young people who

are described as delinquent or partially delinquent to achieve a conventional adaptation. . . .

The assumption of youth agencies was that youth gangs were viable or adaptive and could be re-directed. Counseling and group activities could be useful in persuading youth gang members to give up unlawful behavior. The small gang group or subgroup was to be the center of attention of the street worker.

(1965: 22, 145)

Detached work programmes grew from a historical context reaching back to the mid-nineteenth century, in which, as Brace (1872) reported, charity and church groups – as well as boys' clubs, YMCAs and settlement houses – sought to establish relationships with and programmes for urban youths in trouble or at risk for same. Thrasher spoke of similar efforts in 1927, and the Chicago Area Projects of the 1930s (Kobrin 1959) provided much of the procedural prototype for the youth outreach, detached work programmes which emerged in force in the 1950s and 1960s. And blossom they did. In the fertile context of the social action movements of mid-century America, many US cities developed and put such programming in place. Their goals were diverse and ambitious. The New York City Youth Board (1960), one of the major early programmes (the Street Club Project) during the period, aspired to provide

group work and recreation services to youngsters previously unable to use the traditional, existing facilities; the opportunity to make referrals of gang members for necessary treatment . . . the provision of assistance and guidance in the vocational area; and . . . the education of the community to the fact that . . . members of fighting gangs can be redirected into constructive positive paths.

(1960: 7)

At a more general level, this and many of the detached work programmes which soon followed also held as their broad goals the reduction of anti-social behaviour; friendlier relations with other street gangs, increased participation of a democratic nature within the gang; increased responsibility for self-direction amongst individual gang members, as well as their improved social and personal adjustment; and better relations with the larger community of which the gang was a part.

Most detached work programmes, as the movement evolved, came to the position that their central aspiration was value transformation, a rechannelling of the youth's beliefs and attitudes – and consequently, they hoped, his behaviour – in less anti-social and more pro-social directions.

Four major evaluations of the effectiveness of detached worker, gang intervention programming were conducted during this era: those of the New York City Youth Board Project (New York City Youth Board 1960); the Roxbury Project in Boston (Miller 1975); the Chicago Youth Development Project

(Mattick and Caplan 1962); and the Los Angeles Group Guidance Project (Klein 1968). Each concluded that such programming was ineffective. Yet in each instance, while both implementation plans and later evaluation procedures seem adequate, such was not the case regarding the manner in which worker activities were actually conducted. If this assertion is correct, programme effectiveness remains indeterminate and conclusions regarding outcome efficacy must be suspended. Why do we take this position? There are five reasons:

1 Failure of programme integrity; i.e., the degree to which the intervention as actually implemented corresponded to or followed the intervention programme as planned.
2 Failure of programme intensity; i.e., the intervention's amount, level or dosage.
3 Absence of delinquency-relevant techniques; i.e., lack of direct connectedness between the intervention's procedures and its hoped-for outcome – delinquency reduction.
4 Failure of programme prescriptiveness; i.e., to match technique, worker and youth in a propitiously differential, tailored or individualized manner.
5 Failure of programme comprehensiveness; i.e., to match the multi-source, multi-level nature of delinquency causation with a similarly multi-pronged intervention.

Given these realities of implementation, our view of the efficacy of detached work programming must conclude that its demise was premature, and that the relevant evidence, instead of being interpreted as proof of lack of effectiveness, should more parsimoniously be viewed as indeterminate, generally neither adding to nor detracting from a conclusion of effectiveness or ineffectiveness.

Provision of opportunities

Starting in the mid-1960s, and continuing to the late 1970s, gang intervention programming shifted away from primary emphasis on the worker–youth relationship and attempts to alter youth behaviour by gang re-orientation and value transformation, to a greater concern with *system* change – for example, the enhancement of work, school or family opportunity. This shift in emphasis in gang programming occurred in, and as part of, the broader context of increased legislation and funding for social programming of many types in the United States during this period. This period is often described as the era of opportunities provision, and Spergel *et al*. (1989) describe this intervention strategy as

A series of large scale social resource infusions and efforts to change institutional structures, including schools, job opportunities, political employment . . . in the solution not only of delinquency, but poverty itself. Youth work strategies were regarded as insufficient. Structural strain, lack of resources, and relative deprivation were the key ideas which explained delinquency, including youth gang behavior. The structures of social, and economic means rather than the behavior of gangs and individual youth had to be modified.

(1989: 147)

The proposed relevance of this strategy to gang youth in particular is captured well by Morales (1981):

The gang is a symptom of certain noxious conditions found in society. These conditions often include low wages, unemployment, lack of recreational opportunities, inadequate schools, poor health, deteriorated housing and other factors contributing to urban decay and slums.

(1981: 4)

The need for provision of utilitarian and esteem-enhancing opportunity, of course, was apparent as far back as Thrasher's (1927/1963) work and earlier. What was different in the late 1960s and 1970s was America's willingness to respond to such beliefs with a broad programmatic effort. And indeed, many dozens of varied opportunity-providing programmes followed (see Goldstein 1991 for a comprehensive summary).

With very few exceptions (for example, Klein 1968; Thompson and Jason 1988), opportunities-provision gang programming has not been systematically evaluated. We do not know whether gang youth accept or seek the diverse opportunities provided, nor whether they obtain immediate benefits from them, or wether they result in termination of gang membership, delinquency reduction or determine future life path. There is no shortage of affirming impressionistic and anecdotal support – including a major and highly suggestive forty-five city survey of both law enforcement and non-law enforcement agency views on the effectiveness of opportunity provision and other gang intervention approaches (Spergel et al. 1989). The value of such survey results notwithstanding, the general absence of rigorous evaluation of opportunities-provision gang programming must be emphasized. Klein's (1968) Ladino Hills Project is an important exception; its careful evaluation sets a standard to be aspired to.

Opportunity withdrawal and the rise of deterrence/incarceration

As the 1970s drew to a close, America got tough. A combination of the heavy influx of drugs, growing levels of violence, purported failure of rehabilitative programming, and the rise of political and judicial conservatism, all combined to usher in the era of deterrence/incarceration, and begin ushering out the provision of social, economic and educational opportunity. Opportunity provision is not gone, but it is much less frequently the centrepiece of gang intervention programming. Social control – surveillance, deterrence, arrest, prosecution, incarceration – has largely replaced social improvement as America's pre-eminent approach to gang youth.

> A philosophy of increased social opportunity was replaced by growing conservatism. The gang was viewed as evil, a collecting place for socio-paths who were beyond the capacity of most social institutions to redirect or rehabilitate them. Protection of the community became the key goal.
>
> (Spergel *et al.* 1989: 148)

The deterrence/incarceration strategy came to guide the gang-relevant behaviour not only of law-enforcement personnel, but of others also. In Philadelphia's Crisis Intervention Network programme, in Los Angeles' Community Youth Gang Services, and in the other similar gang crisis inter-vention programmes which sprang up across America, the resource worker, who himself had replaced the detached worker, was in turn replaced by the surveillance/deterrence worker. Working out of radio-dispatched auto-mobiles, and assigned to geographical areas rather than to specific gangs, surveillance/deterrence workers responded to crises, their focus on rumour control, dispute resolution and, most centrally, violence reduction. Maxson and Klein (1983) capture well the essence of this strategy, as they contrast it with the earlier value-transformation approach:

> The transformation model fostered social group work in the streets with empathic and sympathetic orientations toward gang members as well as acceptance of gang misbehavior as far less of a problem than the alienat-ing response of community residents and officials. By contrast, the deterrence model eschews an interest in minor gang predations and con-centrates on the major ones, especially homicide. The worker is, in essence, part of a dramatically energized community control mechanism, a 'firefighter' with a more balanced eye on the consequences as well as the cause of gang violence. Success is measured first in violence reduc-tion, not in group individual change.
>
> (1983: 151)

COMPREHENSIVE PROGRAMMING

Indeed, it is a primary responsibility of society's officialdom to protect its citizens. Gang violence in its diverse and often intense forms must be surveilled, deterred, punished. But much more must be done. Gang youth are *our* youth. They are amongst us now and, even if periodically incarcerated, most will be amongst us in the future. We deserve protection from their preda-tions, but they deserve, too, opportunity to lead satisfying and contributory lives without resorting to individual or group violence. Punishment may have to be employed, but punishment fails to teach new, alternative means to desired goals. In essence, the implementations of the deterrence/incarceration model may indeed be necessary in today's violence-prone America, but they are far from sufficient. What is needed, and hopefully appears to be beginning to emerge, is a less unidimensional and more integrative gang intervention model, one with at least the potential to supplant exclusive employment of deterrence/incarceration. We term it the Comprehensive Model,[4] one which incorporates and seeks to apply prescriptively major features of detached-worker, opportunities-provision and social-control programming. It is a multi-modal, multi-level strategy requiring substantial resources, of diverse types, employed in a co-ordinated manner for its success to be realized. I have documented elsewhere the manner in which aggressive and anti-social behaviour derives from complex causality and, hence, will yield most readily when approached with interventions of parallel complexity and targeting (Goldstein 1983). So, too, for gang aggression and anti-social behaviour. Both the recent California and the New York State Gang Task Force reports give full philosophical and concrete expression to this comprehensive gang intervention strategy.

The California Report (1981) urges adoption and implementation of a broad array of recommendations regarding law enforcement, prosecution, correction, probation/parole, the judicial, legislative, and executive departments, federal agencies, local government, school programming, communities, business, industry and the media. The New York Report concurs with this multi-channel strategy, and urges further that, whatever the mode, interventions adopted must be preventive and not only rehabilitative in thrust; seek not only the reduction of anti-social behaviour, but also the enhancement of pro-social alternatives; be both comprehensive in their coverage and co-ordinated in their implementation; locate themselves in school and other community settings; concern themselves with family, school, employment and recreational domains; seek and be responsive to gang youth input in their planning and conduct; reflect programme integrity, intensity and prescriptiveness; recognize that gangs have potential for, and at times actually have, served in a constructive, socially beneficial manner; and be evaluated rigorously.

In addition to these several diverse recommendations, there is one further way in which comprehensiveness of gang programming may be both profitably conceptualized and operationalized. I refer to greater involvement and utilization of *psychological* knowledge and techniques in helping us better understand the nature of youth gangs, and more effectively reduce their anti-social behaviour. Research and intervention with American gangs have primarily been activities conducted by sociologists, criminologists and criminal justice professionals, and only very rarely by psychologists (for example, Cartwright *et al.* 1975; Goldstein 1991). Nevertheless, I believe psychologists to have a great deal to offer as developers of gang-relevant theory (Bandura 1986; Ellis 1987; Feldman 1977; Nietzel 1979), as developers and evaluators of gang-relevant interventions (Agee 1979; Goldstein and Glick 1987; Gottschalk *et al.*

1987; Grendreau and Ross 1987) and as extrapolators of knowledge from diverse domains of psychology to our understanding of delinquent gangs.

In a recent text (Goldstein 1991), I proposed a series of substantive ways in which clinical, developmental, social and community psychology might profitably be drawn upon, or extrapolated from, towards such gang clarification and intervention goals. Clinical psychology provides diverse theoretical understanding of gang member delinquency in its personality, social learning, neurohormonal and multi-component theories. Developmental psychology examines and elucidates qualities of typical adolescents which appear to exist in exaggerated form in many gang youth: marginality, striving for independence, search for identity, challenge of authority, need for enhancement of self-esteem, focus on peer relationships. Social psychology offers the gang-intervention professional both theory and data concerned with group development, leadership, cohesiveness, communication, conflict and conflict resolution, norm and role development, influence processes, utilization of power, de-individuation, and group-think. Community psychology adds to the pool of information from which gang-relevant extrapolations may be drawn, via its findings regarding natural communities, neighbourhoods, social networks and social support. All of these bodies of psychological knowledge hold potential value for adding to our understanding of why gangs form, why they behave as they do, and how to alter much of their behaviour. Very few such extrapolatory efforts yet have been made and tested, either in practice or research. I feel that their likely value is especially great, and thus enthusiastically encourage such attempts.

Finally I would assert that gang intervention of whatever type is in my view likely to fail unless its strategic planning and tactical implementation involve gang members in a major and sustained way. An accurate and heuristic understanding of gang structure, motivation, perception, aspiration, and both routine and dramatic behaviour cannot be obtained only from the outside looking in. Such understanding will become available if, and only if, substantial input is obtained from gang members themselves. But such input is not easily acquired. Hagedorn and Macon (1988) observe in this regard that

> we are in the absurd position of having very few first hand studies of, but numerous theoretical speculations about, juvenile gangs. . . . One reason is that the vast majority of sociologists and researchers are white, and gangs today are overwhelmingly minority.
>
> (1988: 26–7)

Black, Hispanic, Asian, and other minority youth do indeed constitute a large portion of America's contemporary gang membership. They bring to their gang participation diverse and often culture-specific membership motivations, perceptions, behaviours and beliefs. The meaning of aggression; the perception of gang as family; the gang as a status, honour, or reputation acquisition arena; the gang's duration, cohesiveness, typical and atypical legal and illegal pursuits; its place in the community; and much more about gangs is substantially shaped by cultural traditions and mores.[5]

CONCLUSIONS

Gangs in the United States are growing rapidly in number, breadth of location, drug involvement, amount and lethality of aggression and, more generally, their impact on citizen awareness and concern. I have described their history, their demographies, the purposes they serve their members, their activities, and the nature and sources of their frequent aggression. Intervention efforts have sought value transformation via the widespread use of street gang or detached worker programming, opportunities provision via social infusion programming, and deterrence/incarceration by means of social control, criminal justice procedures. Most promising, in our view, is the period of gang intervention work we may now be entering, that of comprehensive programming. Such programming draws selectively and prescriptively on the full range of available interventions – street work, social programming, the criminal justice system, and more – in a broad effort to meet the diverse needs and aspirations of both gang youth and the larger society of which they are a part.

NOTES

1 This numerical litany of youth participation in gangs should be tempered with the reminder that most youths, even in areas in which gangs are common, do not join gangs. Vigil (1983), for example, estimates that only 4 to 10 per cent of Chicago youth are affiliated with gangs.
2 Membership strongly tends to continue, and often further solidify, when and if the gang youth is incarcerated (Camp and Camp 1985; Jacobs 1974; Lane 1989). Gott (1989), for example, reports that in 1989 approximately 5,000 of the 9,000 youths incarceratd in California Youth Authority facilities were gang members and that, as others have also observed, gang cohesiveness and activity level appear to be substantially accelerated by and during incarceration.
3 The weight of evidence combines to suggest that delinquent gangs in America are indeed behaving in a more violent manner in recent years (Miller 1980; Short 1990). Nevertheless, it is important to note that such an apparent increase may derive, at least in part, from artefactual sources. Media interest in youth gangs ebbs and flows, and tends to be accentuated in direct proportion to youth violence levels. The contemporary increase in such behaviours may be partially just such a media interest effect. The likelihood of this possibility is enhanced by a second potential artefact, the relative absence of reliable sources of gang-relevant information. As Klein and Maxson (1989) note: 'The 1960s gang programs, which permitted detailed description of gang structure and activity patterns, are now largely absent. . . . the current picture is based on evidence that is largely hearsay rather than empirical' (p. 209). Finally, following from the fact that by far the greatest majority of the current gang-relevant information which is available comes from police sources, it becomes possible that information regarding increased gang violence is in part also an artefact of more, and more intensive, activity of police department gang intelligence units.

4 Similar in spirit and, in large measure, in its particulars to Spergel *et al.*'s (1989) approach.

5 A rich literature exists describing in depth the cultural patterns and perspectives of America's ethnic and racial sub-groups – black (Beverly and Stanback 1986; Brown 1978; Glasgow 1980; Helmreich 1973; Keiser 1979; Kochman 1981; Meltzer 1984; Silverstein and Krate 1975; White 1984), Hispanic (Horowitz 1983; Mirande 1987; Moore *et al.* 1978; Quicker 1983; Ramirez 1983; Vigil 1983; Vigil and Long 1990); Asian (Bloodworth 1966; Bresler 1980; Kaplan and Dubro 1986; Meltzer 1980; President's Commission on Organized Crime 1985; Wilson 1970), and others (Hagedorn and Macon 1988; Howard and Scott 1981; Schwartz and Disch 1970). Especially useful in much of this culture-clarifying literature is the opportunity it collectively provides to view the structure, dynamics and purposes of delinquent gangs through the cultural lenses of their members, and the support it implies for the crucial necessity of gang-member inputs for effective gang-member programming.

REFERENCES

Abadinsky, H. (1979) 'Social service in criminal justice', Englewood Cliffs, NJ: Prentice-Hall.

Agee, V. L. (1979) *Treatment of the Violent Incorrigible Adolescent*, Lexington, MA: Lexington.

Ashbury, H. (1927/1971) *The Gangs of New York*, New York: Capricorn Press.

Beverly, C. C. and Stanback, H. J. (1986) 'The black underclass: theory and reality', *The Black Scholar*, 17: 24–31.

Bloodworth, D. (1966) *The Chinese Looking Glass*, New York: Dell.

Bogardus, E. S. (1943) 'Gangs of Mexican-American youth', *Sociology and Social Research*, 28: 55–66.

Brace, C. L. (1872) *Dangerous Classes of New York*, cited in R. H. Bremmer (1976) 'Other people's children', *Journal of Social History*, 16: 83–103.

Bresler, F. (1980) *The Chinese Mafia*, New York: Stein & Day.

Brown, W. K. (1978) 'Black gangs as family extensions', *International Journal of Offenders Therapy and Comparative Criminology*, 22: 39–48.

California Youth Gang Task Force (1981) 'Community Access Team', Sacramento: Youth Gang Task Force.

Camp, G. M. and Camp, C. G. (1985) *Prison Gangs: Their Extent, Nature and Impact on Prisons*, South Salem, NY: Criminal Justice Institute.

Cartwright, D. S., Schwartz, H. and Tomson, B. (1975) *Gang Delinquency*, Monterey, CA: Brooks/Cole.

Clarke, R. V. G. (1977) 'Psychology and crime', *Bulletin of the British Psychological Society*, 30: 280–3.

Cloward, R. A. and Ohlin, L. E. (1960) *Delinquency and Opportunity: A Theory of Delinquent Gangs*, New York: Free Press.

Cohen, A. K. (1955) *Delinquent Boys: The Culture of the Gang*, New York: Free Press.

—— (1966) 'The delinquency subculture', in R. Giallombardo (eds) *Juvenile Delinquency*, New York: Wiley.

Dodge, K. A. and Murphy, R. R. (1984) 'The assessment of social competence in adolescents', in P. Karoly and J. J. Steffen (eds) *Advances in Child Behavior Analysis and Therapy*, vol. 4, New York: Plenum.

Dumpson, J. R. (1949) 'An approach to antisocial street gangs', *Federal Probation*, 13: 22–9.

Ellis, L. (1987) 'Neurohormonal bases of varying tendencies to learn delinquent and criminal behavior', in E. K. Morris and C. J. Braukmann (eds) *Behavioral Approaches to Crime and Delinquency*, New York: Plenum.

Federal Bureau of Investigation (1989) *Uniform Crime Report, 1989*, Washington, DC: Government Printing Office.

Feldman, M. P. (1977) *Criminal Behavior: A Psychological Analysis*, London: Wiley.

Friedman, C. J., Mann, F. and Friedman, A. S. (1975) 'A profile of juvenile street gang members', *Adolescence*, 40: 563–607.

Gardner, S. (1983) *Street Gangs*, New York: Franklin Watts.

Glaser, D. (1956) 'Criminality theories and behavioral images', in D. R. Cressey and D. A. Ward (eds) *Delinquency, Crime, and Social Process*, New York: Harper & Row.

Glasgow, D. G. (1980) *The Black Underclass: Poverty, Unemployment, and Entrapment of Ghetto Youth*, San Francisco: Jossey-Bass.

Goldstein, A. P. (1983) 'United States', in A. P. Goldstein and M. H. Segall (eds) *Aggression in Global Perspective*, Elmsford, NY: Pergamon Press.

—— (1991) *Delinquent Gangs: A Psychological Perspective*, Champaign, IL: Research Press.

Goldstein, A. P. and Glick, B. (1987) *Aggression Replacement Training: A Comprehensive Intervention for Aggressive Youth*, Champaign, IL: Research Press.

Goldstein, A. P. and Segall, M. (1983) *Aggression in Global Perspective*, New York: Pergamon Press.

Gott, R. (1989) 'Juvenile gangs', Presented at Conference on Juvenile Crime, Eastern Kentucky University, May.

Gottschalk, R., Davidson, W. S., Mayer, J. P. and Gensheimer, L. K. (1987) 'Community-based interventions', in H. C. Quay (ed.) *Handbook of Juvenile Delinquency*, New York: Wiley.

Grendreau, P. and Ross, R. R. (1987) 'Revivification of rehabilitation: evidence for the 1980s', *Justice Quarterly*, 4: 349–97.

Hagedorn, J. and Macon, P. (1988) *People and Folks*, Chicago: Lake View Press.

Hardman, D. G. (1967) 'Historical perspectives on gang research', *Journal of Research in Crime and Delinquency*, 4: 5–27.

Helmreich, W. B. (1973) 'Race, sex and gangs', *Society*, 11: 44–50.

Hirschi, T. (1969) *Causes of Delinquency*, Berkeley, CA: University of California Press.

Horowitz, R. (1983) *Honor and the American Dream*, New Brunswick, NJ: Rutgers University Press.

Howard, A. and Scott, R. A. (1981) 'The study of minority groups in complex societies', in R. H. Monroe, R. L. Monroe and B. B. Whiting (eds) *Handbook of Cross-cultural Human Development*, New York: Garland STPM Press.

Jacobs, J. B. (1974) 'Street gangs behind bars', *Social Problems*, 21: 395–408.

Kaplan, D. E. and Dubro, A. (1986) *Yakuza: The Explosive Account of Japan's Criminal Underworld*, Reading, MA: Addison.

Keiser, R. L. (1979) *The Vice Lords: Warriors of the Streets*, New York: Holt, Rinehart & Winston.

Klein, M. W. (1968) 'The Ladino Hills Project', Final report to the Office of Juvenile Delinquency and Youth Development, Washington, DC.

—— (1971) *Street Gangs and Street Workers*, Englewood Cliffs, NJ: Prentice-Hall.

Kobrin, S. (1959) 'The Chicago Area Project: A Twenty-five Year Assessment', *Annals of the American Academy of Political and Social Science*, 322: 136–51.

Kochman, T. (1981) *Black and White Styles in Conflict*, Chicago: University of Chicago Press.

Landesco, J. (1932) 'Crime and the failure of institutions in Chicago's immigrant areas', *Journal of Criminal Law and Criminology* (July): 238–48.

Lane, M. P. (1989) 'Inmate gangs', *Corrections Today* (July): 98–9, 126–8.

McCord, W. and McCord, J. (1959) *Origins of Crime: A New Evaluation of the Cambridge-Somerville Study*, New York: Columbia University Press.

Mattick, H. W. and Caplan, N. S. (1962) *Chicago Youth Development Project: The Chicago Boys Club*, Ann Arbor, MI: Institute for Social Research.

Maxson, C. L. and Klein, M. W. (1983) 'Gangs, why we couldn't stay away', in J. R. Kleugel (ed.) *Evaluating Juvenile Justice*, Newbury Park, CA: Sage.

Meier, R. (1976) 'The new criminology: continuity in criminological theory', *Journal of Criminal Law and Criminology*, 67: 461–9.

Meltzer, M. (1984) *The Chinese Americans*, New York: Thomas Y. Crowell.

Miller, W. B. (1958) 'Lower class culture as a generating milieu of gang delinquency', *Journal of Social Issues*, 14: 5–19.

—— (1974) 'American youth gangs: past and present', in A. Blumberg (ed.) *Current Perspectives on Criminal Behavior*, New York: Alfred A. Knopf.

—— (1975) 'Violence by youth gangs and youth groups as a crime problem in major American cities', Washington, DC: National Institute for Juvenile Justice and Delinquency Prevention.

—— (1980) 'Gangs, groups, and serious youth crime', in D. Shicker and D. H. Kelly (eds) *Critical Issues in Juvenile Delinquency*, Lexington, MA: Lexington Books.

—— (1982) *Crime by Youth Gangs and Groups in the United States*, Washington, DC: National Institute of Juvenile Justice and Delinquency Prevention.

Mirande, A. (1987) *Gringo Justice*, Notre Dame, IN: University of Notre Dame.

Moore, J. W., Garcia, R., Garcia, C., Cerda, L. and Valencia, F. (1978) *Homeboys, Gangs, Drugs, and Prison in the Barrios of Los Angeles*, Philadelphia: Temple University Press.

Moore, J. W., Vigil, D. and Garcia, R. (1983) 'Residence and territory in Chicago gangs', *Social Problems*, 31: 182–94.

Morales, A. (1981) *Treatment of Hispanic Gang Members*, Los Angeles: Neuropsychiatric Institute, University of California.

Needle, J. A. and Stapleton, W. V. (1982) *Police Handling of Youth Gangs*, Washington, DC: National Juvenile Justice Assessment Center.

New York City Youth Board (1960) *Reaching the Fighting Gang*, New York: New York City Youth Board.

New York State Task Force on Juvenile Gangs (1990) *Reaffirming Prevention*, Albany, NY: Division for Youth.

Nietzel, M. T. (1979) *Crime and its Modification*, Elmsford, NY: Pergamon Press.

President's Commission on Law Enforcement and Administration of Justice (1967) *Juvenile Delinquency and Youth Crime*, Washington, DC: US Government Printing Office.

President's Commission on Organized Crime (1985) *Organized Crime of Asian Origin*, Washington, DC: US Government Printing Office.

Puffer, J. A. (1912) *The Boy and His Gang*, Boston: Houghton Mifflin.

Quicker, J. S. (1983) *Seven Decades of Gangs*, Sacramento, CA: State of California Commission on Crime Control and Violence Prevention.

Quinney, R. (1974) *Critique of Legal Order: Crime Control in Capitalist Society*, Boston: Little, Brown.

Ramirez, M. (1983) *Psychology of the Americas*, New York: Pergamon Press.

Reckless, W. C. (1961) *The Crime Problem*, New York: Appleton-Century-Crofts.

Rutter, M. (1971) 'Parent–child separation: psychological effects on the child', *Journal of Child Psychology and Psychiatry*, 12: 233–60.

Schwartz, B. N. and Disch, R. (1970) *White Racism*, New York: Dell.

Shaw, C. R. and McKay, H. D. (1942) *Juvenile Delinquency and Urban Areas: A Study of*

Rates of Delinquents in Relation to Differential Characteristics of Local Communities in American Cities, Chicago: University of Chicago Press.

Short, J. F. (1990) 'New wine in old bottles? Change and continuity in American gangs', in C. R. Huff (ed.) *Gangs in America*, Newbury Park, CA: Sage.

Silverstein, B. and Krate, R. (1975) *Children of the Dark Ghetto*, New York: Praeger.

Spergel, I. (1965) *Street Gang Work: Theory and Practice*, New York: Addison Wesley.

Spergel, I. A., Ross, R. E., Curry, G. D. and Chance, R. (1989) *Youth Gangs: Problem and Response*, Washington, DC: Office of Juvenile Justice and Delinquency Prevention.

Sutherland, E. H. (1937) *Principles of Criminology*, Philadelphia: Lippincott.

Sutherland, E. H. and Cressey, D. R. (1974) *Criminology*, New York: Lippincott.

Sykes, G. M. and Matza, D. (1957) 'Techniques of neutralization: a theory of delinquency', *American Sociological Review*, 22: 664–70.

Tannenbaum, F. (1939) *Crime and the Community*, New York: Columbia University Press.

Thompson, D. W. and Jason, L. A. (1988) 'Street gangs and preventive interventions', *Criminal Justice and Behavior*, 15: 323–33.

Thrasher, F. M. (1927/1963) *The Gang*, Chicago: University of Chicago Press.

Tracy, P. E. (1979) *Subcultural Delinquency: A Comparison of the Incidence and Seriousness of Gang and Nongang Member Offensivity*, Philadelphia: University of Pennysylvania Center for Studies in Criminology and Criminal Law.

Vigil, J. D. (1983) 'Chicago gangs: one response to Mexican urban adaptation in the Los Angeles area', *Urban Anthropology*, 12: 45–75.

Vigil, J. D. and Long, J. M. (1990) 'Emic and etic perspectives on gang culture: the Chicago case', in C. R. Huff (ed.) *Gangs in America*, Newbury Park, CA: Sage.

Wattenberg, W. W. and Balistrieri, J. J. (1950) 'Gang membership and juvenile misconduct', *American Sociological Review*, 15 (Dec.).

White, J. L. (1984) *The Psychology of Blacks*, Englewood Cliffs, NJ: Prentice-Hall.

Wilson, R. W. (1970) *Learning to be Chinese*, Cambridge, MA: MIT Press.

6

WARRIOR VALUES
A socio-historical survey

Barry McCarthy

In any attempt to encompass and explain male violence in its various forms an examination of the warrior role and of warrior values and myths constitutes an essential foundation, although it will not of course be possible to explore in detail the rich anthropological, historical and social psychological sources. I shall begin by examining some common features of warrior values, focusing on traditional cultures, and the relationship between the role of the warrior *per se* and concepts of masculinity in the broader sense. I shall then proceed to trace the evolution of warrior castes in more stratified and 'organized' societies, with the Middle Ages in Europe and in Japan as examples. Next I shall consider the apparent decline in the status of the warrior in the European Renaissance and Enlightenment, before concentrating upon the revival in his fortunes following the nineteenth-century rehabilitation of medievalism, augmented by the Social Darwinist stream of ideas from mid-century onwards. The consequent flood tide of ethnocentric, passionate, popular militarism, which did so much to bring on the First World War, suffered no more than a temporary check in the mud and blood of the trenches before culminating in the terrible apotheosis of romantic nationalist violence that was Nazi Germany, and that ideology's ultimate military expression in the Waffen-SS. Finally, I shall look briefly at war-like elements uncovered by recent social psychological and sociological research on masculinity, and at the current status of warrior values in popular culture. Throughout the chapter I find myself returning repeatedly, I hope not to the point of tedium, to what seems to be an inescapable emergent theme: the almost universal, intimate bond between warrior values and conventional notions of masculinity.

First, what are these 'warrior values'? Not all belligerent cultures or sub-cultures esteem precisely the same attributes and qualities in a fighting man; differences in ecological, technological and religious or ethical variables may lead one group to emphasize one set of behaviours and traits, and another society to highlight others. Cultures without recent first-hand experience of war, but in which the warrior is worshipped at a safe distance, as in most of the economically developed world, may differ from truly war-like societies in their prescriptions for the warrior role. The following categories are derived from a wide survey of cultural models, but they are intended to be heuristic rather than conclusive:

Physical courage The warrior enjoys a fight, is prepared to risk wounds or death, and will if necessary engage superior forces; if death is inevitable he faces it bravely and without flinching.

Endurance The warrior can withstand extremes of climate, pain, hunger and thirst, and fatigue; he will fight on after defeats and reverses, and is not demoralized either by prolonged hard fighting or by captivity.

Strength and skill The warrior is physically robust, fit, and proficient in the use of his weapons; he is also a shrewd tactician and planner, not merely a berserk thug, although an element of frenzy in the desperate heat of battle is to be expected.

Honour The warrior is pre-eminently a 'man of honour'; he keeps his word, is loyal to his leader and to his comrades, and fights honourably without resorting to illegitimate, underhand tricks or ruses; he defends and protects the wounded, the aged and women and children, even the helpless prisoners of the enemy. The warrior is also extremely sensitive to any slight or insult to his own honour or to that of his band or clan, and will respond decisively and forcefully to any such, heedless of risk.

I consider these four to be the common values of the warrior ethos; others, such as altruism, sexual potency, generosity, individual ambition, energy and hearty extroversion I view either as peripheral, or as already included in some form in one or other of the four main categories. As in the case of any value system, the warrior code is aspirational and normative; in practice, derelictions have been and continue to be commonplace. Under the strain and terror of battle courage may wilt and endurance break, and in the shadows away from the battle line itself gross perversions of these values, torture, rape, and murder of noncombatants and prisoners are often the rule rather than the exception.

Before considering the evolution of the warrior and of warrior values I will make a rather obvious, but necessary, observation: by any reasonable sampling of the literature, ancient or modern, documentary or impressionistic, partisan or detached, warfare is an activity in which negative experiences considerably outweigh the positive, both in frequency and in potency. The common psychological elements are striking, whether one reads the memoirs of a Masai recalling the terrors and exhilarations of cattle raids and skirmishes on the East African plains in the 1930s (Saitoti 1986), or the story of an Alsatian volunteer in the German infantry recounting the privations of perhaps the most cataclysmic of all campaigns, the German-Soviet war of 1941–45 (Sajer 1972).

Very few participants appear to enjoy the experience of battle at the time; such 'joy of battle' that is felt rarely survives very long, and few men are able to sustain prolonged exposure to combat without psychological deterioration, and eventually breakdown (S. Marshall 1946; Ingraham and Manning 1980). The pleasures and satisfactions that twentieth-century soldiers report are overwhelmingly those associated with comradeship, and the sensual and aesthetic experiences of survival, when the fighting is, if only temporarily, at a distance: food and drink, sleep, clean clothing and sheets, sexual release, off-duty escapades with comrades, bird-song in the morning or a peaceful sunset without noise or gun-flashes (Holmes 1985). There may sometimes be some dark pleasure in killing, but it is rarely if ever mentioned by soldiers in the immediate aftermath of a fight, and then usually as a technical matter such as satisfaction in hitting a target, in correct performance of a hard-won skill. Blood-lust is not entirely a myth, but it is an elusive phenomenon found more readily in media characterizations of warfare than in real battle, where many men operate in a state of shocked dissociation (S. Marshall 1946; Holmes 1985).

Given that warfare is a tricky business, with many deeply unpleasant accompaniments, what has impelled or attracted young men into the warrior role? Notions of aggressive instincts or drives have proved to be inadequate explanations; cultures differ too widely in the prevalence of aggressive conflict, and indeed, belligerence within a particular society may wax or wane dramatically over a relatively short historical period. It seems reasonable to try to identify a range of possible contributory factors. Material reward, in the form of pay or plunder, may be a significant incentive in some circumstances. Wilson (1978) suggests that primitive ethnocentrism, an exaggerated division of the world into kin and friends on the one side, and aliens on the other, may impel recourse to arms in situations of conflict between traditional cultures. Perceptions of threat from outsiders, whether of massacre or of deprivation of resources, may indeed be significant, or conversely a desire to seize valuable materials currently in the hands of others. One essential ingredient, it seems to me, is a high level of cultural approval and social status for the warrior, including access to valued privileges and perquisites. Ethnographers' reports, across a wide geographical and ecological range, suggest strongly that participation in successful warfare by young men is a key to status and influence within the group, as in the Sambia of New Guinea (Herdt 1982) and to admiration by women and sexual access, as in the Yanomamo of Amazonia (Chagnon 1988), the Samburu (Spencer 1965) and the Masai (Saitoti 1986) of East Africa. Daly and Wilson (1988) observe that having killed an enemy is a mark of status in many pre-state societies, exemplified by such practices as head-hunting and coup-counting, and cite evidence for a similar process at work in the prestige accorded to the successful duellist in the antebellum American South and to the Mafia killer in present-day Sicily.

In many traditional societies the very process of achieving manhood is bound up with the acquisition of martial skills and virtues, although one must not overlook the fact that many of the skills of the warrior, such as proficiency with weapons, as well as courage and endurance, are also required for success in hunting large game, an essential economic enterprise. It is also important to note that hunting is not an activity closely associated with war-like proclivities, as Fromm (1973) points out; there are many examples of hunting peoples who do not practise warfare and have not engaged in it for many generations, at least, such as the Inuit of Arctic Canada (Irwin 1990) and the !Kung Bushmen of the Kalahari Desert (Lee 1979). Over and above the value placed on hunting, however, many traditional cultures prize the explicitly aggressive aspects of manhood embodied in warrior values, with a degree of commonality across widely divergent ecologies that suggests a wide cross-cultural endorsement of war-like activity.

The prevalence of warfare in traditional cultures, past and present, has become an issue of some controversy. Wright's often-cited survey of primitive warfare in a global context (1942) suggested that violent conflict has been a significant aspect of life in the great majority of societies, and his data have been a mainstay of those who argue a sanguinary view of human nature, and of masculine nature in particular. An interesting aspect of Wright's conclusions, which is not so often highlighted, is an apparent tendency for warfare to be least frequent and intense in hunter-gatherer societies, and most prevalent in agricultural and pastoral communities. Van der Dennen (1990), in a more recent and more inclusive inventory, suggests that the proportion of peaceful, or at least predominantly unwarlike peoples, is far greater than Wright's study indicated. The debate becomes rather tortuous, though no less interesting, when one appreciates that terms like 'primitive warfare' are inclusive labels, which subsume a vast range of violent encounters, from the (perhaps mythical) all-out wars of annihilation between genetically distinct hordes beloved of the nineteenth-century race-war apologists (such as Spencer 1873; Bagehot 1884) to small-scale blood-feuding between related clans within the same tribe, or even between families within the same clan. The question of when interpersonal homicide becomes warfare is a difficult one, but presumably inescapable if one is in the business of assessing cultures in terms of belligerence or pacificity: see Eibl-Eibesfeldt (1974), Chagnon (1988) and van der Dennen (1990).

The issue of warfare's prevalence is not a central one for our present purposes, in any case; warrior values may persist and thrive in societies in which war is relatively small-scale or infrequent, provided that fighting can be advantageous in some circumstances. Shaw and Wong (1988) suggest that related individuals banding together in successful conflict with outsiders may gain both individually and indirectly, in terms of well-being of genetically related comrades. Tooby and Cosmides (1988) take this rationale further, by arguing that when perceived probability of success is high, risk of mortality among warriors is seen to be random, and assurance exists that the reproductive resources of the group, plus any gained by victory, will be reallocated among the survivors, then engaging in warfare enhances the average fitness of the group's members. There do appear to be circumstances, however, contrary to the assumptions of resource theorists, when even the most intense cerebration cannot discover any material gain to be obtained from primitive warfare. Even in such cases, however, like that of the endemic warfare practised by some Amazonian Indian groups such as the Yanomamo (Chagnon 1988) and the Waorani (Robarchek and Robarchek 1992), where in the absence of central authority no group can unilaterally cease fighting lest they be slaughtered by their opponents, mere survival requires that combat be conducted as effectively as possible, hence a need for warriors and a warrior ethos to sustain them. The more proficient and well-armed a group's warriors become, the fewer the costs incurred in attacking the enemy, whilst, of course, the effort and resources expended in training and arming warriors is likely to increase the probability of their employment in the event of confrontation with outsiders.

Traditional cultures in which warfare is engaged in most frequently also tend to be highly patriarchal, with a sharp division of labour by sex and a wide gulf between the lifestyles and status of men and women. In such a society, in which boys are normally brought up without frequent contact with men, and consequently have little opportunity to model male behaviour, Segall (1988) suggests that a phenomenon which he calls 'compensatory machoism' operates, as feminine identification and behaviour are harshly stamped out, and the masculine role inculcated. In many cases this is achieved by initiation rituals, in which the boy is removed from the female world, subjected to a range of painful, terrifying and humiliating treatments at the hands of the older males (varying from circumcision to flogging and enforced fellatio), taught masculine skills, and set demanding or dangerous tasks (stealing cattle from neighbouring groups, or killing large and dangerous game, or surviving unaided in the wilderness). Where systematic initiation rites are not a part of the culture, as on Truk (M. Marshall 1979), young males assert their masculinity by themselves, in brawling, sexual assertiveness and other displays.

It is not difficult to appreciate how warrior values are instilled in such a setting: strength, endurance of pain, courage and skill in hunting and fighting are encouraged and praised, while failure, cowardice or passivity bring shame not only to the boy himself, but to his whole family. Success in the warrior role is likely to bring high status within the group, as well as access to wealth and influence, and, in many cases, to a wife. Among the Dodoth of Northern Uganda (Thomas 1965) and the Samburu (Spencer 1965), amongst others, only a proven warrior may marry and have children; on Truk, a youth who avoids or fails in the regular brawls and fights is disdained and ridiculed by the young women (M. Marshall 1979).

Even in those cultures in which warfare is rare or has been long abandoned, there are many instances of stressful initiations into manhood, as amongst the Gisu of Uganda (La Fontaine 1986), or of ritual competitions of strength and skill among the men, with women as interested onlookers, as amongst the Mehinaku of Amazonia (Gregor 1977). Even the pacific !Kung Bushmen of the Kalahari, among whom patriarchy and rigid gender barriers do not operate, subject their young men to a rigorous initiation, involving tests of endurance and hunting skill; proficiency with weapons is valued as a masculine attribute, and strongly associated with sexual prowess (Lee 1979). As we shall see, such connections are also made across a wide range of cultures in the economically developed world, in which active participation in warfare is, for most men, a very remote prospect.

WARRIOR CASTES

In non-state, subsistence cultures, on which I have focused so far, the warrior role tends to encompass all fit males of military age. In more elaborate political-economic systems, with a wide range of occupational specialisms, more-or-less exclusive warrior castes have tended to evolve. In almost every case where this development has occurred the warriors have been accorded, or have secured for themselves, elite status within the society, with high prestige and social privileges. Even in the complex society of the Roman Republic, with its highly trained, professional citizen army of long-service volunteer infantry, an aristocratic officer elite gradually emerged to become a major political force (Keppie 1984), particularly under the later Empire when rival generals, each with the support of his legions, contended for control in a virtually endless series of palace coups. For much of its history of some 700 years the Roman army fought against more traditional warrior cultures of the kind we have already examined: all the menfolk of the tribe or clan in arms, either in offensive raids or in defence of their villages. Roman writers like Julius Caesar and Tacitus often remark upon the courage and ferocity of Gaulish or Teutonic warriors; they also note their indiscipline, impetuosity and lack of operational planning, and 'barbarian' armies many times their own size were repeatedly vanquished by the steady, well-trained, efficiently deployed Roman legions, who fought very much as modern armies do, for pay and gratuity, although comradeship and unit pride developed during a twenty-year enlistment must have played its part, as did the cruel punishments inflicted for any dereliction of duty.

As the Empire gradually succumbed to external pressures and internal decay during the fifth century AD, its territory became the home of a multitude of peoples, indigenous and immigrant, a patchwork of holdings carved out by tribal chiefs and warlords, regions which as the centuries passed became counties, baronies, dukedoms, even empires of a kind, and finally centralized national kingdoms at the close of the Middle Ages, from around 1400 on. The feudal system of land tenure and political-military organization which dominated western and central Europe throughout the medieval period was, at least in its early and 'high' periods (600 to 1300, approximately) pre-eminently a society dominated by a warrior elite whose conduct was more or less influenced by an ever-present church. A vast amount of historical research has been devoted to understanding the nature of European feudal chivalry (see Howard 1976; Mundy 1991); for our purpose it is worth noting that while chivalric traditions varied in detail from Christian Spain to France and England, and especially in the German lands, in essence medieval knighthood closely resembled in many ways the warrior codes of non-state cultures that have already been discussed. Becoming a knight involved a hard apprenticeship in a baronial retinue, and an initiation, usually with powerful religious overtones, in early manhood; marriage was normally delayed until the knight had established his reputation in battle and received a grant of land from his appreciative lord. A worthy knight was fearless in battle, honourable in conduct, and shrewd in advice; aristocratic warriors at all levels, from the most junior esquire to the king or emperor himself, payed homage to the knightly code. In a more complex and hierarchical society than that of the tribe, loyalty was at once even more important and more problematic; at most times in most parts of medieval Europe allegiance to one's immediate feudal lord (and patron) took precedence over any other, until the kings (in Spain, France and England, at least) eventually grew strong enough to subjugate regional magnates and bring the whole military aristocracy under their direct control. By then, as the Middle Ages waned, other complex economic and philosophical changes had sounded the knell of the institution, if not the code, of chivalry.

Two features of the European chivalric code invite further mention, as they provide a vivid contrast, both with the system operating in traditional, subsistence cultures and with later manifestations of warrior values. First, the system of medieval knighthood was, in its developed form, wholly aristocratic. Whilst mercenary warriors of peasant stock (*landsknechte*) flourished in some of the German lands during the later Middle Ages, over most of the Continent the warrior role remained a prerogative of the landed nobility and gentry. The great mass of the rural population (and almost 90 per cent of the people lived on the land or in small country towns) were peasants or serfs of varying levels of unfreedom. Men were required to serve in the feudal levy as archers or pikemen, but did not bear arms in the full sense, as a warrior and a gentleman (from the Latin *gentilis*, noble).

A second point of contrast lies in the role of organized religion. The medieval church claimed, and exercised to the utmost at every opportunity, jurisdiction over every aspect of life, and the chivalric ethos became heavily imbued with religious fervour. While only the naïve can visualize sanctity and piety filling every waking hour of a hard-bitten, struggling knight attempting to maintain or to improve a precarious fiefdom in a Pyrenean valley or a Pomeranian marsh, the sword and the cross bore more than a superficial resemblance in the medieval mind (Mundy 1991). Many bishops and abbots were themselves feudal warlords, with retinues of followers; a number of religious orders had an explicitly military function, amongst them the Knights Templar and the Teutonic Knights, and religious enthusiasm was certainly one salient motive impelling thousands of warriors from western and central

Europe to the periodic invasions of the Middle East that have come to be dignified with the title of Crusades. A close association between faith and force has not, of course, been confined to the world of Christian chivalry; the dramatic expansion of Islam in North Africa and western Asia in the seventh to ninth centuries AD was accomplished by men of the Book who were also men of the sword. Historically and psychologically the alliance of warrior values and religious fervour is an interesting one, religion claiming to mollify and civilize the ferocity of the warrior, while the warrior in turn learns to invoke sacred justification for his martial pursuits.

As one kind of military elite flourished in medieval Europe, an equally striking phenomenon was evolving in Japan, in the samurai code of *bushido*, with a central value system of unquestioning devotion to the lord, and unselfish service to the community. The idealized samurai is the quintessential warrior: unflinching in the face of danger, strong and energetic, cunning in tactics though honourable, proficient with his weapons as well as in the arts of unarmed combat, self-controlled, self-confident and sexually virile. Medieval Japan shared many characteristics with contemporary Europe, essentially lacking continuity of central authority, with local and regional chieftains and warlords ruling by personal charisma, patronage and violence. As in the European chivalric code, *bushido* was a set of guiding principles for those at all levels of the warrior caste; as in chivalry, survival and success are less important to the samurai than honour, and the hero fighting on to the death in hopeless battle is celebrated in both traditions (Morris 1975). The more successful or well-connected members of the samurai caste served the warrior chiefs, many rising to hold lands and castles themselves; the less favoured wandered the land as *ronin*, itinerant mercenaries and no doubt often brigands. For samurai of all types a vast, unbridgeable social gulf existed between themselves and the toiling peasants and fisherfolk; nevertheless, the wandering *ronin* gave rise to the myth of the mysterious, aloof hero, who like the nameless gunfighter in many a western epic, arrives to protect the poor and helpless from merciless villains, disappearing just as mysteriously once the battle is won.

The *bushido* code survived the disappearance of the samurai themselves by the early nineteenth century, and grew in influence to play a central role in the value system of the entire Japanese nation. In its militant aspect it helped to stimulate and sustain Japanese imperialist adventures and expansion, culminating in defeat at the hands of the Allied powers in 1945; in its broader, moral aspect *bushido* remains fundamental to the Japanese conception of masculinity today (Buruma 1984).

In contrast to Japan, where the *bushido* code translated almost effortlessly from feudalism into an industrialized society, in Europe, with its much more lengthy period of transition from the rural, medieval world to that of the twentieth century, the progress of warrior values has been more uncertain. As the European Renaissance of the fifteenth to the seventeenth centuries gave way to the Enlightenment, with a decline in religious conviction and a corresponding elevation of human rationality and a growing belief in progress, the practice of warfare and those who engaged in it underwent a discernible decline in public esteem, which the wars of religion of the sixteenth century and the traumatic savagery of the Thirty Years War (1618–48) can have done little to retard. Rapid economic changes produced a variety of elites, mercantile and professional; status was no longer contingent upon martial prowess. Warrior elites continued in power, to be sure, as in Prussia, and wars continued; many philosophers, exemplified by Thomas Hobbes (1588–1679), advanced a pessimistic view of human nature, but warfare came to be seen by most as an evil, even if an inescapable one, rather than as the *raison d'être* for the ruling classes. Correspondingly, literature and drama, architecture and art tended to celebrate the joys of life rather than death and judgement; the warrior king is still a hero figure in Shakespeare's plays, written at the turn of the sixteenth and seventeenth centuries, but by the late eighteenth one is hard put to find a warrior model in literature or drama that is not a figure of fun, however gently poked. It has been suggested that progressive social movements tend to disparage war-like values and warrior elites alike as embodiments of *anciens régimes*, and the Parliamentarians of the English Civil War (1642–49), the insurgent colonists of the American War of Independence (1775–83), the French Revolutionaries (1789–94) and the Bolsheviks in the Russian Civil War (1917–20) each in their own way struggled with a conflict between distaste for militaristic hierarchy and regimentation and their pressing need for military effectiveness and, ultimately, survival (Ellis 1973). The Soviet regime, though recognizing the need for command and commanders in winning its Civil War victory, resisted the re-introduction of the hated title 'officer' to the Red Army, until driven to the very edge of destruction by the Wehrmacht in 1942 (Erickson 1975).

As well as the general tenor of upper-class life and ideas in seventeenth- and eighteenth-century Europe tending towards a devaluation of the role of the warrior caste, changes in the nature and technology of the battlefield itself had played a significant part in the same process. The medieval warrior was a horseman; even his favourite pastimes (jousting, hunting, falconry) were conducted on horseback, and he led the feudal levy of trudging spearmen and archers from a splendid eighteen-hands' elevation. The massed feudal chivalry was the core of the medieval order of battle, and must indeed have been an awe-inspiring sight, but even at the height of the Middle Ages heavy armoured cavalry was far from invincible. Saracen horsemen on their much lighter, unarmoured ponies gave the crusaders many a bad day, and the power of English longbow archery at Agincourt (1415), taking advantage of a tactical blunder by their adversaries, shattered the mounted French aristocracy in a matter of minutes.

Whatever intimations of mortality such experiences conveyed to the knights-in-arms who came to hear of them seem to have been successfully repressed; as the Middle Ages wore on, armour for man and horse grew ever more elaborate. Within a century or so, however, all had come crashing down, often literally. The invention and proliferation of firearms, both artillery and shoulder-fired, ended the military value of the medieval castle on the one hand, and on the other demoted its occupant to a peripheral role on the field of battle. By the early sixteenth century a plebeian combination of armoured pikemen, musketeers and crude field artillery already dominated the European battlefield; in a straight fight cavalry could cope with none of these, and though it took many a bloody encounter to ram home the lesson, for the rest of its military career (which continued up to, and through, the Second World War) cavalry was effectively restricted to the roles of reconnaissance, raiding and pursuit. Although aristocrats continued to dominate military hierarchies, and officer the infantry and artillery formations that were now the key to victory, they were no longer essential even there, as American and French revolutionary forces were to demonstrate by their victories over the armies of aristocratic reaction.

INTO THE TWENTIETH CENTURY: ROMANTICISM AND RACISM

The relative devaluation of the warrior and of his martial virtues that characterized the eighteenth century in Europe proved short-lived; in the nineteenth and early twentieth centuries enormous changes in the nature of society and of ideas were to lead to a rapid and destructive resurgence in the status of the warrior and of war, whose effects are very much still with us. I can do no more than summarize these socio-cultural changes here; they fall into three main categories – literary-artistic, philosophical and demographic.

The literary-artistic movement we call Romanticism is itself beyond our present scope (see Halsted 1965) but its general tenor is a consistent one: partly in reaction against the mechanism and rationalism of eighteenth-century thought, Romanticists in poetry, drama, music and the visual arts celebrated the human imagination, the unconscious mind, and the natural environment. Many looked back to a (largely fanciful) medieval world, an Arthurian fantasy of magic, gallantry, purity of good and of evil. In Germany, in particular, Romantics eulogized a mythical, pre-classical, pagan, Teutonic warrior cult. This Romantic medievalism spanned the century, from the poetry of Keats and the novels of Sir Walter Scott in the early years to the Pre-Raphaelites' paintings and the operas of Wagner in the middle and later decades. To a great extent this was a cult of the hero, and heroic deeds and quests pervade much of nineteenth-century western culture at all levels, from legends of Robin Hood and William Tell to Jesse James. At the turn of the century, the two main literary-artistic obsessions of the adolescent Adolf Hitler were Wagner's operas, especially his darkly Teutonic Ring cycle, and the adventure stories of a writer of sensationalist westerns, Karl May (Toland 1976).

114

Coinciding with its discovery of an idealized medieval past and the glorification of heroism in the present, the nineteenth century displayed, from around its mid-point, an increasing obsession with philosophies of struggle and of survival, often with crudely racist and bellicose concomitants. A large and vocal Social Darwinist movement (whose themes often owed little to Darwin's own ideas) was immensely influential in shaping the thinking of politicians and popular writers, and via the latter, that of the general public. From a welter of often unsystematic and unsubstantiated assertions and dogmas a few interrelated features are noteworthy (see van der Dennen (1990) for a survey of Social Darwinist ideas on war):

First, the claim that some races or ethnic groups are innately superior to others, and that the so-called 'Aryan race' is superior to all;

Second, the notion of innate hostility of every race or ethnic group to every other;

Third, the idea of war as a crucial instrument of group selection, eliminating the weakest and least 'fit' groups while increasing the organisation and cultural development of the victorious ones.

Through such notions the Darwinian concept of 'survival of the fittest' came, by the early twentieth century, to imply 'survival of the strongest', rather than reproductive success in terms of adaptiveness (Barash and Lipton 1985). Such a doctrine could, and did, serve to justify colonial domination and territorial expansion at the expense of 'inferior' peoples.

A third development in nineteenth-century society that bears significantly on the revival of esteem for warrior values arises from profound demographic changes that accompanied scientific and technological progress, as societies recently rural came to acquire a largely urban character, with substantial population growth following industrialization and major improvements in public health and hygiene. Virtually universal compulsory primary education from mid-century on produced large populations literate enough to consume the usually sensational, chauvinistic and often scaremongering articles that filled the burgeoning popular press. In every European country and in the United States the political establishments imbued the popular mind, via press and education systems, with simplistic, exaggerated notions of national achievements and worth, and contrasting images of foreign nations and peoples that emphasized negative attributes: rivalry, cruelty, ignorance, godlessness, cowardice. With universal male suffrage prevalent by the beginning of the twentieth century politicians who had eagerly stoked the fires of bellicose patriotism now found themselves susceptible in turn to pressure from these excitable, passionate and crudely nationalistic electorates, even in semi-autocracies like the German and Austrian empires. Both the Franco-Prussian War of 1870–71 and the Spanish-American conflict of 1898 were given a crucial initial impetus by media-manipulated popular outrage, and once the mobilization procedures of the respective European powers had begun to click into gear in July and August 1914 an irresistible surge of raw popular enthusiasm made the descent into war unstoppable (Tuchman 1962).

A number of converging socio-historical processes, then, had by the turn of the twentieth century produced a renewed idealization of the warrior, and a powerful identification of manly masculinity with the warrior values of courage, endurance and honourable combat. Few populations in history can have been so eager to participate in battle as were the young men of Europe, cheered on ecstatically by their womenfolk, in August 1914 (Tuchman 1962); their joy is preserved forever in grainy newspaper photos and on jerky, silent newsreels. A glance through an anthology of English poems written at the outbreak of that war is revealing (Gardner 1964): Rupert Brooke thanking God for wakening him 'from sleeping', glad to leave 'all the little emptiness of love' for a glorious life, or death, in battle; W. N. Hodgson praising those who were going out 'to do the work of men'. Brooke died in 1915; Hodgson survived a little longer, to be killed on the Somme in 1916.

With a supreme, almost (from an Olympian perspective) a delicious irony, the war those men strode out to was to prove spectacularly unsuited to purple-prose heroics. The adoption of rifled firearms from the 1860s onward had dramatically increased the range, accuracy and penetrative power of projectiles, whilst the parallel development of new types of explosives, far more potent than gunpowder, had made artillery in particular the new 'Queen of the Battlefield' (Coffman 1968). In combination, these two innovations rendered traditional warfare, as it had been fought at least since late medieval times, well-nigh obsolete. Close-quarters fighting, with sword, bayonet or even pistol, had become essentially an anachronism; massed ranks of colourfully uniformed infantry and columns of cavalry with gleaming brass and plumed helmets were converted almost instantaneously into bloody debris and flying scraps of tissue, as machine guns engaged them at 1,000 yards or the new rapid-firing field artillery at 5,000.

When the fashionable doctrine of the irresistible offensive, as expressed in the tactical manuals, collided with the new facts of battle, the outcome was a slaughter so nightmarish and so prolonged that by its end a deep and cynical disillusionment had replaced early enthusiasm. In many participant nations, in particular France, exhaustion and dread of war persisted long after the end of the conflict. In defeated Germany, however, a peculiar alchemy of humiliation, confusion, economic distress and a still-powerful militarist ethos contributed to the ascendancy, within two decades, of an ideology which fused in dramatic form all the crucial ingredients of popular Romantic culture: notions of blood-and-soil tribal origins, ideas of racial purity and struggle derived from Social Darwinism as well as from an older tradition of anti-semitism, and a determination to mobilize and manipulate mass feeling, all wedded to a passionate desire to undo the outcome of 1914–1918 and to learn its military lessons.

In its reactivation of German martial enthusiasm the Nazi regime

116

concentrated on those aspects of warrior values that had survived, and even flourished, in the trenches: comradeship, the solidarity and mutual support of the small group, individual initiative and endurance. Military doctrine emphasized the avoidance of trench-warfare stalemate, and concentrated on the new offensive power and mobility conferred by the development of armoured vehicles (Seaton 1982). The success of this re-orientation is seen in its most dramatic form in the Waffen-SS, probably the most-studied military entity in recent history. Nominally under the authority of Reichsführer-SS Himmler, the Waffen-SS always remained under the operational control of the army, but kept the training and indoctrination of recruits within its own hands. The force grew rapidly with the outbreak of war in 1939 to attain a total of some thirty-five divisions, or half a million men, by 1945, including (strangely, in view of its openly racist ideology) Croatian, Latvian and Russian formations. At the core of the Waffen-SS were its seven *Panzer* and ten *Panzergrenadier* divisions, predominantly German in composition although containing a substantial number of Belgian, Dutch, Alsatian and Scandinavian volunteers; these units are generally acknowledged to have been amongst the most formidable in the history of warfare (Stein 1966).

Part of the tactical success achieved by the Waffen-SS was undoubtedly due to the priority these divisions enjoyed in the allocation of the best and latest equipment. Much of the explanation, however, must lie in their *esprit de corps* and the adherence of the troopers to a powerful and brutal warrior code, stressing unit solidarity, loyalty to the Führer, and obligation to the *Volk*. At Himmler's instigation, identification with the Teutonic Knights of medieval history and legend was made explicit; recruits were exhorted to see themselves as a modern, mechanized knightly order, spearheading the German people's struggle to destroy the Jewish/Bolshevik menace and carve out *Lebensraum* on the Eastern steppes. Volunteer enlistment, a rigorous training regime, a strong emphasis upon medieval symbolism and ceremonial, and a much less formal relationship between officers and men than in the regular army all contributed to produce an exceptionally high level of camaraderie and unit identification in Waffen-SS divisions, which in turn was reflected in their battle performance, especially in adversity (Stein 1966; Hastings 1981). These same factors must also have contributed to these units' dreadful record of cruelty and wholesale murder of prisoners and noncombatants; strong in-group sentiment combined with a dehumanizing ideology produced a particularly lethal reaction in the Waffen-SS, but a degree of callousness to the fate of 'outsiders' and a tendency to drastic retaliation for any injury to 'one of our own' is characteristic of elite military units the world over.

CONTEMPORARY PERSPECTIVES ON WARRIOR VALUES

Nearly fifty years on, other wars and warriors continue to thrive, both in fact and in fantasy. There is a persistent fascination with the trappings and technology of warfare, as evidenced by the mass consumption in the West of TV coverage of the 1991 Gulf War, the immense popularity of books on military history and exploits (with the Waffen-SS, in particular, enjoying a strong and steady following), and an enormous world-wide market for film and video representations of combat, in every guise from primeval warrior epics to futuristic battles on distant planets. In a bizarre, and one can only assume, a deeply misguided development, life has come to imitate art, with groups like the Colombian cocaine gangs claiming to obtain valuable tactical instruction from video extravaganzas starring Chuck Norris and Sylvester Stallone (Salazar 1992).

In all this proliferation of the warrior as entertainment, women continue to play a peripheral part, as they have always done in active warfare itself. A discussion of how and why the warrior role has never included females to any significant extent is beyond our present scope, but any movement towards opening military combat roles to women – and this is under way in several armies – must at least acknowledge the link between warrior values and stereotypically male role norms, if necessary adaptations are to be made. Masculine role prescriptions continue to emphasize qualities which are often little more than slightly diluted versions of warrior values; Marsh *et al.* (1978) and Dyck (1980) demonstrated this in their studies of young males' attitudes to toughness, fighting and brawling in England and Canada, respectively. In a review of ethnographic data from modern cultures as diverse as Mexico, Algeria, Spain and the Balkans, Gilmore (1990) identified common masculine themes of assertiveness, energy, physical and moral courage and sexual performance. Recent social psychological investigations show a very similar pattern. In the United States, Brannon and Juni (1984), in a factor analysis of young males' questionnaire responses, identified four main clusters of norms which they labelled 'avoidance of femininity', 'independence and self-confidence', 'achieving status' and 'aggressiveness'. A similar investigation by Thompson and Pleck (1987) revealed three norm-clusters: a need to achieve status and respect; mental, emotional and physical toughness; and avoidance of feminine activities and occupations.

I think I have demonstrated that sustained involvement by a group or society in lethal combat requires the evolution or adoption of some system of warrior values. Contemporary male role prescriptions seem well suited to be the foundation of such a code; they may not, of course, be so well adapted to other, perhaps more progressive, life paths.

REFERENCES

Bagehot, W. (1884) *Physics and Politics: Thoughts on the Application of the Principles of Natural Selection and Inheritance to Political Society*, 2nd edn, New York: Appleton.
Barash, D. P. and Lipton, J. E. (1985) *The Caveman and the Bomb: Human Nature, Evolution, and Nuclear War*, New York: McGraw-Hill.

Brannon, R. and Juni, S. (1984) 'A scale for measuring attitudes about masculinity', *Psychological Documents*, 14: 6–7.

Buruma, I. (1984) *Behind the Mask: On Sexual Demons, Sacred Mothers, Transvestites, Gangsters, Drifters and Other Japanese Cult Heroes*, New York: Pantheon Books.

Chagnon, N. A. (1988) 'Life histories, blood revenge and warfare in a tribal population', *Science*, 239: 985–92.

Coffman, E. M. (1968) *The War to End all Wars*, New York: Oxford University Press.

Daly, M. and Wilson, M. (1988) *Homicide*, New York: Aldine de Gruyter.

Dennen, J. van der (1990) 'Primitive war and the Ethnological Inventory Project', in J. van der Dennen and V. Falger (eds) *Sociobiology and Conflict*, London: Chapman & Hall.

Dyck, N. (1980) 'Booze, barrooms and scrapping: masculinity and violence in a western Canadian town', *Canadian Journal of Anthropology*, 1: 191–8.

Eibl-Eibesfeldt, I. (1974) 'The myth of the aggression-free hunter and gatherer society', in R. L. Holloway (ed.) *Primate Aggression, Territoriality and Xenophobia*, New York: Academic Press.

Ellis, J. (1973) *Armies in Revolution*, London: Croom Helm.

Erickson, J. (1975) *The Road to Stalingrad: Stalin's War with Germany*, vol. 1, London: Weidenfeld & Nicolson.

Fromm, E. (1973) *The Anatomy of Human Destructiveness*, New York: Holt, Rinehart & Winston.

Gardner, B. (1964) *Up the Line to Death: The War Poets 1914–1918*, London: Methuen.

Gilmore, D. D. (1990) *Manhood in the Making: Cultural Concepts of Masculinity*, New Haven: Yale University Press.

Gregor, T. (1977) *Mehinaku: The Drama of Daily Life in a Brazilian Indian Village*, Chicago: University of Chicago Press.

Halsted, J. L. (1965) *Romanticism*, Boston: Houghton Mifflin.

Hastings, M. (1981) *Das Reich*, London: Michael Joseph.

Herdt, G. H. (1982) 'Fetish and fantasy in Sambia initiation', in G. H. Herdt (ed.) *Rituals of Manhood*, Berkeley: University of California Press.

Holmes, R. (1985) *Firing Line*, London: Jonathan Cape.

Howard, M. (1976) *War in European History*, Oxford: Oxford University Press.

Ingraham, L. A. and Manning, F. J. (1980) 'Psychiatric battle casualties: the missing column in a war without replacements', *Military Review*, 60(8): 19–29.

Irwin, C. (1990) 'The Inuit and the evolution of limited group conflict', in J. van der Dennen and V. Falger (eds) *Sociobiology and Conflict*, London: Chapman & Hall.

Keppie, L. (1984) *The Making of the Roman Army*, London: Batsford.

La Fontaine, J. (1986) *Initiation*, Manchester: University of Manchester Press.

Lee, R. B. (1979) *The !Kung San: Men, Women and Work in a Foraging Society*, Cambridge: Cambridge University Press.

Marsh, P., Rosser, E. and Harre, R. (1978) *The Rules of Disorder*, London: Routledge.

Marshall, M. (1979) *Weekend Warriors*, Palo Alto, CA: Mayfield.

Marshall, S. L. A. (1946) *Men Against Fire*, New York: William Morrow.

Morris, I. (1975) *The Nobility of Failure: Tragic Heroes in the History of Japan*, New York: Holt, Rinehart & Winston.

Mundy, J. H. (1991) *Europe in the High Middle Ages 1150–1309*, 2nd edn, New York: Longman.

Robarchek, C. A. and Robarchek, C. (1992) 'Cultures of war and peace', in J. Silverberg and J. P. Grey (eds) *Aggression and Peacefulness in Humans and other Primates*, New York: Oxford University Press.

Saitoti, T. O. (1986) *The Worlds of a Masai Warrior: An Autobiography*, Berkeley: University of California Press.

Sajer, G. (1972) *The Forgotten Soldier*, New York: Ballantine.

Salazar, A. (1992) *Born to Die in Medellin*, London: Latin American Bureau.

Seaton, A. (1982) *The German Army 1933–1945*, London: Weidenfeld & Nicolson.

Segall, M. H. (1988) 'Cultural roots of aggressive behaviour', in M. H. Bond (ed.) *The Cross-cultural Challenge to Social Psychology*, Newbury Park, CA: Sage.

Shaw, R. P. and Wong, Y. (1988) *Genetic Seeds of Warfare: Evolution, Nationalism and Patriotism*, London: Unwin Hyman.

Spencer, H. (1873) *The Study of Sociology*, New York: Appleton.

Spencer, P. (1965) *The Samburu*, Berkeley: University of California Press.

Stein, G. (1966) *The Waffen-SS at War*, Oxford: Oxford University Press.

Thomas, E. M. (1965) *Warrior Herdsmen*, New York: Knopf.

Thompson, E. H., Jr and Pleck, J. H. (1987) 'The structure of male role norms', in M. S. Kimmel (ed.) *Changing Men: New Directions in Research on Men and Masculinity*, Newbury Park, CA: Sage.

Toland, J. (1976) *Adolf Hitler*, New York: Ballantine.

Tooby, J. and Cosmides, L. (1988) 'The evolution of war and its cognitive foundations', *Proceedings of the Institute of Evolution Studies*, 88: 1–15.

Tuchman, B. (1962) *The Guns of August*, London: Constable.

Wilson, E. O. (1978) *On Human Nature*, Cambridge, MA: Harvard University Press.

Wright, Q. (1942) *A Study of War*, Chicago: University of Chicago Press.

7

VIOLENCE BETWEEN MEN

John Archer

This chapter concerns the type of violence that occurs between individual or small groups of men. It therefore excludes organized violence on the level of the formal or informal group, which was covered in the two previous chapters. I first consider the relative frequency of these violent conflicts, compared to those between women; the evidence is necessarily indirect, involving records of homicide and other violent crimes, and a limited number of self-report studies. I then examine the demographic characteristics of the participants, to show that violence is more common amongst young men at the margins of society's institutions. I then consider where the violence occurs and the meanings of the context for the participants.

This leads to a consideration of the precipitating events, which often appear trivial at first sight. Such events, which are perceived as identity threats, may lead to the other person's quickly avoiding further involvement by apologizing or escaping; alternatively, they may initiate an aggressive exchange culminating in homicide. During the course of the exchange, verbal insults, threats and commands are issued – transforming the initial cause of the dispute into something more connected to self-esteem and reputation. A progression from lesser to greater acts of aggression is also found in animal fights, and principles which have been applied to their escalation are also relevant to human exchanges. Nevertheless, there are two aspects of human inter-male fights which are not found in animals: the involvement of alcohol and the use of weapons. These transform the nature of the exchange, and make homicide more likely.

Male violence is acted out against a background of beliefs about the importance of aggressive and violent acts for maintaining status in the male group and a sense of masculine identity. In the final section, I consider how violence forms part of traditional masculinity, and its importance is exaggerated in macho cultures.

THE EXTENT OF INTER-MALE VIOLENCE

Homicide statistics from the United States show that whereas a female victim is more likely to be killed by her husband, a man is more likely to be killed by another man outside the family. These statistics indicate the two principal features of male violence: within the home, it occurs towards women who are intimate partners; and outside the home, it occurs towards other men.

Daly and Wilson (1988) listed thirty-five studies which provide figures for same-sex homicides, mostly from various times during the twentieth century (but also from thirteenth- and fourteenth-century England, and nineteenth-century America). Although North American studies were well represented, the geographical location of the other studies was widespread, including Iceland, Germany, Denmark, India, Brazil, Zaïre, Botswana and Kenya. The sample size varied from 10 to over 3,000. In all studies except one, male homicide accounted for over 91 per cent of same-sex homicides. The exception contained fifteen killings by women, all involving dependent children.

A subsequent analysis (Daly and Wilson 1990) involved only cases where the killer and victim were unrelated, and included three large-scale studies (from the United States, United Kingdom and Canada). The proportion of male to female killings was found to be even larger than before. Aggregating the twenty studies shows that 97.2 per cent of 13,680 same-sex homicides were between men. What is striking about the figures in both reviews is their consistency across countries and cultures, and from the limited data available, during different historical times.

Analysis of homicide statistics has its drawbacks, since we are relying on cases of violence that have resulted in a culpable killing and have found their way into official statistics. Nevertheless, considering the difficulties in obtaining a representative sample of incidents of physical aggression between members of the same sex, they remain the most useful source of information. They have, as Daly and Wilson (1988) realized, one considerable advantage over studies involving a wider range of physical aggression: violence culminating in death is nearly always treated seriously, so that there will be less selective reporting than for lesser acts of violence.

Although there are likely to be biases in those non-lethal acts of physical aggression that result in prosecution, official figures can still provide supplementary information on the extent of male and female same-sex violence. For example, FBI crime statistics for the year 1971 show that males were the offenders in 90 per cent of cases (Harries 1974). Dobash and Dobash (1977–78) analysed police records of more than 3,000 cases involving violence from Glasgow and Edinburgh. Men were the offenders in 91.4 per cent of cases: 51.8 per cent involved inter-male violence, and in 39.5 per cent a woman was the victim. Only 32 of the 1,489 cases of inter-male violence occurred towards a family member (whereas 841 of the 1,136 male assaults on women were to a family member, 75.8 per cent of which were to their wives).

Self-report studies of delinquency have shown a higher proportion of female involvement in aggressive behaviour than the crime figures suggest (Campbell 1986b). Campbell found frequent involvement in fighting at some point in the past lives of British schoolgirls and in two samples of female offenders. A minority said they had been involved in more serious acts of violence. Although we have to be wary of the accuracy of such self-reports, the study does at least look beyond crime statistics for evidence on physical aggression. In the present context, it is unfortunate that there were only female respondents.

Gergen (1990) asked 150 male and female American undergraduates questions about their involvement in physical aggression and playful fighting ('horseplay') over the previous three years. The results were expressed in terms of mean scores (reflecting both numbers of items and their frequencies) for the two types of activity: males showed more than twice as much physical aggression to other males than females did to other females. When the frequency of specific actions was considered, men showed most of these more frequently: for example, 60 per cent had punched, 57 per cent shoved, 52 per cent had had a physical fight and 40 per cent hit another with an object. These figures compared with 12–18 per cent for the same items amongst the women. Some actions were more characteristic of female aggression: these were scratching (36 versus 18 per cent), pinching (13 versus 11 per cent) and kicking (19 versus 13 per cent). The first two are, of course, stereotypically feminine acts. Overall, this study found that women used physical aggression less often to their own sex than men did to theirs, and that they used less damaging acts when they did aggress.

Gladue (1991a) based a questionnaire on one developed by Olweus *et al.* (1980) for adolescents, which had shown high reliability with peer ratings. He factor analysed data from male and female students separately, and found the same factor structure in each case, although the order of these factors was different: physical aggression accounted for 32.6 per cent of the variance amongst the men and only 5.6 per cent amongst the women. Men scored 0.8 of a standard deviation higher than women for physical aggression in this study, and 1.01 higher in another sample (Gladue 1991b). Although the inventory did not specify the sex of the antagonist, the items on this sub-scale were such that one would expect them to refer to within-sex aggression (for example, 'When another person picks a fight with me, I fight back').

A rather different self-report method was used by Felson (1984). He interviewed samples of the general population, ex-offenders and ex-psychiatric patients from Albany County, New York. They were asked to provide detailed descriptions of an aggressive social interaction in each of four categories of severity: where anger, but no overt aggression, was provoked; where verbal aggression occurred; where a physical exchange, involving hitting with the fist or slapping, took place; and where a weapon (knife or gun) had been involved. Their analysis showed that conflicts were more likely to

123

lead to physical violence when they involved two men than when they involved two women or a woman and a man.

The studies described so far all involve people's accounts of their violent acts, and they provide some, albeit limited, evidence that men show substantially more physical aggression to other men than women do to other women. Nevertheless, it is well known that considerations of self-presentation affect the relationship between the rhetoric and underlying actions so as to distort accounts in various ways (Marsh 1982). This is particularly likely to be the case with young males, whose social talk – or 'bullshitting' – provides a way of enhancing status in their group (although filling out an anonymous questionnaire would reduce this influence). Two possible ways of seeking to overcome this problem are, first, to seek accounts from people not involved in the conflict (for example, Felson *et al.* 1986), and, secondly, to try to carry out direct observations of fighting.

The second of these is extremely difficult to carry out in the community. It is therefore hardly surprising that there are few such direct observational studies outside of institutions. Graham *et al.* (1980) reported the results of barroom aggressive incidents in Vancouver. During 303 two-hour observation periods, there were 160 such incidents, ranging from mild insults to physical exchanges. Unfortunately, their study did not provide information on the relative frequency amongst men and women, or even on the proportions of men and women found in the bars. Depp (1976) observed violent behaviour over 10 months in a mental hospital in Washington, DC, and found that although the sex ratio was about equal, violence was more likely to be between males (who accounted for 63 per cent of the assailants and 62 per cent of the victims). Most female assaults were to other females.

Overall, the various sources of evidence on within-sex aggression indicate that the most severe forms of violence – including homicide – occur mostly between males. All forms of physical aggression – with the exception of some less damaging forms such as scratching and pinching – occur more frequently between men than women. The large magnitude of the sex differences in physical aggression contrasts with much smaller differences between the sexes found in psychological studies of aggression (Eagley and Steffen 1986: chap. 1), which concentrate on laboratory simulations, questionnaires and some field experiments.

THE DEMOGRAPHIC AND SOCIETAL FEATURES OF MALE VIOLENCE

It is not just men who are more likely to commit violent acts to other men, but men of a certain age range. It is well known that most violent crime is committed by young men. Based on FBI reports, Harries (1974) indicated that 59.2 per cent of violent crime in the United States (in 1971) was committed by males under 24 years of age, and a further 22.4 per cent by those between 25 and 34. Figures for same-sex homicides in Canada, the United Kingdom, Chicago and Detroit (between 1965 and 1986) showed very pronounced peaks between 24 and 27 years of age (Daly and Wilson 1990: 92–3).

Various explanations have been offered for this concentration at younger ages. They include the following: Darwin's theory of sexual selection predicts that inter-male competition will be most pronounced when sexual activity is highest (Daly and Wilson 1988, 1990; see Chapter 14); the high concentration of testosterone in young males may promote aggression as it does in many other birds and mammals (see Chapter 13); the exercise of power erupts into overt violence where status and identity are uncertain (Tedeschi *et al.* 1977; see Chapter 16); cultural values in young male groups are likely to involve exaggerated emphasis on masculinity being attained through violent and risky activities (for example, Beynon 1989; Chapters 5 and 14). As indicated in Chapter 1, these are not necessarily competing explanations. Some operate on different levels of analysis, and others concentrate on one important influence while neglecting another. A full understanding of male violence is likely to arise from a synthesis of these different possible influences (Chapter 18).

Inter-male violence is more likely to occur amongst those who are outside the mainstream institutions of paid employment and marriage. Homicide figures for Detroit in 1972 indicate that unemployed men are over-represented by about four times amongst both offenders and their victims. Unmarried men are also over-represented, but only by about 60 per cent (Daly and Wilson 1988). Farrington *et al.* (1982) found that working-class boys who reported most fights were likely to be from poorer backgrounds, and to have unstable employment records. Again, an evolutionary explanation can be offered, on this occasion the riskiness of the strategy being matched to the lack of alternative ways of obtaining resources and status (Daly and Wilson 1990; Chapter 14).

CONTEXT

As Campbell (1986a) pointed out, the reported rate for assaults is much higher in cities than in rural areas in the United States, thus confirming the general impression people have about the relative safety of cities and country areas. Most assaults occur in low-income neighbourhoods, and around half take place in outside locations near the home of the victim, principally the street (Harries 1974): this follows from the large proportion of assaults that result from arguments between friends or acquaintances.

The context in which acts of violence occur can be understood in terms of the lives of the people who live there (Campbell 1986a). The main reason that the streets of poor urban areas are the places where much inter-male violence occurs is because they are designated as male territory, particularly in US black and Hispanic cultures. Such cultures show a high degree of gender-role polarization, which is accompanied by antagonism between the sexes and their spatial segregation. For various reasons, men spend a lot of time out of the home, in a male subculture composed of individuals seeking to make a living in differing ways, often outside the law.

The stereotype of the western film, of fights, brawls and shoot-outs occurring in the local saloon, has only a partial basis in reality. Harries (1974) reported that 5.7 per cent of homicides occurred in taverns or liquor stores. This is still disproportionate to the time people spend there compared to other locations, although the overall figure masks large differences between individual bars and pubs (Marsh 1980; Felson *et al.* 1986). Daly and Wilson (1988) noted that in other places and at other times (for example, in nineteenth-century Phila-delphia), the typical homicide arose from a brawl or quarrel in a drinking environment. In contemporary times, many arguments and disputes begin in bars and continue as violent exchanges in adjoining car parks and streets (Farrington *et al.* 1982). Two features would seem to be important in consider-ing bars as locations for inter-male violence: the cognitive effects of alcohol and the masculine tradition of bars. I shall discuss the first of these in a later section.

Considering the masculine tradition of the bar, Felson *et al.* (1986) noted that this creates the opportunity for conflict by bringing together in one location a violence-prone section of the community; namely, young males. Bars are also places where issues of social control are problematic: for example, disputes may arise from turns on pool tables and other games, who should be served and, above all, over refusal by the bartender to serve a customer. The bartender may not be recognized as a legitimate source of authority, and some may handle conflict insensitively owing to intoxication (Marsh 1980). Thus the bar is a place where rights and obligations may not be clear-cut, leaving it open for people to view the situation from the perspective of a personal set of values.

Felson *et al.* (1986) interviewed bartenders and bar-owners in the Albany area of New York and around Dublin about instances of verbal and physical aggression in their bars. The most common source of conflict was refusal to serve a customer; fights over the opposite sex, insults and disruptive behaviour were also common reasons for conflict. As expected, aggressive exchanges occurred more commonly amongst men than women. The best predictor of both verbal and physical aggression was the average age of the patrons: the younger they were, the more likely there was to be both verbal and physical aggression, and violent exchanges. Aggressive customers were also less likely to be regulars at the bar. Younger males were more likely to escalate from verbal to physical aggression, and in the United States this applied particu-larly to those who were drunk.

The studies described in this section identify certain locations where males – particularly younger working-class males – congregate as being the places where fights are most likely to occur. In the next two sections, we look at the reasons why aggressive exchanges start, and how they progress when they are under way.

PRECIPITATING ACTS

The immediately preceding cause of physical aggression between adult males is usually an escalating series of hostile verbal acts including insults and threats. The original source of the conflict is often apparently trivial when viewed in retrospect – and the violence which results appears out of all proportion to what started it. We therefore have to consider not just the precipitating act, but also the subsequent exchange. The need to do this can be illustrated by the classic study of the motives for murder by Wolfgang (1958). He analysed the files of the Philadelphia Police Department during the period 1948–52. As Daly and Wilson (1988) noted, the most frequent category was, in Wolfgang's words, 'an altercation of relatively trivial origin; insult, curse, jostling, etc.'. Subsequent studies have found similar results (Daly and Wilson 1988), and they are at first sight puzzling. However, to label the acts 'trivial' reveals more about some researchers' inability to understand them than about their meaning to the participants (Campbell 1986a; Daly and Wilson 1988). Not only is this meaning of crucial importance, but its significance becomes transformed during the social exchange which follows it.

In this context, most commentators have emphasized the impact of violation of social rules, and how these are accentuated by verbal threats and insults, so that the dispute becomes one about reputation and social identity. Both Campbell (1986a) and Daly and Wilson (1988) point out that these are of much greater importance in male groups where the impact of the law or moral restraints are weak or absent. Under such circumstances 'a man's reputation depends in part upon the maintenance of a credible threat of violence' (Daly and Wilson 1988: 128).

Examples of the need to 'establish a reputation' as a hard man by violence can be found in autobiographical accounts of men living under these conditions. A good example is the quote from John Allen in Anne Campbell's chapter. Jimmy Boyle was brought up in the old working-class area of Glasgow and moved from boys' gangs, to petty break-ins and minor violence, finally graduating to a more serious career in violent crime. Of his early gang fights, he said: 'The one giving out the most stitches got the reputation. It also made others think twice before coming near you' (Boyle 1977: 67). About a later time, he wrote: 'I was busy thieving and fighting, still trying to gain a position for myself, which I already had, but couldn't recognise' (p. 85). Daly and Wilson considered a wider range of historical and cross-cultural evidence to show that having killed other men is often considered a status asset. They go further to suggest that this generally applies in pre-state societies.

Daly and Wilson's argument is that status or reputation gained in this way is crucial amongst male groups, since anyone not able to project himself physically will be helpless to stop his possessions – and his women – being taken by any other man who cares to try. From an evolutionary perspective, men in this position would leave few, if any, offspring (except of course under the protected conditions of today). This analysis provides a reason why apparently trivial altercations should have such violent outcomes. They are not really about trivial matters, but about the relative status of the protagonists: one of them cannot back down without rendering himself subordinate and less powerful in the social group. He has to save face.

Berkowitz (1982) has argued that emphasizing social position ignores anger as an instigator of aggression. In his interview studies of the causes of violence amongst men convicted of assault, he found that most incidents involved angry reactions to insults and threats, without apparent thought of the social impact of these reactions (Berkowitz 1978, 1986). Farrington *et al.* (1982) asked a sample of British working-class males, aged 18 to 19, to give an account of the most vicious fight in which they had been involved. These consisted either of individual or group confrontations, and the two categories showed a number of differences: individual fights were less likely to occur in a pub or street, and more likely to arise from a provocation that caused anger, such as an insult to the person or his partner. Such findings were used by Berkowitz to argue that an immediate reaction to an aversive event rather than striving for status is the cause of inter-male violence in many instances.

Nevertheless, the generation of anger is not necessarily incompatible with a status-management interpretation (Campbell, personal communication). Anger is the emotion associated with feeling challenged and humiliated; that is, it is generated by a threat to the person's sense of identity. Where there is a group fight, the immediate cause is likely to be more instrumental, and the fight more obviously related to reputation, which is also important for identity.

In many cases, trivial disputes between men escalate into damaging fights when there is no obvious necessity for the protagonists to gain or keep a reputation as 'someone who takes no shit'. Anger is again the mediating emotion. Many of the common precipitating events for homicide and other serious acts of violence, such as sexual jealousy, territorial or property disputes (Daly and Wilson 1990), provoke aggression amongst a wide cross-section of the male population. In other cases, the issue is one which is personally important to one of the protagonists, but not necessarily to his status in a community or peer group.

Daily newspapers often contain reports of such disputes which have ended in tragedy, even in countries where guns are not widely owned, such as the United Kingdom. The following three very sad examples come from the London newspaper *The Guardian*. The first involved a dispute between two neighbours over smoke from a barbecue, and led to one being fatally stabbed by the other. The second involved a dispute over a parking space, in which a lorry driver punched a greengrocer, who fell, fractured his skull and died. The third involved a 60-year-old man who stabbed to death his friend, aged 70, who had accused him of cheating at dominoes. We cannot say that winning such disputes was necessary to maintain status amongst a community or peer group. Instead, they involve a more personal sense of self-esteem, which is no less important than maintaining or losing face in a group, and is likely to have similar origins in the evolution of the male psyche (Chapter 14).

Blanchard and Blanchard (1989) viewed human aggression as being caused by violations of a sense of ownership (resource disputes) or by a violation of a complex and abstract set of rights and obligations. Felson (1984) reached a similar conclusion: he synthesized three existing theoretical approaches to human aggression – impression management, coercive power and punishment – to suggest that aggressive interactions normally begin when people violate norms or orders. Whether overt aggression is avoided or whether there is a progression to violence depends on the social interaction which follows the initial violation, as indicated in the next section. But as far as the precipitating event is concerned, there is a range of value systems that are likely to be central to a person's sense of self: they include important personal relationships, home, cherished possessions, religious and cultural beliefs, and other sources of status and identity which maintain a feeling of self-worth. Input discrepant with any of these is likely to initiate an aggressive exchange (Archer 1976, 1988). Sometimes this reaction will be generally understood; for example, in the case of sexual jealousy or a threat to important possessions. In other cases, it will be more personal, such as insulting someone's favourite football team. In other cases, it will be widely understood by people holding a particular belief, but not at all by those who do not share the belief (for example, the death threat to the British writer Salman Rushdie).

AGGRESSION AS A SOCIAL INTERACTION

We can only obtain a limited view by concentrating on precipitating events, since aggressive behaviour occurs in the context of a social exchange between two people (Felson 1984; Campbell 1986a). We therefore have to consider the interaction to which the initial event leads. The same provocation may in one case produce nothing further, and in another lead to death.

The aggressive exchanges of both humans and animals can be viewed as a series of 'moves' which escalate the conflict from threats to physically damaging acts, until one protagonist gives up. Since the study of animal fights has revealed a number of general principles, it is worth digressing to consider these principles, and whether they also apply to humans. Archer (1988: 159–208) provides a fuller description, the present discussion being restricted to outlining the general approach and briefly describing three specific theoretical models.

Fighting is widespread in the animal kingdom, and most animals have a range of aggressive activities in their repertoire; the aggressive exchange often begins at a distance, with the protagonists exchanging distinctive displays; these are 'low-cost' in terms of the energy expended and the risk of damage. If one or other animal does not withdraw, the exchange progresses to more intense activities involving closer contact and a higher risk of damage, the process of escalation. Fights stop when one animal abruptly ceases fighting, leaving the other one victorious.

To explain the evolutionary origins of many aspects of animal fighting, including escalation, Maynard Smith (1974, 1976, 1982) used a branch of applied mathematics called 'game theory'. This provides a logical framework for investigating the consequences of different fighting strategies relative to the others available in that population. It is necessary to use such a framework when considering the evolution of social behaviour, because, unlike non-social actions such as food-foraging, the consequences for fitness depend crucially on form and frequency of the strategies used by other animals.

Game theory enables the consequences of each type of interaction to be calculated from a pay-off matrix. The effectiveness of a particular strategy will depend on the other strategies, the costs incurred against each type of opponent (notably injuries), and the benefits of winning the conflict (in terms of resources). Since this is an evolutionary analysis, the consequences are expressed in terms of relative fitness; that is, their contribution to survival and reproduction. The outcome of each simulation is a change in the composition of the population, and this carries on through successive simulations (that is, generations), until a stable mix of strategies is reached. This equilibrium will only be stable providing the costs, benefits and types of fighting strategies remain constant.

These sorts of simulations were used to address a number of questions about the evolution of animal fights. One of the earliest was why many species used what ethologists called 'ritualized fighting' – threat displays rather than attack with a deadly weapon. The Hawk-Dove model (Maynard Smith 1976, 1982) showed that the evolution of ritualized or 'limited war' contests arose from the danger of retaliation in cases where both animals had damaging weapons, thus confirming the insight of Geist (1966). Fights between animals which do not possess dangerous weapons, such as toads and newts, are unrestrained: they escalate to high-intensity acts very quickly. This is also the case where the benefits of winning are high. Putting these two variables together, Maynard Smith (1982) showed that if there is no cost through time or energy expenditure, the probability of a rapidly escalated – rather than a ritualized – strategy evolving would be given by V/C where V is the benefit obtained from winning and C is the cost of injury.

The Hawk-Dove model makes a number of simplifying assumptions. Parker (1974) introduced a refinement in the form of the concept of assessment. He showed that any animal which, in advance of fighting, could assess its opponent's likely fighting ability would be at a selective advantage. It could withdraw without damage if its opponent's fighting ability ('Resource Holding Power' or RHP) was higher than its own, and attack with a high probability of winning if it were lower than its own. This would reduce the risk of fighting. Animals commonly use cues such as size, weapons or vocal capacity to assess their opponent's RHP (Archer 1988: 166–71). Parker's model extended the understanding of animal displays to recognize that they involve more than signalling possible intentions through the threat displays identified by ethologists (Archer 1992a: 176–200). Displays also advertise fighting prowess, and generally do so in a way that is difficult to mimic.

A model devised by Enquist *et al.* (1990) concerns two animals differing in RHP but having little or no information about this at the start of the fight. Escalation can be seen as a series of moves in an information-gathering process. Low-intensity acts provide only unreliable information about RHP, since they are not costly to perform and hence can be mimicked. High-intensity acts provide reliable information but are costly to perform. This Sequential Assessment model views the sequence as a process of statistical sampling, the aim of which is progressively to acquire more accurate information at the lowest possible cost. The decision on whether to keep escalating is based on the information available at each point. So far, tests of this model with fish (Enquist *et al.* 1990) indicate that its predictions are supported.

This account of game-theory models provides only a flavour of some of the more important models put forward in a diverse and active field. Although the original purpose was to provide a method for simulating the process of natural selection, once the concept of RHP had been introduced, models were also concerned with the way costs and benefits influenced decisions during fights: by being able to assess cues related to fitness, the animal was able to base its immediate decisions on these, and hence show flexibility.

We now return from this digression to ask what game-theory models can contribute to the understanding of human aggressive exchanges. First of all, it is apparent that humans are not a species which is endowed with dangerous natural weapons. We have neither teeth, claws nor horns; muscular strength is much less than that of our nearest relative, the chimpanzee. It follows from Maynard Smith's V/C rule that a stable, evolved strategy in early hominids would be to escalate fairly rapidly in an aggressive exchange, rather than showing the caution of an animal with dangerous weapons (Archer 1988). We would therefore not expect the ritualized roaring contests found in stags or the pushing contests found in some fish.

Nevertheless, this provides only a broad comparison with other animals. In practice, the detailed form of each exchange will, as in other species, depend on assessments. It is clear that fights between men seldom occur suddenly, and that they progress through a series of escalating 'moves' just as they do in other animals. Human aggressive interactions also show the non-verbal displays of hostile intent found in animals (Archer 1992a: 176–200), and shouting and posturing which serve to exaggerate and to assess RHP (Blanchard and Blanchard 1989). It is widely recognized that perceived size and strength are important for deciding whether a physical challenge is appropriate, and this is formalized in the weight categories used for boxing contests. What is unique to human aggressive exchanges is the use of language, and the specific role of insults, challenges and face-saving.

I shall use two studies to illustrate the dynamics of aggressive exchanges between men. The first (Luckenbill 1977) analysed the transactions leading to criminal homicides in seventy cases reconstructed from official records covering the period 1963–72 in a part of California. Although this study also included violent acts towards women, it is clear that these are very different, and that Luckenbill's attempts to generalize from inter-male violence were forced and misleading (Dobash and Dobash 1984). Murder was a culmination of an interchange between offender and victim resembling what Goffman (1967) had termed a 'character contest'. This refers to a confrontation in which one or both protagonists seek to save face at the other's expense by not backing down when confronted by accusations, insults, threats or challenges.

These exchanges, like animal fights, took a sequential form involving a series of 'moves'. The eventual victim began by issuing what the offender deemed to be an offensive move. At this point various replies were possible, but in most of these homicide cases, it was met by anger and verbal aggression or a physical challenge. In 14 per cent of exchanges physical aggression started here, but the typical case involved an escalating series of verbal and physical moves, including threats to kill the other. Once this sequence has begun, to break off would demonstrate weakness, so a 'working agreement' is entered into that violence is a suitable or desirable way of settling the contest. This often occurred when the victim would not comply with the offender's challenge or command, for example 'to shut up' or to apologize. In other cases, there was a counter-challenge, such as 'make me', and calling the other's bluff.

Once the sequence reached a commitment to physical aggression, in 64 per cent of cases the subsequent offender left the field to get a weapon, or an improvised weapon such as bottle or baseball bat. Daly and Wilson (1988) described several examples where the subsequent offender had been defeated in a fight, and then left temporarily, only to return with a gun.

Two differences are immediately apparent between this description and the sequence of moves in an animal fight. In animals a pragmatic decision is made on the basis of assessment of the fighting ability of the opponent and the importance of the resource over which they are fighting; but in human males, it seems that face-saving becomes itself a valuable 'resource' over which to fight and the stakes are increased accordingly. I shall offer some suggestions as to why this is so when considering the next study. A second difference is the involvement of weapons, which drastically alters assessments of fighting ability, and enables the loser of a fight to avenge defeat in a lethal way. I shall return to weapons later.

A second study of aggressive exchanges, by Felson (1984), was based on the self-reports of a community sample and of ex-offenders (see above). Each exchange began with a perceived offence. This was greeted by what Felson termed 'orders', requests or commands, to which either refusals to comply or reproaches (such as accusations or complaints) were made. At this point, an account or explanation of conduct was likely to be forthcoming, but it was generally ineffective when it followed rather than preceded the reproach. Alternatively, insults were given, thereby attacking the other person's reputation or identity. These were followed by verbal threats and, in violent exchanges, by physical attacks. Submission and mediation by a third party occur at the end of the sequence. Felson found no differences between the early parts of sequences which culminated in different levels of aggressive behaviour, namely, anger but no action, verbal abuse, a fist fight or a fight involving a weapon. These findings suggest that it is the sequence of inter-actions rather than the initial provoking act that determines the level of escalation, paralleling the importance of assessment in animals.

These and similar studies (for example, Felson and Steadman 1983) describe an escalating sequence, with the perceived need to save face or reputation by entering into a physical exchange arising at a particular point. What seems to be important in determining whether this point is reached is the extent to which a protagonist's self-esteem is threatened by the exchange (Campbell 1986a). As indicated above, this raises the stakes, and is equivalent to animals fighting over a more valuable resource. For a member of a marginal group, challenged in the presence of acquaintances he sees every day, performance will be crucially important for reputation, and hence self-esteem. Campbell (1986a) noted that marginal males will have fewer alternative ways of establishing self-esteem: they are likely to be unemployed, excluded from their households for much of the time, and generally to have little access to recognized sources of status. Reputation gained in conflicts therefore becomes a crucial resource.

There are two important influences which tend to transform mere assaults into homicides. They are alcohol and weapons. They also most clearly distinguish human from animal fights.

A large proportion of homicide assailants and victims have been drinking alcohol. Its influence is probably mediated in a variety of ways, direct and indirect. Gibbs (1986) summarized the cognitive effects of alcohol which are most likely to enhance aggression and to facilitate escalation. They include a narrowing of the perceptual field, so that specific actions are not seen in a wider context; effects on intellectual and verbal abilities which decrease the likelihood that accounts of actions will be provided and accepted; and an accentuated feeling of power and self-importance which makes perceived rule violation by others more likely, and one's own identity more easily threatened. Indirect influences include the situation where much drinking occurs, the bar, which has its own formal and informal rules, that are easily violated. Other situational influences were emphasized by Felson *et al.* (1986) in their study of bars, notably that a violence-prone section of the population is concentrated together.

A striking feature of the violent exchanges described by Daly and Wilson

(1988) is that they often culminate in homicide because one of the individuals has a gun, or goes to fetch one. In the United Kingdom, many street or club fights become life-threatening because one or other protagonist has a knife (for example, Hetherington 1992). The use of weapons in an otherwise unplanned fight which began with an argument can suddenly alter the balance of the opponents and end the fight in a tragic way. The chances of death resulting from aggravated assault when a gun is used is several times higher than for a knife, even though the gun is typically only fired once (Campbell 1986a).

It is instructive to view both weapons and alcohol in terms of game-theory models. If alcohol heightens a person's sense of their own power and import-ance, it will upset rational assessment of the opponent's fighting ability. As Billy Connolly put it in a song about Scottish drinking habits: 'Stone cold sober they come in like Mickey Rooney / Three pints later they go barging out like big John Wayne' (BBC TV programme, 17 August 1978). If alcohol increases awareness of rule-violation by others, it will accentuate the perceived importance of what is at stake in the dispute. By narrowing perception of cues surrounding the conflict, and lessening the impact of verbal accounts, it will decrease the influence of factors which tend to inhibit escalation. Alcohol will therefore accentuate the person's assessment of their own ability, increase the perceived value of what is at stake, and in other ways reduce inhibitions on the escalation process.

Game-theory models predict that animals with dangerous natural weapons typically show cautious fighting strategies, characterized by displays at a distance and trials of strength in which their damaging weapons are not used, before escalating to using the weapons (Archer 1988). Since unarmed humans lack natural weapons, we should expect them overall to have fewer constraints. Nevertheless, we would also expect to see assessment sequences, even if these are not the life-or-death matters they might be for red deer. However, a crucial question is whether evolved assessment rules can encompass arte-factual as well as natural weapons. The evidence suggests they can – but up to a point. Weapons such as sticks and stones are likely to have been around from early in hominid evolution. Even if they were not, the danger posed by such weapons, and others such as knives and swords, would be quickly learnt, and incorporated into the assessment sequence.

This applies to weapons which are openly displayed and do not operate at a distance. Where they are concealed and brought out at a crucial stage in the fight, any assessment will have been based on false information. Where one protagonist has a gun, the opponent will not be able to withdraw from its effective range of action. Here too the evolved assessment sequence will have been bypassed.

Campbell (1986a) raised the intriguing possibility that the predominant strategy in a population would change from one based on a fair fight to one based on immediate attack if the proportion of gun-owners were high. She derived this from an early game-theory model (Maynard Smith and Price

1983) which did not involve the assessment sequence; that is, it was concerned only with modelling evolutionary change. This raises two issues. The first is whether the logic of natural selection is transferable to people's subjective assessment of the most effective strategy to use in the face of different proportions of two or more strategies. The second is that the possession of a gun is not really a strategy, but an enabling device for a strategy. The model of Maynard Smith and Price (1983) showed the superiority of conditional over pure strategies. The presence of a gun allows the person the option of a dangerous move in a conditional strategy. To some extent, the widespread possession of guns takes away the point of an assessment phase, and renders the earlier games such as 'Hawk-Dove' more appropriate. But this will only happen when it is widely understood that most people carry weapons. Under other circumstances, as indicated above, guns are likely to upset the basis for rational decisions made during an escalating aggressive exchange.

MASCULINE VALUES AND MALE VIOLENCE

At various places in the preceding discussion I have referred to the importance of a masculine subculture for encouraging violent exchanges between men. The occurrence of such exchanges in locations such as the street or a bar, the importance of the exchange for face-saving and self-esteem, and the role of the audience in accentuating this process all reflect shared beliefs or social representations of masculinity.

Perhaps the most important feature of masculinity is that it is an achieved rather than an ascribed status. It arises from behaving in a particular way. During childhood, a boy can be ostracized because he does not or cannot reach acceptable standards of masculine behaviour; on the other hand, some girls may achieve honorary masculinity through being skilled at boys' games and activities (Archer 1992b). A boy's self-esteem is derived from taking part in a range of physical activities, and there is emphasis on toughness for defining status (see Chapter 16). During adulthood, self-esteem is derived from a wider range of activities, notably occupational achievement. As we have seen, for men in marginal urban communities this source of status is generally not available. Status arises from challenges and counter-challenges within the male street community.

Several studies have sought to measure the perceived components of masculinity in a questionnaire format. For example, Thompson and Pleck (1986) devised a 'male role norm scale' by asking college men to rate fifty-seven belief statements about men's expected behaviour (such as 'A man should not disclose pains'). The original list came from an earlier scale which comprised the following four clusters of items: avoidance of femininity, achieving status, cultivating independence and self-confidence, and a willingness to be aggressive.

Thompson and Pleck found that scores on their items clustered on three factors. The first involved gaining status and the respect of others; the second, self-reliance and toughness; and the third, avoidance of femininity. There were low but significant correlations between these three factors. Items concerning aggression were loaded on the second factor, and included 'A man should be ready to fight', and 'Fists are sometimes necessary'. Items indicating mental toughness ('I like a guy who does not complain'), and a liking for danger ('A real man enjoys a bit of danger') were also located there.

These scales represent beliefs about men's expected behaviour; that is, stereotypic attributes. The student sample used by Thompson and Pleck did not endorse them very strongly for themselves, but other evidence (see below) indicates that endorsement of such values is related to behaviour. On the face of it, the attributes describe a traditional pattern of masculine values. In modern western societies, they are often referred to as 'macho' attributes when displayed in middle-class circles. Although the term 'macho' is derived from the Spanish *'machismo'*, to prove one's masculinity by courageous action, a wider range of attributes is usually meant by the term. These include aggressiveness, toughness and risk-taking, which have been highlighted in this chapter, but also viewing women as sex objects (see Chapter 11). In a street or pre-state community, such a man will be successful in obtaining resources; he will also obtain sexual access to women where they are typically guarded or protected by men (Daly and Wilson 1988). Such attributes will also be valued in occupations such as the army and the police where physical attributes, fighting ability, toughness and courage are valued, but there will always be a tension between the street cop or 'squaddie' and those in a managerial role. Amongst the educated classes in western societies, the full expression of macho attributes will be curtailed, and status sought in other ways, as indicated above. Fights and taking physical risks are likely to be counter-productive, and macho sexual values unacceptable to emancipated women.

Mosher and Sirkin (1984) constructed a rating scale (the Hypermasculinity Inventory or HMI) to measure what they called 'a macho personality constellation'. The items on their scale were derived from conversations among all-male peer groups of US men, and involved three sub-scales. Factor analysis showed that the scale measured an overall constellation, with three highly intercorrelated components. These were callous sexual attitudes, conceptions of violence as manly, and viewing danger as exciting. These sub-scales obviously overlap with those discussed above in relation to the male role norm scale: only callous sexual attitudes were not represented there. It does, however, represent a common feature of conversations in young male groups (Mosher and Sirkin 1984).

High scores on the HMI were related to a history of sexual aggression, and arousal on exposure to rape imagery (Mosher and Anderson 1986), self-reported juvenile delinquency, alcohol and other drug intake, and driving while intoxicated (Mosher and Sirkin 1984). They were also related to scores on more general gender-trait and attitude scales (Archer and Rhodes 1989). Examination of the HMI sub-scales indicates that one component, conceptions of violence as manly, predicts violent behaviour towards other men, and another, callous sexual attitudes, predicts sexual violence towards women (because it legitimizes such violence by denigrating women and selectively interpreting their responses).

One drawback of the rating-scale approach is that it only captures some surface aspects of what is a coherent set of cultural values. Ideally, rating-scale items need to be integrated with other approaches lest they become separated from the underlying culture. In western societies, we should expect such values to be endorsed most strongly where a legal and moral framework is weak or absent, such as prison communities, the urban underclass, soldiers at war, and criminal subcultures (for example, Beynon 1989; Boyle 1977; McVicar 1982). Macho values may also be attractive for a wider range of young men, who partially act them out while driving a car, or playing contact sports, or in the form of acts of bravado or sexist banter in all-male groups. Alternatively, they may indulge in fantasy, no doubt fuelled by the constant outpouring of films that reflect exaggeratedly macho values. Occasionally, alienated young men act out the fictional portrayal of macho acts of violence in a dramatic way. In the United Kingdom, Michael Ryan, the Hungerford multiple killer of 1987, is perhaps the best-known example.

In this section, I have concentrated on describing those aspects of traditional masculine and macho values which are most related to violence between men. This leaves open a number of questions, foremost among them the extent to which they reflect only culturally acquired values, or whether they also reflect a traditional pattern of masculinity that was evolutionarily important. I would endorse Daly and Wilson's view that such attributes were necessary for survival and reproduction in pre-state communities. However, it is likely that attributes useful for supporting this traditional pattern of masculinity now actually conflict with the achievement of occupational status in the modern state. This, anyway, is the view of Dabbs (1992) in seeking to explain why serum testosterone levels were inversely related to occupational status in a large sample of US men. I shall return to this general issue in Chapter 16, on power explanations of male violence.

CONCLUSIONS

It is clear from several types of evidence that same-sex physical aggression is more common between men than women, and this becomes more pronounced with severe forms of violence. Young men at the margins of society are particularly prone to violent fights, and these mostly occur on the streets around where the protagonists live, and also in and around bars and other places selling alcohol. Violent acts usually develop from an escalating exchange of verbal aggression and minor physical acts. The exchange begins with an event which one of the protagonists perceives as an identity threat. Although this often appears trivial to outsiders, or even to the protagonists in retrospect, it initiates a series of threats, insults and commands which transform the nature of the dispute into one which arouses anger through perceived threats to personal self-esteem or becomes a matter of face-saving and reputation.

The series of events in such exchanges parallel the escalation of aggressive acts found in animal fights, and the application of game theory to these has revealed a number of principles which can be applied to human fights. These include the importance of assessing the opponent in advance of physical aggression, and matching escalation to what is at stake in the fight. In the human case, face-saving and reputation operate to inflate greatly the perceived value of winning the fight. Alcohol and weapons are both common in homicide cases: the first will distort the assessment process, and inflate the importance of the dispute, and the second will make any assessment dangerously unreliable.

The cultural background to inter-male violence concerns a set of beliefs about the importance of toughness and physical aggression for masculinity, which was probably appropriate throughout human evolution, and is still widely applicable today. Among the educated western middle class, such values are given the somewhat negative level of 'macho', and if carried too far may be counter-productive for attaining status in the modern world.

ACKNOWLEDGEMENTS

I would like to thank Anne Campbell for her helpful comments on this chapter, which was written while I was a Simon Industrial and Professional Fellow at the University of Manchester, 1991–92.

REFERENCES

Archer, J. (1976) 'The organization of aggression and fear in vertebrates', in P. P. G. Bateson and P. Klopfer (eds) *Perspectives in Ethology 2*, New York: Plenum, pp. 231–98.
—— (1988) *The Behavioural Biology of Aggression*, Cambridge and New York: Cambridge University Press.
—— (1990) 'The influence of testosterone on human aggression', *British Journal of Psychology*, 82: 1–28.
—— (1992a) *Ethology and Human Development*, Hemel Hempstead, UK: Harvester Wheatsheaf.
—— (1992b) 'Childhood gender roles: social context and organisation', in H. McGurk (ed.) *Childhood Social Development: Contemporary Perspectives*, Hove, UK, and Hillsdale, NJ: Erlbaum, pp. 31–61.
Archer, J. and Rhodes, C. (1989) 'The relationship between gender-related traits and attitudes', *British Journal of Social Psychology*, 28: 149–57.
Berkowitz, L. (1978) 'Is criminal violence normative behavior? hostile and instrumental aggression in violent incidents', *Journal of Research in Crime and Delinquency*, 15: 148–61.
—— (1982) 'Violence and rule-following behaviour', in P. Marsh and A. Campbell (eds) *Aggression and Violence*, Oxford: Blackwell, pp. 91–101.

———— (1986) 'Some varieties of human aggression: criminal violence as coercion, rule-following, impression management and impulsive behavior', in A. Campbell and J. J. Gibbs (eds) *Violent Transactions: The Limits of Personality*, Oxford: Blackwell, pp. 87–103.

Beynon, J. (1989) 'A school for men: an ethnographic case study of routine violence in schooling', in J. Archer and K. Browne (eds) *Human Aggression: Naturalistic Approaches*, London and New York: Routledge, pp. 122–50.

Blanchard, D. C. and Blanchard, R. J. (1989) 'Experimental animal models of aggression: what do they say about human behaviour?', in J. Archer and K. Browne (eds), *Human Aggression: Naturalistic Approaches*, London and New York: Routledge, pp. 94–121.

Boyle, J. (1977) *A Sense of Freedom*, London: Pan Books.

Campbell, A. (1986a) 'The streets and violence', in A. Campbell and J. J. Gibbs (eds), *Violent Transactions: The Limits of Personality*, Oxford: Blackwell, pp. 115–32.

————(1986b) 'Self-report of fighting by females', *British Journal of Criminology*, 26: 28–46.

Dabbs, J. M. Jr. (1992) 'Testosterone and occupational achievement', *Social Forces*, 70: 813–24.

Daly, M. and Wilson, M. (1988) *Homicide*, New York: Aldine de Gruyter.

———— (1990) 'Killing the competition: female/female and male/male competition', *Human Nature*, 1: 81–107.

Depp, F. C. (1976) 'Violent behavior patterns on psychiatric wards', *Aggressive Behavior*, 2: 295–306.

Dobash, R. E. and Dobash, R. P. (1977–8) 'Wives: the "appropriate" victims of marital violence', *Victimology: An International Journal*, 2: 426–42.

———— (1984) 'The nature and antecedents of violent events', *British Journal of Criminology*, 24: 269–88.

Eagly, A. and Steffen, V. J. (1986) 'Gender and aggressive behavior: a meta-analytic review of the social psychological literature', *Psychological Bulletin*, 100: 309–30.

Enquist, M., Leimar, O., Ljungberg, T., Mallner, Y. and Segerdahl, N. (1990) 'A test of the sequential assessment game: fighting in the cichlid fish *Nannacara anomala*', *Animal Behaviour*, 40: 1–14.

Farrington, D. P., Berkowitz, L. and West, D. J. (1982) 'Differences between individual and group fights', *British Journal of Social Psychology*, 21: 323–33.

Felson, R. B. (1984) 'Patterns of aggressive social interactions', in A. Mummendey (ed.) *Social Psychology of Aggression: From Individual Behavior to Social Interaction*, Berlin: Springer-Verlag, pp. 107–26.

Felson, R. B., Baccaglini, W. and Gmelch, G. (1986) 'Bar-room brawls: aggression and violence in Irish and American bars', in A. Campbell and J. J. Gibbs (eds) *Violent Transactions: The Limits of Personality*, Oxford: Blackwell, pp. 153–66.

Felson, R. B. and Steadman, H. J. (1983) 'Situational factors in disputes leading to criminal violence', *Criminology*, 21: 59–74.

Geist, V. (1966) 'The evolution of horn-like organs', *Behaviour*, 27: 175–214.

Gergen, M. (1990) 'Beyond the evil empire: horseplay and aggression', *Aggressive Behavior*, 16: 381–98.

Gibbs, J. J. (1986) 'Alcohol consumption, cognition and context: examining tavern violence', in A. Campbell and J. J. Gibbs (eds) *Violent Transactions: The Limits of Personality*, Oxford: Blackwell, pp. 133–51.

Gladue, B. A. (1991a) 'Qualitative and quantitative sex differences in self-reported aggressive behavioral characteristics', *Psychological Reports*, 68: 675–84.

———— (1991b) 'Aggressive behavioral characteristics, hormones, and sexual orientation in men and women', *Aggressive Behavior*, 17: 313–26.

Goffman, E. (1967) *Interactional Ritual: Essays on Face-to-Face Behavior*, New York: Doubleday.

Graham, K., La Rocque, L., Yetman, R., Ross, T. J. and Guistra, E. (1980) 'Aggression and barroom environments', *Journal of Studies in Alcohol*, 41: 277–92.

Harries, K. (1974) *The Geography of Crime and Justice*, New York: McGraw-Hill.

Hetherington, P. (1992) 'Winning back streets from hard men of Glasgow', *The Guardian*, London (29 June), p. 24.

Luckenbill, D. F. (1977) 'Criminal homicide as a situated transaction', *Social Problems*, 25: 176–86.

McVicar, J. (1982) 'Violence in prisons', in P. Marsh and A. Campbell (eds) *Aggression and Violence*, Oxford: Blackwell, pp. 200–14.

Marsh, P. (1980) 'Violence at the pub', *New Society*, 52: 210–12.

—— (1982) 'Rhetorics of violence', in P. Marsh and A. Campbell (eds) *Aggression and Violence*, Oxford: Blackwell, pp. 102–17.

Maynard Smith, J. (1974) 'The theory of games and the evolution of animal conflicts', *Journal of Theoretical Biology*, 47: 209–21.

—— (1976) 'Evolution and the theory of games', *American Scientist*, 64: 41–5.

—— (1982) *Evolution and the Theory of Games*, Cambridge and New York: Cambridge University Press.

Maynard Smith, J. and Price, G. R. (1973) 'The logic of animal conflict', *Nature*, 246: 15–18.

Mosher, D. L. and Anderson, R. D. (1986) 'Macho personality, sexual aggression, and reactions to guided imagery of realistic rape', *Journal of Research in Personality*, 20: 77–94.

Mosher, D. L. and Sirkin, M. (1984) 'Measuring a macho personality constellation', *Journal of Research in Personality*, 18: 150–63.

Olweus, D., Matteson, A., Schalling, D. and Low, H. (1980) 'Testosterone, aggression, physical and personality dimensions in normal adolescent males', *Psychosomatic Medicine*, 42: 253–69.

Parker, G. A. (1974) 'Assessment strategy and the evolution of fighting behavior', *Journal of Theoretical Biology*, 47: 223–43.

Tedeschi, J. T., Gaes, G. G. and Rivera, A. N. (1977) 'Aggression and the use of coercive power', *Journal of Social Issues*, 33: 101–25.

Thompson, E. H. and Pleck, J. H. (1986) 'The structure of male role norms', *American Behavioral Scientist*, 29: 531–43.

Wolfgang, M. E. (1958) *Patterns of Criminal Homicide*, Philadelphia, PA: University of Pennsylvania Press.

Part III

VIOLENCE TOWARDS WOMEN AND CHILDREN

8

PUTTING RELATIONSHIP AGGRESSION IN ITS PLACE

Contextualizing some recent research

Robin Goodwin

A brief glance at recent social psychology journals shows that the study of aggression in close relationships has increased markedly over the last decade. Researchers working in this area have examined a number of different aspects of such aggression and a variety of possible causal and contributing factors (Gryl *et al.* 1991; Stets and Pirog-Good 1990). Recent work has concentrated on the examination of dyadic variables, focusing on compliance-gaining behaviour (Gordon and Donat 1992), communication skills (Burgoyne and Spitzberg 1992) and relationship dimensions such as love and ambivalence (Gryl *et al.* 1991). It now seems that between 50 per cent (Breslin *et al.* 1990) and 60 per cent (Marshall and Rose 1987) of those questioned have been the recipients of physical aggression, and whilst these figures vary with the stage of the relationship being analysed (Shotland 1989, 1992), the methodologies used (George *et al.* 1992) and the definition of 'physical aggression' (George *et al.* 1992), there can be little doubt that relationship aggression is frequently persistent and severe, often occurring within a context of intimidation and violence (Dobash *et al.* 1992). In this chapter, both sexual and non-sexual aggression will be considered in arguing that relationship aggression research has become too atextual, ignoring not only its meaning to the participants involved but also the social, cultural and historical frameworks within which such aggression is located.

PROBLEMS WITH THE 'COUNTING' APPROACH

A first objection to much of the present research is the failure of many investigators to embed their descriptions of what occurs in a relationship in the participant's own phenomenological world. Consider some recent research on aggression in dating relationships. Here, simple lists of aggressive behaviour predominate, although they actually tell us very little about what is going on in the mind of the aggressor – or indeed the victim. The widely used Conflict Tactics Scales (Straus 1979) involve only the form and frequency of aggressive acts. The acts are taken out of context (Dobash *et al.* 1992; Walker 1990), so that it is difficult to tell whether they are minor or severe in terms of their consequences. Such research is often labelled 'marital violence' or 'dating violence', without addressing this issue (see Chapter 1). Thus, intention and consequences are often ignored, although 'being hit' by a 5-foot pensioner is likely to have very different psychological (and physical) consequences from being hit by a 6-foot-6 boxer. The results of this approach are frequently misleading, and have led to mistaken claims about the sexual similarity in rates of relationship aggression and the misinterpretation of the consequences of particular, even narrowly defined, acts (Dobash *et al.* 1992: see also Chapter 1 of this volume).

Given the complex interrelationship between any couple, it is doubtful whether a simple 'shopping list' approach can ever be appropriate for revealing the meaning of any particular violent action (cf. Dobash *et al.* 1992). What is needed instead is a series of in-depth investigations which contextualize the aggression in terms of the relationship as a whole; they would explore themes such as the couple's needs and commitments, and the sequences of emotions which may precede and follow a violent action. Variables could be examined in terms of 'chains of interactions' as proposed in the interdependence model of Kelley *et al.* (1983). Here, relationship interactions are seen as existing in 'causal loops', with each individual's chain of affect, thought and action producing further effects both within their own chain and also in their partner's chain. In the first case this might be a further thought about whether a violent action would have a particular effect, followed by an apology: in the second, a sense of anguish may be followed by a thought that 'I have to leave this man'. This 'chaining' process continues throughout the present and subsequent interactions. This approach provides a rich descriptive account of the complex interrelationship between action, thought, affect and interpretation that characterizes any relationship process. Multiple methods can be used to collect the data, including 'speak aloud' techniques, diaries and in-depth interviews.

Any investigation using this framework is necessarily extremely complex. Other models, more specifically concerned with relationship aggression, may also be valuable for phenomenological investigations. Riggs and O'Leary (1989) proposed a three-stage cognitive model which aims to explain the incidence of courtship aggression. Its first set of predictors examines *who* will become aggressive. This comprises constructs found to be significant predictors in previous research: (1) exposure to models of aggression in intimate relationships (including the parent's own aggression towards the child); (2) acceptance of aggression as an appropriate response to conflict, stress or threat; (3) personality factors; (4) arousal; (5) prior use of aggression/coercion.

The second set of predictors in Riggs and O'Leary's model is concerned with predicting *when* aggression will occur. Here the other's use of aggression, stress, alcohol and relationship conflict have all been deemed important in previous investigations. Physical location could also be considered here: certain collegiate institutions and occupations, for example, may draw more sexually aggressive males, who then receive support for their aggression from their similar peers (Shotland 1992). The perceived stage of the relationship is also likely to be significant, although the partners may hold quite different views on exactly *which* stage they have reached (Shotland 1989).

The third set of predictors concerns perceptions about the *likely outcome* of any aggression: clearly, the greater the expectation of a positive outcome (winning the argument, regaining lost control) the greater the likelihood of aggression, although these perceptions are likely to be obscured by an uncertainty about the long-term consequences of aggression.

Both the sets of predictors and/or the overall structure of models such as that of Riggs and O'Leary can be best employed by qualitative researchers, who might use particular sets of predictors as valuable heuristics within the context of unstructured interviews or related methods. Rather than resorting to simple listings of aggressive acts, researchers could use such sets of predictors as a means of prompting respondents to provide more detailed information about the exact sequencing of aggressive interactions, and thus more appropriately address the subjective experience of the respondent, and the complexity of relationship aggression.

THE CULTURAL AND HISTORICAL CONTEXT OF AGGRESSION

Just as many psychological researchers have ignored the individual phenomenology of their research participants, so, too, have they ignored the wider societal structure in which aggression takes place. Sexual and non-sexual aggression have often been considered as separate spheres of research, but here the themes converge in illustrating the need for a macro-perspective on relationship aggression.

First, consider *non-sexual* aggression by partners in a relationship, aggression which can often have very serious physical consequences, including homicide. What counts as aggression is never a straightforward issue (Duck 1988), and it may be that the contextual and situational factors involved are such that potential aggressors never see their acts as 'aggressive'. Within a marriage, individuals will differ in terms of peer support, such that certain acts seen as 'unacceptable' within the sphere of one peer group become more 'acceptable' in another. The consequences of this aggression, too, may be of lesser significance when other structural variables – such as the availability of alternatives and investment – are prominent. Such factors are likely to supersede considerations such as relationship rewards and costs when determining the continuance of the relationship (Nye 1979).

The subjective meaning of any aggression to the relationship may also differ between the sexes. Thus, whereas both men and women are equally likely to use minor aggression in their relationship, women are likely to resort to aggression only once a critical level of stress has been reached: men's aggression is more instrumental and aimed at achieving a particular goal (Campbell and Muncer Chapter 17). Evidence from both social psychology and socio-biology suggests that men and women have different sets of responses and motives for their acts of aggression, and are likely to behave in accordance with these (Dobash *et al.* 1992). Overall, however, both sexes may be susceptible to a broader environmental effect: Straus (1983) has argued that the environment in which relationship conflict occurs is influenced by external factors such as national hostilities at a time of war. Such external aggression may help precipitate a wider aggressiveness within the society at large.

According to White and Sorensen (1992: 188), 'Cultural attitudes guide the definition, assessment and study of sexual assault.'

In the study of *sexual* aggression, sociological – and particularly feminist – perspectives have long stressed the manner in which learned patterns of attitudes and behaviour, gender-role socialization and coercive cognitive schema perpetuate sexual aggression (Buckhart and Fromuth 1991). Thus the sociologist Steve Box, in his book *Power, Crime and Mystification* (1983) speaks of five different categories of relationship 'rape', and includes such violent acts as 'seduction turned rape' and 'exploitation rape', tying each within the social framework in which they take place. Society in general, he claims, prepares the male for his potential 'rapist' role, and provides a whole 'cultural library of excuses' to forgive his misdemeanours. At the same time, however, male rapists are viewed by the population at large as extreme psychopaths, strange freaks who are somehow 'outside' of society, whilst the woman is, at least implicitly, given some of the blame for the attack (White and Sorensen 1992; Wilson and Daly 1992).

This wider perspective has, however, often been unconvincingly applied by psychologists working on sexual abuse. Thus research into the acceptance of 'rape myths' such as 'women really want to be taken by force' (for example, Burt 1980) has treated these myths as just another individual-level variable, to be placed alongside others in predicting an individual's proclivity to aggression. Treatment of rape myths at this level ignores the wider social representations of these beliefs and their historical context – as well as the findings that most serious acts of aggression are perpetuated by men (Dobash *et al.* 1992; see also Chapter 1 of this volume). Other studies on 'token resistance' (where a woman will say 'no' when she really means 'yes') have tended to exaggerate the frequency of token resistance by asking, 'Have you ever employed such resistance?' (for instance, Muehlenhard and Hollabaugh 1988). This has tended to obscure the finding that very few women (less than 20 per cent) will *consistently* use such a strategy (Muehlenhard 1988), and can only help perpetuate the stereotypical role of the man as sexual aggressor and the woman as the passive recipient, who is just playing 'hard to get' (Gordon and Donat 1992).

The wider, *cross-cultural perspective* on relationship aggression has also been rarely explored in the literature. One immediately notable aspect of the dating-aggression literature is that it is only Americans who 'date'. Such a term is uncommon in Britain and even less meaningful in cultures where 'dating behaviour' is not permitted. Psychological research on relationship aggression is, like most psychological research, dominated by what Jahoda (1986: 24) calls 'Homo Americanus'.

Cross-cultural contextualization has a number of advantages (Levinson 1989). First, the familiar meaning issue: aggression in the relationship has different meanings in different cultural contexts. To quote Levinson (1989: 10) 'wife beating means different things . . . in different societies'. It may not be very profound, but it is all too easy to forget that the rules of relationship may differ not only within stages of a relationship but also in different cultures (Gelles and Cornell 1983; Mushanga 1983).

Secondly, a cross-cultural perspective is important for testing different theoretical perspectives. Levinson (1989) offers nine theoretical perspectives for research on family aggression, many of which are best validated within a cross-cultural context. Finally, and perhaps most challengingly, cross-cultural perspectives may inform us how to prevent aggression by identifying societies in which aggression does not occur. The study of such societies can help determine both the legal and normative frameworks which may limit the possibilities for violence.

Cultural differences can be located along a number of possible theoretical constructs, but the most widely used is that of individualism-collectivism (Triandis *et al.* 1988). The United States and the United Kingdom are generally considered to be good examples of 'individualistic cultures' (Gudykunst and Ting-Toomey 1988), and it is here that the majority of research is located. However, research on personal relationships across cultures indicates a whole variety of differences between cultures falling at different points on this divide in terms of how they conceptualize relationships and how roles and behaviours within these relationships are defined (Bond 1988).

Two examples from the sexual aggression literature illustrate this. One concerns the rules that govern the initial dating process. Gordon and Donat (1992) argue that the strong ethos of social exchange in US (individualist) society may lead certain men to feel that once they have kept 'their' side of 'the bargain' (having paid for a meal, driven the woman around in an expensive car), then their partner should also keep hers (namely, engage in sexual intercourse). Failure to do so may lead to the man feeling 'justified' in sexually assaulting the woman. In most collectivist societies, however, the value of direct social exchange is less evident, with interaction governed by broader values reflecting the collective goals of the community (Leung 1988). In these societies we would thus anticipate that such an ethos of reciprocal exchange would be less common.

A second, related example is the way in which women in individualist societies are frequently caught in a 'double-bind' situation, being both attracted to their partner but having to deal with the possibility of unwanted advances (Burgoyne and Spitzberg 1992). This situation often leads to equivocation, misunderstanding and potential aggression. Such problems are, of course, less likely to occur in societies where outside parties closely regulate the possibility and nature of premarital interactions (for example, Iran: Hanassab and Tidwell 1989). This may explain why rape is reported less amongst Hispanic women in North America, who usually originate from the collectivist societies of South America (Sorensen and Siegel 1992). Here, patriarchal values obviously reduce the threat of date-rape, not only by limiting the opportunity for the woman to engage in unescorted dating, but also by strongly forbidding acts of sexual aggression against members of the in-group (that is, the same culture) (Sorensen and Siegel 1992). Interestingly, aggression against out-group members (including those from the dominant culture) may be less subject to restraint.

Turning to the incidence of rape in general, Sanday (1981) has distinguished between 'rape-prone' societies, where sexual assault by men or women is either permitted or ignored (18 per cent of the societies she studied), and 'rape-free' societies, where rape is practically unknown (47 per cent of the societies studied). Using ethnographic accounts from 156 societies (originally published by Murdock and White 1969), rape-prone societies were characterized by the theme of women as property, and were predominantly violent societies, where both inter- and intra-group aggression is common. Rape-free societies were distinguished by notions of equality and a belief in the complementarity of men and women. Sanday's careful data provide powerful support for her argument that

> rape in tribal societies is part of a cultural configuration that includes interpersonal violence, male dominance and sexual exploitation . . . rape is not an integral part of male nature but the means by which men programmed for violence express their sexual selves.

(pp. 25f)

A final example deals with non-sexual assault, and points to how differences in cross-cultural perceptions of close relationships make relationship intervention across cultures a difficult procedure. Levinson (1989) cites the case of Christian missionaries in Brazil who, in discouraging divorce, managed to keep together many couples who were clearly unsuited. The available evidence suggests that this contributed, inadvertently, towards a marked increase in wife-beating.

A further dimension is that of historical variation. Changes in both the definition and social judgement of sexual assault, for example, have varied throughout time, although women have consistently attracted at least some of the blame (Donat and D'Emilio 1992). Thus during the times of slavery in

Colonial America, it was deemed 'impossible' to rape black women because of their inherent 'sexual' nature, and there were no penalties for abuse of black women by white men (Wyatt 1992). Furthermore, black women were seen as possessions, and the legal framework encouraged sex between black women and white men (but not vice versa) as a means of producing more slaves. Seen in this context, it is not surprising that African-American women, even nowadays, are less likely than white Americans to report sexual assault to the relevant authorities, anticipating a lack of community and societal support if they do so, a pessimism supported by evidence from police and courtroom procedures (Borque 1989). At the same time, African women are more likely than their white counterparts to see sexual assault as an inevitable part of their lives. This may encourage them to make less effort to guard against its occurrence, thus perpetuating the risk of attack.

At the present time, we have little knowledge about how either sexual or non-sexual aggression in relationships may mirror broader social changes. The first study on courtship aggression, for example, did not appear until the early 1980s (Makepeace 1981), and thus previous comparative indices of frequency are unavailable. Social change within a society can have a number of different effects, contributing to either a decrease or increase in aggression or changes in the definition and/or frequency of such aggression. For example, the late 1920s saw an attempt by the Soviet authorities in Central Asia to overturn the sexual inequalities of Muslim society by giving women new civil rights and creating a new and more sympathetic legal system (Massell 1968). The results, however, were a backlash of hostility against women, including the raping and killing of the (newly) unveiled, denounced as traitors to tradition (Massell 1968). This led to a rapid reversal of Soviet policy in these matters, and an at least tacit recognition of traditional Muslim domestic values. A knowledge of such historical patterns is vital in allowing us to understand how particular social groups may interpret violent activities, and will thus help us obtain a greater accuracy in estimating the incidence of aggression and in constructing appropriate preventive strategies.

CONCLUSIONS

In this chapter I have argued that psychologists and sociologists working in the field of relationship aggression should go further in their attempts to contextualize relationship aggression. Some recognition of this wider perspective is now evident in dealing with one particular area of aggression – rape – and a recent edition of the *Journal of Social Issues* (vol. 48, no. 1, 1992) attempted to explore the 'social roots' of this aggression by explicitly considering historical and legal contexts, definitions of sexual assault and racial and ethnic differences (Sorensen and White 1992). Despite the originality of the papers in this volume, however, both the historical and ethnic perspectives were located within the United States, and the studies reported largely ignored the techniques developed by cultural psychologists for examining inter-group differences (for example, Poortinga 1989). This makes the reliability of the informants' responses a problematic issue, and calls for further research that adopts a truly international perspective.

It is this author's contention that future 'contextualization' needs to be yet more adventurous, using innovative methodologies to explore fully the wealth of social, political and cultural interactions which form this widespread phenomenon. Future research should provide more subjective accounts, perhaps adopting interdependence theory for such a purpose. At the same time, a phenomenological emphasis should not detract from an interest in structural forces which may help provide some of the 'ammunition' for the subjective experience of the aggressor by providing the context in which certain behaviour is seen as 'appropriate', and in which certain 'excuses' become viable. Finally, all this must be seen from the perspective of culture, and within a historical setting. Such research is not easy, and is likely to necessitate the use of a range of methodologies which go beyond the standard questionnaire designs employed for most of the work on relationship aggression. However, without such a perspective it seems unlikely that we can fully understand all the forces involved in relationship aggression, and will thus remain unable to suggest truly effective remedies for its amelioration.

REFERENCES

Bond, M. (1988) *The Cross-cultural Challenge to Social Psychology*, Newbury Park, CA: Sage.

Borque, L. (1989) *Defining Rape*, Durham, NC: Duke University Press.

Box, S. (1983) *Power, Crime and Mystification*, London: Tavistock.

Breslin, F. C., Riggs, D. S., O'Leary, K. D. and Arias, I. (1990) 'Expected and actual consequences of dating aggression', *Journal of Interpersonal Violence*, 5: 247–58.

Buckhart, B. and Fromuth, M. (1991) 'Individual and social psychological understandings of sexual coercion', in E. Gruerholz and M. Koralewski (eds) *Sexual Coercion: A Sourcebook on its Nature, Causes and Prevention*, Lexington, MA: Lexington Books.

Burgoyne, S. and Spitzberg, B. (1992) 'An examination of communication strategies and tactics used in potential date rape episodes', Paper presented at the Sixth International Conference on Personal Relationships, Maine, USA (July).

Burt, M. (1980) 'Cultural myths and supports for rape', *Journal of Personality and Social Psychology*, 18: 217–30.

Dobash, R. P., Dobash, R. E., Wilson, M. and Daly, M. (1992) 'The myth of sexual symmetry in marital violence', *Social Problems*, 39: 71–91.

Donat, P. and D'Emilio, J. (1992) 'A feminist redefinition of rape and sexual assault: historical foundations and change', *Journal of Social Issues*, 48: 9–22.

Duck, S. (1988) *Relating to Others*, Milton Keynes: Open University Press.

Gelles, R. and Cornell, C. (1983) 'Summing up', in R. Gelles and C. Cornell, *International Perspectives on Family Violence*, Lexington, MA: Lexington Books, pp. 161–2.

George, L., Winfield, I. and Blazer, D. (1992) 'Sociocultural factors in sexual assault:

a comparison of two representative samples of women', *Journal of Social Issues*, 48: 105–15.

Gordon, S. and Donat, P. (1992) 'Social exchange and influence strategies in dyadic communication: applications to research on acquaintance rape', Paper presented at the Sixth International Conference on Personal Relationships, Maine, USA (July).

Gryl, F., Stith, S. and Bird, G. (1991) 'Close dating relationships among college students: differences by use of violence and by gender', *Journal of Social and Personal Relationships*, 8: 243–64.

Gudykunst, W. and Ting-Toomey, S. (1988) *Culture and Interpersonal Communication*, Newbury Park, CA: Sage.

Hanassab, S. and Tidwell, R. (1989) 'Cross-cultural perspective on dating relationship of young Iranian women: a pilot study', *Counselling Psychology Quarterly*, 2: 113–21.

Jahoda, G. (1986) 'Nature, culture and social psychology', *European Journal of Social Psychology*, 16: 17–30.

Kelley, H. Deocheid, C., Christensen, A., Harvey, J., Huston, T., Levinger, G., McClintock, E., Peplau, A. and Peterson, D. (1983) *Close Relationships*, San Francisco: Freeman.

Leung, K. (1988) 'Theoretical advances in justice behaviour: some cross-cultural input', in M. Bond (ed.) *The Cross-cultural Challenge to Social Psychology*, Newbury Park, CA: Sage.

Levinson, D. (1989) *Family Violence in Cross-cultural Perspective*, Newbury Park, CA: Sage.

Makepeace, J. (1981) 'Courtship violence among college students', *Family Relations*, 30: 97–102.

Marshall, L. and Rose, P. (1987) 'Gender, stress and violence in the adult relationships of a sample of college students', *Journal of Social and Personal Relationships*, 4: 299–316.

Massell, G. (1968) 'Law as an instrument of revolutionary change in a traditional milieu', *Law and Society Review*, 2: 179–28.

Muehlenhard, C. (1988) ' "Nice women" don't say yes and "real men" don't say "no": how miscommunication and the double standard can cause sexual problems', *Women and Therapy*, 7: 95–108.

Muehlenhard, C. and Hollabaugh, L. (1988) 'Do women sometimes say no when they mean yes? the prevalence and correlates of women's token resistance to sex', *Journal of Personality and Social Psychology*, 54: 872–9.

Murdock, G. and White, D. (1969) 'Standard cross-cultural sample', *Ethology*, 8: 329–69.

Mushanga, T. (1983) 'Wife victimization in East and Central Africa', in R. Gelles and C. Cornell, *International Perspectives on Family Violence*, Lexington, MA: Lexington Books, pp. 139–45.

Nye, F. (1979) 'Choice, exchange and the family', in W. Burr *et al.* (eds) *Contemporary Theories and the family*, vol. 2, New York: Free Press.

Poortinga, Y. (1989) 'Equivalence of cross-cultural data: an overview of basic issues', *International Journal of Psychology*, 24: 737–56.

Riggs, D. and O'Leary, K. (1989) 'A theoretical model of courtship aggression', in M. Pirog-Good and J. Stets (eds) *Violence in Dating Relationships: Emerging Social Issues*, New York: Praeger, pp. 53–72.

Sanday, P. (1981) 'The socio-cultural context of rape: a cross-cultural study', *Journal of Social Issues*, 37: 5–27.

Shotland, R. (1989) 'A model of the causes of date rape in developing and close relationships', in C. Hendrick (ed.) *Close Relationships*, Newbury Park, CA: Sage, chap. 10, pp. 247–70.

——— (1992) 'A theory of courtship rape: part 2', *Journal of Social Issues*, 48: 127–43.

Sorensen, S. and Siegel, J. (1992) 'Gender, ethnicity, and sexual assault: findings from a Los Angeles study', *Journal of Social Issues*, 48: 93–104.

Sorensen, S. and White, J. (1992) 'Adult sexual assault: overview of research', *Journal of Social Issues*, 48: 1–8.

Stets, J. and Pirog-Good, M. (1990) 'Interpersonal control and courtship aggression', *Journal of Social and Personal Relationships*, 7: 371–94.

Straus, M. (1979) 'Measuring intrafamily conflict and violence: the conflict tactics (CT) scale', *Journal of Marriage and the Family*, 41: 75–88.

—— (1983) 'Societal morphogenesis and intrafamily violence in cross-cultural perspective', in R. Gelles and C. Cornell, *International Perspectives on Family Violence*, Lexington, MA: Lexington Books, pp. 27–43.

Triandis, H., Bontempo, R., Villareal, M., Asai, M. and Lucca, N. (1988) 'Individualism and collectivism: cross-cultural perspectives on self–ingroup relationships', *Journal of Personality and Social Psychology*, 54: 323–38.

Walker, L. (1990) 'Response to Mills and Mould', *American Psychologist*, 45: 676–7.

White, J. and Sorensen, S. (1992) 'A sociocultural view of sexual assault: from discrepancy to diversity', *Journal of Social Issues*, 48: 187–95.

Wilson, M. and Daly, M. (1992) 'The man who mistook his wife for a chattel', in J. Barkow, L. Cosmides and J. Tooley (eds) *The Adapted Mind*, Oxford: Oxford University Press.

Wyatt, G. (1992) 'The sociocultural context of African American and white American women's rape', *Journal of Social Issues*, 48: 77–91.

9

MARITAL VIOLENCE
An interactional perspective
Neil Frude

THE DANGEROUS PARTNER

Estimates of the incidence of violence within marital and cohabiting relationships vary greatly, the variation mainly reflecting the criteria used to define
'violence' (see Chapters 1 and 8). Thus, according to the two national US
surveys conducted by Straus and his colleagues (Straus *et al.* 1980; Straus and
Gelles 1986), if slapping, pushing and grabbing (as well as more serious forms
of attack) are included, then the yearly incidence figure is 16 per cent of
couples. If minor forms are excluded, however, then the one-year incidence
(for both the 1975 and the 1985 survey) is in the region of 6 per cent.

Although many women attack their male partner (some surveys appear to
show that slightly *more* wives than husbands indulge in some form of aggressive
behaviour towards their partner), it is clear that many more women than men
are injured as a result of marital violence (Chapter 1). Aggressive behaviour
by women is injurious in relatively few cases, and much is retaliatory
(Saunders 1986; see Dobash *et al.* 1992, for an analysis of marital violence by
male and female perpetrators). Many women sustain serious injuries as a
result of attacks by their partner, and Stark and Flitcraft (1988) suggest that
battering is the single most common source of serious injury to women, being
responsible for more injuries than road accidents, muggings and rape
combined. Thus although both husbands and wives might be said to be
'aggressive', many more husbands than wives are 'violent'.

EXPLANATORY PERSPECTIVES

One approach to the explanation of marital violence focuses on cultural norms
and attitudes. It is held that society condones and even encourages male
brutality within the home as a way of maintaining the cultural status quo and
supporting male dominance or patriarchy. Thus, according to the feminist/
social stratification explanation (for example, Dobash and Dobash 1979),
violence by husbands reflects general patterns of societal resource allocation
and power (for a detailed consideration, see Chapter 16).

A second approach focuses on psychological and family interaction processes. Accepting that cultural factors are relevant, it treats violence by husbands as 'deviant' (rather than 'accepted') forms of behaviour, reflecting the assailant's anger and lack of inhibition. The 'psychiatric' variant of this explanation accounts for violence in terms of the personality or the psychopathology of the perpetrator, whereas the 'interactional' variant offers an explanation in terms of the relationship and interactions between the assailant and the victim. The interactional approach explains the role of societal factors such as poverty and unemployment in terms of the effects these have on individuals and couples.

Thus one of the major distinctions between the 'societal' and 'interactional' views of marital violence relates to the issue of whether such behaviour is 'within' or 'outside' societal norms. Is it tenable to view violence by husbands as 'accepted'? It may be true that little significance is generally attached to pushes and pulls, but the view that *violence* by husbands is accepted or encouraged is difficult to maintain. Few people approve of husbands beating up their wives and, for almost all social groups, it would be totally unacceptable for a man to admit to (let alone boast about) the fact that he had injured his wife. Perpetrators often go to considerable lengths to hide the effects of their violence. Victims, too, often hide the fact that they have been beaten by their husband. A wife may strive to conceal her victimization from other people (her friends, or her own family, for example) as a way of protecting her husband from condemnation and ostracism. Abuse by husbands is usually confined to the home, the presence of other people usually acting as a powerful inhibitor. When a husband's brutality *is* revealed then his actions are almost universally condemned and sympathy is extended to the victim. Thus there is little evidence to support the view that violence by husbands is condoned or 'approved of'. (For a different view of this crime see Chapter 16 on power explanations).

Psychological (as against some sociological) accounts of violence by husbands treat such incidents of brutality as 'extreme', 'unusual' and 'deviant'. Rather than suggesting that violence towards wives is a normal or 'natural' act of 'men within this society', psychological explanations seek to explain why, despite the social condemnation of such behaviour, so many men do engage in wife-beating. The interactional view seeks an explanation in terms of characteristics of the relationship and the interpersonal dynamics of couples involved in violent incidents. This focus on the couple, rather than on the aggressor, often leads to a misunderstanding, particularly with regard to the role assigned to the victim. According to the interactional view, the victim's behaviour (for example, a woman complaining about her husband's gambling) may 'trigger' or 'provoke' the anger that results in violence. This, however, is not to *blame* the victim for the attack, or to detract from the aggressor's culpability. Although the victim's behaviour is often said to provoke the assault, this does not provide a *justification* for the brutal attack.

154

The responsibility for the assault clearly rests with the assailant, and it rests *solely* with the assailant, except in those very few cases in which the victim may be said to have deliberately provoked the attack.

The interactional view does not ignore societal variables, but explains their role in terms of the effects that they have on the attitudes, beliefs and behaviours of both the assailant and the victim. The term 'violent couple' is best avoided, since it might be taken to imply that both partners play a similar role in the violence that occurs. In fact their roles are very different (although they are, in some ways, 'complementary'). If assailant-victim couples are regarded as deviant and exceptional (although by no means rare) then attention needs to be paid to the ways in which their relationships and interactions differ from those of other couples.

In this chapter I shall first review some of the evidence relating to the characteristics of assailant-victim couples before considering in some detail the dynamics of violent incidents.

ASSAILANT-VICTIM COUPLES

Many different variables have been shown to be associated with a relatively high frequency of marital abuse. These include demographic characteristics, personality features of the assailant and the victim, and couple characteristics. A comprehensive account of the origins and nature of marital violence should therefore include reference to the relevant variables at each of these levels. Furthermore, what is needed is an integrated model which combines factors from different levels to provide a causal narrative.

One way in which this can be achieved is to focus on the assailant-victim couple as the primary unit. The personality characteristics of each of the partners are now seen in the context of how they affect the couple relationship and the interaction between the partners. The impact of 'social environment' variables, such as crowded living conditions, poverty and unemployment, can also be understood in terms of how they affect the couple.

Thus to focus on the couple does not imply a denial of the important causal contribution of either social variables or the personalities of the individuals involved. But, rather than explaining violence principally as either a societal phenomenon or as an act by an individual, the interactional approach focuses on the interaction between the assailant and the victim. Individual characteristics and societal factors are important inasmuch as they affect the relationship between the partners and the ways in which they interact.

The notion of 'causal distance' is useful in an attempt to provide an integrated account of marital violence. 'Poverty' and 'unemployment' are causally distant from marital violence, for example, whereas marital conflict is much closer. To explain why poverty is associated with a higher risk of marital abuse, this 'distal' variable needs to be viewed in relation to mediating variables. For example, it might be judged that poverty leads to fewer resources, that this produces competition, which generates conflict, and that conflict may lead to violence. It is not difficult to generate such causal narratives, but ideally the generation and verification of such models would be based on data derived from wide-ranging empirical research. Various statistical tools (path analysis, Lisrel and so on) are available to aid this task.

Societal factors

Many factors in the social environment are relevant to an explanation of marital violence, including social norms relating to marriage and cohabitation, economic conditions, and social policies relating to violence within families. Pattison (1985) concludes from a review of relevant research that all forms of family violence have certain social factors in common: violent styles of family interaction; economic hardship; male dominance; the sanctioning of violence or lack of integrative social norms in a community; isolation of a couple or family; and drug and alcohol abuse.

There has been a good deal of discussion on how all of these affect assaultive behaviour. To illustrate the way in which an interactional analysis may include a consideration of such variables we will focus on just one small aspect of the societal 'contribution' by considering the issue of the relationship between marital violence and the complex variable labelled 'social class'.

Although marital violence occurs in all sections of society, there is convincing evidence to suggest that there is a higher prevalence in lower socio-economic groups (for example, Sugarman and Hotaling 1989; Hotaling and Sugarman 1990). Several explanations have been put forward to explain this association. Social class is related to economic resources, housing conditions and educational level, among many other variables, and any one of these can be used as the basis for explaining some part of the relationship between social class and marital violence. Thus couples facing economic and environmental distress are likely to become frustrated and may engage in frequent struggles over the allocation of their limited resources. Conflict over the allocation of shared resources is likely to be particularly intense where the joint resources are meagre. Affluent couples may fight over 'luxuries', their basic needs being catered for with relatively little difficulty, but severe deprivation may lead to conflict over basic commodities. If there is conflict between a wife who wants money to buy clothing for children, and a husband who wishes to spend some of the money on recreational activities such as drinking or gambling, then a high level of conflict may be expected.

A similar scenario can be depicted for other variables within the composite 'social class', including poor living conditions and lack of employment. Thus couples with limited living space may engage in more conflict over 'territory' than those with ample space. In crowded conditions one partner's activity is likely to interfere with or prevent the preferred activity of the other. Disputes over noise, sleeping, television and so on are clearly more likely when a couple share very limited space than when they have sufficient room to carry out their activities independently.

Unemployment not only brings loss of income and status but also increases the partners' isolation from outside social contact and brings them into close contact for prolonged periods. This can produce chronic irritation, particularly if living conditions are cramped. There may be disputes over who is to 'blame' for the lack of employment, and a partner who has lost self-esteem by virtue of his or her unemployment may feel under attack by the other. With few resources available to break up the day, and with little to look forward to, both partners may become bored and irritable, and in such circumstances a husband's anger may be vented on his unfortunate wife.

Thus, rather than simply stating the fact that social class appears to be associated with a relatively high level of marital violence, we need to understand *why* this association holds. It is easy to suggest ways in which 'distant' variables may be linked to marital violence, but the issue needs to be informed by empirical research.

In principle, a single violent incident could be identified as a result of situational factors, individual psychological factors, and couple relationship factors, with multiple causal chains stretching back from each of these. Within the highly complex causal narrative which would constitute a total explanation of the event, elements of social conditions, social policy, political events and shifts in social history would certainly have a part to play. In practice, of course, such an exhaustive narrative could never be compiled. Any feasible account of a violent incident will simply highlight a number of dominant and proximal elements. Some of these can be identified from detailed case studies that include accounts by perpetrators and victims. Important elements which recur across cases can also be identified through research which seeks out differences by comparing populations in which violence is or is not a feature. Such correlational research has dominated the field and has produced an impressive array of characteristics which differentiate couples (and individuals). Although many of these are likely to reflect the results of violence, it is likely that others will be found to play an important causal role. However, this is an area in which it is important not to think in too 'linear' a fashion. Like other complex social phenomena, the links between factors implicated in marital violence include feedback loops, eddies and reverberations. This is an area in which a 'systemic approach' to understanding certainly has much to offer.

Marital factors

Many studies have compared assailant-victim couples and couples for whom violence is not a feature of the relationship. Differences have been found between such groups in the stability of the relationship, power structure and, particularly, the way in which conflict is dealt with.

157

The rate of 'marital' abuse has been found to be significantly higher for cohabiting than for married couples (Ellis 1989; Stets and Straus 1989). A number of explanations for this phenomenon have been put forward, including the following: cohabiting relationships may be less well defined, leading to frequent fights over power, rules and roles; cohabiting relationships may suffer increased strain and increased social isolation; cohabiting relationships may be subject to lower social control than marital relationships. Many other explanations are possible (and, clearly, several factors may contribute), but the examples given illustrate the way in which a demographic 'fact', rather than offering an explanation for marital abuse, actually raises questions that need an explanation.

A number of other marital factors have consistently emerged from the research studies as having clear associations with marital violence. We will consider (1) relationship dissatisfaction, (2) the couple's power relationship, and (3) couple conflict style.

Relationship dissatisfaction

It is hardly surprising to find that those involved in marital abuse express low satisfaction with their relationship (Rosenbaum and O'Leary 1981; Hurlbert *et al.* 1991). Dissatisfaction is likely to be a *consequence* of violence (particularly for the victim), but may also contribute to the risk of abuse. A husband who is dissatisfied with his wife, or with their relationship, is likely to judge her actions in a negative way. This may then lead to anger, and the husband may have relatively few inhibitions about expressing his anger in an aggressive act. Thus the link between marital dissatisfaction and marital violence is likely to be circular. And as a result of the vicious circle the extent of the violence is likely to escalate over time (Meredith *et al.* 1986).

Gove *et al.* (1990) provide an interesting analysis of the relationship between 'the provisions of marriage' and marital violence. There is now a substantial body of evidence showing that those who are married typically fare better in terms of psychological and physical well-being than those who are without partners. Marriage provides certain benefits that help individuals to cope with stress and to maintain their self-esteem. In a positive relationship, the partner's actions help to build and maintain the individual's 'assumptive world'. If a man judges that his wife is unsupportive, or believes that she is failing to provide him with the attention, consideration, power or privileges that he 'deserves', then, according to this account, the husband is likely to feel aggrieved and hostile and may become violent. Individuals invest substantially in the marital relationship, and it is a significant source of an individual's definition of self and estimation of self-worth. When the relationship fails to repay the investment, or when the partner's actions undermine an individual's self-esteem, high levels of conflict and anger are likely to be generated.

The couple's power relationship

'Resource theory' (Goode 1971) suggests that when people have few resources or little capacity to exert control in other ways they tend to resort to physical violence as a means of influencing others. This might lead to the prediction that a man who has little prestige, social rank or earning power compared to his wife would be likely to use brute force to reassert control. Straus (1990) and Hornung *et al.* (1981) did find that a wide status difference between the partners was associated with a higher frequency of violence, particularly if the man had lower status than his wife. Coleman and Straus (1986) classified more than 2,000 couples as male-dominant, female-dominant, or egalitarian ('divided power'). The lowest rates of conflict and violence were found for egalitarian couples. There was also relatively little conflict and violence in male-dominant and female-dominant families where partners shared a consensus about the legitimacy of the prevailing power structure. High rates of violence were found, particularly, in male-dominant and female-dominant couples where the power structure was a matter of disagreement.

Couple conflict style

Assailant-victim couples have a high level of 'ambient conflict', a background of marital tension, hostility and frequent rows, which sometimes peak as episodes of injurious attack (Sugarman and Hotaling 1989; Hotaling and Sugarman 1990; Goldsmith 1990). Many couples develop a particular style of conflict engagement and escalation that can be identified across different situations, and it is hardly surprising to find that distressed couples and assailant-victim couples tend to engage in ineffective and dangerous conflict strategies.

Straus (1974) found that physical violence was more likely to occur in marital relationships in which rational problem-solving strategies were rarely employed, and Lloyd (1990) found that violent couples were less likely to use problem-solving, discussion or negotiation, and that their conflicts were characterized by high levels of anger and verbal attack. Conflicts were typically unresolved and few apologies were given. In a study of laboratory-based conflicts, Margolin *et al.* (1988) found that physically abusive husbands were more offensive towards their wives than non-abusive husbands. They used more hostile gestures (including pointing, arm-waving and threatening actions) and more hostile verbal behaviours (including angry vocalizations, sarcasm, nagging and accusations). However, there were also differences in the behaviours of the two groups of wives, with the physically abused wives being judged as more offensive in their verbal behaviour.

Faced with experimental conflict-resolution tasks, distressed couples find less agreement and engage in more negative behaviours than do non-distressed couples. Jacobson (1981) suggested that individuals in distressed marriages frequently attempt to control their partner's behaviour by using aversive control tactics such as withdrawing rewards or administering punishments. Bornstein and Bornstein (1985) concluded from their review that partners in distressed marriages make more complaints and criticisms than those in non-distressed marriages. They also tend to resort readily to sarcasm, and their communications are more likely to be uncontrolled and 'uncensored'. Thus some couples rapidly engage in conflict escalation and fight 'below the belt', frequently attacking the partner's self-esteem and steering an argument towards what Gelles (1987) refers to as 'incendiary topics'. Some couples make a swift transition from the verbal to the physical, and this, together with other negative conflict tactics, is predictive of marital violence.

Personality factors

Having examined some of the research evidence regarding assailant-victim couples it can be seen that a number of characteristics differentiate such couples from others. Furthermore, the differences identified are easy to incorporate into a model of marital violence. It is not difficult to see how dissatisfaction with the marital relationship, inequitable power distribution between the partners, and particular types of conflict style may increase the risk of violence within the home. We have also explored the issue of how the social situation may adversely affect the couple. In a sense, social conditions 'feed into' the couple's relationship and affect the partners' interaction. But in addition to such 'input' to the couple 'from above' (that is, at the social level), there is also 'input from below' (namely, at the level of the individual partners). It would be expected that personality characteristics of the individuals would affect the couple relationship and the interactions between the partners. We therefore need to consider, even if briefly, some of the evidence relating to the personality of abusive husbands and their victim wives.

The first aspect of this which deserves consideration is that of the 'aggressiveness' of abusive husbands. Those who beat their wives also tend to be aggressive towards other people. For example, many men who abuse their wives are also physically abusive towards their children. Support for the view that men who beat their wives share many of the same characteristics as those who are aggressive outside the home comes from a study by Maiuro et al. (1988). This team found little difference on various measures of aggressiveness between a group of men involved in domestic violence and a group which had been involved in attacks outside the home. The authors suggest that anger is a key emotion in the psychological profile of the domestic batterer as well as that of the 'street fighter', and that there is little to support an 'ideological separation' of marital abuse from other types of assaultive behaviour.

Besides aggressiveness and a potential for anger, a number of other characteristics are associated with marital assault, including low self-esteem (Telch and Lindquist 1984; Goldstein and Rosenbaum 1985), a tendency towards sexual jealousy, the holding of traditional ('sexist') attitudes towards women and marriage, and 'need for power' (Rosenbaum and O'Leary 1981; Mason and Blankenship 1987). The implications of these for male violence are explored in other chapters (for example, 11, 14 and 16).

The personality of the victim has also been the subject of a number of studies. Several have identified differences between battered wives and other women, notably in such aspects as anxiety, depression and low self-esteem. Undoubtedly, in many cases such differences may be accounted for by the different marital experiences of the two groups, but some studies have also found that wives in physically abusive relationships tend to be critical and 'verbally offensive', and that they engage in high levels of overt negative behaviours during conflictual episodes (Margolin *et al.* 1988).

Thus, although an interactional account of marital violence focuses principally on the interaction of the couple, it does not ignore either the characteristics of the partners as individuals or the social variables that affect couple interaction.

So far we have presented a picture of the 'ambient' characteristics of the relationships of assailant-victim couples, and these present a picture of potentially dangerous situations that seem likely to give rise to sporadic incidents of intense violence. We now shift our attention, employing a much shorter time-base, to consider what may happen within such a 'dangerous' relationship to trigger an injurious assault.

THE VIOLENT INCIDENT

In trying to understand how particular incidents of violence occur it is useful to bear in mind the distinction between hostile and instrumental violence. Hostile violence is driven by anger and has as its principal motive that of causing harm to the victim. Instrumental violence is driven not by anger but by a desire for certain 'gains'. Thus a mugger is violent in order to steal money; a youth may assault another in order to gain or maintain social standing before his peers.

Some incidents of marital violence are best explained as examples of instrumental aggression. A husband may be violent towards his wife, for example, because he believes that violence will enable him to 'get his own way'. Thus some cases of violent marital rape could be explained in this way, as could a violent attack used to obtain money. More generally, the use of violence may instigate or maintain 'a reign of terror' which gives the husband power to dominate his wife and the freedom to do as he wishes. Instrumental violence may be used strategically to 'teach' the wife that a beating will follow if she criticizes, protests, makes claims on resources, or refuses any demand. Many different strategies are used to gain compliance, not all of them violent. It is instructive to consider what might lead a person to accede to another's wish. A wife, for example, might agree to have sex with her husband when she is not feeling in a sexual mood because she wishes to accommodate, because she feels obliged ('a sense of duty'), or because she fears the consequences of a refusal. A husband, in order to gain compliance from his wife in such a situation, may use a variety of strategies, including a gentle attempt at persuasion, the incitement of feelings of 'duty' ('claiming rights') or the use of physical power tactics ('instilling fear'). Different men use different strategies, and some have few inhibitions about using coercion and fear in order to bring about a wife's compliance. Threats of physical violence (explicit or implicit) will often be sufficient to ensure such compliance, but such a fear regime is likely to have been established, and may be maintained, by a series of physical attacks.

While some incidents of marital violence are undoubtedly instrumental in nature, the majority appear to be examples of hostile aggression, with the husband's attack reflecting his feelings of intense anger. Sometimes the anger that leads a husband to attack his wife will have been generated in another context. Thus a husband who is angry at having lost a bet, or who has been annoyed by someone at work, may displace this anger and attack his wife. A person who is already angry tends to become annoyed very easily, and thus a particular action by the partner that would normally pass unnoticed might attract a violent response.

Gelles (1987) maintains that the assailant's action is almost always 'spontaneous' (that is, that it is rarely planned or strategic), that it is almost always 'rational' from the abuser's perspective, and that it is almost always 'interactional' (generally arising as a reaction to some aspect of the victim's behaviour or from an initial non-violent interaction between the perpetrator and the victim). The suggestion that the victim plays a key role in precipitating the attack does *not* mean, of course, that the victim is *responsible* for the violence. The victim's action is typically a necessary but not sufficient condition for the abusive response. Other necessary conditions include the man's negative interpretation of the victim's action, his anger and his lack of inhibition about being violent towards his wife.

According to one analysis, almost all of the situations that generate anger can be analysed in terms of some combination of perceived 'irritants', 'costs' and 'transgressions' (Frude 1980, 1989). Assailants' statements during violent incidents, as reported by victims and assailants themselves, provide numerous illustrations of these elements at work (for example, Roy 1977, 1982; Dobash and Dobash 1979; Pahl 1985; Gelles 1987).

Marital partners often find each other irritating. A husband who finds his wife's appearance, vocal tones and habits irritating is likely to become angry, although such characteristics alone would rarely be sufficient to precipitate an attack. Much more important are the elements of 'cost' and 'transgression'. 'Cost' covers a wide range, including material costs (such as money), effort costs (like having to do a chore), and losses in self-esteem and so on. As social exchange theorists have pointed out (Nye 1982), marital partners engage in frequent high-tariff exchanges. They have to 'play' or 'compete' for limited resources, and many duties, tasks and chores have to be allocated between them. Such 'zero-sum games' often generate conflicts of interest. Thus a husband might be angered by being refused sex, by being denied access to money held by his wife, or by being asked to carry out a chore. His self-esteem may be threatened if his wife complains about his inability to provide adequately for the family, his lack of interest in the children or his laziness, if she insults him by calling him 'stupid' or 'wasteful', or if she taunts him about his untidiness or his lack of sexual prowess.

'Transgressions' are actions that break a rule, and perceived transgressions are especially important in the provocation of angry responses. The rules that operate within couple relationships are numerous and vary to some extent from couple to couple (Argyle and Henderson 1985). The terms 'should' and 'should not' signal accusations regarding transgressions and often feature prominently in marital conflicts. Partners have many expectations of each other, and one partner's 'unreasonable' failure to fulfil an expectation may lead to disappointment or anger. A dispute about rule-breaking may focus on whether a rule has actually been broken (whether, for example, the wife behaved in a flirtatious way) or may focus on the legitimacy of a rule (a wife may agree that she was being flirtatious but feel that this was justified because she had no intention of being unfaithful). Those who judge that their partner has broken a rule are likely to become angry, but they will regard their anger as 'just' and may feel that some degree of 'chastisement' is reasonable.

If a husband accuses his wife, for example, of disloyalty, laziness or infidelity, this initial verbal complaint may produce a defensive reply, or a counter-accusation. In many cases an initial complaint will lead to a verbal fight, and once a conflictual interaction has begun it will often escalate, with words and actions becoming progressively harsher. At some stage other issues are likely to be brought into the dispute. Marital violence often results from a verbal conflict that escalates until a blow is aimed. Patterson and Hops (1972), for example, found that victims and aggressors usually exchanged a series of preliminary verbal attacks and counter-attacks (which the authors refer to as 'coercion spirals'), before physical violence erupted. The conflict episode need not be prolonged, and on some occasions aggression may follow from a single comment or action that the assailant finds particularly annoying.

Partners are generally aware of the kinds of comment that will cause the most distress to the other. They may use this knowledge to avoid 'stepping on the other's toes', but in many cases the knowledge of sensitive topics is used to provide ammunition for an all-out verbal attack. There may be little verbal sparring before a rapid onslaught of insults and disparagements focuses on the opponent's personality, family of origin or other sensitive areas. Long-standing issues of dispute may be brought to the surface whenever a row erupts. The general verbal free-for-all involved in this type of conflict is likely to instigate extremely high levels of anger in both partners. An enraged response, or even cold detachment, may cause extreme irritation. Each partner is likely to judge the other as 'attacking', both in terms of what they say and how they say it, insults and accusations are likely to be seen as rule-breaking (that is, as 'transgressions'), and, for both partners, the other's behaviour is likely to be seen as justifying a counter-attack.

Gelles found that marital abuse was generally triggered by some verbal behaviour of the victim, including nagging, criticizing, name-calling, and gibes about status or sexual performance. He noted that a criticism sometimes touched a particularly sore point, as when a woman berates her husband for his inability to find a job or his lack of sexual stamina. Such verbal triggers often reflect the victim's state of stress, anxiety, disappointment and harassment. Partners become experts at attacking the other's weaknesses, and when they are angry they are liable to 'go for the jugular' and to 'hit below the belt'. Such 'unfairness' is likely to be seen by the partner as outrageous and offensive and may thus be taken by the assailant as a justification for his violent attack.

Whether or not the situation escalates to physical violence will depend to some degree on how the wife responds to the mounting tension of the interaction. Some victims report particular strategies that they use in an attempt to avoid a violent attack. Some respond passively, whereas others try to counter the threat of aggression by making a 'pre-emptive strike'. They may be physically violent or verbally aggressive, or threaten to leave, to call the police or to tell relatives. Sometimes such 'defensive' moves have the opposite effect of that intended. Rather than inhibiting the aggressor, they may generate intense anger and increase the risk that the confrontation will end in a violent attack.

Themes of violent marital encounters

Certain topics frequently recur as themes in episodes of marital violence. Arguments sometimes start over trivial issues and then escalate. Often, issues relating to major long-standing grievances or disputes come to the fore. Sometimes the fundamental controversy is obvious from the content of the verbal battle, but in many cases the matters addressed in the argument will cover a deeper, implicit problem (such as a dispute over power or commitment to the relationship). Complaints and disputes that eventually lead to violence often focus on such topics as child discipline, meals, chores and alcohol, as well as two areas that we will examine in more detail – sexual issues and money (Roy 1977, 1982; Dobash and Dobash 1979; Pahl 1985). These two are particularly relevant to an evolutionary perspective on male violence (Chapter 14).

Sexual issues

Sexual issues are often the source of quarrels that result in violence. Partners in distressed relationships often have different expectations about sexual interaction (how frequently they should have sexual contact, for example, or what types of behaviour are exciting and permissible). Gelles (1987) found that complaints about frigidity or impotence frequently led to violent attacks. A woman who is told that she is 'cold', or a man whose sexual prowess is called into question is likely to respond in an exaggerated fashion. Sometimes a fundamental difficulty in the relationship will have repercussions in the couple's sexual relations, and such changes may become the focus of violent quarrels.

Accusations of infidelity are also powerful triggers of aggression. Whether or not the accusation is justified, jealous arguments over suspected affairs often end in violence. Such violence may follow a prolonged interrogation of the partner who is suspected of cheating. A man may become violent because he suspects that his wife has been unfaithful to him or because he has been accused by his wife of cheating on her. A jealous husband may be super-vigilant for signs of infidelity and draw conclusions of flirtatious behaviour or an affair from meagre cues. Thus a woman who dresses up for an evening out may be accused of trying to attract other men.

Money

Some conflicts can be seen primarily as fights over resources such as money or free time. Most couples have limited finances, and there are certain tasks and chores that have to be performed by one or the other. The benefits that one person derives from personal expenditure represent a cost to the other person, and there may be endless wrangles about the fair allocation of money, chores and privileges. It is within this framework that the impact of poverty can be understood as increasing the risk of violence. Partners are likely to differ in their priorities, so that if a husband spends money (particularly if the wife judges that it has been 'wasted' on gambling, for example, or alcohol), the wife is likely to complain. In such circumstances, a husband's frustration and guilt about having wasted resources may make him extremely aggravated, and the complaint, especially if it is 'undiplomatic' in tone, is likely to provoke extreme rage. If a complaint is made about money spent on alcohol or other drugs while the 'offender' is still intoxicated then the situation may prove especially dangerous.

The role of alcohol

Many reports suggest that the consumption of alcohol greatly increases the risk of marital violence (Leonard and Jacob 1988). There are a number of explanations of why alcohol tends to make situations dangerous. Intoxication reduces the accuracy of social judgement and leads to behaviour that is likely to attract complaints (a general condemnation of the drunkenness, for example, a criticism about the money wasted on drink, or a specific protest about some aspect of drunken behaviour). Some people respond particularly aggressively to complaints when they have been drinking. The effect of alcohol in reducing inhibitions may also increase the likelihood that the angry person will attack in a violent and uncontrolled way. Gelles (1987) suggested that some men might deliberately use alcohol to provide an excuse, after the event, of why they beat up their wife. Alcohol, he claims, provides people with 'time out' from normal moral judgements and allows for 'deviance disavowal' by both the attacker and the victim ('it wasn't really me/him, it was the drink'). Thus he suggests that some individuals become intoxicated in order to carry out the violent act. Sedlak (1988) concluded that the use of alcohol by abusive men is often such an important factor that dealing with the drink problem can be a highly effective way of intervening in many cases of wife abuse.

The form of violence

Violent attacks take many different forms, some forms being much more dangerous than others. Marital abuse may involve a kick, a punch to the stomach, a punch to the head, or an all-out battering with multiple blows to vulnerable parts of the body. The precise form of the abuse is partly deter-mined by the degree of anger. Extreme anger may lead to an 'all-out' attack, while lower levels of anger may preserve some degree of control, so that the assault results in less serious injury. Some men follow their own idiosyncratic guidelines about what forms of aggression are 'legitimate' (examples of such rules are: 'never hit a woman in the chest' or 'only a coward kicks someone when they're down'), and others specifically avoid inflicting injuries, such as a black eye, that will later draw attention to their brutality.

The form of aggression sometimes follows previously uttered threats, as if the verbal threat provides a cue for the precise form of action used. Sometimes there is an instrumental aspect to the aggression, as when a woman who is screaming has a pillow held to her face, or symbolic elements may be involved, as when a man hits a woman in the face so that 'no one else will look at her'. Gelles (1987) suggests that specific techniques of family violence tend to be passed on from one generation to the next. Thus a man who was punched as a child, and witnessed his father punching the mother, would perhaps be more likely to punch his wife than to kick her. A particular form of aggressive action may become habitual, although the severity with which it is used will vary with the circumstances and the attacker's degree of anger.

CONCLUSION

In this chapter I have considered marital violence from an interactional per-spective. The fact that my explanation involves both the assailant and the victim does not imply that both are equally responsible. In the vast majority of cases the responsibility for marital *violence* lies with the husband (the assailant).

The purpose of the chapter has been to sketch a model of marital abuse, focusing on the couple, but not ignoring the important contribution of variables at the 'societal' and 'individual' levels. A model is not a theory, but can help to provide an understanding of the phenomenon. Such understanding has a significance of its own, but models also have a practical significance; for example, in pointing ways towards effective treatment and prevention. Frude (1991) has used the model outlined in this chapter to consider such applied aspects. One simple conclusion that illustrates the practical significance of the interactional model of marital abuse is that treatment can involve not only interventions with the assailant but also with the victim. Thus in a number of couple-based intervention programmes, strategies are aimed simultaneously at modifying the couple's interaction patterns, teaching the assaultive husband anger-control techniques, and helping the victim to develop her own protection plan (for example, Brygger and Edeleson 1987). A comprehensive model, incorporating social variables, also allows for the possibility that powerful intervention procedures may involve changes in family support services, police practices, and social policies (Farrington 1986; Sherman and Berk 1984; Parker 1985).

REFERENCES

Argyle, M. and Henderson, M. (1985) *The Anatomy of Relationships*, Harmondsworth, UK: Penguin.

Bornstein, P. H. and Bornstein, M. T. (1985) *Marital Therapy: A Behavioral-Communications Approach*, New York: Pergamon Press.

Brygger, M. P. and Edeleson, J. L. (1987) 'The Domestic Abuse Project: a multi-systems intervention in woman battering', *Journal of Interpersonal Violence*, 2: 324–36.

Coleman, D. H. and Straus, M. A. (1986) 'Marital power, conflict and violence in a nationally representative sample of American couples', *Violence and Victims*, 1: 141–57.

Dobash, R. E. and Dobash, R. (1979) *Violence against Wives*, New York: Free Press.

Dobash, R. P., Dobash, R. E., Wilson, M. and Daly, M. (1992) 'The myth of sexual symmetry in marital violence', *Social Problems*, 39: 71–91.

Ellis, D. (1989) 'Male abuse of a married or cohabiting female partner: the application of sociological theory to research findings', *Violence and Victims*, 4: 235–55.

Farrington, K. (1986) 'The application of stress theory to the study of family violence: principles, problems and prospects', *Journal of Family Violence*, 1: 131–47.

Frude, N. J. (1980) 'Child abuse as aggression', in N. Frude (ed.) *Psychological Approaches to Child Abuse*, London: Batsford.

—— (1989) 'The physical abuse of children', in K. Howells and C. Hollin (eds) *Clinical Approaches to Violence*, Chichester, UK: Wiley.

—— (1991) *Understanding Family Problems: A Psychological Analysis*, Chichester, UK: Wiley.

Gelles, R. J. (1987) *The Violent Home: Updated Edition*, Beverly Hills, CA: Sage.

Goldsmith, H. R. (1990) 'Men who abuse their spouses: an approach to assessing future risk', *Journal of Offender Counseling, Services and Rehabilitation*, 15: 45–56.

Goldstein, D. and Rosenbaum, A. (1985) 'An evaluation of the self-esteem of maritally violent men', *Family Relations Journal of Applied Family and Child Studies*, 34: 425–8.

Goode, W. J. (1971) 'Force and violence in the family', *Journal of Marriage and the Family*, 33: 624–57.

Gove, W. R., Style, C. B. and Hughes, M. (1990) 'The effect of marriage on the well-being of adults: a theoretical analysis', *Journal of Family Issues*, 11: 4–35.

Hornung, C., McCullough, B. and Sugimoto, T. (1981) 'Status relationships in marriage: risk factors in spouse abuse', *Journal of Marriage and the Family*, 43: 675–92.

Hotaling, G. T. and Sugarman, D. B. (1990) 'A risk marker analysis of assaulted wives', *Journal of Family Violence*, 5: 1–13.

Hurlbert, D. F., Whittaker, K. E. and Munoz, C. J. (1991) 'Etiological characteristics of abusive husbands', *Military Medicine*, 156: 670–5.

Jacobson, N. S. (1981) 'Behavioral marital therapy', in A. S. Gurman and D. P. Kniskern (eds) *Handbook of Family Therapy*, New York: Brunner/Mazel.

Jacobson, N. S., McDonald, D. W., Follete, W. C. and Berley, R. A. (1985) 'Attributional processes in distressed and non-distressed married couples', *Cognitive Therapy and Reseach*, 9: 35–50.

Leonard, K. E. and Jacob, T. (1988) 'Alcohol, alcoholism and family violence', in V. B. Van Hasselt, R. L. Morrison, A. S. Bellack and M. Hersen (eds) *Handbook of Family Violence*, New York: Plenum.

Lloyd, S. A. (1990) 'Conflict types and strategies in violent marriages', *Journal of Family Violence*, 5: 269–84.

Maiuro, R. D., Cohn, T. S., Vitaliano, P. P., Wanger, B. C. and Zegree, J. B. (1988) 'Anger hostility and depression in domestically violent versus generally assaultive men and nonviolent control subjects', *Journal of Consulting and Clinical Psychology*, 56: 17–23.

Margolin, G., John, R. S. and Gleberman, L. (1988) 'Affective responses to conflictual discussion in violent and nonviolent couples', *Journal of Consulting and Clinical Psychology*, 56: 24–33.

Mason, A. and Blankenship, V. (1987) 'Power and affiliation motivation, stress and abuse in intimate relationships', *Journal of Personality and Social Psychology*, 52: 203–10.

Meredith, W. H., Abbott, D. A. and Adams, S. L. (1986) 'Family violence: its relation to marital and parental satisfaction and family strengths', *Journal of Family Violence*, 1: 299–305.

Nye, F. I. (1982) *Family Relationships: Rewards and Costs*, Beverly Hills, CA: Sage.

Pahl, J. (ed.) (1985) *Private Violence and Public Policy: The Needs of Battered Women and the Response of the Public Services*, London: Routledge & Kegan Paul.

Parker, S. (1985) 'The legal background', in J. Pahl, *Private Violence and Public Policy: The Needs of Battered Women and the Response of the Public Services*, London: Routledge & Kegan Paul.

Patterson, G. R. and Hops, H. (1972) 'Coercion, a game for two: intervention techniques for marital conflict', in R. E. Ulrich and P. T. Mountjoy (eds) *The Experimental Analysis of Social Behavior*, New York: Appleton-Century-Crofts.

Pattison, E. M. (1985) 'Violent marriages', *Medical Aspects of Human Sexuality* 19: 57–74.

Rosenbaum, A. and O'Leary, K. D. (1981) 'Marital violence: characteristics of abusive couples', *Journal of Consulting and Clinical Psychology*, 49: 63–71.

Roy, M. (1977) *Battered Women: Psycho-sociological Study of Domestic Violence*, New York: Van Nostrand Reinhold.

—— (ed.) (1982) *The Abusing Partner: An Analysis of Domestic Battering*, New York: Van Nostrand Reinhold.

Saunders, D. G. (1986) 'When battered women use violence: husband abuse or self defense?' *Violence and Victims*, 1: 47–60.

Sedlak, A. J. (1988) 'Prevention of wife abuse', in V. B. Van Hasselt, R. L. Morrison, A. S. Bellack and M. Hersen (eds) *Handbook of Family Violence*, New York: Plenum.

Sherman, L. W. and Berk, R. A. (1984) 'The specific deterrents of arrest for domestic assault', *American Sociological Review*, 49: 261–72.

Stark, E. and Flitcraft, A. (1988) 'Violence among intimates: an epidemiological review', in V. B. Van Hasselt, R. L. Morrison, A. S. Bellack and M. Hersen (eds) *Handbook of Family Violence*, New York: Plenum.

Stets, J. E. and Straus, M. A. (1989) 'The marriage license as a hitting license: a comparison of assaults in dating, cohabiting, and married couples', *Journal of Family Violence*, 4: 161–80.

Straus, M. A. (1974) 'Leveling, civility, and violence in the family', *Journal of Marriage and the Family*, 36: 13–29.

—— (1980) 'Social stress and marital violence in a national sample of American families', in F. Wright, C. Bahn and R. W. Reiber (eds) *Forensic Psychology and Psychiatry: Annals of the New York Academy of Science*, 347: 229–50.

Straus, M. A. and Gelles, R. J. (1986) 'Societal change and family violence from 1975 to 1985 as revealed by two national surveys', *Journal of Marriage and the Family*, 48: 445–79.

Straus, M. A., Gelles, R. J. and Steinmetz, S. K. (1980) *Behind Closed Doors: Violence in American Families*, New York: Doubleday.

Sugarman, D. B. and Hotaling, G. T. (1989) 'Violent men in intimate relationships: an analysis of risk markers', *Journal of Applied Social Psychology*, 19: 1034–48.

Telch, C. F. and Lindquist, C. U. (1984) 'Violent versus nonviolent couples: a comparison of patterns', *Psychotherapy*, 21: 242–8.

10

SEXUAL VIOLENCE AGAINST WOMEN

Characteristics of typical perpetrators

Paul Pollard

Recent studies on the frequency with which women report experiencing sexual aggression have revealed alarmingly high figures. For instance, Mary Koss and colleagues, using a survey instrument developed by Koss and Oros (1982) and validated by Koss and Gidyez (1985), obtained data from a large national sample of US undergraduate students. Among respondents 15.4 per cent reported having been raped since the age of 14; this figure rose to 27 per cent when attempted rapes were included. Over half of these attacks were committed on dates, and very few were reported to the police (Koss et al. 1988; Koss et al. 1987). Koss and her colleagues found substantial additional reports of unwanted intercourse following verbal coercion.

With respect to samples of the general public, Russell (1982) and Koss et al. (1990) found that 24 and 21 per cent, respectively, of respondents reported having been raped, although other reported rape frequencies from North America have been much lower, between 6 and 8 per cent (for example, Brickman and Briere 1984; Divasto et al. 1984; Kilpatrick et al. 1985). Studies reporting lower frequencies have, however, typically used more restricted definitions of rape: they have often focused on reports of 'crimes', and it is therefore unlikely that they detected cases of non-stranger sexual aggression. The authors themselves have usually suggested that their findings are underestimates. Local samples of undergraduates have produced similarly high figures to those of Koss et al. (1987), with between 12 and 17 per cent of respondents reporting having been raped (for example, Coller and Resick 1987; Copenhaver and Grauerholz 1991; Hall and Flannery 1984; Jenkins and Dambrot 1987; Kanin 1957; Kanin and Parcell 1977; Miller and Marshall 1987; Muehlenhard and Linton 1987).

There is no reason to believe that this picture is restricted to North America. Hall (1985) reported a large-scale study in London in which 17 per cent of the respondents reported having been raped. Gavey (1991) administered the Koss survey to New Zealand undergraduates. She found that 14 per cent reported a rape and 25 per cent reported a rape or attempted rape. Consistent with the

170

US surveys, Gavey found that most cases of victimization were within heterosexual relationships. An unpublished study by Beattie (1992) found that 10 per cent of UK undergraduates reported a rape and 19 per cent reported rape or attempted rape.

These surveys reveal a frequency of rape of epidemic proportions. Yet it is primarily a hidden crime. For instance, in Beattie's study only 2 per cent of rape survivors had reported to the police, and a third had told no one at all. Given the very large proportion of rapes by non-strangers, this lack of reporting can, at least in part, be traced to public attitudes about rape amongst intimates that will lead to what has been referred to as 'secondary victimization' of survivors (for example, J. E. Williams 1984). Chambers and Millar (1987) provide some potent examples of this in (Scottish) court settings, with transcripts of cross-examinations that are clearly hostile. There are several reasons why a dating interaction is associated with a high risk of sexual aggression. For example, Weis and Borges (1975) pointed out that dating norms socialize men to be sexually assertive and women to be resistant, but resistance is difficult because women are also socialized to be non-aggressive. Lewin (1985) also identified dating norms as conducive to rape, and argued that 'until the ideology of male supremacy is overcome and sex is no longer played as a game that he wins and she loses, the rate of unwanted intercourse will continue to be high' (p. 192).

Several studies, using vignettes depicting sexual aggression, have found that subjects are less likely to define enforced intercourse as rape, and/or to attribute more responsibility for the attack to the victim, as a function of prior romantic involvement or prior mutually consenting sexual activity (Bridges 1991; Bridges and McGrail 1989; Jenkins and Dambrot 1987; Johnson and Jackson 1988; Johnson et al. 1989; Klemmack and Klemmack 1976; L'Armand and Pepitone 1982; Quackenbush 1989; Shotland and Goodstein 1983). There is also evidence that rape survivors themselves are less likely to define enforced intercourse as rape in such situations (Koss 1985; L. S. Williams 1984). In such cases, the victim is seen as more willing (Check and Malamuth 1983, 1984), and the attack may be seen as justifiable in certain situations that may have led the man to 'expect' intercourse (Fischer 1986a, 1987; Muehlenhard et al. 1985; Muehlenhard and MacNaughton 1988).

It is important to note that, although people may view unwanted intercourse as less serious in this situation (and possibly not even as 'real' rape), there is reason to believe that its traumatic effects are no less serious than those experienced by survivors of stranger rapes (for example, Koss and Burkhart 1989; Koss et al. 1988). Given this, the very high frequencies of largely unreported non-stranger rape indicate an alarming number of criminals and victims who are not brought to the attention of the criminal justice system. Convicted offenders are thus an atypical sample of rapists. Stranger rapists are too highly represented and, although child sexual offenders may be 'crime specialists', persons convicted of sex offences against adults usually have convictions for other offences as well (for example, Hall 1988; Hall and Proctor 1987). By contrast, the 'typical' rapist is an acquaintance, probably an intimate, of the victim, does not have a criminal background, and has not been reported to the police. To find out more about such rapists, researchers have used self-report techniques to identify them. In the next section, I describe how this is done.

DETECTING NON-DETECTED RAPISTS: 'RAPE PROCLIVITY'

The two main measures that have been used are self-reports of actual previous offending and hypothetical estimates of the likelihood of offending in the future.

Several studies, initiated by Neil Malamuth and co-workers, have used self-report indices of the likelihood that a subject would rape a woman if they could be sure that they would not be punished. These are given usually on five-point scales and, typically, subjects indicating the lowest scale response ('not at all likely') are classified as 'low LR' and other subjects are classified as 'high LR', indicating *some* self-reported proclivity towards rape. Malamuth (1981) reported that across several studies (published in the early 1980s), the proportion of high LR subjects was 35 per cent. However, as some people, particularly date-rapists, may not actually label the act as rape, the specific question about rape used in these studies is probably an underestimate of the proportion of male college students who believe that they would engage in sexually aggressive acts. Briere and Malamuth (1983) asked subjects not only for their likelihood of rape if they would not be punished and no one would know, but also (embedded in distractor items) the likelihood of their 'forcing a female to do something she didn't really want to do'. Among the subjects 30 per cent indicated some likelihood of rape and a further 30 per cent indicated some likelihood of force (LF). In a study by Smeaton and Byrne (1987) subjects viewed aggressive or erotic films with one of six female confederates and were asked to indicate on a five-point scale how likely they would be 'to push the person with whom you participated in this experiment farther than she says she wants to go sexually'. Of the sample, 71 per cent indicated some likelihood on this measure.

Koss *et al.* (1987) found that 7.7 per cent of men reported having engaged in rape or attempted rape since the age of 14. A further 7.2 per cent reported coercing a female into intercourse, primarily by continual argument and pressure. Although 15 per cent of males thus reported at least one completed or uncompleted attempt to have intercourse with an unwilling female, this was notably lower than the proportion of females (39 per cent) who reported being the recipients of such aggression. Only 25 per cent of males (as opposed to 54 per cent of females) reported any form of enforced behaviour. Koss *et al.* (1987) point out that the difference between male and female reports could be due to the males intentionally withholding disclosure, and/or to their failing to perceive in some cases that the female is unwilling. Alternatively, the difference could be due to a smaller number of males being involved in a greater number of attacks. This would, in fact, be expected if one takes the not unreasonable view that some males are more prone to aggression than others but that all females are more or less equally likely to be aggressed against. Several other studies have also found that females report receiving more sexual aggression than males report inflicting (for example, Gwartney-Gibbs et al. 1987; Jenkins and Dambrot 1987; Muehlenhard and Linton 1987).

Some studies report comparatively low frequencies for self-reported enforced intercourse. Muehlenhard and Falcon (1990) and Greendlinger and Byrne (1987) found that 1.5 per cent of their samples reported having used physical force to obtain intercourse. However, the former study found that 34 per cent reported use of intentional intoxification or coercion and, in Greendlinger and Byrne's study, 23 per cent said that they had had sex against a woman's will because they had 'become so excited you could not control yourself'. Presumably, many if not all of the latter would have involved some form of force. Similarly, Koss and Oros (1982), Peterson and Franzese (1987), and Petty and Dawson (1989) found 21–23 per cent of males reporting that they had engaged in intercourse with an unwilling female because they were so sexually aroused that 'they couldn't stop', even though these studies found much lower incidences of reported explicit use of force. In a study by Mosher and Anderson (1986), 75 per cent admitted purposeful use of drugs or alcohol in order to lower the woman's ability to resist. Also, coercive behaviours such as 'saying things you didn't mean' to obtain intercourse are frequently reported and, in many studies, most subjects report some form of sexual aggression (for example, 78 per cent in Muehlenhard and Linton 1987). One study that appears to have produced somewhat lower reported frequencies is that by Miller and Marshall (1987) who sampled two universities, one in the South and one in the Midwest. About 1 per cent reported use of physical force and 6 per cent reported intercourse because they were too aroused to stop.

Self-reported frequencies of male sexual aggression are presumably likely to be under-reports due to self-presentational effects, even when responses are anonymous. I have thus not reported all frequency results here, nor made any attempt to compare studies to derive some 'best estimate'. The important point is that there are sufficient reports to obtain meaningful relations with other measures. The frequencies vary quite considerably, but no studies reveal a very low proportion of reported aggression and some reveal very high frequencies.

The validity of these measures would be difficult to demonstrate definitively, but there is some relevant evidence. Self-reports of aggression have been found to correlate with LR ratings (Malamuth 1989; Murphy et al. 1986; Petty and Dawson 1989; Smeaton and Byrne 1987, although not significantly by Greendlinger and Byrne 1987). There is therefore reasonable indication that they are measuring the same thing. This point is further reinforced by the fact that other measures that correlate with LR also correlate with self-reported aggression, and vice versa. For this reason, if similar findings have been reported, I shall sometimes use the term 'rape proclivity' to refer to (either or) both types of measure.

One item of strong evidence for their validity is that both measures correlate with arousal to rape depictions (Malamuth and Check 1980a; Malamuth *et al.* 1980; Malamuth *et al.* 1986; Mosher and Anderson 1986). LR measures have also been linked with greater use of sexually violent pornography (Demare *et al.* 1988). The results of Malamuth and Check (1983) indicate that LR is a particularly important variable in arousal to rape. Low LR subjects reported equal arousal to non-rape and rape descriptions when the latter indicated that the victim suffered involuntary arousal (a 'disinhibition' effect previously reported by Malamuth and Check (1980a, 1980b) and Malamuth *et al.* (1980), but high LR subjects showed *higher* levels of arousal to the 'rape plus victim arousal' story than to a story involving the woman's consent and enjoyment.

CORRELATES OF RAPE PROCLIVITY

Correlates with sexual activity

Abel *et al.* (1976) gave some examples of 'heterosocial-heterosexual' skills training programmes for convicted rapists, and noted that

> the premise of such skills training is that rapists may be sexually aroused by women, but unless they can carry out the preliminary conversation, flirting, and other dating skills antecedent to a relationship, they will not have the opportunity to become involved sexually with the female (except by rape).

> (1976: 103)

In fact, studies have failed to find reliable differences in heterosexual skills between convicted rapists and appropriate controls (Overholser and Beck 1986; Segal and Marshall 1985a, 1985b), but the quotation does illustrate popular (and presumably early clinical) assumptions that rape is mediated by frustration due to lack of sexual access to females. This can be viewed as a 'folk theory' about the causes of sexual aggression.

Although finding attitudinal correlates of LR ratings, Briere and Malamuth (1983) discovered no relationship between LR and ratings of the following: (1) current sex life and relationships with the opposite sex, (2) importance and pleasantness of, and knowledge about, sex, (3) sexual conservatism or inhibitions, or (4) use of, and reaction to, pornography – although Denmare *et al.* (1988) did find a relationship for violent pornography. Malamuth *et al.* (1986) similarly found no relation between a variety of sexual measures and self-reported arousal to force orientated sexual depictions. The failure to find relations between rape proclivity and a range of sexual ratings reinforces the

174

view that rape has little or nothing to do with sexual frustration or maladjustment. Although Briere *et al.* (1985) did find a small number of relationships between sexual and attitudinal variables, this was only the case for three of the thirty-six possible relationships explored. The only significant 'sexual' finding that appears reliable is that extent of previous sexual experience is *positively* related to both LR ratings (Briere and Malamuth 1983) and self-reported sexual aggression (Kanin 1984, 1985; Malamuth 1986; Malamuth *et al.* 1991). Again this is at odds with a 'frustration' explanation. Davis and Leitenberg (1987) similarly concluded that the literature on adolescent sex offenders does not support the idea that lack of sexual experience is positively related to offending.

Further evidence against the view that rape is a result of lack of sexual access due to low social skills is provided by the data of Muehlenhard and Falcon (1990). They found that heterosocially skilled males were more likely to report having engaged in both consenting intercourse, and verbal or alcohol coerced intercourse, than were low-skilled males, but that heterosocial skill was unrelated to reported forced intercourse. Thus the more heterosocially competent males used this ability to increase their frequency of verbal coercion, but did not physically aggress any less. Muehlenhard and Falcon suggest that social skills training for convicted rapists could be even counterproductive, as 'improving a rapist's heterosocial skill without changing his attitudes might simply add verbal sexual coercion to his repertoire of coercive sexual behaviors' (1990: 256).

Personality correlates

Another 'folk theory' is that sexual aggressors are mentally unstable. Ryan (1988) asked subjects to write an example of a typical rape and found that most of these scripts depicted a prototypical 'blitz' rape by a stranger, frequently with reference to the attacker's mental instability. Hollin and Howells (1987) asked subjects from a variety of British populations to rate the importance of mental instability, defective education, parents, excitement, alienation (for example, unemployment) and temptation as causative factors in 'young people's' crimes. They found that mental instability was rated as the most important causal factor in sexual assault, and the least important in the case of robbery and burglary, although a second experiment comparing newspaper accounts of a rape and a robbery did not fully replicate this finding. Giacopassi and Dull (1986) found that 75 per cent of an undergraduate sample expressed agreement with the statement 'most rapists have severe psychological problems'. Instability would thus appear to be the generally expected correlate of rape proclivity.

Some personality correlates of rape proclivity have been investigated. Self-reported previous sexual aggression and/or LR ratings are associated with general aggressive tendencies (Greendlinger and Byrne 1987; Petty and

Dawson 1989), psychoticism (Malamuth and Check 1983, 1985; Malamuth 1986; Murphy *et al.* 1986; although not Koss *et al.* 1985), a ('disinhibition') measure of self-control (Lisak and Roth 1988), impulsivity (Petty and Dawson 1989), and (negatively) with responsibility and socialization (Rapaport and Burkhart 1984). A fairly frequent finding is intergender hostility (e.g. Malamuth *et al.* 1991).

What relationships are found suggest that more sexually aggressive males tend to be more generally aggressive and antisocial, and less sympathetic to other people, although, in general, personality correlates are weak, and the characteristics identified are not of a nature to be classified as consistent with the 'mentally unstable' stereotype of rape offenders. Petty and Dawson (1989) specifically pointed out that, although subjects they identified as higher offenders did have elevated scores on several personality characteristics, they were not outside the normal range. Hall *et al.* (1986) reported that attitudinal correlates were much stronger, and few studies have found personality correlates to be as important as attitudinal ones. Koss *et al.* (1985) found no relation between self-reported aggression and several antisocial measures. However, both Hall *et al.* (1986) and Rapaport and Burkhart (1984) suggested that some antisocial tendency may be necessary to translate rape-supportive attitudes into behaviour.

Attitudinal correlates

General samples

In considering attitudinal correlates of rape proclivity, it will be useful to review briefly research on what are referred to as 'rape-tolerant' attitudes. Brownmiller (1975) argued that there are a variety of beliefs prevalent in the population that legitimize rape. For instance, she listed several 'rape myths' such as: 'all women want to be raped', 'no woman can be raped against her will', and 'she was asking for it' (1975: 311). Burt (1980) devised a Rape Myth Acceptance (RMA) scale, incorporating these beliefs and others, and studied the relationship between acceptance of 'cultural myths' about rape and more general attitudes about male/female interaction. Using a large random sample of the Minnesota general public, she found considerable adherence to these rape myths.

She found that the three main correlates of RMA, for both males and females, were as follows: 'Acceptance of Interpersonal Violence' (AIV) – 'the notion that force and coercion are legitimate ways to gain compliance and specifically that they are legitimate in intimate and sexual relationships; Adversarial Sexual Beliefs (ASB) – 'the expectation that sexual relationships are fundamentally exploitative', 'distrust of the opposite sex'; and Sex-Role Stereotyping (SRS). These were correlated with one another, as well as with RMA. Thus Burt found that RMA was associated with a cluster of beliefs, which could be referred to as 'traditional' views about male/female interactions. She argued that these views, by apparently promoting rape myths, produce a rape-supportive culture. This conclusion is consistent with Sanday's (1981) argument, based on cross-cultural comparisons, that the less females are accorded equal status in a society, the higher the prevalence of rape.

US studies of rape myths (measured by Burt's, or similar, scales) have consistently found that males accept them more than females (Check and Malamuth 1983; Costin 1985; Dull and Giacopassi 1987; Feild 1978; Giacopassi and Dull 1986; Hamilton and Yee 1990; Jenkins and Dambrot 1987; Margolin et al. 1989; Muehlenhard and Linton 1987; Ward 1988). Outside the United States, this sex difference has been reported in the United Kingdom, West Germany and Israel (Costin and Schwarz 1987; although Krahe 1988 found no sex differences in samples in the United Kingdom and Germany), Singapore (Ward 1988), and Hong Kong (Lee and Cheung 1991). The relationship Burt found between RMA and general beliefs about the rights and roles of women in society (the SRS scale) is particularly important as it clearly relates rape-supportive beliefs to traditional cultural attitudes about the secondary role of women. This relationship has been consistently reported in a range of studies (Check and Malamuth 1983, 1985; Costin 1985; Costin and Schwarz 1987; Feild 1978; Hall et al. 1986; Mayerson and Taylor 1987; Murphy et al. 1986; Schwartz and Brand 1983), usually using either Burt's SRS scale or the Attitudes Towards Women Scale (AWS; Spence et al. 1973).

This research has clearly identified some societal beliefs that provide what Burt (1980) has referred to as a 'rape-supportive' culture, consistent with the more theoretical analyses of writers such as Brownmiller (1975). Additionally, males have generally been found to hold these beliefs more than females. Similarly, experimental research in the attribution paradigm has identified various factors that lead to victim blame, and has found that typically males, and subjects with more traditional sex-role views, make judgements that are less 'pro-victim' than do females and subjects with less traditional views (for a review, see Pollard 1992).

Attitudinal correlates of rape proclivity

LR has been found to be associated with tendencies to blame the victim in a rape scenario, greater belief that victims may enjoy sexual violence, and Burt's RMA, AIV and ASB scales (Briere and Malamuth 1983; Check and Malamuth 1985; Hamilton and Yee 1990; Malamuth 1989; Malamuth and Check 1985; Pryor 1987; Quackenbush 1989; Tieger 1981). Check and Malamuth (1983) found a clear relation between LR and traditional sex-role views – some likelihood of rape being reported by 44 per cent of high SRS, as compared to 12 per cent of low SRS, males. However, a discriminant analysis performed by Demare et al. (1988) suggested that relations between LR and RMA, ASB and the AWS may be mediated by the correlations between these

177

variables and the AIV scale. Briere (1987) asked undergraduates to indicate the likelihood of their (non-sexually) aggressing against a future wife and found this to be related to scores on both the AIV and the AWS.

Similar relations have been found between attitudes and self-reported history of aggression. Jenkins and Dambrot (1987) found self-reported sexual aggression to be related to victim blame in a (date) rape scenario, greater belief that the victim desired intercourse, less agreement that it was a rape, and less agreement that the rapist behaved violently. Rapaport and Burkhart (1984) and Muehlenhard and Linton (1987) both found a correlation between undergraduates' self-reported previous history of sexual aggression and Burt's AIV and ASB scales. Muehlenhard and Falcon (1990), Muehlenhard and Linton (1987), and Peterson and Franzese (1987) (although not Murphy *et al.* 1986 or Rapaport and Burkhart 1984) found a relation between self-reported sexual aggression and traditional sex-role views. Crossman *et al.* (1990) found a comparable relation for the extent of severe (though not minor) marital abuse. Koss *et al.* (1985), using adaptations of Burt's scales, concluded that

> the more sexually aggressive a man had been, the more likely he was to attribute adversarial qualities to interpersonal relationships, to accept sex role stereotypes, to believe myths about rape, to feel that rape prevention is the woman's responsibility, and to view as normal an intermingling of aggression and sexuality.

(1985: 989)

The above studies have identified a cluster of interrelated beliefs that correlate with rape proclivity: greater belief in rape myths, traditional sex-role attitudes, greater victim blame, and attitudes supportive of interpersonal violence. As the quote from Koss *et al.* (1985) illustrates, these relate to the linking of sexual aggression with traditional male socialization about the appropriateness of male aggression and dominance. For instance, Check and Malamuth (1983) found that high SRS males were non-significantly *more* aroused to a rape than to a consenting depiction, even though the victim was clearly shown to be distressed. Similarly, male subjects high on the hypermasculinity ('macho') scale (Mosher and Sirkin 1984) have been found to report greater frequencies of past, and greater likelihood of future, sexual aggression (Mosher and Anderson 1986; Muehlenhard and Falcon 1990; Smeaton and Byrne 1987). Males with more 'traditional' attitudes tend to believe that women enjoy, and are responsible for, sexual aggression, and that such aggression is legitimate, and they report more arousal to, and proclivity towards, sexual violence. Smeaton and Byrne (1987) have suggested that the 'macho' male is particularly fearful about the adequacy of his masculinity and that sexual access to females is of primary importance in this respect. This type of male, with his strong beliefs in the legitimacy of male dominance, may thus be particularly likely to aggress when sexual advances are rejected.

Sexual aggression has been linked to general measures of dominance and

178

power motivation (Lisak and Roth 1988; Petty and Dawson 1989), and Malamuth and Check (1983, 1985) found LR ratings and rape-supportive beliefs to be correlated with a measure of power motivation in sexual interaction. This was derived from a questionnaire that assesses motivations for engaging in sexual acts, an example of a power motivation question being 'I enjoy the conquest'. Malamuth (1986) has similarly shown a relation between self-reported previous aggression and the dominance sub-scale of the power motivation measure. Hendrick *et al.* (1985) observed that men generally tend to link power and sex more than do women. For instance, males were less likely than females to disagree with the statement 'To create sexual desire in someone is one of the best ways to dominate that person'.

The role of power and dominance in sexual aggression is further illustrated by Greendlinger and Byrne's (1987) finding that LR and reported aggression are correlated with use of forced or violent sexual fantasies, and also with Silbert and Pines's (1984) report that prostitutes who revealed their profession to a rapist and offered to submit were more severely injured. Rapists 'became furious at hearing the woman say she was a prostitute, . . . insisting on taking her by force. In order to reassert their own control, assailants then became extremely violent' (1984: 864). Dominance appears to have been the primary motive in these attacks. This relationship between power and aggression is apparently not limited to sexual abuse, since Mason and Blankenship (1987) found that males with a high need for power reported considerably more physical abuse of their ongoing partners than did those low in power motivation.

The influence of sexually aggressive peers

As it is very likely that the attitudes and behaviours of young males will be strongly influenced by peer-group norms, this variable merits particular attention. Alder (1985) identified the presence of sexually aggressive friends as of particular importance in predicting sexual aggression. In her study, this factor was the best of three predictive factors, the others being rape-supportive attitudes and service in Vietnam (a variety of demographic factors were not predictive of aggression). Further, factors interacted such that having sexually aggressive friends appeared to be a necessary component (that is, rape-supportive attitudes and Vietnam service had little effect if subjects did not have sexually aggressive peers). Gwartney-Gibbs *et al.* (1987) found that almost twice as many males with sexually aggressive peers reported coercive or enforced intercourse than did males with no sexually aggressive peers. Petty and Dawson (1989) found reported sexual aggression to be related to desires to be held in high esteem by acquaintances ('social recognition'), and suggested that 'This characteristic may play an important part in maintaining sexual aggression by men through peer pressure' (1989: 360). Conversely, Heilbrun and Loftus (1986) found reported sexual aggression to be (marginally) negatively related to reports that the person had ever felt pressure from male peers about the degree of sexual intimacy he could achieve. However, this discrepancy may be due to the fact that Heilbrun and Loftus asked about the respondents' feelings rather than about their friends' behaviour. Members of an aggressive group may be the most reluctant to admit pressure from anybody.

Further indication of the importance of peer-group norms emerges from the studies of Kanin, in interviews with 87 respondents (in a sample of 341) who reported having attempted to gain enforced intercourse (1969), and with 71 who had volunteered to be interviewed about a self-reported completed rape 'over the last ten years'. (These 71 respondents were compared with a selected control group who did not report instances of sexual aggression: Kanin 1984, 1985.) All these rapes were during dates and most involved some immediately prior sexual contact, usually genital. It should be noted, however, that possible misunderstandings about the females' motives do not appear to have been a significant contributory factor, as the couple had often engaged in similar levels of sexual activity on prior dates, and in most cases the female had stated a level beyond which she did not wish to proceed. Even so, most of the offenders attributed some amount of blame to the victim and saw their crime as, although wrong, not meriting severe punishment.

Kanin described these offenders as sexual predators, being much more sexually active than controls and having on previous occasions used similar levels of (successfully resisted) force in attempting intercourse, and also having used a variety of other coercive strategies. Most, for instance, reported having used attempts at intoxification. Peer-group influences were said to provide 'a culture where sexual access is of paramount importance in the maintenance of self-esteem' (Kanin 1985: 224). Friends were reported as providing much more pressure for sexual activity, and as being more likely to condone sexual aggression in certain situations, than were friends of control subjects. Of the self-reported rapists 41 per cent had engaged in group male intercourse with a female and 67 per cent had had intercourse with a female 'recommended as sexually congenial' by a friend (as compared to 7 per cent and 13 per cent of their controls), again attesting to the sexually predatory nature of their social network.

Attitudes of convicted rapists

Although convicted offenders are a small, atypical sub-sample of rapists, particularly in that they tend to be stranger rapists who were reported to the police and have records of other criminal offences, it is of some interest to compare attitudes in convicted populations to see whether similar themes emerge.

Feild (1978) found that convicted rapists showed more RMA than a general public sample on five of the eight factors on his scale. However, although the general public sample was very large (over 1,000), there were only twenty convicted rapists and these were from a state mental hospital and were thus presumably particularly exceptional. Burt (1983) asked thirty-six convicted rapists who were voluntarily on a treatment programme, and a large random sample, to make judgements about the male attacker in various scenarios involving physical assault on a female victim. For the violent assault that caused the victim to be hospitalized for several days, only 35 per cent of the general sample (and 20 per cent of the rapists) said that *no* behaviour would justify it when asked what the victim 'might have done to deserve what happened to her'. Of the general sample 46 per cent, and 73 per cent of the rapists, offered one or more possible explanations as to why she may have 'deserved' the assault. Although this study did identify some differences between convicted rapists and others, it should be noted that Burt interpreted her results as showing that the convicted rapists were simply more ready to 'select and organize the culturally available excuses and explanations' (1983: 134). In other words, although the convicted offenders were more ready to offer justifications, they were providing explanations that many of the general public also cited.

Non-incarcerated samples differ from convicted rapists in many ways, and therefore cannot be considered as true controls. Hall *et al.* (1986) compared twenty-seven convicted rapists, nineteen men convicted of assault or armed robbery, and a control group of thirty men, matched on age and race only. The control group showed significantly less RMA than the other groups, but the offender groups did not differ. Overholser and Beck (1986) found no significant difference in the level of RMA between their groups of convicted rapists, child-molesters, non-incarcerated controls, and 'minimal dater' students (students who reported low frequencies of dating). The power of this study was low, however (twelve subjects per group). Sattem *et al.* (1984) similarly found no overall differences between (child and adult) sex offenders, other offenders and controls (group numbers thirty-three, fifty-two and thirty-four), and reported that, if anything, the sex offenders were *less* sex-role stereotyped. With a rather larger sample (114 convicted rapists and 75 other offender controls), Marolla and Scully (1986) obtained a very small, marginally significant, difference in RMA scores. However, they found no differences in scores on the Attitudes Towards Women Scale, scores on Burt's Acceptance of Interpersonal Violence scale, and on judgements about whether a rape vignette should be defined as rape and how much fault should be attributed to the victim. In general, then, studies have failed to detect significant attitudinal differences between convicted rapists and other types of offenders.

Although there were few differences between responses of convicted rapists and controls to the scales used by Marolla and Scully, detailed interviews with the convicts produced some revealing findings. Scully and Marolla (1984, 1985) provide a variety of quotations, the sheer callousness of which, in general, is very striking. Running through most of the accounts were the themes of power, conquest and the enjoyment of impersonal sex. As the authors put it, 'through rape men can experience power and avoid the emotions related to intimacy and tenderness' (1985: 259). Although the act was seen as an expression of masculine power and will, many rapists did not see their crime as having been 'really' a rape. Over a quarter of the seventy-nine who did not deny contact with the victim said that she either seduced them or at least was willing and made some advances. An equal number claimed that, although the victim did not express willingness, she did not 'resist enough' and thus had really meant 'yes' (in several of these cases the victim had been threatened with a weapon!); thirty-one claimed that the victim had enjoyed her ordeal. Another theme apparent in the accounts of thirty-two rapists was reference to the victim's past sexual behaviour, with the implication that assault on non-monogamous sexually active women does not really count as rape. The authors point out that the belief that 'nice girls don't get raped' leads to a conclusion that the victim probably had a 'bad reputation' and must have 'asked for it' in some way.

As the authors acknowledge, these men had good reason to atempt to justify their behaviour, and thus may have been inventing 'excuses', but the interest is in the consistency of the justifications. They were drawing upon a culturally shared set of excuses that reflect the general rape myths suggested by Brown-miller. However, given Marolla and Scully's results, the convicts were pre-sumably not particularly discrepant in these views from males in the control group.

In view of the findings that belief in rape myths, traditional sex-role atti-tudes, acceptance of interpersonal violence, and associated attitudes are related to unconvicted offending, it might seem surprising that convicted rapists do not generally differ from other offender control groups in these beliefs. However, this apparent discrepancy is resolved if account is taken of the fact that serious offenders in general may be highly socialized to the masculine role that promotes sexual aggression. As Marolla and Scully (1986) concluded about their offender groups:

> They have been socialized to accept and even anticipate a certain degree of physical violence between men and women. Both groups indicated a history of physically abusing women close to them 'at least occasionally'. Many believed women enjoy being hurt or dominated by men. Over two thirds of the sample believed women cause their own rape by their actions and choice of clothing.
>
> (1986: 352)

In other words, sexual offending can be seen as related to a socialized 'male view of the world', which probably characterizes other serious offenders. Both rapist and other offender groups can thus be seen as having high proclivity towards sexual aggression, which accounts for the lack of attitudinal differ-ences. The offender controls were not convicted for rape either because not all males with these views will necessarily have offended, or (as in the undergraduate studies) because they had not been caught.

DISCUSSION

Correlates of sexual aggression

In the previous sections, the following variables were found to be consistently related to self-reported sexual aggression: greater sexual arousal to rape depictions, greater sexual experience and number of sexual partners, more adherence to 'rape-tolerant' attitudes, some personality correlates – particularly inter-gender hostility – and a sexually exploitive peer group. The identification of a cluster of rape-related variables indicates that individual differences exist in the general male population that may typify males more likely to engage in sexual aggression.

Malamuth (1986) found that several variables predictive of sexual aggression interact rather than have an additive effect, a fact also noted by Alder (1985) using a more limited number of predictors. Malamuth's regression analysis showed that presence of several variables had more predictive power than would be implied by a summation of their individual predictive power, which was generally low. Thus a sexually experienced male, with a tendency to be aroused by rape depictions, and scoring above average on measures of power and dominance motivation for sex, inter-gender hostility and psychoticism, would be particularly likely to be prone to sexual aggression; whereas no reliable prediction could be made about males having some but not all of these factors.

Malamuth *et al.* (1991) have extended the above analysis with structural equation modelling of data from male respondents in the national survey conducted by Mary Koss and co-workers. The two main proximal determinants of sexual aggression were 'sexual promiscuity' (age at first intercourse and number of partners) and 'hostile masculinity' (measured by three scales including hostility towards women and adversarial sexual beliefs). The latter also predicted non-sexual aggression towards women, and high levels of both produced particularly high levels of both sexual and non-sexual aggression. The latter finding supports Malamuth's (1986) results that stressed the importance of interactions, and the model of Malamuth *et al.* (1991) was said to fit the earlier data very well.

Sexual and non-sexual aggression were also predicted by peer delinquency, attitudes supporting violence (RMA, AIV and ASB), and a history of child abuse and parental violence. However, the analysis revealed these variables to be indirect in their influence, in that attitudes strongly affected hostile masculinity, whereas parental violence and child abuse affected delinquency, which in turn strongly affected promiscuity. This study has gone some way towards identifying the factors related to sexual aggression. The typical highly sexually

aggressive male is particularly focused on a high frequency of sexual interactions with an attendant hostility towards women. Attitudinal and peer-
group influences discussed earlier can be viewed as background variables that
encourage the creation of such personalities.

In Malamuth's (1986) study, only a small proportion (less than 10 per cent)
of the participants fell into the high-likelihood category. However, given the
prevalence of sexual aggression revealed by both male and female self-report
data, it is clearly not the case that sexual aggressors form a small sub-group of
the male population. It was not the case, for instance, that the remaining 90
per cent of subjects showed no proclivity for aggression. They simply showed
less proclivity, which was not reliably predictable if only some of the 'risk
factors' were present. Thus, although the findings of Malamuth (1986) and
Malamuth *et al.* (1991) suggested that there may be a small sub-group who are
highly prone to aggression, in general the male population cannot be divided
into those who may, or may not, sexually aggress. However, although all
males probably have some proclivity to sexual aggression, particularly at
lower levels, the 'macho' male, whose sense of self-worth is bolstered by the
pursuit of dominance and exploitation of the opposite sex, is particularly likely
to translate his basic misogyny into sexual violence.

Hostile or instrumental aggression?

One might object to the findings on non-convicted offenders on the grounds
that self-reported past or future rape proclivity may not reflect actual
behaviour. However, more direct evidence has been provided by Malamuth
(1983), who measured males' arousal to rape depictions and also assessed their
'attitudes facilitating violence' (RMA and AIV scales). A week later, as part of
an ostensibly unrelated study, participants were given the opportunity to
deliver aversive noise to a female confederate in a pseudo-ESP experiment.
Arousal to rape descriptions and 'rape-supportive' attitudes were related to
each other, but also proved to be independent predictors of aggression in the
ESP study. Self-report data corroborated the fact that the motivation for the
punishment level was a desire to hurt the woman. A similar study by
Malamuth (1988) found laboratory aggression to be predicted by AIV,
psychoticism and the dominance motive for sex. Arousal to a rape depiction,
although correlated, was not a significant predictor of aggression, and,
perhaps, surprisingly, high SRS scores predicted significantly *less* aggression,
although they also predicted less reward. In the 1988 study, the predictors of
aggression against female targets were unrelated to aggression against males.
These studies thus clearly implicate factors correlated with self-reports of sexual
aggression as also associated with experimentally measured sex-specific aggression. As Malamuth (1988) pointed out, self-report measures of sexual aggression and laboratory analogues have complementary strengths and weaknesses,
but the finding of similar relations for both constitutes strong evidence.

Apart from providing converging evidence for the validity of findings based on self-reported sexual aggression, there is another important aspect to this laboratory work, as it is essentially based on the assumption that a laboratory analogue of sexual aggression does not require an explicit sexual component. That noise aggression in the laboratory is predicted by the same factors that predict naturally occurring sexual aggression, together with the fact that these factors do not predict males' aggression against males, clearly supports this assumption.

An early view of sexual aggression, that focused on hostile aggression, was that only a small sub-group of males would be aroused by sexual violence. For instance, several studies found that convicted rapists showed equal arousal to depictions of consenting sex and rape, whereas controls showed lower arousal to the rape depictions (for example, Abel *et al.* 1977; Barbaree *et al.* 1979). There was also some specific evidence that some convicted sex offenders were more sexually aroused by non-sexual aggression against women (for example, Abel *et al.* 1977; Quinsey *et al.* 1984). People who showed equal arousal to rape depictions were originally generally conceived as being particularly aroused by the aggressive cues implicit in the material. From this point of view, rape was clearly viewed as an aggressive, rather than sexual act – the aggression having some reward in its own right, rather than being simply an (instrumental) 'means to an end'.

However, later studies using more representative samples of convicted offenders have found that they also show reduced arousal to rape depictions (for example, Baxter *et al.* 1986; Hall 1989; Hall *et al.* 1988; Murphy *et al.* 1984). Although Murphy *et al.* interpreted their findings as due to possible problems with their physiological measures, the other authors argued that earlier findings were a function of testing extremely disturbed criminals. If a small number of seriously deviant offenders show a sexual preference for rape, then their arousal will inflate group means and lead to the conclusion that there are no differences across the sample.

From the latter perspective, although convicted sex offenders show a variety of arousal patterns (Barbaree and Marshall 1991) and there is reasonable evidence that there are a few severely psychologically disturbed males who have a sexual preference for rape, for the vast majority of males, including convicted sex offenders, sexual arousal to forced intercourse tends to be inhibited by the negative cues. However, research using 'normal' (undergraduate) males with no convictions has shown that this inhibition can be 'disinhibited' under a variety of circumstances. Specifically, undergraduates have been found to show equal arousal to rape and consenting depictions when the rape victim is said to be involuntarily aroused (Malamuth and Check 1980a, 1980b) and when the participant has been angered by a female (Yates *et al.* 1984), and decreased inhibition when the participant has consumed alcohol (Barbaree *et al.* 1983).

Apart from the case of the very small number of disturbed 'sexual-preference' rapists, the question of whether aggression is hostile or instrumental could be viewed as a function of the disinhibitors involved. This would apply particularly to the majority of non-convicted rapists. Although anger would support a 'hostile' interpretation, some attitudinal effects are less easy to view entirely from this perspective. Thus the 'disinhibition of (normal) inhibition' perspective may be less conducive to a purely hostile interpretation of sexual aggression than was the earlier 'sexual preference' viewpoint. However, it is relevant to note that attitudinal effects have been found to be mediated by hostility (Malamuth *et al.* 1991) and it may thus be the case that hostility is necessary for disinhibition to occur.

Hamilton and Yee (1990) have recently specifically raised the issue of whether sexual aggression is more often instrumental (that is, in pursuit of sexual gratification) than hostile. Both motives had been identified in convicted rapists' accounts but, as most rapes are not of the type which lead to conviction, it is quite possible that the typical rape (namely, by an intimate or close acquaintance) is characterized primarily by one type of aggression. Further, the apparent motive for many non-stranger rapes involving dates or friends would appear to be sexual access, rather than hostility towards women in general or the victim in particular. One may feel, for instance, that in many date rapes the attacker would have been equally content had the victim consented. Ellis (1991) argued that, given that self-reports of sexual aggression are linked with reports of a wide range of exploitative and coercive strategies to gain intercourse, viewing rape as a 'pseudo-sexual' act that is a goal in itself rather than a tactic is difficult 'unless one were to assume that male attempts to get their dates drunk, lying about loving them, and so forth also lacked sexual motivation' (1991: 632).

Hamilton and Yee (1990) pointed out that their finding that proclivity for sexual aggression is inversely related to perception of the harm done to the victim is inconsistent with a 'hostile aggression' view. In their study, males who knew more about the traumatic effects of rape were less likely to be sexual aggressors. The authors argue that

> If rape is to be conceptualized as a form of hostile aggression – if, that is, the motivation for rape is anger or hostility towards women – then realizing that victimized women truly suffer should increase the likelihood of performing the act. If, however, rape is instrumental aggression then realization of victim suffering should decrease rape propensity.
>
> (1990: 119)

A related view has been expressed by Kanin (1985), who argued that the 'sexually predatory' socialization identified in his rapists' peer group led the aggressors to be relatively sexually deprived, even though they reported being about seven times more sexually active than controls. From this, he concluded that these rapes were primarily sexual, rather than aggressive, in motivation, and that aggression may be more characteristic of the type of stranger rape that leads to conviction. In my view, this interpretation is too superficial. Kanin points out that sexual access was of particular importance to the maintenance of these rapists' self-esteem, which echoes Smeaton and Byrne's comment on the relation between sexual access and perceived masculinity. The peer-group emphasis on sexuality was an aspect of male values that legitimized competition for dominance and peer esteem via the sexual exploitation of females. Thus, although these rapists might well have been quite content with consenting intercourse, the power and dominance expressed via the intercourse (whether consenting or not) should not be ignored.

From the above point of view, for certain types of male in particular, and arguably for many males in general, even consenting sexual relations are expressions of power and dominance and mediate both personal and peer-group perceptions of fulfilment of their masculine role. Heavily socialized, particularly 'macho' males will see aggression as a legitimate method of achieving this goal, as will individuals high on aggressive or other antisocial tendencies. The general exploitative view of obtaining consenting intercourse will thus easily translate into a specifically aggressive approach to obtaining enforced intercourse. Is this instrumental or hostile? In the short term, it can be characterized as instrumental in that sexual access is the immediate priority. However, the finding of Malamuth *et al.* (1991) that promiscuity was a poor predictor unless the person also had high levels of hostile masculinity strongly suggests that for sexual aggressors hostility is involved in the desire for sexual access. Also, in the long term the overriding intention is to display superiority and dominance via exploitation of others. Technically, this could still be viewed as instrumental, but this should not lead us to overlook the essential hostility towards others involved in this view of the world.

In line with this conclusion is the finding that self-reported sexual and non-sexual aggression against females are related (Malamuth *et al.* 1991), and the finding that reports of marital rape are almost always linked with reports of other forms of abuse (for example, Hanneke *et al.* 1986). Self-reported proclivity to sexual aggression has been found to be correlated with general aggression (Greendlinger and Byrne 1987; Petty and Dawson 1989) and, more specifically, with measures of inter-gender hostility or misanthropy (Lisak and Roth 1988; Malamuth 1983, 1986, 1989; Malamuth *et al.* 1991; Peterson and Franzese 1987), and with relatively greater sexual attraction to pictures of emotionally distressed females (Heilbrun and Loftus 1986). The key role of *aggression* in sexual aggression, especially hostile aggression specifically towards females, has thus been demonstrated in a variety of ways, with some specific indication that the aggression is based on a desire to hurt.

Implications for future research

It is clear that most rapes are committed by 'psychologically normal' males, whose aggression may be both tacitly condoned by their immediate peer group, and more indirectly condoned by attitudes that are prevalent in society generally. I think it follows from this that, although interventions with convicted rapists, who may often have severe psychological problems, may be primarily the province of clinical psychologists, this is not the case for interventions aimed at reducing sexual aggression generally. Given the strong relation between rape-supportive attitudes and rape proclivity, a starting point would be for studies of informational interventions that may change attitudes, although later work would need to ensure that improved attitudes were eventually reflected in less aggression. There are some indications in the literature that such interventions may be successful. Hamilton and Yee (1990) found knowledge about the traumatic effects of rape to be negatively related to rape proclivity, although the direction of causality is unclear. Exposure to a course (Fischer 1986b), or one piece of information (Johnson *et al.* 1989), about women's rights has been found to produce less rape-tolerant attitudes, as has information contradicting rape myths following exposure to rape pornography (Check and Malamuth 1984; Donnerstein and Berkowitz 1981; Malamuth and Check 1984). Research on these types of interventions seems a particularly fruitful way forward.

REFERENCES

Abel, G. G., Barlow, D. H., Blanchard, E. B. and Guild, D. (1977) 'The components of rapists' sexual arousal', *Archives of General Psychiatry*, 34: 895–903.

Abel, G. G., Blanchard, E. B. and Becker, J. V. (1976) 'Psychological treatment of rapists', in M. J. Walker and S. L. Brodsky (eds) *Sexual Assault*, Lexington, MA: Lexington Books.

Alder, C. (1985) 'An exploration of self-reported sexually aggressive behavior', *Crime and Delinquency*, 31: 306–31.

Barbaree, H. E. and Marshall, W. L. (1991) 'The role of male sexual arousal in rape: six models', *Journal of Consulting and Clinical Psychology*, 59: 621–30.

Barbaree, H. E., Marshall, W. L. and Lanthier, R. D. (1979) 'Deviant sexual arousal in rapists', *Behavior Research and Therapy*, 17: 215–22.

Barbaree, H. E., Marshall, W. L., Yates, E. and Lightfoot, L. O. (1983) 'Alcohol intoxification and deviant sexual arousal in male social drinkers', *Behavior Research and Therapy*, 21: 365–73.

Baxter, D. J., Barbaree, H. E. and Marshall, W. L. (1986) 'Sexual responses to consenting and forced sex in a large sample of rapists and nonrapists', *Behavior Research and Therapy*, 24: 513–20.

Beattie, V. L. (1992) 'Analysis of the results of a survey on sexual violence in the UK', Unpublished manuscript, Cambridge Women's Forum.

Brickman, J. and Briere, J. (1984) 'Incidence of rape and sexual assault in an urban Canadian population', *International Journal of Women's Studies*, 7: 195–206.

Bridges, J. S. (1991) 'Perceptions of adult and stranger rape: a difference in sex role expectations and rape-supporting beliefs', *Sex Roles*, 24: 291–307.

Bridges, J. S. and McGrail, C. A. (1989) 'Attributions of responsibility for date and stranger rape', *Sex Roles*, 21: 273–86.

Briere, J. (1987) 'Predicting self-reported likelihood of battering: attitudes and childhood experiences', *Journal of Research in Personality*, 21: 61–9.

Briere, J. and Malamuth, N. M. (1983) 'Self-reported likelihood of sexually aggressive behavior: attitudinal versus sexual explanations', *Journal of Research in Personality*, 17: 315–23.

Briere, J., Malamuth, N. and Check, J. V. P. (1985) 'Sexuality and rape-supportive beliefs', *International Journal of Women's Studies*, 8: 398–403.

Brownmiller, S. (1975) *Against our Will: Men, Women, and Rape*, New York: Simon & Schuster.

Burt, M. R. (1980) 'Cultural myths and support for rape', *Journal of Personality and Social Psychology*, 38: 217–30.

—— (1983) 'Justifying personal violence: a comparison of rapists and the general public', *Victimology: An International Journal*, 8: 131–50.

Chambers, G. and Millar, A. (1987) 'Proving sexual assault: prosecuting the offender or persecuting the victim?', in P. Carlen and A. Worrall (eds) *Gender, Crime, and Justice*, Milton Keynes, UK: Open University Press.

Check, J. V. P. and Malamuth, N. M. (1983) 'Sex role stereotyping and reactions to depictions of stranger versus acquaintance rape', *Journal of Personality and Social Psychology*, 45: 344–56.

—— (1984) 'Can there be positive effects of participation in pornography experiments?', *Journal of Sex Research*, 20: 14–31.

—— (1985) 'An empirical assessment of some feminist hypotheses about rape', *International Journal of Women's Studies*, 8: 414–23.

Coller, S. A. and Resick, P. A. (1987) 'Women's attributions of responsibility for date rape: the influence of empathy and sex-role stereotyping', *Violence and Victims*, 2: 115–25.

Copenhaver, S. and Grauerholz, E. (1991) 'Sexual victimization among sorority women: exploring the link between sexual violence and institutional practices', *Sex Roles*, 24: 31–41.

Costin, F. (1985) 'Beliefs about rape and women's social roles', *Archives of Sexual Behavior*, 14: 319–25.

Costin, F. and Schwarz, N. (1987) 'Beliefs about rape and women's social roles: a four-nation study', *Journal of Interpersonal Violence*, 2: 46–56.

Crossman, R. K., Stith, S. M. and Bender, M. M. (1990) 'Sex role egalitarianism and marital violence', *Sex Roles*, 22: 293–304.

Davis, G. E. and Leitenberg, H. (1987) 'Adolescent sex offenders', *Psychological Bulletin*, 101: 417–27.

Demare, D., Briere, J. and Lips, H. M. (1988) 'Violent pornography and self-reported likelihood of sexual aggression', *Journal of Research in Personality*, 22: 140–53.

Divasto, P. V., Kaufman, A., Rosner, L., Jackson, R., Christy, J., Pearson, S. and Burgett, T. (1984) 'The prevalence of sexually stressful events among females in the general population', *Archives of Sexual Behavior*, 13: 59–67.

Donnerstein, E. and Berkowitz, L. (1981) 'Victim reactions in aggressive erotic films as a factor in violence against women', *Journal of Personality and Social Psychology*, 41: 710–24.

Dull, R. T. and Giacopassi, D. J. (1987) 'Demographic correlates of sexual and dating attitudes', *Criminal Justice and Behavior*, 14: 175–93.

Ellis, L. (1991) 'A synthesized (biosocial) theory of rape', *Journal of Consulting and Clinical Psychology*, 59: 631–42.

Feild, H. S. (1978) 'Attitudes toward rape: a comparative analysis of police, rapists, crisis counselors, and citizens', *Journal of Personality and Social Psychology*, 36: 156–79.

Fischer, G. J. (1986a) 'College student attitudes toward forcible date rape: 1. Cognitive predictors', *Archives of Sexual Behavior*, 15: 457–66.

—— (1986b) 'College student attitudes toward forcible date rape: changes after taking a human sexuality course', *Journal of Sex Education and Therapy*, 12: 42–6.

—— (1987) 'Hispanic and majority student attitudes toward forcible date rape as a function of differences in attitudes toward women', *Sex Roles*, 17: 93–101.

Gavey, N. (1991) 'Sexual victimization prevalence among New Zealand university students', *Journal of Consulting and Clinical Psychology*, 59: 464–6.

Giacopassi, D. J. and Dull, R. T. (1986) 'Gender and racial differences in the acceptance of rape myths within a college population', *Sex Roles*, 15: 63–75.

Greendlinger, V. and Byrne, D. (1987) 'Coercive sexual fantasies of college men as predictors of self-reported likelihood to rape and overt sexual aggression', *Journal of Sex Research*, 23: 1–11.

Gwartney-Gibbs, P. A., Stockard, J. and Bohmer, S. (1987) 'Learning courtship aggression: the influence of parents, peers, and personal experiences', *Family Relations*, 36: 276–82.

Hall, E. R. and Flannery, P. J. (1984) 'Prevalence and correlates of sexual assault experiences in adolescents', *Victimology: An International Journal*, 9: 398–406.

Hall, E. R., Howard, J. A. and Boezio, S. L. (1986) 'Tolerance of rape: a sexist or antisocial attitude?', *Psychology of Women Quarterly*, 10: 101–18.

Hall, G. C. N. (1988) 'Criminal behavior as a function of clinical and actuarial variables in a sexual offender population', *Journal of Consulting and Clinical Psychology*, 56: 773–5.

—— (1989) 'Self-reported hostility as a function of offence characteristics and response style in a sexual offender population', *Journal of Consulting and Clinical Psychology*, 57: 306–8.

Hall, G. C. N. and Proctor, W. C. (1987) 'Criminological predictors of recidivism in a sexual offender population', *Journal of Consulting and Clinical Psychology*, 55: 111–12.

Hall, G. C. N., Proctor, W. C. and Nelson, G. M. (1988) 'Validity of physiological measures of pedophilic sexual arousal in a sexual offender population', *Journal of Consulting and Clinical Psychology*, 56: 118–22.

Hall, R. E. (1985) *Ask any Woman: A London Inquiry into Rape and Sexual Assault*, London: Falling Wall Press.

Hamilton, M. and Yee, J. (1990) 'Rape knowledge and propensity to rape', *Journal of Research in Personality*, 24: 111–22.

Hanneke, C. R., Shields, N. M. and McCall, G. J. (1986) 'Assessing the prevalence of marital rape', *Journal of Interpersonal Violence*, 1: 350–62.

Heilbrun, A. B., Jr. and Loftus, M. P. (1986) 'The role of sadism and peer pressure in the sexual aggression of male college students', *Journal of Sex Research*, 22: 320–32.

Hendrick, S., Hendrick, C., Slapion-Foote, M. J. and Foote, F. H. (1985) 'Gender differences in sexual attitudes', *Journal of Personality and Social Psychology*, 48: 1630–42.

Hollin, C. R. and Howells, K. (1987) 'Lay explanations of delinquency: global or offence-specific?', *British Journal of Social Psychology*, 26: 203–10.

Jenkins, M. J. and Dambrot, F. H. (1987) 'The attribution of date rape: observers' attitudes and sexual experiences and the dating situation', *Journal of Applied Social Psychology*, 17: 875–95.

Johnson, J. D. and Jackson, L. A., Jr. (1988) 'Assessing the effects of factors that might underlie the differential perception of acquaintance and stranger rape', *Sex Roles*, 19: 37–45.

Johnson, J. D., Jackson, L. A. and Smith, G. J. (1989) 'The role of ambiguity and gender in mediating the effects of salient cognitions', *Personality and Social Psychology Bulletin*, 15: 52–60.

Kanin, E. J. (1957) 'Male aggression in dating – courtship relations', *American Journal of Sociology*, 63: 197–204.

—— (1969) 'Selected dyadic aspects of male sex aggression', *Journal of Sex Research*, 5: 12–28.

—— (1984) 'Date rape: unofficial criminals and victims', *Victimology: An International Journal*, 9: 95–108.

—— (1985) 'Date rapists: differential sexual socialization and relative deprivation', *Archives of Sexual Behavior*, 14: 219–31.

Kanin, E. J. and Parcell, S. R. (1977) 'Sexual aggression: a second look at the offended female', *Archives of Sexual Behavior*, 6: 67–76.

Kilpatrick, D. G., Best, C. L., Veronen, L. J., Amick, A. E., Villeponteaux, L. A. and Ruff, G. A. (1985) 'Mental health correlates of criminal victimization: a random community survey', *Journal of Consulting and Clinical Psychology*, 53: 866–73.

Klemmack, S. H. and Klemmack, D. L. (1976) 'The social definition of rape', in M. J. Walker and S. L. Brodsky (eds) *Sexual Assault*, Lexington, MA: Lexington Books.

Koss, M. P. (1985) 'The hidden rape victim: personality, attitudinal, and situational characteristics', *Psychology of Women Quarterly*, 9: 193–212.

Koss, M. P. and Burkhart, B. R. (1989) 'A conceptual analysis of rape victimization: long-term effects and implications for treatment', *Psychology of Women Quarterly*, 13: 27–40.

Koss, M. P., Dinero, T. E., Seibel, C. A. and Cox, S. L. (1988) 'Stranger and acquaintance rape: are there differences in the victim's experience?', *Psychology of Women Quarterly*, 12: 1–24.

Koss, M. P. and Gidycz, C. A. (1985) 'Sexual experiences survey: reliability and validity', *Journal of Consulting and Clinical Psychology*, 53: 422–3.

Koss, M. P., Gidycz, C. A. and Wisniewski, N. (1987) 'The scope of rape: incidence and prevalence of sexual aggression and victimization in a national sample of higher education students', *Journal of Consulting and Clinical Psychology*, 55: 162–70.

Koss, M. P., Leonard, K. E., Beezley, D. A. and Oros, C. J. (1985) 'Nonstranger sexual aggression: a discriminant analysis of the psychological characteristics of undetected offenders', *Sex Roles*, 12: 981–92.

Koss, M. P. and Oros, C. J. (1982) 'Sexual experiences survey: a research instrument investigating sexual aggression and victimization', *Journal of Consulting and Clinical Psychology*, 50: 455–7.

Koss, M. P., Woodruff, W. J. and Koss, P. G. (1990) 'Relation of criminal victimization to health perceptions among women medical patients', *Journal of Consulting and Clinical Psychology*, 58: 147–52.

Krahe, B. (1988) 'Victim and observer characteristics as determinants of responsibility attributions to victims of rape', *Journal of Applied Social Psychology*, 18: 50–8.

L'Armand, K. and Pepitone, A. (1982) 'Judgments of rape: a study of victim–rapist relationship and victim sexual history', *Personality and Social Psychology Bulletin*, 8: 134–9.

Lee, H-C. B. and Cheung, F. M. (1991) 'The Attitudes toward Rape Victims scale: reliability and validity in a Chinese context', *Sex Roles*, 24: 599–603.

Lewin, M. (1985) 'Unwanted intercourse: the difficulty of saying no', *Psychology of Women Quarterly*, 9: 184–92.

Lisak, D. and Roth, S. (1988) 'Motivational factors in non-incarcerated sexually aggressive men', *Journal of Personality and Social Psychology*, 55: 795–802.

Malamuth, N. M. (1981) 'Rape proclivity among males', *Journal of Social Issues*, 37(4): 138–57.

—— (1983) 'Factors associated with rape as predictors of laboratory aggression against women', *Journal of Personality and Social Psychology*, 45: 432–42.

—— (1986) 'Predictors of naturalistic sexual aggression', *Journal of Personality and Social Psychology*, 50: 953–62.

—— (1988) 'Predicting laboratory aggression against female and male targets: implications for sexual aggression', *Journal of Research in Personality*, 22: 474–95.

—— (1989) 'The Attraction to Sexual Aggression scale: part two', *Journal of Sex Research*, 26: 324–54.

Malamuth, N. M. and Check, J. V. P. (1980a) 'Sexual arousal to rape and consenting depictions: the importance of the woman's arousal', *Journal of Abnormal Psychology*, 89: 763–6.

—— (1980b) 'Penile tumescence and perceptual responses to rape as a function of victim's perceived reactions', *Journal of Applied Social Psychology*, 10: 528–47.

—— (1983) 'Sexual arousal to rape depictions: individual differences', *Journal of Abnormal Psychology*, 92: 55–67.

—— (1984) 'Debriefing effectiveness following exposure to pornographic rape depictions', *Journal of Sex Research*, 20: 1–13.

—— (1985) 'The effects of aggressive pornography on beliefs in rape myths: individual differences', *Journal of Research in Personality*, 19: 299–320.

Malamuth, N. M., Check, J. V. P. and Briere, J. (1986) 'Sexual arousal in response to aggression: ideological, aggressive and sexual correlates', *Journal of Personality and Social Psychology*, 50: 330–40.

Malamuth, N. M., Haber, S. and Feshbach, S. (1980) 'Testing hypotheses regarding rape: exposure to sexual violence, sex differences, and the "normality" of rapists', *Journal of Research in Personality*, 14: 121–37.

Malamuth, N. M., Heim, M. and Feshbach, S. (1980) 'Sexual responsiveness of college students to rape depictions: inhibitory and disinhibitory effects', *Journal of Personality and Social Psychology*, 38: 399–408.

Malamuth, N. M., Sockloskie, R. J., Koss, M. P. and Tanaka, J. S. (1991) 'Characteristics of aggressors against women: testing a model using a national sample of college students', *Journal of Consulting and Clinical Psychology*, 59: 670–81.

Margolin, L., Miller, M. and Moran, P. B. (1989) 'When a kiss is not just a kiss: relating violations of consent in kissing to rape myth acceptance', *Sex Roles*, 20: 231–43.

Marolla, J. and Scully, D. (1986) 'Attitudes toward women, violence, and rape: a comparison of convicted rapists and other felons', *Deviant Behavior*, 7: 337–55.

Mason, A. and Blankenship, V. (1987) 'Power and affiliation motivation, stress, and abuse in intimate relationships', *Journal of Personality and Social Psychology*, 52: 203–10.

Mayerson, S. E. and Taylor, D. A. (1987) 'The effects of rape myth pornography on women's attitudes and the mediating role of sex role stereotyping', *Sex Roles*, 17: 321–38.

Miller, B. and Marshall, J. C. (1987) 'Coercive sex on the university campus', *Journal of College Student Personnel*, 28: 38–47.

Mosher, D. L. and Anderson, R. D. (1986) 'Macho personality, sexual aggression, and reactions to guided imagery of realistic rape', *Journal of Research in Personality*, 20: 77–94.

Mosher, D. L. and Sirkin, M. (1984) 'Measuring a macho personality constellation', *Journal of Research in Personality*, 18: 150–63.

Muehlenhard, C. L. and Falcon, P. L. (1990) 'Men's heterosocial skill and attitudes toward women as predictors of verbal sexual coercion and forceful rape', *Sex Roles*, 23: 241–59.

Muehlenhard, C. L., Friedman, D. E. and Thomas, C. M. (1985) 'Is date rape justifiable? the effects of dating activity, who initiated, who paid, and men's attitudes toward women', *Psychology of Women Quarterly*, 9: 297–310.

Muehlenhard, C. L. and Linton, M. A. (1987) 'Date rape and sexual aggression in dating situations: incidence and risk factors', *Journal of Counseling Psychology*, 34: 186–96.

Muehlenhard, C. L. and MacNaughton, J. S. (1988) 'Women's beliefs about women who "lead men on" ', *Journal of Social and Clinical Psychology*, 7: 65–79.

Murphy, W. D., Coleman, E. M. and Haynes, M. R. (1986) 'Factors related to coercive sexual behavior in a nonclinical sample of males', *Violence and Victims*, 1: 255–78.

Murphy, W. D., Krisak, J., Stalgaitis, S. and Anderson, K. (1984) 'The use of penile tumescence measures with incarcerated rapists: further validity issues', *Archives of Sexual Behavior*, 13: 545–54.

Overholser, J. C. and Beck, S. (1986) 'Multimethod assessment of rapists, child molesters, and three control groups on behavioral and psychological measures', *Journal of Consulting and Clinical Psychology*, 54: 682–7.

Peterson, S. A. and Franzese, B. (1987) 'Correlates of college men's sexual abuse of women', *Journal of College Student Personnel*, 28: 223–8.

Petty, G. M. Jr. and Dawson, B. (1989) 'Sexual aggression in normal men: incidence, beliefs, and personality characteristics', *Personality and Individual Differences*, 10: 355–62.

Pollard, P. (1992) 'Judgments about victims and attackers in depicted rapes: a review', *British Journal of Social Psychology*, 31: 307–26.

Pryor, J. B. (1987) 'Sexual harassment proclivities in men', *Sex Roles*, 17: 269–90.

Quackenbush, R. L. (1989) 'A comparison of androgynous, masculine sex-typed, and undifferentiated males on dimensions of attitudes toward rape', *Journal of Research in Personality*, 23: 318–42.

Quinsey, V. L., Chaplin, T. C. and Upfold, D. (1984) 'Sexual arousal to nonsexual violence and sadomasochistic themes among rapists and non sex offenders', *Journal of Consulting and Clinical Psychology*, 52: 651–7.

Rapaport, K. and Burkhart, B. (1984) 'Personality and attitudinal characteristics of sexually coercive college males', *Journal of Abnormal Psychology*, 93: 216–21.

Russell, D. E. H. (1982) 'The prevalence and incidence of forcible rape and attempted rape of females', *Victimology: An International Journal*, 7: 81–93.

Ryan, K. M. (1988) 'Rape and seduction scripts', *Psychology of Women Quarterly*, 12: 237–45.

Sanday, P. R. (1981) 'The socio-cultural context of rape', *Journal of Social Issues*, 37(4): 5–27.

Sattem, L., Savells, J. and Murray, E. (1984) 'Sex role stereotypes and commitment to rape', *Sex Roles*, 11: 849–60.

Schwartz, N. and Brand, J. F. (1983) 'Effects of salience of rape on sex role attitudes, trust, and self-esteem in non-raped women', *European Journal of Social Psychology*, 13: 71–6.

Sculley, D. and Marolla, J. (1984) 'Convicted rapists' vocabulary of motive: excuses and justifications', *Social Problems*, 31: 530–44.

—— (1985) ' "Riding the bull at Gilley's": convicted rapists describe the rewards of rape', *Social Problems*, 32: 251–63.

Segal, Z. V. and Marshall, W. L. (1985a) 'Heterosexual social skills in a population of rapists and child molesters', *Journal of Consulting and Clinical Psychology*, 53: 55–63.

—— (1985b) 'Self-report and behavioral assertion in two groups of sexual offenders', *Journal of Behavior Therapy and Experimental Psychiatry*, 16: 223–9.

Shotland, R. L. and Goodstein, L. (1983) 'Just because she doesn't want to doesn't mean it's rape: an experimentally based causal model of the perception of rape in a dating situation', *Social Psychology Quarterly*, 46: 220–32.

Silbert, M. H. and Pines, A. M. (1984) 'Pornography and sexual abuse of women', *Sex Roles*, 10: 857–68.

Smeaton, G. and Byrne, D. (1987) 'The effects of R rated violence and erotica, individual differences, and victim characteristics on acquaintance rape proclivity', *Journal of Research in Personality*, 21: 171–84.

Spence, J. T., Helmreich, R. and Stapp, J. (1973) 'A short version of the Attitudes Toward Women Scale (AWS)', *Bulletin of the Psychonomic Society*, 2: 219–20.

Tieger, T. (1981) 'Self-rated likelihood of raping and the social perception of rape', *Journal of Research in personality*, 15: 147–58.

Ward, C. (1988) 'The Attitudes Toward Rape Victims Scale: construction, validation, and cross-cultural applicability', *Psychology of Women Quarterly*, 12: 127–46.

Weis, K. and Borges, S. S. (1975) 'Victimology and rape: the case of the legitimate victim', in G. Schultz (ed.) *Rape Victimology*, Springfield, IL: C. C. Thomas.

Williams, J. E. (1984) 'Secondary victimization: confronting public attitudes about rape', *Victimology: An International Journal*, 9: 66–81.

Williams, L. S. (1984) 'The classic rape: when do victims report?', *Social Problems*, 31: 459–67.

Yates, E., Barbaree, H. E. and Marshall, W. L. (1984) 'Anger and deviant sexual arousal', *Behavior Therapy*, 15: 287–94.

11

FAMILY VIOLENCE IN A SOCIAL CONTEXT

Factors relating to male abuse of children

Bernice Andrews

In this chapter I shall consider some of the social circumstances that might increase the likelihood of male violence directed at children. Both physical and sexual abuse of children are considered in relation to the stability and nature of family life surrounding such experiences.

Investigations of the social causes of child abuse have considered both biography and current social context. Early adverse family experiences, in particular having been abused oneself, have been widely implicated as increasing the likelihood of adult physical and sexual child abuse (for example, Widom 1989; Tierney and Corwin 1983). With regard to current social context, demographic factors such as age, income level and employment status have been associated with child abuse (Creighton and Noyes 1989; Straus and Smith 1990). Family structure (American Humane Association 1984; Creighton and Noyes 1989; Wilson and Daly 1987) and current life stress (for example, Finkelhor 1980; Straus *et al.* 1980) have also been implicated as factors that increase the risk of both forms of child abuse.

But how much is known specifically about *male* violence towards children? Whilst it is recognized that the vast majority of perpetrators of sexual abuse are male, the extent to which men are involved in child physical abuse is not altogether clear. Reviews have been critical of the literature on child abuse and neglect in respect of the over-emphasis on the role of mothers in such a process (Martin 1983; Phares and Compas 1992; Stark and Flitcraft 1988; Wolfe 1985). In Wolfe's (1985) review he reported that studies up to that time had almost entirely involved samples of mothers only. Since then, although the majority of the existing research into the characteristics of abusive parents is still exclusively concerned with mothers, some investigators have started to consider the role of the father in child abuse. Studies have shown that fathers of abused children have higher rates of psychiatric disturbance than controls, particularly personality disorders and alcoholism (Reid *et al.* 1987; Rogeness *et al.* 1986). However, these studies do not reveal the extent to which social context influences men to abuse children, nor do they shed any light on the degree to which physical child abuse is a male, as opposed to a female, problem.

There are two sources of evidence concerning the proportions of males and females involved in the physical abuse of children. One source is nationally representative surveys of physical aggression, the other is epidemiological studies of known abusive families. In the oft-cited nationally representative surveys of Murray Straus and his colleagues (see Chapters 1–8), carried out in the United States, women were as likely as men to report physical aggression within family settings, according to their criteria for such acts, which include punching, kicking and hitting with an implement (see Straus and Gelles 1990). This was as true for child abuse as it was for spouse abuse. Indeed, in the first survey that was carried out, women were significantly more likely than men to report physical aggression towards their children, although this difference was no longer apparent in the second survey ten years later (Straus and Smith 1990). However, these findings are at odds with those from the studies of known abusers. In a large national study in the United States perpetrators of child physical abuse were 1.5 times more likely to be male than female (American Humane Association 1984 [cited in Wolfe 1987]). In the United Kingdom, a recent study by the NSPCC showed that men and women were equally as likely to be implicated in cases of physical injury to children. However, men were approximately twice as likely as women to be implicated when the rate was adjusted for who the child was living with at the time (Creighton and Noyes 1989).

Both methods of ascertaining sex differences in child abuse described in the above studies have potential sources of bias. Although the survey method is likely to be representative of the general population, questioning people about whether or not they have used physical aggression is bound to be unreliable, as many would not want to admit to what may be seen as illegal acts. There is evidence of lack of reliability in reporting violence from the spouse abuse literature. Agreement between husbands' and wives' reports of the occurrence of spouse abuse has been shown to be modest or low (Jouriles and O'Leary 1985, but see Dobash et al. 1992). In addition, studies of spouse abuse have shown that men minimize reports of violence (Dutton 1986; Edeleson and Brygger 1986). A central problem specific to studies of Straus et al. involves the use of the Conflict Tactics Scale (CTS), the questionnaire used to ascertain the occurrence of violent acts. The scale has been criticized on the grounds that it does not take into account the meaning, intention and consequences of so-called violent acts (for example, O'Leary et al. 1989; Dobash et al. 1992; see also Goodwin, this volume). With regard to marital violence, O'Leary and his colleagues make the point that 'women's aggression engenders less fear . . . and inflicts less physical harm . . . than men's aggression' (O'Leary et al. 1989: 267).

The difficulties in interpreting the results of studies of known or convicted perpetrators concerns the generalizability of the findings to all perpetrators. It is often the most vulnerable who come to the attention of local authorities and other detection agencies. For example, young people are probably more likely to be detected through lack of experience in covering their tracks, and mothers who are usually the primary caregivers are more likely than fathers to come to the attention of welfare agencies, especially if they are showing signs of mental distress. It appears therefore that biases in data collection favour men, inasmuch as their degree of involvement in physical child abuse may in fact be higher than research has so far shown.

How then should we investigate the occurrence of male violence towards children and the social context in which it occurs? One issue concerns the best group to target for research; another concerns social factors in need of investigation. With regard to the first, given the problems associated with obtaining information from potential perpetrators in representative samples and known perpetrators in samples that may be unrepresentative, an alternative strategy may be to identify and question victims in representative samples about their experiences. With regard to the second issue, surveys have already shown that the incidence of social stressors, such as poverty and unemployment, are associated with a high rate of reported violent acts to children from both men and women (Straus *et al*. 1980; Straus and Smith 1990). The question then is whether there are particular circumstances that specifically influence the occurrence of child abuse by males.

One such circumstance may involve the parental situation. As children usually stay in the custody of their natural mother when couples separate, one context which may favour the occurrence of male abuse is where children are living with the natural mother and a stepfather, or father substitute. In fact families comprising one natural and one step-parent are over-represented in large-scale surveys of known child abusers both in the United States and the United Kingdom (Creighton and Noyes 1989; Wilson and Daly 1987). Wilson and Daly (1987) interpret their findings within an evolutionary perspective. They argue that conflict is more likely to occur between step-parents and stepchildren than between natural parents and their children because

> The welfare of offspring (a token of their probability of eventual fitness) is reward enough for altruistic natural parents, but not for nonrelatives. Substitute parents are likely to feel exploited and resentful unless they have contractual guarantees of more proximal reciprocities.
>
> (Wilson and Daly 1987: 229)

However, a different argument may be needed to explain why step-parents should be over-represented as sexual abusers of children (Creighton and Noyes 1989) – perhaps involving weaker incest taboos in non-blood relatives – as child sexual abuse is not usually seen as the result of adult–child conflict. Another problem with Wilson and Daly's explanation concerns who is actually abusing children in reconstituted families. Studies have not always identified who perpetrates abuse within this context so it cannot necessarily be assumed that it is the step-parent.

Another explanation may involve the relatively vulnerable position of the stepchild. It has been argued that the natural mother's commitment to consolidating a new relationship may be to the detriment of her children, possibly due to her lack of availability for them (Tierney and Corwin 1983). Therefore, the behaviour or mental state of the primary caregiver may be another circumstance that is conducive to male abuse of children, regardless of the type of family arrangement, as this could influence the extent to which the child is vulnerable to abuse from others (Henderson 1972).

This brief review of existing research into the social contexts which influence the occurrence of male abuse of children points to gaps and contradictions in existing knowledge. It was therefore decided to investigate in further detail the extent to which family structure and maternal affect and behaviour influence the likelihood of adult male child abuse. The research also took into account the degree to which men are implicated in the physical abuse of children. The rest of the chapter focuses on this investigation.

BACKGROUND TO THE STUDY

The material to be reported is drawn from a sample of 101 mothers aged between 32 and 56, and 75 of their daughters aged between 15 and 25, living in Islington, an inner city area of London. The mothers were a sub-sample of women who had taken part in a longitudinal community study which explored social and biographical factors relating to the onset and course of depressive disorder (Brown et al. 1986; Andrews and Brown 1988a, 1988b). The present cross-sectional study, started seven years later, was concerned with intergenerational differences and transmission of such vulnerability factors in women. The sub-sample was chosen because they had at least one daughter between the ages of 15 and 25 in the study period. For further details of sample selection, see Andrews et al. (1990).

One particular focus of the research concerned the antecedents and consequences of early adverse childhood experiences such as parental neglect and emotional, physical and sexual abuse occurring before the age of 17. Information about early family life was therefore collected in considerable detail from both generations. One situation which has been linked to poor mothering is maternal depression (Andrews et al. 1990; Weissman and Paykel 1974; Pound et al. 1984), and chronic and recurrent disorders in the mother were shown to be highly related to reports of physical and sexual abuse by male family members in the younger sample of daughters (Andrews et al. 1990). One of the aims of the present analysis was to explore this result in further detail and see if it could be replicated in the older generation of women. Another aim was to investigate the relation of family structure to the occurrence of abuse by males in both generations. However, the first task was to identify the perpetrators of any reported abuse.

DO MEN AND WOMEN PHYSICALLY ABUSE CHILDREN IN EQUAL PROPORTION?

Overall, 31 per cent (31/101) of the mothers and 28 per cent (21/75) of their daughters reported being physically or sexually abused before the age of 17. Physical abuse was reported by 27 per cent (27/101) of mothers and 16 per cent (12/75) of daughter, and sexual abuse by 12 per cent (12/101) of mothers and 15 per cent (11/75) of daughters. To ensure confidentiality and reduce bias in reporting, mothers and daughters were seen separately by different interviewers. The criteria for inclusion in the abuse categories were fairly stringent. Reports of physical violence at the hands of a family member were rated only where they were a feature of childhood and not a one-off occurrence. Following Straus's severe violence index (Straus *et al.* 1980), being punched or kicked and being hit with an instrument such as a stick or a belt were included, but milder acts of physical chastisement such as being slapped, pushed or shoved were not. All reports of sexual abuse before the age of 17 were included, whether or not they involved a family member, as long as the incidents involved direct physical contact of the sexual parts of the respondent.

Table 11.1 identifies the perpetrators of physical and sexual abuse amongst those who reported such abuse in childhood.

Table 11.1 Perpetrators of abuse amongst women with experiences of physical or sexual abuse in childhood

Mothers	Physical abuse (n = 27) % abusing	Sexual abuse (n = 12) % abusing
Both parents	30	0
Mother without father	13	0
Father without mother	56	25
Other alone	0	75

Daughters	Physical abuse (n = 12) % abusing	Sexual abuse (n = 11) % abusing
Both parents	17	0
Mother without father	17	0
Father without mother	67	27
Other alone	0	73

None of the mothers or daughters reporting sexual abuse had been abused by a mother or mother substitute. All had been abused by males – 50 per cent of the sexually abused mothers implicated a family member; 25 per cent, someone known to them; and 25 per cent were strangers. Forty-five per cent of the sexually abused daughters implicated a family member; 10 per cent, someone known to them, and 45 per cent were strangers.

But to what extent were males implicated in physical abuse in the family? Table 11.1 shows that proportionally more fathers than mothers were implicated by both the mothers and daughters in the study who had been physically abused in childhood. Eighty-six per cent and 84 per cent of the abused mothers and daughters respectively reported abuse from a father or step/surrogate father and 43 per cent and 34 per cent respectively reported abuse from a mother or a step/surrogate mother.

These results show that a high proportion of males were implicated in reports of childhood abuse by the women in the study. This justifies and sets the scene for the next stage of the analysis which investigates the social context of male abuse of children.

MALE ABUSE IN RELATION TO MATERNAL AFFECT AND BEHAVIOUR

Maternal affect

The first part of the analysis was to consider whether maternal depression and other psychiatric disorders were associated with an increased risk of male abuse in childhood. With regard to the measurement of maternal depression, we had a reliable independent measure of the mothers of the daughters in the sample, as the clinical state of the mothers had been assessed at four contacts in an eight-year period, using a well-established, standardized clinical interview, the Present State Examination (Wing *et al.* 1974). Each interview covered the period since they had last been seen. Their psychiatric history before the eight-year study period was covered with an additional set of questions. Women were included as having had an episode of disorder at a 'case' level outside the study period if they had been a psychiatric in-patient or out-patient or if they had been prescribed anti-depressant medication by a GP.

The assessment of the clinical state of the sample of mothers' own mothers was dependent on their responses to questions about whether their own mothers had suffered with their nerves or had been depressed, or had had a drink problem when the woman was a child. A rating of maternal disorder was only made where the woman reported that her mother had had a severe drink problem or had received medication or other psychiatric treatment.

The vast majority of psychiatric disorder assessed in the mothers of both generations of women involved depression, and overall there was a strong relationship between such maternal disorders and abuse. Sixty-nine per cent (9/13) of the mothers who reported that their mother had had a disorder when they were children also reported physical or sexual abuse in childhood, compared with 23 per cent (19/84) of those whose mothers had not had a disorder, $X^2 = 9.74$, $p < 0.01$ (data were missing on maternal disorder for those of the mothers). Amongst the daughters, 62 per cent (13/21) whose mothers had been assessed as having a chronic recurrent psychiatric disorder reported abuse in childhood, compard with 15 per cent (8/54) whose mothers had not been so assessed, $X^2 = 14.37$, $p < 0.001$. But who was perpetrating the abuse when the mother was depressed? Table 11.2 shows that the most likely candidate for both generations of women was the father or father substitute. There also appears to be a tendency for others outside the family to abuse when the mother is depressed, and this difference is significant in the mother cohort.

Table 11.2 Who perpetrates abuse when the mother is depressed?

Mother cohort			
Disorder in mother	% abused by mother	% abused by father	% abused by other
Yes	8 (1/13)	46 (6/13)	23 (2/13)
No	10 (8/84)	17 (14/84)	4 (3/84)
	$X^2 = 0.09$	$X^2 = 4.31^*$	$X^2 = 4.40^*$
Daughter cohort			
Disorder in mother	% abused by mother	% abused by father	% abused by other
Yes	14 (3/21)	43 (9/21)	19 (4/21)
No	2 (1/54)	4 (2/54)	9 (5/54)
	$X^2 = 2.49$	$X^2 = 15.52^{**}$	$X^2 = 0.6$

* $p < 0.05$
** $p < 0.001$

Does maternal psychiatric disorder increase the risk of both physical and sexual abuse from males? In the mother sample, the reported rate of sexual abuse amongst those whose own mothers had had a disorder was significantly higher than those whose mothers had not had a disorder – 38 per cent (5/13) compared with 6 per cent (5/84), $X^2 = 9.59$, $p < 0.01$. The rate of reported physical abuse by a father or stepfather was higher amongst those whose mothers had suffered from a disorder, but not significantly so – 38 per cent (5/84) compared with 17 per cent (14/84) of the other women, $X^2 = 2.15$. The daughters whose mothers had been assessed as having a chronic or recurrent disorder reported a significantly higher rate of physical abuse by a father or stepfather than the other daughters – 43 per cent (9/21) compared with 6 per cent (3/54) $X^2 = 13$, p<0.001. However, the relationship between sexual abuse and maternal disorder was not as strong – 24 per cent (5/21) with mothers with disorders had been sexually abused compared with 11 per cent (6/54) of the other daughters, $X^2 = 1.06$, ns.

Maternal behaviour

It is of interest that maternal psychiatric disorder was not significantly associated with maternal abuse in either cohort, although there was a weak relationship in the daughter sample. There was, however, a strong relationship between maternal disorder and reports of neglect or antipathy from the mother in both generations. Neglect or what has been termed 'lack of care' (Andrews and Brown 1988a, 1988b) was rated where there was evidence of marked indifference based on actual instances of neglect, or marked lack of control based on reports of the amount of supervision provided by the primary caregiver (most usually the mother). Antipathy was rated where there was evidence of high hostility, dislike, exclusion and/or disapproval from the mother, based on specific behavioural indicators (Andrews *et al.* 1990). Sixty-nine per cent (9/13) of the mothers who reported their mothers had had a disorder when they were children reported such poor mothering, compared with 23 per cent (19/84) of the other women, $X^2 = 9.74$, p<0.01. Amongst the daughters, 57 per cent (12/21) whose mothers had been assessed as having a chronic or recurrent psychiatric disorder in the daughter's childhood reported neglect or antipathy from her, compared with 19 per cent (10/54) whose mothers had not been so assessed, $X^2 = 9.09$, p<0.01. Such poor mothering was also associated with reports of having been abused in childhood by fathers or other males – 45 per cent (14/31) of the mothers reporting such mothering also reported male abuse in childhood compared with 17 per cent (12/70) without such mothering, $X^2 = 5.99$, p<0.025. For the daughters 48 per cent (10/21) with poor mothering reported male abuse compared with 17 per cent (9/54) of the others, $X^2 = 6.1$, p<0.025.

MALE ABUSE AND FAMILY STRUCTURE

Having established that maternal depression and poor mothering are associated with reports of physical and/or sexual abuse by a male in childhood in the two generations, the final step was to consider whether family structure was also related to risk of such abuse. Three different types of family arrangement were distinguished: (1) where the respondent had lived with a natural parent and step-parent or non-related parent substitute at some time in childhood; (2) where she had lived with just one natural parent alone at some time in childhood, and (3) where she had always lived with both natural parents (one mother whose parents had died early had lived with a succession of relatives

Table 11.3 Women abused by males in childhood by predominant family composition in childhood (percentages)

Mother cohort	% physically abused	% sexually abused	% any male abuse
Family composition			
1 Natural parent and step-parent[1]	29 (2/7)	29 (2/7)	29 (2/7)
2 One natural parent	7 (1/14)	21 (3/14)	21 (3/14)
3 Both natural parents	22 (17/76)	9 (7/76)	28 (21/76)
	$X^2 = 1.96$ 2 df	$X^2 = 3.45$ 2 df	$X^2 = 1.38$ 2 df

[1] Excludes 3 living with stepmothers.

Daughter cohort	% physically abused	% sexually abused	% any male abuse
Family composition			
1 Natural parent and step-parent[1]	11 (2/18)	33 (6/18)	39 (7/18)
2 One natural parent	22 (4/18)	11 (2/18)	28 (5/18)
3 Both natural parents	10 (4/39)	8 (3/39)	18 (7/39)
	$X^2 = 1.18$ 2 df	$X^2 = 6.70*$ 2 df	$X^2 = 2.92$ 2 df

*$p < 0.05$

from an early age and she was excluded from any analysis). Within these family arrangements, rates of abuse from anyone, male or female, reported by mothers were: 40 per cent (4/10) living with a natural parent and step-parent, 29 per cent (4/14) living with one natural parent, and 29 per cent (22/76) living with both natural parents, $X^2 = 0.5$, 2df, ns. Rates of abuse for the daughters were: 39 per cent living with a natural parent and step-parent, 33 per cent living with one natural parent and 21 per cent (8/39) living with both natural parents, $X^2 = 2.39$, 2df, ns. It was, however, necessary to consider the rates of *male* abuse in these different arrangements. Table 11.3 echoes the above results, showing that, overall, the different types of family composition in childhood were not related to the reported incidence of abuse from males in either cohort. Rates of physical abuse by males were lowest for the mothers who had lived in single-parent households as children, whilst they were highest for the daughters (Table 11.3), although these differences were not significant. Close examination of the data showed that the one case of male physical abuse reported by a mother brought up in a single-parent household and the four by the daughters all involved the natural father as the perpetrator, and in all but one the abuse occurred before the parents separated. As male physical abuse appeared likely to occur before parental separation, it is plausible that it is reflecting general conflict within the family prior to marital breakup. The lower rate of male physical abuse amongst the mothers brought up by one parent might therefore be explained by the finding that the majority (9/14) had lost a parent through death rather than through their parents' marital disruption. This is in contrast to the daughters brought up by one parent, all of whom had parents who had separated.

Turning now to sexual abuse, those daughters who had lived with a stepfather were significantly more likely to have reported sexual abuse than daughters living with one natural parent only or both natural parents. But only two of the six sexually abused girls living with a stepfather or father substitute reported that they had been abused by him. One of the remaining four had been abused by her grandfather, and the other three had suffered non-repeated sexual assaults by friends or strangers. In the mother cohort, there were no significant differences between the different family arrangements in rates of early sexual abuse, although those who had lived with both natural parents reported the lowest rate. Of the two who had been sexually abused while living with a stepfather, one had been abused by him, the other by a stranger.

DISCUSSION AND CONCLUSIONS

What can the results of these investigations tell us about male violence towards children? With regard to physical abuse, so far the predominant focus in child physical abuse research has been on the mother, but the findings suggest that male physical abuse of children within the family is a problem that should be taken seriously by both researchers and practitioners. In both generations, fathers or father substitutes were implicated twice as often as mothers in reports of physical abuse in childhood.

None of the women in the study reported being sexually abused in childhood by a female. This finding is in accord with large-scale representative community surveys that have shown the vast majority of perpetrators reported by victims of child sexual abuse to be males (Baker and Duncan 1985; Finkelhor et al. 1990; Russell 1983; Seigel et al. 1987).

In these two samples of younger and older women, the predominant family arrangement in childhood was not a particularly strong indicator of reports of abuse by males. Although there was a modest relationship between male sexual abuse and having been brought up with a stepfather, the finding was not wholly explained by a lack of taboo against incestuous contact among non-blood relatives. Only three of the eight mothers and daughters who had been sexually abused within such a family setting were actually abused by their stepfather.

Another explanation involves the relatively vulnerable position of children brought up in step-parent homes due to lifestyles involved with seeking a new spouse and later remarriage. It has been suggested that this may involve increased contact with adults and decreased supervision (Tierney and Corwin 1983). However, the mothers and daughters in this study brought up with a step-parent were no more likely than those brought up in other family arrangements to report maternal neglect (or indeed maternal depression).

The criteria for neglect involved evidence of severe emotional and material deprivation, and it is possible that more subtle forms of parental uninvolvement may be implicated. That being said, it should be remembered that the relationship of family composition to sexual abuse was weak, and not significant in the sample of mothers, and family composition was not significantly related to male physical abuse in either cohort.

These findings are at odds with those of non-representative studies of known child abusers (Creighton and Noyes 1989; Wilson and Daly 1988). However, the sample sizes may have been too small to detect significant differences, particularly in view of the limited numbers in the step- and single-parent categories of family composition. It is therefore possible that with larger numbers differences would have emerged.

Another explanation for the contradiction in findings may be that step-parents are more likely than natural fathers to be suspected of child abuse because of their position in the family, and the pressure against disclosing abuse may be stronger in intact families. But whatever the explanation, the present results suggest it is important to look for explanations of male violence towards children in contexts that are common to all types of family composition.

The study provided ample proof that such contexts exist. Both generations of women were more likely to report male abuse in their childhoods when their mothers had been depressed, or had some other psychiatric disorder, or where they had been subjected to poor mothering, a factor highly related to the mother's mental state. A recent review of the literature has pointed out that, in general, studies of maternal depression and child development have ignored the role of the father (Downey and Coyne 1990), and researchers in this field have been accused of 'mother bashing' (Downey and Coyne 1990; Phares and Compas 1992). The current findings confirm that fathers should be considered in such investigations.

Unfortunately, there was no independent assessment of maternal disorder in childhood in the mother sample, and it could be argued that reports of parental maltreatment and maternal disorder could have been confounded, inasmuch as reports of maternal disorder may have influenced responses to subsequent questions about the quality of maternal care. However, daughters were not questioned about their mothers' mental state, as assessment of maternal disorder in the daughter sample was made from material collected from their mothers. As the results for both samples were remarkably similar, the findings for the mothers can be interpreted with some confidence.

Another objection to the methods used to obtain these results involves the validity of retrospective reports of childhood experiences (see Widom 1989). However, the sample of daughters were sufficiently close to their childhood to report a reasonably accurate picture of early family life. Furthermore, a recent comprehensive review (Brewin *et al.* 1993) came to the conclusion that adult reports of childhood were likely to be reasonably valid provided they were restricted to factual accounts of significant episodes occurring after the period of infant amnesia and for which the individual was sufficiently well placed to know about.

It finally remains to consider just why mothers' mental state and behaviour should increase the risk of abuse by males, particularly fathers and father substitutes. With regard to maternal mental state, one possible explanation is that women with mental disorders, particularly depression, are more often married to men with psychiatric problems and personality disorders (Merikangas and Spiker 1982; Rutter and Quinton 1984), and such men have been shown to be more likely to abuse their children (Reid *et al.* 1987; Rogeness *et al.* 1986). An alternative but not incompatible explanation, regarding both maternal depression and mothering behaviour relates to the finding in this study that women with depression and other disorders are likely to show impairment in their parental role, and because of this it is probable that they are less likely to protect children from fathers and others who have abusive tendencies.

From a wider social perspective we may interpret the results as evidence for the abuse of power (Finkelhor 1983). Finkelhor points out that the common definition of abuse involves situations where a more powerful person takes advantage of a less powerful one. But even within these situations, there is evidence that

> the most common patterns in family abuse are not merely for the more powerful to abuse the less powerful, but for the most powerful to abuse the least. . . . Abuse tends to gravitate toward the relationships of *greatest power differential.*

> (Finkelhor 1983: 18)

This principle is particularly clear in the case of child sexual abuse where the most common form is for males in positions of authority to victimize girls in subordinate positions (Finkelhor 1979). Male abuse of boys is much less common, and abuse of boys or girls by females is extremely rare. With regard to physical abuse of children, studies have shown that the youngest groups are over-represented (Creighton and Noyes 1989; Straus *et al.* 1980) and, in teenage years, girls are more likely to be abused than boys (Creighton and Noyes 1989).

The findings presented confirm this pattern, and show more males than females to be implicated in the abuse of the women in the study when they were children. Those with the least maternal protection in childhood were also the most likely to have suffered abuse at the hands of males. This is not to suggest that all men will abuse children, given the chance. With reference to what is already known about circumstances leading to child abuse, a diathesis/stress model seems most reasonable: those suffering stressful life circumstances, and who have abusive tendencies, possibly as a result of childhood experiences or poor mental health, will seek out and abuse the easiest targets.

These results go some way towards elucidating the relationship between social factors and the male abuse of children. The samples were small, and all female, and replication is necessary in larger, more heterogeneous samples. However, it is noteworthy that the pattern of results was consistent across two different samples of younger and older women. Keeping in mind the need for replication, the research has important implications for those involved in identifying both children at risk of abuse and their potential perpetrators.

ACKNOWLEDGEMENT

This research was supported by the Economic and Social Research Council.

REFERENCES

American Humane Association (1984) *Trends in Child Abuse and Neglect: A National Perspective*, Denver, CO: Author.

Andrews, B. and Brown, G. W. (1988a) 'Marital violence in the community: a biographical approach', *British Journal of Psychiatry*, 153: 305–12.

——— (1988b) 'Social support, onset of depression and personality: an exploratory analysis', *Social Psychiatry and Psychiatric Epidemiology*, 23: 99–108.

Andrews, B., Brown, G. W. and Creasey, L. (1990) 'Integrational links between psychiatric disorder in mothers and daughters: the role of parenting experiences', *Journal of Child Psychology and Psychiatry*, 31: 1115–29.

Baker, A. W. and Duncan, S. P. (1985) 'Child sexual abuse: a study of prevalence in Great Britain', *Child Abuse and Neglect*, 9: 457–67.

Brewin, C. R., Andrews, B. and Gotlib, I. H. (1993) 'Psychopathology and early childhood experience: a reappraisal of retrospective reports', *Psychological Bulletin*, 113, 82–98.

Brown, G. W., Andrews, B., Harris, T., Adler, Z. and Bridge, L. (1986) 'Social support, self-esteem and depression', *Psychological Medicine*, 16: 813–31.

Creighton, S. J. and Noyes, P. (1989) *Child Abuse Trends in England and Wales 1983–1987*, London: NSPCC.

Dobash, R. P., Dobash, R. E., Wilson, M. and Daly, M. (1992) 'The myth of sexual symmetry in marital violence', *Social Problems*, 39: 71–91.

Downey, G. and Coyne, J. C. (1990) 'Children of depressed parents: an integrative review', *Psychological Bulletin*, 108: 50–76.

Dutton, D. G. (1986) 'Wife assaulters' explanations for assault: the neutralization of self-punishment', *Canadian Journal of Behavioral Science*, 18: 381–90.

Edeleson, J. L. and Brygger, M. P. (1986) 'Gender differences in self-reporting of battering incidences', *Family Relations*, 35: 377–82.

Finkelhor, D. (1979) *Sexually Victimized Children*, New York: Free Press.

—— (1980) 'Risk factors in the sexual victimization of children', *Child Abuse and Neglect* 6: 94–102.

—— (1983) 'Common features of family abuse', in D. Finkelhor (ed.) *The Dark Side of Families: Current Family Violence Research*, London: Sage, pp. 17–28.

Finkelhor, D., Hotaling, G., Lewis, I. A. and Smith, C. (1990) 'Sexual abuse in a national survey of adult men and women: prevalence, characteristics and risk factors', *Child Abuse and Neglect*, 14: 19–28.

Henderson, D. (1972) 'Incest: a synthesis of data', *Canadian Psychiatric Association Journal*, 17: 299–313.

Jouriles, E. N. and O'Leary, K. D. (1985) 'Interspousal reliability of reports of marital violence', *Journal of Consulting and Clinical Psychology*, 53: 419–29.

Martin, J. (1983) 'Maternal and paternal abuse of children: theoretical and research perspectives', in D. Finkelhor (ed.) *The Dark Side of Families: Current Family Violence Research*, London: Sage, pp. 293–304.

Merikangas, K. R. and Spiker, D. G. (1982) 'Assortative mating among in-patients with primary affective disorder', *Psychological Medicine*, 12: 753–64.

O'Leary, K. D., Barling, J., Arias, I. and Rosenbaum, A. (1989) 'Prevalence and stability of physical aggression between spouses: a longitudinal analysis', *Journal of Consulting and Clinical Psychology*, 57: 263–8.

Phares, V. and Compas, B. E. (1992) 'The role of fathers in child and adolescent psychopathology: make room for daddy', *Psychological Bulletin*, 111: 387–412.

Pound, A., Cox, A. D., Puckering, C. and Mills, M. (1984) 'The impact of maternal depression on young children', in J. Stevenson (ed.) *Recent Research in Developmental Psychopathology (Journal of Child Psychology and Psychiatry*, Monograph Supplement No. 4), Oxford: Pergamon, pp. 3–10.

Reid, J. B., Kavanagh, K. and Baldwin, D. V. (1987) 'Abusive parents' perceptions of child problem behaviors: an example of parental bias', *Journal of Abnormal Child Psychology* 15: 457–66.

Rogeness, G. A., Amrung, S. A., Macedo, C. A., Harris, W. R. and Fisher, C. (1986) 'Psychopathology in abused or neglected children', *Journal of the American Academy of Child Psychiatry*, 25: 659–65.

Russell, D. E. H. (1983) 'The incidence and prevalence of intrafamilial and extrafamilial sexual abuse of female children', *Child Abuse and Neglect*, 7: 133–46.

Rutter, M. and Quinton, D. (1984) 'Parental psychiatric disorder: effects on children', *Psychological Medicine*, 14: 853–81.

Seigel, J. M., Sorenson, S. B., Golding, J. M., Burnam, M. A. and Stein, J. A. (1987) 'The prevalence of childhood sexual assault: the Los Angeles epidemiologic catchment area project', *American Journal of Epidemiology*, 126: 1141–53.

Stark, E. and Flitcraft, A. H. (1988) 'Women and children at risk: a feminist perspective on child abuse', *International Journal of Health Services*, 18: 97–118.

Straus, M. A. and Gelles, R. J. (1990) *Physical Violence in American Families*, London: Transaction.

Straus, M., Gelles, R. and Steinmetz, S. (1980) *Behind Closed Doors: Violence in the American Family*, New York: Anchor.

Straus, M. and Smith, S. (1990) 'Family patterns of child abuse', in M. A. Straus and R. J. Gelles (eds) *Physical Violence in American Families*, London: Transaction, pp. 245–61.

Tierney, K. J. and Corwin, D. L. (1983) 'Exploring intrafamilial child sexual abuse: a systems approach', in D. Finkelhor (ed.) *The Dark Side of Families: Current Family Violence Research*, London: Sage, pp. 102–16.

Weissman, M. M. and Paykel, E. S. (1974) *The Depressed Woman: A Study of Social Relationships*, Chicago: University of Chicago Press.

Widom, C. S. (1989) 'Does violence beget violence? a critical examination of the literature', *Psychological Bulletin*, 106: 3–28.

Wilson, M. and Daly, M. (1987) 'Risk of maltreatment of children living with step-parents', in R. J. Gelles and J. B. Lancaster (eds) *Child Abuse and Neglect: Biosocial Dimensions*, New York: Aldine de Gruyter, pp. 215–32.

Wing, J. K., Cooper, J. E. and Sartorius, N. (1974) *The Measurement and Classification of Psychiatric Symptoms*, Cambridge: Cambridge University Press.

Wolfe, D. A. (1985) 'Child-abusive parents: an empirical review and analysis', *Psychological Bulletin*, 97: 462–82.

—— (1987) *Child Abuse: Implications for Child Development and Psychopathology*, London: Sage.

12

CHILD SEXUAL ABUSE

Kevin Browne

Early sexual experiences may be classified into two types: those that are 'desired' events an individual personally wants to happen, and those that are 'unwanted' events where an individual is forced or feels obliged to participate. The concept of 'desired' sexual life events in childhood and adolescence has received little attention from researchers, especially in relation to their long-term psychological effects. By contrast, the topic of 'unwanted' sexual life events experienced by children and adolescents has been the subject of intense investigation and, according to much of the literature, early sexual maltreatment can have lasting negative effects (for example, Peters 1988).

This chapter investigates the concept of child sexual abuse and the characteristics of individuals who seek sexual activities with children. Special emphasis is given to the influence of early sexual experiences on adult cognitions and behaviour. The chapter is concerned exclusively with males, as it is currently thought that over 80 per cent of sexual acts with children are perpetrated by men and that female sex offenders present somewhat differently from men (Finkelhor 1979; Russell 1983; Jehu 1988; Finkelhor *et al.* 1990; Kennedy and Manwell 1992).

THE EXTENT OF EARLY SEXUAL MALTREATMENT

Kempe (1980) defines sexual abuse as 'The involvement of dependent, developmentally immature children and adolescents in sexual activities that they do not fully comprehend, to which they are unable to give informed consent or that violate the social taboos of family roles' (p. 198). Using this definition, Mrazek *et al.* (1981) conducted a postal survey of relevant professionals in the United Kingdom. They revealed that 1,065 reported cases of sexual abuse could be classified into three types:

Type 1 Battered children whose injuries were primarily in the genital area (4 per cent);

Type 2 Children who have experienced attempted or actual intercourse and/or other inappropriate genital contact with an adult (68 per cent);

Type 3 Children who have in some other way been involved with adult sexual
activities, for example, child pornography (16 per cent).

Using this classification of child sexual abuse there is no doubt that the phenomenon is as old as human society. In fact, child prostitution is documented to
have been common in Roman times and child molestation is said to have been
the rule rather than the exception in the sixteenth, seventeenth and eighteenth
centuries, at least in Europe (Aires 1962). There are even folk-tales depicting
incestuous relations (Goodwin 1988).

Over the course of the last decade the problem of child sexual abuse has
become more fully realized. There has been heightened media and public
awareness of its extent and the traumatic and distressing consequences for
many 'victims'. The publicity has attracted a variety of reactions, from over-
zealous investigation through to denial and disbelief (for example, Cleveland
Inquiry, Butler-Sloss 1988).

Whether there has been a true increase in the prevalence of child sexual
abuse in recent times is unknown. The fact is that there has been an explosion
in the reporting of the incidence of child sexual abuse, both in North America
(Finkelhor 1979; Greenberg 1979; Waterman and Lusk 1986; Goodwin 1988)
and in the United Kingdom (Creighton and Noyes 1989). Creighton and
Noyes (1989) confirm an increasing trend in the reported incidence of child
sexual abuse for England and Wales. Between 1983 and 1987 the number of
child sexual abuse cases dealt with by the NSPCC rose by 800 per cent, from
0.08 to 0.65 per thousand children (1,255 cases). In Northern Ireland the
observed incidence rate in 1987 was one in 1,000 children, which was half that
reported for the United States (Kennedy and Manwell 1992).

The current situation, according to the latest figures available from the
Department of Health in England (1991), is that 5,900 children (0.55 per
1,000) under 18 years of age are reported to have been sexually abused as
defined above. These figures represent 13 per cent of the total number of
maltreated children on Child Protection registers in England and Wales as
recorded on 31 March 1991. However, it is likely that these figures from the
NSPCC and DOH are biased towards intrafamilial abuse and exclude a large
proportion of child sexual assault by strangers, friends and neighbours. Retrospective surveys of adults and teenagers give an even more alarming picture of
the exploitation of children for the sexual gratification of adults.

Estimates of the number of children who are victims of sexual assault vary
according to the sample studied and the definition used. Peters et al. (1986)
describe the range of estimates from a review of North American studies of 6
to 62 per cent for females and 3 to 31 per cent for males. Bagley and King's
(1990) review of recent prevalence studies report figures of 11 to 45 per cent
for females and 6 to 9 per cent for males.

Sexually exploitative acts are generally classified into two categories:

1 *Non-contact abuse*: exposure of genital organs, showing and/or talking about pornographic material;
2 *Contact abuse*: genital touching and fondling, attempted or actual penetration (oral, anal or vaginal).

Overall, most of non-contact and contact abuse to children and adolescents is perpetrated by someone outside the immediate family (Russell 1983; Baker and Duncan 1985; Wyatt and Peters 1986). In California, it has been claimed that, in the broadest sense, one in two women have experienced some form of non-contact abuse by the time they have reached 18 years of age, whereas one in three women report 'unwanted' contact abuse experiences during childhood and adolescence (Russell 1983). In Canada, one in six women report unwanted sexual touching before they reached adulthood (Jehu 1988). Community-based studies in the United Kingdom (Hall 1985; Baker and Duncan 1985) give similar prevalence figures for adverse sexual experiences of between 11 and 12 per cent for females and 8 per cent for males, whilst clinically based studies (Hanks *et al.* 1988) give evidence of an increasing proportion of preschool victims of sexual abuse.

Evidence of the high rates of *contact* abuse has been provided by a US National Survey of Adult Men and Women (Finkelhor *et al.* 1990), which found that 27 per cent of women and 16 per cent of men reported sexual victimization in childhood, 20 per cent of women and 5 per cent of men had a history of unwanted sexual contact and 15 per cent of women and 10 per cent of men reported unwanted attempted or actual sexual intercourse.

CHARACTERISTICS OF THE OFFENDERS

The vast majority of child sex abusers (80–95 per cent) are male (Siegal *et al.* 1987; Finkelhor 1986; Jehu 1988; see Chapter 11). However, evidence does exist for the presence of female abusers, especially for male victims (Fritz *et al.* 1981). The most common age of the offender is between 35 and 40 years (Fitch 1962; Herman and Hirschman 1981), although there is growing evidence for adolescent offenders, peer and sibling abuse (Finkelhor 1979; Bentovim *et al.* 1988; Watkins and Bentovim 1992).

Mrazek *et al.* (1981) state that 57 per cent of child sex abuse is perpetrated outside the family, but only 25 per cent of the time by strangers. In between 75 and 90 per cent of cases the victim is abused by someone known to the child (Hunter *et al.* 1985; Childline 1988). Natural fathers are responsible for the abuse in 20 per cent of cases, stepfathers 12 per cent and natural mothers 2 per cent (Mrazek *et al.* 1981).

Victim surveys

From interviews with individuals who had experienced sexual abuse as children, Finkelhor (1986) determined the patterns of offences. The most common type of assault for both male and female children was found to be genital fondling or kissing of the child's genitals, followed by experiences involving masturbation and exhibitionism. Sexual activities involving penetration were less often reported.

Most individuals (60 per cent) described a single unpleasant experience. They consequently avoided the perpetrator or told a parent or guardian, who prevented it happening again. Other individuals described sexual assaults on an episodic or regular basis, the average being thirty-one weeks for female victims. This finding may be related to the fact that almost half the female victims were abused by a member of the family, and for a further third the offender was known to them. By contrast, only one-fifth of male victims were abused by a family member, but half knew their abuser.

Certain family factors have been associated with the risk of both intra-familial and extrafamilial child sex abuse (Russell 1983; Finkelhor and Baron 1986; Finkelhor 1986; see Andrews, this volume). These include:

- single or separated parent family;
- step-parent or cohabitee in the family;
- maternal caregiver disabled or ill;
- maternal caregiver employed outside the home;
- child victim has poor relationship with parent(s);
- child victim is emotionally abused within the family;
- child victim is physically abused or severely physically punished within the family.

There are close links between wife abuse and the sexual maltreatment of children in the home (Julian and Mohr 1979; Dietz and Craft 1980; Truesdell et al. 1986). The importance of these risk factors are that they influence the child's personality and behaviour, especially when the child is also a witness to wife abuse (Jaffe et al. 1990). Children from disruptive homes may become socially withdrawn, shy, unsure and show low self-esteem. Such children are especially vulnerable to the initial advances of a child sex offender. Indeed, sex offenders report these components of child behaviour to be attractive and act as a signal for possible recruitment (Browne 1992b).

Offender surveys

Findings from offender studies also give the impression that many child sexual assaults go unreported. On average, men convicted of sex offences against children claim five more undetected sexual assaults for which they were never apprehended or caught (Groth et al. 1982b).

Berliner and Conte (1990) and Conte et al. (1989) studied the offenders in twenty-three cases of child sexual abuse who gave clear descriptions of how they targeted and exploited children. They described three stages of 'grooming' the child:

- sexualization of an existing relationship;
- justification of the abuser's behaviour;
- final co-operation; where the offender seeks to keep the child involved in the relationship but prevents them telling others about it.

The offenders pointed out how they would play on the child's needs (such as affection). The children would sometimes fail to see themselves as victims of sexual exploitation until later.

A number of approaches to classifying child sexual abusers has been reported. These focus on the nature of the offence or some characteristic of the offender. Groth *et al.* (1982a) distinguishes between child rapists and child molesters. The rapists are characterized by the use of force, and this is linked to violent emotions similar to adult rape. By contrast, molesters coerce their victim into sexual activity for their own sexual gratification.

Howells (1981) further dichotomizes child molesters into (1) *'preference molesters'* – men with a stable and consistent interest in sexual activities with children with little concern for adult relationships (paedophiles); and (2) *'situational molesters'* – who form adult sexual relationships but impulsively seek sexual activities with children in an inconsistent way. It has been suggested that this dichotomy may be seen as a dimension of offender behaviour (Lanyon 1986).

Frequently a distinction is made between incestuous and non-incestuous offenders (for example, Herman 1981). This is to some extent a false dichotomy because research shows that one in two incestuous fathers also abuse children outside the family and one in five admit to raping mature women (Conte 1985). Obviously, incestuous parents find children sexually arousing, and perhaps those children in their own family are the most available. Another classification that is often made is homosexual and heterosexual child sex offenders. However, it is unclear as to whether these sexual preferences are constant over time or relate to adult sexual interactions (Freund and Langevin 1976).

Personality and behaviour problems of child sex offenders

A number of specific problems in the personality and behaviour of child sex offenders has been identified. However, these psychological disturbances are not unique to perpetrators of child sexual assaults and many are shown by other groups, such as violent offenders. The psychological disturbances consistently reported for child sex offenders have been reviewed by Conte (1985) and Overholser and Beck (1986). They may be summarized as follows:

- alcohol and drug abuse;
- depression;
- poor self-concept;
- low-self-esteem;

- relationship problems;
- poor impulse control;
- poor anger management;
- fear of negative evaluation;
- highly stereotypic views of sex roles and behaviour.

Blackburn (1983) claims that severe personality disorders that attract the label 'psychopath' are more highly represented among perpetrators of violent and sex offences. Nevertheless, there is little evidence for biologically related explanations (see Chapter 13). Thiessen (1990) points out that the hormonal activity associated with full maturity increases the probability of extreme violence during a rape but cannot be considered to cause sex crimes.

There is a suggestion that learning disability is associated with sexual assaults. Studies have shown that male offenders with learning disabilities are four to six times more likely to commit a sexual offence than other male offenders (Tutt 1971). However, the sexual assaults of males with learning disabilities are 'clumsy, impulsive expressions of sexual feelings rather than violent acts' shown by other perpetrators of sexual crimes (Hollin 1992: 99). For example, the sex offences are usually with an unknown victim, unplanned and poorly executed (Gilby et al. 1989).

The higher rates of sex offences amongst males with learning disabilities may relate to a lack of social competence. Howells (1986) points out that consenting sex with an adult requires a degree of social skill. He suggests that those adults with impaired social skills may find it difficult to form a sexual relationship with an adult partner and in some cases resort to children. Indeed, a number of studies have found that child molesters are poor in social perception and social performance in comparison to others (for example Overholser and Beck 1986; Segal and Marshall 1985).

Models of child molesting

Conte (1985) asserts that 'there is *no* currently verified profile of the typical adult who sexually abuses children'. He nevertheless goes on to offer five dimensions that are commonly observed in child sex offenders:

- Denial that a personal problem exists;
- Sexual arousal to children;
- Sexual fantasy involving children;
- Social skill deficits;
- Distorted attitudes and beliefs about sexual activities with children (see p. 223, Table 12.2).

From a much broader perspective Finkelhor (1986) has formulated a model which includes individual, familial, social and cultural concepts. The model consists of four complementary processes that create sexual interest in children.

1 *Emotional congruence* Children are easily dominated and the offender is immature, has low self-esteem and is possibly aggressive due to adherence to the masculine stereotype (see Chapter 7).
2 *Sexual arousal* Children are sexually arousing due to personal experience and socialization of the offender. There is a predisposition to use child pornography with masturbation and develop a learnt physiological arousal to children.
3 *Blockage* There are problems in forming relationships with adult women which are related to attitudes towards sex, sexual anxiety and poor social skills.
4 *Disinhibition* The offender is able to overcome his inhibitions through drugs, alcohol, cognitive distortions and fantasies. Situational stress may also disrupt inhibiting feelings.

The use of such models promotes a better understanding of child molesters and helps to determine the degree of dangerousness of the individual and whether (further) imprisonment is necessary in order to protect children in the community (Hollin 1989).

THE CONSEQUENCES OF CHILD SEXUAL ABUSE

Studies aimed at establishing links between characteristics of child sexual abuse and subsequent trauma displayed by the victim are mainly American in origin. Finkelhor (1986), for example, provided a useful model encompassing characteristics of child sexual abuse which result in long-term trauma into four traumatizing dynamics:

• traumatic sexualization;
• betrayal;
• powerlessness;
• stigmatization.

Each victim's experience of abuse will differ and their response to it will be determined by their own personal resources and perspective on life, a wide range of different long-term effects can be observed (see Table 12.1).

Finkelhor (1986) maintains that some effects may be a result of more than one dynamic. For example, depression can be a function of a sense of betrayal or powerlessness. Thus, it is important to understand how a victim relates to their abusive experiences and their offender. This makes the prediction of trauma associated with child sexual abuse very difficult, and much ambiguity exists as to how abuse characteristics influence trauma.

Table 12.1 Psychological response patterns amongst victims

Emotional	*Behavioural*
Fear	Aggressive behaviour
Anxiety	Suicidal behaviour
Intrusion	Substance abuse
Depression	Impaired social functioning
Self-esteem disturbances	Personality disorders
Anger	
Guilt and shame	
Cognitive	*Interpersonal*
Perceptual disturbances	Sexuality problems
(hallucinations, illusions, flashbacks,	Relationship problems
depersonalization, dissociation)	Revictimization
	Victim becomes offender
Biological	
Physiological hyper-arousal	
Somatic disturbances	

Source: Adapted from McCann *et al.* 1988: 538

Traumatic sexualization

Most consensus seems to be in relation to the increased traumatizing effects of multiple perpetrators and extended duration of child sexual abuse. It is suggested that a victim suffering abuse at the hands of several different perpetrators is more likely to blame themselves rather than the offender (Peters 1988; Briere 1988).

Whether the type of abusive act consistently influences trauma is uncertain (Finkelhor 1979), but evidence for increased trauma and mental health problems resulting from more serious contact, particularly vaginal, anal and oral penetration, receives most support (Russell 1986; Bagley and Ramsey 1986). Extensive examples of the physical trauma associated with sexual abuse of very young children is also being reported (Hanks *et al.* 1988).

The consequences of the age of the victim at the time the abuse occurs are uncertain. Effects at different ages are difficult to quantify and may be more qualitative in nature, in accordance with the stage of development achieved by the victim (Friedrich 1988). Nevertheless, most evidence suggests that young victims suffer the greatest trauma (Baker and Duncan 1985; Russell 1986), although some claim that increased trauma may be associated with increasing age of the victim, as a product of social and emotional maturity and understanding (Peters 1988; Burgess 1985).

Meiselman (1978) found more cases of 'seriously disturbed' children amongst those who had been abused under the age of 12, in comparison to adolescents aged 12 and over. Steele and Alexander (1981) suggest that sexual abuse is only less harmful to older children when undue coercion or violence is absent. It is assumed that adolescents who have had a non-abusive childhood will have a more integrated personality and therefore more inner resources to cope with an abusive experience as a teenager.

Trauma resulting from the relationship between the victim and the perpetrator is suggested to be the product of the degree of 'closeness' or 'quality' of the relationship (Finkelhor 1979; Conte and Shuerman 1987). However, increased age of the offender (Bagley 1988), and the perpetrator being male (Russell 1986) also seem to have a significant traumatizing effect.

Betrayal

Anna Freud (1981) postulated that intrafamilial sexual abuse is more traumatic for the child due to the degree of trust and unquestioning power inherent in family relationships. Whereas Baker and Duncan (1985) claimed that abuse by strangers results in less long-term trauma when the child victim can tell parents, be believed and not be held responsible for the abuse.

The post-abusive environment is also documented as having a significant effect on child sexual abuse victims (Kempe and Kempe 1978; Silver and Wortman 1980). Greenwald *et al.* (1990) found that psychological distress was nevertheless greater in sexual abuse victims compared to a non-abused sample even when parental support was present. However, Bagley and Ramsey (1986) and Fromuth (1986) demonstrated the positive effects of parental support for the later psychological adjustment of sexual abuse victims. Furthermore, Wyatt and Mickey (1988) found 'self-attribution' was high in women who had not disclosed their own experiences of child sexual abuse due to fear of not being believed. It has been suggested that therapy and rehabilitation of the family in incest cases is only possible where the mother believes the child and the incestuous father accepts full responsibility for what has happened (Bentovim 1991).

Powerlessness

The use of force to initiate or perpetuate abuse is ambiguous with regard to its traumatizing effects. Some studies show the presence of force as one of the most influential abuse characteristics predicting adverse outcome (Finkelhor 1979; Russell 1986). This can be explained by the direct traumatizing effects of violence itself, a point illustrated by the effect of the physical abuse of children. The ambiguity arises from the fact that force may prove traumatic initially but its presence could alleviate guilt on a longer-term basis (MacFarlane 1983).

If the abuse is co-coercive and non-aggressive, guilty feelings can emerge in the victim related to pleasurable physical sensations, feeling responsible for the abuse and the mistaken belief that the abuser could have been stopped.

218

Stigmatization

With respect to the sex of the victim, male victims may suffer trauma, directly through the homosexual nature of the act and indirectly through the effect of inhibition to disclose (Nasjleti 1986). They may also be subject to more serious sexual acts (Hanks *et al.* 1988). In an American community survey, Finkelhor *et al.* (1990) found that 42 per cent of girls compared to 33 per cent of boys had disclosed an incident of child sexual abuse occurring to them. This variation is believed to be largely the product of societally based gender roles. Finkelhor (1979) postulated that our society casts men as sexually active and women as sexually passive, thus attributing more consent and less exploitation into male victims. Indeed, Pierce and Pierce (1985), in a sample of child sexual abuse victims, found that 12 per cent of boys compared to 3 per cent of girls were believed to have encouraged their sexual abuse.

Nevertheless, four out of five victims of intrafamilial child sexual abuse are female (Mrazek *et al.* 1981; Bentovim *et al.* 1988; Childline 1988). Thus, females may be traumatized through stigma and betrayal (Finkelhor 1979; Baker and Duncan 1985).

Long-term trauma is especially a product of the victim's feelings of stigmatization and low self-esteem (Finkelhor 1984, 1986). Such feelings may themselves be the result of societal definitions of appropriate sexual behaviour. For example, there are tribes in New Guinea which practise incestuous oral intercourse as part of an initiation process for pre-pubescent boys without any apparent ill effect on their socio-emotional development (Ford and Beach 1951). Some writers suggest that early sexual experiences may do minimal harm to a child. For example, Kinsey *et al.* (1953) stated, 'It is difficult to understand why a child, except for cultural conditioning, should be disturbed at having its genitalia touched or disturbed at seeing the genitalia of other persons, or disturbed at even more specific sexual contacts.' West (1984) goes as far as to say that adult–child sexual relationships may be 'positive' for the child.

By contrast, there is growing evidence (Reiss 1967; Davenport *et al.* 1993) which suggests that a very clear hierarchy of sexual 'seriousness' exists in western culture from kissing, through touching breasts, touching genitals and finally to intercourse. In this context, Finkelhor (1988) states that sometimes the fact of having been abused is only recognized in retrospect as children learn more about socially appropriate sexual behaviour. This may result in anxious feelings and trauma about sexual events that the child did not previously comprehend.

VICTIM RESPONSES TO CHILD SEXUAL ABUSE

The general conclusions to be drawn from clinical observations and research on personal trauma are that short-term effects are largely behavioural and a direct reflection of age-inappropriate sexual contact, whereas long-term effects can be considered to be a manifestation of short-term effects coloured by other life events, personality characteristics and the psychological maturation of the victim.

The most important impact of child sexual abuse for the child victim is an overwhelming sense of anxiety which can interfere with the development of self-esteem and influence self-perception (Kilgore 1988). In incestuous relationships a young child may still preserve the idea of good parents or care-givers; therefore, the emotions of love and hate towards an abuser can exist simultaneously. Winnicott (1961) claims that effects of child sex abuse are long-lasting because the critical periods of learning through play and social interaction have been spoiled.

In North America, at least a quarter of child sexual abuse carries a legacy of serious, long-term psychological harm (Bagley and King 1990). Therefore, the prevalence of child sexual abuse is even higher amongst men and women seeking help with psychological problems. Nearly as many as one in two people who 'walk in' for counselling recollect sexual abuse as children (Briere and Runtz 1986), and a similar figure is reported for drug abusers (Benward and Densen Gerber 1975). Not surprisingly, 90 per cent of people attending a sexual dysfunction clinic report being a child victim of sexual abuse (Baisden and Baisden 1979). At least eight out of ten psychiatric patients with person-ality disorders have been victims of sexual maltreatment as children (Bliss 1984; Coons and Milstein 1986; Herman *et al.* 1989; Lobel 1992) and six out of ten schizophrenic in-patients have also suffered such experiences (Friedman and Harrison 1984).

Similar findings have been reported in the United Kingdom for men and women suffering from psychological distress both in the community and in psychiatric hospitals (Metcalf *et al.* 1990; Mullen *et al.* 1988). For example, just over half (51 per cent) of patients being treated for eating disorders reported adverse sexual experiences in childhood (Oppenheimer *et al.* 1985).

FROM VICTIM TO OFFENDER

A recognition of the influences of sexual abuse on the behaviour of individuals later in life has been one of the factors that has challenged the assumption that delinquent and anti-social acts are in some way inherent in the individual (Eysenck 1964). There is an increased awareness that childhood sexual victimization can involve physical, psychological and sexual components (Groth and Burgess 1979, 1980), any of which can have long-lasting effects on the behaviour and cognitions of the victim (Peters 1988).

The effects can include feelings of depression, low self-esteem, powerless-ness, loss of control and lack of trust in others (Peters 1988; Jehu 1988; Watkins and Bentovim 1992). The victim may experience difficulties in managing emotions and feelings in relation to others and show poor social skills (Steele and Alexander 1981), or may express their distress through abuse of drugs and alcohol (Watkins and Bentovim 1992). However, Rogers and Terry (1984) suggested that some behavioural responses appear to be much more common in male victims. These are (1) confusion of sexual identity, (2) inappropriate reassertions of masculinity and (3) the recapitulating victim experiences. Thus, sexually abused boys have a higher probability of homosexual activity (Finkelhor 1984; Johnson and Shrier 1987), aggressive and antisocial behaviour (Summit 1983) and becoming a perpetrator of sexual abuse (Cantwell 1988; Watkins and Bentovim 1992).

The fact that some victims may experience difficulties in expressing emotions and trust is important, as this may form the basis of later problems in adulthood. These problems may be triggered by critical events in an individual's life, such as developing a sexual relationship, having children and so on. Painful feelings about the past may affect current behaviour, sometimes resulting in the victim becoming an offender (Search 1988). Thus, it is important to address questions about the existence of a possible relationship between early negative sexual experience and sexual offending. Indeed, it has been reported that adults with a history of child sexual abuse have more long-term emotional, behavioural and interpersonal problems than victims of any other form of child maltreatment (Bagley and MacDonald 1984; Egeland 1988; Freud 1981).

Summit (1983) claimed that male victims of sexual abuse are more likely than female victims to externalize their inner rage and hostility and hence harm others rather than themselves. This can result in juvenile delinquency and/or crime. A recent review of prospective studies on sexually abused boys indicated that one in five go on to molest other children sexually (Watkins and Bentovim 1992). Retrospective studies of adult sex offenders provide further evidence for the long-term nature of a victim-to-perpetrator cycle. Groth and Burgess (1979) found that one-third of the 106 child molesters in their study reported some form of sexual trauma in their childhood. Faller (1989) also found that 27 per cent of incestuous fathers and stepfathers had been sexually abused as children.

The victim-to-perpetrator pattern seems to be particularly relevant to child molesters and paedophiles, with 56–57 per cent reporting adverse sexual experiences as children in comparison to between 5 and 23 per cent of rapists (Pithers et al. 1988; Seghorn et al. 1987). Furthermore, retrospective studies have also revealed that 60–80 per cent of adult child sex offenders began molesting children as adolescents (Groth et al. 1982b), and it has been estimated that adolescents perpetrate 50 per cent of the sex crimes against boys and 15–20 per cent of offences against girls (Rogers and Terry 1984).

The victim-to-offender pattern is not limited to sexual offences; for example, 14 per cent of male and 50 per cent of female adolescent fire-setters have a history of child sexual abuse (Epps and Swaffer 1993).

THE SEXUAL ASSAULT CYCLE AND COGNITIVE DISTORTIONS

The concept of a victim to perpetrator pattern is helpful for understanding both sexual dysfunction and deviance, and their relationship to cognitive distortions. In particular, it is relevant to the stages of offending, namely, the fantasy of child sex, planning the act and the actual child sexual molestation, which have been termed the 'sexual assault cycle' (Ryan *et al.* 1987).

The idea of a sexual assault cycle was originally developed by Ryan *et al.* (1987) at the adolescent treatment centre in Denver. The cycle provides a framework for young offenders to understand the cognitive, behavioural, physiological, psychological and situational factors that relate to their offences. According to Ryan and colleagues, elements of the cycle include the following: negative self-image, predicting rejection, perceived helplessness and isolation, fantasy, planning sexual offence, and post-offence feelings such as loss of control.

Abel *et al.* (1987, 1989) suggest that cognitive distortions develop during childhood and adolescence, and these may be understood through a Social Learning Theory model. For example, offenders may use 'grooming' strategies that they themselves experienced as part of their own victimizing experiences as children, and there may exist a dynamic process for the parallel development of cognitive distortions and grooming practices. One of the cognitive distortions that offenders often hold is a belief that the reason children do not tell about their abusive experiences is because they enjoy the activity (Abel *et al.* 1987, 1989). A therapist might highlight the inconsistency of this belief with the offender's practice of using strategies to ensure secrecy as part of the grooming process. A therapist might also confront the offender's distorted view that children do not physically resist the assault because they enjoy the activity, with the evidence that the offender uses bribes and threats to discourage such resistance.

Little has been written about whether cognitive distortions differ between sex offenders, other offenders and the general population. This is despite the fact that an unexpectedly high rate of sexual interest in children has been identified in a university, male undergraduate sample. Briere and Runtz (1989) surveyed the sexual interest in children of male students with the intention of predicting potential indices of paedophilia in a non-forensic sample. They found that 21 per cent reported sexual attraction to some small children, 9 per cent having sexual fantasies involving children, 5 per cent admitted masturbating to these fantasies and 7 per cent indicated some likelihood of having sex with a child if they could avoid detection and punishment. A similar finding was also made by Tieger (1981). He discovered that of a group of 172 male university students, 64 indicated some likelihood of raping if they could be certain that they would not be caught.

Browne (1993) further investigated the relationship between early sexual experiences, adult cognitions and sexual activities with children in 122 male medical students. They were compared to twelve convicted male sex offenders on their responses to the Abel and Becker Cognition Scale (Abel *et al.* 1989) and the Sex Life Event Questionnaire (Browne 1992a). Analysis showed that child sex offenders held more distorted beliefs than students (Table 12.2), although 9 per cent of the students had cognitive distortions similar to those possessed by the sex offenders. Overall, 22 per cent of the male students reported 'unwanted sexual experiences' during childhood and adolescence, 6 per cent of whom were under 11 years old when they occurred. By contrast, 92 per cent of the sex offenders indicated adverse sexual experiences under 11 years of age which, unlike the students, involved penetration and group sexual activities.

Table 12.2 Comparison of offenders and students on factor scores of the Abel and Becker Cognitive Scale

Factor	Content	P value chi²
A	Child–adult sex helps the child and enhances the child–adult relationship	.05
B	Children initiate child–adult sex for specific reasons, when they inquire about sex they would also like to experience sex.	.001
C	Adults initiate child–adult sex for specific reasons, such as to teach the child about sex.	.001
D	The child's behaviour and lack of resistance show their desire for child–adult sex.	.001
E	Adults can predict when child–adult sex will damage the child and genital fondling is not really sex so no harm is done.	.01
F	Child–adult sex is or will be acceptable to society in the future.	N.S.

Source: From Browne and Carlyle 1993

NB Child sex offenders show significantly more cognitive distortions on factors A to E. For factor F both offenders and male undergraduates believe child–adult sex will *not* be acceptable to society in future.

The validity of comparing convicted sex offenders with male medical students may be questioned. However, it has previously been indicated that educational levels are not a factor in the prevalence of sexual victimization (Russell 1984). Similarly, research on sex offenders has concluded that the committing of sex offences is not related to the educational level of the individuals concerned (Groth and Burgess 1980). Overall, these findings raise the question of the influences and factors that are present in our society that may be associated with or underpin the development of distorted attitudes towards sexuality. The prevalence of cognitive distortions associated with sexual activities with children is unknown.

THE DEVELOPMENT OF CHILD SEXUAL ASSAULTS

Abel *et al.* (1989) has espoused a social learning framework for understanding how child molesters develop cognitive distortions (see Table 12.2) that allow the offender to justify his on-going sexual abuse of a child. Such distortions are likely to play a part in how sex offenders recruit and maintain child victims and in how they respond to the child's resistance.

Ryan (1989) described how one of the dysfunctional responses to experiences of child sexual abuse may be an increased risk of becoming sexually abusive, and explored parallels in the treatment of victims and offenders. One of these parallels is a feeling of helplessness, which is exacerbated by the secrecy surrounding sexual abuse and can lead to maladaptive coping mechanisms such as 'acting out' and destructive behaviour directed at both self and others.

Rasmussen *et al.* (1992), proposed that sexually victimized children have three possible 'trauma outcome processes': (1) they may express and work through feelings associated with trauma to the point of acceptance or resolution (recovery); (2) they may develop self-destructive behaviour (self-victimization); and (3) they may identify with their aggressor and display assaultive behaviour against others (assault). Sexually aggressive behaviour, more often seen in males, may be an attempt to recreate past trauma and victimizing experiences in ways which lead to developing mastery and control over the associated feelings (Breer 1987). Indeed, Ryan (1989) views the sexual assault cycle as 'a predictable pattern of negative feelings, cognitive disorders, and control-seeking behaviours which lead up to a sexual offense' (p. 328).

CONCLUSION

Recently, considerable time and effort have been put into the development of prevention programmes for children. Davro (1991) reviews the evidence on how effective 'strengthening the child' is in preventing child sexual abuse. She also reviews work on the idea of 'strengthening parents or guardians' in ways of better parental care to enhance the child's self-esteem and confidence which protect the child from the initial advances of the sexual offender. This review has emphasized the need for mental health professionals to consider the prevalence and prevention of child sexual abuse in males. It would be a grave mistake to ignore the long-term consequences that promote sexual crimes in this generation and the next.

REFERENCES

Abel, G., Becker, J., Mittelman, M., Cunningham-Rather, J., Rouleau, J. and Murphy, W. (1987) 'Self-reported sex crimes of non-incarcerated paraphiliacs', *Journal of Interpersonal Violence*, 2: 3–25.

Abel, G., Gore, D., Holland, C., Comp, N., Becker, J. and Rathner, J. (1989) 'The measurement of cognitive distortions of child molesters', *Annals of Sex Research*, 2: 135–53.

Aires, P. (1962) *Centuries of Childhood*, New York: Basic Books.

Bagley, C. (1988) 'Depression, self-esteem and suicidal behaviour as sequels of sexual abuse in childhood: research and therapy', in M. Rothey and G. Cameron (eds) *Child Maltreatment: Expanded Conceptions of Helping*, Ontario: Wilford Launer University Press.

Bagley, C. and King, K. (1990) *Child Sexual Abuse: The Search for Healing*, London: Tavistock/Routledge.

Bagley, C. and MacDonald, M. (1984) 'Adult mental health sequels of child sexual abuse, physical abuse and neglect in maternally separated children', *Canadian Journal of Community Mental Health*, 3 (Spring): 15–26.

Bagley, C. and Ramsey, R. (1986) 'Sexual abuse in childhood: psychological outcomes and implications for social work practice', in J. Gripton and M. Valentich (eds) *Social Work Practice in Sexual Problems*, New York: Hamworth Press, pp. 33–47.

Baisden, M. J. and Baisden, J. R. (1979) 'A profile of women who seek counselling for sexual dysfunction', *American Journal of Family Therapy*, 7: 68–76.

Baker, A. W. and Duncan, S. P. (1985) 'Child sexual abuse: a study of prevalence in Britain', *Child Abuse and Neglect*, 8: 457–67.

Bentovim, A. (1991) 'Clinical work with families in which child sexual abuse has occurred', in C. Hollin and K. Howells (eds) *Clinical Approaches to Sex Offenders and Their Victims*, Chichester: Wiley.

Bentovim, A., Elton, A., Hildebrand, J., Tranter, M. and Vizard, E. (1988) *Child Sexual Abuse within the Family (Assessment and Treatment)*, London: Wright.

Benward, J. and Denson Gerber, J. (1975) 'Incest as a causative factor in anti-social behaviour: an exploratory study', *Contemporary Drug Problems*, 4: 323–40.

Berliner, L. and Conte, J. (1990) 'The process of victimisation: the victim's perspective', *Child Abuse and Neglect*, 14: 29–40.

Blackburn, R. (1983) 'Psychopathy, delinquency and crime', in A. Gale and J. Edwards (eds) *Physiological Correlates of Human Behaviour*, vol. 3, *Individual Differences and Psychopathology*, London: Academic Press.

Bliss, E. L. (1984) 'A symptom profile of patients with multiple personalities including MMPI results', *Journal of Nervous and Mental Disease*, 172: 197–202.

Breer, W. (1987) *The Adolescent Molester*, Springfield, IL: C. Thomas.

Briere, J. (1988) 'The long term clinical correlates of childhood sexual victimisation', in R. A. Prentley and V. L. Quinsey *Human Sexual Aggression: Current Perspectives*, Annals of the New York Academy of Sciences, vol. 528: 327–34.

Briere, J. and Runtz, M. (1986) 'Suicidal thoughts and behaviour in former sexual abuse victims', *Canadian Journal of Behavioral Sciences*, 18: 414–23.

—— (1989) 'University males' sexual interest in children', *Child Abuse and Neglect*, 13: 65–75.

Browne, K. D. (1992a) *The Sexual Life Event Scale*, School of Psychology, Birmingham University, Unpublished.

—— (1992b) 'Sex offenders' strategies for victimising children: an investigation of the "grooming" strategies that sex offenders use to select, recruit and maintain children in victimising situations', *Proceedings of the 9th International Congress on Child Abuse and Neglect*, Chicago, September 1992 (Abstract No. ID566), International Society for Prevention of Child Abuse (ISPCAN), Chicago.

Browne, K. D. and Carlyle, J. (1993) 'The early sexual exploitation and adult cognitions of child sex offenders in comparison to non-offenders', *Youth Treatment*, 1(1): in press.

Burgess, A. W. (1985) 'Sexual victimisation of adolescents', in A. W. Burgess (ed.) *Rape and Sexual Assault: A Research Handbook*, New York: Garland Publishing, pp. 123–38.

Butler-Sloss, E. (1988) *Report of the Inquiry into Child Abuse in Cleveland*, 1987, Cm. 412, London: HMSO.

Cantwell, H. B. (1988) 'Child sexual abuse: very young perpetrators', *Child Abuse and Neglect*, 12: 579–82.

Childline (1988) *Childline: The First Year*, London: Childline.

Conte, J. (1985) 'Clinical dimensions of adult sexual interest in children', *Behavioral Sciences and the Law*, 3: 341–54.

Conte, J. and Shuerman, J. R. (1987) 'Factors associated with an increased impact of child sexual abuse', *Child Abuse and Neglect*, 11: 201–11.

Conte, J., Wolff, S. and Smith, T. (1989) 'What sexual offenders tell us about prevention', *Child Abuse and Neglect*, 13: 293–301.

Coons, P. M. and Milstein, V. (1986) 'Psychosexual disturbances in multiple personality: characteristic etiology and treatment', *Journal of Clinical Psychology*, 47: 106–10.

Creighton, S. J. and Noyes, P. (1989) *Child Abuse Trends in England and Wales, 1983–1987*, NSPCC (July).

Davro, D. (1991) 'Prevention programs', in C. Hollin and K. Howells (eds) *Clinical Approaches to Sex Offenders and their Victims*, Chichester: Wiley.

Davenport, C. F., Browne, K. D. and Palmer, R. (1993) 'Opinions on the traumatising effects of child sexual abuse: evidence for consensus', *Child Abuse and Neglect*, 17 (in press).

Department of Health (1991) *Children and Young Persons on Child Protection Registers Year Ending 31st March 1991, England*, Department of Health Personal Social Services Local Authority Statistics, London: HMSO.

Dietz, C. A. and Craft, J. L. (1980) 'Family dynamics of incest: a new perspective', *Social Casework*, 61: 602–9.

Egeland, B. (1988) 'Intergenerational continuity in parental maltreatment of children', in K. D. Browne, C. Davies and P. Stratton (eds) *Early Prediction and Prevention of Child Abuse*, Chichester: Wiley, pp. 87–99.

Epps, K. and Swaffer, T. (1993) 'Adolescent fire-setters', *Journal of Forensic Psychiatry* (in submission).

Eysenck, H. J. (1964) *Crime and Personality*, London: Penguin.

Faller, K. C. (1989) 'Why sexual abuse? an exploration of the intergenerational hypothesis', *Child Abuse and Neglect*, 13: 543–8.

Finkelhor, D. (1979) *Sexually Victimised Children*, New York: Free Press.

—— (1984) *Child Sexual Abuse: New Theory and Research*, New York: Free Press.

—— (1986) *A Source Book on Child Sexual Abuse*, Beverly Hills, CA: Sage.

—— (1988) 'The trauma of child sexual abuse: two models', in G. Wyatt and G. Powell (eds) *The Lasting Effects of Child Sexual Abuse*, Beverly Hills, CA: Sage, pp. 61–82.

Finkelhor, D. and Baron, L. (1986) 'Risk factors for child sexual abuse', *Journal of Interpersonal Violence*, 1: 43–71.

Finkelhor, D., Hotaling, G., Lewis, I. A. and Smith, C. (1990) 'Sexual abuse in a National Survey of Adult Men and Women: prevalence, characteristics and risk-factors', *Child Abuse and Neglect*, 14: 19–28.

Fitch, Z. H. (1962) 'Men convicted of sexual offences against children: a descriptive follow-up study', *British Journal of Criminology*, 3: 18–37.

Ford, C. S. and Beach, F. (1951) *Patterns of Sexual Behaviour*, New York: Harper & Row.

Freud, A. (1981) 'A psychoanalyst's view of sexual abuse by parents', in P. Beezley,

P. Mrazek and C. H. Kempe, *Sexually Abused Children and their Families*, Oxford: Pergamon Press, pp. 33–4.

Freund, K. and Langevin, R. (1976) 'Bisexuality in homosexual paedophilia', *Archives of Sexual Behaviour*, 5: 415–23.

Friedman, S. and Harrison, G. (1984) 'Sexual histories, attitudes and behaviour of schizophrenic and "normal" women', *Archives of Sexual Behaviour*, 13: 555–67.

Friedrich, W. N. (1988) 'Behaviour problems in sexually abused children: an adaptational perspective', in G. Wyatt and G. Powell (eds) *Lasting Effects of Child Sexual Abuse*, Beverly Hills, CA: Sage.

Fritz, G. S., Stoll, K. and Wagner, N. N. (1981) 'A comparison of males and females who were sexually molested as children', *Journal of Sex and Marital Therapy*, 7: 54–9 (Spring).

Fromuth, M. E. (1986) 'The relationship of childhood sexual abuse with late psychological and adjustment in a sample of college women', *Child Abuse and Neglect*, 10: 5–15.

Gilby, R., Woolf, L. and Goldberg, B. (1989) 'Mentally retarded adolescent sex offenders: a survey and pilot study', *Canadian Journal of Psychiatry*, 34: 542–8.

Goodwin, Z. M. (1988) 'Obstacles to policy making about incest: some cautionary folktales', in G. Wyatt and G. Powell (eds) *Lasting Effects of Child Sexual Abuse*, New York: Sage, pp. 21–38.

Greenberg, N. H. (1979) 'The epidemiology of childhood sexual abuse', *Paediatric Annals*, 3(15): 289–99.

Greenwald, E., Leitenberg, H., Cado, S. and Tarram, M. J. (1990) 'Childhood sexual abuse: long-term effects on psychological and sexual functioning in a non-clinical and non-student sample of adult women', *Child Abuse and Neglect*, 14: 503–13.

Groth, N. and Burgess, A. (1979) 'Sexual trauma in the life histories of rapists and child molesters', *Victimology*, 1: 10–16.

—— (1980) 'Male rape: offenders and victims', *American Journal of Psychiatry*, 137: 807–10.

Groth, N., Hobson, W. and Garry, T. (1982a) 'The child sexual molester: clinical observations', in J. Conte and D. Shore (eds) *Social Work and Child Sexual Abuse*, New York: Hamworth.

Groth, N., Longo, R. and McFadin, J. (1982) 'Undetected recidivism among rapists and child molesters', *Crime and Delinquency*, 128: 450–8.

Hall, R. E. (1985) *Ask Any Woman: A London Inquiry into Rape and Sexual Assault*, London: Falling Wall Press.

Hanks, H., Hobbs, C. and Wynne, J. (1988) 'Early signs and recognition of sexual abuse in the pre-school child', in K. Browne, C. Davies and P. Stratton (eds) *Early Prediction and Prevention of Child Abuse*, London: Wiley, pp. 139–60.

Herman, J. L. (1981) *Father–Daughter Incest*, Cambridge, MA: Harvard University Press.

Herman, J. L., Perry, J. C. and van der Kilk, B. A. (1989) 'Childhood trauma in borderline personality disorder', *American Journal of Psychiatry*, 146: 490–5.

Herman, J. and Hirschman, L. (1981) 'Families at risk for father–daughter incest', *American Journal of Psychiatry*, 138: 967–70.

Hollin, C. R. (1989) *Psychology and Crime: An Introduction to Criminological Psychology*, London: Routledge.

—— (1992) *Criminal Behaviour: A Psychological Approach to Explanation and Prevention*, London: Falmer Press, p. 99.

Howells, K. (1981) 'Adult sexual interest in children: considerations relevant to theories of etiology', in M. Cook and K. Howells (eds) *Adult Sexual Interest in Children*, London: Academic Press.

227

—— (1986) 'Social skills training and criminal and antisocial behaviour in adults', in C. Hollin and P. Trower (eds) *Handbook of Social Skills Training*, vol. 1, *Applications Across the Life Span*, Oxford: Pergamon.

Hunter, P. S., Kilstrom, N. and Loda, F. (1985) 'Sexually abused children: identifying masked presentations in a medical setting', *Child Abuse and Neglect*, 9: 17–25.

Jaffe, P. G., Wolfe, D. A. and Wilson, S. K. (1990) *Children of Battered Women*, Beverly Hills, CA: Sage.

Jehu, D. (1988) *Beyond Sexual Abuse: Therapy with Women Who Were Childhood Victims*, Chichester: Wiley.

Johnson, R. L. and Shrier, D. (1987) 'Past sexual victimisation by females of male patients in an adolescent medicine clinic population', *American Journal of Psychiatry*, 144: 650–2.

Julian, V. and Mohr, C. (1979) 'Father–daughter incest: a profile of the offender', *Victimology*, 4: 10–17.

Kempe, C. H. (1980) 'Incest and other forms of sexual abuse', in C. H. Kempe and R. E. Helfer (eds) *The Battered Child*, 3rd edn, Chicago: University of Chicago Press, pp. 198–214.

Kempe, R. S. and Kempe, C. H. (1978) *Child Abuse*, London: Fontana/Open Books.

Kennedy, M. T. and Manwell, M. K. (1992) 'The pattern of child sexual abuse in Northern Ireland', *Child Abuse Review*, 1(2): 89–101.

Kilgore, L. C. (1988) 'Effects of early childhood sexual abuse on self and ego development', *Social Casework: The Journal of Contemporary Social Work*, 9: 224–30.

Kinsey, A. C., Pomeroy, W. B., Martin, C. E. and Gebhard, P. (1953) *Sexual Behaviour in the Human Female*, 116, Philadelphia and London: Saunders.

Lanyon, R. I. (1986) 'Theory and treatment in child molestation', *Journal of Consulting and Clinical Psychology*, 54: 176–82.

Lobel, C. M. (1992) 'Relationship between childhood sexual abuse and borderline personality disorder in women psychiatric inpatients', *Journal of Child Sexual Abuse*, 1: 63–80.

McCann, I. L., Sakheim, D. K. and Abrahamson, D. J. (1988) 'Trauma and victimisation: a model of psychological adaptation', *The Counselling Psychologist*, 16: 531–94.

MacFarlane, K. (1983) 'Program considerations in the treatment of incest offenders', in S. G. Greer and I. R. Stuart (eds) *The Sexual Aggressor: Current Perspectives on Treatment*, New York: Nostrand Reinhold Group.

Meiselman, K. C. (1978) *Incest: A Psychological Study of Causes and Effects with Treatment Recommendations*, San Francisco: Jossey Bass.

Metcalf, M., Oppenheimer, R., Digron, A. and Palmer, R. L. (1990) 'Childhood sexual experiences reported by male psychiatric patients', *Psychological Medicine*, 20: 925–9.

Mrazek, P., Lynch, M. and Bentovim, A. (1981) 'Sexual abuse of children in the United Kingdom', *Child Abuse and Neglect*, 7: 147–53.

Mullen, P., Walton, V., Romans-Clarkson, S. and Herbison, G. (1988) 'Impact of sexual and physical abuse on women's mental health', *The Lancet*, 16 April, 841–5.

Nasjleti, M. (1986) 'Suffering in silence: the male incest victim', in D. C. Haden (ed.) *Out of Harm's Way: Readings on Child Sexual Abuse, its Prevention and Treatment*, Phoenix, AZ: Onyx Press, pp. 67–71.

Oppenheimer, R., Howells, K., Palmer, R. and Chaloner, D. (1985) 'Adverse sexual experience in childhood and clinical eating disorders: a preliminary description', *Journal of Psychiatric Research*, 19: 357–61.

Overholser, J. and Beck, S. (1986) 'Multimethod assessment of rapists, child molesters and three control groups on behavioural and psychological measures', *Journal of Consulting and Clinical Psychology*, 54: 682–7.

Peters, S. D. (1988) 'Child sexual abuse and later psychological problems', in G. Wyatt and G. Powell (eds) *Lasting Effects of Child Sexual Abuse*, Beverly Hills, CA: Sage, pp. 101–18.

Peters, S., Wyatt, G. and Finkelhor, D. (1986) 'Prevalence', in D. Finkelhor (ed.) *A Sourcebook on Child Sexual Abuse*, Beverly Hills, CA: Sage.

Pierce, R. and Pierce, L. H. (1985) 'The sexually abused child: a comparison of male and female victims', *Child Abuse and Neglect*, 9: 191–9.

Pithers, W. D., Kashima, K. M., Cumming, G. F. and Beal, L. F. (1988) 'Relapse prevention: a method of enhancing maintenance of change in sex offenders', in A. C. Salter (ed.) *Treating Child Sex Offenders and Victims: A Practical Guide*, Beverly Hills, CA: Sage.

Rasmussen, L., Burton, J. and Christopherson, B. (1992) 'Precursors to offending and the trauma outcome process in sexually reactive children', *Journal of Child Sexual Abuse*, 1: 33–48.

Reiss, I. L. (1967) *The Social Context of Pre-marital Permissiveness*, New York: Holt, Rinehart.

Rogers, C. M. and Terry, T. (1984) 'Clinical intervention with boy victims of sexual abuse', in I. R. Stuart and J. G. Greer (eds) *Victims of Sexual Aggression: Men, Women and Children*, New York: Van Nostrand Reinhold, pp. 91–103.

Russell, D. E. (1983) 'The incidence and prevalence of intrafamilial sexual abuse of female children', *Child Abuse and Neglect*, 7: 133–46.

—— (1984) *Sexual Exploitation*, London: Sage.

—— (1986) *The Secret Trauma: Incest in the Lives of Girls and Women*, New York: Basic Books.

Ryan, G. (1989) 'Victim to victimizer: rethinking victim treatment', *Journal of Interpersonal Violence*, 4: 325–41.

Ryan, G., Lane, S., Davis, J. and Isaac, C. (1987) 'Juvenile sexual offenders: development and correction', *Child Abuse and Neglect*, 11: 385–95.

Search, G. (1988) *The Last Taboo: Sexual Abuse of Children*, Harmondsworth, UK: Penguin Books.

Segal, Z. V. and Marshall, W. L. (1985) 'Heterosexual social skills in a population of rapists and child molesters', *Journal of Consulting and Clinical Psychology*, 53: 55–63.

Seghorn, T. K., Prentky, R. A. and Boucher, R. J. (1987) 'Childhood sexual abuse in the lives of sexually aggressive offenders', *Journal of the American Academy of Child and Adolescent Psychiatry*, 26: 262–7.

Siegal, J. M., Sorensor, S. B., Golding, J. M., Burman, N. A. and Stein, J. A. (1987) 'The prevalence of sexual assault: the Los Angeles Epidemiologic Catchment Area Project', *American Journal of Epidemiology*, 126: 1141–53.

Silver, R. L. and Wortman, C. B. (1980) 'Coping with undesirable life events', in J. Garber and M. E. P. Seligman (eds) *Human Helplessness Theory and Applications*, New York: Academic Press.

Steele, B. F. and Alexander, H. (1981) 'Long-term effects of sexual abuse in childhood', in P. B. Mrazek and C. H. Kempe (eds) *Sexually Abused Children and their Families*, New York: Pergamon Press.

Summit, R. C. (1983) 'The child sexual accommodation syndrome', *Child Abuse and Neglect*, 7: 177–93.

Thiessen, D. (1990) 'Hormonal correlates of sexual aggression', in L. Ellis and H. Hoffman (eds) *Crime in Biological, Social and Moral Contexts*, New York: Praeger.

Tieger, T. (1981) 'Self-rated likelihood of raping and the social perception of rape', *Journal of Research in Personality*, 15: 147–58.

Truesdell, D., McNeil, J. and Deschner, J. (1986) 'Incidence of wife abuse in incestuous families', *Social Work*, 31: 138–40.

Tutt, N. (1971) 'The subnormal offender', *British Journal of Mental Subnormality*, 17: 42–7.

Waterman, J. and Lusk, R. (1986) 'Scope of the problem', in K. MacFarlane, J. Waterman, S. Conerley, L. Damon, M. Durfree and S. Long (eds) *Sexual Abuse of Young Children*, New York: Guilford Press, pp. 3–12.

Watkins, B. and Bentovim, A. (1992) 'The sexual abuse of male children and adolescents: a review of current research', *Journal of Child Psychology and Psychiatry*, 33: 197–248.

West, D. J. (1984) 'The victim's contribution to sexual assault', in J. Hopkins (ed.) *Perspectives on Rape and Sexual Assault*, London: Harper & Row, pp. 1–14.

Winnicott, D. (1961) *Home is Where We Start From*, Harmondsworth, UK: Penguin.

Wyatt, G. E. and Mickey, M. R. (1988) 'The support by parents and others as it mediates the effects of child sexual abuse: an exploratory study', in G. E. Wyatt and G. J. Powell (eds) *Lasting Effects of Child Sexual Abuse*, Beverly Hills, CA: Sage, pp. 211–26.

Wyatt, G. E. and Peters, S. D. (1986) 'Issues on the deprivation of child sexual abuse in prevalence research', *Child Abuse and Neglect*, 10: 231–51.

Part IV

EXPLANATIONS AND THEORETICAL PERSPECTIVES

13

GENETIC AND HORMONAL INFLUENCES ON MALE VIOLENCE

Angela K. Turner

In many non-human animals, genes and hormones have clear effects on the aggressive behaviour of males (Huntingford and Turner 1987; Archer 1988). In highly social mammals such as many of the primates, their effects are less clear-cut, because social and experiential factors come into play. Human society is much more complex than that of any other primate. We would therefore expect these influences to be particularly important in shaping our own behaviour. Uniquely human attributes – notably, our cultures and languages – further affect our behaviour; for example, by justifying some forms of aggression and condemning others. Purely biological factors are therefore likely to have a relatively minor role, particularly in large-scale, group-organized aggression such as warfare.

Many studies have, nevertheless, investigated possible links between human aggression and biological factors. Of particular interest has been the question why human males are more aggressive and more frequently involved in antisocial and criminal behaviour than females. Many studies have indicated that, across cultures, males are generally more assertive, less inhibited in expressing anger and more likely to use physical aggression (Archer and Lloyd 1985). Men are also more likely to commit crimes: in a survey of crime in thirty-one countries between 1962 and 1980, for example, men accounted for about 87 per cent of all arrests and 90 per cent of arrests for homicide (Simon and Baxter 1989).

Genetic and hormonal factors have been suggested as possible causes of this difference in behaviour between the sexes. Males, for example, normally possess one Y chromosome and one X chromosome in contrast to the usual two X chromosomes of women, and they have higher plasma levels of the sex hormone testosterone. However, environmental factors, such as the different ways in which boys and girls are brought up and the gender-role expectations of parents and society, have also been implicated in augmenting or causing differences between males and females. Several recent reviews and critical commentaries have provided detailed coverage of this area, so that the present chapter will form an overview based on these sources (for example, Archer and Lloyd 1985; Wilson and Herrnstein 1985; Mednick *et al.* 1987; Plomin *et al.* 1990; Archer 1991).

GENES AND VIOLENCE

Methodological issues

Selective breeding is known to influence the expression of aggressive behaviour in a wide range of non-human animals from crickets to dogs (for a review, see Huntingford and Turner 1987). A number of animals, such as dogs, cockerels and Siamese fighting fish, have been bred to be more or less aggressive than normal. Amongst the various breeds of dog, for example, beagles are bred to be docile and terriers to be fierce. Mice can be selectively bred to attack more quickly than normal when two males are introduced into a neutral arena, and aggressiveness clearly runs in mouse families (van Oortmersson and Bakker 1981; Cairns *et al.* 1983).

Whereas it is a simple matter to breed other animals such as dogs selectively for aggressiveness, and thereby demonstrate a genetic influence, when it comes to humans we cannot do this and so have to examine indirect evidence. Evidence for an effect of genetic variation on human male aggression and violent behaviour comes from several lines of research: family studies; studies of twins; studies of adopted children; and studies of the behaviour of men with genetic abnormalities. There are problems with many of these studies, making interpretation of the results difficult. These problems will be outlined in the relevant sections, but I shall first discuss two general issues.

A particular problem with studies of aggression in human males is how to measure it. Aggression in humans is poorly defined; the word is used for different types of emotion and behaviour such as assertiveness, teasing, feelings of anger, verbal aggression and violent acts. One could also include organized aggression such as warfare, but such phenomena are unlikely to have simple biological causes; genetic and hormonal influences are more likely to be seen at the level of individual aggression. There are complications, also, of how the behaviour is interpreted; thus violence may be seen to be justified in one context but not in another. In searching for genetic variation in aggression, researchers have used mainly questionnaire surveys and official statistics of antisocial behaviour such as records of arrest for particular crimes. Some studies have obtained ratings of aggressive behaviour from peers, teachers and parents; others have used self-reports of aggressive feelings and behaviour. These vary, however, in what they attempt to measure. The Buss-Durkee hostility inventory, for example, provides data on aggressive thoughts and acts, and the Straus Conflict Tactics Scale measures how frequently particular acts of aggression are used.

A second general problem occurs in measuring the genetic component of aggressive behaviour. The proportion of the variability in a behavioural trait that is due to genetic effects is known as the 'heritability'. This is a widely used statistic in genetic studies but it has limitations (see Hay 1985). Heritability estimates are valid only for the particular sample of the population being studied, at the time it is studied. In addition, heritability estimates will be affected by changes in environmental variation. Improved education, for example, may reduce environmental variation in, and hence increase the estimated heritability of, cognitive abilities. A further problem with heritability estimates is the assumption that genetic and environmental effects can be added together, which ignores interactions between these factors.

There have been few studies of genetic variation in aggressive behaviour itself in human males; most interest has focused on the broader issue of heredity and crime with a view to understanding and, perhaps, preventing or controlling criminal behaviour. The idea that criminality may be genetically determined has a long history. From an examination of their features, Lombroso (1918, cited in Walters and White 1989) concluded that criminals were genetic throwbacks to an earlier stage of human evolution, and Sheldon (1942, cited in Walters and White 1989) related body build to criminality, muscular mesomorphs apparently being prone to such behaviour. Since then, many investigators have continued the search for a genetic basis to criminality. These studies are usually concerned with wide categories of antisocial behaviour rather than aggression or violence. Such all-inclusive categories as delinquency or criminality include types of behaviour such as fare-dodging and motoring offences whose motivation is unlikely to be aggressive, and studies of them do not even usually differentiate between violent and non-violent crimes. Any genetic influence on violent behaviour is thus likely to be masked. Even when violence is considered, the measures used are inconsistent; some studies use a variety of self or peer ratings of aggression, for example, whereas others use a history of violent crimes. Criminality is also not a consistently defined phenomenon; its definition varies with time and across cultures. Finally, if studies use official records of convictions for crimes, then those individuals who evade arrest will be under-represented and certain individuals, such as those from ethnic minorities, may be over-represented. There are also a number of other problems with these studies, including biased sources of data and sampling, small sample sizes, lack of control groups and inadequate statistics (Walters and White 1989; Fishbein 1990).

Early studies looked at whether children resemble their parents and siblings in their behaviour and criminal tendencies. Such inter-generational similarities are evident, but one can say little about how they are transmitted because family members share both genes and many environmental experiences.

Twin studies may be more informative about possible genetic effects than family studies. They involve a comparison of identical (or monozygotic) and non-identical, fraternal (or dizygotic) twins. Identical twins share an identical set of genes, whereas fraternal twins share only half their genes, on average, as do any other two siblings. Hence one can estimate what proportion of the phenotypic variation in a behavioural trait is due to genetic factors (the heritability of the trait) and how much to environmental factors, given that the twins are brought up in the same way. If, for example, aggressive behaviour is more similar amongst identical than amongst fraternal twins, then one can attribute a genetic component to that behaviour. There are problems, however, with observing which categories twins belong to, and this applies particularly to the earliest studies. Studies may also be biased because identical twins may be over-represented; the family experiences of identical twins may be more similar than those of fraternal twins; identical twins may be given special treatment so that they become more similar than they would otherwise have been; and they may commit criminal acts together (Christiansen 1977; Rowe 1983).

Adoption studies may help disentangle the influences of genes and rearing environment. The behaviour of adoptees is compared with that of their biological parents (with whom they share half their genes but no or little familial experience) and their adoptive parents (whose family environment may influence their behaviour but whose genes will not). There are problems with such studies, however (see, for example, Hutchings and Mednick 1975). A couple with a recent history of antisocial or criminal behaviour would not normally be allowed to adopt a child, so studies assessing the effect of variation in the adopted child's family environment on the child's behaviour are restricted. Similarly, an adopted child may be more likely anyway to come from a home where a biological parent is antisocial or criminal. Adoption agencies may also try to match the families of adoptee and adoptive parents. In addition, if children are not adopted as very young babies their behaviour may be influenced to some extent by their experiences with their biological parents as well as by their shared genes.

Some evidence for a genetic basis to aggressive behaviour also comes from studying people with genetic abnormalities. These people may show up differences in behaviour from the normal population that can be attributed to the genetic defect. Genetic abnormalities, such as the mutation producing Lesch-Nyhan's disease, can result in abnormal aggressive behaviour (Palmour 1983). Lesch-Nyhans is an X-linked recessive disorder in which purine metabolism is affected owing to the deficiency of an enzyme HPRT; patients compulsively mutilate themselves and show outbursts of physical aggression towards others. In this case there is a clear-cut link between a genetic abnormality and aggressive behaviour. Another genetic link with aggressive behaviour was suspected in the late 1960s and 1970s. Because men with an X and a Y chromosome are more aggressive than women, who have two X chromosomes, the possession of an extra Y chromosome was thought to lead to hyper-aggressiveness. However, psychological studies have shown that XYY men are no more likely than the normal XY male to be aggressive in a situation of conflict (Schiavi et al. 1984). They are slightly over-represented in prison populations, but their criminality is not particularly aggressive and is likely to be a result of their generally low intelligence and poor school performance rather than the possession of an extra Y chromosome. Studies of genetic abnormalities such as Lesch-Nyhan's disease and abnormal chromosome numbers may provide useful insights into the working of genes, but these conditions are rare and can explain little of the variation in aggressive and criminal behaviour seen in the general population (only about one male in 1,000, for example, is XYY). The next section on evidence for genetic variation in aggression therefore concentrates on twin and adoption studies.

Evidence for genetic effects

Various personality traits, particularly those relating to sociability, emotionality and activity, seem to have a heritable component (see, for example, Goldsmith 1983; Hay 1985). Twin studies indicate that 40–50 per cent of the variation in many traits may be genetic. Some of these inheritable aspects of personality, such as low intelligence, impulsiveness, hyperactivity, sensation-seeking, neuroticism and emotionality, may predispose certain boys and men, in certain environments, to be aggressive, antisocial or even criminal (Rutter and Giller 1983; Rowe 1986; Cloninger 1987).

If one looks at studies of aggression itself, however, the evidence for a genetic influence is scanty and conflicting (for reviews, see Loehlin *et al.* 1988; Plomin *et al.* 1990). Several studies have been carried out on adolescent and adult twins, all using different sorts of self-report questionnaires. Canter (1973) found no significant difference between nine identical and fourteen fraternal male twins measured on Fould's hostility scale, suggesting no genetic effect. Vandenberg (1967) also found no difference between fifty identical and thirty-eight fraternal twins using Stern's Activities Index. A study on Finnish male twins (Partanen *et al.* 1966), based on a self-report score developed by the authors, revealed only small differences between the two types of twin (within-class correlations were 0.25 for 157 identical and 0.16 for 189 fraternal twins). Loehlin and Nichols (1976) obtained similar low correlations using another self-report scale on a sample of male high-school twins (217 identical and 137 fraternal). Other studies, however, obtained substantial heritability estimates in line with those of other personality traits. Rushton *et al.* (1986) assessed aggressiveness and assertiveness with the aggressiveness scale from the Interpersonal Behavior Survey in ninety identical and forty-six fraternal male twins, obtaining heritability estimates of 0.34 and 0.36, respectively (within-class correlations were 0.33 for identical and 0.16 for fraternal twins for aggressiveness, and 0.44 and 0.26, respectively, for assertiveness). Tellegen *et al.* (1988) calculated a heritability estimate of 0.44 for aggression in a study of a mixed sample of 331 male and female twins using the aggression scale from the Multidimensional Personality Questionnaire (within-class correlations were 0.43 for identical and 0.14 for fraternal twins).

Studies on young children give no clearer a picture. Owen and Sines (1970) studied twenty-one 6–14-year-olds using a projective measure of aggression from the Missouri Children's Picture Series but did not obtain a statistically significant result. O'Connor *et al.* (1980) found evidence of high heritability for bullying rated by parents in a study of eighty-four male and female twins with an average age of 7.6 years (within-class correlations were 0.72 for identical and 0.42 for fraternal twins). In another study in which aggressive behaviour of thirty-eight male and female twins aged 4–7 years was rated from the mothers' observations of their children, the heritability was also high (within-class correlations of 0.65 for identical and 0.35 for fraternal twins; Ghodsian-Carpey and Baker 1987). The only direct observational study, in which aggressive behaviour was measured as the number and intensity of hits to a Bobo clown in the laboratory, showed no genetic component (Plomin *et al.* 1981), but the 'aggression' may anyway have been rough-and-tumble play, which is not aggressively motivated (Smith 1989).

Several studies have investigated the relative contribution of genes and environment to more extreme antisocial behaviour, including delinquency and criminality. Antisocial personality disorder in men and conduct disorder in boys incorporate elements of aggressive behaviour such as fighting but also truancy, problems at school, failure to keep a job or to sustain a marriage, and drug abuse. These disorders seem to run in families, and adoption studies suggest a genetic component (Cadoret 1978, 1982; Cadoret *et al.* 1987). In one study, aggressive conduct disorder in adopted children was related to anti-social personality disorder in their biological but not adoptive parents (Jary and Stewart 1985).

In contrast, there may be little genetic influence on delinquency. In studies of twins reared together, where one twin is delinquent the other often is as well. Concordance rates (that is, where both twins are similar with respect to the trait under study) in four such studies of delinquency amongst boys (see Cloninger and Gottesman 1987; Dilalla and Gottesman 1989) ranged from 80 to 100 per cent for fifty-five pairs of identical twins. However, the authors pointed out that the thirty pairs of fraternal twins also had a high concordance level, of 71–78 per cent, indicating an important influence of the environment shared by the twins and only a small genetic effect. A self-report study of sixty-one identical and thirty-eight fraternal male twins (Rowe 1983) also showed both genetic and shared family effects on delinquent behaviour: twins may influence each other by committing delinquent acts together, for example. In a study of delinquent adopted children less than 12 years old, however, there was no clear genetic effect of the biological parents' criminality on the behaviour of the adopted sons (Bohman 1972), suggesting that delinquency and criminality are not closely related.

The apparently small genetic effect on delinquency in general may arise because delinquency, on a minor and infrequent scale, is common amongst boys anyway (Rutter and Giller 1983). In West and Farrington's (1973) study of boys in inner London, for example, 82 per cent of boys aged 14–17 had broken windows of empty houses and 90 per cent had travelled on public transport without paying the proper fare. In contrast, serious and repeated delinquency was much rarer in this study; only 10 per cent of boys had broken into a house to steal something and 22 per cent had used a weapon in a fight.

If there is a genetic effect, it may apply to a minority of boys and these may continue to behave criminally throughout adolescence and into adulthood, whereas the majority of delinquent behaviour may be influenced by the boy's environment, such as the attitudes and behaviour of peers, and is eventually outgrown (DiLalla and Gottesman 1989, and references therein), although childhood delinquency and adulthood criminality may also have quite different causes (Cloninger and Gottesman 1987).

In contrast to delinquency, criminality amongst men seems to involve a more substantial genetic predisposition (for reviews, see Wilson and Herrnstein 1985; Mednick *et al.* 1987; Fishbein 1990). A survey of six studies of criminality in male twins showed a range of concordance rates of 34–76 per cent for criminal behaviour in 216 pairs of identical twins, much higher than the 18–54 per cent for the 301 pairs of fraternal twins (Cloninger and Gottesman 1987; DiLalla and Gottesman 1989). Surprisingly, however, non-violent crime seems to have a higher genetic predisposition than violent crime. In Christiansen's (1977, updated in Cloninger and Gottesman 1987) Danish study of 4,997 male twins, the heritability estimate was 0.78 for property crimes but only 0.50 for crimes against a person which would have involved an element of aggression. However, there was a more important shared environment effect for the latter and little overlap in genetic predisposition for the two categories of crime (Cloninger and Gottesman 1987).

Adoption studies of criminal behaviour also suggest a genetic component to criminality. Adoptees (thirty-seven males and females) of criminal biological mothers in a study in Iowa were more likely than a control group to be convicted of a crime when they were adult and to be diagnosed as antisocial (Crowe 1975). The crimes of both the mothers and the children were mainly non-violent, however, such as prostitution, larceny and forgery. Bohman *et al.* (1982) also found a relationship between convictions for property crimes in male adoptees and their biological parents in Sweden. In a Danish study (Mednick *et al.* 1987) of court convictions of 4,065 male adoptees aged 15 or more years, 25 per cent of those with both criminal biological and adoptive parents and 20 per cent of those with a criminal biological parent had also been convicted of a crime. In contrast, only 15 per cent of those with only a criminal adoptive parent and 14 per cent of those with no criminal parents, biological or adoptive, were criminal themselves. The relationship between convictions of adoptees and biological parents was particularly strong for habitual offenders, recidivistic fathers having recidivistic sons. The effects of biological and adoptive parents were additive. The adoptees probably had little experience of the criminal behaviour of an adoptive parent because the latter were mostly one-time offenders and had not offended for at least five years before the adoption; criminal biological parents, on the other hand, were frequently habitual criminals. There was a difference between property and violent crimes, however, the percentage of sons convicted being positively related to the number of convictions of their biological parent for property crimes but not for violent crimes, supporting the results from twin studies that violent behaviour has only a small genetic component.

Genetic and environmental effects

Studies on human males suggest that there is at most a small genetic component to aggression, delinquency and violent behaviour but a greater one for personality traits associated with such behaviour and for criminality of a non-violent nature. The biological mechanisms translating the message in the genes into antisocial or criminal behaviour are not known. There is clearly no simple aggressive gene effect. Many genes are likely to be involved, and each may have a weak effect on aggressive behaviour. These effects may come about in many different ways; for example, by changing the pattern of development of behaviour, by varying the production and metabolism of hormones and neurotransmitters, by affecting the peripheral and central nervous system and sensory pathways, or by changing the appearance of the individual, such as its size, which would affect its probability of initiating and winning fights (Huntingford and Turner 1987). Some of these factors are considered in more detail in the next section.

These genetic influences vary along a continuum from being a direct effect on some aspect of behaviour to more indirect or general routes (Anastasi 1958; Bateson 1976). A direct genetic effect on aggression, for example, may determine how quickly an individual responds to provocation. Aggression may also be influenced indirectly; for example, via a man's size and strength which may affect the way he behaves and how others react to him. There may also be a more general genetic effect on behaviour; for example, increasing overall activity and hence the likelihood of an individual becoming involved in a situation of conflict.

Environmental and other biological factors mediate genetic effects to varying degrees, and a genetic predisposition for a particular behavioural trait may not necessarily be expressed, except in a particular environment. Thus boys with a genetic predisposition for antisocial behaviour may not behave antisocially if they also have a high IQ or if they grow up in a secure family environment (Cadoret 1982; Moffitt et al. 1989; Fishbein 1990). Criminal tendencies, with a genetic component, may become apparent only in certain situations; for example, in adoption studies, if an adoptive father is also criminal the adopted son may have more opportunity and more reinforcement to engage in criminal behaviour. Social reactions are important in mediating genetic effects – for example, on the appearance of an individual. Thus members of some ethnic minorities may be more likely to be arrested purely on their looks. Facial features, too, are popularly associated with certain types of criminal: in one study, both civilians and police officers 'matched' photos of faces with supposed crimes such as mugging, company fraud and drug possession, even though none of the photos portrayed people convicted of a crime (Bull and Green 1980).

For humans, there is substantial evidence for environmental factors affecting aggressive behaviour, particularly factors in the home, such as parental attitudes, parental discipline, role models and television violence (for example, Eron 1982; Widom 1989; Perry *et al*. 1990; Simons *et al*. 1991), but neither environmental nor biological factors can be viewed in isolation. At first, a child has little control over his environment, but as he grows he can, to a greater or lesser extent, create his own environment, selecting certain situations, responding to and reinforcing his own behaviour, and evoking certain reactions from others (Scarr and McCartney 1983). Thus an aggressive boy may seek out hostile situations and reinforce his aggression, and may evoke hostile reactions from others; he may, for example, choose to watch violent television programmes, he may elicit harsh punishment from his parents and he may be the cause of problems in the family which themselves are predictors of delinquency (Mednick *et al*. 1984; Rowe and Osgood 1984; Caspi *et al*. 1987; Rowe and Rodgers 1989; Plomin *et al*. 1990).

Neural and physiological factors in aggression

As mentioned above, genes may influence aggression by their effects on the peripheral and central nervous system and brain chemistry. A variety of neural and physiological factors, some of which may have a genetic component, have been associated with delinquent and criminal behaviour. Mental abnormalities and central nervous system impairment, for example, may impair learning to inhibit antisocial behaviour, and frontal lobe deficits are associated with increased irritability and loss of concern for one's actions (Buikhuisen 1987). Slow alpha waves have been suggested as a predictor of delinquency (Mednick *et al*. 1981); they may be associated with low arousal and impaired avoidance learning (Volavka 1987). Some studies suggest a link between criminal, delinquent or sociopathic behaviour and, as well as slow alpha waves, low physiological responses during stress, high cardiovascular response prior to shock and low anxiety levels (reviewed in Venables 1987). Low arousal leads to lack of fear, which in turn inhibits release of pituitary hormones such as vasopressin that would increase avoidance learning. Hare (1978) suggested that individuals with these traits are consequently good at coping with impending stress so that emotional situations appear to have little impact on them; such a response may be mediated both genetically and by experience. There may be a genetic component to physiological factors such as alpha waves (Volavka 1987); but there are also clear environmental influences. For example, Mednick *et al*. (1988) found that boys with minor physical anomalies due to stressful birth factors, which may have damaged the development of the brain, were more likely to have committed a violent offence by the time they were 21, although only if they came from an unstable family background (see review in Moffitt *et al*. 1989).

Several biochemical differences have been found between certain groups of criminals, compared with non-criminal controls. Studies of habitually violent men have suggested a slight link between their violence and low levels of blood cholesterol, enhanced secretion of insulin and low levels of serotonin (see review in Virkkunen 1987). An inhibitory effect of serotonin on aggression is in agreement with studies on laboratory animals (for example, Sheard 1983). High levels of noradrenaline have also been associated with a history of violent behaviour (Rubin 1987). Changes in blood and brain chemistry, however, may also result from, rather than cause, aggressive behaviour and they may also be influenced by diet or toxins such as lead in the environment, and especially by the consumption of alcohol or drugs.

Other genetic effects on behaviour may come about by changing the production and metabolism of hormones. Whether hormones affect aggressive behaviour in humans is considered in the next section.

HORMONES AND VIOLENCE

Hormones in other animals

Although hormones are widely involved in the expression of aggressive behaviour in vertebrates, they work in several different ways (Huntingford and Turner 1987). During the development of the foetus, androgens (that is, 'male hormones' such as testosterone) have an organizing effect on morphology, particularly on the form of the genitals and on structures in the nervous system controlling later sex-typical behaviour. These neural influences are typically shown after puberty and include variations in the aggressiveness of the adult animal. During puberty and throughout adulthood, testosterone and other related hormones directly influence features associated with aggression, such as body size and scent production, as well as influencing parts of the central nervous system concerned with the control of aggression. In influencing sexual and aggressive behaviour typical of males, testosterone acts after conversion to oestrogenic metabolites at its site of action.

Amongst male mammals, an increase in the level of testosterone is sometimes associated with an increase in aggressive behaviour during the mating period; for example, during the rut of red deer and other ungulates (see, for instance, Clutton-Brock et al. 1982). But this is not universally so. The link between testosterone and aggression is most clearly seen in males that fight directly over access to females. Castration in such species reduces the animal's aggressiveness, and giving the castrated male testosterone reinstates it. In many social species, however, particularly primates, access to females depends on the male's status, which remains the same for long periods, and is not linked to the mating period. In these species, testosterone levels and fighting are dissociated. Castration does not make tamarin, rhesus or talapoin monkeys, for example, less aggressive, and administering testosterone to them does not consistently make them more aggressive or lead to a rise in their status (Wilson and Vessey 1968; Dixson and Herbert 1977; Epple 1978, 1981; Gordon et al. 1979). Rather, in male primates generally, aggression and status are determined largely by current social factors and the past experience of the individual (Dixson 1980). High-ranking animals are not necessarily the most aggressive animals; a low-ranking animal will defer to a higher-ranking one without any aggression being shown. At puberty, too, status and aggression depend primarily on social factors. In a fight between males of similar size and status, the male with the higher androgen levels may be favoured, but in the general life of a primate society, androgens play a minor role (Dixson 1980).

A complication in determining whether androgens affect aggressiveness is that androgen levels may be affected by the consequences of fighting. In rats, for example, testosterone levels can increase in winners of fights and fall in the losers (Schuurman 1980); in squirrel and talapoin monkeys testosterone levels vary with changes in status and are higher in dominant males than in subordinates (Coe et al. 1979; Eberhart et al. 1980). Thus androgen levels can be high as a result of aggression rather than high levels of androgens being the cause of aggression. Concurrent measures of aggressiveness and androgen levels will not be able to distinguish the direction of a possible causal link.

Adrenal hormones have the opposite role to androgens, high levels being associated with submissive behaviour. In rats, for example, ACTH and glucocorticoids increase during a fight, but more so and for longer in the eventual loser (Schuurman 1980). These hormones are also associated with status in primates; thus, baboons have low glucocorticoid levels when they become dominant (Sapolsky 1982). Other hormones are also associated with aggressive behaviour in laboratory animals (Huntingford and Turner 1987). For example, in mice vasopressin increases submissiveness, possibly by promoting avoidance learning (Roche and Leshner 1979). Fighting itself, however, produces changes in output of these substances and these changes may affect future behaviour.

Humans are very social primates, so as in other primates, we would not expect androgens and other hormones to have a simple, clear-cut effect on their level of aggression. In other animals, testosterone levels and aggression can be investigated by surgery and replacement doses of hormones. In humans, however, we have to rely on indirect evidence that has problems of interpretation. This evidence includes studies of children whose mothers were given hormones during pregnancy to prevent miscarriage, correlations of behaviour with plasma levels of testosterone and other hormones, manipulations of hormone levels in adults – for example, to treat sex offenders – and studies of individuals with abnormal hormone levels.

Foetal hormones

Early exposure to sex hormones appears to have at most a slight effect on assertiveness and aggressive behaviour in humans (for reviews, see Meyer-

Bahlburg 1981; Mazur 1983; Archer 1991). Children who are genetically insensitive to testosterone tend to be less assertive, as are children exposed as foetuses to progesterone (administered to prevent miscarriage). In one study, both boys and girls exposed to progestogens (which are androgenic) as foetuses (again to prevent miscarriage) were more likely to choose an aggressive response to certain situations than their unexposed siblings (Reinisch 1981), but Ehrhardt and her colleagues (1989) found no effect of early exposure of progestogens in a study of women. These studies are beset with problems of interpretation, however. Sample sizes are small, measures of aggression indirect (Archer 1991), the pregnancy disorders themselves may have affected the development of the foetus, and the physique and gender identity of the child may have influenced with whom and how he or she interacted, complicating any direct effect of the sex hormones (Archer and Lloyd 1985; Donovan 1985). In a different type of study, Jacklin et al. (1983) found a relationship between testosterone and progesterone levels in the umbilical cord blood of male foetuses and the child's boldness at between 6 and 18 months old but it is not clear if the hormones measured came from the mother or the foetus.

Hormones at puberty

For pubertal boys, the evidence for an effect of testosterone on aggressive behaviour is sparse but positive (see Archer 1991 and references therein). Olweus (1987, and references therein) reported positive correlations between testosterone levels and self- and peer-assessed scores of verbal and physical aggression for 15–17-year-old boys, the correlations being highest for items that involved a response to provocation such as fighting back when another boy starts a fight. Testosterone levels also correlated positively with impatience and irritability. Olweus concluded from an analysis of these data that boys with high testosterone levels are more intolerant of being frustrated and so are more likely to behave antisocially. He used path analysis to examine whether plasma testosterone levels have causal effects on his measures of aggression. Path analysis involves producing a model (a set of equations) to represent causal relations between the measured variables; standardized partial regression coefficients (path coefficients) are calculated to assess the causal effect of a variable on another, when other variables are held constant. The results suggested that testosterone has a direct causal effect on provoked aggression and an indirect, slight effect on unprovoked aggression through its effect on the boy's tolerance of being frustrated. Kreuz and Rose (1972) suggested that testosterone acts as an additional factor in adolescents already socially predisposed to antisocial behaviour. They based this suggestion on data from twenty-one male prisoners (aged 19–32): those with a history of violent or aggressive offences in adolescence had higher testosterone levels than those with a history of other offences and there was a negative correlation (-0.65, $P<0.01$) between age at first conviction for violent crimes and plasma testosterone, a large effect compared with the results of later studies.

Hormones in adults

Several studies have investigated whether there is a relationship between plasma testosterone levels and aggressive behaviour in adults. These have recently been reviewed by Rubin (1987) and Archer (1991). The results have been variable, some showing no effect, others a positive one. Overall there seems to be only a very weak relationship between testosterone and various ratings of aggressive behaviour. Self-assessed ratings of aggression were particularly poorly associated with testosterone levels, but the association was better when the assessment was done by the men's peers (Archer 1991). Archer calculated weighted mean correlations for studies that were comparable: for five studies that used the Buss-Durkee Hostility Inventory (a self-report measure of aggressiveness) the weighted correlation was only 0.115 (P<0.05, with a combined sample size of 230); for Factor II of the Buss-Durkee Hostility Inventory, which indicates direct and indirect hostility, the weighted mean correlation from six studies was 0.15 (P<0.025, with a sample size of 180). For studies in which aggressiveness was rated by peers or other people in the person's social environment (excluding one with a large pre-pubertal sample), the correlation was higher at 0.38 (P<0.001, with a sample size of 125). Regressions between testosterone levels and measures of aggression have also failed to find a clear link, although sample sizes have been small (Archer 1991). Studies involving a comparison between violent male prisoners and non-violent prisoners or non-criminals have shown a more consistent association between testosterone levels and history of violence (Rubin 1987; Archer 1991). Ratings of dominance, rather than hostility, and other personality traits such as sensation-seeking, also generally show weak associations with testosterone levels (Ehrenkranz et al. 1974; Daitzman and Zuckerman 1980; Schalling 1987; Dabbs et al. 1990; Gray et al. 1991).

As with the studies on foetal androgens, studies of adults are open to a number of criticisms, as Archer (1991) and Rubin (1987) have pointed out. First, there is a wide variation in the methodologies used, the measure of aggression and testosterone and the type of subject, making overall conclusions difficult. Secondly, psychological measures of aggression, particularly by the subject, are likely to be poor indicators of long-term behavioural traits. Thirdly, measurement of testosterone has often ignored diurnal variation. In addition, variation between individuals in sensitivity to testosterone may need to be taken into account.

Even abnormally low or high levels of sex hormones fail to have clear and consistent effects on aggression in humans. Castration and anti-androgenic drugs such as cyproterone acetate and medroxyprogesterone acetate reduce the incidence of sexual aggression and other aberrant sexual behaviour such as paedophilia and transvestism, but they have little or no effect on non-sexual violence (for reviews, see Meyer-Bahlburg 1981; Rubin 1987). High doses of anabolic steroids, taken by athletes to improve their performance, can increase aggressive behaviour (Haupt and Rovere 1984; Choi *et al*. 1990), but testosterone replacement therapy for prepubertal hypogonadism does not consistently increase aggressiveness (Rubin 1987).

Other hormones also seem to have marginal associations with aggressive behaviour in humans. Olweus (1987) found negative correlations between adrenaline and hostility ratings for boys at puberty, particularly for peer ratings of unprovoked aggressive acts ($r = -0.44$). Cortisol is associated with anxiety, depression and introversion, and may inhibit violent behaviour: in a study of 113 adolescent male prison inmates, there was an association between testosterone levels and the violence of the crime committed, this being significant only for prisoners with levels of cortisol below the median ($r = 0.28$, $P < 0.05$), and a multiple-regression analysis showed that the correlation decreased as cortisol concentrations increased (Dabbs *et al*. 1991). However, the effect was small, with only about 8 per cent of variance being accounted for by testosterone and its interaction with cortisol.

Effects of aggression on hormones

A major problem with studies on the effect of hormones on aggression is that, as already mentioned for other animals, being aggressive or experiencing aggression also affects hormone levels. Thus correlations between, for example, testosterone and hostility ratings cannot reveal which is the cause and which the effect. There may be a change in production of the hormone following an experience of aggression rather than high hormone levels causing the aggression. In addition, if high testosterone levels do have a causal effect on certain personality traits such as assertiveness and sensation-seeking, then individuals with high levels may further increase those levels by winning encounters (Schalling 1987). Some studies have shown elevated levels of testosterone subsequent to the subjects' engaging in competitive sports, which may be thought of as involving an element of aggression or a rise in status of the winner (see Archer 1991 for a review). Scaramella and Brown (1978) found that hockey players who responded to threat aggressively had higher levels than unaggressive ones; previous experience of winning at judo, but not an immediate win or loss, correlated with changes in testosterone levels over a bout in the study by Salvador *et al*. (1985); and testosterone increased in tennis players and wrestlers but especially in winners (Mazur and Lamb 1980; Elias 1981).

CONCLUSIONS

Although the evidence is still sparse and open to interpretation, there is some suggestion of substantial genetic effects on personality traits such as

246

emotionality, sensation-seeking and impulsiveness that may in turn affect aggressive and antisocial behaviour, whereas a genetic component to aggressive and violent behaviour itself and to delinquency seems to be small. The evidence for an effect of hormones on aggression in humans, either early in development or at and after puberty, is also sparse and inconclusive. Positive associations have been found between testosterone and aggression, particularly when assessed by other people in the individuals' environment, but these are difficult to interpret because of the effects of aggressive behaviour on hormone levels.

There are clearly no simple genetic or hormonal factors that can explain the variation in aggressive and antisocial behaviour between individuals or the difference in such behaviour between males and females. Nor for that matter can environmental influences alone provide explanations. There are complex interactions between genetic, hormonal and environmental factors. A boy grows up learning gender roles – that is, how males and females are expected to behave (Archer and Lloyd 1985) – while his personality, for example, determines how he responds to situations and the sort of environment he grows up in. Testosterone may have an additional effect at puberty on how he reacts to provocation. Indirect effects also need to be considered: thus a boy's appearance and size will affect how others react to him.

Past studies have clearly had many conceptual and methodological problems and have not yet given definitive results. However, they have suggested several reasons for individual variation in, and predictors of, aggressive and antisocial behaviour, even if these are mainly weak ones, and they are beginning to provide a theoretical framework for future work. Much work still remains to be done, however, before we understand the causes, and have reliable predictors, of aggressive and antisocial behaviour.

ACKNOWLEDGEMENT

I am grateful to John Archer for helpful comments on earlier drafts of this chapter.

REFERENCES

Anastasi, A. (1958) 'Heredity, environment, and the question "How?" ', *Psychological Review*, 65: 197–208.

Archer, J. (1988) *The Behavioural Biology of Aggression*, Cambridge: Cambridge University Press.

—— (1991) 'The influence of testosterone on human aggression', *British Journal of Psychology*, 82: 1–28.

Archer, J. and Lloyd, B. B. (1985) *Sex and Gender*, New York: Cambridge University Press.

Bateson, P. P. G. (1976) 'Specificity and the origins of behavior', *Advances in the Study of Behavior*, 6: 1–20.

Bohman, M. (1972) 'A study of adopted children, their background, environment and adjustment', *Acta Paediatrica Scandinavica*, 61: 90–7.

Bohman, M., Cloninger, C., Sigvardsson, S. and von Knorring, A. L. (1982) 'Predisposition to petty criminality in Swedish adoptees: genetic and environmental heterogeneity', *Archives of General Psychiatry*, 39: 1233–41.

Buikhuisen, W. (1987) 'Cerebral dysfunctions and persistent juvenile delinquency', in S. S. Mednick, T. E. Moffitt and S. A. Stack (eds) *The Causes of Crime: New Biological Approaches*, Cambridge: Cambridge University Press.

Bull, R. H. and Green, J. (1980) 'The relationship between physical appearance and criminality', *Medicine, Science and the Law*, 20: 79–83.

Cadoret, R. J. (1978) 'Psychopathy in adopted away offspring of biological parents with antisocial behavior', *Archives of General Psychiatry*, 35: 176–84.

—— (1982) 'Genotype–environment interaction in antisocial behavior', *Psychological Medicine*, 12: 235–9.

Cadoret, R. J., Troughton, E. and O'Gorman, T. W. (1987) 'Genetic and environmental factors in alcohol abuse and antisocial personality', *Journal of Studies on Alcohol*, 48: 1–8.

Cairns, R. B., MacCombie, D. J. and Hood, K. E. (1983) 'A developmental-genetic analysis of aggressive behaviour in mice. 1. Behavioural outcomes', *Journal of Comparative Psychology*, 97: 69–89.

Canter, S. (1973) 'Personality traits in twins', in G. Claridge, S. Canter and W. I. Hume (eds) *Personality Differences and Biological Variations*, New York: Pergamon Press.

Caspi, A., Elder, G. H., Jr and Bem, D. J. (1987) 'Moving against the world: life-course patterns of explosive children', *Developmental Psychology*, 23: 308–13.

Choi, P. Y. L., Parrott, A. C. and Cowan, D. (1990) 'High dose anabolic steroids in strength athletes: effects on hostility and aggression', *Human Psychopharmacology, Clinical and Experimental*, 5: 349–56.

Christiansen, K. O. (1977) 'A preliminary study of criminality among twins', in S. A. Mednick and K. O. Christiansen (eds) *Biosocial Bases of Criminal Behavior*, New York: Gardner Press.

Cloninger, C. R. (1987) 'Pharmacological approaches to the treatment of antisocial behavior', in S. A. Mednick, T. E. Mofitt and S. A. Stack (eds) *The Causes of Crime: New Biological Approaches*, Cambridge: Cambridge University Press.

Cloninger, C. R. and Gottesman, I. I. (1987) 'Genetic and environmental factors in antisocial behavior disorders', in S. A. Mednick, T. E. Mofitt and S. A. Stack (eds) *The Causes of Crime: New Biological Approaches*, Cambridge: Cambridge University Press.

Clutton-Brock, T. H., Guinness, F. E. and Albon, S. D. (1982) *Red Deer: Behaviour and Ecology of Two Sexes*, Edinburgh: Edinburgh University Press.

Coe, C. L., Mendoza, S. P. and Levine, S. (1979) 'Social status constrains the stress response in the squirrel monkey', *Physiology and Behavior*, 23: 633–8.

Crowe, R. R. (1975) 'An adoptive study of psychopathy: preliminary results from arrest records and psychiatric hospital records', in R. R. Fieve, D. Rosenthal and H. Brill (eds) *Genetic Research in Psychiatry*, Baltimore, MD: Johns Hopkins University Press.

Dabbs, J. M., Jr, de la Rue, D. and Williams, P. M. (1990) 'Testosterone and occupational choice: actors, ministers, and other men', *Journal of Personality and Social Psychology*, 59: 1261–5.

Dabbs, J. M., Jr, Jurkovic, G. J. and Frady, R. L. (1991) 'Salivary testosterone and cortisol among late adolescent male offenders', *Journal of Abnormal Child Psychology*, 19: 469–78.

Daitzman, R. and Zuckerman, M. (1980) 'Disinhibitory sensation seeking, personality and gonadal hormones', *Personality and Individual Differences*, 1: 103–10.

Dilalla, L. F. and Gottesman, I. I. (1989) 'Heterogeneity of causes for delinquency and criminality: lifespan perspectives', *Development and Psychopathology*, 1: 339–49.

Dixson, A. F. (1980) 'Androgens and aggressive behaviour in primates: a review', *Aggressive Behavior*, 6: 37–67.

Dixson, A. F. and Herbert, J. (1977) 'Testosterone, aggressive behavior and dominance rank in captive adult male talapoin monkeys', *Physiology and Behavior*, 18: 539–43.

Donovan, B. T. (1985) *Hormones and Human Behaviour*, Cambridge: Cambridge University Press.

Eberhart, J. A., Keverne, E. B. and Meller, R. E. (1980) 'Social influences on plasma testosterone levels in male talapoin monkeys', *Hormones and Behavior*, 14: 246–66.

Ehrenkranz, J., Bliss, E. and Sheard, M. H. (1974) 'Plasma testosterone: correlation with aggressive behavior and social dominance in man', *Psychosomatic Medicine*, 36: 469–75.

Ehrhardt, A. A., Meyer-Bahlburg, H. F. L., Rosen, L. R., Feldman, J. F., Veridiano, N. P., Elken, E. J. and McEwan, B. S. (1989) 'The development of gender-related behavior in females following prenatal exposure to diethylstilbestrol (DES)', *Hormones and Behavior*, 23: 526–41.

Elias, M. (1981) 'Serum cortisol, testosterone and testosterone-binding globulin responses in competitive fighting in human males', *Aggressive Behavior*, 7: 215–24.

Epple, G. (1978) 'Lack of effects of castration on scent marking, displays and aggression in a South American primate (*Saguinus fuscicollis*)', *Hormones and Behavior*, 11: 139–50.

—— (1981) 'Effects of prepubertal castration on the development of scent glands, scent marking and aggression in the saddle-backed tamarin (*Saguinus fuscicollis*)', *Hormones and Behavior*, 15: 54–67.

Eron, L. D. (1982) 'Parent–child interaction, television violence and aggression in children', *American Psychologist*, 37: 197–211.

Fishbein, D. H. (1990) 'Biological perspectives in criminology', *Criminology*, 28: 27–72.

Ghodsian-Carpey, J. and Baker, L. A. (1987) 'Genetic and environmental influences on aggression in 4- to 7-year-old twins', *Aggressive Behavior*, 13: 173–86.

Goldsmith, H. H. (1983) 'Genetic influences on personality from infancy to adulthood', *Child Development*, 54: 331–55.

Gordon, T. P., Rose, R. M., Grady, C. L. and Bernstein, I. (1979) 'Effects of increased testosterone secretion on the behaviour of adult male rhesus monkeys living in a social group', *Folia Primatologia*, 32: 149–60.

Gray, A., Jackson, D. N. and McKinlay, J. B. (1991) 'The relation between dominance, anger, and hormones in normally aging men: results from the Massachusetts male aging study', *Psychosomatic Medicine*, 53: 375–85.

Hare, R. D. (1978) 'Electrodermal and cardiovascular correlates of psychopathy', in R. D. Hare and D. Schalling (eds) *Psychopathic Behavior: Approaches to Research*, New York: John Wiley.

Haupt, H. A. and Rovere, G. D. (1984) 'Anabolic steroids: a review of the literature', *American Journal of Sports Medicine*, 12: 469–84.

Hay, D. (1985) *Essentials of Behaviour Genetics*, Oxford: Blackwell Scientific Publications.

Huntingford, F. A. and Turner, A. K. (1987) *Animal Conflict*, London: Chapman & Hall.

Hutchings, B. and Mednick, S. A. (1975) 'Registered criminality in the adoptive and biological parents of registered male criminal adoptees', in R. R. Fieve, D.

Rosenthal and H. Brill (eds) *Genetic Research in Psychiatry*, Baltimore, MD: Johns Hopkins University Press.

Jacklin, C. N., Maccoby, E. E. and Doering, C. H. (1983) 'Noenatal sex-steroid hormones and timidity in 6–18-month-old boys and girls', *Developmental Psychobiology*, 16: 163–8.

Jary, M. L. and Stewart, M. A. (1985) 'Psychiatric disorder in the parents of adopted children with aggressive conduct disorder', *Neuropsychobiology*, 13: 7–11.

Kreuz, L. E. and Rose, R. M. (1972) 'Assessment of aggressive behaviour and plasma testosterone in a young criminal population', *Psychosomatic Medicine*, 34: 321–32.

Loehlin, J. C. and Nichols, R. C. (1976) *Heredity, Environment and Personality*, Austin: University of Texas Press.

Loehlin, J. C., Willerman, L. and Horn, J. M. (1988) 'Human behavior genetics', *Annual Review of Psychology*, 39: 101–33.

Lombroso, C. (1918) *Crime, its Causes and Remedies*, Boston: Little, Brown.

Mazur, A. (1983) 'Hormones, aggression and dominance in humans', in B. B. Svare (ed.) *Hormones and Aggressive Behavior*, New York: Plenum Press.

Mazur, A. and Lamb, T. A. (1980) 'Testosterone, status and mood in human males', *Hormones and Behavior*, 14: 236–46.

Mednick, S. A., Brennan, P. and Kandel, E. (1988) 'Predisposition to violence', *Aggressive Behavior*, 14: 25–33.

Mednick, S. A., Gabrielli, W. F., Jr and Hutchings, B. (1984) 'Genetic influences in criminal convictions: evidence from an adoption cohort', *Science*, 224: 891–4.

—— (1987) 'Genetic factors in the etiology of criminal behavior', in S. A. Mednick, T. E. Moffitt and S. A. Stack (eds) *The Causes of Crime: New Biological Approaches*, Cambridge: Cambridge University Press.

Mednick, S. A., Volavka, J., Gabrielli, W. F. and Itil, T. M. (1981) 'EEG as a predictor of antisocial behavior', *Criminology*, 19: 219–22.

Meyer-Bahlburg, H. F. L. (1981) 'Androgens and human aggression', in P. F. Brain and D. Benton (eds) *The Biology of Aggression*, Rockville, MD: Sijthoff & Noordhoff.

Moffitt, T. E., Mednick, S. A. and Gabrielli, W. F., Jr (1989) 'Predicting careers of criminal violence: descriptive data and predispositional factors', in D. A. Brizar and M. Crowner (eds) *Current Approaches to the Prediction of Violence*, Washington, DC: American Psychiatric Press.

O'Connor, M., Foch, T. T., Sherry, T. and Plomin, R. (1980) 'A twin study of specific behavioral problems of socialization as viewed by parents', *Journal of Abnormal Child Psychology*, 8: 189–99.

Olweus, D. (1987) 'Testosterone and adrenaline: aggressive antisocial behavior in normal adolescent males', in S. A. Mednick, T. E. Moffitt and S. A. Stack (eds) *The Causes of Crime: New Biological Approaches*, Cambridge: Cambridge University Press.

Owen, D. and Sines, J. O. (1970) 'Heritability of personality in children', *Behavior Genetics*, 1: 235–48.

Palmour, R. M. (1983) 'Genetic models for the study of aggressive behavior', *Progress in Neuro-Psychopharmacology and Biological Psychiatry*, 7: 513–17.

Partanen, J., Bruun, K. and Markkanen, T. (1966) *Inheritance of Drinking Behavior, a Study on Intelligence, Personality, and Use of Alcohol of Adult Twins*, Helsinki: The Finnish Foundation for Alcohol Research.

Perry, D. G., Perry, L. C. and Boldizar, J. P. (1990) 'Learning of aggression', in M. Lewis and S. M. Miller (eds) *Handbook of Developmental Psychopathology*, New York: Plenum Press.

Plomin, R., Foch, T. T. and Rowe, D. C. (1981) 'Bobo clown aggression in childhood: environment not genes', *Journal of Research in Personality*, 15: 331–42.

Plomin, R., Nitz, K. and Rowe, D. C. (1990) 'Behavioral genetics and aggressive behavior in childhood', in M. Lewis and S. M. Miller (eds) *Handbook of Developmental Psychopathology*, New York: Plenum Press.

Reinisch, J. M. (1981) 'Prenatal exposure to synthetic progestins increases potential for aggression in humans', *Science*, 211: 1171–3.

Roche, K. E. and Leshner, A. I. (1979) 'ACTH and vasopressin immediately after a defeat increase future submissiveness in mice', *Science*, 204: 1343–4.

Rowe, D. C. (1983) 'Biometrical genetic models of self-reported delinquent behavior: a twin study', *Behavior Genetics*, 13: 473–89.

—— (1986) 'Genetic and environmental components of antisocial behavior: a study of 265 twin pairs', *Criminology*, 24: 513–32.

Rowe, D. C. and Osgood, D. W. (1984) 'Heredity and sociological theories of delinquency: a reconsideration', *American Sociological Review*, 49: 526–40.

Rowe, D. C. and Rodgers, J. L. (1989) 'Behavioral genetics, adolescent deviance, and "d": contributions and issues', in G. R. Adams, R. Montemayor and T. P. Gullotta (eds) *Biology of Adolescent Behavior and Development*, Newbury Park, CA: Sage.

Rubin, R. T. (1987) 'The neuroendocrinology and neurochemistry of antisocial behavior', in S. A. Mednick, T. E. Moffitt and S. A. Stack (eds) *The Causes of Crime: New Biological Approaches*, Cambridge: Cambridge University Press.

Rushton, J. P., Fulker, D. W., Neale, M. C., Nias, D. K. B. and Eysenck, H. J. (1986) 'Altruism and aggression: individual differences are substantially heritable', *Journal of Personality and Social Psychology*, 50: 1192–8.

Rutter, M. and Giller, H. (1983) *Juvenile Delinquency: Trends and Perspectives*, Harmondsworth, UK: Penguin.

Salvador, A., Simon, V., Suay, F. and Llorens, L. (1985) 'Testosterone and cortisol responses to competitive fighting in human males: a pilot study', *Aggressive Behavior*, 13: 9–13.

Sapolsky, R. M. (1982) 'The endocrine stress-response and social status in the wild baboon', *Hormones and Behavior*, 16: 279–92.

Scaramella, T. J. and Brown, W. A. (1978) 'Serum testosterone and aggressiveness in hockey players', *Psychosomatic Medicine*, 40: 262–5.

Scarr, S. and McCartney, K. (1983) 'How people make their own environments: a theory of genotype–environment effects', *Child Development*, 54: 424–35.

Schalling, D. (1987) 'Personality correlates of plasma testosterone levels in young delinquents: an example of person–situation interaction?', in S. A. Mednick, T. E. Moffitt and S. A. Stack (eds) *The Causes of Crime: New Biological Approaches*, Cambridge: Cambridge University Press.

Schiavi, R. C., Theilgaard, A., Owen, D. R. and White, D. (1984) 'Sex chromosome anomalies, hormones and aggressivity', *Archives of General Psychiatry*, 41: 93–9.

Schuurman, T. (1980) 'Hormonal correlates of agonistic behaviour in adult male rats', *Progress in Brain Research*, 53: 415–20.

Sheard, M. H. (1983) 'Aggressive behavior: effects of neural modulation by serotonin', in E. C. Simmel, M. E. Hahn and J. K. Walter (eds) *Aggressive Behavior: Genetic and Neural Approaches*, Hillsdale, NJ: Erlbaum.

Sheldon, W. (1942) *The Varieties of Temperament: A Psychology of Constitutional Differences*, New York: Harper & Row.

Simon, R. J. and Baxter, S. (1989) 'Gender and violent crime', in N. A. Weiner and M. E. Wolfgang (eds) *Violent Crime, Violent Criminals*, London: Sage.

Simons, R. L., Whitbeck, L. B., Conger, R. D. and Win Chyi-In (1991) 'Intergenerational transmission of harsh parenting', *Developmental Psychology*, 27: 159–71.

Smith, P. K. (1989) 'Ethological approaches to the study of aggression in children', in

J. Archer and K. Browne (eds) *Human Aggression: Naturalistic Approaches*, London: Routledge.

Tellegen, A., Lykken, D. T., Bouchard, T. J., Wilcox, K., Segal, N. and Rich, S. (1988) 'Personality similarity in twins reared apart and together', *Journal of Personality and Social Psychology*, 54: 1031–9.

Vandenberg, S. G. (1967) 'Heredity factors in normal personality traits (as measured by inventories)', in J. Wortis (ed.) *Recent Advances in Biological Psychiatry*, New York: Plenum Press.

van Oortmerssen, G. A. and Bakker, T. C. M. (1981) 'Artificial selection for short and long attack latencies in wild *Mus musculus domesticus*', *Behaviour Genetics*, 11: 115–26.

Venables, P. H. (1987) 'Autonomic nervous system factors in criminal behavior', in S. A. Mednick, T. E. Moffitt and S. A. Stack (eds) *The Causes of Crime: New Biological Approaches*, Cambridge: Cambridge University Press.

Virkunnen, M. (1987) 'Metabolic dysfunction among habitually violent offenders: reactive hypoglycemia and cholesterol levels', in S. A. Mednick, T. E. Moffitt and S. A. Stack (eds) *The Causes of Crime: New Biological Approaches*, Cambridge: Cambridge University Press.

Volavka, J. (1987) 'Electroencephalogram among criminals', in S. A. Mednick, T. E. Moffitt and S. A. Stack (eds) *The Causes of Crime: New Biological Approaches*, Cambridge: Cambridge University Press.

Walters, G. D. and White, T. W. (1989) 'Heredity and crime: bad genes or bad research?', *Criminology*, 27: 455–86.

West, D. J. and Farrington, D. P. (1973) *Who Becomes Delinquent?*, London: Heinemann Educational.

Widom, C. S. (1989) 'Child abuse, neglect, and violent criminal behavior', in D. A. Brizar and M. Crowner (eds) *Current Approaches to the Prediction of Violence*, Washington, DC: American Psychiatric Press.

Wilson, A. P. and Vessey, S. H. (1968) 'Behaviour of free-ranging castrated rhesus monkeys', *Folia Primatologia*, 9: 1–14.

Wilson, J. Q. and Herrnstein, R. J. (1985) *Crime and Human Nature*, New York: Simon & Schuster.

14

EVOLUTIONARY PSYCHOLOGY OF MALE VIOLENCE

Martin Daly and Margo Wilson

What explains a behavioural phenomenon like male violence? The sorts of answers offered by psychologists and evolutionary biologists often sound radically different. Psychologists, even comparative psychologists, seldom pay much attention to evolutionary theory, and it is often suggested that the 'proximate causal' (mechanistic and developmental) explanations of behaviour sought by psychologists are qualitatively distinct from and incommensurate with the 'ultimate' (functional and selectional) explanations sought by evolutionists. We disagree. In this chapter, we argue that the evolutionary approach can provide valuable guidance to psychological investigations, illustrating this thesis with particular (but not exclusive) reference to our own studies of homicide. Evolutionary models suggest many novel hypotheses about risk patterns in family violence, about sex differences, about individual differences, and about changes over the lifespan.

AN EVOLUTIONARY APPROACH TO PSYCHOLOGY

Animals like ourselves are hugely complex systems. The more we learn about our thousands of constituent chemicals, cell types, tissues and physiological processes, the more we marvel at the system's intricacy and functional integrity. How can such adaptive organization have come into being?

Charles Darwin and Alfred Russel Wallace provided science's generally accepted answer to this question more than a century ago, when they discovered the process that Darwin called 'natural selection'. Adaptation arises in populations of reproducing organisms because random variation is ceaselessly generated and then winnowed by non-random differential survival and reproduction, with the result that the more adaptive forms proliferate while their alternatives perish. Every living creature has been shaped by such a history of Darwinian selection, and so has every complex functioning constituent part of every living creature. (Biologists note that there are additional sources of evolutionary change besides selection, including mutation, migration, drift and catastrophe. However, only selection generates functional complexity.) The enterprise of elucidating the functional designs that selection has imparted to organisms and their constituent parts has lately come to be called 'adaptationism'. Adaptationism is the cornerstone of biological discovery (Mayr 1983).

This idea of elucidating the parts of organisms as evolved adaptations may be more readily grasped with a morphological example. Imagine that we discover the fossil jaw of some unknown creature. What can we infer from its teeth? If their surfaces look suitable for grinding, rather than puncturing or shearing, we may infer that our extinct creature must have partaken of grindable food. This inference derives partly from considerations of efficient 'design', and partly from observation of the diets of living creatures (comparative evidence and analogy). It is important to note that this inference is not merely a pat conclusion and the end of the matter. Rather, its status is that of a hypothesis from which we can derive further implications that will subject it to potential disconfirmation. We can predict that a grinding tooth should articulate in a certain way with another; we can predict muscle attachments appropriate to the hypothesized grinding action; we can predict certain patterns of wear. And as each predicted detail – improbable under competing hypotheses – is confirmed, we become increasingly confident that we have attributed the correct adaptive function to the tooth.

The complex functional parts of living creatures with which psychology is primarily concerned are not their teeth but their 'minds'. The catch is that minds are private, and yet scientific method requires public verifiability. Thus, the data of psychological science are necessarily the mind's behavioural manifestations, and psychological hypotheses are necessarily claims about the processes and mechanisms that produce individual behaviour. Those processes and mechanisms comprise the 'psyche'. We may then define 'evolutionary psychology' as *the science that studies the psyche in the light of current knowledge and theory about the evolutionary processes that created it.*

There can be no doubt that Darwinian selection has shaped our psyches, just as it has our bodies, but elucidating the evolved species-typical components of the human mind and their adaptive functions is not as straightforward a task as deciding that molars are for grinding. Nevertheless, it is arguably the most fundamental task of psychology and psychiatry. What is the nature of the human psyche? Increasingly, answers are being sought in the form of evolved functional subunits of the brain and mind. Are there sexually differentiated aptitudes or interests that can be understood as adaptations to sexually differentiated impacts of natural and sexual selection on ancestral women and men? Are there specific parts of the brain dedicated to specific tasks like face recognition? Can psychiatric disorders like agoraphobia be better understood by considering them to reflect emotional and behavioural adaptations to genuine threats in past environments? Are there specialized mental 'algorithms' for reasoning about co-operation, conflict and threat? Buoyed by neuroscience's burgeoning knowledge of the structural and functional complexity of the brain, and by cognitive science's discovery of multiple mental 'modules' with different information-processing rules appropriate to different content domains, evolutionary psychologists are at last abandoning the sterile theoretical 'parsimony' of recent decades to investigate the psyche's intricacy (for example, Barkow *et al.* 1992). The contribution of Darwinism to this enterprise resides in the recognition that *selection (differential reproductive success or, more precisely, differential success in replicating genes) has been the arbiter of adaptation, with the result that our most basic motives and emotions, appetites, aversions and modes of information processing are interpretable as contributors to relative reproductive success and hence genetic posterity (sometimes called 'fitness') in the environments in which we evolved.*

We owe the term 'fitness' not to Darwin, but to the sociologist Herbert Spencer, who epitomized the theory of natural selection as 'survival of the fittest'. Even Darwin and Wallace adopted Spencer's phrase, but it has produced a lot of misunderstanding. Evolutionists have used the term 'fitness' in several slightly different senses, none of which corresponds to its vernacular meaning of physical condition (see Dawkins 1982). We shall use it as a shorthand for *the expected value (in the statistical sense, and in a natural environment) of a phenotypic design's success in promoting the relative replicative success of its bearer's genes, in competition with their alleles.*

The 'survival' in 'survival of the fittest' is no more to be taken literally than the 'fitness'. When we speak of the 'survival value' of adaptive characteristics, we naturally think of those devices that help the individual find food, conserve energy, dodge predators and fend off disease. But personal survival is not the bottom line on the natural selective ledger. Over generations, it is successful traits that 'survive', not individuals, and this sort of long-term survival depends not merely on the longevity of those carrying the trait, but on the abundance of their progeny. Should a more risk-prone and violent type of male appear in a population of risk-averse pacifists, for example, and should the new type tend to fertilize more females but die younger than the old, then that new type will supplant the old by natural selection, and male lifespan will decline.

A common claim in general treatises on motivation is that people and other animals attend to their survival needs first, and that only when these are satisfied do they turn to the gratification of other 'inessential' drives like sex. Many observations seem to affirm such a hierarchy of needs, and it is easy to see why that should be so. Death terminates one's capacity to promote one's fitness; if inclinations have been shaped by natural selection, life should almost always be preferred to death. But life is valued because of its historical contributions to fitness, and not as an end in itself. Without this insight, we cannot understand why animals ever take risks. A stickleback fish guarding a nest full of eggs, for example, will stand his ground against an approaching predator longer and dart at the predator more bravely, the more eggs he has in the nest (Pressley 1981). In effect, the greater fitness value of a larger brood elevates the statistical probability of death that the little fish is prepared to incur. What evolutionary reasoning suggests is that all evolved motivational mechanisms, including our own, have been designed to expend the organism's very life in the pursuit of genetic posterity.

Of course, psychologists have long engaged in theorizing about adolescent crises and Oedipal conflicts, about self-esteem and attribution processes, about short-term buffers and retrieval mechanisms, penis envy, group dynamics and synaptic plasticity, and have managed to do so without an evolutionary thought in their heads. Nevertheless, what all these psychologists, whether psychoanalyst or behaviourist, reductionist or holist, have been trying to do is to formulate theories in terms of concepts that rise above the culturally and historically particular so as to capture something more lasting and basic. Their preferred levels and domains of theorizing are clearly diverse, but all have been seeking to characterize human nature. This is true even of those who insist that plasticity and cultural variability make human nature a worthless concept, since their theoretical constructs, such as 'sex-role socialization', 'attribution processes', 'attitude change' and 'developmental plasticity', are still formulated at a level of abstraction that is clearly intended to transcend cross-cultural variations. Theorists who rely on such concepts would be disconcerted to learn, say, that Papuans do not *have* 'attitudes'.

When psychologists succeed in focusing on truly basic components of human nature, such as appetites and aversions, motives and emotions that are characteristic of our species (or of one sex or life stage), then they are necessarily dealing with evolved mechanisms which have been shaped by a history of natural and sexual selection to achieve certain ends. This is not a proposition about which there is any substantive controversy. There are probably few psychologists who would quarrel with the claim that the psyche has evolved by selection. Until recently, however, even fewer derived direction or inspiration from evolutionary theory, and that has been psychology's misfortune. As we shall illustrate below, the discovery and analysis of the mental mechanisms underlying behaviour can be greatly facilitated by explicit consideration of what evolutionary biologists know about the process of evolution by selection.

TELEOLOGY AND FUNCTIONAL DESIGN

An impediment to evolutionary sophistication within psychology has been a suspicion of explanations that invoke ends. Even those psychologists who study highly specialized domain-specific mechanisms often insist that only proximate causal questions are 'scientific' and that asking 'why' is futile. It seems that many psychologists are convinced that the victory of Newton's blind physics over Aristotle's teleology contains a message for any aspiring science, a message which has been characterized by Sober (1983) as 'the idea that a science progresses by replacing teleological concepts with ones that are untainted by ideas of goals, plans, and purposes' (p. 115). Sober proceeds to argue that this positivist philosophical view of how psychology should mature 'received further impetus from the Darwinian revolution in biology', because Darwin replaced a purposeful creator with a blind mechanism. But if Sober is correct in claiming that the Darwinian revolution provided an impetus to psychology's misplaced physics envy, then that influence was ironic indeed, and psychologists badly misunderstood Darwinism's real implications. By providing a fully materialistic explanation for the obvious but previously incomprehensible fact that living things have 'goals, plans, and purposes' instantiated in their structures, Darwin's nineteenth-century discovery of natural selection actually rendered doctrinaire antagonism to purposive concepts obsolete!

Darwin's theory made teleological reasoning scientific, by showing that the consequences of biological phenomena constitute an essential part of their explanation: *what they achieve is in a specific, concrete sense why they exist*. The fact that psychologists persisted in their rejection of purposive concepts is sad testimony to their continuing lack of familiarity with the basic conceptual framework of the life sciences. Those, like Tolman (1932), who tried to reinstate such concepts, were inspired more by the manifest purposes of their subject animals than by the philosophical legitimization of functional explanation that Darwinism provides, and the later revival of concepts like 'plans' in cognitive science was inspired more by cybernetics and servomechanisms than by an understanding of evolutionary adaptation. Thus, most psychologists have continued to operate with only a superficial understanding of the psyche's objectives and hence of its functional organization. And yet in practice, psychological scientists, while scorning the explicit functional theorizing of evolutionists, have always, inevitably, relied on their intuitive understandings of aspects of the purposive organization of their subjects' psyches.

Consider the control of feeding behaviour. The proximal 'goal' of feeding might be identified as the inhibition of a central motivational mechanism; for example, by gut-load messages and blood sugar cues. But a catalogue of relevant physiological processes is not a fully adequate account of the feeding animal's objectives. All efforts to understand the integrated function of the complex motivational system that controls feeding gain direction from functional assumptions about what the system is '*for*': the physiology and psychology of feeding exists *in order to* extract utilizable energy from foodstuffs and maintain energy balance. These are the presumed purposes of feeding, and although they correspond to nothing that can be measured or identified in the machinery regulating feeding, the assumption that this is what the nuts and bolts under investigation are 'for' crucially guides the research.

Thus, physiological psychologists studying feeding proceed on the assumption that the mechanisms under study are adaptively designed. Students of sensation and perception, memory, motor control and so forth inevitably do the same. The reason why this assumption of adaptation is sound – and hence the reason why these psychologists' research strategies are successful – resides in Darwinism. Nevertheless, even researchers in 'biological' psychology often

257

know astonishingly little about evolution by selection, the process that shaped the systems they study.

SELECTIONAL THINKING FOR THE RESEARCH PSYCHOLOGIST

So what? We may grant that psychological research relies on intuitive understandings of the functional organization of psychological mechanisms, but what does it matter that the researchers know little about the historical processes that engender functional organization? In an important paper advocating a Darwinian psychology, Symons (1987) has argued that such ignorance of (or inattention to) Darwinian theory is a serious impediment to psychological theorizing and research only in certain special domains. The Darwinian perspective tells us that 'energy balance' or even 'survival' is no more the animal's ultimate objective than is a gut-load because all of these things are adaptive only in so far as they are convertible to reproductive gains, but Symons maintains that this insight, although correct, is often superfluous. For example:

> Selectional thinking sheds little light on perceptual-constancy mechanisms because an ideal design for such a mechanism probably would be the same whether the mechanism's ultimate goal was to promote the survival of genes, individual human bodies, or *Homo sapiens*; for precisely the same reason, selectional thinking sheds little light on organismic goals as vague as *not being hungry* or *not being frightened*.
>
> (Symons 1987: 130)

There is merit to this argument, but Symons has overstated it. The state of '*not being hungry*', for example, can*not* be adequately analysed if one imagines that the organism's objective is mere energy balance, or even personal survival. Consider the fact that animals exhibit 'adaptive anorexias': the mechanisms determining the inclination to feed are sensitive not only to cues of internal energy reserves, but also to cues of the expected fitness costs of taking time away from other adaptive activities such as incubation in order to feed (Mrosovsky and Sherry 1980; Sherry *et al.* 1980). Selectional thinking was crucial to these discoveries.

The same goes for Symons's other example. Selectional thinking is in fact essential for understanding what situations will engender the goal state of '*not being frightened*'. Recall the stickleback guarding his nest more bravely the more eggs it contains. One correlate of brood size which might be the cue modulating fear versus bravery in this case is carbon-dioxide production by the eggs, and if so, then it is likely that this cue will prove to mitigate fearfulness only in egg-guarding males. Without the basic Darwinian insight that even personal survival is a subordinate objective to that of genetic posterity, one could never understand – and would be unlikely ever to discover – this sort of contextual variation in the determination of fearfulness.

Thus, although the design of a mechanism for something like perceptual constancy may indeed be studied and explained without explicit recourse to Darwinism, as Symons maintains, it does not follow that psychologists can safely treat familiarity with current developments in evolutionary biology as an expendable luxury. By paying explicit attention to adaptive significance and selective forces, evolutionists attain well-founded expectations about which proximate causal cues are likely to affect animals, and about what sorts of contingencies, priorities and combinatorial information processing algorithms are likely to be instantiated in the architecture of the psyche.

Not that Darwinism is itself a motivational theory. A common error is to suppose that evolutionary theory is isomorphic with an account of goals and drives: that fitness is what animals strive for, and that the thwarting of reproductive ends will elicit counter-measures. In fact, fitness plays a quite different role in evolutionary theory from the role that self-esteem or a target level of blood glucose or some other 'goal' plays in a psychological theory. When the fitness consequences of behaviour are invoked to explain it, they are invoked not as direct objectives or motivators, but as explanations of *why* particular more proximal objectives and motivators have evolved to play their particular roles in the causal control of behaviour, with particular domains of relevance, and why they are calibrated as they are and not otherwise. This crucial point is consistently misunderstood by those social scientists who point to vasectomies or adoptions as evidence against evolutionary ideas, and, ironically, it has been misunderstood by some evolutionists, too (Tooby and Cosmides 1990a). Selection designs organisms to cope with particular adaptive problems which have been sufficiently persistent across generations, both in their essential forms and in their significance, to elicit a solution. These evolved solutions necessarily entail contingent responsiveness to environmental features that *were* statistical predictors of the average fitness consequences of alternative courses of action in the past. Adaptation is not prospective. The apparent purpose in organismic design depends upon the persistence of essential features of past environments.

FUNCTIONAL DESIGN FEATURES SOLVE SPECIFIC ADAPTIVE PROBLEMS

In successful natural sciences, the controversial issues that excite the greatest interest are those that are resolvable by discovery, such that there is an accumulation of knowledge and understanding which transcends factional dispute. By this criterion, psychology has been successful in only some of its sub-fields. Perhaps the most successful has been the study of sensation and perception. This area has made great progress by its identification and exploration of species-typical information-processing mechanisms with specific functions: boundary completion and object delineation, computation of relative motion, auditory localization, recognition of specific prey species, and so forth. As this list illustrates, the claim of functionality is not necessarily a claim of narrow special purpose. Although some perceptual mechanisms, such as the frog's retinal 'bug detector', may indeed be highly specific in their uses, others are exploited in multiple domains. A creature with the visual pigments and attendant neural information-processing equipment necessary for discriminating hues, for example, may use its colour vision to find food, to detect predators, and to assess the health of suitors. Nevertheless, the claim of functionality does constitute a claim that the mechanism in question is complexly organized to solve some significant adaptive problem, whether that problem is as general as movement detection or as specific as bug detection. It is surely no accident that this relatively successful sub-field of psychology divides its subject matter into functional mechanisms that correspond to adaptive problems posed by natural environments (Tooby and Cosmides 1992).

The history of certain other sub-fields, such as social psychology, looks more like a succession of fashions than a cumulative growth of understanding. Social psychologists have postulated functions, too, in the sense that they have repeatedly attributed broad, basic objectives to the social psyche – things like the maintenance of Heiderian 'balance', 'self-actualization', escape from 'cognitive dissonance', and so forth – and they have then attributed social phenomena to the pursuit of those objectives. Unfortunately, social psychology's hypotheses about the psyche's basic objectives have usually been formulated without reference to the adaptive problems that the social psyche must solve if it is to promote fitness. Little wonder, then, that these social psychological constructs simply fall out of fashion, rather than being validated as essential components of the social psyche upon which to build the next wave of research.

This lack of progress cannot be explained by arguing that the adaptive problems of social life are especially obscure. Unlike social psychologists, behavioural ecologists and socio-biologists have made rapid, cumulative progress in understanding social phenomena in non-human animals (and plants), because they have organized their inquiries around the adaptive problems that social life presents, problems such as mate selection, kin recognition, optimal allocation of parental investments, and assessments of the prowess and intentions of rivals.

In the past thirty years, there has in fact been a revolution in understanding of the evolution of social phenomena, inspired both by Hamilton's (1964) demonstration that selection creates adaptations that are not merely effectively *reproductive* but effectively *'nepotistic'*, and by Williams's (1966) devastating critique of naïve group-level adaptationism (discussed below). Psychologists and other social scientists have been regrettably slow to appreciate this revolution, largely because of their attachment to a false dichotomy of 'social' versus 'biological' explanations. Subscribers to this false dichotomy equate 'biology' with its purely mechanistic sub-disciplines (genetics, endocrinology, neurology), and think of biological influences as intrinsic and irremediable (a *non sequitur* even within the misguided terms of this framework), to be contrasted with extrinsic and remediable social influences. Moreover, since putative 'biological' influences are invariant and constraining, those who propose their existence (the 'nature' crowd) are unmasked as pessimists and reactionaries, while the advocates of 'alternative' social influences (the 'nurture' crowd) are optimists and progressives. This ideology, predicated on profound incomprehension of evolutionary biology, pervades the social sciences, where it is often accepted by 'nature' advocates as thoroughly and thoughtlessly as by their 'nurture' foes.

A presumption of this prevalent world-view is that biology (falsely defined as the study of the invariant 'innate') is mute about all aspects of sociality and behaviour manifesting developmentally, experientially and circumstantially contingent variations. The very demonstration of any such contingency is seen as an exercise in the alternative, anti-biological mode of explanation. The irony is that *developmentally, experientially and circumstantially contingent variation is precisely what evolutionary biological theories of social phenomena are about*.

Exactly what *sorts* of contingent social responsiveness would we expect selection to favour, in what circumstances, and why? These are the issues that occupy theorists of social evolution. What social, demographic and ecological variables would be expected to influence social development, how, and why? Mechanistic details about the roles of hormones and particular neural structures constitute valuable 'proximate causal' accounts both of the immediate controls of action and of how such action changes with puberty or rank or particular social and material circumstances. But beyond this, evolutionists are concerned with the question why extant proximate causal controls and observed patterns of developmentally, experientially and circumstantially contingent behavioural responsiveness take particular forms and not others. Exemplary theoretical work specifically concerning the strategic logic of the contingent control of aggression and violence includes that of Hamilton (1979), Maynard Smith (1974), Mock (1987), O'Connor (1978), Parker (1974) and Popp and DeVore (1979). Knowing exactly how certain stimuli evoke particular physiological processes and how these in turn play a causal role in violence is valuable knowledge, to be sure, but it does not address the functional question of why the creature in question has evolved to aggress in this but not that life stage or situation. And without addressing such functional questions, scientists have no sound basis for estimating how generalizable (across species, sexes, life stages and circumstances) the causal links discovered in a particular programme of proximate causal research are likely to be.

'Nature' versus 'nurture' and 'social' versus 'biological' are profoundly misguided and unproductive dichotomies. But it does not follow that there are no genuine substantive issues lurking behind the controversies that are misformulated in these terms. Symons (1987, 1992) has argued persuasively that the genuine issue of contention in many such murky debates concerns the

261

specificity of evolved adaptations. Where a 'nativist' might see lifespan development as a complex evolved succession of aptitudes and inclinations appropriate to the changing adaptive problems posed by infantile, juvenile, courting, parenting and post-reproductive life stages, for example, an 'environmentalist' sees these aptitudes as by-products of one or a few general-purpose adaptations such as 'learning'. A much more productive way to frame the issues than the usual 'nature–nurture' debate is then to ask *whether the evolved elements or procedures of the mind are relatively numerous, specific and complex, or relatively few, general and simple*. The former view or polarity may thus be called the *'domain-specific'* position and the latter the *'domain-general'*. These are fairer and more constructive labels than 'nativist' and 'environmentalist', since the more sophisticated advocates of both polarities are confirmed developmental interactionists.

The pendulum in psychology has been swinging toward the domain-specific view at least since Chomsky (1959) called halt to the excesses of behaviourist parsimony and hubris, as embodied in Skinner's (1957) *Verbal Behavior*. That pendulum swing has continued for decades, under the influence of (1) discoveries in cognitive neuroscience, and (2) a growing appreciation of the computational complexity of the many things our minds do easily, engendered by the difficulties encountered in simulating those talents in artificial intelligence algorithms (Tooby and Cosmides 1992). But the pendulum will not soon be swinging back towards domain-general formulations. Although it is unquestionably possible to go too far in postulating domain-specific adaptations, mainstream psychology still has a long way to go to escape the unrealistically domain-general assumptions of its behaviourist past. Moreover, the psychological concepts and hypotheses that have become established dogma in adjacent social sciences are often vestiges of the heyday of the most extreme domain-general behaviourism.

The obsolete behaviourist model of 'general process learning theory', for example, continues to be invoked by social scientists as an explanation for the complex facts of lifespan development. After reviewing some interesting evidence that the affect associated with 'adrenaline highs' shifts from positive to negative over the lifespan, for example, Gove (1985) adds the gratuitous claim that this change is understandable as resulting from conditioning, since 'adrenaline highs are paired with substantial risk and thus anxiety' (p. 134). This pseudo-explanation is gratuitous not only because it no more explains why 'adrenaline highs' should become negative than why 'anxiety' should become positive; more importantly, the lifespan changes that Gove reviews clearly do not track the number of adrenaline-anxiety pairings, as an explanation in terms of general process learning theory would require. (Moreover, Gove's explanation takes no account of the substantial sex differences in the phenomena he reviews.) Similarly, Baldwin (1984) argued that the rapid post-adolescent diminution in crime and violence can be understood as reflecting a predictable decline in 'the sensory rewards of thrill and adventure seeking'

(p. 1326) 'due to habituation' (p. 1327). As Symons (1987) has responded to an analogous proposal about waning sexual interest in familiar partners, 'an actual neural process, habituation, becomes a metaphor for boredom. The problem with this metaphor is that it also explains why koalas become bored eating eucalyptus leaves' (p. 137). Appeals to domain-general concepts like 'learning', 'habituation' and 'reinforcement' are commonly mistaken for explanations of developmental patterns, but they are at best re-descriptions of the phenomena begging explanation (Cosmides and Tooby, 1987, 1989; Symons 1987; Tooby and Cosmides 1989). Because of its domain-general pretensions, learning theory offers no insight into the reasons why familiarity breeds attachment in one domain and loss of interest in another. The domain-specific ways in which classes of experience affect development are themselves targets of selection over evolutionary time, leading to strategically organized ontogenies.

VIOLENCE CANNOT BE DISMISSED AS PATHOLOGY

Violence is abhorrent. It produces pain, misery, premature death and countless sorts of injustice. Violence is so aversive that merely witnessing an instance can be literally sickening, and most of us are powerfully motivated to avoid violence-prone individuals 'like the plague'. It is therefore but a short leap to the metaphorical characterization of violence itself as a sort of 'sickness' or 'dysfunction'. However, this dismissal of violence as pathology cannot be sustained.

To an evolutionist, pathologies are failures of anatomical, physiological and psychological mechanisms and processes, such that the compromised mechanisms and processes exhibit reduced effectiveness in achieving the adaptive functions for which they evolved. Pathologies may be divided into nonadaptive failures due to mishap or senescent decay, and failures due to subversion by biotic agents with antagonistic interests. Violence cannot be dismissed as either sort of pathology.

Consider first those pathologies that are the consequences of discrete mishaps. Prototypical is a bone fracture, the literal breakage of an evolved entity, destroying its functionality. Clearly, violence cannot be understood as a maladaptive product of damage to the organism, analogous to fracture. It is true that damage to particular brain structures can lead to pathologies *of* violence (for example, Elliott 1992; Weiger and Bear 1988), but these are predicated upon the existence of neural organization *for* the generation of adaptively organized violence. (It is worth noting parenthetically that even genuine pathologies like fracture can be illuminated by evolutionary functional considerations. For example, the statistical risk of fractures in ancestral environments has presumably played a natural selective role in the evolution of various anatomical, psychological and physiological adaptations and parameter settings – diverse attributes such as bone hardness and diameter, the fear of heights, and the allocation of physiological resources to repair and regeneration – with consequences for the present forms and frequencies of fractures.)

Many other pathologies represent senescent decay in those lucky enough to have escaped early mortality sources. Senescent pathologies are deteriorations of evolved mechanisms and processes due to such age-related hazards as mechanical wear, gumming-up of passages, transcription errors in cell replication, and accumulation of toxic substances. Senescent pathologies are best understood as the by-products of processes which have been naturally selected for their positive fitness consequences at earlier life stages (Williams 1957; Williams and Nesse 1991). Violence is obviously not explicable as a pathology of this sort, either. In fact, in the human case, the most violent demographic class is young adult males, and it is no accident that this is also the most physically formidable demographic class (Daly and Wilson 1990).

Another major class of pathologies is those induced by disease organisms (pathogens and parasites). A crucial question in this case is whether particular symptoms reflect defensive responses by the host rather than a failure of the host's adaptive machinery (see Williams and Nesse 1991); fever, for example, was long misunderstood as pathology when it is in fact a complex, regulated host defence. Other disease symptoms certainly are failures of the host's adaptive machinery: pathological manifestations induced as epiphenomena of the disease organism's activities, which, like fractures, are not themselves adaptations but whose likelihood affects the evolution of counter-adaptations. Still other disease-induced attributes may represent adaptations 'for' the disease organism's own replication or dispersion, hence entail usurpation of the host's evolved machinery to promote the fitness of an alien genome (Dawkins 1982). A possible example is the biting frenzy of animals infected with rabies, who behave as if motivated to transmit the disease. But again, as in brain-damage-induced violent states, the disease exploits organized violent action already in the host animal's behavioural repertoire, rather than creating it *de novo*.

VIOLENCE AS COMPLEX ADAPTATION

What justifies the interpretation of violence as an instance of evolved adaptation? In the spirit of the classical examples of adaptations such as the vertebrate eye (Dawkins 1986; Williams 1992), the answer must be apparent functional 'design'. If the attributes of violence are too well suited to intelligible (that is, fitness-promoting) objectives to be dismissed as an accidental by-product of other adaptations, then we must conclude that violence has been shaped by a history of selection.

The evidence for functional design of violence is multifarious. In the first place, its elicitors are typically threats to fitness and its effects are typically to counter those threats. Animals (including people) react violently to usurpation of essential resources by rivals, and they direct their violence against those rivals. Moreover, those who initiate violence typically do so where there is some means to the end of fitness to be gained. Aggression occurs where territories are limited, when one's *own* offspring are under threat, when food is scarce, and in the context of mating competition (Archer 1988; Huntingford and Turner 1987). Unmated males of many species, for example, challenge conspecific males who are guarding fertilizable females (the limiting resource for male fitness), and in such cases (for example, many hoofed mammals) success in violent contests is highly predictive of mating success. Especially telling is the seasonal shutdown of the entire complex of psychological, physiological and morphological machinery used in such contests. In certain cases, once all the adult females are pregnant and there are no more perquisites of dominance, weapons are literally shed and males who raged at the sight of one another forage side-by-side. Thus, a growing area of empirical and theoretical work in behavioural ecology concerns the question of when and to what degree animals *should* be willing to incur risk to self in aggressive encounters (for example, Enquist and Leimar 1990). A sort of 'ecological task analysis' addresses the selective milieu: what are the conditional determinants of the expected fitness consequences of fight versus flight, and of escalation? Research, then, addresses whether the animal exhibits contingent responsiveness to available cues of the probable costs and benefits of alternative actions, and with what degree of adaptive fit.

In addition to contextual appropriateness, the motivational states of readiness for violence (angry arousal, rage) entail postures appropriate for attack and defence, and complex psychophysiological mobilization for effective agonistic action (Archer 1988; Huntingford and Turner 1987). There are morphological structures that function only or primarily as intraspecific weapons, and they are often sexually differentiated and characteristic of delimited life stages, as cost-benefit analyses of aggressive escalation suggest they should be. There is neural machinery dedicated to aggression and this too is often sexually differentiated (for example, Hines *et al.* 1992). Moreover, the sexual differentiation of physical aggression is itself variable across species, and the magnitude of sex differences in both overt weaponry and in intrasexual aggressive behaviour is predictably related to the degree of effective polygyny of the breeding system (Daly and Wilson 1983). All of these facts testify to the potency of natural and sexual selection in shaping the anatomy and psychology of intrasexual aggression.

That aggressive behaviour is an instance of evolved adaptation rather than pathology was the central proposition of the Nobel Prize-winning ethologist Konrad Lorenz's famous (and much vilified) 1966 book *On Aggression*. In that limited claim, he was indubitably correct. Unfortunately, however, Lorenz's naïve assumptions about group-level adaptation undermined his analysis, which consistently downplayed aggression's self-interested competitive function in favour of far-fetched notions of collective utility.

An understanding of evolution by selection suggests not simply that adaptive attributes exist to promote reproduction, but that they exist to promote success in reproductive *competition*: evolutionary change occurs because some phenotypes out-reproduce others. Darwin clearly understood that selection is essentially a process of intraspecific competition, but until the 1960s most animal behaviourists were inclined to equate adaptation with social harmony (but see Tinbergen 1953 and Lack 1954 as exceptions). The shared objective of conspecific animals was presumed to be the 'perpetuation of the species', a very different ultimate objective from that of the competitive ascendancy of one's genotypic elements over their alleles.

According to the idea of group-level adaptation that Lorenz and others espoused, attributes such as aggression somehow serve the interests of a whole species. The presumed functions of aggression included assuring that only the healthiest males breed and that individuals are adequately spaced to avoid over-exploitation of their food resources. This notion that adaptations should have evolved to serve the interests of whole species rather than the separate and conflicting interests of individuals is the formerly popular fallacy of *naïve group adaptationism*.

Naïve group adaptationism was a *fallacy* because its conception of adaptive function had no logical connection with the selective process responsible for generating adaptations: there is no reason why the differential survival and reproductive success of phenotypically variable individuals should tend to produce adaptations whose beneficiaries are populations. And it was *naïve* because its adherents offered no compelling counter-arguments to the orthodox Darwinian view, whose inconsistency with the fallacy went unrecognized for decades. Wynne-Edwards (1962) finally made group adaptationism *non*-naïve, by perceiving that group-level adaptations are not expected products of orthodox Darwinian processes and proposing that they arise by a countervailing process of selection at the between-group level. Wynne-Edwards's 'group selection' theory was useful in highlighting the theoretical problems faced by naïve group adaptationists, but it had numerous flaws (see Williams 1966, 1971) and is now discarded. Contemporary evolutionary biologists no longer consider the concept of group-level adaptation to have much general significance, and aggressive violence in particular is now almost universally interpreted as self-interested competitive behaviour whose effects on entire populations are seldom salutary and are in any event irrelevant to the selective forces shaping and maintaining it.

In retrospect, naïve group adaptationism provides a cautionary tale of the extent to which prevailing assumptions can influence not just our interpretations of behavioural phenomena but even our ability to recognize their existence. Lorenz was so blithely convinced that all evolved attributes function to 'preserve the species' as to assert (1966: 38) that the 'aim of aggression' is never lethal, a claim he attributed to 'objective observation of animals' rather than to any theoretical predilections of his own. Arguing in this vein, Lorenz effectively ruled out the considerable evidence that animals are frequently killed by conspecifics as indicative of pathology or 'mishap' and hence unworthy of investigation by biologists interested in adaptation. Lethality was thus eliminated by fiat from Lorenz's analysis of intraspecific aggression and became invisible to his readers. He continues to be cited in popular works as having documented the sub-lethal restraint of animal aggression in natural environments and the unique murderousness of mankind, notions which are now and were in 1966 wildly at odds with actual observations of animal conflict in the field.

RELATIONSHIP-SPECIFIC CONTEXTS OF VIOLENT CONFLICTS

Widespread evidence of animal conflicts is hardly surprising to an evolutionist. Reproductive competitors are in conflict in so far as either's expected fitness (that is, statistically expected in environments of selection) can be enhanced at the other's expense. Competition refers to any conflict of interests in which one party's possession or use of a mutually desired resource precludes the other party's possession or use of the same. Competition is not necessarily confrontational, but confrontational conflict is one particularly clear case of a competitive situation in which an escalation of conflict tactics increases the danger both to one's antagonist and to oneself. Some limited resources are not worth risking one's life or even expending much time for, but others are crucial. As the variance in attained utility increases, the costs that competitors are willing to incur in the pursuit of victory increase as well, and competition can become deadly (for example, Daly and Wilson 1988a; Enquist and Leimar 1990). However, the costs of violent confrontational conflict can be high even for the 'winner', a consideration which reduces the efficacy of using violence. The costs can include increased risk of own morbidity and mortality from injuries sustained or from reduced vigilance where risk of predation or attack is non-trivial. In the case of humans, the costs of harming others by assault or other intentional means include risk of subsequent harm to self or relatives from the vengeful relatives of your victim (Daly and Wilson 1988a).

The relationship-specificity of human violence bespeaks its functionality: circumstances eliciting it are threats to fitness, and the targets of violence are generally not merely those available but those with whom assailants have substantive conflict (for example, Daly and Wilson 1982), and hence have something to gain by subduing them. Threats to fitness as a result of others' actions depend not only on the nature of the threats but also on the relationship and the reproductive value of the parties, and on the alternative avenues to fitness of each. The utility of using violence to protect, defend or promote fitness in past environments can be discerned by an analysis of the complex functionality of morphology and psychology, as illustrated by the stag's antlers which serve no other function than competition amongst rivals for access to females (Clutton-Brock et al. 1982), the male scorpionfly's 'rape' clasper used solely to restrain uncooperative females (Thornhill and Sauer 1991), and the mitigated fear of the male three-spined stickleback in defence of his young (Pressley 1981).

(a) Same-sex rivals

In general, competitive conflict is predominantly a same-sex affair because same-sex individuals are usually more similar in the resources they desire than are opposite-sex individuals. In particular, opposite-sex individuals are often the 'resource' being competed for, especially in male–male conflicts. (We discuss the evolutionary rationale for sex differences in the substantive issues of conflict below, under the heading 'Why males, in particular?'.)

Sexual rivalry is a ubiquitous and sometimes deadly source of conflict in the human animal. A substantial proportion of homicides can be construed as the outcome of dangerous confrontational competition amongst men over women (Daly and Wilson 1988a); these men are most likely to belong to the demographic category of unmarried 15–34-year-olds (Daly and Wilson 1990; Wilson and Daly 1985, 1993b).

The social and economic conditions of the US urban underclass are the very kinds of social circumstances where risk-taking, discounting the future, confrontational competition and violence might be expected since life expectancy is relatively short and there are a limited number of 'legal' avenues to social and economic success for people who are socially, economically and politically disenfranchised from the mainstream society. There is a substantial literature on evolved decision-making under variable conditions of risk, where risk is defined as variance in the magnitude of pay-offs for a given course of action (Real and Caraco 1986). Rather than simply maximizing the expected (mean) return in some desired commodity, such as food, animals should be – and demonstrably are – sensitive to variance as well. Risk in the sense of an acceptance of some probability of death or injury is a distinct but related concept. Dangerous acts are adaptive choices if positive fitness consequences are large enough and probable enough to offset the possible negative consequences (Maynard Smith 1982). Selection can favour competitive tactics that entail increasing danger to oneself as the fitness pay-offs for success versus failure in the competition become more disparate. Disdain of danger to oneself is especially to be expected where available risk-averse alternatives are likely to produce a fitness of zero: if opting out of dangerous competition maximizes longevity but never permits the accrual of sufficient resources to reproduce, then selection will favour opting in (Rubin and Paul 1979).

Men also have frequently formed alliances with other men to compete with other coalitions of men (that is, warfare) to acquire wives (for example, Chagnon 1988, 1992). More typically, potentially lethal conflicts between coalitions of men are the result of competition over material and social resources which in turn can be used to obtain wives (for instance, Betzig 1985;

Cohen and Machalek 1988; Harcourt and de Waal 1992; see also McCarthy, this volume, for a discussion of values associated with aggressive coalitions from a socio-historical perspective).

(b) Sexual conflict

Competition amongst same-sex rivals is not the only context for violent conflicts. Men assault wives – the very resource for which rivals compete. The use of a credible threat of violence can effectively deter rivals, but it can also deter a wife from pursuing courses of action that are not in a man's interests. Marital partners are not competitors like same-sex rivals, but as genetically unrelated individuals their commonality of interests is largely limited to their overlapping interests in the welfare of joint offspring. The likely sources of marital conflict predictive of substantial fitness consequences in past environments include sexual infidelity (and risk of cuckoldry in the case of men), and desertion, as well as conflicts over the allocation of parental effort, and conflict over each partner's nepotistic interest in the welfare of own kin (Daly and Wilson 1988a; Wilson 1989; Wilson and Daly 1992). The one source of conflict that applies to men and not women is the risk of unwittingly misdirecting parental effort to another man's offspring.

The use of violence by men against wives is ubiquitous. But the contexts in which husbands commonly assault wives are remarkably few: in response to a wife's sexual infidelity (or cues thereof), or a wife's unilateral decision to terminate the relationship (or cues thereof), as well as to 'discipline' a 'too independent' wife, and in response to other factors (perhaps his own infidelity or paranoia) that activate male sexual jealousy mechanisms (for example, Daly et al. 1982; Daly and Wilson 1988a; Wilson and Daly 1992; Dobash and Dobash 1979; Campbell 1992; Counts 1991; Counts et al. 1992; Polk and Ranson 1991). We propose that the particular cues and circumstances which inspire men to use violence against their partners reflect a domain-specific masculine psychology which evolved in a social milieu in which assaults and threats of violence functioned to deter wives from pursuing alternative reproductive opportunities, which would have represented substantial threats to husbands' fitness by misdirecting parental investment and loss of mating opportunities to reproductive competitors.

Another obvious context for sexual conflict in which violence is used by men against women is rape (Thornhill and Thornhill 1983, 1992; Smuts 1992). Perhaps the most costly threat to a woman's fitness throughout history was loss of the opportunity to choose who is likely to sire her offspring, thereby depriving her of the opportunity both to have her children sired by a man with desirable phenotypic qualities and to have her children benefit from the time, effort and resources of a father. Since these are substantial costs, the sexual psychology of women may be expected to manifest adapted design features reflecting the past costs and benefits of accepting or rejecting particular sexual partners (Thornhill and Thornhill 1990). Undesired sexual encounters are resisted by women, and use of violence by men can be a very effective means of controlling the reluctant victim. The fitness costs of any single act of sexual intercourse have always been less for men than for women, which suggests that the evolved sexual psychology of men is likely to be less discriminating regarding choice of partner for a single sexual opportunity than that of women (Daly and Wilson 1983; Symons 1979). Another design feature of male sexual psychology which is relevant to the occurrence of rape is the apparent disregard of women's unwillingness as indicated by the use of coercion to achieve copulation. The ability of the male to remain sexually competent in such circumstances presumably reflects the past fitness benefits of pursuing and achieving copulation in the face of female resistance (Thornhill and Thornhill 1992).

(c) Parent–offspring conflict

Genetic relatedness is a predictor of reduced conflict and enhanced co-operation because the genetic posterities of blood relatives co-vary (are promoted by common exigencies) in direct proportion to their degree of relatedness. It follows that blood kin should be relatively unlikely to perceive their interests as conflicting and hence relatively immune from violence. However, in order to assess whether this is really so, one needs some sort of unbiased assay of severe violence and some sort of denominator representing 'opportunity'. One approach that we have employed is to study homicide cases involving members of the same household. We have used homicides as an assay of conflict because they are manifestations of conflict least contaminated by biases of detection or reporting, and because the universe of potential victims can be specified by confining attention to household members. Given the prevailing household compositions in Detroit in 1972, for example, co-residents unrelated to the killer by blood, whether spouses or not, were more than eleven times more likely to be slain than the co-residing genetic relatives (Daly and Wilson 1982).

(i) Step-relationships

A particularly apt comparison for assessing effects of perceived relatedness on conflict is a comparison of parent–offspring relationship and surrogates thereof. Parental solicitude has evolved to expend animals' resources (and even their lives) in enhancing the reproductive prospects of their descendants (Trivers 1972; Daly and Wilson 1980, 1987). It is therefore not surprising that parental solicitude evolves to be discriminative with respect to predictors of the offspring's probable contribution to the parent's genetic posterity. One implication is that substitute parents will often care less profoundly for 'their' children than will genetic parents, and the risk of maltreatment may be expected to be greater for stepchildren than for genetic offspring. In fact, there is over-representation of step-families in child-abuse samples (Daly and Wilson 1981, 1985, 1987, 1993), in samples of child homicides perpetrated by parents (Daly and Wilson 1988b), amongst children dying before the age of 15 (Hill and Kaplan 1988), and amongst children with head and other injuries (Wadsworth et al. 1983; Fergusson et al. 1972).

In view of the costs of prolonged 'parental' investment in non-relatives, it may seem remarkable that step-relationships are ever peaceful. However, violent hostility is rarer than friendly relations even amongst non-relatives; people thrive by the maintenance of networks of social reciprocity and by establishing reputations for fairness and generosity that will make them attractive exchange partners (Alexander 1987). Furthermore, the likely social (and mortality) costs of harming other people's grandchildren and nephews and nieces can be a very effective deterrent to the use of violence against a mate's children from a prior union.

(ii) Genetic parent–offspring relationships

Even though offspring are the parents' means to genetic posterity, parent–offspring conflict is an endemic feature of sexually reproducing organisms because the allocation of resources and efforts that would maximize a parent's genetic posterity seldom matches that which would maximize that of a particular offspring (Trivers 1974). In some circumstances, an offspring's reproductive prospects (according to cues that were predictive in the species' environment of evolutionary adaptation) may be insufficient to offset that offspring's detrimental effect on the parent's capacity to pursue other adaptive action, in which case parental solicitude may be expected to fail (Daly and Wilson 1987; Wilson and Daly 1993b). There are at least four classes of circumstances in which we might anticipate some reluctance to invest in a newborn: (1) doubt that the offspring is the putative parent's own; (2) indications of poor offspring quality and reduced reproductive value; (3) all those extrinsic circumstances such as food scarcity, lack of social support, and needs of older but still nursing offspring, that would have made a child unlikely to survive during human evolutionary history; and (4) where the present child's demands compromise alternative reproductive options of the parents. The great majority of ethnographic accounts of infanticide in non-industrial societies reflect one or another of these categories of strategic allocation of life-time parental effort (Bugos and McCarthy 1984; Dickemann 1975; Daly and Wilson 1984, 1988a; Wilson and Daly 1993). Variations in the risk of physical and sexual abuse of own offspring also reflect cues of these four classes of circumstantial predictors of the fitness value of offspring to the parents (Wilson et al. 1980; Daly and Wilson 1981, 1985). However, abuse does not otherwise match any criteria for adaptive action. Abusive parents commonly persist in inflicting damage upon their wards, while continuing to invest in them. This is hardly an efficient strategy of parental effort allocation. Rather, we consider that the variable risk of child abuse is a non-adaptive reflection of the socially contingent responsiveness of an evolved discriminative parental psychology, exhibiting predictable relationships to several independent variables that were historically predictive of the child's expected contribution to parental fitness.

VIOLENT AGGRESSIVITY AS A PERSONALITY VARIABLE

It is everyone's experience that individuals vary greatly in their likelihood of becoming angry or in inclination to use violence. Why this should be so is a conundrum from an evolutionary perspective. Selection favours an optimal species-typical (and sex- and lifestage-typical) facultative design, so it is challenging to address the question of individual differences in personality from an adaptationist perspective (Buss 1991; Tooby and Cosmides 1990b). Whereas there is much individual variation in use of violence in within-group competitive conflicts, there probably is less variation in inclination to use violence against threatening out-groups. And even amongst those individuals disinclined to participate in aggressive coalitions, the social costs of pacifism in the face of a popular war can often assure participation.

So why does violent aggressivity seem to be a 'personality' variable? That is, why is facultative violence not in everyone's repertoire? One plausible answer is that facultativeness is developmental; experientially based expertise in the use of violence makes it more available as a social tool. Use of violence without expertise in processing of subtle changes in the social and physical dynamics of a violent or potentially violent confrontation can be costly with respect to social reputation (for example, Coie *et al.* 1991; Dodge *et al.* 1990b), injury and even death. It would seem that prior effective experience in the use of threats and assaults increases the expected utility and hence the probability of using violence again.

The social utilities of threats and assaults depend on the relationship-specific conflicts, the social contexts and the parties' skill in using violence as a tool. A cross-cultural analysis of non-state societies revealed that parents and others were more likely explicitly to promote the expression of aggressivity, strength, skilled use of weapons and tolerance of pain amongst male youths in those societies which have repeatedly engaged in war in recent history than in non-warring societies (Low 1989). Within western industrialized nations such as the United States, there is some evidence that adult use of violence is facilitated by childhood experiences of violence as victims or as witnesses (for example, Widom 1989a, 1989b; Dodge *et al.* 1990; see also Hoffman, Ireland and Widom, this volume). Longitudinal studies of juvenile delinquents and career criminals reveal a prior history of various social transgressions including physical violence (for instance, Wilson and Herrnstein 1985; Farrington 1991; Tonry *et al.* 1991). In natural environments of lifelong relations with a few hundred people and no powerful central authority or modern weapons, the role of a feared and dangerous character probably must be total: if a man is not prepared to intimidate other men, it may be foolish to beat and threaten women and children. Potentially lethal vengeful action by the victim's relatives is likely wherever the state has usurped the role of arbiter and justice (for example, Daly and Wilson 1988a).

Frequency-dependent maintenance of polymorphism in violent aggressivity is also theoretically possible but not very plausible. Although there have been specialized 'castes' of warriors throughout history (see McCarthy, this volume), this phenomenon is not akin to a frequency-dependent polymorphism in which the fitness benefits are dependent on the relative proportion of alternative morphs in the population (as is the case with male and female morphs). Furthermore, the degree of individual variability in violent aggressivity that we see in contemporary mass society may be an evolutionary novelty, because of relaxed selection (extreme variability in a trait is selected against if the fitness consequences are impactful) and the evolutionarily novel social circumstance that new acquaintances can be unknown (anonymity of personal history).

Psychiatrists have identified a personality disorder which is particularly likely to engage in violent aggressivity: the antisocial personality (American Psychiatric Association 1987). The diagnostic criteria for antisocial personality include a history of 'conduct disorder' and 'attention-deficit hyperactive disorder' prior to age 15 and a continued pattern of 'irresponsible and anti-social behavior' into adulthood. Juvenile delinquents and career criminals are routinely diagnosed as having an antisocial personality (for example, Robins 1979; Robins and Rutter 1990; Moffitt 1990). There are apparently a number of reliable risk factors other than arrests associated with the development and maintenance of the antisocial personality, including poverty, maleness, early maturity, poor school performance, parental criminal history and psycho-pathology, and lone mother *in loco parentis* (for instance, Tonry *et al.* 1991; Robins and Rutter 1990; Moffitt 1990; Schonfeld *et al.* 1988; Tremblay *et al.* 1992; Loeber 1990). These risk factors for the antisocial personality largely overlap the risk factors for juvenile delinquency and violent crime (for example, Hagan 1990b; Messner and Tardiff 1986; Messner and Sampson 1991; Parker 1989; Sampson 1987). Moreover, these same risk factors charac-terize underclass urban communities (for instance, Wilson and Aponte 1985).

The existence of two or more personality types need not reflect a basic poly-morphism, since both may be manifestations of the same universal – but socially and experientially contingent – psychology. A universal human psychology which uses violence in response to cues of its utility may then develop into the 'antisocial personality' type in those social circumstances where there is intense competition amongst rivals who have a limited number of effective alternatives to compete (see also Turner, this volume). We would therefore expect that the demographic characteristics and the social contexts in which the antisocial personality type is found would correspond to the expected cues for risk-proneness of an evolved risk-sensitive socially competitive psychology. In addition, the particular individuals most likely to be identified by psychiatrists as suffering from the antisocial personality disorder (in so far as this diagnosis is not merely pejorative or invalid) may be those in whom the psychological mechanisms are not appropriately modulated by relevant context-specific cues because of 'errors' in information-processing (for example, Dodge *et al.* 1990c).

WHY MALES, IN PARTICULAR?

There is a cross-culturally universal sex difference in human use of physical violence, whether it be fist fights or homicides, warfare or the slaughter of non-human animals (for example, Daly and Wilson 1988a; Murdock 1967; see also Chapter 1). There is no evidence even suggesting that this sex difference is contravened anywhere, notwithstanding the perennial appeal of such fantasies as the ancient Greek legend of the Amazons and Margaret Mead's (1935) just-so stories of sex-role reversal in New Guinea (see Daly and Wilson 1988a). The competent use of violent skills contributes quite directly to male fitness: both successful warriors (for example, Matthiessen 1962; Chagnon 1988) and successful game hunters (Kaplan and Hill 1985) have converted their successes into sexual, marital and reproductive success. Violent behaviour is risky behaviour, of course, but the greater variance in fitness amongst males than amongst females (Bateman 1948; Trivers 1972) and the male's greater likelihood of going to his grave without descendants (Ellison 1985) make for a sexually differentiated selective circumstance favouring greater risk-proneness in same-sex competition amongst men than amongst women (Alexander 1979; Daly and Wilson 1990; Wilson and Daly 1985).

Men have evolved the morphological, physiological and psychological means to be effective users of violence. In modern nations in which the state has usurped the legitimate use of violence, we can easily lose sight of the general utility of a credible threat of violence, but in pre-state societies, such a threat was essential if one's rivals were to be deterred from violating one's interests. And a credible threat must be a genuine threat, which can at least occasionally be exercised. In many tribal societies, violent capability is one essential component of the reputation needed to acquire and maintain status and power (Chagnon 1988, 1992; Daly and Wilson 1988a). (And of course if evolved violent capabilities are better developed in men than in women initially or primarily because of sex differential intensity of same-sex competition, it is hardly surprising that men should also sometimes make use of their superior violent capabilities in their conflicts with women.)

These considerations are generally overlooked by those who embrace the false dichotomy of social and biological explanations for violence. Reviewers of biological factors typically discuss hormonal effects, Y chromosomes, sexually differentiated body builds, and the supposed generality of greater male aggressivity amongst non-human animals (for example, Burrowes *et al.* 1988; Mednick *et al.* 1982; Wilson and Herrnstein 1985). Others deny that the relevance of these factors has been demonstrated, and propose, as an alternative 'social' explanation, that sex differences are caused by people's differential treatment of girls versus boys and women versus men. Occasionally explicit (for example, Adler 1975; Eagley and Steffen 1986; Hagan 1990a; Tieger 1980), but more often implied, is the proposition that women and men would behave identically if treated identically. The common practice of invoking 'sex roles in our society' when discussing sex differences carries the additional implication, whether intended or unwitting, that the differences under consideration are absent or reversed in other societies. In the case of violence, neither of these propositions has any evidentiary basis or coherent theoretical rationale (Daly and Wilson 1988a; Klama 1988).

Our species-typical sex difference in violent aggression is one which we share with other effectively polygynous mammals, and its link with effective polygyny is well understood (Trivers 1972; Williams 1966). By 'effective polygyny', we refer to a breeding system in which the variance in fitness amongst males exceeds that amongst females (Clutton-Brock 1988; Daly and Wilson 1983). Diverse threads of morphological, physiological, developmental and psychological evidence are consistent in indicating that hominid evolution has been characterized by a moderate degree of effective polygyny (Alexander 1979; Alexander *et al.* 1979; Daly and Wilson 1983, 1988a; Symons 1979). Effective polygyny is a circumstance conducive to the evolution of a male psychology more combative and risk-prone than that of females.

The reason why departures from effective monogamy are associated with the evolution of sex differences in risky competitiveness is that high variance means relatively great rewards for success and penalties for failure: males in effectively polygynous species have a higher maximal reproductive success than females, but they also have a higher probability of dying without issue. Greater variance in rewards favours greater acceptance of risk in their pursuit. Women compete, too, and may even kill one another in the process, but their lesser fitness variance has generally meant that they have little to gain, and at least something to lose, by dangerous tactics. (Note, too, that differential taste for risky confrontational competition need not imply a domain-general sex difference in tolerating danger; females might well be found to tolerate greater risk than males in defence of children, for example.)

What makes the comparative evidence relevant to the human case is the body of theory and data linking cross-species diversity in sexual differentiation of behaviour and morphology to ecology, demography and mating system. The point is not some typological claim about the significance of maleness (or androgens or Y chromosomes) across the animal kingdom; in fact, the familiar sex difference in belligerence is reversed in precisely those species in which the fitness variance differential is reversed; namely, in effectively polyandrous species such as spotted sandpipers (Colwell and Oring 1989; Maxson and Oring 1980; but see Oring *et al.* 1991), Wilson's phalaropes (Colwell and Oring 1988) and jacanas (Stephens 1982; Emlen *et al.* 1989). In comparative perspective, *Homo sapiens* is an effectively polygynous primate, and more specifically, one whose degree of effective polygyny – more than the gibbon's, for example, but much less than the gorilla's – is intelligibly related to the magnitude of sex differences in maturation, senescence and body size.

This is not to say that the precise magnitudes of sex differences in violent competitive behaviour are predictable from available theories of sexual selection and comparative considerations. We are, after all, a biparental species, and only slightly effectively polygynous and dimorphic as compared to many other mammals. What are now required are theories of the contingent control of competitive inclinations sufficiently precise to predict the variable magnitude of sex differences in behaviour. Theoretical modelling and research are needed to determine whether even small sex differences in fitness variance, such as those likely to have been characteristic of our foraging ancestors, could be sufficient to account for large sex differences in risk-proneness and mortality.

Alternatively, an adequate explanation of the large human sex difference in violent competition may have to focus upon peculiarities of this species. Perhaps the human propensity to coalitional aggression and deterrent vengeance has raised the premium on masculine competitive preoccupations and skills beyond what is demanded of less socially complex animal species (Alexander 1971; Chagnon 1988; Harcourt and de Waal 1992). Perhaps a hunting specialization has incidentally elevated men's violent capabilities so that the cost-benefit structure of male–male versus female–female conflicts is more different than it would be if the sexes foraged similarly. Perhaps contemporary weapon technology somehow amplifies sex differences in lethal outcomes which were less extreme in the environments in which the human social psyche evolved (though the cross-cultural evidence provides no particular reason to believe this). Transforming such speculations into testable theories is a challenge which will require (at the least) strategic modelling (Tooby and DeVore 1987) and explicit postulation of empirically demonstrable psychological mechanisms. We also need to develop theories of facultative variation in conflictual inclinations in response to demographic and ecological factors. The intensities of male–male and female–female competition vary inversely with one another in relation to operational sex ratio variation and attendant competition for mates (Emlen and Oring 1977), for example; competition also varies in relation to cohort size (Easterlin 1980; Cohen and Land 1987), and, between societies, in relation to modes of subsistence and the monopolizability of resources (Flinn and Low 1986).

THE YOUNG MALE SYNDROME

Men in young adulthood are the principal perpetrators of potentially lethal violence and its principal victims, too (for example, Chapter 7 this volume; Block 1987; Daly and Wilson 1988a, 1990; Hirschi and Gottfredson 1983; Hewlett 1988; Holinger 1987; Steffensmeier *et al.* 1989; Tittle 1988; Wilson and Daly 1985, 1992). This is especially so where rates of lethal violence are high, because cases in which victim and killer are unrelated young men constitute the most volatile component of variable homicide rates (Block 1975; Daly and Wilson 1989). Many homicides arise out of social conflicts amongst acquaintances in which either party might have killed the other, with the result that victim and killer populations are similar demographically (Wilson and Daly 1985). Accident victimization risk tends to parallel homicide victimization and perpetration (Holinger 1987; Wilson and Daly 1985). Maleness, youth and poor economic circumstances and prospects are all predictive of relatively dangerous or reckless behavioural inclinations.

We have already discussed the utilitarian logic by which poverty and poor prospects favour risk-proneness: as Bob Dylan (1965) put it, 'when you got nothing, you got nothing to lose'. But the relationship between youth and risk-proneness requires further explanation. Why should it be young men – at the peak of their physical capabilities and in the very stage of life at which mortality from disease and defect is lowest – who are maximally risk-prone and vulnerable to violent death? All else equal, might we not expect increasing age to be associated with increasing disdain for one's own safety? And as for gender, why should not young women respond as desperately as young men to their no less desperate circumstances? It is a fact so familiar as to seem ordinary that the very demographic class that is most formidable in violence (young adult males) is also most vulnerable thereto, but it is a remarkable fact none the less and one in need of explanation.

We propose that the requisite explanation lies in the social demands and agendas that confronted ancestral men and women in particular life stages (see also Gardner 1993; Rogers 1993; Rubin and Paul 1979). Young men are both especially formidable and especially risk-prone because they constitute the demographic class upon which there was the most intense selection for confrontational competitive capabilities amongst our ancestors.

In the foraging societies in which the human psyche evolved, the young man who would acquire a wife had to display prowess in hunting and warfare and a capacity to defend his interests, to women and to any men who might hinder or facilitate his ambitions. Moreover, although young adulthood is an especially competitive stage for any male mammal, human social complexity can make the consequences of differential performance in that stage enduring and hence even more crucial. In most effectively polygynous animals, a male's continuing success is dependent upon his continuing competitive prowess; a senior stag must remain as aggressive and dangerous as the young bucks, or

277

he is finished (Clutton-Brock *et al.* 1982). But in people, ubiquitous practices of long-term paternal and nepotistic investment, solidary kin groups, between-group hostilities and coalitional reciprocity create an arena within which individual reputations have lasting effects.

The hypothesis that competitive success or failure in early adulthood has been an especially strong determinant of total lifetime fitness in men in ancestral environments as compared to other male mammals warrants empirical investigation; early competitive performance may have major long-term consequences in other creatures, too. Our general argument about sex- and life-stage-specific competitive inclinations having been shaped by sexual selection does not require that people be special in these matters. People are clearly special, however, in that individuals have reputations, which are consensually built up and transmitted amongst one's acquaintances and affect one's social fortunes. Demonstrations of competence in the face of danger reap reputational (and perhaps direct material) rewards whose utility persists over the rest of the lifespan. Successful risk-taking is admired (for example, Fishbain *et al.* 1987; Moore 1972; Wilson and Daly 1985), and much dangerous and violent behaviour by young men functions as social display facilitated by the presence of an audience to impress (Daly and Wilson 1988a; Jackson and Gray 1976; Rothe 1987; Wilson and Daly 1985).

Several other lines of evidence about lifespan development support the idea that young men constitute a demographic class specialized by a history of selection for maximal competitive effort. Changes in muscle strength which are apparently unrelated to exercise, for example, show characteristic sex-specific patterns: male strength increases abruptly at puberty and only slightly in the following decade (McComas *et al.* 1973); strength subsequently declines gradually in adults of both sexes, but especially in men (Murray *et al.* 1985). Aerobic capacity is likewise maximal and maximally sexually differentiated in the teens and twenties (for example, Shephard 1986). Sex differences in various sorts of motor performance favouring males tend generally to increase around puberty, but this is much more striking with respect to measures of strength and quick energetic bursts than in measures of balance and precision (Thomas and French 1985).

Not only are young men the most physically formidable of human demographic classes; they also appear to be psychologically specialized to embrace danger and confrontational competition. In various activities, young men have been found to especially be motivated by competition and especially undeterred by danger to self (for example, Bell 1992; Bell and Bell 1993; Gove 1985; Holinger 1987; Jonah 1986; Kandel 1980; Lyng 1990; Tonkin 1987; Wilson and Daly 1985). 'Age is by far the most powerful predictor of the cessation of those forms of deviant behavior that involve substantial risk and/or physically demanding behavior,' begins Walter Gove (1985: 115), in a provocative chapter in which he asserts that his own discipline of sociology has no handle on age or sex differences in 'deviance' and argues the need for 'a biopsychosocial perspective'. Gove reviewed much intriguing but sketchy evidence of lifespan developmental changes in motives, tastes and attitudes in such spheres as competitiveness, self-absorption, moralizing, need for approval, emotionality and stimulation-seeking, all of which seem to reflect a declining appetite and/or aptitude for risk and competition over the course of adulthood. Unfortunately, although Gove offered a rich characterization of these lifespan changes, he offered no functional (strategic) interpretation of them, and gratuitously implied that lifespan development constitutes a progression from inferior to superior attributes rather than a series of life-stage-appropriate phenotypes. (See Alexander 1987, for a critique and re-evaluation of similarly gerontocentric accounts of 'moral development'.)

It is interesting to inquire how age- and sex-related variations in effective risk-proneness are instantiated psychologically. Wilson and Herrnstein (1985) argued from diverse evidence that men who engage in predatory violence and other risky criminal activity have different 'time-horizons' than law-abiding men, weighing the near future relatively heavily against the long term; what they failed to note is that facultative adjustment of one's personal time-horizons could be an adaptive response to predictive information about one's prospects for longevity and eventual success (Gardner 1993; Rogers 1993). Many other psychological processes of potential relevance can be envisaged. One could become more risk-prone as a result of one or more of the following: intensified desire for the fruits of success; intensified fear of the stigma of non-participation; finding the adrenalin rush of danger pleasurable in itself; underestimating objective dangers; overestimating one's competence; or ceasing to care whether one lives or dies. Several of these processes appear to be relevant to the risk-proneness of young men. As drivers, for example, they both underestimate objective risks and overestimate their own skills, as compared to older drivers (Brown and Groeger 1988; Finn and Bragg 1986; Matthews and Moran 1986). Apparent disdain for their own lives might be inferred from the fact that men's suicide rates maximally surpass women's in young adulthood (for example, Gardner 1993; Holinger 1987). Gove (1985) also provided some evidence that the pleasure derived from skilled encounters with danger diminishes with age (see also Lyng 1990).

An alternative to the hypothesis that men have evolved an adaptive lifespan schedule of risk-proneness is that age patterns are entirely the result of changes in relevant circumstances which happen to be correlated with age. Mated status, for example, would be expected to inspire a reduction in dangerous behaviour, because access to mates is a principal issue inspiring competition and married men have more to lose than their single counterparts. One might therefore hypothesize that the decline in violence with age is entirely accounted for by increases in the proportion married. Marital status is indeed related to the probability of committing homicide, but age effects remain conspicuous when married and unmarried men are distinguished (Daly and Wilson 1990; Wilson and Daly 1985).

This question of whether age (or sex) effects would evaporate if associated circumstances were factored out appears to be the substantive point of contention behind much of the confusing debate about social versus biological explanations. If 15-year-olds and 50-year-olds were found to differ solely as a result of differences in the frequencies at which they encounter specific situations, and not in their responses thereto, then the idea of an evolved schedule of life-stage-appropriate psychology would be superfluous. But then so would any notion of post-pubertal development. Presumably no one defends such an extreme version of environmental determinism: even the most enthusiastic sociological critic of psychological reductionism recognizes that cumulative experience changes people. What is less often recognized is that some sort of complex functional theory of lifespan development is necessary to account for the particular ways in which experiences matter.

Despite considerable research on risk perception, subjective probability and the heuristics of decision-making (for example, Kahneman *et al*. 1982; Nisbett and Ross 1980; Slovic 1987), differences in responding as a function of age or sex have hitherto been treated largely as 'noise' rather than as meaningful phenomena. Moreover, the distinction between outcomes impacting directly on the decision-maker and those more hypothetical or impacting on someone else has been trivialized. Researchers in this area often maintain that heuristics fail as formally logical inference but probably serve well enough. However, we cannot judge how well or poorly our heuristics serve our purposes until we specify those purposes (for example, Cosmides 1989; Cosmides and Tooby 1992). Decision theorists have yet to address the functional significance of domain-specific decision processes in any depth, presumably because they lack a fundamental theory of self-interest from which to derive predictions about the utilities and subjective costs of alternative consequences of one's decisions. One may recognize, for example, that death is a major cost and that an appreciable risk thereof is thus likely to be a major deterrent, without apprehending that psyches may evolve to treat the 'genetic death' of non-reproduction as an equally negative outcome. A sexually selected appetite for confrontational competition can be adaptive even where it entails a high risk of mortality.

CONCLUDING REMARKS

An evolutionary psychological view of people does not imply that they are irrational automata, but rather that their behaviour is the result of decision processes with a cost-benefit structure that instantiates age-, sex- and circumstance-specific valuations of various classes of material and social goods. Evolutionary models of the lifespan agendas of men and women indicate how behavioural control mechanisms must be strategically organized in order to have achieved adaptive ends in ancestral environments, and this way of thinking can direct the attention of psychologists to relevant variables and processes. Knowing what the mind has been 'designed' by selection to achieve affords numerous hints about its probable organization.

ACKNOWLEDGEMENTS

Our research on homicide has been supported by the Harry Frank Guggenheim Foundation, the Social Sciences and Humanities Research Council of Canada, the North Atlantic Treaty Organization, and the Natural Sciences and Engineering Research Council of Canada.

REFERENCES

Adler, F. (1975) *Sisters in Crime*, New York: McGraw-Hill.

Alexander, R. D. (1971) 'The search for an evolutionary philosophy of man', *Proceedings of the Royal Society of Victoria*, 84: 99–120.

—— (1979) *Darwinism and Human Affairs*, Seattle, WA: University of Washington Press.

—— (1987) *The Biology of Moral Systems*, Hawthorne, NY: Aldine de Gruyter.

Alexander, R. D., Hoogland, J. L., Howard, R. D., Noonan, K. M. and Sherman, P. W. (1979) 'Sexual dimorphisms and breeding systems in pinnipeds, ungulates, primates and humans', in N. A. Chagnon and W. Irons (eds) *Evolutionary Biology and Human Social Behavior*, North Scituate, MA: Duxbury.

American Psychiatric Association (1987) *Diagnostic and Statistical Manual of Mental Disorders*, 3rd edn, revised, Washington, DC: American Psychiatric Association.

Archer, J. (1988) *The Behavioural Biology of Aggression*, New York: Cambridge University Press.

Baldwin, J. D. (1984) 'Thrill and adventure seeking and the age distribution of crime: comment on Hirschi and Gottfredson', *American Journal of Sociology*, 90: 1326–30.

Barkow, J. H., Cosmides, L. and Tooby, J. (1992) *The Adapted Mind*, New York: Oxford University Press.

Bateman, A. J. (1948) 'Intra-sexual selection in *Drosophila*', *Heredity*, 2: 349–68.

Bell, N. J. and Bell, R. W. (eds) (1993) *Adolescent Risk Taking*, Newbury Park, CA: Sage.

Betzig, L. L. (1985) *Despotism and Differential Reproduction: A Darwinian View of History*, Hawthorne, NY: Aldine de Gruyter.

Block, C. R. (1987) *Homicide in Chicago*, Chicago: Loyola University Press.

Block, R. (1975) 'Homicide in Chicago: a nine-year study (1965–1973)', *Journal of Criminal Law and Criminology*, 66: 496–510.

Brown, I. D. and Groeger, J. A. (1988) 'Risk perception and decision taking during the transition between novice and experienced driver status', *Ergonomics*, 31: 585–97.

Bugos, P. E. and McCarthy, L. M. (1984) 'Ayoreo infanticide: a case study', in G. Hausfater and S. B. Hrdy (eds) *Infanticide: Comparative and Evolutionary Perspectives*, New York: Aldine de Gruyter.

Burrowes, K. L., Hales, R. E. and Arrington, E. (1988) 'Research on the biologic aspects of violence', *Psychiatric Clinics of North America*, 11: 499–509.

Buss, D. M. (1991) 'Evolutionary personality psychology', *Annual Review of Psychology*, 42: 459–91.

Campbell, J. C. (1992) 'If I can't have you, no one can: issues of power and control in homicide of female partners', in J. Radford and D. E. H. Russell (eds) *Femicide: The Politics of Woman Killing*, New York: Twayne.

Chagnon, N. A. (1988) 'Life histories, blood revenge, and warfare in a tribal population', *Science*, 239: 985–92.

—— (1992) *Yanomamö: The Last Days of Eden*, San Diego, CA: Harcourt Brace Jovanovich.

Chomsky, N. (1959) 'Review of Skinner's *'Verbal Behavior'*, *Language*, 35: 26–58.

Clutton-Brock, T. H. (1988) *Reproductive Success*, Chicago: University of Chicago Press.

Clutton-Brock, T. H., Guinness, F. E., Albon, S. D. (1982) *Red Deer*, Chicago: University of Chicago Press.

Cohen, L. E. and Land, K. C. (1987) 'Age structure and crime: symmetry versus asymmetry and the projection of crime rates through the 1990s', *American Sociological Review*, 52: 170–83.

Cohen, L. E. and Machalek, R. (1988) 'A general theory of expropriative crime: an evolutionary ecological approach', *American Journal of Sociology*, 94: 465–501.

Coie, J. D., Dodge, K. A., Terry, R. and Wright, V. (1991) 'The role of aggression in peer relations: an analysis of aggression episodes in boys' play groups', *Child Development*, 62: 812–26.

Colwell, M. A. and Oring, L. W. (1988) 'Wing fluttering display by incubating male Wilson's phalaropes', *Canadian Journal of Zoology*, 66: 2315–17.

—— (1989) 'Extra-pair mating in the spotted sandpiper: a female mate acquisition tactic', *Animal Behaviour*, 38: 675–84.

Cosmides, L. (1989) 'The logic of social exchange: has natural selection shaped how humans reason? studies with the Wason selection task', *Cognition*, 31: 187–276.

Cosmides, L. and Tooby, J. (1987) 'From evolution to behavior: evolutionary psychology as the missing link', in J. Dupré (ed.) *The Latest on the Best: Essays on Evolution and Optimality*, Cambridge, MA: MIT Press.

—— (1989) 'Evolutionary psychology and the generation of culture, part II: case study: a computational theory of social exchange', *Ethology and Sociobiology*, 10: 51–98.

—— (1992) 'Cognitive adaptations for social exchange', in J. H. Barkow, L. Cosmides and J. Tooby (1992) *The Adapted Mind*, New York: Oxford University Press.

Counts, D. A. (1991) 'Domestic violence in Oceania', Special issue of *Pacific Studies*, 13.

Counts, D. A., Brown, J. and Campbell, J. C. (1992) *Sanctions and Sanctuary: Cultural Perspectives on the Beating of Wives*, Boulder, CO: Westview Press.

Daly, M. and Wilson, M. (1980) 'Discriminative parental solicitude: a biological perspective', *Journal of Marriage and the Family*, 42: 277–88.

—— (1981) 'Abuse and neglect of children in evolutionary perspective', in R. D. Alexander and D. W. Tinkle (eds) *Natural Selection and Social Behavior*, New York: Chiron.

—— (1982) 'Homicide and kinship', *American Anthropologist*, 84: 372–8.

—— (1983) *Sex, Evolution and Behavior*, Belmont, CA: Wadsworth.

—— (1984) 'A sociobiological analysis of human infanticide', in G. Hausfater and S. B. Hrdy (eds) *Infanticide: Comparative and Evolutionary Perspectives*, New York: Aldine de Gruyter.

—— (1985) 'Child abuse and other risks of not living with both parents', *Ethology and Sociobiology*, 6: 197–210.

—— (1987) 'The Darwinian psychology of discriminative parental solicitude', *Nebraska Symposium on Motivation*, 35: 91–144.

—— (1988a) *Homicide*, Hawthorne, NY: Aldine de Gruyter.

—— (1988b) 'Evolutionary social psychology and family homicide', *Science*, 242: 519–24.

—— (1989) 'Homicide and cultural evolution', *Ethology and Sociobiology*, 10: 99–110.

——— (1990) 'Killing the competition: female/female and male/male homicide', *Human Nature*, 1: 81–107.

——— (1993) 'Stepparenthood and the evolved psychology of discriminative parental solicitude', in S. Parmigiani and F. S. vom Saal (eds) *Infanticide and Parental Care*, London: Harwood Academic Publishers.

Daly, M., Wilson, M. and Weghorst, S. J. (1982) 'Male sexual jealousy', *Ethology and Sociobiology*, 3: 11–27.

Dawkins, R. (1982) *The Extended Phenotype*, San Francisco: Freeman.

——— (1986) *The Blind Watchmaker*, New York: Norton.

Dickeman, M. (1985) 'Demographic consequences of infanticide in man', *Annual Review of Ecology and Systematics*, 6: 107–37.

Dobash, R. E. and Dobash, R. P. (1979) *Violence Against Wives: A Case Against the Patriarchy*, New York: Free Press.

Dodge, K. A., Bates, J. E. and Pettit, G. S. (1990a) 'Mechanisms in the cycle of violence', *Science*, 250: 1678–83.

Dodge, K. A., Coie, J. D., Pettit, G. S. and Price, J. M. (1990b) 'Peer status and aggression in boys' groups: developmental and contextual analyses', *Child Development*, 61: 1289–309.

Dodge, K. A., Price, J. M. and Bachorowski, J.-A. (1990c) 'Hostile attributional biases in severely aggressive adolescents', *Journal of Abnormal Psychology*, 99: 385–92.

Dylan, B. (1965) 'Like a rolling stone', Warner Brothers Music.

Eagley, A. H. and Steffen, V. J. (1986) 'Gender and aggressive behavior: a meta-analytic review of the social psychological literature', *Psychological Bulletin*, 100: 309–30.

Easterlin, R. A. (1986) *Birth and Fortune*, New York: Basic Books.

Elliott, F. A. (1992) 'Violence. The neurologic contribution: an overview', *Archives of Neurology*, 49: 595–603.

Ellison, P. T. (1985) 'Lineal inheritance and lineal extinction', *Behavioral and Brain Sciences*, 8: 672.

Emlen, S. T., Demong, N. J. and Emlen, D. J. (1989) 'Experimental induction of infanticide in female Wattled Jacanas', *Auk*, 106: 1–7.

Emlen, S. T. and Oring, L. W. (1977) 'Ecology, sexual selection and the evolution of mating systems', *Science*, 197: 215–23.

Enquist, M. and Leimar, O. (1990) 'The evolution of fatal fighting', *Animal Behaviour*, 39: 1–9.

Farrington, D. P. (1991) *Childhood Aggression and Adult Violence: Early Precursors and Later-life Outcomes*, Cambridge: Cambridge University Press.

Fergusson, D. M., Fleming, J. and O'Neill, D. P. (1972) *Child Abuse in New Zealand*, Wellington, New Zealand: Government of New Zealand Printer.

Finn, P. and Bragg, B. W. E. (1986) 'Perception of the risk of an accident by young and older drivers', *Accident Analysis and Prevention*, 18: 289–98.

Fishbain, D. A., Fletcher, J. R., Aldrich, T. E. and Davis, J. H. (1987) 'Relationship between Russian roulette deaths and risk-taking behavior: a controlled study', *American Journal of Psychiatry*, 144: 463–567.

Flinn, M. V. and Low, B. S. (1986) 'Resource distribution, social competition, and mating patterns in human societies', in D. I. Rubenstein and R. W. Wrangham (eds) *Ecological Aspects of Social Evolution*, Princeton, NJ: Princeton University Press.

Gardner, W. (1993) 'A life-span theory of risk-taking', in N. J. Bell and R. W. Bell (eds) *Adolescent Risk Taking*, Newbury Park, CA: Sage.

Gove, W. R. (1985) 'The effect of age and gender on deviant behavior: a biopsycho-social perspective', in A. S. Rossi (ed.) *Gender and the Life Course*, New York: Aldine.

Hagan, J. (1990a) 'The structuration of gender and deviance: a power-control theory of vulnerability to crime and the search for deviant exit roles', *Canadian Review of Sociology and Anthropology*, 27: 137–56.

—— (1990b) 'Destiny and drift: subcultural preferences, status attainments, and the risks and rewards of youth', *American Sociological Review*, 56: 567–82.

Hamilton, W. D. (1964) 'The genetical evolution of social behaviour, I and II', *Journal of Theoretical Biology*, 7: 1–52.

—— (1979) 'Wingless and fighting males in fig wasps and other insects', in M. S. Blum and N. A. Blum (eds) *Sexual Selection and Reproductive Competition in Insects*, New York: Academic Press.

Harcourt, A. H. and de Waal, F. B. M. (1992) *Coalitions and Alliances in Humans and other Animals*, New York: Oxford University Press.

Hewlett, B. S. (1988) 'Sexual selection and paternal investment among Aka pygmies', in L. Betzig, M. Borgerhoff Mulder and P. Turke (eds) *Human Reproductive Behaviour*, Cambridge: Cambridge University Press.

Hill, K. and Kaplan, H. (1988) 'Tradeoffs in male and female reproductive strategies among the Ache, Part 2', in L. Betzig, M. Borgerhoff Mulder and P. Turke (eds) *Human Reproductive Behaviour*, Cambridge: Cambridge University Press.

Hines, M., Allen, L. S. and Gorski, R. A. (1992) 'Sex differences in subregions of the medial nucleus of the amygdala and the bed nucleus of the stria terminalis of the rat', *Brain Research*, 579: 321–6.

Hirschi, T. and Gottfredson, M. (1983) 'Age and the explanation of crime', *American Journal of Sociology*, 89: 552–84.

Holinger, P. C. (1987) *Violent Deaths in the United States*, New York: Guilford Press.

Huntingford, F. and Turner, A. (1987) *Animal Conflict*, London: Chapman & Hall.

Jackson, T. T. and Gray, M. (1976) 'Field study of risk-taking behavior of automobile drivers', *Perceptual and Motor Skills*, 43: 471–4.

Jonah, B. A. (1986) 'Accident risk and risk-taking behaviour among young drivers', *Accident Analysis and Prevention*, 18: 255–71.

Kahneman, D., Slovic, P. and Tversky, A. (1982) *Judgment under Uncertainty: Heuristics and Biases*, New York: Cambridge University Press.

Kandel, D. B. (1980) 'Drug and drinking behavior among youth', *Annual Review of Sociology*, 6: 235–85.

Kaplan, H. and Hill, K. (1985) 'Hunting ability and reproductive success among male Ache foragers: preliminary results', *Current Anthropology*, 26: 131–3.

Klama, J. (1988) *Aggression: The Myth of the Beast Within*, New York: Wiley.

Lack, D. (1954) *The Natural Regulation of Animal Numbers*, Oxford: Oxford University Press.

Loeber, R. (1990) 'Development and risk factors of juvenile antisocial behavior and delinquency', *Clinical Psychology Review*, 10: 1–41.

Lorenz, K. Z. (1966) *On Aggression*, New York: Harcourt, Brace & World.

Low, B. S. (1989) 'Cross-cultural patterns in the training of children: an evolutionary perspective', *Journal of Comparative Psychology*, 103: 311–19.

Lyng, S. (1990) 'Edgework: a social psychological analysis of voluntary risk taking', *American Journal of Sociology*, 95: 851–86.

McComas, A. J., Sica, R. E. P. and Petito, F. (1973) 'Muscle strength in boys of different ages', *Journal of Neurology, Neurosurgery and Psychiatry*, 36: 171–3.

Matthews, M. L. and Moran, A. R. (1986) 'Age differences in male drivers' perception of accident risk: the role of perceived driving ability', *Accident Analysis and Prevention*, 18: 299–313.

Matthiessen, P. (1962) *Under the Mountain Wall: A Chronicle of Two Seasons in the Stone Age*, New York: Viking.

Maxson, S. J. and Oring, L. W. (1980) 'Breeding season time and energy budgets of the polyandrous spotted sandpiper', *Behaviour*, 74: 200–63.

Maynard Smith, J. (1974) 'The theory of games and the evolution of animal conflict', *Journal of Theoretical Biology*, 47: 209–22.

—— (1982) *Evolution and the Theory of Games*, Cambridge: Cambridge University Press.

Mayr, E. (1983) 'How to carry out the adaptationist program?', *American Naturalist*, 121: 324–34.

Mead, M. (1935) *Sex and Temperament in Three Primitive Societies*, New York: Morrow.

Mednick, S. A., Pollock, V., Volavka, J. and Gabrielli, W. F. (1982) 'Biology and violence', in M. E. Wolfgang and N. A. Weiner (eds) *Criminal Violence*, Beverly Hills, CA: Sage.

Messner, S. F. and Sampson, R. J. (1991) 'The sex ratio, family disruption, and rates of violent crime: the paradox of demographic structure', *Social Forces*, 69: 693–713.

Messner, S. F. and Tardiff, K. (1986) 'Economic inequality and levels of homicide: an analysis of urban neighbourhoods', *Criminology*, 24: 297–317.

Mock, D. W. (1987) 'Siblicide, parent–offspring conflict, and unequal parental investment by egrets and herons', *Behavioral Ecology and Sociobiology*, 20: 247–56.

Moffitt, T. E. (1990) 'Juvenile delinquency and attention deficit disorder: boys' developmental trajectories from age 3 to age 15', *Child Development*, 61: 893–910.

Moore, R. J. (1972) 'Canadian adolescents and the challenge to demonstrate competence at personal physical risk', *Adolescence*, 7: 245–64.

Mrosovsky, N. and Sherry, D. F. (1980) 'Animal anorexias', *Science*, 207: 837–42.

Murdock, G. P. (1967) *Ethnographic Atlas*, Pittsburgh, PA: University of Pittsburgh Press.

Murray, M. P., Duthie, E. H., Gambert, S. R., Sepic, S. B. and Mollinger, L.A. (1985) 'Age-related differences in knee muscle strength in normal women', *Journal of Gerontology*, 40: 275–80.

Nisbett, R. and Ross, L. (1980) *Human Inference: Strategies and Shortcomings of Social Judgment*, Englewood Cliffs, NJ: Prentice-Hall.

O'Connor, R. J. (1978) 'Brood reduction in birds: selection for fratricide, infanticide, and suicide?', *Animal Behaviour*, 26: 79–96.

Oring, L. W., Colwell, M. A. and Reed, J. M. (1991) 'Lifetime reproductive success in the spotted sandpiper (*Actitis macularia*): sex differences and variance components', *Behavioral Ecology and Sociobiology*, 28: 425–32.

Parker, G. A. (1974) 'Assessment strategy and the evolution of animal conflicts', *Journal of Theoretical Biology*, 47: 223–43.

Parker, R. N. (1989) 'Poverty, subculture of violence, and type of homicide', *Social Forces*, 47: 983–1007.

Polk, K. and Ranson, D. (1991) 'The role of gender in intimate violence', *Australia and New Zealand Journal of Criminology*, 24: 15–24.

Popp, J. L. and DeVore, I. (1979) 'Aggressive competition and social dominance theory', in D. A. Hamburg and E. R. McCown (eds) *The Great Apes*, Menlo Park, CA: Benjamin/Cummings.

Pressley, P. H. (1981) 'Parental effort and the evolution of nest-guarding tactics in the threespine stickleback, *Gasterosteus aculeatus* L.', *Evolution*, 35: 282–95.

Real, L. and Caraco, T. (1986) 'Risk and foraging in stochastic environments', *Annual Review of Ecology and Systematics*, 17: 371–90.

Robins, L. N. (1979) 'Follow-up studies', in H. C. Quay and J. S. Werry (eds) *Psychopathological Disorders of Childhood*, New York: John Wiley.

Robins, L. N. and Rutter, M. R. (1990) *Straight and Devious Pathways to Adulthood*, Cambridge: Cambridge University Press.

Rogers, A. (1993) 'Evolution of time preference by natural selection', Unpublished manuscript.

Rothe, J. P. (1987) *Rethinking Young Drivers*, North Vancouver: Insurance Corporation of British Columbia.

Rubin, P. H. and Paul, C. W. (1979) 'An evolutionary model of taste for risk', *Economic Inquiry*, 17: 585–96.

Sampson, R. J. (1987) 'Urban black violence: the effect of male joblessness and family disruption', *American Journal of Sociology*, 93: 348–82.

Schonfeld, I. S., Shaffer, D., O'Connor, P. and Portney, S. (1988) 'Conduct disorder and cognitive functioning: testing three causal hypotheses', *Child Development*, 59: 993–1007.

Shephard, R. J. (1986) *Fitness of a Nation*, Basel: Karger.

Sherry, D. F., Mrosovsky, N. and Hogan, J. A. (1980) 'Weight loss and anorexia during incubation in birds', *Journal of Comparative and Physiological Psychology*, 94: 89–98.

Skinner, B. F. (1957) *Verbal Behavior*, New York: Appleton-Century-Crofts.

Slovic, P. (1987) 'Perception of risk', *Science*, 236: 280–5.

Smuts, B. (1992) 'Male aggression against women: an evolutionary perspective', *Human Nature*, 3: 1–44.

Sober, E. (1983) 'Mentalism and behaviorism in comparative psychology', in D. W. Rajecki (ed.) *Comparing Behavior*, Hillsdale, NJ: Erlbaum.

Steffensmeier, D. J., Allan, E. A., Harer, M. D. and Streifel, C. (1989) 'Age and the distribution of crime', *American Journal of Sociology*, 94: 803–31.

Stephens, M. L. (1982) 'Mate takeover and possible infanticide by a female northern jacana (*Jacana spinosa*)', *Animal Behaviour*, 30: 1253–4.

Symons, D. (1979) *The Evolution of Human Sexuality*, New York: Oxford University Press.

—— (1987) 'If we're all Darwinians, what's the fuss about?', in C. B. Crawford, M. F. Smith and D. L. Krebs (eds) *Sociobiology and Psychology*, Hillsdale, NJ: Erlbaum.

—— (1992) 'On the use and misuse of Darwinism in the study of human behavior', in J. H. Barkow, L. Cosmides and J. Tooby (eds) *The Adapted Mind*, New York: Oxford University Press.

Thomas, J. R. and French, K. E. (1985) 'Gender differences across age in motor performance: a meta-analysis', *Psychological Bulletin*, 98: 260–82.

Thornhill, N. W. and Thornhill, R. (1990) 'Evolutionary analysis of psychological pain of rape victims I: the effects of victim's age and marital status', *Ethology and Sociobiology*, 11: 155–76.

Thornhill, R. and Sauer, K. P. (1991) 'The notal organ of the scorpionfly (*Panorpa vulgaris*): an adaptation to coerce mating duration', *Behavioral Ecology*, 2: 156–64.

Thornhill, R. and Thornhill, N. W. (1983) 'Human rape: an evolutionary analysis', *Ethology and Sociobiology*, 4: 137–73.

—— (1992) 'The evolutionary psychology of men's coercive sexuality', *Behavioral and Brain Sciences*, 15: 363–421.

Tieger, T. (1980) 'On the biological basis of sex differences in aggression', *Child Development*, 51: 943–63.

Tinbergen, N. (1953) *Social Behaviour in Animals*, London: Methuen.

Tittle, C. R. (1988) 'Two empirical regularities (maybe) in search of an explanation: commentary on the age/crime debate', *Criminology*, 26: 75–85.

Tolman, E. C. (1932) *Purposive Behavior in Animals and Man*, New York: Appleton-Century-Crofts.

Tonkin, R. S. (1987) 'Adolescent risk-taking behavior', *Journal of Adolescent Health Care*, 8: 213–20.

Tonry, M. H., Ohlin, L. E. and Farrington, D. P. (1991) *Human Development and Criminal Behavior*, New York: Springer-Verlag.

Tooby, J. and Cosmides, L. (1989) 'Evolutionary psychology and the generation of culture, Part 1: Theoretical considerations', *Ethology and Sociobiology*, 10: 29–51.

—— (1990a) 'The past explains the present: emotional adaptations and the structure of ancestral environments', *Ethology and Sociobiology*, 11: 375–424.

—— (1990b) 'On the universality of human nature and the uniqueness of the individual: the role of genetics and adaptation', *Journal of Personality*, 58: 17–67.

—— (1992) 'The psychological foundations of culture', in J. H. Barkow, L. Cosmides and J. Tooby (eds) The Adapted Mind, New York: Oxford University Press.

Tooby, J. and DeVore, I. (1987) 'The reconstruction of hominid behavioral evolution through strategic modeling', in W. G. Kinzey (ed.) *The Evolution of Human Behavior: Primate Models*, Albany, NY: SUNY Press.

Tremblay, R. E., Masse, B., Perron, D., Leblanc, M., Schwartzman, A. E. and Ledingham, J. E. (1992) 'Early disruptive behavior, poor school achievement, delinquent behavior, and delinquent personality: longitudinal analyses', *Journal of Consulting and Clinical Psychology*, 60: 64–72.

Trivers, R. L. (1972) 'Parental investment and sexual selection', in B. Campbell (ed.) *Sexual Selection and the Descent of Man 1871–1971*, Chicago: Aldine.

—— (1974) 'Parent–offspring conflict', *American Zoologist*, 14: 249–64.

Wadsworth, J., Burnell, I., Taylor, B. and Butler, N. (1983) 'Family type and accidents in preschool children', *Journal of Epidemiology and Community Health*, 37: 100–4.

Weiger, W. A. and Bear, D. M. (1988) 'An approach to the neurology of aggression', *Journal of Psychiatric Research*, 22: 85–98.

Widom, C. S. (1989a) 'The cycle of violence', *Science*, 244: 160–6.

—— (1989b) 'Does violence beget violence? a critical examination of the literature', *Psychological Bulletin*, 106: 3–28.

Williams, G. C. (1957) 'Pleiotropy, natural selection, and the evolution of senescence', *Evolution*, 11: 398–411.

—— (1966) *Adaptation and Natural Selection*, Princeton, NJ: Princeton University Press.

—— (1971) *Group Selection*, Chicago: Aldine/Atherton.

—— (1992) *Natural Selection: Domains, Levels and Challenges*, New York: Oxford University Press.

Williams, G. C. and Nesse, R. (1991) 'The dawn of Darwinian medicine', *Quarterly Review of Biology*, 66: 1–22.

Wilson, J. Q. and Herrnstein, R. J. (1985) *Human Nature*, New York: Simon & Schuster.

Wilson, M. (1989) 'Marital conflict and homicide in evolutionary perspective', in R. W. Bell and N. J. Bell (eds) *Sociobiology and the Social Sciences*, Lubbock, TX: Texas Technical University Press.

Wilson, M. and Daly, M. (1985) 'Competitiveness, risk-taking and violence: the young male syndrome', *Ethology and Sociobiology*, 6: 59–73.

—— (1992) 'The man who mistook his wife for a chattel', in J. H. Barkow, L. Cosmides and J. Tooby (eds) *The Adapted Mind*, New York: Oxford University Press.

—— (1993a) 'The psychology of parenting in evolutionary perspective and the case of human filicide', in S. Parmigiani and F. S. vom Saal (eds) *Infanticide and Parental Care*, London: Harwood Academic Publishers.

—— (1993b) 'Lethal confrontational violence among young men', in N. J. Bell and R. W. Bell (eds) *Adolescent Risk Taking*, Newbury Park, CA: Sage.

Wilson, M., Daly, M. and Weghorst, S. J. (1980) 'Household composition and the risk of child abuse and neglect', *Journal of Biosocial Science*, 12: 333–40.
Wilson, W. J. and Aponte, R. (1985) 'Urban poverty', *American Sociological Review*, 11: 231–58.
Wynne-Edwards, V. C. (1962) *Animal Dispersion in Relation to Social Behaviour*, Edinburgh: Oliver & Boyd.

15

TRADITIONAL SOCIALIZATION
THEORIES OF VIOLENCE
A critical examination

*John P. Hoffmann, Timothy O. Ireland and
Cathy Spatz Widom*[1]

This chapter presents a critical examination of traditional socialization theories of violent behaviour. A fundamental assumption, which we believe reflects the theoretical and empirical literature to be discussed, is that explanations of violence are generally explanations of male violence. Studies of violent offenders are typically studies of males (for example, Lewis *et al.* 1989). Males are also the sole focus of many self-report studies of criminal violence (for instance, Capaldi and Patterson 1992). We make these assertions at the beginning of this chapter to provide a framework for the discussion that follows.

Originally, we intended to focus on violence, defined by Weiner, Zahn and Sagi (1990: xiii) as 'physical force or threat of physical force that results in physical or nonphysical harm to one or more persons . . . against the will or without the consent of the other person or persons'. However, in examining the major theories included in the discussion here, we found that much of the research and relevant theorizing draws heavily on the aggression literature. With a strict adherence to only theories of violence, this chapter would be extremely brief. With the inclusion of theories of aggression, the field is more adequately represented. We have opted to take a pragmatic approach and to include theories of aggression and violence in our considerations. None the less, it should be stressed at the outset that aggression is not synonymous with violence, although it is beyond the scope of this chapter to discuss this issue (see Kleinig 1991 and Introduction to this volume).

The chapter is organized into two parts. The first part briefly reviews and evaluates major traditional socialization theories of aggression and violence, while the second part presents a number of issues which we believe require further theoretical and empirical attention in the future. We have restricted our discussion to traditional socialization theories of aggression and violence. A discussion of biological theories of violence is omitted from this chapter not because we believe they are irrelevant or unimportant (Widom 1991) but because they are addressed elsewhere in this volume (Chapter 13).

TRADITIONAL SOCIALIZATION THEORIES OF VIOLENCE

Since, according to psychoanalytic theory, aggression is a natural drive that can lead to violent responses, the important task for this approach is to explain how these impulses – defined as discharges of psychic energy from the id – are controlled by other aspects of the personality, specifically the ego (Pulkkinen 1986). Although early psychoanalytic explanations for excessively aggressive behaviour focused on an 'out-of-control' id, studies of delinquents by Redl and Wineman (1951, 1952; see also Redl and Toch 1979) suggested that the most appropriate focus is the ego. Ego development is considered the primary controlling mechanism over natural impulses such as aggression. When the ego is inappropriately developed, due either to faulty maturation or socialization (see Erikson 1950), impulsivity, anxiety and less control over aggression may be the consequences (Redl and Toch 1979). According to this approach, impaired ego development occurs with inadequate socialization. This is supported by studies of violent criminal offenders which indicate that they tend to come from cruel, harsh, conflict-ridden homes (for example, Farrington 1991; Arbuthnot et al. 1987).

Others have suggested that development of the ego should not be viewed as a simple continuum with an improperly developed ego at one end and a well-developed ego at the other. More often than not, face-to-face violence and criminal behaviour have been equated with an undercontrolled individual. However, Block and Gjerde (1986) have argued that both an undercontrolled or an overcontrolled ego may result in aggression or violence. Block and Gjerde point to some evidence indicating that extremely violent criminals are more controlled than either non-assaultive criminals or normal individuals (Megargee 1970; Block and Gjerde 1986). Thus, a simple explanation of improper ego development may be misleading for understanding violent behaviour.

Berkowitz's (1969, 1989) frustration-aggression theory specifies that frustrating experiences act as instigators of aggressive behaviour, heightening the 'drive level and thereby presumably sparking aggressive behavior' (Eron 1987: 436). In contrast to the psychoanalytic perspective, individuals are motivated to behave aggressively by a frustration-instigated drive rather than by innate aggressive forces.

Although frustration was originally conceptualized as a necessary condition for aggression, it is clear that aggressive responses follow from a number of other conditions in addition to frustration, and aggression is only one of several potential responses to frustration (Bandura 1973). In more recent revisions of the original theory, Berkowitz (1989) has called attention to the findings that aggressive cues (for example, guns) and negative affect are also often required before frustration results in aggressive or violent responses. Again, this is an example of how a theory of aggressive behaviour is consistent with an image of a violent male. Typically, because males use guns and weapons, they are exposed to and have experience with instigators of aggression. Furthermore, for some young males, guns are the 'great equalizer' (Silberman 1978): 'If you feel like you're nothing, a gun can make you feel like a king' (p. 60).

Another aspect of frustration-aggression theory is that inhibition of aggression may cause displacement to occur, so that it is directed at objects (such as spouses or children) that offer a decreased threat of punishment. An additional component of this theoretical approach has postulated that direct or vicarious aggression may reduce further aggression (through the process of catharsis); however, there is only limited evidence in support of this view (see Bandura 1973; Hokanson 1970; Parke and Slaby 1983).

Probably the most prominent of the socialization theories is that which has been labelled 'social learning' by Bandura (1973, 1977). In contrast to inner drives, or aggression in response to certain frustrating situations, Bandura described the origins of behaviour in the learning environment of the individual. Learning occurs through direct reinforcement (rewards and punishments) and observation; it can be directly experienced or result from observing another's behaviour. In order for observation to become behaviour, one must retain the behaviour in memory. The symbols of the behaviour that reside in memory must then be converted into actions similar to the observed behaviour. This is often limited by the skill level of the individual. Finally, repeating the behaviour is governed by whether it causes reinforcement or punishment, and whether there is sufficient motivation for the actor to undertake the behaviour (Bandura 1977).

Recognizing that many models in a person's life influence behaviour, Bandura (1973) identified three in particular that affect criminal behaviour: family, subculture (such as peer groups), and culture (for example, symbols such as television and movies). One may therefore learn violent behaviour through modelling or renforcement of behaviour in the family (see, for instance, Gully et al. 1981; Kalmuss 1984; Roopnarine et al. 1988; Farrington 1991), in peer groups (for example, Cairns and Cairns 1991), and from television and movies (Huesmann et al. 1992; National Institute of Mental Health 1982; Eron et al. 1972; Goldstein 1986; see, however, Freedman 1992, 1984).

Another component of Bandura's theory involves the concepts of self-regulation and self-efficacy. Individuals develop beliefs about their abilities and, in turn, the evaluation of beliefs influences whether or not certain types of behaviour are attempted, and whether they provide reinforcement for future behaviour. For example, people who see aggression or violence as a source of pride or self-esteem may act out violently in order 'to experience the self-satisfaction that is associated with acting aggressively' (Parke and Slaby 1983: 556). Again, this is a good example of theory development closely aligned with male violence. For males, violent crimes such as robbery and rape often represent attempts to feel masculine and powerful – to control, when in fact these young males often are unable to legitimately fulfil societal expectations for the traditional male role (see also Chapters 7 and 14). Silberman (1978) described robbery as a group activity where participation demonstrates and reinforces a young man's virility and manhood to his peers: 'People got to prove things to people. My partner didn't think I could do it' (p. 56); youths turn to robbery to prove things to themselves as well as to others. 'I just like the feeling of the dude, you know . . . like if I had a .38 right now, I can make you do just about anything I wanted you to do, see, and you couldn't do nothing about it' (p. 56).

Social learning theory emphasizes a reciprocal relationship between personal (self-regulation and self-efficacy) and situational characteristics in explaining aggression (Bandura 1986). To a certain extent, research supports general principles of social learning theory. Children, for example, will imitate adults who punch dolls, especially when the observers are angry and when the aggression appears justified (Bandura 1973). Adults who as children observed hitting between their parents are more likely to be involved in severe marital aggression, even more so than those who were hit as teenagers by their parents (Kalmuss 1984).

Examinations of the effects of witnessing family violence on males and females have produced equivocal results. However, while Gelles (1976) found that physical aggression in the childhood family increased the likelihood that men would perpetrate and women would be victimized by marital aggression, Pagelow (1981) found that exposure to the father beating the mother was related to a man's subsequent commission of wife abuse but not to a woman being victimized by such abuse. Ulbrich and Huber (1981) demonstrated that exposure to parent–parent hitting related to men's but not to women's attitudes towards husbands hitting their wives. And Kalmuss (1984) found that exposure to the father hitting the mother increased the likelihood of husband-to-wife *and* wife-to-husband severe aggression in the next generation. Kalmuss's (1984) findings in particular provide a clear challenge to the long-held notion that children imitate the same-sex parent more than an opposite-sex model. In addition, modelling theory would have a difficult time explaining the fact that although females are more likely to be sexually abused than males, they rarely commit sexual abuse as adults (Chapter 12).

More recent work on aggression that further elaborates social learning theory is exemplified by the writings of Eron and his colleagues and Patterson. Patterson's work is based upon a sample of boys, whereas Eron's longitudinal study involves males and females.

Eron (1987) contends that one of the most important determinants of aggression is a lack of support from parents. Parents teach and reinforce aggression. When this is coupled with poor parental management techniques, such as harsh discipline, children may acquire few skills beyond aggression

(Eron et al. 1991). Excessively harsh or inconsistent discipline, for example, especially when combined with coercive and hostile parenting approaches, provides models of aggression that are reinforced if few alternatives are present (such as induction) (Eron 1987; Morton 1987). These factors are also related to violent offending in adulthood (Farrington 1991).

Patterson (Patterson 1982; Patterson et al. 1989, 1991) has called attention to the effects of parental and family processes on aggression and antisocial behaviour in boys. Patterson's group found that families of aggressive boys are marked by high levels of coercive behaviour on the part of parents and children. Parents in these families tend to be harsh and inconsistent in their approach to discipline, less positively involved with their children, and less effective at supervising their children's activities (Patterson et al. 1989; Patterson and Dishion 1985; Loeber and Dishion 1983; see also Morton 1987). Positive parenting is noticeably absent (Snyder and Patterson 1987).

Patterson asserts that the family trains the child to perform antisocial acts through interactions between parent and child that are repeatedly coercive and often escalate to the point of physical attacks. The child learns to apply coercive behaviour to escape aversive situations and eventually learns to control situations with other family members through coercive interactions. Aggression is thus reinforced (Patterson et al. 1991). Moreover, children in these families are provided with few pro-social skills, and consequently coercion becomes normative (Patterson et al. 1989).

Cognitive aspects of social development have received increased attention in recent years, although it has only recently been applied to the study of aggression and violence from a social learning perspective (Perry et al. 1986). Bandura's (1986) social cognitive theory, for example, argues for a triadic reciprocal model that includes behaviour, environment, cognition and other personal attributes. This model also allows for both biological and environmental processes to influence behaviour; that is, social learning within the confines of biological capabilities.

The cognitive perspective offers a significant shift in theoretical development surrounding aggression. The theories focusing on internal explanations generally offer a unidirectional causal model in which personal attributes affect behaviour, with those personal attributes appearing during infancy and early childhood having an influence throughout the life cycle. While theorists such as Patterson (1982) suggest a reciprocal relationship between the individual and the environment, there is often a failure to take into account the individual's perceptions of capabilities and knowledge of consequences. Bandura's (1986) modifications argue that behaviour should not be considered as a purely endogenous variable, but rather as one that has a transactional relationship with both the environment and the individual.

Recent research on the development of aggressiveness and antisocial behaviour has taken this more transactional approach. For example, this line of thinking has been examined extensively by Cairns et al. (1989); Dodge and his colleagues (Dodge 1980, 1991; Dodge and Newman 1981; Dodge *et al.* 1990; Dodge and Tomlin 1987; Steinberg and Dodge 1983; Weiss *et al.* 1992); and Perry *et al.* (1986, 1989). Perry *et al.* (1986), for example, examined two aspects of cognition that may influence a child's decision to employ aggression or violence: perceptions of self-efficacy, which refer to a child's perception of ability to perform the aggressive activity, and response outcome expectancies, which refer to a child's belief about the reinforcing or punishing consequences of aggression. They concluded that both factors need to be taken into account by cognitive models of aggression.

Dodge's research indicates that aggressive children attribute more hostile intentions to others than non-aggressive children, and also interpret aggression as positive (Dodge 1980, 1991; Dodge and Newman 1981; Dodge *et al.* 1990; Dodge and Tomlin 1987; Steinberg and Dodge 1983; Weiss *et al.* 1992). These research findings suggest that aggressive children tend to have deficient social processing capabilities and a lack of behavioural strategies to settle interpersonal disputes. Interestingly, research on adult violent offenders also indicates that they tend to overattribute hostile intentions to others, and see aggression in a favourable light (Toch 1969).

Integration of each of these areas of cognitive research on aggression may eventually increase the overall efficacy of a cognitive theory on aggression. Perry *et al.* (1986) argued that the attributional bias model being developed by Dodge may be further explicated if self-efficacy and response outcome expectancies are taken into consideration. They contended that even in the presence of attributional bias 'it seems unlikely that children who erroneously interpret provocation by others as hostility will respond aggressively unless they expect an aggressive response to be successful in eliminating their aversive state or otherwise improve their plight' (Perry *et al.* 1986: 708). Moreover, research by Cairns *et al.* (1989) suggests the importance of employing longitudinal data to assess whether one's cognitive abilities converge between self-assessment and other-assessment in terms of aggression. This convergence may act to increase a child's perception of his ability to perform the aggression, and a child's perception that such behaviour is expected. This is particularly appropriate as an explanation of male violence. When boys are encouraged to be violent and have the physical capability to be so, aggressiveness is likely to appear.

In sum, traditional theories have increasingly recognized the importance of a cognitive component to explanations of violence. However, theories of violence, developed primarily with and for male subjects, remain theories of male violence. Although this work provides an important foundation for understanding aggressive and violent behaviour, we now highlight a number of research and theoretical issues which we believe merit scholarly consideration in the future.

FUTURE RESEARCH AND THEORETICAL ISSUES

(1) Traditional socialization theories are designed to explain antisocial behaviour, aggression and delinquency. To what extent are these theories adequate explanations for violent behaviour? Is violence aetiologically similar to aggression (that is, is it the manifestation of extreme aggression?) or do the origins and developmental processes for violence and aggression differ?

Some light can be shed upon the relationship between antisocial behaviour, delinquency, aggression and violence by examining the literature on the general versus specific nature of problem behaviour. Recent empirical research supports both the notions of commonality and specificity in problem behaviour. Aggression (Cairns *et al.* 1989; Huesmann *et al.* 1984; Olweus 1979) and antisocial behaviour (Loeber 1982; Patterson 1992) have consistently been identified as relatively time-stable traits, suggesting a thread of commonality between aggression/antisocial behaviour and delinquency (Farrington 1986; Patterson *et al.* 1992; Roff and Wirt 1984), criminality (Farrington 1986, 1989, 1991; Roff and Wirt 1984), and violence (Capaldi and Patterson 1992; Farrington 1989, 1991). Capaldi and Patterson (1992), Farrington (1989) and Hamparian *et al.* (1978) have similarly concluded that 'aggression and violence are elements of a more general antisocial tendency and that the predictors of aggression and violence are similar to the predictors of antisocial and criminal behavior in general' (Farrington 1989: 1).

Although there is considerable consensus that theories of aggression and antisocial behaviour are relevant for violent behaviour as well, we question whether a reliance on models of antisocial and aggressive behaviour adequately address violent behaviour. Although aggression and violence have similar covariates, the possibility remains that unique theoretical contributions (specificity) will discriminate between aggression and violence, and generalized delinquency and violence.

If in fact violence can be considered aggravated aggression (Megargee 1982), or physical aggression (Straus 1991), the question is: what factors lead some aggressive individuals to engage in violent behaviour? For example, the frustration-aggression hypothesis fails to explain why some frustrating stimuli lead a few individuals to seek violent responses. Berkowitz's (1989) recent reformulation suggests that frustration leads to negative affect which then leads to aggression. But this does not explain specific violent responses to negative affect. Empirical evaluations of this reformulation suggest that other factors (such as being the target of aggression) mediate the relationship between negative affect and violent behaviour, suggesting a need to consider the violent actor's cognitive interpretations of an aggressive situation (Felson 1992). Thus, research is needed on situational components and how one is socialized to respond to these components. One the other hand, Bandura (1979) identified a range of instigational mechanisms that may lead to violent responses. These include physical assaults, verbal threats and insults, and aversive conditions of life. Further understanding of how individuals are socialized to respond to these instigators is required since not all individuals respond through violent means.

(2) Do traditional socialization theories adequately incorporate a developmental perspective?

Although more recent theories have, at least to some degree, implicitly incorporated a developmental orientation, psychoanalytic theory clearly ignores the changing conditions of the individual and the environment as he or she passes through time. In addition, social learning theories 'view life patterns as largely the product of childhood socialization' and ignore preceding physiological events and subsequent social experiences in adulthood (Bandura 1986: 28).

While implicit recognition of developmental processes appears in some theoretical work, little contemporary theory-building explicitly address developmental concerns (Farrington *et al.* 1990; Loeber and Le Blanc 1990). Recently, however, several researchers have incorporated developmental processes into specific theoretical models. For example, Patterson and his colleagues have proposed a theoretical model to explain different patterns of onset of antisocial behaviour (Patterson *et al.* 1989). Patterson (1992) proposed a model analogous to a chimera in which the same general construct takes on different, additional manifestations as it passes through time, the end result being related to the original, but at the same time different. Sampson and Laub (1990) have also emphasized de-escalation and desistance of criminal behaviour in a theory of informal social control.

Cairns and Cairns (1986) suggested that the lack of theory construction across ontogeny may be attributable, in part, to the short-term nature of many studies. In addition, incorporation of developmental considerations into theories of delinquency and crime has met with stiff resistance from those proposing a static model to explain deviant behaviours (Wilson and Herrnstein 1985; Gottfredson and Hirschi 1986, 1990).

Very little developmental research has been undertaken to explain violent behaviour, however. Another neglected area of research deals with the identification of stages (Kandel 1989) or stepping-stones (Farrington 1986) to violent offending. Although a number of studies have identified sequences or stages of general offending behaviour, Loeber and Le Blanc (1990) concluded that there is scant available information on this issue. Furthermore, although one would expect that violent behaviour occurs at a later stage in the sequence, there is a dearth of relevant empirical evidence. Nevertheless, since several studies have found evidence of aetiological commonality among types of problem behaviour, it is very likely that there is some developmental pattern or patterns involved in the path to violent behaviour.

Similarly, the relationship between early onset of antisocial and delinquent behaviour and subsequent violent behaviour (Nagin and Farrington 1992) has not been adequately addressed. While a number of researchers have concluded that early age of first arrest is one of the best predictors of future chronic offending (Farrington *et al.* 1990; Blumstein *et al.* 1986), others have reported that multiple offending is one of the best predictors for violent offending (Capaldi and Patterson 1992; Farrington 1989).

Those who eschew the developmental perspective suggest that early onset is not causally related to persistent offending, but reflects a time-stable antisocial construct, 'criminal propensity' (Gottfredson and Hirschi 1990). Recent empirical research suggests that early onset may be 'an extension of a pattern of high rates of antisocial acts already in place in late childhood' (Patterson *et al.* 1992: 350). Nagin and Farrington (1992) address this specific question and find no causal relationship between early onset and subsequent offending. Rather, their findings support the presence of a time-stable individual difference in criminal potential with early onset reflecting a selection process, not a causal relationship (Nagin and Farrington 1992). In light of the relative stability of aggression and antisocial behaviour (Eron *et al.* 1987; Lefkowitz *et al.* 1977; Olweus 1979), these findings imply that aggression may not be causally related to violent behaviour, but rather both may have the same determinants. This line of research, which indirectly questions whether aggression is causally related to violence or whether aggression and violence are different manifestations of some underlying construct, warrants greater research attention.

Although current research suggests the presence of a stable construct affecting both onset and persistence of offending, additional empirical questions related to the developmental perspective deserve attention. For example, in a recent analysis of violent offending, Rivera and Widom (1990) found that more than a third of the sample of violent offenders had no arrests for violence in childhood (up to the age of 18 years), but had arrests for violence as adults. The more traditional pattern of early onset violent offenders represented 37 per cent of the group of violent offenders. The remaining third were individuals with non-violent arrests as juveniles and violent arrests as adults. Fully 63 per cent of this sample of violent offenders became violent as adults.

Thus, there may very well be different pathways to violence, some of which begin with traditional manifestations of antisocial and violent behaviour. For others, however, there may be other factors which provoke violence at later points in life. Most existing research assumes that it is early starters and chronic offenders who become violent.

Some recent research suggests that there are at least two pathways to delinquency: an early-starter and a late-starter model (Farrington 1986; Farrington *et al.* 1990; Huizinga *et al.* 1991; Loeber 1988; Loeber *et al.* 1991; Nagin and Farrington 1992; Patterson *et al.* 1989; Patterson and Yoerger 1991). Loeber (1988) proposes three pathways for delinquents which are to some degree dependent upon whether the individual was an early starter or a late starter (sec also Farrington *et al.* 1990; Loeber and Le Blanc 1990). Aggressive versatile youth are early starters and are involved in property crime, illicit drug use and violent crime; non-aggressive antisocial youths have somewhat later onset and are involved in property crime and illicit drug use; and the third path involves only drug users who have the latest onset and no antecedent conduct problems (Loeber 1988; Farrington *et al.* 1990; Kandel 1989; Loeber and Le Blanc 1990).

Different developmental pathways for violent behaviour have direct implications for socialization theories. Psychoanalytic theorists as well as traditional social learning theorists would need to account for at least two different paths towards aggression or violence, although current explanations fall short. On the other hand, Patterson *et al.* (1989) have made explicit attempts to incorporate different pathways (early and late starters) into their coercion model.

We argue that a developmental perspective offers fertile ground for empirical research and theoretical explanations of violent behaviour. In addition, the introduction of cognitive aspects into research on aggression and violence further suggests the need to incorporate developmental components. Cognition is developmental in nature, and maturation of cognitive processes occurs along a relatively consistent continuum, with changes taking place with greater frequency during the early years and slowing down as the individual reaches adulthood (Kagan 1976).

Research on criminal and aggressive behaviour which considers the developmental nature of cognitive capabilities is beginning to appear. For example, Cairns *et al.* (1989) include cognitive elements into their examination of the relationship between childhood aggression and early adolescent aggression.

In addition, there may be a need for a re-conceptualization of the 'stages of development' approach. Kagan (1976: 121) offers an alternative interpretation of stages in the light of cognitive functioning by suggesting that

> it may be useful to regard basic cognitive competencies as having long developmental histories. Each of the basic cognitive processes . . . emerges in very narrow problem contexts early in development. With growth, each is applied – or generalized – to an increasing array of contexts until that competence is reliably activated in most relevant problem situations.

The difficulty in identifying stages of offending, and the occurrence of violent behaviour, may in part be explained by varying levels of cognitive development within the offending population.

(3) A broadening of traditional theorizing on violence is needed to include the role of the family and peer group.

In recent years, the scope of research has begun to broaden in an attempt to account for both the individual level and micro-level structural determinants of aggression and violence. Much has been written about the role of family in the aetiology of aggression and violence (see, for example, Capaldi and Patterson 1992; Fagan and Wexler 1987; Kruttschnitt *et al.* 1986; Patterson

298

et al. 1989; Olweus 1980), in particular the role of familial physical abuse, sexual abuse and neglect in predicting subsequent violent behaviour (Lewis *et al.* 1989; Widom 1989a, 1989b, 1989c).

This latter line of research consistently reports that maltreatment places children at greater risk for delinquency, criminality and violence (see Andrews; Browne, this volume). For example, in a direct test of the 'cycle of violence' hypothesis, Widom (1989d) found that physical abuse as a child led significantly to later violent criminal behaviour, when other relevant demographic variables such as age, sex and race were held constant. However, being *neglected* as a child also showed a significant relation to later violent criminal behaviour, and the type of abuse was not as powerful a predictor of violent criminal behaviour as the demographic characteristics. Furthermore, the majority of abused and neglected children did not have arrests for violence as juveniles or adults.

Research on the intergenerational transmission of violence is in its early stages. Although a traditional social learning or modelling approach provides an obvious explanation for the intergenerational transmission of violence, the model is challenged by the findings that not all physically abused children become violent offenders. In addition, other factors lead to violent behaviour, since the neglected children were also at increased risk. Research and theory are needed which incorporate the complexity of these and similar findings.

Although much family research has focused upon the relationship between the parent(s) and the child, the role of siblings (Hamparian *et al.* 1978; Patterson 1986) and violence between parents (Cappell and Heiner 1991; Kalmuss 1984) also needs further consideration.

Similarly, there is a need to consider the role of peers in the aetiology of violence. Peers have been consistently treated as major covariates in the study of delinquency (Warr and Stafford 1992; cf. Cairns and Cairns 1991). Therefore, it seems logical to suggest that deviant peers may play an important role in the onset or maintenance of violent behaviour. Deviant peers may reinforce a time-table antisocial predisposition, or they may causally influence violent behaviour. In either case, peers provide a social mechanism that affects aggressive and violent behaviour.

(4) Greater attention needs to be placed on the role of environmental factors or social context variables in explanations of violence.

Future research needs to take into account the social context or macro-level variables, such as socio-economic status, degree of urbanism, over-crowding, and other community factors which have often been excluded from traditional socialization theories (but see Chapter 9). Each of these variables may be involved in the occurrence of solidarity or multiple violent events.

For example, isolation from non-violent models may facilitate violent responses. If exposure is limited to violent models in the home, amongst peers and in the neighbourhood, the likelihood of violent responses in an ambiguous situation may increase (cf. Fagan *et al*. 1986; Cairns and Cairns 1991; Patterson *et al*. 1989; Short and Strodtbeck 1974). Social learning theory's emphasis on facilitative and maintenance mechanisms can be helpful here, but so far it has failed to identify specific variables.

Pro-social skills provide one potential protective mechanism from violent adaptations (Eron and Huesmann 1989). Pro-social skills include the ability or motivation to perform actions that directly benefit other individuals or groups of individuals (Eisenberg and Mussen 1989; Staub 1986). Obviously, pro-social behaviour is at odds with violent behaviour, and thus the acquisition of such skills may act to inhibit or provide alternatives to violent or aggressive behaviour (see also Gilbert, this volume).

The relationship between pro-social skills and aggression is complex and evidence is mixed; moreover, the relationship with violence is unknown (Staub 1986). According to some studies, pro-social behaviour amongst young children is positively related to aggression (Eisenberg and Mussen 1989), but this probably reflects assertiveness and not expressive aggression – see Dodge (1991) and Smith (1989) for distinctions. Empirical studies suggest that as pro-social skills are acquired, aggressiveness (in particular, extreme aggressiveness) tends to dissipate (Feshbach and Feshbach 1982). Whether such acquisition translates into protective measures against violence is unknown. None the less, when assessing the socialization of aggression and violence, it is important to consider the role of pro-social skills and behaviour since these are socialized from a young age (Grusec and Dix 1986), and may provide individuals with alternatives to violent responses. Further research is needed to study individuals who survive or overcome environmental conditions or violent social contexts that often as not lead to negative outcomes.

(5) There is a dearth of violence theory which takes into account gender.

We have asserted that much of the literature on socialization processes applies to *male* models of aggression and violence, rather than violent behaviour in general. Hopefully, it is apparent that far more is known about antisocial and aggressive behaviour amongst males than females (Loeber 1992). In part, this is due to the higher prevalence and frequency rates for problem behaviour, such as conduct disorder, aggression, delinquency, criminality and violence, in males than females (Widom 1984). For example, Chesney-Lind (1987) reports that virtually all sources of data reveal that more males than females engage in delinquency and violence, and they engage in such behaviour with greater frequency (see also Chapters 1, 7 and 14). Much of the longitudinal research on crime and delinquency examines only males (for example, Farrington 1986; Le Blanc and Frechette 1989; Patterson *et al*. 1989), or fails to provide separate analyses for males and females (Huizinga *et al*. 1991). Consequently, in both theoretical writings and empirical research, sex differences have not been addressed (Farrington 1986; Loeber *et al*. 1991; Patterson *et al*. 1989; Sampson and Laub 1990).

Generally, the literature on sex differences in delinquency and criminality assumes a social learning model based upon differential socialization or gender roles (Widom 1984; Eagly and Steffen 1986, but see Daly and Wilson, this volume). One central proposition offered to explain the gender gap in delinquency and crime is that males are socialized from an early age to be more physical and to engage in more rough-and-tumble play (see Chapter 2) than females. In at least one study, males were found to be punished physically more harshly (Eron and Huesmann 1989). Aggression amongst boys is reinforced to a greater extent by peers and by those in authority. The general social learning approach has also been linked with opportunity. This variation on social learning theory argues that not only are males socialized into aggression, but because of differential levels of parental monitoring and supervision, males also have greater opportunities to engage in delinquent and criminal behaviour (Maccoby 1986).

Recent examinations of sex differences in aggressive behaviour have provided support for an elaborated social learning model. Although traditional social learning models anticipate lower levels of predictability for females with conduct disorders because of the 'social disapproval of overt aggressive expression in girls' (Cairns and Cairns 1986, citing Kagan and Moss 1962), Cairns and Cairns (1986) and Robins (1986) suggest that the presence of a low prevalence female behaviour (for example, conduct disorder) might better predict later problems (such as violence) in females than in males.

Robins (1986) finds support for the latter hypothesis, but only when examining subsequent externalizing and internalizing behaviour. Loeber (1992: 269) also reports a 'gender paradox':

> once females engage in patterned problem behavior, the predictability of later delinquency is as high as that of males, although some studies have shown higher predictability. Conduct disordered females are also at a higher risk than males for developing comorbid conditions.

The presence of such a paradox suggests that there may be more at work than socialization processes. Certain females, even when social stigma is greater than that for males engaging in identical behaviour, are at greater rather than lesser risk for future problem behaviour, when compared to their male counterparts. Thus, other factors, such as cognitive functioning, must be considered in future research.

(6) Traditional socialization theories fail to adequately integrate consideration of the target of the violence. Violence against whom?

Another area of research suggests the need to take into account the sex of the target of aggression. Eagley and Steffen (1986), in a meta-analytic review of literature on adult aggression, and the research on elementary schoolchildren by Perry *et al.* (1986), indicated that females (compared to males) estimate greater harm to the victim, and higher levels of guilt or anxiety from aggressive behaviour. Perry *et al.* (1986) suggested that this differential 'empathy inhibitor' may be attributable to sex of the target: respondents are typically requested to picture aggression against someone of the same sex. In subsequent analyses using different data, Perry *et al.* (1989) reported that the sex difference in terms of victims' suffering diminishes greatly when sex of the target is taken into account, but that, unexpectedly, more guilt ensues when aggressing against boys rather than girls. This suggests that the sex of the potential victim plays a role in determining whether aggression will be employed.

A related issue which has not received enough attention is Bandura's (1973) distinction between *learning* and *utilizing* aggressive behaviour. Bandura suggested that boys and girls both learn aggressive behaviour, but that the factors which determine whether an individual performs the learned behaviour differ. The actual performance is based largely upon an individual's perception of the functional value of the behaviour and the risk of punishment. Condry and Ross (1985) examined the origin of individual perceptions and found them to be grounded in differential socialization processes for boys and girls. They reported that observers of identical aggressive interactions between two boys and between two girls consistently rated the boy–boy interaction favourably, and the girl–girl interaction unfavourably. Boys, engaging in the same aggressive behaviour as girls, were consistently assessed as less aggressive. That is, the boy–boy behaviour was de-emphasized, while the girl–girl behaviour was overemphasized. This indicates that differential use of aggression by the two sexes is in part attributable to differential responses by authority figures, and that, in all likelihood, males and females learn what is sex-appropriate behaviour through reinforcement cues. Finally, Cairns *et al.* (1989) report convergence over time for assessment of aggression between self-ratings and other-ratings for boys into a single construct of direct confrontation. However, for girls, this convergence does not occur; rather, a new arrangement of self-ratings and other-ratings appears as two independent constructs: direct confrontation and social aggression (ostracism). This line of thinking suggests that males and females develop different aggression strategies and that traditional examinations of delinquency and violent outcomes include females engaged in direct confrontation, and ignores females utilizing other forms of aggression. This issue is explored in more detail in the chapter by Ahmad and Smith on bullying.

CONCLUSION

After briefly summarizing major socialization theories of aggression and violence, we call attention to six issues that we believe merit attention in future research and theory on violence. To summarize, these include: (1) the extent to which traditional socialization theories designed to explain antisocial behaviour, aggression and delinquency can adequately explain violent behaviour; (2) the extent to which traditional socialization theories adequately incorporate a developmental perspective; (3) the need for a broadening of traditional theorizing in the area of violence to include the role of the family and peer group; (4) the need for greater attention to the role of environmental factors and/or social context variables; (5) the dearth of violence theory which takes into account sex differences; and (6) the failure of traditional socialization theories adequately to consider the target of the violence.

We conclude that sex differences in aggressive and violent behaviour are far more complex than originally conceived. Although social learning models may account for some of these differences, future research needs to focus on sex differences in perceptions of self-efficacy and response-outcome expectancies and type of aggressiveness and violence examined. There is also a critical need for creative methodologies for studying violent individuals (Widom 1989a). Population-based samples are limited because exceptionally large samples would be necessary to identify a sufficient number of violent offenders to permit adequate statistical analysis. This drawback, particularly if one wanted to study developmental sequences using longitudinal designs, makes research on violence exceedingly difficult, time-consuming and expensive. One possible alternative strategy is to use a case-control approach (Schlesselman 1982; Loftin and McDowall 1988). By identifying a group of violent individuals, and comparing them to a control group, a large number of risk factors may be assessed in an efficient and economical fashion. Thus, the factors that place individuals at risk for violent behaviour may be better identified.

NOTE

1 Authorship was determined by alphabetical order.

REFERENCES

Arbuthnot, J., Gordon, D. A. and Jurkovic, G. (1987) 'Personality', in H. C. Quay (ed.) *Handbook of Juvenile Delinquency*, New York: John Wiley & Sons.

Bandura, A. (1973) *Aggression: A Social Learning Analysis*, Englewood Cliffs, NJ: Prentice-Hall.

—— (1977) *Social Learning Theory*, Englewood Cliffs, NJ: Prentice-Hall.

—— (1979) 'The social learning perspective', in H. Toch (ed.) *Psychology of Crime and Criminal Justice*, New York: Holt, Rinehart & Winston.

—— (1986) *Social Foundations of Thoughts and Action: A Social Cognitive Theory*, Englewood Cliffs, NJ: Prentice-Hall.

Berkowitz, L. (1969) 'The frustration-aggression hypothesis revisited', in L. Berkowitz (ed.) *Roots of Aggression: A Re-examination of the Frustration-Aggression Hypothesis*, New York: Atherton Press.

—— (1989) 'Frustration-aggression hypothesis: examination and reformulation', *Psychological Bulletin*, 106: 59–73.

Block, J. and Gjerde, P. F. (1986) 'Distinguishing between antisocial behavior and undercontrol', in D. Olweus, J. Block and M. Radke-Yarrow (eds) *Development of Antisocial and Prosocial Behavior Research, Theories, and Issues*, New York: Academic Press.

Blumstein, A., Cohen, J., Roth, J. and Visher, C. (1986) (eds) *Criminal Careers and Career Criminals*, Washington, DC: National Academy Press.

Cairns, R. B. and Cairns, B. D. (1986) 'The development-interactional view of social behavior: four issues of adolescent aggression', in D. Olweus, J. Block and M. Radke-Yarrow (eds) *The Development of Antisocial and Prosocial Behavior*, New York: Academic Press.

—— (1991) 'Social cognition and social networks: a developmental perspective', in D. J. Pepler and K. Rubin (eds) *The Development and Treatment of Childhood Aggression*, Hillsdale, NJ: Lawrence Erlbaum.

Cairns, R. B., Cairns, B. D., Neckerman, N. J., Ferguson, L. L. and Gariepy, J. (1989) 'Growth and aggression: 1. Childhood to early adolescence', *Developmental Psychology*, 25: 320–30.

Capaldi, D. M. and Patterson, G. R. (1992) 'Is violence a selective trajectory or part of a deviant life style?', Unpublished manuscript, Oregon Social Learning Center.

Cappell, C. and Heiner, R. (1991) 'The intergenerational transmission of family aggression', *Journal of Family Violence*, 5: 135–52.

Chesney-Lind, M. (1987) 'Girls and violence: an exploration of the gender gap in serious delinquent behavior', in D. H. Crowell, I. M. Evans and C. R. O'Donnell (eds) *Childhood Aggression and Violence: Sources of Influence, Prevention, and Control*, New York: Plenum Press.

Condry, J. C. and Ross, D. F. (1985) 'Sex and aggression: the influence of gender label on the perception of aggression in children', *Child Development*, 56: 225–33.

Dodge, K. A. (1980) 'Social cognition and children's aggressive behavior', *Child Development*, 51: 162–70.

—— (1991) 'The structure and function of reactive and proactive aggression', in D. J. Pepler and K. Rubin (eds) *The Development and Treatment of Childhood Aggression*, Hillsdale, NJ: Lawrence Erlbaum.

Dodge, K. A., Bates, J. E. and Pettit, G. S. (1990) 'Mechanisms in the cycle of violence', *Science*, 250: 1678–83.

Dodge, K. A. and Newman, J. P. (1981) 'Biased decision making processes in aggressive boys', *Journal of Abnormal Psychology*, 90: 375–9.

Dodge, K. A. and Tomlin, A. M. (1987) 'Utilization of self-schemas as a mechanism of interpersonal bias in aggressive children', *Social Cognition*, 5: 280–300.

Eagley, A. H. and Steffen, V. J. (1986) 'Gender and aggressive behavior: a meta-analytic review of the social psychological literature', *Psychological Bulletin*, 100: 309–30.

Eisenberg, N. and Mussen, P. H. (1989) *The Roots of Prosocial Behavior in Children*, Cambridge: Cambridge University Press.

Erikson, E. H. (1950) *Childhood and Society*, New York: W. W. Norton.

Eron, L. D. (1987) 'The development of aggressive behavior from the perspective of a developing behaviorism', *American Psychologist*, 42: 435–42.

Eron, L. D. and Huesmann, L. R. (1989) 'The genesis of gender differences in aggression', in M. A. Luszcz and T. Nettelbeck (eds) *Psychological Development: Perspectives Across the Life-span*, North-Holland: Elsevier Science.

Eron, L. D., Huesmann, L. R., Dobow, E., Romanoff, R. and Yarmel, P. W. (1987) 'Aggression and its correlates over 22 years', in D. H. Crowell, I. M. Evans and C. R. O'Donnell (eds) *Childhood Aggression and Violence: Sources of Influence, Prevention, and Control*, New York: Plenum Press.

Eron, L. D., Huesmann, L. R., Lefkowitz, M. M. and Walder, L. O. (1972) 'Does television violence cause aggression?', *American Psychologist*, 27: 253–63.

Eron, L. D., Huesmann, L. R. and Zelli, A. (1991) 'The role of parental variables in the learning of aggression', in D. J. Pepler and K. Rubin (eds) *The Development and*

Treatment of Childhood Aggression, Hillsdale, NJ: Lawrence Erlbaum.

Fagan, J., Piper, E. and Moore, M. (1986) 'Violent delinquents and urban youths', *Criminology*, 24: 439–71.

Fagan, J. and Wexler, S. (1987) 'Family origins of violent delinquents', *Criminology*, 25: 643–69.

Farrington, D. P. (1986) 'Stepping stones to adult criminal careers', in D. Olweus, J. Block and M. Radke-Yarrow (eds) *Development of Antisocial and Prosocial Behavior: Research, Theories, and Issues*, New York: Academic Press.

—— (1989) 'Early predictors of adolescent aggression and adult violence', *Violence and Victims*, 4: 79–100.

—— (1991) 'Childhood aggression and adult violence: early precursors and later-life outcomes', in D. J. Pepler and K. Rubin (eds) *The Development and Treatment of Childhood Aggression*, Hillsdale, NJ: Lawrence Erlbaum.

Farrington, D. P., Loeber, R., Elliott, D., Hawkins, J. D., Kandel, D., Klein, M., McCord, J., Rowe, D. and Tremblay, R. (1990) 'Advancing the knowledge about the onset of delinquency and crime', in B. B. Lahey and A. E. Kazdin (eds) *Advances in Clinical Child Psychology*, vol. 13, New York: Plenum Press.

Felson, R. B. (1992) ' "Kick 'em when they're down": explanations of the relationship between stress and interpersonal aggression and violence', *Sociological Quarterly*, 33: 1–16.

Feshbach, N. D. and Feshbach, S. (1982) 'Empathy training and the regulation of aggression: potentialities and limitations', *Academic Psychological Bulletin*, 4: 399–413.

Freedman, J. L. (1984) 'Effect of television violence on aggressiveness', *Psychological Bulletin*, 96: 227–46.

—— (1992) 'Television violence and aggression: what psychologists should tell the public', in P. Suedfeld and P. E. Tetlock (eds) *Psychology and Public Policy*, New York: Hemisphere.

Gelles, R. J. (1976) *Family Violence*, Beverly Hills, CA: Sage.

Goldstein, J. H. (1986) *Aggression and Crimes of Violence*, 2nd edn, Oxford: Oxford University Press.

Gottfredson, M. and Hirschi, T. (1986) 'The true value of lambda would appear to be zero: an essay on career criminals, criminal careers, selective incapacitation, cohort studies, and related topics', *Criminology*, 24: 213–34.

—— (1990) *A General Theory of Crime*, Palo Alto, CA: Stanford University Press.

Grusec, J. E. and Dix, T. (1986) 'The socialization of prosocial behavior: theory and reality', in C. Zahn-Waxler, E. M. Cummings and R. Ianotti (eds) *Altruism and Aggression: Biological and Social Origins*, Cambridge: Cambridge University Press.

Gully, K. J., Dengerink, H. A., Pepping, M. and Bergstrom, D. (1981) 'Research note: sibling contribution to violent behaviour', *Journal of Marriage and the Family*, 333–7.

Hamparian, D. M., Schuster, R., Dintz, S. and Conrad, J. P. (1978) *The Violent Few: A Study of Dangerous Juvenile Offenders*, Lexington, MA: D.C. Heath & Co.

Hokanson, J. E. (1970) 'Psychophysiological evaluations of the catharsis-hypothesis', in E. I. Megargee and J. E. Hokanson (eds) *The Dynamics of Aggression*, New York: Harper & Row.

Huesmann, L. R., Eron, L. D., Berkowitz, L. and Chaffee, S. (1992) 'The effects of television violence on aggression: a reply to a skeptic', in P. Suedfeld and P. E. Tetlock (eds) *Psychology and Public Policy*, New York: Hemisphere.

Huesmann, L. R., Eron, L. D., Lefkowitz, M. M. and Walder, L. O. (1984) 'The stability of aggression over time and generation', *Developmental Psychology*, 20: 1120–34.

Huizinga, D., Esbensen, F. and Weiher, A. W. (1991) 'Are there multiple paths to delinquency', *Journal of Criminal Law and Criminology*, 82: 83–118.

Kagan, J. (1976) 'New views on cognitive development', *Journal of Youth and Adolescence*, 5: 113–29.

Kagan, J. and Moss, H. A. (1962) *Birth to Maturity: A Study in Psychological Development*, New York: Wiley.

Kalmuss, D. (1984) 'The intergenerational transmission of marital aggression', *Journal of Marriage and the Family*, 47: 11–19.

Kandel, D. B. (1989) 'Issues of sequencing of adolescent drug use and other problem behavior', *Drugs and Society*, 3: 54–76.

Kleinig, J. (1991) 'Conceptual cannibalism: the social scientific appropriation of ordinary discourse', in *Social Interactionist Approaches to Violence: The Albany Conference*, 5 and 6 April, Albany, NY: Department of Sociology, University at Albany.

Kruttschnitt, C., Heath, L. and Ward, D. A. (1986) 'Family violence, television viewing habits, and other adolescent experiences related to violent criminal behavior', *Criminology*, 24: 235–67.

Le Blanc, M. and Frechette, M. (1989) *Male Criminal Activity from Childhood Through Youth: Multilevel and Developmental Perspectives*, New York: Springer-Verlag.

Lefkowitz, M. M., Eron, L. D., Walder, L. O. and Huesmann, L. R. (1977) *Growing Up to be Violent: A Longitudinal Study of the Development of Aggression*, New York: Pergamon Press.

Lewis, D. O., Lovely, R., Yeager, C. and Femina, D. D. (1989) 'Toward a theory of the genesis of violence: a follow-up study of delinquents', *Journal of the American Academy of Child and Adolescent Psychiatry*, 28: 431–6.

Loeber, R. (1982) 'The stability of antisocial and delinquent child behavior: a review', *Child Development*, 53: 1431–46.

—— (1988) 'Natural histories of conduct problems, delinquency, and associated substance abuse: evidence for developmental progressions', in B. B. Lahey and A. E. Kazdin (eds) *Advances in Clinical Child Psychology*, vol. 11, New York: Plenum Press.

—— (1992) 'Developmental interactions between juvenile disruptive behavior, comorbid conditions, and their risk factors', *Recueil des Etudes commandées par le Group de Travail pour les Jeunes*, Montreal, Quebec: Ministère de la Santé et des Services Sociaux.

Loeber, R. and Dishion, T. J. (1983) 'Early predictors of male delinquency: a review', *Psychological Bulletin*, 94: 68–99.

Loeber, R. and Le Blanc, M. (1990) 'Toward a developmental criminology', in M. Tonry and N. Morris (eds) *Crime and Justice: A Review of Research*, vol. 12, Chicago, IL: University of Chicago Press.

Loeber, R., Stouthamer-Loeber, M., van Kammen, W. and Farrington, D. P. (1991) 'Initiation, escalation, and desistance in juvenile offending and their correlates', *Journal of Criminal Law and Criminology*, 82: 36–82.

Loftin, C. and McDowall, D. (1988) 'The analysis of case-control studies in criminology', *Journal of Quantitative Criminology*, 4: 85–98.

Maccoby, E. E. (1986) 'Social groupings in childhood: their relationship to prosocial and antisocial behavior in boys and girls', in D. Olweus, J. Block and M. Radke-Yarrow (eds) *Development of Antisocial and Prosocial Behavior Research, Theories, and Issues*, New York: Academic Press.

Megargee, E. I. (1970) 'Undercontrolled and overcontrolled personality types in extreme antisocial aggression', in E. I. Megargee and J. E. Hokanson (eds) *The Dynamics of Aggression*, New York: Harper & Row.

—— (1982) 'Psychological determinants and correlates of criminal violence', in

M. E. Wolfgang, N. A. Weiner and P. J. Cook (eds) *Criminal Violence*, Beverly Hills, CA: Sage.

Morton, T. (1987) 'Childhood aggression in the context of family interaction', in D. H. Crowell, I. M. Evans and C. R. O'Donnell (eds) *Childhood Aggression and Violence: Sources of Influence, Prevention, and Control*, New York: Plenum Press.

Nagin, D. S. and Farrington, D. P. (1992) 'The onset and persistence of offending', *Criminology*, 30: 501–23.

National Institute of Mental Health (1982) *Television and Behavior: Ten Years of Scientific Progress and Implications for the Eighties*, Washington, DC: US Government Printing Office.

Olweus, D. (1979) 'Stability of aggressive reaction patterns in males: a review', *Psychological Bulletin*, 86: 852–75.

—— (1980) 'Familial and temperamental determinants of aggressive behavior in adolescent boys: a causal analysis', *Developmental Psychology*, 16: 644–60.

Pagelow, M. D. (1984) 'Factors affecting women's decisions to leave violent relationships', *Journal of Family Issues*, 2: 39–414.

Parke, R. D. and Slaby, R. G. (1983) 'The development of aggression', in E. M. Hetherington (ed.) *Handbook of Child Psychology*, vol. IV, *Socialization, Personality Development, and Social Development*, New York: John Wiley & Sons.

Patterson, G. R. (1982) *Coercive Family Process*, Eugene, OR: Castalia Press.

—— (1986) 'The contribution of siblings to training for fighting: a microsocial analysis', in D. Olweus, J. Block and M. Radke-Yarrow (eds) *Development of Antisocial and Prosocial Behavior Research, Theories, and Issues*, New York: Academic Press.

—— (1992) 'Orderly change in a stable world: the antisocial trait as a chimera', Unpublished manuscript, Oregon Social Learning Center.

Patterson, G. R., Capaldi, D. and Bank, L. (1991) 'An early starter model for predicting delinquency', in D. J. Pepler and K. Rubin (eds) *The Development and Treatment of Childhood Aggression*, Hillsdale, NJ: Lawrence Erlbaum.

Patterson, G. R., Crosby, L. and Vuchinich, S. (1992) 'Predicting risk for early police arrest', *Journal of Quantitative Criminology*, 8: 335–55.

Patterson, G. R., DeBaryshe, B. D. and Ramsey, E. (1989) 'A developmental perspective on antisocial behavior', *American Psychologist*, 44: 329–35.

Patterson, G. R. and Dishion, T. J. (1985) 'Contributions of family and peers to delinquency', *Criminology*, 23: 63–79.

Patterson, G. R. and Yoerger, K. (1991) 'Developmental models for delinquent behavior', Paper presented at NATO Advanced Study Institute, Crime and Mental Disorder, Ciocco, Italy.

Perry, D. G., Perry, L. C. and Rasmussen, P. (1986) 'Cognitive social learning mediators of aggression', *Child Development*, 57: 700–11.

Perry, D. G., Perry, L. C. and Weiss, R. J. (1989) 'Sex differences in the consequences that children anticipate for aggression', *Developmental Psychology*, 25: 312–19.

Pulkkinen, L. (1986) 'The role of impulse control in the development of antisocial and prosocial behavior', in D. Olweus, J. Block and M. Radke-Yarrow (eds) *Development of Antisocial and Prosocial Behavior Research, Theories, and Issues*, New York: Academic Press.

Redl, F. and Toch, H. (1979) 'The psychoanalytic perspective', in H. Toch (ed.) *Psychology of Crime and Criminal Justice*, New York: Holt, Rinehart & Winston.

Redl, F. and Wineman, D. (1951) *Children who Hate: The Disorganization and Breakdown of Behavior Controls*, New York: The Free Press.

—— (1952) *Controls from Within: Techniques for the Treatment of the Aggressive Child*, New York: The Free Press.

Rivera, B. and Widom, C. S. (1990) 'Childhood victimization and violent offending', *Violence and Victims*, 5: 19–35.

Robins, L. N. (1986) 'The consequences of conduct disorders in girls', in D. Olweus, J. Block and M. Radke-Yarrow (eds) *Development of Antisocial and Prosocial Behavior: Research, Theories, and Issues*, New York: Academic Press.

Roff, D. J. and Wirt, R. D. (1984) 'Childhood aggression and social adjustments as antecedents of delinquency', *Journal of Abnormal Child Psychology*, 12: 111–26.

Roopnarine, J. L., Cochran, D. and Mounts, N. S. (1988) 'Traditional psychological theories and socialization during middle and early childhood: an attempt at reconceptualization', in T. D. Yawkey and J. E. Johnson (eds) *Integrative Processes and Socialization: Early to Middle Childhood*, Hillsdale, NJ: Lawrence Erlbaum.

Sampson, R. J. and Laub, J. H. (1990) 'Crime and deviance over the life course: the salience of adult social bonds', *American Sociological Review*, 55: 609–27.

Schlesselman, J. J. (1982) *Case-Control Studies*, Oxford: Oxford University Press.

Short, J. F. and Strodtbeck, F. L. (1974) *Group Process and Gang Delinquency*, Chicago, IL: University of Chicago Press.

Silberman, C. E. (1978) *Criminal Violence, Criminal Justice*, New York: Random House.

Smith, P. K. (1989) 'Ethological approaches to the study of aggression in children', in J. Archer and K. Browne (eds) *Human Aggression: Naturalistic Approaches*, London: Routledge.

Snyder, J. and Patterson, G. R. (1987) 'Family interaction and delinquent behavior', in H. C. Quay (ed.) *Handbook of Juvenile Delinquency*, New York: John Wiley & Sons.

Staub, E. (1986) 'A conception of the determinants and development of altruism and aggression: motives, the self, and the environment', in C. Zahn-Waxler, E. M. Cummings and R. Ianotti (eds) *Altruism and Aggression: Biological and Social Origins*, Cambridge: Cambridge University Press.

Steinberg, M. S. and Dodge, K. A. (1983) 'Attributional bias in aggressive boys and girls', *Journal of Social and Clinical Psychology*, 1: 312–22.

Straus, M. A. (1991) 'Punishment of children and violence and other crime in adulthood', *Social Problems*, 38: 133–54.

Toch, H. (1969) *Violent Men: An Inquiry into the Psychology of Violence*, Chicago, IL: Aldine.

Ulbrich, P. and Huber, J. (1981) 'Observing parental aggression: distribution and effects', *Journal of Marriage and the Family*, 43: 623–31.

Warr, M. and Stafford, M. (1991) 'The influences of delinquent peers: what they think or what they do?', *Criminology*, 29: 851–66.

Weiner, N. A., Zahn, M. A. and Sagi, R. J. (eds) (1990) *Violence: Patterns, Causes, Public Policy*, New York: Harcourt Brace Jovanovich.

Weiss, B., Dodge, K. A., Bates, J. E. and Pettit, G. S. (1992) 'Some consequences of early harsh discipline: aggressiveness, and a maladaptive social information processing style', *Child Development*, 63: 1321–35.

Widom, C. S. (1984) 'Sex roles, criminality, and psychopathology', in C. S. Widom (ed.) *Sex Roles and Psychopathology*, New York: Plenum Press.

—— (1989a) 'Does violence beget violence? a critical examination of the literature', *Psychological Bulletin*, 106: 3–28.

—— (1989b) 'Child abuse, neglect, and violent criminal behavior', *Criminology*, 27: 251–70.

—— (1989c) 'The intergenerational transmission of violence', in N. Weiner and M. E. Wolfgang (eds) *Pathways to Criminal Violence*, Newbury Park, CA: Sage, pp. 137–201.

—— (1989d) 'The cycle of violence', *Science*, 244: 160–6.
—— (1991) 'A tail on an untold tale: response to "Biological and genetic contributors to violence – Widom's untold tale" ', *Psychological Bulletin*, 109: 130–2.
Wilson, J. Q. and R. Herrnstein (1985) *Crime and Human Nature*, New York: Simon & Schuster.

16

POWER AND MALE VIOLENCE

John Archer

The central aspect of feminist analyses of women's position in society is that men hold the positions of power and women do not (for example, Wilkinson 1986). Although Kitzinger (1991) has argued that power has been neglected by many feminist psychologists, this criticism applies less to those who have been concerned with male violence: it is but a short step from a general recognition of the importance of power for analysing the position of women in society to explaining men's violence towards women in the same terms. As Walker (1989) put it:

> The feminist political agenda analysis has reframed the problem of violence against women as one of misuse of power by men who have been socialized into believing that they have a right to control the women in their lives, even through violent means.

> (p. 695)

Thus violence towards women is seen as following from men's greater control of access to all sorts of resources, force being one of several strategies used to exercise this power. In the case of rape, violence is used to override a woman's sexual choices, rendering her completely degraded and powerless even over her own body. (It should be noted that this explanation is concerned with societal power, and not with whether the immediate goal of rape is primarily sexual or to foster a feeling of power in the rapist: see Chapters 1 and 11; similarly, it is not necessary for a violent husband to feel powerful each time he attacks his wife.) Feminist power explanations are therefore relevant to the pattern of violence between the sexes; namely, why there are more battered wives than battered husbands and why men rape (Chapters 8, 9 and 11). On the other hand, they have little or nothing to say about why men are violent to other men (Chapters 5 to 7).

Violence between males has also been viewed within a power framework, albeit one which involves a more limited view of power, one derived from the concept of dominance hierarchies in animals. This takes us to a different area of investigation, concerning social comparisons and status relations between men. Since I shall argue that there are some common threads joining together these two sorts of male power, this chapter is concerned with both types of power explanation. I shall begin by considering some general points from theoretical analyses of power which are relevant to both explanations. This is followed by a discussion of feminist theories of power which account for violence against women, and then the status explanation of inter-male violence. Links between these two sorts of male power are explored, and finally I consider their origins, both evolutionary and cultural.

THE CONCEPT OF POWER

Clegg (1989) began his analysis of the concept of power by stating that 'There is no such thing as an all-embracing concept of power' (p. xv). 'Power', and related terms such as 'status', have been used in a variety of ways in the social and political sciences. It is not possible to consider all the complex issues in this chapter. I shall confine myself to those which are relevant to the two sorts of male power.

Clegg traced the roots of most modern thinking about power to Hobbes, and a rival strand in the earlier writings of Machiavelli. Hobbes was concerned with what power is, and his answer to this question was framed by the way in which power was exercised by the British sovereign in the seventeenth century. He saw power in terms of direct control by a personal monarch, the result of which was a moral order and a civil society: rights became extended to others from the central sovereign. Hobbes's tradition led to modern North American political scientists taking an individualistic view of power, involving the subordination of others' preferences to one's own. This is an interpersonal view of power, those in an elite position simply having a greater concentration of power.

The limitations of this position were set out in a number of critical works (see Clegg 1989). The importance of distinguishing structural and interpersonal power led to the viewing of power in terms of different levels of analysis, the whole society, the organization and the personal relationship (for example, Ragins and Sundstrom 1989). Structural power – that which resides in the state and organizations – is an important basis for feminist explanations of male violence towards women. These emphasize the patriarchal structure of society, which encourages and legitimizes the use of violence by men towards their wives, through an ideological and legal framework. In contrast, power at an interpersonal level, concerning relationships between individuals in circumstances where the influence of structural power is minimal, has been emphasized when considering inter-male violence. Here motives concerned with personal status in a peer group, rather than power legitimized by societal structures, is foremost.

The Hobbesian view is also limited because it is restricted to an agentic view of power. The powerful exercise power by ensuring that their own preferences and interests are enacted at the expense of those of the less powerful. Of

311

course, force and threat of force are compelling ways of bringing this about. However, this is not the only way in which power operates. Lukes (1974) distinguished three forms of power, which he termed the one-, two- and three-dimensional views respectively. The one-dimensional view concerns an overt conflict of interest, and concentrates on the individual's behaviour. The two-dimensional view introduced the notion of 'nondecision', the means through which demands for change can be muted; put another way, it involves control over the agenda, the keeping of certain issues out of the realm of overt disputes. The three-dimensional view introduces control over how people perceive their interests and wants: it is a form of power which prevents people from having grievances by shaping their perceptions and preferences so that they accept the existing order: it coincides with concepts such as 'false consciousness', which are open to the criticism that they represent ways of dismissing people's stated aspirations, and hence of not taking them seriously (Clegg 1989).

In contrast to the Hobbesian concern with the structure of power, Machiavelli wrote about strategies of power, how power was enacted. This concern is particularly pertinent to the relation between power and violence. Machiavelli realized that although violence or the threat of violence was central to the concept of power, there was no simple relation between the two. To be effective, violence should be used sparingly and appropriately; power could operate more effectively by securing consent. From this vantage point, too much violence may indicate a weakness of power. This analysis enables us to understand why only some husbands show violence towards their wives, despite male power being structural. It also enables us to understand why male violence is more likely where there is a lessening of legal and organizational power, and where there is no recognized informal power structure to replace it. Again, there is a weakness of power.

I have indicated some of the ways in which these general principles can be applied to male violence. In the next two sections, I consider first power explanations of violence towards women, and, secondly, inter-male violence.

POWER EXPLANATIONS OF MALE VIOLENCE AGAINST WOMEN

Statements by some feminist writers – for example, Hanmer (1978) and Walker (quoted in the Introduction) – see the power explanation as following from a specific ideology: it represents a particular way of looking at the problem rather than being a scientific hypothesis to be tested against alternatives. However, other writers, such as Dobash and Dobash (1977–78) and Yllo (1983) have treated the power explanation as a hypothesis, and this is the position I shall adopt in this chapter.

Explaining male violence towards women in terms of the gendered power relations in society as a whole is not the most obvious explanation to strike the non-feminist mind, which is more attuned to examining the characteristics of those men who are particularly violent. However, a persuasive argument can be made out for the power explanation. Let us first consider some alternatives.

As I have just intimated, one common approach is to view male violence as an aberrant or deviant pattern of behaviour, to seek to characterize rapists and violent husbands as morally or psychologically different from other men. This approach has informed many of the older studies of rape, which sought to examine differences between convicted rapists and 'normal' men. However, it became no longer tenable when the widespread nature of rape was uncovered (for example, Koss and Oros 1982; Hall 1985; Koss 1990; see Chapter 11). In the case of physical violence, situational influences such as stress, or early experiences of family violence, have been identified as predisposing certain men towards violence (Gelles 1972, 1987). The limitations of a perspective which characterizes spousal violence in terms of the individual's circumstances or background become apparent when the history of encouragement and legitimization of such acts is recognized (Dobash and Dobash 1977–78, 1980).

An alternative view, mentioned in passing by Gilbert (1990), is a different type of power explanation, one which is restricted to the level of individual interactions. Gilbert argued that where the rule of law is weakly represented – as in most private settings, including the family – dominance relations will be left to the individuals concerned. If there are few inhibitions about using violence to settle conflicts, husbands will be able to dominate their wives by violence or threats of violence. This reflects a view of marital violence characteristic of researchers who came to the subject from an interest in marital relationships, such as Steinmetz (1977) and Straus *et al.* (1980).

It can be called the 'Lord of the Flies' view of marital violence, since it parallels the Hobbesian view of human behaviour depicted in William Golding's novel: take away the civilized rule of law, and human beings will revert to a power struggle based on ability to use force. I think there is much to recommend this view in other contexts, for example, when considering institutions such as boarding schools and prisons. Although it is undoubtedly the case that an imbalance of size and strength is necessary for husbands to be able to hit their wives with impunity in the short term (Steinmetz 1977), as a complete explanation it misses a crucial consideration: over the centuries, the rule of law has *encouraged* wife-beating, and what we see today is the legacy of this encouragement.

The view that wife-beating has existed for centuries in our culture as an acceptable and even desirable part of the patriarchal family system was persuasively put by Dobash and Dobash (1977–78). They argued that, from the viewpoint of traditional ideology, backed up by centuries of religious and legal support, wives are the 'appropriate' victims of any family violence. Their discussion was confined to severe systematic assaults and homicides, so it is clear that they were dealing with violence, rather than a wider range of aggressive acts (see Chapter 1).

The beginning of legal marriage in Roman times was associated with the

313

complete subjugation of wives, so that they held the position of slaves without property rights and were subject completely to control by their husbands. This control included the right, even the duty, to beat the wife if she did not adhere to the code of behaviour expected of her. Murder of the wife for adultery – and other forms of 'misbehaviour' such as drinking wine – was accepted and even encouraged.

Christianity incorporated this view of the legitimacy of the power of husbands over their wives, and in Europe both church and state maintained it through the centuries. Likewise, wife-beating was accepted as an appropriate way of enforcing such power. In several European countries, the law specified the ways in which the husband could 'chastise' his wife. Adultery was widely viewed as justifying severe violence, even murder; in France it was considered legitimate for a husband to break the nose of a 'scolding wife'.

Gradually, severe assaults became restricted, and a distinction was drawn between brutal and ordinary assaults. This distinction maintained the legitimacy of wife-beating, while at the same time delineating its boundaries, in much the same way that child cruelty legislation did for violence against children. Dobash and Dobash argued that present-day marital violence by men towards their wives or partners remains as part of this historical tradition, and serves the same function: it is an attempt to establish or maintain power over the wife when her behaviour becomes unacceptable to the man. From their own interviews with battered wives, they found that violence occurred when there had been a perceived challenge to the husband's authority or control, unfulfilled expectations about domestic work being the commonest source of conflict, followed by possessiveness and sexual jealousy (Dobash and Dobash 1984): often the precipitating event was a seemingly innocuous occurrence, such as a late meal or talking to another man. But they become understandable if we recognize that the ideologies and social arrangements which explicitly supported wife-beating in the past are still present today. As Dobash and Dobash (1977–78) put it: 'Wives may no longer be the legitimate victims of social violence, but in social terms they are still the "appropriate" victims' (p. 438). Other studies indicate that violence occurs in circumstances where the husband's feeling of control and authority is likely to be challenged, for example, during arguments over money, sexual problems and jealousy, the wife's desire to work, the husband's unemployment and the wife's drinking alcohol (Roy 1977).

Of course, social circumstances have changed, so that a woman may now have the option to leave the abusive relationship, or to go to the police or a refuge, or to take legal proceedings herself. However, all of these have considerable costs (for example, Strube 1988; Miller and Simpson 1991) and are only chosen by a minority of abused women. In many communities the ideology which supports male authority will be widely shared and deep-rooted, so that there will be informal support for the husband's authority from the extended family and wider community. This becomes apparent when the law seeks to eliminate the oppression of women, and with it wife-beating, as happened in Muslim areas of Soviet Central Asia in the late 1920s (Massell 1968). As a reaction to such measures, a reign of terror was initiated against those women who had tried to exercise their rights, and against representatives of the Soviet regime. In such cases, men's greater size and strength would have been an important ingredient in helping this to happen (Goode 1971), but it is unlikely to have been fully successful in the face of determined action by the agents of law and order.

I have highlighted the argument presented by Dobash and Dobash because it is the most coherent and persuasive version of the patriarchal power hypothesis. The one drawback, referred to earlier, is that it is *both* a feminist analysis *and* a hypothesis. This means that for some it has the status of dogma and is tied to a particular type of methodology (notably, involving the rejection of quantification). Both of these obstruct the testing of it as a hypothesis. This point was realised by Yllo (1983) who explicitly criticized the link between feminist theory and qualitative methodology, dear to the hearts of many feminists.

Yllo and Straus (1984) investigated the societal power hypothesis by examining the association between violence and the overall status of women in different US states amongst a sample of over 2,000 husbands and wives. Women's status was assessed from their legal, economic, educational and political rights in that state. Overall, this showed a curvilinear relationship with marital violence. Where women's status was low there was more violence, but violence decreased as status increased up to high levels, where there was again an increase in violence. A measure of patriarchal norms, consisting of attitudes to decision-making in the family, showed a linear relationship with marital violence: the more egalitarian the normative climate in that state, the lower the rate of violence towards wives. These seemingly inconsistent findings were reconciled by a further analysis which showed that the highest rates of violence occurred where there was normative support for men making the family decisions yet the structural status of women was higher. Here there was an inconsistency between women's status in educational, economic and political life and social norms which viewed men as dominant over their wives. As indicated later in this section, these are the conditions under which power will tend to be enforced by violence.

Levinson (1989) has provided a broader cross-cultural analysis of the relationship between structural power and wife-beating by examining data from ninety small-scale and peasant societies throughout the world. Economic inequality between the sexes, combined with male dominance in family decisions and restrictions on divorce, were strong predictors of wife-beating – thus supporting the structural power hypothesis without the complications noted in Yllo's research.

Can we explain how power at a structural level becomes the exercise of violence at the individual level? In answering this question, there are two separate issues: first, how it is that power in a structural sense is filtered down to individual actions; and secondly, why some men and not others show violence towards women.

How can structural power explain individual acts? Several analyses of sex differences in social behaviour have argued that a recognition of status inequalities directly affects the way in which men and women interact at an interpersonal level. For example, Henley (1977) has analysed the expressions and gestures by men towards women and concluded that they correspond to those generally shown by higher-status individuals to lower-status ones. In this case, there is presumably a recognition by the people concerned of the status inequality between them, from which feelings and actions arise. These inter-actions mirror others between people who differ in power and status. Eagley (1983) has suggested that sex differences in influenceability also follow from wider status inequalities between men and women. In such explanations, the precise way in which structural power influences individual actions is not clearly specified.

In suggesting that several aspects of boys' and girls' gender roles can be explained in terms of structural power (Archer 1992b), I argued that research on intergroup relations (for example, Tajfel 1982; Brown 1988) can bridge the gap between the two levels of analysis. In particular, studies involving the consequences for individuals of belonging to groups which differ in status are particularly relevant. Perhaps the most important finding from this research for the present discussion is that, for members of a lower-status group, inter-actions with members of a higher-status group will lead to a lowering of self-esteem (Brown 1988). This gives some clue to the way in which power on a societal level can filter down to affect an individual's behaviour and feelings. But it obviously leaves the detailed picture unexplored.

Another way of examining the individual manifestations of societal power is to explore people's feelings of power. Griffin (1991) asked a sample of young people about the ways in which they felt powerful or powerless as a woman or man or in general. Over half the women said they felt powerlessness as a woman due to threats of violence by men or by actual incidences of harass-ment and abuse by men. The perpetrators of actual assaults ranged from male relatives and friends to strangers. Sexual harassment was viewed as con-nected, and also inducing a feeling of powerlessness. Some women saw sexual violence – and male power in general – as a result of the male's greater size and strength, and some men (15 per cent) also mentioned physical strength as a source of masculine power. Other women viewed sexual violence as a result of its implied legitimization (for example, in media images) in a patriarchal society. There were therefore commonsense interpretations which corres-ponded to two of the explanations put forward by researchers to elucidate violence against women.

None of the sample of forty-eight men reported the threat of violence towards women as a source of masculine power. In fact, several argued that men were more likely to be attacked in the street than were women. Griffin concluded that structural positions of power and the use of sexual violence and harassment by some men do not necessarily mean that men in general *feel* a sense of power over women.

Griffin's findings showed that many women experienced a feeling of powerlessness which was directly connected to the threat of male violence or sexual harassment. In contrast, the men did not see their potential to harm women in this way as a source of their feeling powerful. In view of the findings from intergroup relations research indicating that status inequalities affect features such as self-esteem, it seems likely that simply asking people about their feelings of power taps only one aspect of the way in which structural power is translated into the psychological domain.

Once the societal context of violence towards women has been understood, we are still left with explaining why some men but not others show violence towards women. In the previous section, I referred to analyses of power derived from Machiavelli (Clegg 1989), which viewed violence as revealing a weakness in power. Similarly, modern theorists such as Tedeschi *et al.* (1977) see coercion as the mode of influence of last resort (cf. a similar view of rape by Felson 1993).

From this perspective, we should expect violence towards women to occur when the power of the husband is low or is threatened in some way. The findings of Yllo and Straus (see above) support this view in a broad sense, in that marital violence was pronounced in states where there was a disparity between women's relatively high public status and men's more traditional normative beliefs. Researchers on family relationships have also emphasized the relative status of members of a married couple in relation to marital violence (for example, Goode 1971). Gelles (1972) and O'Brien (1971) focused on cases where the husband has lower status than the wife through lack of money or educational achievement.

As indicated earlier, Dobash and Dobash (1977–78, 1984) concluded that husbands used violence when there were real or perceived challenges to their authority or control over their wives. Such findings indicate that we need to consider not only threats to authority in an objective sense (namely, inequalities between husband and wife in money or education or occupation), but the perception of actions as threats to the man's authority. Here, we enter the fragile world of the male ego. We would need to consider both the individual man's conception of his wife's marital obligations, and the importance of these being maintained for his self-esteem. In Chapter 7, I discussed theoretical models of aggression which viewed it as a reaction to discrepancies between events in the outside world and personally important expectations, and extended this view to include concepts of property, rights and obligations. If these concepts incorporate traditional and patriarchal views of male power, together with a belief that it is legitimate to use physical violence when they are not fulfilled by the spouse, we have all the ingredients necessary for systematic violence by the husband. The costs and difficulties for the wife of leaving such a relationship complete the picture. The implications of this view are that individual attitudes endorsing male supremacy and the legitimacy of violence will be predictive of male violence. I shall return to this issue in a later section, since it also ties in with inter-male violence.

DOMINANCE, STATUS AND INTER-MALE VIOLENCE

Explaining inter-male violence takes us to a different form of power, that exercised on an individual level. The analysis of this type of power, often referred to as 'dominance', can remain on the level of Lukes's one-dimensional view of power, which involves an overt conflict of interests, and concentrates on the individuals' behaviour.

The concept of dominance was introduced to describe the behaviour of animals, and later transferred to observational and peer-rating studies of children, principally boys (Archer 1992a: 128–48; see Chapter 3). The term has been used in two senses (Hinde 1978). The first, 'dominance hierarchy', refers to the overall pattern of relations between individuals in a group, and the second, dyadic dominance, refers to the pattern of power relationships between pairs of individuals (Archer 1992a: 129). Dominance has also been applied to adults, although here the emphasis is on the person's subjective sense of his or her own rank, and the consequences for mood of losing or enhancing perceived rank (Gilbert 1990). In these cases, social evaluation and comparison are important, and the use of physical aggression to settle dominance disputes is rare under many modern conditions.

Weisfeld (Chapter 3) views not only adults but also children and animals as showing a specific form of aggression motivated by the desire to achieve dominance over another individual. In contrast, I have maintained (Archer 1988, 1992a) that dominance is only a description of the consequences of conflicts between individuals, of the regularities in their competitive relationships. The reasons that they fight in the first place is another matter, and it is a mistake to view the consequences as a motive. This mistake arises from transferring the human notion of status to animal conflicts (Appleby 1985). Two crucial issues are, first, whether animals have a concept of status (I shall later argue that they do not), and secondly, whether status provides a motive for all inter-male disputes (again I shall argue that it does not).

Leaving aside this usage for the present, dominance describes the pattern of power relations in small groups of individuals, usually in settings where these arise from the individuals' interactions rather than as part of a higher-level structure imposed on them. That is why the concept is mainly applicable to groups of social animals and to children. It also applies to groups of adolescent and adult men in 'Lord of the Flies' settings, where the outside rule of law, or mutually agreed constraints, are absent or weakly operating. For example, McVicar (1982) described how non-compliance with officials was carried over from the outside world into prison, leading to a system of social relations being worked out between the inmates, with violence forming the main sanction. Weisfeld (Chapter 3) also indicates the physically based dominance relations formed in street youth gangs, again where outside constraints are weak.

The way I have used the concept of 'dominance' is as a description of a pattern of relationships, arising from conflicts between individuals, which are shown in many animal species (Archer 1976, 1988). From such disputes, animals learn to recognize those they can defeat, and those which can defeat them. They modify their behaviour, and the resulting pattern is what the observer describes as a dominance order, although in many cases it will not be the linear hierarchy which has often been assumed (Appleby 1985; Archer 1992a: 134–40).

This observed pattern will not necessarily be reflected in the knowledge that the individual animal or child possesses of his or her own dominance relations. As Appleby (1985) put it: 'A hen will quickly learn which of her flockmates she can beat, and which can beat her. So she knows which birds she can steal from, and which she should avoid' (p. 18). Such knowledge is a very different matter from knowledge of one's place in the pattern of dominance relation-ships, which we can call 'status'. As Appleby (1985) went on to say: 'She *(the hen)* does not need to know her rank in the hierarchy, or even that there is a hierarchy, for us to be able to describe one in the group.' This is the crucial point: in general, researchers have exaggerated the extent to which animals have knowledge of their place in the overall pattern of dominance. They only need to possess the more limited knowledge described by Appleby. Knowledge of status in the way that humans use the term is a higher-level concept, and we would need to turn to research on the cognitive abilities of animals and children to find out when it is likely to occur (Archer 1992a: 201–26).

In the case of animals, there is little or no direct evidence of the ability to understand the concept of status, as opposed to behaving to particular indi-viduals or classes of individuals in a dominant or a subordinate manner. Some field studies may indicate awareness of rank in baboons and vervet monkeys. When supplanting one another in competition over grooming access, the monkeys appear to agree on the ranking of the most preferred partners: but this and similar data from other monkeys is all indirect and inferential (Silverberg and Gray 1992), and therefore open to other interpretations. Cognitive abilities such as seriation and transitive inference which would be necessary for inferring overall ordering of a sequence from pairs within that sequence have been claimed for some primates, notably the chimpanzee (Cheney and Seyfarth 1990), but other researchers (for example, Doré and Dumas 1987) are more cautious. Even if such abilities were established, it would be a different matter from inferring the possession of conceptual knowledge about status. In the case of children, there is more definite research evidence on their abilities to conceptualize other children's dominance capabilities.

Edelman and Omark (1973) showed that US nursery school children (ages 3 to 4 years) could understand the term 'tough' by showing their muscles or pretending to hit, but at first they applied it egocentrically: when members of a pair were asked who was the toughest, both children often replied 'me'. At this age, there was below-chance-level agreement as to the relative toughness of pairs of other children in the class. A year later they showed much higher-than-chance levels, around 70 per cent, which was maintained at ages 6 to 8 years.

In a follow-up study, Omark and Edelman (1975) found that there was a high level of agreement about the toughness-ranking of themselves in relation to other children from 6 years of age, and a greater consensus about the perception of other children's dominance relations. Although girls were less concerned with relative toughness when describing their same-sex pairs than were boys, they were still able to rank the boys in their class in much the same way that the boys themselves did.

These and a number of studies carried out since in several countries (for example, Omark et al. 1975; see Boulton and Smith 1990) show that the concept of toughness (or 'strength' in the United Kingdom) is a salient one at the pre-operational level. At these ages there is only low agreement about the ranking of other children in the social group (Boulton and Smith 1990). From the ages of 6 to 7 upwards, shared social representations of status become apparent, although children consistently overrank themselves (Omark et al. 1975) and other children whom they like (Boulton and Smith 1990).

It seems likely that more complex notions of status and reputation develop from these early concepts of who is tough or strong in a social group. The elaboration of such notions into concern with a wider range of attributes, such as coolness, autonomy and commanding respect, has been described for black and Hispanic males in urban areas of the United States (Campbell 1986). This takes us away from power which is a simple consequence of individual inter-actions (as is dominance in animals) to a form of positional or notional power which is understood and recognized throughout the social group. Neverthe-less, even in primate social groups, dominance becomes complicated by alliances (de Waal 1984) and kinship (for example, Datta 1988; Johnson 1987), leading some researchers to refer to primate social relations in terms normally used only for humans, such as 'chimpanzee politics' (de Waal 1982).

Even if it becomes recognized throughout a social group (hence taking on some aspects of formal status), this form of power nevertheless emerges from individual interactions, and small-scale alliances, rather than from established structures. Power derived in this way is inherently unstable, since it is based on the ability to keep it through violence or threat of violence. Those who have power are always having to protect it or to take pre-emptive action, and they are subject to being usurped by those willing to challenge them. One way of overcoming this is to seek to legitimize and justify the power by institutional-izing it. Indeed, state power is likely to have originated in such a way.

In contrast, male power over women is much more stable and is deeply intrenched in historically ancient forms of legitimization. Since it is a form of power which is in the individual interest of all men, it does not suffer from the instability shown by inter-male competitive power. That is why men's power over women can be described in such global terms as 'the patriarchy'.

Essentially, violence towards women is one way of enforcing overall male supremacy when this is perceived to be challenged. Although some acts of inter-male violence may arise directly out of a status challenge, this cannot provide a complete explanation for all cases (Chapter 7). It may explain why a dispute about another matter escalates into violence: the conflict becomes transferred from one about, say, money, into a dispute about identity and status, through a process of argument and insults and challenges (for example, Felson 1984; Campbell 1986).

INTEGRATING DIFFERENT FORMS OF MALE VIOLENCE

We have seen that two very different types of power explanation have been advanced to explain male violence towards women and towards other men. One concerns structural power legitimizing violence towards wives, and the other concerns a power struggle between men at an interpersonal level. In this section, I shall argue that the two are linked. First, they are linked empirically, through evidence that those men who show violence towards wives and partners are also likely to show violence outside the home, for example, in bars, schools or the workplace (Fagan *et al.* 1983), i.e. the sorts of violence considered in Chapter 7. Cross-culturally, severe wife-beating is associated with a broader pattern of using violence to resolve interpersonal conflicts (Levinson 1989).

A second link is in terms of shared beliefs. I shall argue that in western societies, men who are likely to show violence both towards their wives and towards other men share a set of ideological beliefs which entails a certain view of manhood, involving on the one hand preoccupation with achieving and maintaining status, through fighting and risk-taking, and on the other viewing women as property whose behaviour has to be controlled, violence being a legitimate way of doing so. These beliefs may be marginalized in western intellectual circles, but I would argue that they are deep-rooted historically as prescriptions and justifications of masculine behaviour which strongly involves the striving for and exercise of power. We have merely glimpsed at one aspect of these values in connection with the history of wife-beating. They are also implicated in violence towards other men (Chapter 7) and sexual aggression (Chapter 11).

Beliefs about masculinity prescribe the behaviour of men by offering a set of standards – or role-related behaviour – to which to aspire, and a set of actions which are prohibited by sanctions. From early in life, avoidance of femininity is an important motivation for young boys. I have argued that this stems from a recognition of the greater structural power of males in society (Archer 1989, 1992b). Similarly, aspiring to be 'tough' is an important motivation for young boys, to be replaced by achievement in a wider sense later in life (for example, Weisfeld et al. 1980, 1987). All of these aspirations, reflecting prescriptions for behaviour, are related to male power – the first emphasizing the importance of not being feminine, and the other two the importance of competing with other men for status.

In societies and in sub-cultures where the separation of male and female worlds is most pronounced, these sorts of values will be emphasized. An extreme and aberrant – not to mention abhorrent – example was cited by Daly and Wilson (1988). It concerned the man who supposedly has the world record for siring children (888). Moulay Ismail the Bloodthirsty, emperor of Morocco in the early eighteenth century, was highly competitive with other men in a direct physical sense: he reputedly killed 30,000 of them; he also kept a harem of 500 young women, each completely isolated and guarded by a eunuch and a female slave.

Domination over women and physical interpersonal competition are two prominent aspects of a loose set of masculine values referred to in western societies as 'macho values'. I described these, and rating scales designed to measure them, in Chapter 7. High scores on the 'Hypermasculinity Inventory' were associated with both sexual violence towards women (Mosher and Anderson 1986), and violent behaviour towards other men (Mosher and Sirkin 1984). I argued that although in modern western societies educated men pursue goals in a less physical manner, the impact of these more basic values will be reduced but none the less present, especially in subcultures where fighting ability and physical courage are necessary.

These values promote both more intense interpersonal competition between men, and domination of men over women. They represent a legitimization of both inter-male power struggles, in that these are seen as the proper activities of 'real men', and of male domination over women, in that this is how 'real men' treat women. They also encourage the use of violence in achieving these aims. In both senses they help us to understand the link between inter-male violence towards women, both physical and sexual.

In our society, many men do not subscribe to such values, or at least only partially do so. It is likely that those who endorse such values in modern western societies are those for whom other – less risky – strategies for obtaining material resources and mates are not so readily available. In terms of a power analysis, this again represents a 'weakness of power'. Of typical American murders, Daly and Wilson (1988) stated: 'Most of the victims, like most of the offenders, were nobodies: unpropertied and unmarried, little educated, often unemployed' (p. 124).

Nevertheless, this is unlikely to be the whole story: macho values have a partial appeal to a wider section of the community, through socialization into a macho subculture (for example, Beynon 1989), or because they are attractive to younger males and those drawn to risk-taking. In their evolutionary analysis, Daly and Wilson (1988, 1990, this volume) portray such values as appealing to certain aspects of the male psyche which have been shaped by natural selection, a psyche (in their words) 'obsessed with social comparisons, with the need for achievement, and with the desire to gain control over the reproductive capacities of women' (1988: 136).

They claim in effect that macho behaviour can be viewed as directly resulting from our evolved tendencies. While I agree that this is partly the case, it is not necessarily the whole story, and indeed represents a pessimistic view of men. Other evidence indicates a measure of flexibility about male behaviour. For example, Daly and Wilson (1988: 136) themselves argue that inter-male competition and risk-taking is most pronounced amongst men who have 'nothing to lose'. Conversely, it will be less pronounced amongst those who have alternative routes to resources and status.

Another likely source of flexibility arises from developmental influences. Here the socio-biological concept of alternative reproductive strategies has been used. This term refers to the conditions of rearing providing cues about the sort of behaviour which will be adaptive during adulthood, and altering development accordingly (see Archer 1992a: 116–17). Draper and Harpending (1982, 1987) used it to argue that in societies where fathers are absent during childhood, there is rearing by peers from an early age, which for boys involves intense aggressive competition, dominance relationships and antagonism towards women. This fits the boy for a society where machismo is at a premium, whereas in societies where men are less competitive and more parental, these characteristics are less evident. This hypothesis, supported by cross-cultural comparisons, involves a more flexible view of the male psyche than that implied by Daly and Wilson's quotation.

THE EVOLUTIONARY ORIGINS OF POWER

The concept of power is concerned with one individual's interests being exercised at the expense of another's. In the natural world, when one individual achieves goals related to fitness at the expense of another individual doing so, this is referred to as ecological competition (for example, MacArthur 1972; Wilson 1975). It forms the basis of changes in the composition of genes in the population throughout successive generations, namely, natural selection. The means through which ecological competition is achieved are various: a plant may outgrow another variety; the males of many animal species possess mechanisms for blocking or removing the sperm of rivals (for example, Parker 1970, 1984; Smith 1984). The best-known form of competition in the animal world is of course aggression, the active interference with a rival over a short space of time (Archer 1988).

Dominance relations occur where one animal recognizes that another individual or class of individuals is capable of defeating it in any contest over fitness-related interests (Archer 1992a: 128–9). This widens the scope of ecological competition so that it coincides with notions of human power on an interpersonal level. This would correspond to the power relations among a small group, based on force or the threat of force. As indicated earlier, in humans, a clear *concept* of status is possible, thereby elaborating this form of power into a reputation or acknowledged position within a wider group or community.

As elaborated in Chapter 14 (by Daly and Wilson), Darwin (1871) identified the process of sexual selection as involving competition between males for access to receptive females, and choice by females of males with adaptive characteristics. Trivers (1972) outlined the reasons why sexual selection usually took these forms. These analyses provide an overall reason why interindividual competition and dominance relations are more likely to be found amongst males than females. However, they are by no means inevitable consequences of natural selection: sexual selection can take many forms besides aggressive inter-male competition. I have already mentioned sperm competition; another alternative is avoidance of overt competition by adopting alternative mating tactics (Archer 1992a: 114). There are also conditions where biparental rearing is necessary for offspring survival, and inter-male competition is much reduced, as in the so-called monogamous birds and mammals (see below). Under some conditions, females are the more competitive sex.

Judging by the degree of sexual dimorphism in humans, and the range of mating patterns (Archer 1992a: 160–1), it is likely that inter-male competition was an important feature in human evolution, but that it was not as pronounced as in polygynous species such as baboons and elephant seals (cf. Chapter 14 by Daly and Wilson, who reach the same conclusion; others have argued that monogamy is the basic human pattern).

When considering the evolutionary origins of men's structural power over women, we need also to consider the conflicting reproductive interests of males and females. Simplifying the situation somewhat, we can characterize the optimum strategy for males as fertilizing as many females as possible, and for the female as limiting the access of males so as to choose the fittest one available. This is the general picture derived from Darwin's theory of sexual selection. However, as indicated above, it will be complicated where both sexes need to engage in parental care. Here the range of females available to the male is reduced, and the choice of the female restricted: however, recent studies of 'extra-pair copulations' (EPC) in birds (Mock and Fujioka 1990) suggest that even in an apparently monogamous mating system, the sexes still show different sexual inclinations: females will, if possible, copulate with a more attractive male (namely, one with greater fitness than her mate), whereas males will take any chance to copulate with another female.

Even in apparently monogamous species, therefore, males and females have different reproductive interests. These are more pronounced if there is a tendency towards polygamy, as indicated for humans. There is evidence from a variety of species, including Old World Monkeys and apes (Smuts 1992), that the male will, if possible, seek to impose his optimum strategy on the female by force (Parker 1974). This takes various forms, such as attacking oestrous females, guarding them after copulation, or herding females over longer periods of time; in some cases (such as the orang-utan), the male uses force to achieve copulation itself (Smuts 1992). Since this will remove female choice entirely, it is likely that female strategies have evolved in most cases to counter the widespread occurrence of such forced copulations. This argument hinges on females who do not retain choice of males leaving less fit offspring than those who retain choice (Archer 1992c; see also Gowaty 1992). Indeed, there will be selective pressures more generally to resist male coercion: currently there is disagreement about how effective these have been in non-human primates (Gowaty 1992; Smuts 1992).

These considerations provide the background for human evolution and history. As Smuts (1992) put it: 'Male reproductive striving is the ultimate cause of male dominance over women; men's superior fighting ability is simply one means to this end' (p. 28). This ultimate cause has, however, resulted not in a single form of male–female relations, but in a variety of patterns, adapted to the social and ecological circumstances. Smuts (1992) proposed several hypotheses to account for variations in men's aggression towards women across different cultures. For example, she suggested that wife-beating would be highest where female alliances were weak, where kin were unwilling, and/or unable, to protect the wife, where there were strong male alliances, where male relations were not egalitarian, and where husbands controlled family resources. These hypotheses were derived from an appreciation of the selection pressures that have produced the varying patterns of male–female relations in non-human primate societies. Smuts went on to assess them in terms of human cross-cultural evidence.

This approach enables men's domination over women to be understood in terms of the conflicting reproductive interests of the two sexes and men's ability to impose their interests over those of women by force (partly through their being bigger and stronger, partly through male alliances, and partly through mammalian reproduction limiting women's freedom of action). This approach also identifies the specific conditions under which the costs of such a male strategy will be counter-productive, and those under which female counter-strategies will be successful. It provides a socio-ecological framework for understanding cross-cultural variation, of the sort which can be used to understand animal societies (for example, Crook 1970). It can also be extended to consider the impact of modern technological and cultural changes on male domination: contraception, baby food, universal education and the mass media are just some of the influences which have paved the way for the feminist challenge to the patriarchy.

Nevertheless, in the human case, cultural institutions mediate or transform the relationship between ecology and social relations (Hinde 1987; Crook 1992). In the present case, it is clear that most traditional cultural beliefs about gender (outlined in the previous section) actively encourage male domination, and the use of violence as a way of enforcing this ideology (Dobash and Dobash 1977–78, 1980; Smuts 1992). A potent way of enforcing male interests is to build them into religious beliefs, and hence to legitimize them as coming from a higher authority. In modern western societies, the sorts of technological and cultural innovations referred to above have combined with the partial breakdown of religious and family authority, to produce a challenge to the traditional pattern of male control over women's reproductive lives.

For men to be able to enact such power over women in traditional societies, there also needed to be a separation of the worlds of men and women, and the control of women's world by that of men. Separation of public and private spheres is pronounced in many parts of the world today, men controlling the public spheres where they strive for status and power amongst themselves, and the private involving mainly females and having little or no public status. Repeated pregnancy, child-rearing and lack of education (or a different education) all made (or make) it easier to keep women out of the public sphere. Their relative isolation in family groups, in the absence of the mass media, would have prevented political organization.

Thus the positions of formal power could readily come to be exclusively male. In the traditional world it has been unnecessary for men to exert power over women in the public sphere: those who are in the workforce are in subordinate, often spatially separated, positions. In any case it was clear that the world of work was a male domain. The entry of women into male occupations provides a challenge to this authority which is met with various ways of seeking to denigrate women and their work, such as sexual harassment (for example, Ott 1989). In the private world of the family, where women had considerable informal influence, there has always been direct contact between male and female, and therefore there has always been a perceived need to enforce male authority. Ideological justification of a 'woman's place', backed up by the legitimization of violence towards women, facilitated the exercise of male power in the private sphere.

CONCLUSIONS

In this chapter, I have considered two very different types of power explanations for male violence: the structural explanation of violence towards women, and the interpersonal status explanation of inter-male violence. I concluded that the first did indeed provide an appropriate general explanation of why it is women who are the major recipients of marital violence. However, a subsidiary explanation was acquired to explain why certain men and not others were violent towards women: this involved the use of violence when women's behaviour challenged the specific expectations held by their husbands about

326

how 'their' wife should behave. The second explanation concerned the exercise of male power through violence under conditions of minimal structural power.

I argued that the two explanations are linked because men who hold certain masculine or 'macho' values are likely to seek to exercise power over other men and over women through violence. Such values vary within and across cultures, but it is likely that they tap certain views about masculinity widely held in the traditional world.

Finally, I discussed the possible evolutionary and historical origins of male power. Inter-male dominance relations are readily understood in terms of the process of sexual selection. Structural power by men over women reflect two considerations: first, there is a conflict of interests between the optimum reproductive strategies of males and females; secondly, through socio-ecological and cultural conditions, men have been able to control the reproductive interests of women, by force if necessary.

ACKNOWLEDGEMENTS

I would like to thank Anne Campbell for her helpful comments on this chapter, which was written while I was a Simon Industrial and Professional Fellow at the University of Manchester 1991–92.

REFERENCES

Appleby, M. C. (1985) 'Hawks, doves . . . and chickens', *New Scientist*, 105(1438): 16–18.

Archer, J. (1976) 'The organization of aggression and fear in vertebrates', in P. P. G. Bateson and P. Klopfer (eds) *Perspectives in Ethology*, 2, New York: Plenum, pp. 231–98.

—— (1988) *The Behavioural Biology of Aggression*, Cambridge and New York: Cambridge University Press.

—— (1989) 'Childhood gender roles: structure and development', *The Psychologist: Bulletin of the British Psychological Society*, 2: 367–70.

—— (1992a) *Ethology and Human Development*, Hemel Hempstead, UK: Harvester Wheatsheaf.

—— (1992b) 'Childhood gender roles: social context and organisation', in H. McGurk (ed.) *Childhood Social Development: Contemporary Perspectives*, Hove, UK, and Hillsdale, NJ: Erlbaum, pp. 31–61.

—— (1992c) 'Mating tactics are complex and involve females too', *The Behavioral and Brain Sciences*, 15: 379–80 (commentary on Thornhill and Thornhill).

Beynon, J. (1989) 'A school for men: an ethnographic case study of routine violence in schooling', in J. Archer and K. Browne (eds) *Human Aggression: Naturalistic Approaches*, London and New York: Routledge, pp. 122–50.

Boulton, M. J. and Smith, P. K. (1990) 'Affective bias in children's perceptions of dominance relationships', *Child Development*, 61: 221–9.

Brown, R. (1988) *Group Processes: Dynamics Within and Between Groups*, Oxford: Blackwell.

Campbell, A. (1986) 'The streets and violence', in A. Campbell and J. J. Gibbs (eds)

Violent Transactions: The Limits of Personality, Oxford: Blackwell, pp. 115–32.

Cheney, D. L. and Seyfarth, R. M. (1990) *How Monkeys See the World: Inside the Mind of Another Species*, Chicago and London: University of Chicago Press.

Clegg, S. R. (1989) *Frameworks of Power*, London and Newbury Park, CA: Sage.

Crook, J. H. (1970) 'The socio-ecology of primates', in J. H. Crook (ed.) *Social Behaviour in Birds and Mammals*, London and New York: Academic Press, pp. 103–66.

—— (1992) 'Ecology and culture in the adaptive radiation of Tibetan speaking peoples in the Himalayas', Primate Society Osmand Hill Lecture, presented at the Joint Association for the Study of Animal Behaviour/Primate Society of Great Britain, Winter meeting, 3–4 Dec., held at the Zoological Society of London.

Daly, M. and Wilson, M. (1988) *Homicide*, New York: Aldine de Gruyter.

—— (1990) 'Killing the competition: female/female and male/male competition', *Human Nature*, 1: 81–107.

Darwin, C. (1871) *The Descent of Man, and Selection in Relation to Sex*, London: Murray.

Datta, S. (1988) 'The acquisition of dominance among free-ranging rhesus monkey siblings', *Animal Behaviour*, 36: 754–72.

de Waal, F. B. M. (1982) *Chimpanzee Politics*, London: Jonathan Cape.

—— (1984) 'Sex differences in the formation of coalitions among chimpanzees', *Ethology and Sociobiology*, 5: 239–55.

Dobash, R. E. and Dobash, R. P. (1977–78) 'Wives: the "appropriate" victims of marital violence', *Victimology: An International Journal*, 2: 426–42.

—— (1980) *Violence Against Wives: A Case Against the Patriarchy*, London: Open Books.

—— (1984) 'The nature and antecedents of violent events', *British Journal of Criminology*, 24: 269–88.

Doré, F. Y. and Dumas, C. (1987) 'Psychology of animal cognition: Piagetian studies', *Psychological Bulletin*, 102: 219–33.

Draper, P. and Harpending, H. (1982) 'Father absence and reproductive strategy: an evolutionary perspective', *Journal of Anthropology Research*, 38: 255–73.

—— (1987) 'A sociobiological perspective on the development of human reproductive strategies', in K. B. MacDonald (ed.) *Sociobiological Perspectives on Human Development*, New York and Berlin: Springer-Verlag, pp. 340–72.

Eagly, A. H. (1983) 'Gender and social influence: a social psychological analysis', *American Psychologist*, 38: 971–81.

Edelman, M. S. and Omark, D. R. (1973) 'Dominance hierarchies in young children', *Social Science Information*, 12(1): 103–10.

Fagan, J. A., Stewart, D. K. and Hansen, K. V. (1983) 'Violent men or violent husbands? background factors and situational correlates', in D. Finkelhor, R. J. Gelles, G. T. Hotaling and M. A. Straus (eds) *The Dark Side of Families*, Beverly Hills, CA, and London: Sage, pp. 49–67.

Felson, R. B. (1984) 'Patterns of aggressive social interactions', in A. Mummendey (ed.) *Social Psychology of Aggression: From Individual Behavior to Social Interaction*, Berlin: Springer-Verlag, pp. 107–26.

—— (1993) 'Sexual coercion: a social interactionist approach', in R. B. Felson and J. T. Tedeschi (eds) *Aggression and Violence: Social Interactionist Perspectives*, American Psychological Association.

Gelles, R. J. (1972) *The Violent Home*, Beverly Hills, CA: Sage.

—— (1987) *The Violent Home*, 2nd edn, Beverly Hills, CA: Sage.

Gilbert, P. (1990) 'Changes: rank, status and mood', in S. Fisher and C. L. Cooper (eds) *On the Move: The Psychology of Change and Transition*, New York: Wiley, pp. 33–52.

Goode, W. J. (1971) 'Force and violence in the family', *Journal of Marriage and the Family*, 33: 624–36.

Gowaty, P. A. (1992) 'Evolutionary biology and feminism', *Human Nature*, 3: 217–49.

Griffin, C. (1991) 'Experiencing power: dimensions of gender, race and class', *British Psychological Society, Psychology of Women Section Newsletter*, 8: 43–58.

Hall, R. E. (1985) *Ask Any Woman: A London Inquiry into Rape and Sexual Assault*, London: Falling Wall Press.

Hanmer, J. (1978) 'Violence and the social control of women', in G. Littlejohn, B. Smart, J. Wakeford and N. Yuval-Davis (eds) *Power and the State*, London: Croom-Helm, pp. 217–38.

Henley, N. M. (1977) *Body Politics: Power, Sex and Non-verbal Communication*, Englewood-Cliffs, NJ: Prentice-Hall.

Hinde, R. A. (1978) 'Dominance and role – two concepts with dual meanings', *Journal of Social and Biological Structures*, 1: 27–38.

—— (1987) *Individuals, Relationships and Culture: Links Between Ethology and the Social Sciences*, Cambridge and New York: Cambridge University Press.

Johnson, J. A. (1987) 'Dominance rank in juvenile olive baboons, *Papio anubis*: the influence of gender, size, maternal rank and orphaning', *Animal Behaviour*, 35: 1694–708.

Kitzinger, S. (1991) 'Feminism, psychology and the paradox of power', *Feminism and Psychology*, 1: 111–29.

Koss, M. P. (1990) 'The women's mental health research agenda: violence against women', *American Psychologist*, 45: 374–80.

Koss, M. P. and Oros, C. J. (1982) 'Sexual experiences survey: a research instrument investigating sexual aggression and victimization', *Journal of Consulting and Clinical Psychology*, 50: 455–7.

Levinson, D. (1989) *Family Violence in Cross-Cultural Perspective*, Newbury Park, CA, and London: Sage.

Lukes, S. (1974) *Power: A Radical View*, London: Macmillan.

MacArthur, R. H. (1972) *Geographical Ecology: Patterns in the Distribution of Species*, New York: Harper & Row.

McVicar, J. (1982) 'Violence in prisons', in P. Marsh and A. Campbell (eds) *Aggression and Violence*, Oxford: Blackwell, pp. 200–14.

Massell, G. W. (1968) 'Law as an instrument of revolutionary change in a traditional milieu: the case of Soviet Central Asia', *Law and Society Review*, 11: 179–228.

Miller, S. L. and Simpson, S. S. (1991) 'Courtship violence and social control: does it matter?', *Law and Society Review*, 25: 335–65.

Mock, D. W. and Fujioka, M. (1990) 'Monogamy and long-term pair bonding in vertebrates', *Trends in Ecology and Evolution*, 5: 39–43.

Mosher, D. L. and Anderson, R. D. (1986) 'Macho personality, sexual aggression, and reactions to guided imagery of realistic rape', *Journal of Research in Personality*, 20: 77–94.

Mosher, D. L. and Sirkin, M. (1984) 'Measuring a macho personality constellation', *Journal of Research in Personality*, 18: 150–63.

O'Brien, J. (1971) 'Violence in divorce-prone families', *Journal of Marriage and the Family*, 33: 692–8.

Omark, D. R. and Edelman, M. S. (1975) 'A comparison of status hierarchies in young children: an ethological approach', *Social Science Information*, 14(5): 87–107.

Omark, D. R., Omark, M. and Edelman, M. S. (1975) 'Formation of dominance hierarchies in young children', in T. Williams (ed.) *Psychological Anthropology*, Chicago: Aldine, pp. 289–315.

Ott, E. M. (1989) 'Effects of the male–female ratio at work: police women and male nurses', *Psychology of Women Quarterly*, 13: 41–57.

Parker, G. A. (1970) 'Sperm competition and its evolutionary consequences in the insects', *Biological Reviews*, 45: 525–67.

—— (1974) 'Courtship persistence and female-guarding as male time-investment strategies', *Behaviour*, 48: 157–84.

—— (1984) 'Sperm competition and the evolution of animal mating strategies', in R. L. Smith (ed.) *Sperm Competition and the Evolution of Animal Mating Systems*, New York and London: Academic Press, pp. 1–60.

Ragins, B. R. and Sundstrom, E. (1989) 'Gender and power in organizations: a longitudinal perspective', *Psychological Bulletin*, 105: 51–88.

Roy, M. (1977) 'A current survey of 150 cases', in M. Roy (ed.) *Battered Women: A Psychological Study of Domestic Violence*, New York: Van Nostrand, pp. 25–44.

Silverberg, J. and Gray, J. P. (1992) 'Violence and peacefulness as behavioral potentialities of primates', in J. Silverberg and J. P. Gray (eds) *Aggression and Peacefulness in Humans and Other Primates*, New York: Oxford University Press, pp. 1–36.

Smith, R. L. (1984) 'Human sperm competition', in R. L. Smith (ed.) *Sperm Competition and the Evolution of Animal Mating Systems*, New York and London: Academic Press, pp. 601–59.

Smuts, B. (1992) 'Male aggression against women: an evolutionary perspective', *Human Nature*, 3: 1–44.

Steinmetz, S. (1977) 'Wifebeating, husbandbeating: a comparison of the use of physical violence between spouses to resolve marital fights', in M. Roy (ed.) *Battered Women: A Psychosociological Study of Domestic Violence*, New York: Van Nostrand, pp. 63–72.

Straus, M., Gelles, R. and Steinmetz, S. (1980) *Behind Closed Doors: Violence in the American Family*, New York: Anchor Press.

Strube, M. J. (1988) 'The decision to leave an abusive relationship: empirical evidence and theoretical issues', *Psychological Bulletin*, 104: 236–50.

Tajfel, H. (1982) 'Social psychology of intergroup relations', *Annual Review of Psychology*, 33: 1–39.

Tedeschi, J. T., Gaes, G. G. and Rivera, A. N. (1977) 'Aggression and the use of coercive power', *Journal of Social Issues*, 33: 101–25.

Trivers, R. L. (1972) 'Parental investment and sexual selection', in B. Campbell (ed.) *Sexual Selection and the Descent of Man*, Chicago: Aldine, pp. 136–79.

Walker, L. E. A. (1989) 'Psychology and violence against women', *American Psychologist*, 44: 659–702.

Weisfeld, G. E., Muczenski, D. M., Weisfeld, C. C. and Omark, D. R. (1987) 'Stability of boys' social success among peers over an eleven-year period', in J. A. Meacham (ed.) *Interpersonal Relations: Family, Peers and Friends*, Basel: Karger, pp. 58–80.

Weisfeld, G. E., Omark, D. R. and Cronin, C. L. (1980) 'A longitudinal and cross-sectional study of dominance relations in boys', in D. R. Omark, F. F. Strayer and D. G. Freedman (eds) *Dominance Relations: An Ethological View of Human Conflict and Social Interaction*, New York and London: Garland STPM Press, pp. 205–16.

Wilkinson, S. (1986) 'Introduction', in S. Wilkinson (ed.) *Feminist Social Psychology: Developing Theory and Practice*, Milton Keynes and Philadelphia, PA: Open University Press, pp. 1–6.

Wilson, E. O. (1975) *Sociobiology: The New Synthesis*, Cambridge, MA: Harvard University Press.

Yllo, K. A. (1983) 'Using a feminist approach in quantitative research', in D. Finkelhor, R. J. Gelles, G. T. Hotaling and M. A. Straus (eds) *The Dark Side of Families*, Beverly Hills, CA, and London: Sage, pp. 277–88.

Yllo, K. A. and Straus, M. A. (1984) 'The impact of structural inequality and sexist family norms on rates of wife-beating', *Journal of International and Comparative Social Welfare*, 1: 16–29.

17

MEN AND THE MEANING OF VIOLENCE

Anne Campbell and Steven Muncer

It is men who commit 90 per cent of violent crime (see Chapter 1). Violence and the male sex are virtually synonymous – the two are interwoven seamlessly in our minds as part of the natural order of things. Yet women are not devoid of the capacity for anger and aggression. As infants they cry and display temper tantrums as often as boys (Goodenough 1931) and in adulthood they experience anger as frequently and as intensely as do men (Frost and Averill 1982; Tavris 1989). In this chapter we want to examine the differences between men's and women's understanding of aggression in order to focus on how men's interpretation makes them much more likely to engage in violent behaviour. The behavioural differences between the sexes, we believe, can be traced to the distinctive social representations or implicit theories that they hold about the meaning of aggression.

Male violence is marvellously heterogeneous in form. It manifests itself in acts as disparate as robbery, assault, football hooliganism, school bullying, date rape and pub brawls. Yet as diverse as these behaviours may appear to be, they share certain common features. They all serve a clear instrumental purpose – they achieve interpersonal ends. Robbery is about monetary gain but it is also about the effective use of threat as a means of interpersonal control (Katz 1988; Lejeune 1977). Assaults are character contests in which neither participant will back down for fear of losing face (Luckenbill 1977). Bullying is about the achievement of social status through the humiliation of peers (Besag 1980). Saturday afternoons provide football hooligans with a forum in which they can demonstrate courage and loyalty between the mundane weeks of stultifying work and anonymity (Marsh *et al* 1978). Date rape is about the use of force to coerce compliance for purposes of sexual gratification or the exercise of power (Felson 1993). Drunken brawls as often as not result from power struggles between customers and bar staff about who has the right to regulate behaviour in the pub (Felson *et al*. 1986; Marsh and Campbell 1979). No matter how much the media plays up the idea of 'senseless' or 'mindless' violence, it is clear to the actors involved and to the researchers who study them that the behaviour is in fact goal-directed and functional despite its prohibited criminal status. Violence, amongst some men, serves to demonstrate their control over others and in that control resides power and so self-esteem.

SEX AND THE UNDERSTANDING OF AGGRESSION

Violence and aggression differ principally in their outcomes. Violence results in actual bodily injury which is subject to criminal prosecution. Aggression encompasses a variety of verbal, emotional as well as physical attacks that share in common the actor's intent to hurt or control and the victim's desire to avoid these outcomes. But in terms of the motives espoused by the male actors, violence and aggression share much in common. Listen to John Allen (1978: 181, 183), a convicted violent criminal explaining his position on the crime of robbery and on the intimately related issue of self-esteem:

> You know when people are going to rip you off. You know when some-body up to something. They give theirself away, the way they look or the way they act or the way they talk. The amount of money really don't make no difference: *you just can't let them get out on you.* It don't matter who you are or what you are; they'll try, and you gotta stop them. At all times you gotta stop them. . . . *You got to maintain who you are at all times. You do it for the people watching.* I remember one time in Lorton the psychiatrist asked me, 'Do you sometimes grow weary of portraying the image of a tough guy?' And I say 'Yeah, I really do.' Because you can't let your guard down. Once you start one way, people expect this of you at all times. This thing where you just had to show you had the heart, you could do it.

Now listen to the words of a Wall Street broker and a New York journalist (from Campbell 1993), men with no history of criminal violence but with normal exposure to male conflicts, discussing what aggression means to them:

Mike: I want that guy to know I'm going to beat him and I want him to back down. I don't want to hit him. I want that guy to be the guy to say 'OK we're not going to fight'. *I want to maintain my self-respect.* That's the kind of person I am. . . . *I just want to get one up on him* and walk away and go 'Haha'.

Robert: But do you do it for the other guys? I think sometimes I'm like that. There comes a point where I don't know if I do it for me or for the acceptance. I think maybe you first start doing it for yourself and you really get pissed off and you get in there and start something. And then you realize that people are listening. And it's kind of uplifting because *you're on-stage*, you know? Everyone is going 'Ooh, look at that over there'. You enjoy the fact that people are watching and all. You feel good. You feel like 'I have some power here. I have some-thing over them.'

These texts come from speakers with very different backgrounds. They differ in race, social class, family backgrounds and life opportunities, but as men they share a great deal when it comes to the subject of aggression. They inhabit a world beset with threat from other men. The perception of threat sets in motion a zero-sum game in which self-esteem is either won or lost. To back down from challenge means that the game is lost before it has begun, so, for these men, there is no alternative but to enter the fray. Once committed to the contest, public honour in the form of audience expectation raises the stakes above mere private self-esteem. Violence is not relished for its own sake – Mike hopes that the other guy will back down and John Allen gets tired of living up to his fearless image – but when challenged it is the only conceivable response.

Analysis of men talking about aggression suggests that they view it as an instrumental act concerned with issues of interpersonal control (Campbell and Muncer 1987). This view is also taken by many academic accounts of aggression which can be united under the general rubric of instrumental theories. They focus upon the consequences of aggression in terms of social or material rewards accruing to the actor. The proposed rewards include coercive power (Tedeschi *et al.* 1974), social control (Black 1983), normative approval (Wolfgang and Ferracuti 1967), self-esteem (Toch 1969), the management of identity (Felson 1982, 1984; Athens 1977) and a variety of other social and material reinforcers such as the acquisition of territory, money and peer approval (Bandura 1973). Though differing in their specifics, these theories share a common concern with aggression as a personally functional and learned behaviour with a clear focus upon the interpersonal context and rewards for aggression.

In recent years instrumental theories have become so widely accepted that their assertions about the motivations for aggression seem self-evident. But by contrasting them with a very different theoretical position – expressive theories – we can see more clearly the unique properties of such a view. Expressive theories focus upon the build-up of drive, stress or arousal which is discharged through aggressive action. Theorists such as Freud (1946), Lorenz (1966), Storr (1968) and the Yale group (Dollard *et al.* 1939) are particularly concerned with the motivational component that energizes or potentiates the behaviour. Others have devoted more attention to the discharge mechanisms by which this drive is expressed in aggressive action. Candidates include catharsis (Freud 1946), genetically linked deficiency in learning (Eysenck 1964), inadequate imposition of external social control (Gottfredson and Hirschi 1990), environmental cues (Berkowitz 1965), failure of cognitive guidance at high levels of arousal (Zillmann 1979) and deficient ego functions (Perls 1969; Redl and Toch 1986). Expressive theories share a belief in aggression as socially and personally dysfunctional and a concern with the intra-psychic rather than interpersonal dynamics of the act.

If we listen to women speaking about violence, expressive concerns feature very prominently in their talk. The following extract is from a New York woman in her mid-twenties:

Karen: We had a really terrible fight. It probably was about nothing important. *I can't remember what it was about.* But it did terminate with him going in and taking a shower and I was so furious. I just sort of whirled around and tried to pick up the phone. *I don't know if I wanted to throw it* but I knew it wasn't going to go far enough. So I picked up this frying pan that was right there and I tossed it right through the curtain. I didn't even think about it and then he came out dripping, holding the frying pan. And he said 'You could have killed me. You could have killed me, do you know that?' I still didn't realize I could have killed him because I didn't feel like I wanted to kill him. I mean it wasn't even in my head at the time I was throwing it. *I could have flung it against the wall.* I did fling it at him but it wasn't that I was thinking 'I am going to aim for his head or someplace else'. I just threw it. I can do that. I really have a very blind kind of rage sometimes when *I seem to get really crazy.*

In this text, there is little to suggest that her aggression is about maintaining self-esteem or demonstrating control. Control features in the role of *self-control* and specifically in the consequences of its breakdown. So powerful is the impact of the erupting anger that she remembers little of what preceded the fight or of the aims of her actions. She clearly recalls the terrifying potential of her aggression – the possibility that she could have killed someone – but insists that this was not her motivation. She needed to discharge her anger and frustration and realizes that she could have achieved the same effect by throwing something at the wall. She was in the throes of a blind rage which took possession of her, making her temporarily 'crazy'. Whereas in instrumental accounts of aggression acts are directed at physically incapacitating the challenger, in expressive accounts they are about the discharge of anger. In the former the actor must maintain a level of control in order effectively to subdue his challenger, but in the latter the actor's behaviour is seen as out of control as if she were possessed by some demonic force.

SOCIAL REPRESENTATIONS OF AGGRESSION

Before elaborating upon the consequences of the social representations of aggression held by men and women, we shall digress briefly to clarify the concept of 'social representation'. The term was coined by Moscovici (1976) in his seminal work tracing the diffusion of psychoanalytic theory into modern lay consciousness. Derived from Durkheim's (1953) 'collective' and 'individual' representations, the term was designed to capture the middle ground between sociology and psychology by focusing upon social representations which 'are shared by many individuals and as such constitute a *social*

335

reality which can influence *individual* behaviour' (Jaspars and Fraser 1984: 104). Moscovici has been deliberately evasive in defining the term (Farr 1987), but has perhaps come closest in this quotation:

> cognitive systems with a logic and language of their own. . . . They do not represent simply 'opinions about', 'images of' or 'attitudes towards' but 'theories' or 'branches of knowledge' in their own right, for the discovery and organization of reality. . . . Systems of values, ideas and practices with a two-fold function; first, to establish an order which will enable individuals to orientate themselves in their material and social world and to master it; secondly, to enable communication to take place among members of a community by providing them with a code for social exchange and a code for naming and classifying unambiguously the various aspects of their world and their individual and group history.
>
> (Moscovici, p. xiii, in his foreword to Herzlich 1973)

Because social representations are explanatory and interpretative devices, they appear to share some common ground with attribution theory and problem-solving. Yet they differ fundamentally; the latter are constructivist in approach whereas the former focus upon social transmission. Constructivist approaches maintain that consensus amongst persons with regard to, for example, moral judgement or causal attribution results from similar methods of problem-solving. They further assume that there are optimal solutions to such problems, that the development of problem-solving is internally generated and that the outcome of development is perfect intellectual autonomy. Development is social only to the extent that the problems to be solved may be social in nature. Such theories 'assume that each individual has arrived independently at an objective understanding of the same reality' (Emler 1987: 376). Emler goes on to argue that life is simply too short for the individual discovery of many non-obvious causal connections and that the consensus that people achieve arises from the cultural dissemination of social representations. Children acquire 'currently employed and acknowledged ways of thinking and talking within the social system to which (they) belong'. Recent research (Campbell *et al.* 1992; Campbell *et al.* 1993; Campbell and Muncer, forthcoming) has confirmed quantitatively, using more than 450 subjects, the significant correlation between being male and showing a preference for an instrumental interpretation of aggression. The prevalence of two distinct representations of aggression associated with sex precludes the notion of 'optimal solutions' to attributional dilemmas. Each model does a good job of accounting for the facts of social life since the act of holding a given model tends to encourage selective attention to variables which confirm it (Moscovici 1981). In addition, the relationship between sex and preference for instrumental or expressive representations suggests that either (1) the sexes have distinct problem-solving styles which independently lead men in one attributional direction and women in another, or (2) that part of gender socialization entails the acquisition of appropriate social representations of specific phenomena, including aggression. We favour this latter interpretation.

It is likely that gendered differences in social representations of aggression may be traced to contemporary structural factors and to the socialization experiences of boys and girls. Men and women differ in the mundane occupational and social roles that they hold. Men's work legitimates the controlled use of aggression (Eagly and Steffen 1986; Eagly 1987). In the world of business it is used as a means of encouraging competition and maintaining hierarchies of power while in the military it is actively trained and encouraged. Women occupy subordinate work positions often in professions which encourage caring and support (teaching, nursing, social work). These same qualities are also called upon in their domestic work as homemakers and mothers. In both cases the expression of aggression is strongly discouraged. For women both the nature of their work roles and their lesser power are consonant with an expressive view of aggression as a dysfunctional force to be controlled, while for men an instrumental interpretation of aggression gels with its function as a source of social influence and personal power (Bakan 1966; Gilligan 1982; Parson and Bales 1955).

Developmentally, the aggression of boys and girls is not differentially sanctioned by mothers (Maccoby 1980; Newson and Newson 1968). The critical differences between the sexes seem to lie in their peer-group experiences (Maccoby 1988). Boys' peer groups are larger, more public and organized hierarchically (Archer 1992). Language is used as a means of achieving status within the group, as is physical aggression in the early years (Maltz and Borker 1982). Aggression is a particularly potent means of evoking a response from male peers (Fagot and Hagan 1985; Fagot et al. 1985). In the peer group boys learn that aggression is critical in asserting interpersonal control and achieving respect, and this message is clearly reinforced on television where popular male 'superheroes' employ violence as a legitimate and socially applauded means of controlling the villains. Girls, on the other hand, typically have one or two best friends, construct their friendships more privately and avoid direct confrontation as a means of settling disputes (Archer 1992). Language is a means of establishing bonds and cementing friendship through self-disclosure rather than a combative device. Outright aggression tends to produce not censure but a lack of response (Fagot and Hagan 1985; Lloyd and Smith 1986). Girls learn that aggression is both ineffective as a means of interpersonal influence and a threat to the harmony of relationships.

We turn now to a consideration of the implications of gendered social representations for male and female involvement in criminal violence. There are significant variations in the sex ratio in violent crime as a function of specific offence (Kruttschnitt 1990). Self-reported and official data indicate that robbery is the most predominantly male form of violent crime (with the exception of rape). In contrast, national surveys of spousal violence show that men and women admit to similar numbers of aggressive acts toward their spouses. How can a theory of differential social representations of aggression interpret data in each of these two areas?

ROBBERY

Robbery is the most frequent stranger-to-stranger crime in the United States and it is a largely male enterprise. There are between ten and fifteen male robberies for every one committed by a female (Hindelang *et al*. 1979; Laub and McDermott 1985). Robbery – defined as theft employing force or the threat of force – is perhaps the prototype of instrumental violence. It is an act characterized by the absence of anger (indeed the absence of any relationship between the parties involved), where the principal goal is monetary and the secondary benefits include the symbolic humiliation of the victim and consequently a sense of power and mastery on the part of the criminal (Gabor *et al*. 1987; Lejeune 1977; Luckenbill 1981; Walsh 1986). Such an act by its nature appeals to a masculine and instrumental understanding of aggression and is foreign to women's expressive representation of aggression. But before considering the merits of such an argument, let us first look at four alternative explanations of the sex imbalance in this crime.

Robbery requires the use or potential use of *physical strength*. Studies suggest that in adolescence ghetto youth perfect the art of yoking (grabbing an unsuspecting peer round the neck with a bent arm) as part of routine street games (Allen 1978; Katz 1988) and that in adulthood many robbers display a marked concern with their physical fitness and physique (Walsh 1986). Perhaps it is merely women's lesser strength that deters them from engaging in robbery? Such a straightforward proposal, however, presupposes that the only potential victims of robbery are males. If a female robber were to restrict her 'marks' to other females she would be at no more of a physical disadvantage than would a male in a same-sex confrontation. In fact, 53 per cent of victims of female robbers are male, suggesting that such women do not fear the physical disparity between them (Fortune *et al*. 1980; Girouard 1988). In addition, the physical strength argument should also apply to all forms of violent crime. Yet the sex imbalance for robbery is considerably higher than for assault or domestic violence (Laub and McDermott 1985; Straus and Gelles 1990). Furthermore, the disparity in physical strength can easily be equalized by the use of a gun or other lethal weapon. Clearly, women are able to gain access to firearms since in domestic homicides guns are used equally by men and women (Cook 1982).

Perhaps women lack the *motives* for robbery. Interviews with robbers unambiguously endorse the speedy acquisition of money as the chief motive for the crime. Yet in the United States it is women, not men, who form the bulk of those living below the poverty line; the sex ratio for poverty is 1.51:1. Amongst blacks, who are disproportionately represented in poverty statistics, half of all children under 18 live with their mothers only, and half of these families are below the poverty line. With child-support payments erratic or non-existent, scant day-care facilities for those who want to work and the lower average wage earned by women, surely it is women who have the greater financial motive for robbery. Yet an analysis of sex differentials in crime trends from 1930 to 1980 indicates that there has been no change for robbery in spite of the fact that the differential for other property crimes rose steadily from 7 to 32 per cent over the same period (Steffensmeier and Cobb 1981). Women, especially those in poverty, are not adverse to crime. Forty per cent of female arrests are for shoplifting, forgery and fraud. But though women engage in property crime and in violent assaults, they rarely combine both in the act of robbery.

The thrill of robbery is often cited as a secondary motive for the crime (Gabor et al. 1987; Katz 1988; Lejeune 1977; Walsh 1986). But we should be cautious in uncritically accepting such verbal reports by offenders. The term tends to imply a risky confrontation between equal adversaries, whereas this is rarely the case (Harlow 1987). Fifty per cent of robberies are by multiple offenders, 50 per cent use weapons, one-third are committed against women and a further one-third against children under 15 or older people over 50 years of age. In addition, the offender has the clear advantage of surprise. The rhetorical presentation of robbery as 'risky business' serves to perpetuate a romantic myth about the equality of the parties involved and so to offer grounds for self-congratulation on the part of the successful robber. It is doubtful if a robbery is any more dangerous to the offender than is the act of prostitution engaged in largely by women. Thrill seems to be an inadequate basis for explaining the gender imbalance in robbery.

A vital element in crime commission is *opportunity*. The majority of robberies – about 70 per cent – are situational or opportunistic acts occurring without prior planning (Gabor et al. 1987; Nugent et al. 1989). The typical robbery occurs on the street after dark in the inner city. Ethnographic studies portray inner-city streets as the territory of men – there are few 'street corner' women (Anderson 1978; Campbell 1986; Hannerz 1969; Liebow 1967). Unemployed and irregularly employed men gather on the stoops to while away the long hours with beer and conversation. Playful and not-so-playful masculine banter centres on the demonstration of essential qualities such as 'coolness' (autonomy and grace under pressure), 'smartness' (the ability to dupe or con others) and 'heart' (courage). These qualities are seen to coalesce in the crime of robbery. Robberies often occur as a result of peer pressure and a determination not to chicken out – what Fagot and Hagan (1985), in a quite different context, have eloquently termed 'the tyranny of the male group'. If women are simply absent from such settings, perhaps this explains their desistance from robbery. The problem with such an explanation is that women are not absent. At least one-third of victims are women, and if they are present as victims (Harlow 1987), they must be also present as potential criminals.

Even if they are excluded from the male groups in which robberies are spawned there is nothing to prevent them from conspiring in their apartments to engage in planned robberies. Yet the ratio of planned to spontaneous robberies amongst women who do rob is the same as that of men (Fortune *et al.* 1980; Girouard 1988). Opportunities for crime can be created where there is a desire, but we believe women do not see robbery as an option because of their different orientation to the meaning of aggression.

A robbery has been described by Luckenbill (1981) as a four-stage process: the offender establishes co-presence with the victim, he announces the robbery and is taken seriously, he takes the goods and then makes his escape. Perhaps women's difficulty lies in their *lack of credibility* at the second stage of the process – they are unable to convince the victim that they are in earnest and that they will use force if required. Some data suggest that this may be the case. Women are more likely than men to use incapacitating force on the victim probably in an attempt to convince the victim of the seriousness of the encounter (Harlow 1987). (There is an inverse relation between weapon use and injury in robbery for the obvious reason that the presence of a knife or gun is usually successful in subduing the victim; see Cook 1986. Because women are less likely to carry guns, they must find other means of instilling fear.) Apparently this tactic is effective, because women and men are identical in the rate of 'success' in robbery. Though credibility may present a problem to the female robber, it is clearly not an insurmountable one.

Katz (1988: 247) came close to summarizing our position when he noted, 'Unless it is given sense as a way of elaborating, perhaps celebrating, distinctively male forms of action and ways of being . . . stickup has almost no appeal at all.' We want to be more specific about these 'male forms of action', identifying them as the embodiment of the far end of the continuum of an instrumental representation of aggression. Robbers are men who use aggression to material and social ends with such frequency that it becomes a way of life. Robbers have a higher rate of recidivism than other serious criminals; a three-year follow-up study of arrestees indicated that 44 per cent of robbers were re-arrested for robbery (Cook and Nagin 1979). Nor do they confine themselves to robbery; violent predators identified in one study had high rates of involvement in robbery, assault and drug offences (Chaiken and Chaiken 1982). All three form part of a lifestyle characterized by exploitation and material hedonism. With respect to the former, ethnographic studies and biographies indicate a highly antagonistic and competitive view of other men. Because of this marked distrust and their aversion to being the underdog, the prevailing attitude seems to be 'Get them before they get you'. Because of this acute awareness of the ignominy of being conned or duped, such men take pride in their ability to humiliate others (Toch 1969). Cutting or diluting drugs, pimping, conning and robbing are all ways of 'getting over on someone'. Robbery holds a particular attraction since in the critical moment of the transaction, the victim is humiliated not only into submission but also into

340

giving up his money. The rewards are both monetary and social. By insisting at a rhetorical level that it is an even contest (despite the obvious advantages which the robber possesses, including the element of surprise and weaponry), the robber can augment his self-esteem by demonstrating his capacity to terrorize and subdue.

At the same time the financial rewards not only reinforce the act itself but also support a hedonistic lifestyle which in addition confers a particular social identity. One study found that 76 per cent of robbers spend the proceeds on clothes, cars, holidays and travel (Gabor *et al.* 1987). Ethnographic work endorses this finding, noting the cycle of 'earning and burning' in which parties, drug-taking, womanizing and shopping sprees follow robberies and necessitate further stick-ups (Allen 1978; Williamson 1965; Willwerth 1974). For young men from areas of urban blight, such a lifestyle sets them apart from those around them and confirms their relative 'smartness'.

Such cold-blooded use of aggression is foreign to most women. For them, anger is a necessary (though far from sufficient) condition for aggression, and violence is only comprehensible in the context of at least a minimal relationship between the parties. Women may be driven to violence by frustration, jealousy or abuse, but not by poverty or a need to demonstrate material or physical superiority. The equation of money, control and social status is a masculine one, as is the use of violence as a means to these ends.

DOMESTIC VIOLENCE

In 1975 and in 1985 two national probability samples of intact couples were interviewed about their involvement in domestic violence (Straus *et al.* 1980; Straus and Gelles 1990). Approximately 16 per cent of all married couples had experienced physical aggression in the year prior to the survey; 28 per cent had experienced physical aggression at some point in their relationship. More controversially, 3.8 per cent of women and 4.6 per cent of men were the victims of severe violence. It appears that wives are as aggressive as husbands in the private domain of the home and in dating relationships (Archer and Ray 1989; Cate *et al.* 1982; Marshall and Rose 1987), although this parity does not extend to injuries sustained (Stark *et al.* 1979; Straus 1989).

There has been no shortage of empirical data and theorizing about wife-beaters. The predominant explanation of their behaviour is in terms of their need to maintain power and control (Dobash and Dobash 1979; Dutton and Strachen 1987; Kantor and Straus 1987; McClelland 1975). This is consonant with an instrumental framework for male aggression generally, and indeed Fagan *et al.* (1983) found that males with arrests for stranger violence were the most frequent and severe wife-abusers.

Those who support a power motivation theory of wife assault offer data from a variety of measures. Structurally, wife-beating is more common where status differentials in education or occupational status place the husband in an inferior position to the wife (Coleman and Straus 1986; Gelles 1974). Attempts to assert or maintain control over decision-making, social relations, family finances and spouse's freedom of movement have all been identified as salient factors in wife-beating (Frieze and Browne 1989; Frieze and McHugh 1981; Pagelow 1984; Walker 1984), as well as attempts to compensate for deficits in power outside the home (Frieze and Browne 1989). Bowker (1983) concluded that male subcultures play a role in supporting wife-beating; men who are most integrated into peer subcultures which support patriarchal dominance of the family are more severe in their domestic violence. Personality measures have endorsed a connection between wife-beating and low self-esteem (Ganley and Harris 1978; Pagelow 1984), jealousy (Bowker 1983; Davidson 1978), depression (Shields *et al.* 1988), need for control (Elbow 1977) and poor verbal skills (Novaco 1976; Rosenbaum and O'Leary 1981), all of which offer either tangential or direct support for a power motivation theory.

Developmentally, exposure to violence as a child is a powerful precursor of adult domestic violence in men (Caesar 1988; Fagan *et al.* 1983; Gelles 1974; Hotaling and Sugarman 1986; Pagelow 1984; Rosenbaum and O'Leary 1981). Boys in violent families acquire an instrumental theory of violence through modelling, vicarious and, ultimately, direct reinforcement (Bandura 1973; Pagelow 1984). Sonkin and Durphy (1985) note that men use violence in the home because it is effective in allowing them to win arguments and control situations. The 'gratifications' described by criminologists (Bowker 1983; Herzberger 1983) translate simply into psychologists' reinforcers. These include the power to control the spouse's behaviour, increases in feelings of power and self-esteem, denial of dependence, and physical rewards such as access to economic resources and sexual gratification (Bowker 1983; Browne 1987; Frieze 1983; Shields *et al.* 1988). The literature, then, is very largely in agreement that male violence in the home is an instrumental act aimed at asserting or maintaining control and that men who beat their wives are most likely to be those who in terms of marital power structure, personality, sex-role adherence or peer-group affiliation have a particular sensitivity to issues of masculine control.

Very little has been written on the causes of aggression by wives. Indeed, the primary responses to the well-replicated finding that similar percentages of women and men admit to at least one act of serious violence in the preceding year have been to question the validity of the measures (Pleck *et al.* 1977–78), to minimize the importance of this area of inquiry (Berk *et al.* 1981) or to assert that violence by wives is a defensive response to male-initiated violence (Saunders 1986). Straus (1980) used the national survey data to estimate that at most 50 per cent of acts of female domestic violence could be considered to be acts of self-defence.

If women view aggression as an expressive act involving loss of self-control (rather than attempts at control over others), then aggression is most likely when stress or frustration is high and/or when self-control is low. We believe that both these elements of the female 'violence equation' are affected in marriage. 'Push' forces are heightened in the domestic arena. Despite women's increased involvement in the workforce, they are frequently employed in part-time or short-term jobs as a means of augmenting the family income and work is an adjunct to rather than a replacement of their major arena of responsibility – the home. This is particularly true of mothers, who, despite increases in husbands' 'helping out', remain the primary caretakers of children. Although the major focus for many women is their family and home, male dominance in domestic decision-making remains high. Added to this is the day-to-day responsibility of child-rearing, a 24-hour-a-day job usually without vacations. Self-report data and community studies indicate higher levels of stress and neurotic symptoms amongst women compared to men (Fujita *et al.* 1991; Gove and Tudor 1973; Dohrenwend and Dohrenwend 1976). Sex differences in the relation between stress and domestic aggression also lend support to an expressive aggression position (Straus and Gelles 1990). Men's violence increases regularly as a function of stress. Women's violence remains considerably lower than men's until a high level of stress is present, when their violence shows a dramatic increase. This is in line with the assertion that women suppress their stress more effectively until some critical level is reached. Another very significant factor in stress is the behaviour of husbands. In discussing marital homicide we shall raise more fully the traumatic long-term effects of physical abuse and alcoholism by husbands.

What factors might contribute to a failure of self-control by women in the domestic arena? We believe that the critical variable may be privacy. Although we argue that women internalize behavioural restraint in the form of self-control, there is no denying the powerful additional force of public surveillance. Public aggression by women involves the potential for negative evaluation by the audience as well as the woman herself. In private this source of censure is lacking. She is still subject to her husband's evaluation of her behaviour, but we believe that two factors are relevant here. First, the private nature of marriage may erode public standards of gender-appropriate behaviour. Secondly, if the message which women attempt to convey by aggression is a plea for help, then it is the husband to whom it is usually directed. If women are announcing that their daily life is intolerable, then it is the husband who has the principal power to alter it for the better. In support of this expressive interpretation of female aggression we again note that women, more than men, engage in a range of acts not all of which involve injury. Indeed, women are more likely to cry rather than hit in domestic disputes (Averill 1982; Campbell and Muncer 1987; Straus *et al.* 1980). The aim is to issue a plea for help rather than, as with men, to coerce by the use of force.

Approximately 40 per cent of family homicides are committed by women. Yet a comparison of male and female spouse-killers indicates that 'the motivations of women who commit marital homicide differ significantly from male

343

homicide perpetrators' (Fagan and Browne 1990). Wolfgang (1967) and Wilbanks (1983) both found that men who were killed by their wives were more likely to have beaten their spouses (60 per cent) than were women who were killed by their husbands (5 per cent). Browne (1987) compared women who killed in marital relationships with other women in abusive relationships who did not kill. The factors which differentiated the groups were those associated with the extremity of the *husbands'* behaviour. Women who killed lived with men who drank daily, used street drugs, had threatened them with murder, physically attacked them more frequently, more severely and caused more serious injuries. From an expressive aggression perspective, the salient dimension of the women's experience is the traumatic build-up of stress. The husband's ability to restrain her movement and to isolate her from social and legal assistance, combined with the constant threat and use of violence, leads to the build-up of an intolerable level of stress in which self-control snaps and lethal violence ensues.

Contrast this scenario with accounts of men who kill their wives. Several studies (Browne 1987; Gelles 1974; Luckenbill 1977) suggest that male spousal homicide is the result of an escalating series of events in which the wife fails to obey orders or challenges his self-esteem or power. Katz (1988) and Zahn (1989) suggest that homicide is the culmination of a series of attempts to regain control over the wife's behaviour or affections. Men who kill can be characterized as demanding that the wife 'Do what I tell you to do'. Women who kill seem to be saying, 'I can't take this any more.' Though the result in both cases is equally tragic, these two messages are quite distinct and a predictable result of men and women's differing understanding of aggression.

DIVERSITY IN MEN'S REPRESENTATIONS

In this chapter we have focused heavily on gendered, socially transmitted ways of thinking as the basis of behavioural differences between men and women in aggression and violence. But there is variation within sex in representations of aggression – not all men subscribe to an instrumental view of aggression. Social representations are cultural phenomena, not biological requirements; there is no necessary link between masculinity and instrumentality. What, then, are the social factors that might explain variation between men in their understanding of aggression?

Social representations of aggression (and indeed a variety of other social phenomena) provide the cognitive glue that holds together social structural variables on the one hand and individual action on the other. Relative *power* is perhaps the most politically visible and contentious aspect of the differences between the sexes. And power differentials are also relevant to the use of instrumental aggression amongst men. As Hannah Arendt (1970: 56) notes: 'Power and violence are opposites; where one rules absolutely the other is absent. Violence appears when power is in jeopardy.' So instrumental approaches to aggression may be the hallmark of those men whose positions are under threat – the office bully, the dispensable middle manager, the estranged husband – rather than amongst those whose power is institutionalized and confirmed. For those who are confident of their power, the use or threat of force is a line of last resort against resistant subordinates in the workplace or the home.

Outright violence between equals as a route to interpersonal power is more likely where the means for achieving legitimate respect and recognition are absent, where the subculture itself encourages violence as a route to community esteem and where formal social control is weak (see Archer, Chapter 7). These conditions, tied to both *social class and age*, are most likely to be met amongst teenagers, economically disadvantaged groups and criminal subcultures and in societies where the rule of law has broken down (Brownfield 1986). Reciprocally middle-class lifestyles are likely to engender a more expressive orientation to aggression and violence. Emphasis is placed upon the demonstration of superiority through organized competition in education and professional life (David and Brannon 1976). This socially sanctioned means of demonstrating worth and gaining respect actively debars direct aggression and violence except within the rule-governed arena of the Rugby pitch or the boxing ring. Boys who reject middle-class values of academic success and upward social mobility as 'sissy' may be more likely to seek status through direct physical confrontation (Cohen 1955; Willis 1977, 1978).

Differences in orientation to aggression may also be tied to *social roles*. Men and women differ in their typical daily occupations, with women overrepresented in caring roles whereas men are more likely to be engaged in competitive and even confrontational daily activities like policing, the armed forces and business. Those whose daily life involves the support and nurturing of others are more likely to view aggression as destructive and self-indulgent, whereas mundane involvement in coercion and competition meshes with a more instrumental attitude. We found in a recent study (Campbell and Muncer, forthcoming) that male and female nurses held a more expressive view of aggression than did army personnel of both sexes. Men engaged in a traditionally 'female' caring occupation viewed aggression very much like their women co-workers, whereas men in the army were by far the most instrumental in their view of aggression. From the viewpoint of social change, opening up new avenues of work to both sexes is likely to result in alterations in the typical gender patterns of social representations of aggression. To the extent that men assume increasing responsibility for child care, for example, we might expect a corresponding shift in their attitude towards violence compared to men who remain in the traditionally competitive and individualistic world of business.

Though power, class, age and role can be identified as potential mediators of individuals' orientation towards aggression, they are in the real world often interdependent both between and within sexes. Middle-class, middle-aged men are more likely to hold jobs in business with in-built power. Working-class boys are more likely to be unemployed and to reside in areas where the demonstration of physical prowess is accepted as a source of status. To tease out the factors that influence the way in which men view aggression is a formidable task, but, if it is true that social representations are not merely interpretive but generative, it will be a worthwhile one. If men were to relinquish the idea that aggression is a legitimate means of social coercion and a source of status, a range of social problems from schoolyard bullying and domestic violence to terrorism and international conflicts might be brought under control.

REFERENCES

Allen, J. (1978) *Assault with a Deadly Weapon: The Autobiography of a Street Criminal*, New York: McGraw-Hill.

Anderson, E. (1978) *A Place on the Corner*, Chicago: Chicago University Press.

Archer, J. (1992) 'Childhood gender roles: social context and organization', in J. McGurk (ed.) *Childhood Social Development: Contemporary Perspectives*, Hillsdale, NJ: Lawrence Erlbaum.

Archer, J. and Ray, N. (1989) 'Dating violence in the United Kingdom: a preliminary study', *Aggressive Behaviour*, 15: 337–43.

Arendt, H. (1970) *On Violence*, New York: Harcourt Brace & World.

Athens, L. H. (1977) *Violent Criminal Acts and Actors: A Symbolic Interactionist Study*, Boston, MA: Routledge & Kegan Paul.

Averill, J. (1982) *Anger and Aggression: An Essay on Emotion*, New York: Springer-Verlag.

Bakan, D. (1966) *The Duality of Human Existence*, Boston: Beacon Press.

Bandura, A. (1973) *Aggression: A Social Learning Analysis*, Englewood Cliffs, NJ: Prentice-Hall.

Berk, R., Berk, S., Loseke, D. and Rauma, D. (1981) 'Mutual combat and other family violence myths', in D. Finkelhor, R. Gelles, G. Hotaling and M. Straus (eds) *The Dark Side of Families: Current Family Violence Research*, Beverly Hills, CA: Sage.

Berkowitz, L. (1965) 'The concept of aggressive drive: some additional considerations', in L. Berkowitz (ed.) *Advances in Experimental Social Psychology*, vol. 2, New York: Academic Press.

Besag, V. E. (1980) *Bullies and Victims*, Milton Keynes, UK: Open University Press.

Black, D. (1983) 'Crime as social control', *American Sociological Review*, 48(1): 34–55.

Bowker, L. (1983) *Beating Wife Beating*, Lexington, MA: D. C. Heath.

Browne, A. (1987) *When Battered Women Kill*, New York: Macmillan/Free Press.

Brownfield, D. (1986) 'Social class and violent behavior', *Criminology*, 24: 421–38.

Caesar, P. L. (1988) 'Exposure to violence in families of origin amoung wife abusers and maritally nonviolent men', *Violence and Victims*, 3(1): 49–64.

Campbell, A. (1986) 'The streets and violence', in A. Campbell and J. Gibbs (eds) *Violent Transactions: The Limits of Personality*, Oxford and Boston: Basil Blackwell.

—— (1993) *Men, Women and Aggression*, New York: Basic Books.

Campbell, A. and Muncer, S. (1987) 'Models of anger and aggression in the social talk of women and men', *Journal for the Theory of Social Behaviour*, 17: 489–512.

—— (forthcoming) 'Sex differences in aggression: social representations and social roles', *British Journal of Social Psychology*.

Campbell, A., Muncer, S. and Coyle, E. (1992) 'Social representations of aggression as an explanation of gender differences: a preliminary study', *Aggressive Behaviour*, 18(1): 95–108.

Campbell, A., Muncer, S. and Gorman, B. (1993) 'Sex and social representations of aggression: a communal-agentic analysis', *Aggressive Behavior*, 19: 125–36.

Cate, R. M., Henton, J. M., Koval, J., Christopher, F. S. and Lloyd, S. (1982) 'Premarital abuse: a social psychological perspective', *Journal of Family Issues*, 3: 79–90.

Chaiken, J. M. and Chaiken, M. R. (1982) *Varieties of Criminal Behaviour*, Santa Monica, CA: Rand Corporation.

Cohen, A. (1955) *Delinquent Boys: The Subculture of the Gang*, London: Collier Macmillan.

Coleman, D. H. and Straus, M. A. (1986) 'Marital power, conflict and violence in a nationally representative sample of American couples', *Violence and Victims*, 1(2): 141–57.

Cook, P. J. (1982) 'The role of firearms in violent crime: an interpretive review of the literature', in M. E. Wolfgang and N. A. Weiner (eds) *Criminal Violence*, Beverly Hills, CA: Sage.

—— (1986) 'The relationship between victim resistance and injury in noncommercial robbery', *Journal of Legal Studies*, 15: 405–16.

Cook, P. J. and Nagin, D. (1979) *Does the Weapon Matter?* Washington, DC: Institute for Law and Social Research.

David, D. and Brannon, R. (1976) 'The male sex-role: our culture's blueprint of masculinity and what it's done for us lately', in D. David and R. Brannon (eds) *The Forty-nine Percent Majority: The Male Sex-role*, Reading, MA: Addison-Wesley.

Davidson, J. (1978) *Conjugal Crime*, New York: Hawthorne Books.

Dobash, R. E. and Dobash, R. P. (1979) *Violence Against Wives: A Case Against Patriarchy*, New York: Free Press.

Dohrenwend, B. P. and Dohrenwend, B. S. (1976) 'Sex differences in psychiatric disorders', *American Journal of Sociology*, 81: 1447–71.

Dollard, J., Doob, L. W., Miller, N. E., Mowrer, O. H. and Sears, R. R. (1939) *Frustration and Aggression*, New Haven, CT: Yale University Press.

Durkheim, E. (1953) 'Individual and collective representations', in E. Durkheim (ed.) *Sociology and Philosophy*, London: Cohen & West.

Dutton, D. G. and Strachan, C. E. (1987) 'Motivational needs for power and dominance as differentiating variables of assaultive and non-assaultive male populations', *Violence and Victims*, 2: 145–56.

Eagly, A. (1987) *Sex Differences in Social Behaviour: A Social Role Analysis*, Hillsdale, NJ: Lawrence Erlbaum.

Eagly, A. H. and Steffen, V. J. (1986) 'Gender and aggressive behaviour: a meta-analytic review of the social psychological literature', *Psychological Bulletin*, 100: 309–30.

Elbow, M. (1977) 'Theoretical considerations of violent marriages', *Social Casework*, 58: 515–26.

Emler, N. (1987) 'Socio-moral development from the perspective of social representations', *Journal for the Theory of Social Behaviour*, 17: 371–88.

Eysenck, H. J. (1964) *Crime and Personality*, London: Routledge & Kegan Paul.

Fagan, J. and Browne, A. (1990) 'Marital violence: physical aggression between women and men in intimate relationships', Report to the Panel on Understanding and Control of Violent Behaviour, National Academy of Sciences, Washington, DC.

Fagan, J., Stewart, D. and Hansen, K. (1983) 'Violent men or violent husbands? Background factors and situational correlates of domestic and extra-domestic violence', in D. Finkelhor, R. Gelles, G. Hotaling and M. Straus (eds) *The Dark Side of Families*, Beverly Hills, CA: Sage.

Fagot, B. I. and Hagan, R. (1985) 'Aggression in toddlers: responses to the assertive acts of boys and girls', *Sex Roles*, 12(314): 341–51.

Fagot, B., Hagan, R., Leinbach, H. and Kronsberg, S. (1985) 'Differential reactions to the assertive and communicative acts of toddler boys and girls', *Child Development*, 56: 1499–505.

Farr, R. (1987) 'Social representations: a French tradition of research', *Journal for the Theory of Social Behaviour*, 17: 343–70.

Felson, R. B. (1982) 'Impression management and the escalation or aggression and violence', *Social Psychology Quarterly*, 45: 245–54.

—— (1984) 'Patterns of aggressive social interaction', in A. Mummendey (ed.) *Social Psychology of Aggression: From Individual Behavior to Social Interaction*, Berlin: Springer-Verlag.

—— (1993) 'Sexual coercion: an interactionist approach', in R. Felson and J. Tedeschi (eds) *Aggression and Violence: Social Interactionist Perspectives*, Washington, DC: American Psychological Association.

Felson, R. B., Baccaglini, W. and Gmelch, G. (1986) 'Bar room brawls: aggression and violence in Irish and American bars', in A. Campbell and J. Gibbs (eds) *Violent Transactions: The Limits of Personality*, Oxford and Boston: Basil Blackwell.

Fortune, E. P., Vega, M. and Silverman, I. J. (1980) 'A study of female robbers in a southern correctional institution', *Journal of Criminal Justice*, 8: 317–25.

Freud, S. (1946) 'Triebe und triebschicksale', in *Gesammelte Werke*, vol. 10, London: Imago (first published, 1915).

Frieze, I. H. (1983) 'Investigating the causes and consequences of marital rape', *Signs*, 8(3): 532–53.

Frieze, I. H. and Browne, A. (1989) 'Violence in marriage', in L. Ohlin and M. Tonry (eds) *Family Violence*, vol. 11, *Crime and Justice: An Annual Review of Research*, Chicago: University of Chicago Press.

Frieze, I. H. and McHugh, M. C. (1981) 'Violence in relation to power in marriage', Paper presented to the Association for Women in Psychology, Santa Monica, CA.

Frost, W. D. and Averill, J. R. (1982) 'Differences between men and women in the everyday experience of anger', in J. R. Averill, *Anger and Aggression: An Essay on Emotion*, New York: Springer-Verlag, pp. 281–316.

Fujita, F., Diener, E. and Sandvik, E. (1991) 'Gender differences in negative affect and well-being: the case for emotional intensity', *Journal of Personality and Social Psychology*, 61: 427–34.

Gabor, T., Baril, M., Cusson, M., Elie, D., Leblanc, M. and Normandeau, A. (1987) *Armed Robbery: Cops, Robbers and Victims*, Springfield, IL: Charles C. Thomas.

Ganley, A. L. and Harris, L. (1978) 'Domestic violence: issues in designing and implementing programs for male batterers', Paper presented to the American Psychological Association, Toronto, Ont.

Gelles, R. J. (1974) *The Violent Home: A Study of Physical Aggression between Husbands and Wives*, Newbury Park, CA: Sage.

Gilligan, C. (1982) *In a Different Voice: Psychological Theory and Women's Development*, Cambridge, MA: Harvard University Press.

Girouard, D. (1988) 'Les Femmes incarcerées pour vol qualifié, en Quebec, en 1985: importance de leur rôle', *Canadian Journal of Criminology*, April.

Goodenough, F. (1931) *Anger in Young Children*, Minneapolis: University of Minnesota Press.

Gottfredson, M. and Hirschi, T. (1990) *A General Theory of Crime*, Stanford, CA: Stanford University Press.

Gove, W. and Tudor, J. (1973) 'Adult sex roles and mental illness', *American Journal of Sociology*, 78: 812–35.

Gurin, G., Veroff, J. and Feld, S. (1960) *Americans View their Mental Health: A Nationwide Interview Survey*, New York: Basic Books.

Hannerz, M. (1969) *Soulside*, New York: Columbia University Press.

Harlow, C. W. (1987) *Special Report: Robbery Victims*, Washington, DC: Bureau of Justice Statistics.

Herzberger, S. (1983) 'Social cognition and the transmission of abuse', in D. Finkelhor, R. Gelles, G. Hotaling and M. Straus (eds) *The Dark Side of Families*, Beverly Hills, CA: Sage.

Herzlich, C. (1973) *Health and Illness: A Social Psychological Analysis*, London: Academic Press.

Hindelang, M. J., Hirschi, T. and Weis, J. G. (1979) 'Correlates of delinquency', *American Sociological Review*, 44: 995–1014.

—— (1981) *Measuring Delinquency*, Beverly Hills, CA: Sage.

Hotaling, G. T. and Sugarman, D. B. (1986) 'An analysis of risk markers in husband to wife violence: the current state of knowledge', *Violence and Victims*, 1(2): 101–24.

Jaspars, J. M. F. and Fraser, C. (1984) 'Attitudes and social representations', in R. M. Farr and S. Moscovici (eds) *Social Representations*, New York: Cambridge University Press.

Kantor, G. K. and Straus, M. A. (1987) 'The "drunken bum" theory of wife beating', *Social Problems*, 34: 213–31.

Katz, J. (1988) *Seductions of Crime: Moral and Sensual Attractions of Doing Evil*, New York: Basic Books.

Kruttschnitt, C. (1990) 'Gender and interpersonal violence', Washington, DC: Report to the Panel on the Understanding and Control of Violent Behaviour, National Academy of Sciences, Washington, DC.

Laub, J. H. and McDermott, N. J. (1985) 'An analysis of crime by young black women', *Criminology*, 23: 81–98.

Lejeune, R. (1977) 'The management of a mugging', *Urban Life*, 6(2); 123–48.

Liebow, E. (1967) *Tally's Corner*, Boston: Little, Brown.

Lloyd, B. and Smith, C. (1986) 'The effects of age and gender on social behavior in very young children', *British Journal of Social Psychology*, 25: 219–30.

Lorenz, K. (1966) *On Aggression*, London: Methuen.

Luckenbill, D. F. (1977) 'Criminal homicide as a situated transaction', *Social Problems*, 25: 176–86.

—— (1981) 'Generating compliance: the case of robbery', *Urban Life*, 10: 25–46.

McClelland, D. C. (1975) *Power: The Inner Experience*, New York: Irvington Publishers.

Maccoby, E. (1980) *Social Development: Psychological Growth and the Parent–Child Relationship*, New York: Harcourt Brace Jovanovich.

—— (1988) 'Gender as a social category', *Developmental Psychology*, 24: 755–65.

Maltz, D. and Borker, R. (1982) 'A cultural approach to male–female miscommunication', in J. Gumperz (ed.) *Language and Social Identity*, New York: Cambridge University Press.

Marsh, P. and Campbell, A. (1979) *Final Report to Whitbread Ltd*, Oxford: Contemporary Violence Research Centre.

Marsh, P., Rosser, E. and Harre, R. (1978) *The Rules of Disorder*, London: Routledge & Kegan Paul.

Marshall, L. L. and Rose, P. (1987) 'Gender, stress and violence in the adult relationships of a sample of college students', *Journal of Personal and Social Relationships*, 4: 299–316.

Moscovici, S. (1976) *La Psychanalyse: Son image et son public*, Paris: Presses Universitaires de France.

—— (1981) 'On social representations', in J. Forgas (ed.) *Social Cognition: Perspectives on Everyday Understanding*, London: Academic Press.

Newson, J. and Newson, E. (1968) *Four-year-olds in an Urban Community*, London: Allen & Unwin.

Novaco, R. (1976) 'The functions and regulation of the arousal of anger', *American Journal of Psychiatry*, 133(1): 1124–8.

Nugent, S., Burns, D., Wilson, P. and Chappell, D. (1989) *Risks and Rewards in Robbery*, Sydney: Australian Institute of Criminology.

Pagelow, M. D. (1984) *Family Violence*, New York: Praeger.

Parson, T. and Bales, R. F. (1955) *Family Socialization and Interaction Process*, New York: Free Press.

Perls, F. (1969) *In and Out of the Garbage Pail*, Lafayette, CA: Real People's Press.

Pleck, E., Pleck, J., Grossman, M. and Bart, P. (1977–78) 'The battered data syndrome: a reply to Steinmetz' article', *Victimology*, 2: 680–4.

Redl, F. and Toch, H. (1986) 'The psychoanalytic perspective', in H. Toch (ed.) *Psychology of Crime and Criminal Justice*, Prospect Heights, IL: Waveland Press.

Rosenbaum, A. and O'Leary, R. D. (1981) 'Marital violence: characteristics of abusive couples', *Journal of Consulting and Clinical Psychology*, 49: 63–76.

Saunders, D. (1986) 'When battered women use violence: husband-abuse or self-defense?', *Victims and Violence* 1: 47–60.

Shields, N., Hanneke, C. R. and McCall, G. J. (1988) 'Patterns of family and non-family violence: violent husbands and violent men', *Violence and Victims*, 3: 83–98.

Sonkin, D. J. and Durphy, M. (1985) *Learning to Live Without Violence: A Handbook for Men*, 2nd edn, San Francisco: Volcano Press.

Stark, E., Flitcraft, A. and Frazier, W. (1979) 'Medicine and patriarchical violence: the social construction of a private event', *International Journal of Health Services*, 9: 461–93.

Steffensmeier, D. J. and Cobb, M. (1981) 'Sex differences in urban arrest patterns 1934–79', *Social Problems*, 29: 37–50.

Storr, A. (1968) *Human Aggression*, New York: Atheneum.

Straus, M. A. (1980) 'Victims and aggressors in marital violence', *American Behavioral Scientist*, 23(5): 681–704.

—— (1989) 'Assaults by wives on husbands: implications for primary prevention of marital violence', Paper presented to the American Society of Criminology, Reno, NV.

Straus, M. A. and Gelles, R. J. (1990) *Physical Violence in American Families: Risk Factors and Adaptations to Violence in 8,145 Families*, New Brunswick, NJ: Transaction.

Straus, M. A., Gelles, R. J. and Steinmetz, S. (1980) *Behind Closed Doors: Violence in the American Family*, New York: Anchor Press.

Tavris, C. (1989) *Anger: The Misunderstood Emotion*, 2nd edn, New York: Touchstone Books.

Tedeschi, J. T., Smith, R. B. and Brown, R. C. (1974) 'A reinterpretation of research on aggression', *Psychological Bulletin*, 81: 540–62.

Toch, H. (1969) *Violent Men: An Inquiry into the Psychology of Violence*, Chicago: Aldine.

Walker, L. E. (1984) *The Battered Woman Syndrome*, New York: Springer.

Walsh, D. (1986) *Heavy Business: Commercial Burglary and Robbery*, London and Boston: Routledge & Kegan Paul.

Wilbanks, W. (1983) 'The female homicide offender in Dade County, Florida', *Criminal Justice Review*, 8: 9–14.

Williamson, H. (1965) *Hustler! The Autobiography of a Thief*, New York: Doubleday.

Willis, P. (1977) *Learning to Labour*, London: Saxon House.

—— (1978) *Profane Culture*, London: Routledge & Kegan Paul.

Willwerth, J. (1974) *Jones*, New York: M. Evans & Co.

Wolfgang, M. and Ferracuti, F. (1967) *The Subculture of Violence*, New York: Barnes & Noble.

Wolfgang, M. E. (1967) 'A sociological analysis of criminal homicide', in M. E. Wolfgang (ed.) *Studies in Homicide*, New York: Harper & Row.

Zahn, M. A. (1989) 'Homicide in the twentieth century: trends, types and causes', in T. R. Gurr (ed.) *Violence in America*, vol. 1, *The History of Violence*, Beverly Hills, CA: Sage.

Zillmann, D. (1979) *Hostility and Aggression*, Hillsdale, NJ: Lawrence Erlbaum.

18

MALE VIOLENCE
Towards an integration
Paul Gilbert

A cursory look at history shows the enormity of suffering caused by male violence; in the wars, rapes, tortures and beatings that men have perpetrated on their fellow men, women and children. Indeed, male violence may even outrank disease and famine as the major source of human suffering. There is much evidence that many forms of adult pathology relate to a history of abuse, especially at the hand of men. If one wanted to instigate one mental illness prevention programme, then targeting male violence would possibly be the single most significant one. How to do it is the problem.

The guiding framework of this chapter derives from three central concerns. First, to consider how evolution may have shaped certain forms of social behaviour (for example, attachment, ranking) and how violence can be viewed as a potential evolutionary stable strategy for control over resources. Secondly, to suggest that even though our first concern may be valid, phenomena like male violence require complex multi-process models for their explanation; that the linkage between an evolved stable strategy and specific behavioural episodes is complex and must take into consideration factors such as social context, cultural values and development. Thirdly, to suggest that part of the problem of male violence lies in the trivialization of certain pro-social, human strategies, such as empathy, compassion, caring and forgiveness (Levenson 1992; Smail 1987). Such trivialization arises from cultural socio-economic values, family structures, and social relations which construct self-identities and gender scripts around core themes of competitiveness (Miedzian 1992).

The chapter is divided into two main sections. In the first I shall explore ideas that focus on the (violent) individual (namely, that it is something particular about them). In the second section I shall explore an integrative, multi-process, biopsychosocial approach to male violence. From the outset I should stress that such an endeavour is bound to be selective, personal, at times discursive and speculative, and in places a little idiosyncratic.

EXPLANATIONS

Explanations of male violence are embedded in various political, historical and cultural assumptions and basic beliefs about human nature. In western traditions there seem to be two rather polarized positions. One argues that we are by nature basically aggressive, violent and selfish and that there exists in all of us a beast waiting to get out (Klama 1988). Further, the selfish, violent and aggressive traits are somehow more basic, or more at the core of the male mind than, say, love, compassion and morality. Freud's idea of the id is directly related to this view (Ellenberger 1970). It was a dominant myth of the nineteenth century, captured in books like *Dr Jekyll and Mr Hyde* and more recently in *Lord of the Flies*, and plays a major part in some religious ideologies. Against this is the view that our violent and destructive behaviour owes much to the environment and the distortions and deprivations of socialization (Klama 1988; Howell and Willis 1989).

Current evolutionary approaches suggest that this polarization is misleading (Buss 1991; Trivers 1985; MacDonald 1988; Wenegrat 1984). In the first place the brain is not a unitary system but rather consists of a set of mixed social strategies and modular, evaluative systems that evolved to solve certain problems. Goals and strategies that increase the chances of the carrier's genes being represented in subsequent generations are passed on. This is called 'inclusive fitness'. A central concern is the way breeding environments have shaped evolved, stable social behaviours (such as courtship, care of offspring, altruism and so on) over the long term and laid down gene-neural structures that underlie them (Buss 1991; Gardner 1988; MacLean 1985, 1990). Thus evolutionary theorists are concerned with exploring goal-directed systems and their various strategies that are evolutionarily stable (for example, Archer 1988; Barkow *et al.* 1992; Buss 1991; Gilbert 1989, 1992a, 1992b; MacDonald 1988; Trivers 1985; Wenegrat 1984). Generally speaking, our human biosocial goals and strategies represent past solutions to problems posed by selective pressure (see Chisholm (1988) for a good discussion). These focus on problems such as

1 care of offspring, together with the capability to shape the experience of offspring such that they can acquire the knowledge base necessary to live as a viable representative of that species;
2 selecting, attracting and maintaining mates, including successful conception;
3 selecting, attracting and maintaining alliances, including discrimination between in-group or out-group, and ally or non-ally;
4 successfully negotiating social hierarchies and social place.

Reproductive success requires social success in these domains (Gilbert 1989; Nesse 1990), and many of our emotions seem to track social success. Consequently, we tend to feel good when we feel cared for, have a sense of belonging within a group, have access to friends, gain respect and prestige and find a mate. In contrast, negative emotions are associated with not being cared for, feeling alienated from others – an outsider, losing or failing to obtain respect and not finding or losing a desired mate (Nesse 1990). Affects seem set up to help track particular social relationship outcomes. Hence what is rewarding and threatening is not simply learnt but also tracks social success and evolutionarily meaningful goals. Such a view also leads to a theory of the evolution of human needs; for instance, for support, care, attachments, respect, closeness, status and freedom from terror (Gilbert 1989, 1992a, 1992b).

This approach suggests that there are at least three evolved components to the structure of mind; biosocial goals, evolved stable strategies and algorithms.

Biosocial goals

In general, these turn out to be finite, and relate to establishing control over resources. Goals may be experienced as something one is aiming for. Amongst the commonly agreed ones are:

1 *Attachment* between parent and offspring, involving the relationship of caregiving and care-eliciting;
2 *Mate selection* and sexual behaviour, involving courting, conception and mate retention;
3 *Formation of alliances*, involving aggression inhibition, sharing, co-operative and reciprocal behaviour;
4 *Ranking behaviour*, involving gaining and maintaining rank/status and accommodation to those of higher rank.

Strategies

To acquire any of the above biosocial goals one might use various strategies of aggression, deception, appeasement, altruism/helping/caring, or affiliation (or some combination); these seem the most common strategies. Strategies are goal-serving. Thus one does not, say, deceive just for the sake of it, but to achieve some goal (such as gaining and enticing a mate, gaining a job or money). The use of strategies are rewarding or punishing according to how far they move one towards a goal.

Algorithms

These represent information-processing routines. They help direct attentional mechanisms and are the evaluative or reasoning modules; that is how information is evaluated *vis-à-vis* the goal that is being pursued. Typical algorithms are concerned with proximity-distance, reciprocation and detection of cheating, social comparisons (for instance, of same–different as in in-group–out-group and inferior–superior as in ranking).

Thus we can distinguish between (1) what is wanted (the goal); (2) how the person judges how close or how far they are from it (algorithm); and (3) what behaviours (strategies) they will use to get to their goal. Threats and benefits are associated with signals of social success and these in turn can be present within different types of role behaviour.

AGGRESSION AS A HIGHLY VARIABLE STRATEGY

Accidental injury (for example, knocking a person over) is distinguishable from physical aggression because it is arbitrary and has no strategic value. Strategies, however, are like game plans or response rules for achieving goals (Wenegrat 1984). Particular strategies can be used to obtain a variety of different goals. For example, deception may be used to become accepted within a group, to entice a lover, or to make gains in a ranked organization. Affiliative strategies may be used to attract a lover, help a student, care for a child or reduce aggressive behaviour.

In this scheme aggression (like deception) is one potential strategy used to obtain (bisocial) goals or defend against losing them. Different combinations of strategies may be used according to how the cost and benefits of each are evaluated. Consequently, the study of aggression and violence is moving away from assumptions of single motivational systems – because aggression and violence are not goals but strategies. Instead, it aims to understand the contextual, person-environment interactions or, more specifically, an analysis of why physical aggression, as a strategy, is chosen by this particular person in this particular context to achieve this (or these) particular goal(s).

Violence (namely, damaging physical aggression – see Chapter 1) can be used to exert control or when control has been lost (see Campbell and Muncer, this volume). It can be used against others or against the self (as in a violent suicide) or against animals and objects. Violence can be enacted individually or by gangs, groups or nations; it may be the result of personal vendettas, or occur to complete strangers. It can also arise in contexts involving emotional closeness, where the issues of power and control are mixed and confused with needs for intimacy, understanding and complete commitment (Goldner *et al.* 1990). Thus it turns out that in any one episode violence can result from a variety of complex factors.

The variability of violence as a strategy can be seen by considering the following. It may be instrumental and without anger, when securing a resource; or it may be accompanied by negative affect where the motive is frequently a defensive one – for example, involving a threat to self-esteem, reputation or perceived control (see Chapters 7 and 16; Gilbert 1993). There are many different negative affects that can be associated with violence besides anger, such as hostility, anxiety, shame, resentment and envy (Buss 1988) and in everyday language we use labels to distinguish various types of violence –

355

such as 'defensive', 'vindictive', 'malicious', 'spiteful', 'sadistic', 'impulsive', 'vengeful', 'exploitative', 'protective'.

Another distinction is between planned and unplanned acts of violence (which in law are distinguished as premeditated and unpremeditated acts). Planned acts include wars but also any set of activities where an individual sets out, in advance, with the intent of committing acts of violence. Certain rapes fall into this category and have been linked to predatory behaviour (Bailey 1987). As a sexual reproductive strategy, rape combined with murder appears to be highly maladaptive. Some instrumental acts of violence seem to have elements of predatory strategic behaviour attached to them, involving planning, co-ordinating, stalking and waiting for opportunities 'to strike' (MacDonald 1988). Unplanned acts of violence result from the experience of provocation, of being thwarted or disappointed in seeking some goal; they arise in contexts such as frustration, but also from conflicts where there is an 'attack on status' and social standing (face-saving; Daly and Wilson, this volume). In this context it can be an immediate, relatively unplanned, 'lashing-out' response. Here violence can arise quickly following rapid escalations (see Chapter 7). The facilitators and inhibitors of planned an unplanned violence may be different, but they also share some common features.

FACILITATORS AND INHIBITORS

At the individual level, facilitator processes are involved in both planned and unplanned acts of violence (see, for example, Bailey 1987; Goldstein and Keller 1987). They include: (1) *sensitivity to external cues* and stimuli signalling threats and opportunities; (2) *heightened arousal*, increasing the activation of certain affects, frustration tolerance and psychomotor behaviour; (3) *cognitive evaluations* that control judgements such as social comparisons, self-esteem, issues of injustice and 'must'-abation beliefs (from Rational Emotive Theory), such as 'I must have X, you must be to me as I say'; (4) *coping evaluations* and judgements of what is acceptable and likely to obtain rewards or overcome threats; and (5) *coping behaviour* relating to a varied or limited repertoire for resolving conflicts, or obtaining incentives.

Inhibitors include the following: (1) *the costs of violence*; (2) *affect* – for example, anger may cue fear, and hence violence inhibition, or empathy for potential victims may inhibit violence; (3) *cognitive processes* which value empathy, affiliative behaviour and which associate violence with a lowering of self-esteem; (4) *cognitive evaluations*, which reduce the value of certain incentives, and reduce 'I must have' beliefs; (5) *coping behaviour*, especially conflict resolution skills and pro-social behaviour.

Inhibitors that are primarily fear-based might lead to overcontrol, and violent individuals have been distinguished between those who are under-controlled and those who are overcontrolled (Blackburn 1989). Both early learning and culture have major socializing influences on the power and effectiveness of facilitators and inhibitors of aggression and violence (Macdonald 1988).

Escalation–de-escalation

Another way to think of these processes is that in any conflict situation there will be factors that increase a person's tendency to escalate the conflict and processes that increase a person's tendency to de-escalate (Price 1988; see Chapter 7). Such decisions might be operating at different levels in the brain and be in conflict (Price, personal communication). Thus a person might feel intense anger regarding some event, and experience the urge to fight or escalate, but does not do so because of cognitive factors that control it (such as moral concerns and self-evaluations, or evaluations of the risk). Such a person may seethe with resentment but not become violent. The choice of coercion as a strategy and the degree to which a person escalates or de-escalates towards violence are major factors in male violence (Miedzian 1992).

CONFLICTS

Behavioural ecologists (Trivers 1985; Klama 1990) and psychologists (Buck 1988) turn the spotlight away from violence and aggression as a single category and on to conflicts, specific behavioural contexts and coping behaviours. The incentive value of a resource (its evaluated importance) has a powerful influence on escalation–de-escalation and the preparedness to give way or fight (Archer 1988; Daly and Wilson, this volume; Trivers 1985). When we look (as we shall shortly) at cultural influences this factor will be seen to be important. Buddhist philosophy, for example, involves a powerful set of de-escalation beliefs that operate to increase 'the value of life' and demote the importance of (attachment to) many incentives and resources and the use of violence (Crook 1980). Capitalism can operate in the other direction.

Conflicts themselves are complex and there are many different types. In one type, person A and person B are in conflict over a resource Z. Both want the same thing and the loser may leave the field. A only threatens B in so far as B seems in a position to get Z. Provided B does not challenge for the resource, A does not act aggressively and conflict is avoided. Fighting for a territory or food are examples. However, A may actually set out to destroy B. Such unrestrained escalated violent acts are rare in animals but are very common in humans. They are noted in situations of in-group–out-group conflicts; for example, in 'ethnic cleansing' (a hallmark of Nazi atrocities and now growing in Eastern Europe), and at an individual level as murder (Wilson and Daly 1985; Chapter 14). Humans are the only animals which devote much time and energy to making weapons for non-ritualized violence where death and serious injury are the goals.

In a second type of conflict, A wants something that B has or is in a position

357

to give or share; A wants something from, or of, B. This may be labour (as in slavery), attention, help, closeness, sex and so on. The purpose here is to coerce B to act in a certain way in relation to A. Here B cannot simply get away (and de-escalate the conflict) since B actually is the source of the wanted resource. The key issue is that there is no external resource that they are in conflict over, but it is the behaviour of one to another that is the source of conflict (Goldner *et al.* 1990).

ATTRACTIVENESS

Humans very often compete to be seen in a positive light. This type of conflict, which is particularly powerful in humans, relates to third-party competition or competing to gain approval, esteem and status from an admiring audience; it serves to create a positive image in the eyes of others. In this case one competes for preferential treatment from another person or to be seen as special in some way. Pascal (1670) said: 'We do not content ourselves with the life we have in ourselves and in our being, we desire to live an imaginary life in the minds of others, and for this purpose we endeavour to shine.' Thus in humans much effort is put into self-presentation with the desire to create a favourable impression (Baumeister 1982; Goffman 1968). This impression management may be aimed at one's group (or family, friends and alliances), at authority figures, or lovers. To be esteemed by others is to have status or prestige bestowed (Kemper 1988, 1990). Furthermore, this concern lies behind efforts 'to fit in' and identify with group values, which in turn feeds self-esteem and self-identity (Abrams *et al.* 1990; Brown and Lohr 1987).

Attractiveness status depends on social comparison (Suls and Wills 1991). One form derives from a cognitive capacity to judge what a person thinks of someone else and what they think of oneself and then compare the two (Gilbert 1992a, 1992b). For example, a person may be aware that their desired lover may prefer someone else and is fearful of defection so they continually ask, 'Do you love me more than Fred?' At job interviews, examinations, beauty contests and so on, one is in competition with others over the attention of a third party and trying to prove one is more able and more worthy of selection. Here one competes to be seen as more attractive, able, worthy, deserving, capable and so on than others and in this way one is *voluntarily chosen* (Barkow 1975, 1980, 1991). Others are not threatened into choosing the self in preference to competitors but are enticed to choose in one's favour (deception rather than aggression may be a strategy used here). This type of competing, which can be contrasted with rank based on fighting ability (RHP – see Archer 1988 and Chapter 7), has been called Social Attention Holding Power (SAHP – Gilbert, 1989, 1992a, 1992b) to indicate the amount of positive attention and level of positive investments an individual can elicit in relationships.

RANK

As many contributors to this volume point out, violence, conflicts and contests are often related to our internal and social comparative judgements (RHP and SAHP) and relative standing or position. But as noted above, rank is also related to an evaluation of the view others make of oneself. Gaining and losing rank has major effects on emotions and self-esteem (Gilbert 1990, 1992a; Kemper 1988, 1990; Kemper and Collins 1990). Clark (1990) calls these interactions 'micropolitics' and they consume much of our social discourse. Judgements of rank can be made very quickly in interactions (Kalma 1991) and the face and body posture are salient sources of these evaluations (Ohman 1986). Some violent males are very sensitive to how they are 'looked at'. But to gain and maintain rank often occurs at points of conflict. In order to win contests and conflicts, one must use strategies that work; that is, the benefits must outweigh the costs.

There are two basic (but not mutually exclusive) strategies for gaining rank, and hence control over various resources: (1) being seen as powerful and making others submit or avoid challenging out of fear – in other words, showing one's toughness or fighting ability (the authoritarian hierarchy or RHP); (2) being seen as able and talented, desired or positively attractive – that is, demonstrating attributes that are useful to others (the authoritative-affiliative hierarchy or SAHP). In the first, one takes what one wants, in the second one entices the other to give *voluntarily* what is wanted (see Table 18.1).

The way in which ranks can be decided by aggressiveness and coercion have been discussed by others (for example, Weisfeld, Chapter 3; Archer, Chapter 7). Paradoxically, however, some types of violence arise from the desire to create a *good* impression on others in the group. This applies to various forms of ritualized contests such as sports, and where aggressive behaviour may be applauded (for instance, hurling a ball at 90 miles an hour at a batsman's head). Boxing and wrestling are extreme and violent forms: here violence is clearly designed to harm or intimidate – yet the motive is to win approval in the eyes of others. After a contest, conciliatory behaviour may be shown. Yet even in sports such as cricket and soccer, physical intimidation and violence are applauded.

Violence can also be perpetrated as an appeasement strategy. As Milgram (1974) showed, violence can arise from trying to please or comply with a higher authority. At a more complex level, the effort to fit in and be attractive to others may mean that one ignores moral issues (Sabini and Silver 1982).

Attractiveness and social image

As Wilson and Daly (1985, this volume) point out, attractiveness (SAHP), social appearance and image are often major factors in inter-male violence. Attractiveness involves gaining a positive judgement from others, and hence depends on signals sent. What is attractive to others depends crucially on the social context. In one group it might be academic ability, in another physical beauty, in another strength, and in another compassion and caring. These domains are socially constructed, as are their standards for judgement (for instance, slim or fat) and outcomes. Thus selected goals and strategies become the *scripts* for self-presentation and the construction of self-identities, and are often gender-related: for example, that women should be slim and nurturing while men should be muscular and not show vulnerability. Thus a culture can value (reward) demonstrations of strength and violence as acceptable and desirable qualities.

Table 18.1 Types and tactics of ranking behaviour

Ranking		
SELF		OTHER
	Inferior–superior	
	Controlled–controller	

Ranking systems *(tactics/strategies)*		
POWER AGGRESSION		ATTRACTIVENESS
Cohesion		Talent
Threat		Role competence
Authoritarian		Democratic-authoritative
To be obeyed		To be valued
To be reckoned with		To be chosen

If self is construed as losing/inferior
(possible defensive responses)

Shame
Envy
Hostile resentment
Revenge
Depression
Social anxiety
Defeated
Controlled by others
Involuntary subordinate
Internal attack (self-criticism)

The affect that seems linked with loss of attractiveness (SAHP) in the eyes of others, so that one thinks one is seen as weak, bad, incompetent, unable and useless is *shame* (Gilbert 1992a; Kaufman 1989; Scheff 1988), and the consequent damaged identity as *stigma* (Goffman 1968). Thus shame is both an internal experience and a social-relational phenomena (Scheff 1988). These low-status (stigmatizing) labels signal reduced eligibility to engage advantageously in social interactions, and they convey to the self and others that one is in some sense inferior. These create an experience of powerlessness: one is powerless to have a desired impact on others and elicit from them desired interactions. These themes are strongly evoked in the context of violence in intimate relationships (Goldner *et al.* 1990). Men seem to dread the labels 'wimp', 'spineless' and 'gutless' (Miedzian 1992). Although shame-induced depression is one outcome of perceiving oneself to be so labelled (Gilbert 1992a), shame-induced rage, leading to violence, is another. This shame-induced rage seems to be increased if a put-down or loss of status occurs in front of an audience, with consequent damage to the person's reputation, and also if strong needs for closeness are at stake. Psychoanalysts call such experiences narcissistic rage because of the effects of the loss on self-esteem. Shame rage may be extremely important for an understanding of male violence (Tangney *et al.* 1992). In my clinical experience there is nearly always a ruminative component to such violence, with preoccupation of injury done to self, injustice and fantasies of revenge. These are also the hallmarks of shame (Gilbert 1992a; Kaufman 1989).

A failure in the attractiveness game can switch a person from an SAHP strategy to a more coercive (RHP) strategy, especially, as evolutionary theory suggests, if the potential benefits of coercion outweigh the costs. These may differ for males and females (Daly and Wilson, Chapter 14). These can be accentuated in a culture that puts (for males) a low cost on violence and a low value on compassion and the ability to accept losing and defeat gracefully. As we shall see, capitalist culture seems to make losing and giving way, and seeking reconciliation, not signs of maturity but of weakness and inferiority – with very serious costs. To accept defeat is not manly!

Novaco (in press), in his development of an anger scale and explorations of the linkage of anger with violence, suggests that violence relates to a variety of cognitive, behavioural and biological factors, including a susceptibility to feel easily slighted, physiological arousal, a tendency to rumination, a deep sense of harm done and an acceptance of violence as a legitimate response. Apart from acceptance of violence, all these bear centrally on shame (Broucek 1991; Kaufman 1989). Unfortunately, the research on shame (which can often be the parent of violence) and violence has rarely been integrated.

Reconciliation

In one sense, shame-induced rage may continue as a failure of reconciliation. In chimpanzees, reconciliation is of major importance, and aggressive interactions are interspersed with reconciliation. This has the effect that previous adversaries may become allies, at least in close-knit communities (de Waal

1988). The acceptance of reconciliation may do much to reduce vengeful rumination and the desire to retaliate. In therapy we talk of helping patients to 'let go' of anger (Fitzgibbons 1986) and facilitating forgiveness (Enright 1991). But in our wider culture these processes are rarely addressed or promoted. Indeed, fictional representations of violent conflict, for example in films, rarely end in reconciliation. Any efforts by wrong-doers to reconcile is usually shown to be untrustworthy. Moreover, it seems to me that reconciliation and forgiveness are often presented as 'lowering defences' and as a sign of inferiority, weakness or crass stupidity and not manly. Wrong-doers are usually defined as out-group members, such as criminals or deviants. Thus reconciliation may be reserved for in-group members, in order to preserve the cohesion of the group.

Although reconciliation may be reserved for in-group members, it does not always work here either. Clinical experience suggests that many patients, especially those prone to anger and aggression, are very poor at reconciliation, even with family members. Some will not agree to reconcile unless the other totally submits and is humiliated. On the other hand, compliance or even passive aggression may appear as a submissive response, but this is not reconciliation. When face-saving is at issue, peacemaking and reconciliation are not seen as masculine traits. Some families have very poor ways of reconciling or dealing with shame (Fossum and Mason 1989).

In intimate relationships also, certain types of reconciliation can spell trouble. After a violent attack on a lover, a male may collapse into a state of vulnerability and remorse and beg forgiveness from his partner. This collapse is both a sign of the desperation of the male's needs for closeness and to be esteemed by the partner, although this level of need is also a potential source of the violence. During these episodes of being needed, a woman, for various psychological reasons of her own, may have her care-taking (SAHP) and rescuer ideals (Gilbert 1992a) strongly aroused and may find it difficult to separate (Goldner et al. 1990). Female forgiveness of males is prescribed (even expected) in a way quite different from that of males. As far as I know there has been no research of these different aspects of forgiveness. Archer (personal communication) points out that females may have more to lose by not reconciling and forgiving. First, they may have invested much time and effort in the relationship, and leaving and starting again may be a poorer prospect for females than males. Secondly, she may have children whom she would find difficult to support alone. Thirdly, she may have to cope with being pursued by a violent male who may even threaten her life. She may also blame herself for the violence (Andrews and Brewin 1990), which has the effect of subduing her counter-aggression, igniting guilt at leaving and raising doubts about her ability to form non-violent relationships.

Allies, reconciliation and the blind eye

There is another potentially dark side to reconciliation. While in intimate relationships it can set up cycles of reconciling-violent interactions, in non-intimate interactions, reconciled relationships may allow individuals to go unchallenged in their immoral actions. In order to maintain the support of allies, and avoid conflicts we may turn a blind eye to their violence and repression of others. This is a position of grave concern in international politics (Chomsky 1992). In spite of the known atrocities in Iraq, throughout the eighties the west continued to provide support for that country because of its fear of Iran and need for oil. But it raises the whole issue of how we define domains of non-interference, and violence as an 'internal matter'.

Thus there are serious questions to be asked as to why we have a tendency to allow violence in various arenas, including within countries, organizations, religious sub-groups and families, making us essentially bystanders to many forms of violence (Sabini and Silver 1982). Fear (arising from the risks and costs) seems the issue in avoiding personal intervention, but does not explain the failure of law. There is no international law that prohibits torture of indigenous people, for example. Such offences are mainly brought to light by organizations like Amnesty International. The collusion to avoid targeting heads of state and holding them accountable is very noticeable. In these situations (political) self-interest seems more likely. Closer to home, domestic violence is tolerated at a far higher rate than violence against strangers, unless the strangers are seen as out-group members, such as ethnic minorities. Thus the issue of the contexts in which one bestows the power to intervene in violent interactions is a complex but very major issue.

TACTICS OF POWER

Some writers link violence to power. Power has always been a troublesome concept in terms of its definition and function (Dell 1989). But in general, power is about influence and is related to rank (and the complex interplay of RHP and SAHP). The higher the rank the more influence one has (Gilbert 1990). However, neither power nor rank is, in itself, bad. The relation of student to teacher is a ranked relationship – parent to child is another (Hartup 1989) – but these work for the benefit of the student and child.

In its positive context power is put at the disposal of the other(s) and it is concerned with signals of investing in the other (Gilbert 1992a). Investments are social rewards but also belong to what may be called *pro-social safety signals* (Gilbert 1993) because of their general effects on psychobiological functioning and *social relations*. Here are all those signals that convey to an individual that they can rely on others; namely, that others are able and willing to invest in them (Trivers 1985; Gilbert 1992a). Price (1988) used the term 'anathetic signal', meaning that they have the effect of boosting up the receiving person's self-esteem, helping them to feel secure, content and happy.

Investment and self-esteem 'boosting up' signals from social others include *actual rewards* such as acquiring control over resources, being awarded prizes, being helped to obtain a desired incentive – a voluntary bestowing of resources that is pleasurable for the receiver and giver. Also important is *social attention*, such as listening, empathizing, taking interest in, approval, encouraging and acceptance; choosing to be with and *reassurance*, such as helping, offering support or sharing feelings, the positive exchange of facial signals (like smiling), non-verbal behaviour (for example, cuddling) and breaking down a sense of difference between people. These rewarding and reassuring signals encourage exploration and an openness of attention, and affiliation rather than violence (Gilbert 1992a, 1993). Thus in children, aggression and violence over conflicts are less between friends than strangers (Hartup 1989). It is not surprising, then, that many therapies which provide interpersonal relationships where the therapist is empathic, and listens in a friendly, reassuring way, are experienced as helpful and boosting (Frank 1982).

The voluntary giving and receiving of investments promotes an openness to experiences, more complex and creative problem-solving, a greater capacity to integrate information, and more pro-social behaviour (Eisenberg and Mussen 1989; Isen 1990). These signals tend to avoid aggression and are based on mutuality. Groups and relationships functioning in this way have been called hedonic (Chance 1980, 1988) and egalitarian (Power 1991). Also, the message that a previous adversary will become a helper may do much to facilitate reconciliation and reduce vengeful strategies.

However, the tactics of influence and control can operate in very different ways. In some situations we can try to exert control by boosting our own power *at the expense of others*. These often take the form of attacks to reduce the power of others, to put them down. (Interestingly, in our use of language 'putting down' can be used to describe a status reduction, but is also used for killing.)

Put(ting)-down signals can take various forms: *direct attacks* involving violence and physical insults to take or force something from another; *physical threats*, such as ritualized aggression (shouting, screaming, intimidating); *verbal insults and symbolic threats*, such as criticism, sarcasm, jokes and condescending verbal and non-verbal behaviour; *neglect*, ignoring, not listening to or taking notice of, lack of interest; *removal of investment signals*, such as actual or threatened withdrawal of love, attention, support, or help. Removal of sources of investment, separations and defections are common triggers for violence (Trivers 1985).

Eliciting submission from another can have positive effects and increase one's sense of control and influence, self-esteem and status, but by its very nature this way of influencing others will not develop the more pro-social possibilities of a relationship (like openness, mutuality, equality, sharing and moral behaviour), and can have very serious effects on those who are the recipients of neglect, attack and put-down (Gilbert 1992a, 1993). Further, the recipient of put-downs, or the withdrawal of signals of positive value and interest, may switch to violent and coercive tactics.

Overview

It is now clear that violence cannot be explored with single-process models for it involves a complex interplay of a variety of factors. Various distinctions (such as between gang and individual and between planned and unplanned violence) can be made. Further, it was suggested that many types of human conflict concern issues such as (1) coercion, and the ability to induce fearful submission in others; and (2) how attractive one is, in terms of self-presentation and social image (Baumeister 1982): hence the concern is to gain the voluntary investment of others. These tactics are not always easy to separate. I also explored briefly the issue of power and pointed out that the tactics of influence and power can be pro-social or antisocial. The choice of which is selected depends on various factors such as the effectiveness of the relative tactics, their costs and benefits, and the socially constructed values placed on pursuing them. It was noted that in many situations violence can arise from the failure of inhibitors such as empathy and compassion (see also Miller and Eisenberg 1988; Blackburn 1989).

TOWARDS AN INTEGRATION

Violence can be conceptualized in many ways:

- *Physiology*; as the study of hormones and neurotransmitters;
- *Evolutionary function*; as in the descriptions defensive, predatory and competitive (Archer 1988);
- *Development*; as in early family history and socializations and giving rise to personality characteristics such as poor impulse control or personality disorders;
- *Affects*; such as anger and frustration tolerance, and mood states such as depression and paranoia;
- *Cognitive characteristics*; such as attitudes and attributions;
- *Cultural values*; such as gender scripts, needs and tactics of face-saving and the trivialization of others;
- *Socio-economic*; (power) structures and resource allocations.

Further, we can study the antecedents or consequences of violence. All these different approaches add to our understanding of male violence, but it is the *integration* of these various themes that now concerns us. To do this we need some kind of biopsychosocial approach or model that can illuminate multiple processes. Many researchers now accept that, although much of our understanding and theories are based on restricted models of sociobiology, psychology and sociology, we need a more co-operative orientation that integrates data from many different fields (for example, see Hinde and Groebel 1991).

There is in fact a growing effort to derive multi-process models. Feminist writers (for example, Goldner *et al.* 1990) highlight interactions between (1) psychoanalytic – pertaining to the internal life of the person; (2) social learning and modelling; (3) sociopolitical – involving cultural proscriptions of gender behaviour; and (4) systemic – pertaining to the interactional sequences that lead to escalations of conflict and violence. In family therapy the work of Cronen *et al.* (1982) explores the relationship between higher-order organizing scripts and schema for meaning-making. They depict various levels in the organization of the construction of meaning and social behaviour (Table 18.2). Hannah and McAdam (1991) and McAdam and Hannah (1991) have outlined some new developments of this model and how it can be used in clinical work.

Table 18.2 Hierarchically organized meanings

Cultural patterns and scripts are the broad patterns of socially shared discourses that define relational patterns. These patterns locate and educate human experience in the cultural context and legitimize ways of knowing, defining and acting. Gender scripts are located here, for example.

Life scripts are the various repertoires of actions, goals and beliefs that make up a person's sense of self. In this sense they are owned by the person.

Relationships refer to the collective 'we' of interacting persons; they are interpersonal exchanges.

Episodes refer to communication routines that persons view as wholes.

Speech acts (or communication acts) refer to the actual things people do or say to one another.

Content refers to the information that is communicable.

Source: adapted from Cronen *et al.* 1982

The concept of a 'script' is very important here since it contains definition elements that often exist in advance of any specific behaviour. For example, the idea that men should hide their feelings is a cultural script or rule that in part defines manhood and in part defines (and legitimizes) what men should do (and feel and believe) if they are to view themselves, and be viewed, as men (Meth and Pasick 1990; Tejirian 1990). It thereby gives rise to scripted values, behaviour and self-definitions.

From ethology, Hinde (1987, 1989, 1992) developed a different multi-process model for outlining various complex biopsychosocial interactions. These are outlined in Figure 18.1. This model outlines the complex dialectal

interactions between an individual's biological state, the nature of the relationships they seek, the type of relationships they elicit and how all these are
embedded in a socially prescribed set of cultural patterns and values. These
values influence the attributes for gaining or losing attractiveness in the eyes of
others, and facilitate or inhibit (reduce) the advantage to be gained from
violent interactions.

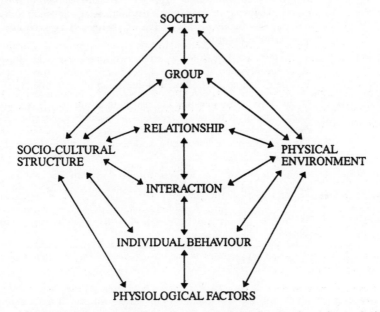

Figure 18.1 The dialectical relations between successive levels of social complexity
Source: Hinde 1992, reproduced with kind permission

The biopsychosocial approach (Gilbert 1992a) is not a theory of human
behaviour but, rather, seeks to outline interacting processes and levels. A brief
description of it is given in Table 18.3. Although theorists are moving away
from simple, single-component process models for understanding human
behaviour, we are still a long way from agreeing on what models are the most
useful, and there are few educational efforts to teach multi-process working.
But with these approaches as our map we can now explore violence as a multi-
process phenomenon.

CULTURE

Culture is transmitted via meaningful communications that outlive the com-
municator and are stored and enacted by others. In humans, our extraordinary capacity for symbolic representations allows us to perform this feat

Table 18.3 Levels of interaction in the biopsychosocial approach

CULTURE	At this level are role possibilities and values that are part of the culture and are transmitted from generation to generation (e.g., designated roles for masculinity, femininity and parenting styles, economic opportunities, religious behaviour, traditions, etc.).
FAMILY	At this level families operate within the values of their own culture and from their own earlier experiences. Their relationships may be supportive/loving or more towards dominating, downing and controlling other family members. These experienced styles become part of a personal history.
SOCIAL	At this level are the quality of current relationships that the individual experiences (family, friends, etc.). For some, significant relationships may be downing, controlling and devaluing of the individual.
PERSONAL	At this level is the person's internal judgements of self and others. Especially important are judgements of negative social comparison, ideals, aspirations and needs (basic personal themes and life scripts). The judgements of inferiority and loss of face are important in violence.
BIOLOGICAL	At this level are the various measurable state factors, such as hormones and neurotransmitter integrity, and variations of brain functioning.
ORGAN	At this level are the specific biological targets of study; e.g., synaptic control.

Source: adapted from Gilbert (1992a)

par excellence. What is handed to us are sets of values for social discourse that moves across generations. Weingartner (1991) suggests that social discourses refer to at least five phenomena:

> (1) A discourse consists of various ideas and practices that share common values; (2) a discourse reflects and constructs a specific world view; (3) there are dominate and subjugated discourses. Dominate discourses contain and constrain what we can feel, think and do; (4) that which is not part of the discourse shapes our experience as critically as the discourse itself; and (5) discourse evolves. Changes of discourse occur when the collective conversations people have about their lives transform culturally available narratives about people's lives.
>
> (1991: 286)

Thus culture, as a process of social discourses and social communications, produces various values concerned with how to create meaning, what to think and enact, and these become a source of self-identity. Taylor's (1992) exhaustive philosophic work on the self explores many of these themes through the ages, and he argues that the subjective meaning of the 'good life' lies behind many of our constructions. He says,

What brings this to light is the essential link between identity and a kind of orientation. To know who you are is to be orientated in a moral space, a space in which questions arise about what is good or bad, what is worth doing and what not, what has meaning and importance for you and what is trivial and secondary.

(1992: 28)

These decisions arise from shared human interactions, which all the time are selecting, developing (or constraining) and moulding from an array of evolved human potentials (Gilbert 1989).

In order to see if culture facilitates male violence we should look for answers to the following questions. First, how does culture educate individuals into understanding themselves and their interpersonal needs? Secondly, does it create multiple arenas for conflicts? Thirdly, if so, what means of conflict resolution does it promote (especially for males)? Fourthly, what messages does culture send to, or create for, losers and those who feel vulnerable? Fifthly, what attributes does it value and devalue? Sixthly, what stance does it take on the mechanisms of control? In my view, in all these domains our modern culture comes out very badly.

Feminists and others have drawn attention to the cultural-historical patterns that not only sanction male violence but also encourage it (Chapter 16). Two central forces are articulated, economics and religion.

Economics

There are various theories concerning how competitive economic structures gradually came to replace the more mutually dependent social structures of hunter-gatherers. The ownership of land and the growing size of groups that agriculture supported gave rise to *accumulation*, rather than sharing, as an economic process (Diamond 1991; Glantz and Pearce 1989). This, together with the growth of warrior classes to defend accumulations and plunder other groups' resources and the formation of male hierarchies to contain and control these warriors, is one view (McCarthy, this volume; Itzkoff 1990; MacDonald 1988). Intense shortages of resources and the loss of coherent values that support co-operative lifestyles is another (Power 1991). It is the interchange between economic structures and evolved strategies, which, though poorly understood, is crucial. Indeed, even in primates (and other animals) it seems that ecology has a very significant effect on various forms of social behaviour, such as co-operative and competitive interactions and relations between the sexes (Power 1991; Van Schaik 1989).

By whatever means it came about, as Marx and many others (Galbraith 1987; Toffler 1991; Smail 1987) have pointed out, capitalist economic structures depend on the creation of winners, losers and owners. Bailey (1987) and MacDonald (1988) argue that this increases predatory behaviour, especially between competing groups. Further, competitive economic structures in large groups, where the genetic and attachment relationships between individuals are low, encourage the exploitation of resources for individual advantage. The market came to be, in essence, the battleground for proficient exploitation. Capitalism has no intrinsic value system over and above the maximization of profit and resource control. Any inhibition on exploitation came from the rules of law and tentative efforts at justice. But in capitalist societies and competitive social systems anything that is exploitable is up for grabs – as our planetary chaos attests. Not only does this lead to the subjugation of individuals and the creation of a class system, defined by work, but also, due in part to the different reproductive strategies of males and females, one group (males) can render the other group (females) into little more than a subordinate class and a resource suitable for exploitation.

When Mike Tyson was imprisoned for rape, it turned out that although he had shown serious emotional problems throughout his adolescence, he was given clear messages that once he was champion of the world he could have any female he wanted (Rendell 1992). Subsequently, his rape and aggressions were not explained by the failures of his guardians, nor the expectations and values he had been given, but by his blackness, maleness, and early life in the ghetto. In speaking of one of his managers, Rendell suggests that

> The only thing Cus D'Amato wanted before he died was another world champion. Nothing was to stand in the way of that goal, least of all any problems at school that Tyson might have, in which D'Amato professed himself to be utterly disinterested.

(1992: 4)

This comment is a mirror to society. Interest in the individual is notably absent provided they can deliver and show themselves able to get results. If, in this struggle, some behave badly, then either we turn a blind eye to it or blame and punish them, labelling them as bad or mad (Levenson 1992). As Campbell and Muncer (this volume) point out, under this sytem of values males become preoccupied with showing that they can meet challenges and beat opponents, be this on the street or on the stock market. This attribute is the one most valued by the capitalist system. It shows itself in many ways, in work and films, and comes over as toughness, determination, 'having bottle', 'the right stuff', and, more cynically, as ruthlessness. A major culture script for males is showing that they are 'up to the job' (Miedzian 1992). Many working with males (for example, Meth and Pasick 1990) note how these scripts become incorporated into gender schema and identities; moreover, they exclude concern about *stereotypically feminine* attributes of self, such as fear, acknowledgement of vulnerability, care and compassion.

Indeed, as Goldner *et al.* (1990) point out, in every culture the division of labour makes gender a pervasive construct that permeates language, religion and socio-economic life. In cultures that require men to be strong and dominant, any personal attribute such as fear and vulnerability must be projected if males are to cope and show themselves up to the business of 'doing the job'. Once females have become the holders of such projections – so that it is they who are the vulnerable and in need of protection or are viewed as inadequate and not 'up to it' – there operates a 'taboo against similarity and the dread of collapse of gender difference operates silently and powerfully in all relations between men and women' (Goldner *et al.* 1990: 348).

These cultural themes and discourses accentuate male archetypal reproductive strategies such that 'striding forth', to do the business and prove oneself in battle (or its modern equivalent) dominates masculine ideals of selfhood. In mythology the prize was often access to a female (or females) and to rule as king. So capitalist economics does indeed, quite purposely, create many arenas for conflict; it is concerned only with winners and has little interest in those who are disadvantaged; it tends to advantage those who can gain power and then exclude others; namely, those who can accumulate and defend their resources rather than sharing them. It stresses the importance of winners and losers, and being tough enough to step on others and even break social moral rules (Baumeister 1991). It also stresses the benefits of greed and does not support people voluntarily limiting themselves. Maximization – of potential, earning power, ownership, wealth and even life experiences – are at the heart of this system: more is better in the 'me first' society. If one deconstructs the capitalist dream with a critical eye, at its heart it appears as freedom to exploit and own and once owned defend it regardless (Galbraith 1987).

Capitalist systems stress differences between people with the specific function of ranking them in terms of their ability to exert control over resources. Now, not all cultures are like this, and in some, reciprocity and mutuality are far more important than gaining competitive advantage (Haviland 1990; Howell and Willis 1989). But in competitive social groups the strategies serving ranking behaviour are advantaged and valued (Gilbert 1989). Males internalize these values and enact them; they become the lens through which the self is evaluated (Meth and Pasick 1990). Even though there is growing evidence that after a certain point it is not the overall level of resources in a community that is linked with health, crime and violence but the disparities within the community (Wilkinson 1992), this seems to have little impact on shifting us to more egalitarian social structures. Those with power and resources rarely vote (in large enough numbers) to share them.

Thus society is split into the haves, have-nots and have-lots, and those who are disadvantaged tend to collapse into more primitive and aggressive, male-dominated social structures: violence is pronounced in young males at the margins of society (Chapter 7). In some of these groups drugs become the only means of gaining advantage. In commenting on the massive violence in the Colombian city, Medellín, Salazar (1992) says,

Drug trafficking has become the major means of social and economic advancement, and the youth of the city consider it the only way to achieve wealth and status. In the hope of eventually breaking into the cartels, boys form contract killing gangs. Almost invariably they end up dead themselves.

(1992: 12)

These cultural forces are dehumanizing and reduce compassionate mechanisms. Any individual attribute – roles, skills or sexuality – is potentially exploitable in the market place. So capitalist cultures have also been seen as the culture of narcissism, in that they have put a high premium on the need to gain advantage over others (Lasch 1985). Potentials for mutual nurturance, compassion, sharing, empathy and a sense of the sanctity of life fall foul of the culture of trivialization in its exploitative dramas (Gilbert 1989; Levenson 1992; Miedzian 1992). It is by way of the trivialization of so many of these human qualities that individuals may come to see themselves in terms of marketable objects, whose self-presentation is everything. They are indeed preoccupied with social comparison and the fear of being losers, of being seen as weak, inferior and powerless, since these are stigmatizing and there is no 'community' to support losers (Frosh 1991; Goffman 1968; Lasch 1985).

Culture turns a blind eye to those who, once in power, use violence and exclusion to maintain their position and wealth. There is also an acceptance and even admiration of vengeful violence; for example, in some of Stephen King's novels, and in films, such as *Death Wish*, *Rambo*, *Batman*, and *Mad Max* and their sequels. They all involve some offence committed by a wrong-doer, and encounters involving ritualized and unritualized aggression. Then – often armed with superhuman powers – the victim comes back to wreak revenge. Inter-male violence is thereby condoned and valued.

The repeated observation of such scenarios is likely to affect people's views of the world and their internalized standards for behaviour. This is especially so if they have few alternative role models or few opportunities to gain control over economic resources. Hence these aggressive role models are likely to have a marked impact on younger males who are poor and are constantly confronted by television advertising that shows them what they do not and cannot have. In my view, our culture is preoccupied with such violence, in part because of the enormous levels of social injustice we tolerate, and the costs imposed on being seen as less able and marginalized.

Very few studies of television violence have been controlled for these social factors. Although the findings on viewing television violence are controversial, there is growing evidence that it has an effect on at least some males (Buck 1988; MacDonald 1988; Miedzian 1992). There are few studies which examine long-term effects of the media on attitudes and how these become related to self-esteem, gender constructs, in-group–out-group identification or the desire and skills for reconciliation. In my own work with the police, they

372

are alarmed that in some – often poor – homes, violent videos are watched by children as young as 3 and 4.

Leadership

The structure of cultural values can also be influenced by key individuals in positions of power (Emler and Hogan 1991). The military junta which promotes repression by the state is an obvious example, and males are often the vehicles for such repression. But the manipulation of economic values is another. The era of the 'me-first' society of Thatcher and Reagan grew out of monetarist theories and right-wing political theory. Leaders themselves may value sharing and compassionate behaviour very little, preferring instead individualistic competitive behaviour. Such traits may be affected by their own personality or even by drugs and mental illness (Freeman 1991). Leaders can have very serious consequences on the structure of cultural and moral values and on economic exchanges within organizations and groups (Emler and Hogan 1991). Efforts to explore how leaders may affect the social structure of society, so that various underclasses are created, are difficult. However, there is evidence that authoritarian attitudes can be manipulated, leading to a more stratified and punitive society (Doty *et al.* 1991).

Religion

There is much we could say about the economic structures that facilitate, encourage or allow violence by default. But there are other factors at work, especially in regard to gender. For various reasons (Archer, Chapter 16; Baumeister 1991) women are in low-status positions in many societies. Once put into these roles, rape and other forms of violence are more likely, and concern with injustices towards those labelled 'low status' is notably absent. But it is more than this. There is also a positive denigration of femininity, a certain contemptuousness, rather than the mere attempt to exclude females from positions of influence: Goldner *et al.* (1990) refer to fear of the collapse of gender difference.

One of the major forces shaping these aspects is religion. Of course religions serve many biological functions. They provide attachment objects, reciprocal relationships and enable large numbers of people to feel part of a group by virtue of shared beliefs (Wenegrat 1990). Yet, many sources of conflict are between groups that differ in religious beliefs rather than genetically. Although at the heart of most religions are messages of love and compassion, their internal structure can work against this, for it is authoritarian. For example, the early Christians inherited ideas from the Greeks that were anti-sex, anti-female and anti-body, and these were linked with authoritarian attitudes (Fisher 1989). Nearly all the major monotheistic religions have a powerful male God who decides the fate of his subjects. Their structure is hierarchical and male-dominated, keeping females out. Moreover, the early history of these religions usually depicts God as some kind of warrior interested in conquest. Their discourses are full of submission to God's will, and efforts to work out his desires so as to find favour, to be attractive, wanted or desired by him (Tejirian 1990). The fear of the powerful male is not only an evolutionary theme but is built into the fabric of many religions; both God and the Devil are males. And for reasons that would fit evolutionary explanations this dominant male God seems particularly interested in, and controlling of, the sexual behaviour of his subjects. Not surprisingly under this archetype the opportunities for positive, sexual, intimate and mutually valuing relationships between males and females may be seriously distorted. Although marriage may reduce inter-male fighting for access to females and offer some stability for child-rearing (MacDonald 1988), the plight of females themselves is ignored and for many years Christian marriage required the woman to 'honour and obey' the male and see him as dominant over her.

There has been extraordinary cruelty by males to females: at their height, witch-burnings are believed to have accounted for over 3 million deaths (Tejirian 1990); the confusion of female sexuality – dividing them into whores and madonnas – and homophobia, culminated in increasing preoccupation with hell, or God's punishment for the disobedient (Tejirian 1990). Most of this had nothing to do with the compassionate and egalitarian messages of Christ. It was later that fear of a dominant male, and victimization of those seen to offend the dominant male, became significant forces that were reintroduced in our culture. Although these aspects were involved in previous religious horrors, they are still active in the human imagination. For example, Sutcliff, who killed thirteen women he believed to be prostitutes, felt that God wanted him to cleanse the world of them.

Whilst evolutionary theory helps us to understand why subordinate males are very cautious and submissive towards those who are dominant and may explain why sexuality and fear are often linked, we still need to recognize how these themes were symbolized into particular values (Tejirian 1990). Blaming females for tempting men into certain sexual practices (a theme going back to the book of Genesis) lets men off. Males are rendered powerless to female desires and this enables them to avoid punishment, a theme many females have complained of in modern law. Moreover, this leads to a sense that women somehow 'deserved it' or had 'invited it' – in other words victim-blaming (see Pollard, Chapter 10).

For these reasons intimacy by males with females and even other males can be both desired but also feared and rendered as bad objects, leading to punishment or contamination. There is cross-cultural evidence that in male-dominated societies, female genital and reproductive processes can be seen as bad, evil, contaminating and disgusting (Gregor 1990), and that shame is located on the object of desire. The phallus, however, is seen as a symbol of power and potency. Whereas television advertising has long been happy with

374

toilet rolls, sanitary-towel advertising is very new! When I was growing up male jokes about female genitals usually involved them as something bad or disgusting. Moreover, sexual violence as in rape often involves acts of defilement.

It is the rendering of an individual or some group as something bad and contaminating (Fisher 1989) that unleashes these acts of defilement. I am not sure how evolutionary theory helps us understand why males collude to take such a negative view of female sexuality and their reproductive biology. One reason might be that, if women can be shamed about their sexuality, then they are less likely actively to use it to attract other males; that is, it is a tactic of male control. Thus if females may choose to defect to higher status or more attractive males, then they must be controlled by shaming them and thus stop them from being openly seductive.

So, for various reasons economic and religious, cultures can take a firm stand against violence or ignore it. Social structures can create many arenas of conflict, give advantage to individualistic rather than reciprocating relationships and make losing a very serious outcome. Further, cultures create gender scripts and domains of empowerment. The competitive capitalist economic culture requires a certain ruthlessness in its dealing with people. Competitive economies often have religions that are focused on a single, dominant, male God. These two social domains give rise to various discourses that can reduce the opportunities for sharing and caring and increase the potential for violent interactions. The mixture of fear and need for control can be explosive.

FAMILIES

We know that learning is essential to many non-human animals, and the young often need some education in order to be able to perform certain activities needed for survival. For example, in lions successful predation requires education and modelling of parental behaviour. In primates the ability to nurture young often relates to the experience of being nurtured (Harlow and Mears 1979).

Early life has a very major impact on biological as well as psychological maturation (Hofer 1981; Henry and Stephens 1977; Meyersburg and Post 1979; Post 1992). Distortions introduced early into a biological maturation process can prove very difficult to repair later in life. For example, primates who have experienced disturbed attachments may appear to make a satisfactory recovery when they are adults, but under conditions of stress they can behave in extreme and disorganized ways.

Cross-cultural evidence does suggest that family structures and interactions vary considerably. In !Kung societies, for example, fathers spend a lot of time with their children in non-authoritarian and playful interactions, so that most do not grow up fearing their fathers (Haviland 1990). This is very different from the father-dominated family structures of western societies, in which the male automatically assumes that as head of the household he is to be obeyed, and is often away from the family for long periods of the day.

Much research shows that serious male violence is often seeded in childhood. Families transmit cultural values and aspirations and these vary cross-culturally, especially with regard to the acceptance of violence and promotion of pro-social behaviour (Buss 1988; Goody 1991; MacDonald 1988). But they also provide the context for biopsychosocial maturation and the formation of identities and gender scripts. Alice Miller (1983) points out that the whole western view of childhood has been riddled with concepts of the need for the child to submit to parental control, preparing them perhaps to live in authoritarian social structures by learning fearful submission. It has often used harsh discipline 'to break the child's spirit'. But whether or not parents abuse their children out of misguided attempts to educate them, or because they know of no better means of conflict resolution, or because of poor frustration tolerance, the effects of violence and neglect against children rings through the generations (Rohner 1986). In many instances, it is the lack of warmth and affiliative behaviour within the family, coupled with parental abuse, which turns out to be the most destructive (Frude 1989).

In many of the histories of violent males one hears the stories of alcoholic, abusive fathers, neglectful and emotional distant parents. The so-called men's movement is beginning to explore father relationships and the appallingly violent and neglectful relationships that many males seem to have had with their fathers. Furthermore, we are beginning to understand the innumerable paradoxes and double-binds that families put on their children (Fossum and Mason 1989; Goldner et al. 1990). Although not every abused male child will become a violent or abusive adult (Kaufman and Zigler 1987), such treatment greatly increases the risk. In abusive families, not only does the child learn to model certain styles of interaction (Fossum and Mason 1989), but also the fear of abuse probably affects the maturing nervous system. Although a history of being abused does not excuse violence, we cannot ignore it. Perhaps one way of reducing violence is to make our cultures much more child-focused, to be aware of children's needs, rather than seeing them as inconvenient to our economic lives. Unfortunately this may mean we have to give up more, rather than have more. Work crèches are still the exception rather than the rule.

Families who express low levels of aggression and high levels of warmth tend to have children who are pro-social, open and trusting (Eisenberg and Mussen 1989; Rohner 1986). Violence is not only inhibited but avoided because it is not valued, while affiliative and co-operative behaviour are valued. Eisenberg and Mussen (1989) have reviewed research on the promotion of caregiving and pro-social behaviour in children; they note a number of factors as being important. These include: personal competency and general well-being; having role models that attend to, value and reward caring behaviour; experiencing benefits of sharing and caring; having opportunities to practise, and having models for developing pro-social forms of conflict resolution. Experiences with punitive and neglectful parenting have detrimental effects on the development of pro-social behaviour.

The internalization of relational styles experienced in early life that results in a sense of self that is fragile, full of mistrust and rage, is still being researched, but we know enough to be clear that early life is a major factor in male violence.

SOCIAL RELATIONSHIPS

Individuals are embedded in social relationships that help to shape their values, identities (Taylor 1992) and gender scripts (Meth and Pasick 1990). Archer (Chapter 7; see also Colman 1991) points out that in some economically disadvantaged sections of society, the sub-group returns to a kind of pre-state structure where males dominate certain territories, have very segregated gender roles and where violence, particularly amongst males, is common. Thus peer-group values are important sources of self-understanding (Abrams *et al.* 1990; Brown and Lohr 1987). Peer groups also shape the relational style, and this accounts for the goals and tactics of influence used between individuals (Weisfeld, this volume). Montagner *et al.* (1988) explored children's peer interactions and distinguished their social relationship style in terms of *affiliative, aggressive* and *fearful*, and combinations of these. Cultures take differing stances on how these three different strategies are developed and woven into the psychology of the child (Goody 1991). In some groups, aggressive demonstrations of strength and toughness are key characteristics for acquiring and maintaining status. However, this depends on the group dynamics, since in affiliative groups, aggressive individuals can be unpopular, though not if the group structure is aggressive (Wright *et al.* 1986).

At the present time the work on peer-group classification and early attachment style with parents has not been integrated, but preliminary data (Troy and Sroufe 1987) suggest that avoidant types are more likely to be either aggressive (that is, victimizers) or subordinate (namely, victim), the anxiously attached child more easily becoming subordinate (a fearful victim) while the secure child more generally becomes affiliative. Further, early experience of attachments will affect affiliation and attachment strategies later in life (Heard and Lake 1986). Those who experience low levels of pro-social interactions are perhaps less likely to seek out and develop affiliative relationships and more likely to express antisocial strategies.

The influence of one's immediate social group can have profound effects on violence, as has been demonstrated for the development of torturers (Williams 1992). As feminists point out, the social group can influence whether the issue of male violence and power abuse are addressed at all. Male violence and styles of competition can be kept firmly off agendas because the issue is seen as too threatening. But the effects of not addressing it can be insidious. For example, there seems a verbal agreement amongst many academics that the person who can pinpoint weakness in an argument is seen as brighter than those who highlight its strengths. Here we speak of the ability to pull apart a particular discourse. Young academics are schooled in these skills. We educate them in the dialectics of polemics. But in many forms of discourses between others, and even in family relationships, the same may apply. Foucault had this to say:

> In the serious play of questions and answers, in the work of reciprocal elucidation, the rights of each person are in some sense immanent in the discussion. They depend only on the dialogue situation. The person asking the questions is merely exercising the right that has been given him; to remain unconvinced, to perceive a contradiction, to require more information, to emphasise different postulates, to point out faulty reasoning, etc. As for the person answering the questions, he too exercises a right that does not go beyond the discussion itself; by the logic of his own discourse he is tied to what he has said earlier, and by the acceptance of dialogue he is tied to the questioning of the other. Questions and answers depend on a game, a game that is at once pleasant and difficult in which each of the two partners takes pains to use only the rights given him by the other and by the accepted form of the dialogue. The polemicist, on the other hand, proceeds encased in privileges that he possesses in advance and will never agree to question. On principle, he possesses rights authorizing him to wage war and making that struggle a just undertaking; the person he confronts is not a partner in the search for truth, but an adversary, an enemy who is wrong, who is harmful and whose very existence constitutes a threat. For him then, the game does not consist of recognizing this person as a subject having the right to speak, but of abolishing him as an interlocutor, from possible dialogue; and his final objective will be, not to come as close as possible to a difficult truth, but to bring about the triumph of the just cause he has been manifestly upholding from the beginning. The polemicist relies on a legitimacy that his adversary is by definition denied.
>
> (1984: 381–2)

I believe that in many situations males, and indeed females, are educated to believe that an ability in polemics is evidence of having 'the right stuff'. This is just one more factor that bears on the internalization of attitudes that are about controlling and winning. The encasement in privileges that one possesses in advance is a source of racism, sexism and ageism.

THE PERSON

There are many ways in which to conceptualize salient person variables related to violence; for example, impulsiveness, poverty of empathy and poor (affiliative) social skills (see above, and Novaco, in press). However, one way is to think of them in terms of the tactics of interpersonal control. For cultural and family reasons, some men do seem to see the world as predominately one of competitive challenge, have very stereotyped and restricted gender scripts, and a focus on the supremacy of men (Meth and Pasick 1990). This in part relates to various beliefs and attitudes, such as

- My worth depends on what I achieve.
- I must prove myself – to myself and to others – that I have what it takes.
- Others can take away from my worth and put me down so I must be vigilant to their challenges.
- Others (and I) are out for what they can get.
- Don't trust others.
- I must not have and must not show feelings of fear, concern or vulnerability.

Some of these attitudes are particularly noted in Type A males (Price 1982). And some Type As are well noted for their more aggressive and competitive behaviours (Table 18.4). Research suggests that Type A has at least two components, hostility and achievement (Price 1982). It is hostility that is related to health issues, while achievement (which can be high in non-hostile types) relates to actual achievements. Gilbert (1989) has argued that the hostile style does not relate to a particular personality type (for example, Type A) but is a superordinate description that covers, amongst others, narcissistic personality and antisocial personality; the key focus is on the experience of life as a competitive struggle, a distrustfulness of others, a trivialization of others' needs, and a readiness to aggress or threaten in conflict situations. For example, Adler (1986) describes the narcissist thus:

> These patients tend to be extremely self-centred, often needing praise and constant recognition in order to feel momentarily good about themselves. Rather than feeling a sense of their own worth or value, they require repeated bolstering from the outside. In their relationships with people, they tend to be exploitative and insensitive to the feelings and needs of others. Their behaviour can be superficially charming on the one hand and arrogant on the other. They expect special privileges from those around them without giving anything in return, yet they can feel easily humiliated or shamed and respond with rage at what they perceive to be criticisms or failure of people to react in the way they wish. . . . Many can elaborate active fantasies about magnificent success in love, sex, beauty, wealth or power. They often devalue people they have previously idolised and tend to split, i.e. see people as either all good or all bad, or alternate between these extremes.
>
> (1986: 430–1)

Adler's description highlights components of such narcissistic characters as being concerned with evaluation of status and with power as well as hostility, the use of others for self-valuing purposes and a comparative lack of the more

Table 18.4 A selected list of common Type A behaviours, attitudes and environmental determinants likely to emerge in group members during group discussions

Overt behaviour	*Hostility*
	Relives anger about past incidents
	Hypersensitivity to criticism
	Argues tenaciously to win small points
	Annoyance at trivial errors of others
	Defensiveness/rationalizations
	Strong opinions
	Challenges validity of statements of others
	Short-tempered
	Edginess
	Time urgency
	Interrupts others
	Poor listener
	Polyphasic behaviour, thoughts
	Rapid, accelerated speech
Environmental determinants	*Trivial situations which are uncontrollable, unexpected*
	Driving a car
	Waiting for someone who is late
	Waiting in a queue
	Interpersonal challenge
	People who talk too much with nothing to say
	Incompetent telephone operators, shop assistants, waitresses/waiters, bank clerks
	Engaged tone on the phone
	Ongoing struggle with family member, work associate
Signs and symptoms of physiological reactivity	Tense body posture
	Fast, jerky movements
	Repetitive movements: knees jiggling, finger tapping
	Expiratory sighing
	Tic-like grimaces
Covert attitudes and beliefs	Egocentrism: dominates conversations, interested in self only
	Suspiciousness: distrusts others' motives
	Competitive: belittles achievements of others, perceives other group members as adversaries
	Resentment: harbours feelings of ill-will
	Prejudice: stereotyped generalizations about groups
	Deterministic world view: believes self to be a pawn of the environment rather than active determiner of fate
	Short-term perspective: deals with problems from immediate consequences
	Belief in inherent injustice: acts like the policeman of the world

Source: Powell and Friedman (1986). Reprinted with kind permission J. Wiley & Sons Ltd

pro-social aspects of human nature such as empathy, moral thinking, and caregiving. Using interpersonal theory, Leary (1957) also described this pattern as narcissistic. Kegan (1982) suggested that a lack of moral development can result in symptom presentations not dissimilar from those noted above. Now we can see how a culture and family experiences, and possibly biological factors, might educate males into this style, but it is still important to recognize that individual differences are useful in the analysis of violence in certain contexts.

Recent work on narcissism suggests that there are a number of related attributes to it, including hostility, grandiosity, dominance and exploitativeness (see Raskin and Terry 1988; Raskin et al. 1991). Wink (1991) suggests two forms of narcissism, one relating to a sense of inferiority and fearfulness, the other related to superiority, exhibitionism and exploitation of others.

What comes out of this research is *the need for control* and at times overcontrol of interpersonal interactions. It is as if such a person never feels secure when attention or resources are focused on anyone else except themselves. The need for control may represent the failure of other mechanisms, such as trust, empathy and moral feelings. Violence becomes the most adaptive solution to that individual if they feel thwarted. But, as Levenson (1992) points out, this style is as much a philosophy of life (or a strategic choice) as a kind of mental abnormality. Thus when we focus on the exploitative and destructive behaviour of individuals, we may label them psychopaths or narcissistic, viewing these as illnesses, deviance or inadequacy. But the cultural acceptance of corporate abuse towards workers, the destruction and exploitation of Third World economies and resources, and above all the arms trade, do not attract the label 'corporate psychopath'.

Shame

There has recently been a growing interest in shame (Lewis 1987; Broucek 1991; Kaufman 1989; Schore 1991; Tangney et al. 1992). Vulnerability to it begins very early in life (Schore 1991), but it is active throughout the life cycle. Gilbert (1992a) referred to shame as the experience of the weak, subordinate self. In my clinical experience with violent men, I find that many are extensively prone to shame and sensitive to their image and its acceptance. Unless they can have their own way they feel shamed, put down and enraged. Even minor criticisms, or refusals by others, can be experienced as a major assault on self-esteem. Sensitivity to shame is one reason that they often refuse to come to therapy.

Shame is beginning to be seen as lying behind not only violence but also many forms of acting-out behaviour. It is closely linked to the issue of rank, and to the experience and fear of powerlessness (Gilbert 1992a). Violence may be enacted in shame-inducing situations, if the person feels able to make it work (that is, can win), and is not deterred by empathy for the victim. Thus

381

status and power – especially over women – play a major role in whether shame-induced rage is acted out or not. Some therapists see many maladaptive marital conflicts as shame-driven (Fossum and Mason 1989).

Another factor is that shame-induced rage can be displaced on to others; that is, 'If you shame me, I will shame you'. The idea that 'all men are potential rapists, or all men think with their dicks', is an effort at 'gender-shaming'. Unfortunately, this leads to counter-rage, increases competitiveness and the desire to avoid or rid oneself of the 'shamer's stare'. Shame, at best, will lead to fearful compliance and secretiveness, not development of compassion or efforts at reparation (Gilbert 1989, 1992a). Thus shaming as a method of changing people is likely to run into serious trouble. In my view, because guilt and shame are related to different mental systems, guilt and empathic awareness may be helpful in treating perpetrators of violence, but not shame. Unfortunately, many of our institutions are shame-based, but if the current evidence on shame is shown to be valid then these institutions are likely to increase rage, competitiveness and narcissistic styles rather than reduce them, and certainly not activate guilt and compassion for others. In many ways ours is a shaming culture (Broucek 1991), and many think shaming is the way to exert control. Certainly, as we begin to address the feminist agendas we should be careful to avoid shame and counter-shaming dialogues.

PHYSIOLOGY

Although I have not the space to explore physiology in any detail here, this is not to demote its importance. As mentioned above, physiological maturation is very much influenced by early relationships (Henry and Stephens 1977; Hofer 1981). Moreover, certain individuals who have suffered from conditions such as attention-deficit disorder may be more prone to violence (see Miedzian 1992). However, at present the physiology of aggression and violence is confusing. There are various biological correlates of violence such as hormones (e.g. testosterone: Archer 1991; Kemper 1990) and neurotransmitters, but these are little more than listings of correlates. 5-HT, for example, is believed to be involved with aggressiveness, but 5-HT and other monoamines have been implicated in just about every psychiatric disorder investigated, particularly depression, anxiety and obsessional disorders. Of course, substance use and abuse have been clearly related to violence. Various brain injuries increase violent behaviour (Buck 1988), and certain areas of the brain such as the amygdala are known to be involved in aggression. Bailey (1987, personal communication) suggests that although violence is a variable strategy, in severe forms of violence there are a number of internal changes: (1) reduced control of behaviour via neocortical structures in preference to 'lower limbic and reptilian structure' control, thereby inhibiting language and rationality; (2) responses become more stereotyped and less flexible; and

(3) with the reduction in control of higher cortical centres, sex differences are maximally accentuated. Further research is needed to illuminate the genetic and neural structures which mediate violent behaviour.

CONCLUSIONS

This chapter has attempted an overview of male violence and at times wandered far afield. I have tried to indicate, like others in this volume, that violence is not one entity but results from an enormous variety of factors. It seems that we cannot understand violence without understanding the loss of the pro-social. Although our pro-social behaviour may be to some extent constrained for biological reasons (for example, tending to be restricted to kin and in-group reciprocating others), it is eminently trainable (Eisenberg and Mussen 1989; MacDonald 1988). Evidence suggests an empathic awareness of harm to the other (Miller and Eisenberg 1988) and a respect for the being of the other both inhibit violence. Therefore, violence is not necessarily or only related to the fact that there is too much of something (such as anger or impulsiveness) but too little of something (like empathy, moral and affiliative interest and skills). Thus the chances of violence may increase when empathic and compassionate (and, more negatively, guilt) mechanisms fail. Various economic and family relationships seem particularly powerful in reducing compassion and the ability to accept defeat gracefully without it becoming a major attack on self-esteem.

Evolutionary explanations can sometimes be taken to mean that this is the way things should be or there is nothing that can be done about it. But the view that we are no more than the puppet of the genes has been refuted by Klama (1988) and many others. We cannot ignore the way in which cultures activate competitive tendencies and create multiple arenas for conflict, with winners and losers. Equally, we cannot ignore what can be done to promote pro-social behaviour (Hinde and Groebel 1991). As soon as we recognize that evolved tendencies are mediated through flexible developmental processes, and are influenced by contextual and environmental indicators of fitness, then the old genetic determinism that sees culture and evolution as alternatives fades away. Increases and decreases in male violence are what culture has made of male strategies (amplifying some and demoting others). But if our reproductive evolution had been different, like that of phalaropes (wading birds with large females who compete for smaller males who guard the eggs), then our culture and laws would be different.

If our planet ends up with the nightmare scenarios of increasing environmental destruction, poverty and violence that some commentators suggest, then in part it will be because of our trivialization of the trainable qualities of compassion, empathy and sharing (Eisenberg and Mussen 1989; Gilbert 1989). Thus, as Hinde and Groebel (1991) point out, many may regard aggression and violence as a more important social problem than pro-social behaviour, but this is a mark of the problem itself.

My point here is that if the absence of empathy and compassion are important in understanding violence, why we do it and why we allow it (Miedzian 1992), then these must be seen as the other side of the violence coin. If males are prone to violence, then what has happened to their compassion? But when cultures make competitive values paramount and trivialize the needs and feelings of others, then compassion may be costly. In my view, the mind is a system of various possibilities, and cultural and family values do much to amplify different potentials from this array (Gilbert 1989).

ACKNOWLEDGEMENTS

I would like to thank Professor J. Archer for his encouragement and advice, Professor K. Baily for very helpful comments on an earlier draft and Mrs H. Howell for discussion of gender issues.

REFERENCES

Abrams, D., Cochrane, S., Hogg, M. A. and Turner, J. C. (1990) 'Knowing what to think by knowing who you are: self categorization and the nature of norm formation, conformity and group polarization', *British Journal of Social Psychology*, 29: 97–119.

Adler, G. (1986) 'Psychotherapy of the narcissistic personality disorder patient', *American Journal of Psychiatry*, 143: 430–6.

Andrews, B. and Brewin, C. R. (1990) 'Attributions of blame for marital violence: a study of antecedents and consequences', *Journal of Family and Marriage*, 52: 757–67.

Archer, J. (1988) *The Behavioural Biology of Aggression*, Cambridge: Cambridge University Press.

—— (1991) 'The influence of testosterone on human aggression', *British Journal of Psychology*, 82: 1–28.

Bailey, K. (1987) *Human Paleopsychology: Applications to Aggression and Pathological Processes*, Hillsdale, NJ: Lawrence Erlbaum Associates.

Barkow, J. H. (1975) 'Prestige and culture: a biosocial interpretation (plus peer review)', *Current Anthropology*, 16: 533–72.

—— (1980) 'Prestige and self-esteem: a biosocial interpretation', in D. R. Omark, D. R. Strayer and J. Freedman (eds) *Dominance Relations: An Ethological View of Social Conflict and Social Interaction*, New York: Garland STPM Press.

—— (1991) 'Precis of Darwin, sex and status: biological approaches to mind and culture (plus peer commentary)', *Behavioral and Brain Sciences*, 14: 295–334.

Barkow, J. H., Cosmides, L. and Tooby, J. (eds) (1992) *The Adapted Mind: Evolutionary Psychology and the Generation of Culture*, New York: Oxford University Press.

Baumeister, R. F. (1982) 'A self-presentational view of social phenomena', *Psychological Bulletin*, 91: 3–21.

—— (1991) *Meanings of Life*, New York: Guilford.

Beck, A. T., Freeman, A. and Associates (1990) *Cognitive Therapy of Personality Disorder*, New York: Guilford.

Blackburn, R. (1989) 'Psychopathology and personality disorder in relation to violence', in K. Howells and C. R. Hollin (eds) *Clinical Approaches to Violence*, Chichester: J. Wiley.

Broucek, F. J. (1991) *Shame and the Self*, New York: Guilford.

Brown, B. B. and Lohr, M. J. (1987) 'Peer-group affiliation and adolescent self-esteem: an integration of ego-identity and symbolic-interaction theories', *Journal of Personality and Social Psychology*, 52: 47–55.

Buck, R. (1988) *Human Motivation and Emotion*, New York: J. Wiley.

Buss, A. H. (1988) *Personality: Evolutionary Heritage and Human Distinctiveness*, Hillsdale, NJ: Lawrence Erlbaum Associates.

Buss, D. M. (1989) 'Sex differences in human mate preference: evolutionary hypotheses tested in 37 cultures', *Brain and Behavioral Sciences*, 12: 1–49.

—— (1991) 'Evolutionary personality psychology', *Annual Review of Psychology*, 42: 459–91.

Chance, M. R. A. (1980) 'An ethological approach assessment of emotion', in R. Plutchik, R. Kellerman and H. Kellerman (eds) *Emotion: Theory Research and Experience*, vol. 1, New York: Academic Press.

—— (1988) 'Introduction', in M. R. A. Chance (ed.) *Social Fabrics of the Mind*, Hove, Sussex: Lawrence Erlbaum Associates.

Chisholm, J. S. (1988) 'Toward a developmental evolutionary ecology of humans', in K. M. MacDonald (ed.) *Sociobiological Perspectives on Human Development*, New York: Springer-Verlag.

Chomsky, N. (1992) *Deterring Democracy*, London: Vintage.

Clark, C. (1990) 'Emotions and micropolitics in everyday life: some patterns and paradoxes of "place" ', in T. D. Kemper (ed.) *Research Agendas in the Sociology of Emotions*, New York: State University of New York Press.

Collins, N. L. and Read, S. J. (1990) 'Adult attachment, working models, and relationship quality in dating couples', *Journal of Personality and Social Psychology*, 58: 644–63.

Colman, A. (1991) 'Psychological evidence in South African murder trials', *The Psychologist*, 4: 482–6.

Cronen, V. E., Johnson, K. M. and Lannamann, J. W. (1982) 'Paradoxes, double binds, and reflexive loops: an alternative theoretical perspective', *Family Process*, 21: 91–112.

Crook, J. H. (1980) *The Evolution of Human Consciousness*, Oxford: Oxford University Press.

de Waal, F. M. B. (1988) 'The reconciled hierarchy', in M. R. A. Chance (ed.) *Social Fabrics of the Mind*, Hove, UK: Lawrence Erlbaum Associates.

Dell, P. (1989) 'Violence and the systemic view: the problem of power', *Family Process*, 28: 1–14.

Diamond, J. (1991) *The Rise and Fall of the Third Chimpanzee: How our Animal Heritage Affects the Way we Live*, London: Vintage.

Doty, R. M., Peterson, B. E. and Winter, D. G. (1991) 'Threat and authoritarianism in the United States, 1978–1987', *Journal of Personality and Social Psychology*, 61: 629–40.

Eibl-Eibesfeldt, I. (1989) *Human Ethology*, New York: Aldine de Gruyter.

Eisenberg, N. and Mussen, P. H. (1989) *The Roots of Prosocial Behavior in Children*, New York: Cambridge University Press.

Ellenberger, H. F. (1970) *The Discovery of the Unconscious: The History and Evolution of Dynamic Psychiatry*, New York: Basic Books.

Emler, N. and Hogan, R. (1991) 'Moral psychology and public policy', in W. M. Kurtines and J. L. Gewirtz (eds) *Handbook of Moral Behavior and Development*, vol. 3, *Application*, Hillsdale, NJ: Lawrence Erlbaum Associates.

Enright, P. D. (1991) 'The moral development of forgiveness', in W. M. Kurtines and J. L. Gewirtz (eds) *Handbook of Moral Behavior and Development*, vol. 1, *Theory*,

Hillsdale, NJ: Lawrence Erlbaum Associates.

Fisher, S. (1989) *Sexual Images of the Self: The Psychology of Erotic Sensations and Illusions*, Hillsdale, NJ: Lawrence Erlbaum Associates.

Fitzgibbons, R. B. (1986) 'The cognitive and emotive uses of forgiveness in the treatment of anger', *Psychotherapy*, 23: 629–33.

Fossum, M. A. and Mason, M. J. (1989) *Facing Shame: Families in Recovery*, New York: Norton Paperbacks.

Foucault, M. (1984) *The Foucault Reader*, P. Rainbow (ed.), Harmondsworth: Penguin.

Frank, J. D. (1982) 'Therapeutic components shared by psychotherapies', in J. H. Harvey and M. M. Parkes (eds) *Psychotherapy Research and Behavior Change*, vol. 1, Washington, DC: American Psychological Association.

Freeman, H. (1991) 'The human brain and political behaviour', *British Journal of Psychiatry*, 159: 19–32.

Frosh, S. (1991) *Identity Crisis, Modernity, Psychoanalysis and the Self*, London: Macmillan.

Frude, N. (1989) 'The physical abuse of children', in K. Howells and C. R. Hollin (eds) *Clinical Approaches to Violence*, Chichester: J. Wiley.

Galbraith, J. K. (1987) *The Affluent Society*, 4th edn, Harmondsworth, UK: Penguin Books.

Gardner, R. (1988) 'Psychiatric infrastructures for intraspecific communication', in M. R. A. Chance (ed.) *Social Fabrics of the Mind*, Hove, Sussex: Lawrence Erlbaum Associates.

Gilbert, P. (1989) *Human Nature and Suffering*, Hove, UK: Lawrence Erlbaum Associates.

—— (1990) 'Changes: rank, status and mood', in S. Fisher and C. L. Cooper (eds) *On the Move: The Psychology of Change and Transition*, Chichester: J. Wiley & Sons.

—— (1992a) *Depression: The Evolution of Powerlessness*, Hove, UK: Lawrence Erlbaum Associates, New York: Guilford.

—— (1992b) 'Defense, safety and biosocial goals in relation to the agonic and hedonic social modes', *World Futures: Journal of General Evolution*, 35: 31–70.

—— (1993) 'Defence and safety: their function in social behaviour and psychopathology', *British Journal of Clinical Psychology*, 32: 131–53.

Gilbert, P. and Trower, P. (1990) 'The evolution and manifestation of social anxiety', in W. R. Crozier (ed.) *Shyness and Embarrassment: Perspectives from Social Psychology*, Cambridge: Cambridge University Press.

Glantz, K. and Pearce, J. K. (1989) *Exiles from Eden: Psychotherapy from an Evolutionary Perspective*, New York: W. W. Norton & Co.

Goffman, E. (1968) *Stigma: Notes on the Management of a Spoiled Identity*, Harmondsworth, UK: Penguin.

Goldner, V., Penn, P., Sheinberg, M. and Walker, G. (1990) 'Love and violence: gender paradoxes in volatile attachments', *Family Process*, 29: 343–64.

Goldstein, A. P. and Keller, H. (1987) *Aggressive Behaviour: Assessment and Intervention*, New York: Pergamon Press.

Goody, E. (1991) 'The learning of prosocial behaviour in small-scale egalitarian societies: and anthropological view', in R. A. Hinde and J. Groebel (eds) *Cooperation and Prosocial Behaviour*, Cambridge: Cambridge University Press.

Greenberg, J. R. and Mitchell, S. A. (1983) *Object Relations in Psychoanalytic Theory*, Cambridge, MA: Harvard University Press.

Gregor, T. (1990) 'Male domination and sexual coercion', in J. W. Stigler, R. A. Shweder and G. Herdt (eds) *Cultural Psychology: Essays in Comparative Human Development*, Cambridge: Cambridge University Press.

Hannah, C. and McAdam, E. (1991) 'Violence, Part 1: Reflections on our work with violence', *Human Systems: Journal of Systemic Consultation and Management*, 2: 201–6.

Harlow, H. F. and Mears, C. (1979) *The Human Model: Primate Perspectives*, New York: Winston & Sons.

Hartup, W. (1989) 'Social relationships and their developmental significance', *American Psychologist*, 44: 120–6.

Haviland, W. A. (1990) *Cultural Anthropology*, 6th edn, New York: Holt, Rinehart & Winston.

Heard, D. H. and Lake, B. (1986) 'The attachment dynamic in adult life', *British Journal of Psychiatry*, 149: 430–8.

Henry, J. P. and Stephens, P. M. (1977) *Stress, Health and the Social Environment: A Sociobiologic Approach to Medicine*, New York: Springer-Verlag.

Hill, J. (1984) 'Human altruism and sociocultural fitness', *Journal of Social and Biological Structures*, 7: 17–35.

Hinde, R. A. (1987) *Individuals, Relationships and Culture: Links between Ethology and the Social Sciences*, Cambridge: Cambridge University Press.

——(1992) 'Developmental psychology in the context of other behavioral sciences', *Developmental Psychology*, 28: 1018–29.

Hinde, R. A. and Groebel, J. (1991) 'Introduction', in R. A. Hinde and J. Groebel (eds) *Cooperation and Prosocial Behaviour*, Cambridge: Cambridge University Press.

Hinde, R. S. (1989) 'Relations between levels of complexity in behavioral sciences', *Journal of Nervous and Mental Disease*, 177: 655–67.

Hofer, M. A. (1981) *The Roots of Human Behavior*, San Francisco: W. H. Freeman.

—— (1984) 'Relationships as regulators: a psychobiologic perspective on bereavement', *Psychosomatic Medicine*, 46: 183–97.

Howell, S. and Willis, R. (1989) (eds) *Societies at Peace: An Anthropological Perspective*, London: Routledge.

Isen, A. M. (1990) 'The influence of positive and negative affect on cognitive organisation: some implications for development', in N. L. Stein, B. Leventhal and T. Trabasco (eds) *Psychological and Biological Approaches to Emotion*, Hillsdale: Lawrence Erlbaum Associates.

Itzkoff, S. W. (1990) *The Making of the Civilized Mind*, New York: Peter Lang.

Kalma, A. (1991) 'Hierarchisation and dominance assessment at first glance', *European Journal of Social Psychology*, 21: 165–81.

Kaufman, G. (1989) *The Psychology of Shame*, New York: Springer.

Kaufman, J. and Zigler, E. (1987) 'Do abused children become abusive parents?', *American Journal of Orthopsychiatry*, 57: 186–92.

Kegan, R. (1982) *The Evolving Self: Problem and Process in Human Development*, Cambridge, MA: Harvard University Press.

Kemper, T. D. (1988) 'The two dimensions of sociality', in M. R. A. Chance (ed.) *Social Fabrics of the Mind*, Hove, UK: Lawrence Erlbaum Associates.

—— (1990) *Social Structure and Testosterone: Explorations of the Socio-Bio-Social Chain*, New Brunswick, NJ: Rutgers University Press.

Kemper, T. D. and Collins, R. (1990) 'Dimensions of microinteraction', *American Journal of Sociology*, 96: 32–68.

Klama, J. (1988) *Aggression: Conflict in Animals and Humans Reconsidered*, Harlow, UK: Longman.

Lasch, C. (1985) *The Minimal Self*, London: Picador.

Leary, T. (1957) *The Interpersonal Diagnosis of Personality*, New York: Ronald Press.

Levenson, M. R. (1992) 'Rethinking psychopathy', *Theory and Psychology*, 2: 51–71.

Lewis, H. B. (1987) 'Introduction: Shame – the "sleeper" in psychopathology', in H. B. Lewis (ed.) *The Role of Shame in Symptom Formation*, Hillsdale, NJ: Lawrence Erlbaum Associates.

McAdam, E. and Hannah, C. (1991) 'Violence – 2: Creating the best context to work with clients who have found themselves in violent situations', *Human Systems: Journal of Systemic Consultation and Management*, 2: 201–6.

MacDonald, K. B. (1988) *Social and Personality Development: An Evolutionary Synthesis*, New York: Plenum Press.

MacLean, P. D. (1985) 'Brain evolution relating to family, play and the separation call', *Archives of General Psychiatry*, 42: 405–17.

—— (1990) *The Triune Brain in Evolution*, New York: Plenum Press.

Meth, R. L. and Pasick, R. S. (1990) *Men in Therapy: The Challenge of Change*, New York: Guilford.

Meyersburg, H. A. and Post, R. M. (1979) 'A holistic developmental view of neural and psychobiological processes: a neurobiologic-psychoanalytic integration', *British Journal of Psychiatry*, 135: 139–55.

Miedzian, M. (1992) *Boys will be Boys: Breaking the Link between Masculinity and Violence*, London: Virago.

Milgram, S. (1974) *Obedience to Authority*, New York: Harper & Row.

Miller, A. (1983) *For Your Own Good: The Roots of Violence in Child-rearing*, London: Virago.

Miller, P. A. and Eisenberg, N. (1988) 'The relation of empathy to aggressive behaviour and externalising/antisocial behaviour', *Psychological Bulletin*, 103: 324–44.

Montagner, H., Restoin, A., Rodriguez, D., Ullman, V., Viala, M., Laurent, D. and Godard, D. (1988) 'Social interactions of young children with peers and their modifications in relation to environmental factors', in M. R. A. Chance (ed.) *Social Fabrics of the Mind*, Hove, UK: Lawrence Erlbaum Associates.

Nesse, R. M. (1990) 'Evolutionary explanations of emotions', *Human Nature*, 1: 261–89.

Novaco, R. W. (in press) 'Anger as a risk factor among the mentally disordered', in J. Monahan and H. Steadman (eds) *Violence and Mental Disorder*, Chicago: Chicago University Press.

Ohman, A. (1986) 'Face the beast and fear the face: animal and social fears as prototypes for evolutionary analyses of emotion', *Psychophysiology*, 23: 123–44.

Pascal, B. (1670) *Pensées: Notes on Religion and Other Subjects*, L. Lafuma (ed.), J. Warrington (trans.), London: Dent.

Post, R. M. (1992) 'Transduction of psychosocial stress into the neurobiology of recurrent affective disorders', *American Journal of Psychiatry*, 149: 999–1010.

Powell, L. H. and Friedman, M. (1986) 'Alteration of Type A behaviour in coronary patients', in M. J. Christie and P. G. Mallet (eds) *The Psychosomatic Approach: Contemporary Practice of Whole-Person Care*, Chichester: Wiley.

Power, M. (1991) *The Egalitarians: Human and Chimpanzee: An Anthropological View of Social Organisation*, Cambridge: Cambridge University Press.

Price, J. S. (1988) 'Alternative channels for negotiating asymmetry in social relationships', in M. R. A. Chance (ed.) *Social Fabrics of the Mind*, Hove, UK: Lawrence Erlbaum Associates.

Price, V. A. (1982) *Type A Behavior Pattern: A Model for Research and Practice*, New York: Academic Press.

Raskin, R., Novacek, J. and Hogan, R. (1991) 'Narcissistic self management', *Journal of Personality and Social Psychology*, 60: 911–18.

Raskin, R. and Terry, H. (1988) 'A principle components analysis of the narcissistic personality inventory and further evidence of its construct validity', *Journal of Personality and Social Psychology*, 54: 890–902.

Rendall, J. (1992) 'Who betrayed Mike Tyson?', *The Independent on Sunday*, 16 Feb., pp. 2–5.

Rohner, R. P. (1986) *The Warmth Dimension: Foundations of Parental Acceptance–Rejection Theory*, Beverly Hills, CA: Sage.

Sabini, J. and Silver, M. (1982) *The Moralities of Everyday Life*, New York: Oxford University Press.

Salazar, A. (1992) 'Born to die in Medellín', *Weekend Guardian*, 1–2 Aug., pp. 12–13.

Scheff, T. J. (1988) 'Shame and conformity: The deference-emotion system', *American Review of Sociology*, 53: 395–406.

Schore, A. N. (1991) 'Early superego development: the emergence of shame and narcissistic affect regulation in the practicing period', *Psychoanalysis and Contemporary Thought: A Quarterly of Integrative and Interdisciplinary Studies*, 14: 187–250.

Smail, D. (1987) *Taking Care: An Alternative to Therapy*, London: J. Dent & Sons.

Suls, S. and Wills, T. A. (1991) *Social Comparison: Contemporary Theory and Research*, Hillsdale, NJ: Lawrence Erlbaum Associates.

Tangney, J. P., Wagner, P., Fletcher, C. and Gramzow, R. (1992) 'Shamed into anger? the relation of shame and guilt to self-reported aggression', *Journal of Personality and Social Psychology*, 62: 669–75.

Taylor, C. (1992) *Sources of the Self: The Making of the Modern Identity*, Cambridge: Cambridge University Press.

Tejirian, E. (1990) *Sexuality and the Devil: Symbols of Love, Power and Fear in Male Psychology*, New York: Routledge.

Tinbergen, N. (1963) 'On the aims and methods of ethology', *Zeitschrift für Tierpsychologie*, 20: 410–33.

Toffler, A. (1991) *Power Shift: Knowledge, Wealth and Violence at the Edge of the 21st Century*, London: Bantam.

Trivers, R. (1985) *Social Evolution*, Menlo Park, CA: Benjamin/Cummings.

Troy, M. and Sroufe, L. A. (1987) 'Victimization among preschoolers: role of attachment relationship history', *Journal of American Academy of Child and Adolescent Psychiatry*, 26: 166–72.

Van Schaik, C. P. (1989) 'The ecology of social relationships amongst female primates', in V. Standen and R. A. Foley (eds) *Comparative Socioecology: The Behavioural Ecology of Humans and Other Animals*, Oxford: Blackwell.

Weingartner, K. (1991) 'The discourses of intimacy: adding a social constructionist and feminist view', *Family Process*, 30: 285–305.

Wenegrat, B. (1984) *Sociobiology and Mental Disorder: A New View*, Menlo Park, CA: Addison-Wesley.

—— (1990) *The Divine Archetype: The Sociobiology and Psychology of Religion*, Lexington, MA: Lexington Books.

Wilkinson, R. G. (1992) 'Income distribution and life expectancy', *British Medical Journal*, 304 (18 Jan.): 165–8.

Williams, L. (1992) 'Torture and the torturer', *The Psychologist*, 5: 305–8.

Wilson, M. and Daly, M. (1985) 'Competitiveness, risk taking, and violence: the young man's syndrome', *Ethology and Sociobiology*, 6: 59–73.

Wink, P. (1991) 'Two faces of narcissism', *Journal of Personality and Social Psychology*, 61: 590–7.

Wright, J. C., Giammarino, M. and Parad, H. W. (1986) 'Social status in small groups: individual-group similarity and social "misfit" ', *Journal of Personality and Social Psychology*, 50: 523–36.

NAME INDEX

SUBJECT INDEX